Lecture Notes in Computer Science

Lecture Notes in Artificial Intelligence 16019

Founding Editor

Jörg Siekmann

Series Editors

Randy Goebel, *University of Alberta, Edmonton, Canada*
Wolfgang Wahlster, *DFKI, Berlin, Germany*
Zhi-Hua Zhou, *Nanjing University, Nanjing, China*

The series Lecture Notes in Artificial Intelligence (LNAI) was established in 1988 as a topical subseries of LNCS devoted to artificial intelligence.

The series publishes state-of-the-art research results at a high level. As with the LNCS mother series, the mission of the series is to serve the international R & D community by providing an invaluable service, mainly focused on the publication of conference and workshop proceedings and postproceedings.

Rita P. Ribeiro · Bernhard Pfahringer ·
Nathalie Japkowicz · Pedro Larrañaga ·
Alípio M. Jorge · Carlos Soares ·
Pedro H. Abreu · João Gama
Editors

Machine Learning and Knowledge Discovery in Databases

Research Track

European Conference, ECML PKDD 2025
Porto, Portugal, September 15–19, 2025
Proceedings, Part VII

Editors
Rita P. Ribeiro ⓘ
University of Porto
Porto, Portugal

Bernhard Pfahringer ⓘ
University of Waikato
Hamilton, Waikato, New Zealand

Nathalie Japkowicz ⓘ
American University
Washington, D.C., WA, USA

Pedro Larrañaga ⓘ
Technical University of Madrid
Boadilla del Monte, Madrid, Spain

Alípio M. Jorge ⓘ
Departamento de Ciência de Computadores
University of Porto
Porto, Portugal

Carlos Soares ⓘ
University of Porto
Porto, Portugal

João Gama ⓘ
University of Porto
Porto, Portugal

Pedro H. Abreu ⓘ
University of Coimbra
Coimbra, Portugal

ISSN 0302-9743   ISSN 1611-3349 (electronic)
Lecture Notes in Artificial Intelligence
ISBN 978-3-032-06108-9   ISBN 978-3-032-06109-6 (eBook)
https://doi.org/10.1007/978-3-032-06109-6

LNCS Sublibrary: SL7 – Artificial Intelligence

© The Editor(s) (if applicable) and The Author(s), under exclusive license
to Springer Nature Switzerland AG 2026
Chapter "Breaking Free: Decoupling Forced Systems with Laplace Neural Networks" is licensed under the terms of the Creative Commons Attribution 4.0 International License (http://creativecommons.org/licenses/by/4.0/). For further details see license information in the chapter.

This work is subject to copyright. All rights are solely and exclusively licensed by the Publisher, whether the whole or part of the material is concerned, specifically the rights of translation, reprinting, reuse of illustrations, recitation, broadcasting, reproduction on microfilms or in any other physical way, and transmission or information storage and retrieval, electronic adaptation, computer software, or by similar or dissimilar methodology now known or hereafter developed.
The use of general descriptive names, registered names, trademarks, service marks, etc. in this publication does not imply, even in the absence of a specific statement, that such names are exempt from the relevant protective laws and regulations and therefore free for general use.
The publisher, the authors and the editors are safe to assume that the advice and information in this book are believed to be true and accurate at the date of publication. Neither the publisher nor the authors or the editors give a warranty, expressed or implied, with respect to the material contained herein or for any errors or omissions that may have been made. The publisher remains neutral with regard to jurisdictional claims in published maps and institutional affiliations.

This Springer imprint is published by the registered company Springer Nature Switzerland AG
The registered company address is: Gewerbestrasse 11, 6330 Cham, Switzerland

If disposing of this product, please recycle the paper.

Preface

The 2025 edition of the European Conference on Machine Learning and Principles and Practice of Knowledge Discovery in Databases (ECML PKDD 2025) was held in the vibrant city of Porto, Portugal on September 15–19, 2025. This marks a significant return of the conference to Porto, following successful editions in 2005 and 2015, underscoring the city's enduring appeal as a hub for scientific exchange.

The annual ECML PKDD conference stands as a premier worldwide platform dedicated to showcasing the latest advancements and fostering insightful discussions in the fields of machine learning and knowledge discovery in databases. Held jointly since 2001, ECML PKDD has firmly established its reputation as the leading European conference in these disciplines. It provides researchers and practitioners with an unparalleled opportunity to exchange knowledge, share innovative ideas, and explore the latest technical advancements. Furthermore, the conference deeply values the synergy between foundational theoretical advances and groundbreaking practical data science applications, actively encouraging contributions that demonstrate how Machine Learning and Data Mining are being effectively employed to address complex real-world challenges.

A Hub for Responsible AI and Cutting-Edge Research

As the technological landscape continues to evolve and societal needs shift, the conference remains committed to adapting to and reflecting these dynamic changes. This year's event saw a robust engagement from the global research community with a substantial increase in the number of submissions.

The three main conference days were organised into five distinct tracks:

- The Research Track received an impressive number of 924 submissions, with 226 papers ultimately accepted, reflecting a highly competitive acceptance rate of 24.5%.
- The Applied Data Science Track received a total of 299 submissions, accepting 74 papers, resulting in an acceptance rate of 24.7%.
- The Journal Track continued to bridge the gap between conference and journal publications, accepting 43 papers (27 for the Machine Learning journal and 16 for the Data Mining and Knowledge Discovery journal) out of 297 submissions.
- The Nectar Track, focusing on recent scientific advances at the frontier of machine learning and data mining, received 30 submissions.
- The Demo Track showcased practical applications and prototypes, accepting 15 papers from a total of 30 submissions.

These proceedings cover the papers accepted in the Research and Applied Data Science tracks.

The high quality and diversity of the accepted papers across all tracks underscore the continued vitality and intellectual breadth of the machine learning and data mining communities. We extend our sincere gratitude to all authors for their valuable contributions, to the program committee members and reviewers for their diligent efforts in ensuring the rigorous double-blind review process, and to the organising committee for their tireless work in making ECML PKDD 2025 a resounding success. We believe these proceedings will serve as a valuable resource, inspiring future research and innovation in these rapidly advancing fields.

This year's conference featured seven insightful keynote talks that focused on crucial and emerging areas within Responsible AI, including trustworthy AI, interpretability, and explainability. The keynotes also explored fundamental theoretical issues, covering causality, neural-symbolic systems, large language models (LLMs), and AI for science. We were honoured to host leading experts who shared their valuable perspectives:

- Cynthia Rudin (Duke University) presented on "Many Good Models Lead to …";
- Elias Bareinboim (Columbia University) discussed "Towards Causal Artificial Intelligence";
- Francisco Herrera (University of Granada) addressed "Not Just a Trend: Institutionalizing XAI for Responsible and Compliant AI Systems";
- Mirella Lapata (University of Edinburgh) explored "Compositional Intelligence: Coordinating Multiple LLMs for Complex Tasks";
- Nuria Oliver (ELLIS Alicante Foundation, Spain) spoke on "Towards a Fairer World: Uncovering and Addressing Human and Algorithmic Biases";
- Pedro Domingos (University of Washington) shared insights on "A Simple Unification of Neural and Symbolic AI"; and
- Sašo Džeroski (Jožef Stefan Institute, Slovenia) presented on "Artificial Intelligence for Science".

Fostering Diversity and Inclusion

Our Diversity and Inclusion initiative proudly awarded 10 scholarship grants of €500 to early-career researchers. These grants enabled individuals from developing countries and communities underrepresented in science and technology to attend the conference, present their work, and become integral members of the ECML PKDD community.

Acknowledging Our Contributors and Supporters

We extend our sincere gratitude to everyone who contributed to making ECML PKDD 2025 such a success. Our heartfelt thanks go to the authors, workshop and tutorial organisers, and all participants for their valuable scientific contributions.

An outstanding conference program would not be possible without the immense dedication and substantial time investment from our area chairs, program committee, and organising committee. The smooth execution of the event was also largely due to the hard work of our many volunteers and session chairs. A special acknowledgement goes to the local organisers for meticulously handling every detail, making the conference a truly memorable experience.

Finally, we are incredibly grateful for the generous financial support from our wonderful sponsors. We also appreciate Springer's ongoing support and Microsoft's provision of their CMT software for conference management, as well as their continued assistance. Our sincere thanks also go to the ECML PKDD Steering Committee for their invaluable advice and guidance over the past two years.

September 2025

João Gama
Pedro H. Abreu
Alípio M. Jorge
Carlos Soares
Rita P. Ribeiro
Pedro Larrañaga
Nathalie Japkowicz
Bernhard Pfahringer
Inês Dutra
Mykola Pechenizkiy
Sepideh Pashami
Paulo Cortez

Organization

Honorary Chair

Pavel Brazdil   University of Porto, Portugal

General Chairs

João Gama	University of Porto, Portugal
Pedro H. Abreu	University of Coimbra, Portugal
Alípio M. Jorge	University of Porto, Portugal
Carlos Soares	University of Porto, Portugal

Research Track Program Chairs

Bernhard Pfahringer	University of Waikato, New Zealand
Nathalie Japkowicz	American University, USA
Pedro Larrañaga	Technical University of Madrid, Spain
Rita P. Ribeiro	University of Porto, Portugal

Applied Data Science Track Program Chairs

Inês Dutra	University of Porto, Portugal
Mykola Pechenisky	TU Eindhoven, The Netherlands
Paulo Cortez	University of Minho, Portugal
Sepideh Pashami	Halmstad University, Sweden

Journal Track Chairs

Ana Carolina Lorena	Instituto Tecnológico de Aeronáutica, Brazil
Arlindo Oliveira	Instituto Superior Técnico, Portugal
Concha Bielza	Technical University of Madrid, Spain
Longbing Cao	Macquarie University, Australia
Tiago Almeida	Federal University of São Carlos, Brazil

Nectar Track Chairs

Ricard Gavaldà Amalfi Analytics, Spain
Riccardo Guidotti University of Pisa, Italy

Demo Track Chairs

Arian Pasquali Faktion, Belgium
Nuno Moniz University of Notre Dame, USA

Local Chairs

Bruno Veloso University of Porto, Portugal
Rita Nogueira INESC TEC, Portugal
Shazia Tabassum INESC TEC, Portugal

Workshop Chairs

Irena Koprinska University of Sydney, Australia
João Mendes Moreira University of Porto, Portugal
Paula Branco University of Ottawa, Canada

Tutorial Chairs

Alicia Troncoso Universidad Pablo de Olavide, Spain
Nikolaj Tatti University of Helsinki, Finland

PhD Forum Chairs

Raquel Sebastião Polytechnic Institute of Viseu, Portugal
Yun Sing Koh University of Auckland, New Zealand

Awards Committee Chairs

André Carvalho   University of São Paulo, Brazil
Amparo Alonso-Betanzos   University of A Coruña, Spain
Katharina Morik   TU Dortmund, Germany
Vítor Santos Costa   University of Porto, Portugal

Proceedings Chairs

João Vinagre   European Commission (JRC), Spain
Miriam Santos   University of Porto, Portugal
Shazia Tabassum   INESC TEC, Portugal

Diversity and Inclusion Chairs

Inês Sousa   Fraunhofer, Portugal
Zahraa Abdallah   University of Bristol, UK

Discovery Challenge Chairs

Carlos Ferreira   Polytechnic Institute of Porto, Portugal
Peter van der Putten   Leiden University, The Netherlands
Rui Camacho   University of Porto, Portugal

Panel Chairs

Pedro H. Abreu   University of Coimbra, Portugal
Paula Brito   University of Porto, Portugal

Publicity Chair

Carlos Ferreira   Polytechnic Institute of Porto, Portugal

Sponsorship Chairs

Mariam Berry   BNP Paribas, France
Nuno Moutinho   University of Porto, Portugal
Rui Teles   Accenture, Portugal

Social Media Chairs

Luis Roque   ZAAI.ai, Portugal
Ricardo Pereira   University of Coimbra, Portugal
Dalila Teixeira   Creative Matter, USA

Web Chair

Thiago Andrade   University of Porto, Portugal

Senior Program Committee – Research Track

Adam Jatowt   University of Innsbruck, Austria
Andrea Passerini   University of Trento, Italy
Anthony Bagnall   University of Southampton, UK
Arno Knobbe   Leiden University, Netherlands
Arno Siebes   Universiteit Utrecht, Netherlands
Arto Klami   University of Helsinki, Finland
Bernhard Pfahringer   University of Waikato, New Zealand
Bettina Berendt   TU Berlin, Germany
Celine Robardet   INSA Lyon, France
Celine Vens   KU Leuven, Belgium
Cesar Ferri   Universitat Politècnica Valencia, Spain
Charalampos Tsourakakis Boston University, USA
Chedy Raissi   Inria, France
Chen Gong   Nanjing University of Science and Technology, China
Danai Koutra   University of Michigan, USA
Dimitrios Gunopulos   University of Athens, Greece
Donato Malerba   Università degli Studi di Bari Aldo Moro, Italy
Dragi Kocev   Jožef Stefan Institute, Slovenia
Dunja Mladenic   Jožef Stefan Institute, Slovenia
Eirini Ntoutsi   Universität der Bundeswehr München, Germany

Emmanuel Müller	TU Dortmund, Germany
Ernestina Menasalvas	Universidad Politécnica de Madrid, Spain
Esther Galbrun	University of Eastern Finland, Finland
Evaggelia Pitoura	University of Ioannina, Greece
Evangelos Papalexakis	University of California, Riverside, USA
Fabio A. Stella	University of Milano-Bicocca, Italy
Fabrizio Costa	Exeter University, UK
Fragkiskos Malliaros	CentraleSupélec, France
Georg Krempl	Utrecht University, Netherlands
Georgiana Ifrim	University College Dublin, Ireland
Gustavo Batista	University of New South Wales, Australia
Heikki Mannila	Aalto University, Finland
Hendrik Blockeel	KU Leuven, Belgium
Henrik Bostrom	KTH Royal Institute of Technology, Sweden
Henry Gouk	University of Edinburgh, UK
Ioannis Katakis	University of Nicosia, Cyprus
Jan N. Van Rijn	LIACS, Leiden University, Netherlands
Jefrey Lijffijt	Ghent University, Belgium
Jerzy Stefanowski	Poznań University of Technology, Poland
Jesse Davis	KU Leuven, Belgium
Jesse Read	Ecole Polytechnique, France
Jessica Lin	George Mason University, USA
Jesus Cerquides	IIIA-CSIC, Spain
Jilles Vreeken	CISPA Helmholtz Center for Information Security, Germany
João Gama	INESC TEC - LIAAD, Portugal
Jörg Wicker	University of Auckland, New Zealand
José Hernández-Orallo	Universitat Politècnica de Valencia, Spain
Junming Shao	University of Electronic Science and Technology of China, China
Kai Puolamaki	University of Helsinki, Finland
Manfred Jaeger	Aalborg University, Denmark
Marius Kloft	TU Kaiserslautern, Germany
Marius Lindauer	Leibniz University Hannover, Germany
Mark Last	Ben-Gurion University of the Negev, Israel
Matthias Renz	University of Kiel, Germany
Matthias Schubert	Ludwig-Maximilians-Universität München, Germany
Michele Lombardi	University of Bologna, Italy
Michèle Sebag	LISN CNRS, France
Nathalie Japkowicz	American University, USA
Paolo Frasconi	Università degli Studi di Firenze, Italy

Parisa Kordjamshidi	Michigan State University, USA
Pasquale Minervini	University of Edinburgh, UK
Pauli Miettinen	University of Eastern Finland, Finland
Pedro Larrañaga	Technical University of Madrid, Spain
Peer Kroger	Christian-Albrechts-Universität Kiel, Germany
Peter Flach	University of Bristol, UK
Ricardo B. Prudencio	Universidade Federal de Pernambuco, Brazil
Rita P. Ribeiro	University of Porto and INESC TEC, Portugal
Salvatore Ruggieri	University of Pisa, Italy
Sebastijan Dumancic	TU Delft, Netherlands
Sibylle Hess	TU Eindhoven, Netherlands
Sicco Verwer	Delft University of Technology, Netherlands
Siegfried Nijssen	Université catholique de Louvain, Belgium
Sophie Fellenz	RPTU Kaiserslautern-Landau, Germany
Stefano Ferilli	University of Bari, Italy
Stratis Ioannidis	Northeastern University, USA
Szymon Jaroszewicz	Polish Academy of Sciences, Poland
Tijl De Bie	Ghent University, Belgium
Ulf Brefeld	Leuphana University of Lüneburg, Germany
Varvara Vetrova	University of Canterbury, New Zealand
Wannes Meert	KU Leuven, Belgium
Wei Ye	Tongji University, China
Wenbin Zhang	Florida International University, USA
Willem Waegeman	Universiteit Gent, Belgium
Wouter Duivesteijn	Technische Universiteit Eindhoven, Netherlands
Xiao Luo	University of California, Los Angeles, USA
Yun Sing Koh	University of Auckland, New Zealand
Zied Bouraoui	CRIL CNRS and Université d'Artois, France

Senior Program Committee – Applied Data Science Track

Albrecht Zimmermann	Université de Caen Normandie, France
Andreas Hotho	University of Würzburg, Germany
Anirban Dasgupta	IIT Gandhinagar, India
Anna Monreale	University of Pisa, Italy
Annalisa Appice	University of Bari Aldo Moro, Italy
Bruno Cremilleux	Université de Caen Normandie, France
Carlotta Domeniconi	George Mason University, USA
Dejing Dou	BCG, USA
Fabio Pinelli	IMT Lucca, Italy
Fuzhen Zhuang	Beihang University, China

Gabor Melli	PredictionWorks, USA
Giuseppe Manco	ICAR-CNR, Italy
Glenn Fung	Independent Researcher, USA
Grzegorz Nalepa	Jagiellonian University, Poland
Hui Xiong	Hong Kong University of Science and Technology (Guangzhou), China
Inês Dutra	University of Porto, Portugal
Ioanna Miliou	Stockholm University, Sweden
Ira Assent	Aarhus University, Denmark
Jiayu Zhou	Michigan State University, USA
Jiliang Tang	Michigan State University, USA
Jingrui He	University of Illinois at Urbana-Champaign, USA
João Gama	INESC TEC - LIAAD, Portugal
Jose A. Gamez	Universidad de Castilla-La Mancha, Spain
Ke Liang	National University of Defense Technology, China
Kurt Driessens	Maastricht University, Netherlands
Lars Kotthoff	University of Wyoming, USA
Liang Sun	Alibaba Group, China
Martin Atzmueller	Osnabrück University and DFKI, Germany
Michael R. Berthold	KNIME, Germany
Michelangelo Ceci	University of Bari, Italy
Min-Ling Zhang	Southeast University, China
Mykola Pechenizkiy	TU Eindhoven, Netherlands
Myra Spiliopoulou	Otto-von-Guericke-Universität Magdeburg, Germany
Niklas Lavesson	Blekinge Institute of Technology, Sweden
Nikolaj Tatti	Helsinki University, Finland
Panagiotis Papapetrou	Stockholm University, Sweden
Paolo Frasconi	Università degli Studi di Firenze, Italy
Paulo Cortez	University of Minho, Portugal
Peggy Cellier	INSA Rennes, IRISA, France
Rayid Ghani	Carnegie Mellon University, USA
Sahar Asadi	King (Microsoft), UK
Sandeep Tata	Google, USA
Sepideh Pashami	Halmstad University, Sweden
Slawomir Nowaczyk	Halmstad University, Sweden
Sriparna Saha	IIT Patna, India
Thomas Liebig	TU Dortmund, Germany
Thomas Seidl	LMU Munich, Germany
Tom Diethe	AstraZeneca, UK
Tony Lindgren	Stockholm University, Sweden

Vincent S. Tseng   National Yang Ming Chiao Tung University, Taiwan
Vítor Santos Costa   Universidade do Porto, Portugal
Xingquan Zhu   Florida Atlantic University, USA
Yi Chang   Jilin University, China
Yinglong Xia   Meta, USA
Yongxin Tong   Beihang University, China
Yun Sing Koh   University of Auckland, New Zealand
Zhaochun Ren   Shandong University, China
Zheng Wang   Alibaba DAMO Academy, China
Zhiwei (Tony) Qin   Lyft, USA

Program Committee – Research Track

Christoph Bergmeir   Monash University, Australia
A. K. M. Mahbubur Rahman   Independent University, Bangladesh
Abdulhakim Qahtan   Utrecht University, Netherlands
Abhishek A.   Fujitsu Research, India
Acar Tamersoy   Microsoft, USA
Ad Feelders   Universiteit Utrecht, Netherlands
Adam Goodge   I2R, A*STAR, Singapore
Adele Jia   China Agricultural University, China
Adem Kikaj   KU Leuven, Belgium
Aditya Mohan   Leibniz Universität Hannover, Germany
Ajay A. Mahimkar   AT&T, USA
Akka Zemmari   Université de Bordeaux, France
Akshay Sethi   MasterCard, USA
Alborz Geramifard   Meta, USA
Alessandro Antonucci   IDSIA, Switzerland
Alessandro Melchiorre   Johannes Kepler University Linz, Austria
Alexander Dockhorn   Leibniz University Hannover, Germany
Alexander Schiendorfer   Technische Hochschule Ingolstadt, Germany
Alexander Schulz   CITEC, Bielefeld University, Germany
Alexandre Termier   Université de Rennes 1, France
Alexandre Verine   Ecole Normale Supérieure - PSL, France
Alexandru C. Mara   Ghent University, Belgium
Ali Ayadi   University of Strasbourg, France
Ali Ismail-Fawaz   IRIMAS, Université de Haute-Alsace, France
Alicja Wieczorkowska   Polish-Japanese Academy of Information Technology, Poland
Alipio M. G. Jorge   INESC TEC/University of Porto, Portugal

Alireza Gharahighehi	KU Leuven, Belgium
Alistair Shilton	Deakin University, Australia
Alneu A. Lopes	University of São Paulo, Brazil
Alper Demir	Izmir University of Economics, Turkey
Alvaro Figueira	CRACS and Universidade do Porto, Portugal
Amal Saadallah	TU Dortmund, Germany
Aman Chadha	Stanford University and Amazon, USA
Amer Krivosija	TU Dortmund, Germany
Amir H. Payberah	KTH Royal Institute of Technology, Sweden
Ammar Shaker	NEC Laboratories Europe, Europe
Ana Rita Nogueira	INESC TEC, Portugal
Anand Paul	Louisiana State University HSC, USA
Anastasios Gounaris	Aristotle University of Thessaloniki, Greece
Andre V. Carreiro	Fraunhofer Portugal AICOS, Portugal
André C. P. L. F. de Carvalho	University of São Paulo, Brazil
Andrea Cossu	University of Pisa, Italy
Andrea Mastropietro	University of Bonn, Germany
Andrea Pugnana	University of Trento, Italy
Andrea Tagarelli	DIMES - UNICAL, Italy
Andreas Bender	LMU Munich, Germany
Andreas Nürnberger	Otto-von-Guericke-Universität Magdeburg, Germany
Andreas Schwung	Fachhochschule Südwestfalen, Germany
Andrei Paleyes	University of Cambridge, UK
Andrzej Skowron	University of Warsaw, Poland
Andy Song	RMIT University, Australia
Angelica Liguori	ICAR-CNR, Italy
Anirban Dasgupta	IIT Gandhinagar, India
Anke Meyer-Baese	Florida State University, USA
Anna Beer	University of Vienna, Austria
Anna Krause	Universität Wurzburg and Chair X Data Science, Germany
Anna Monreale	University of Pisa, Italy
Annelot W. Bosman	Universiteit Leiden, Netherlands
Antoine Caradot	Hubert Curien Laboratory, France
Antonio Bahamonde	University of Oviedo, Spain
Antonio Mastropietro	Università di Pisa, Italy
Antonio Pellicani	Università degli Studi di Bari, Aldo Moro, Italy
Antonis Matakos	Aalto University, Finland
Antti Laaksonen	University of Helsinki, Finland
Aomar Osmani	LIPN-UMR CNRS, France
Aonghus Lawlor	University College Dublin, Ireland

Aparna S. Varde	Montclair State University, USA
Apostolos N. Papadopoulos	Aristotle University of Thessaloniki, Greece
Aritra Konar	KU Leuven, Belgium
Arjun Roy	Freie Universität Berlin, Germany
Arthur Charpentier	UQAM, Canada
Arunas Lipnickas	Kaunas University of Technology, Lithuania
Atsuhiro Takasu	National Institute of Informatics, Japan
Aurora Esteban	University of Cordoba, Spain
Baosheng Zhang	Tsinghua University, China
Barbara Toniella Corradini	University of Florence and University of Siena, Italy
Bardh Prenkaj	Technical University of Munich, Germany
Barry O'Sullivan	University College Cork, Ireland
Beilun Wang	Southeast University, China
Benjamin Halstead	University of Auckland, New Zealand
Benjamin Paassen	Bielefeld University, Germany
Benjamin Quost	Université de Technologie de Compiègne, France
Benoit Frenay	University of Namur, Belgium
Bernardo Moreno Sanchez	University of Helsinki, Finland
Bernhard Pfahringer	University of Waikato, New Zealand
Bertrand Cuissart	University of Caen, France
Bin Liu	Chongqing University of Posts and Telecommunications, China
Bin Shi	Xi'an Jiaotong University, China
Bin Wu	Zhengzhou University, China
Bin Zhou	National University of Defense Technology, China
Bitao Peng	Guangdong University of Foreign Studies, China
Bo Kang	Ghent University, Belgium
Bogdan Cautis	Université Paris-Saclay, France
Bojan Evkoski	Central European University, Hungary
Boshen Shi	Institute of Computing Technology, Chinese Academy of Sciences, China
Boualem Benatallah	Dublin City University, Ireland
Brandon Gower-Winter	Utrecht University, Netherlands
Bunil K. Balabantaray	NIT Meghalaya, India
Carlos Ferreira	INESC TEC, Portugal
Carlos Monserrat-Aranda	Universitat Politècnica de Valencia, Spain
Carson K. Leung	University of Manitoba, Canada
Catarina Silva	University of Coimbra, Portugal
Cecile Capponi	Aix-Marseille University, France
Celine Rouveirol	LIPN Université de Sorbonne Paris Nord, France

Cesar H. G. Andrade	Porto University, Portugal
Chandrajit Bajaj	University of Texas, Austin, USA
Chang Rajani	University of Helsinki, Finland
Charlotte Laclau	Polytechnique Institute, Télécom Paris, France
Charlotte Pelletier	Université de Bretagne du Sud, France
Chen Wang	DATA61, CSIRO, Australia
Cheng Cheng	Carnegie Mellon University, USA
Cheng Xie	Yunnan University, China
Chenglin Wang	East China Normal University, China
Chenwang Wu	University of Science and Technology of China, China
Chiara Pugliese	IIT Institute of National Research Council, Italy
Chien-Liang Liu	National Chiao Tung University, Taiwan
Chihiro Maru	Chuo University, Japan
Chongsheng Zhang	Henan University, China
Christian Beecks	FernUniversität in Hagen, Germany
Christian M. M. Frey	University of Technology Nuremberg, Germany
Christian Hakert	TU Dortmund, Germany
Christine Largeron	LabHC Lyon University, France
Christophe Rigotti	INSA Lyon, France
Christophe Rodrigues	DVRC Pôle universitaire Léonard de Vinci, France
Christos Anagnostopoulos	University of Glasgow, UK
Christos Diou Harokopio	University of Athens, Greece
Chuan Qin	Chinese Academy of Sciences, China
Chunchun Chen	Tongji University, China
Chunyao Song	Nankai University, China
Claire Nedellec	INRAE, MaIAGE, France
Claudio Borile	CENTAI Institute, Italy
Claudio Gallicchio	University of Pisa, Italy
Claudius Zelenka	Kiel University, Germany
Colin Bellinger	NRC and Dalhousie University, Canada
Collin Leiber	Aalto University, Finland
Cong Qi	New Jersey Institute of Technology, USA
Congfeng Cao	University of Amsterdam, Netherlands
Corrado Loglisci	Università degli Studi di Bari, Aldo Moro, Italy
Cuicui Luo	University of Chinese Academy of Sciences, China
Cuneyt G. Akcora	University of Central Florida, USA
Cynthia C. S. Liem	Delft University of Technology, Netherlands
Dalius Matuzevicius	Vilnius Gediminas Technical University, Lithuania

Dan Li	Sun Yat-sen University, China
Danai Koutra	University of Michigan, USA
Dang Nguyen	Deakin University, Australia
Daniel Neider	TU Dortmund, Germany
Daniel Schlor	Universität Würzburg, Germany
Danil Provodin	TU Eindhoven, Netherlands
Danyang Xiao	Sun Yat-sen University, China
Dario Garcia-Gasulla	Barcelona Supercomputing Center (BSC), Spain
Dario Garigliotti	University of Bergen, Norway
Darius Plonis	Vilnius Gediminas Technical University, Lithuania
Dariusz Brzezinski	Poznań University of Technology, Poland
David Gomez	Universidad Politecnica de Madrid, Spain
David Holzmüller	University of Stuttgart, Germany
David Q. Sun	Apple, USA
Davide Evangelista	University of Bologna, Italy
Debo Cheng	University of South Australia, Australia
Deepayan Chakrabarti	University of Texas at Austin, USA
Deng-Bao Wang	Southeast University, China
Denilson Barbosa	University of Alberta, Canada
Denis Huseljic	University of Kassel, Germany
Denis Lukovnikov	Ruhr-Universität Bochum, Germany
Destercke Sebastien	UTC, France
Di Jin	TikTok, USA
Di Wu	Chongqing Institute of Green and Intelligent Technology, Chinese Academy of Sciences, China
Diana Benavides Prado	University of Auckland, New Zealand
Dianhui Wang	Independent Researcher, Australia
Diego Carrera	STMicroelectronics, Switzerland
Diletta Chiaro	Università degli Studi di Napoli Federico II, Italy
Dimitri Staufer	TU Berlin, Germany
Dimitrios Katsaros	University of Thessaly, Greece
Dimitrios Rafailidis	University of Thessaly, France
Dino Ienco	INRAE, France
Dmitry Kobak	University of Tübingen, Germany
Domenico Redavid	University of Bari, Italy
Dominik M. Endres	Philipps-Universität Marburg, Germany
Dominique Gay	Université de La Réunion, France
Dong Li	Baylor University, USA
Duarte Folgado	Fraunhofer Portugal AICOS, Portugal
Duo Xu	Georgia Institute of Technology, USA

Edoardo Serra	Boise State University, USA
Edouard Fouche	Karlsruhe Institute of Technology (KIT), Germany
Eduardo F. Montesuma	Université Paris-Saclay, France
Edward Apeh	Bournemouth University, UK
Edwin Simpson	University of Bristol, UK
Ehsan Aminian	INESC TEC, Portugal
Ekaterina Antonenko	Mines Paris - PSL, France
Eliana Pastor	Politecnico di Torino, Italy
Emanuela Marasco	George Mason University, USA
Emilio Dorigatti	LMU Munich, Germany
Emilio Parrado-Hernandez	Universidad Carlos III de Madrid, Spain
Emmanouil Krasanakis	CERTH, Greece
Emmanouil Panagiotou	Freie Universität Berlin, Germany
Emre Gursoy	Koc University, Turkey
Engelbert Mephu Nguifo	Université Clermont Auvergne, CNRS, LIMOS, France
Eran Treister	Ben-Gurion University of the Negev, Israel
Erasmo Purificato	Otto-von-Guericke Universität Magdeburg, Germany
Erik Novak	Jožef Stefan Institute, Slovenia
Erwan Le Merrer	Inria, France
Esra Akbas	Georgia State University, USA
Esther-Lydia Silva-Ramirez	Universidad de Cadiz, Spain
Evaldas Vaičiukynas	Kaunas University of Technology, Lithuania
Evangelos Kanoulas	University of Amsterdam, Netherlands
Evelin Amorim	INESC TEC, Portugal
Fabian C. Spaeh	Boston University, USA
Fabio Fassetti	Università della Calabria, Italy
Fabio Fumarola	Prometeia, Italy
Fabio Mercorio	University of Milan-Bicocca, Italy
Fabio Vandin	University of Padova, Italy
Fandel Lin	University of Southern California, USA
Federica Granese	Inria, Université Côte d'Azur, France
Federico Baldo	University of Bologna, Italy
Federico Sabbatini	National Institute for Nuclear Physics (INFN), Italy
Feifan Zhang	China Agricultural University, China
Felipe Kenji Nakano	KU Leuven, Belgium
Fernando Martinez-Plumed	Universitat Politècnica de Valencia, Spain
Filipe Rodrigues	Technical University of Denmark (DTU), Denmark

Flavio Giobergia	Politecnico di Torino, Italy
Florent Masseglia	Inria, France
Florian Beck	JKU Linz, Austria
Florian Lemmerich	University of Passau, Germany
Francesca Naretto	University of Pisa, Italy
Francesco Piccialli	University of Naples Federico II, Italy
Francesco Renna	Universidade do Porto, Portugal
Francisco Pereira	DTU, Denmark
Franco Raimondi	Gran Sasso Science Institute, Italy
Frederic Koriche	Université d'Artois, CRIL CNRS, France
Frederic Pennerath	CentraleSupélec - LORIA, France
Furong Peng	Shanxi University, China
Gabriel Marques Tavares	LMU Munich, Germany
Gabriele Sartor	University of Turin, Italy
Gabriele Venturato	KU Leuven, Belgium
Gaetan De Waele	Ghent University, Belgium
Gaia Saveri	University of Trieste, Italy
Gang Li	Deakin University, Australia
Gaoyuan Du	Amazon, USA
Gavin Smith	University of Nottingham, UK
Geming Xia	National University of Defense Technology, China
Geng Zhao	Heidelberg University, Germany
Gennaro Vessio	University of Bari Aldo Moro, Italy
Geoffrey I. Webb	Monash, Australia
Georgia Baltsou	Centre for Research & Technology, Greece
Geraldin Nanfack	Concordia University, Canada
Germain Forestier	University of Haute Alsace, France
Gerrit Grossmann	DFKI, Germany
Gerrit J. J. van den Burg	Alan Turing Institute, UK
Gherardo Varando	Universitat de Valencia, Spain
Giacomo Medda	University of Cagliari, Italy
Gilberto Bernardes	INESC TEC and University of Porto, Portugal
Giorgio Venturin	University of Padova, Italy
Giovanna Castellano	University of Bari Aldo Moro, Italy
Giovanni Ponti	ENEA, Italy
Giovanni Stilo	Università degli Studi dell'Aquila, Italy
Gisele Pappa	UFMG, Brazil
Giuseppe Manco	ICAR-CNR, IT, Italy
Gizem Gezici	Scuola Normale Superiore, Italy
Gjergji Kasneci	TU Munich, Germany
Goreti Marreiros	ISEP/GECAD, Portugal

Graziella De Martino	University of Bari, Aldo Moro, Italy
Grazina Korvel	Vilnius University, Lithuania
Grigorios Tsoumakas	Aristotle University of Thessaloniki, Greece
Guangyin Jin	National University of Defense Technology, China
Guangzhong Sun	University of Science and Technology of China, China
Guanjin Wang	Murdoch University, Australia
Guilherme Weigert	Cassales University of Waikato, New Zealand
Guillaume Derval	UC Louvain - ICTEAM, Belgium
Guorui Quan	University of Manchester, UK
Guoxi Zhang	Beijing Institute of General Artificial Intelligence, China
Gustau Camps-Valls	Universitat de Valencia, Spain
Gustav Sir	Czech Technical University, Czech Republic
Gustavo Batista	University of New South Wales, Australia
Hachem Kadri	Aix-Marseille University, France
Hadi Asghari	Humboldt Institute for Internet and Society, Germany
Haifeng Sun	University of Science and Technology of China, China
Haihui Fan	Institute of Information Engineering, Chinese Academy of Sciences, China
Haizhou Du	Shanghai University of Electric Power, China
Hajer Salem	AUDENSIEL, France
Hakim Hacid	TII, United Arab Emirates
Hamid Bouchachia	Bournemouth University, UK
Han Wang	Xidian University, China
Hang Yu	Shanghai University, China
Hanna Sumita	Institute of Science Tokyo, Japan
Hao Niu	KDDI Research, Japan
Hao Xue	University of New South Wales, Australia
Hao Yan	Carleton University, Canada
Haowen Zhang	Zhejiang Sci-Tech University, China
Harsh Borse	IIT Kharagpur, India
Heitor M. Gomes	Victoria University of Wellington, New Zealand
Helder Oliveira	FCUP and INESC TEC, Portugal
Helge Langseth	Norwegian University of Science and Technology, Norway
Hendrik Blockeel	KU Leuven, Belgium
Henrique O. Marques	University of Southern Denmark, Denmark
Henryk Maciejewski	Wroclaw University of Science and Technology, Poland

Hideaki Ishibashi	Kyushu Institute of Technology, Japan
Hilde J. P. Weerts	Eindhoven University of Technology, Netherlands
Holger Froening	University of Heidelberg, Germany
Holger Karl	HPI, Germany
Hongbo Bo	University of Bristol, UK
Hongyang Chen	Zhejiang Lab, China
Hua Chu	Xidian University, China
Huaiyu Wan	Beijing Jiaotong University, China
Huaming Chen	University of Sydney, Australia
Huandong Wang	Tsinghua University, China
Huanlai Xing	Southwest Jiaotong University, China
Hui Ji	University of Pittsburgh, USA
Hui (Wendy) Wang	Stevens Institute of Technology, USA
Huiping Chen	University of Birmingham, UK
Humberto Bustince	Universidad Publica de Navarra, Spain
Huong Ha	RMIT University, Australia
Idir Benouaret	Epita Research Laboratory, France
Ines Sousa	Fraunhofer AICOS, Portugal
Ingo Thon	Siemens AG, Germany
Inigo Jauregi Unanue	University of Technology Sydney, Australia
Ioannis Sarridis	Centre for Research & Technology, Greece
Issam Falih	Université Clermont Auvergne, CNRS, LIMOS, France
Ivan Vankov	iris.ai, Norway
Ivor Cribben	University of Alberta, Canada
Jaemin Yoo	KAIST, South Korea
Jakir Hossain	University at Buffalo, USA
Jakub Klikowski	Wroclaw University of Science and Technology, Poland
Jalaj Bhandari	Columbia University, USA
Jaleed Khan	University of Oxford, UK
James Goulding	University of Nottingham, UK
Jan Kalina	Czech Academy of Sciences, Czech Republic
Jan P. Mielniczuk	Polish Academy of Sciences, Poland
Jan Ramon	Inria, France
Jan Verwaeren	Ghent University, Belgium
Jannis Brugger	TU Darmstadt, Germany
Jean-Marc Andreoli	Naverlabs Europe, Netherlands
Jedrzej Potoniec	Poznań University of Technology, Poland
Jeronimo Arenas-Garcia	Universidad Carlos III de Madrid, Spain
Jhony H. Giraldo	Télécom Paris, Institut Polytechnique de Paris, France

Jia Cai	Guangdong University of Finance and Economics, China
Jiahui Jin	Southeast University, China
Jiang Zhong	Independent Researcher, China
Jianwu Wang	University of Maryland, Baltimore County, USA
Jiawei Chen	Tianjin University, China
Jiaxin Ding	Shanghai Jiao Tong University, China
Jidong Yuan	Beijing Jiaotong University, China
Jie Song	Zhejiang University, China
Jie Wu	Fudan University, China
Jie Yang	University of Wollongong, China
Jimeng Shi	Florida International University, USA
Jin Chen	Hong Kong University of Science and Technology, China
Jin Liang	South China Normal University, China
Jing Ren	NUDT, China
Jing Wang	Amazon, USA
Jinghui Zhong	South China University of Technology, China
Jingtao Ding	Tsinghua University, China
Jinli Zhang	Beijing University of Technology, China
Jiri Sima	Czech Academy of Sciences, Czech Republic
João Gama	University of Porto, Portugal
Joao Mendes-Moreira	University of Porto, Portugal
Joao Vinagre	European Commission (JRC), Spain
Joaquim Silva	NOVA LINCS, Universidade Nova de Lisboa, Portugal
Jochen De Weerdt	KU Leuven, Belgium
Joe Mellor	University of Edinburgh, UK
Johanne Cohen	LISN-CNRS, France
Johannes Jakubik	IBM Research, USA
John W. Sheppard	Montana State University, USA
Jonata Tyska Carvalho	Federal University of Santa Catarina, Brazil
Jordi Guitart	Barcelona Supercomputing Center (BSC), Spain
Joris Mattheijssens	Ghent University, Belgium
Jose M. Costa Pereira	University of Porto, Portugal
Jose Oramas	University of Antwerp, sqIRL/IDLab, imec, Belgium
Jose Tomas Palma	University of Murcia, Spain
Joydeep Chandra	Indian Institute of Technology, Patna, India
Juan A. Botia	University of Murcia, Spain
Juan Rodriguez	Universidad de Burgos, Spain
Jukka Heikkonen	University of Turku, Finland

Julien Delaunay	Inria, France
Julien Ferry	Polytechnique Montreal, Canada
Julien Perez	EPITA, France
Jun Zhuang	Boise State University, USA
Jun Yu Hou	Nanjing University, China
Junbo Zhang	JD Intelligent Cities Research, USA
Junze Liu	University of California, Irvine, USA
Jurgita Kapočiūtė-Dzikienė	Tilde SIA, University of Latvia and Tilde IT, Vytautas Magnus University, Lithuania
Justina Mandravickaitė	Vytautas Magnus University, Lithuania
Kamil Adamczewski	Max Planck Institute for Intelligent Systems, Germany
Kamil Michal Ksiazek	Jagiellonian University, Poland
Karim Radouane	Université Sorbonne Paris Nord, France
Kary Framing	Umeå University, Sweden
Katerina Taskova	University of Auckland, New Zealand
Katharina Dost	Jožef Stefan Institute, Slovenia
Kaushik Roy	University of South Carolina, USA
Kejia Chen	Nanjing University of Posts and Telecommunications, China
Ken Kobayashi	Tokyo Institute of Technology, Japan
Khaled Mohammed Saifuddin	Northeastern University, USA
Khalid Benabdeslem	Université de Lyon 1, France
Kim Thang Nguyen	LIG, University Grenoble-Alpes, France
Kira Maag	Heinrich-Heine-Universität Düsseldorf, Germany
Koji Maruhashi	Fujitsu Research, Japan
Koyel Mukherjee	Adobe Research, USA
Kristen M. Scott	KU Leuven, Belgium
Krzysztof Ruda	Polish Academy of Sciences, Poland
Krzysztof Slot	Lodz University of Technology, Poland
Kuldeep Singh	Cerence, Germany
Kushankur Ghosh	University of Alberta, Canada
Lamine Diop	EPITA, France
Latifa Oukhellou	IFSTTAR, France
Laurence Park	Western Sydney University, Australia
Laurens Devos	KU Leuven, Belgium
Len Feremans	Universiteit Antwerpen, Belgium
Lena Wiese	Goethe University Frankfurt, Germany
Lenaig Cornanguer	CISPA Helmholtz Center for Information Security, Germany
Lennert De Smet	KU Leuven, Belgium
Lev Reyzin	University of Illinois at Chicago, USA

Li Wang	National University of Defense Technology, China
Liang Du	Shanxi University, China
Lianyong Qi	China University of Petroleum (East China), China
Lijie Hu	King Abdullah University of Science and Technology, Saudi Arabia
Lijing Zhu	Bowling Green State University, USA
Lingling Zhang	Capital Normal University, China
Lingyue Fu	Shanghai Jiao Tong University, China
Linh Le Pham Van	Deakin University, Australia
Livio Bioglio	University of Turin, Italy
Lixing Yu	Yunnan University, China
Liyan Song	Harbin Institute of Technology, China
Longlong Sun	Chang'an University, China
Luca Corbucci	University of Pisa, Italy
Luca Ferragina	University of Calabria, Italy
Luca Romeo	University of Macerata, Italy
Lucas Pereira	LARSyS, Tecnico Lisboa, Portugal
Luciano Caroprese	ICAR-CNR, Italy
Ludovico Boratto	University of Cagliari, Italy
Luis Rei	Jožef Stefan Institute, Slovenia
Mahardhika Pratama	University of South Australia, Australia
Maiju Karjalainen	University of Eastern Finland, Finland
Makoto Onizuka	Osaka University, Japan
Manali Sharma	Samsung, South Korea
Maneet Singh	MasterCard, India
Manuel M. Garcia-Piqueras	Universidad de Castilla La Mancha, Spain
Manuele Bicego	University of Verona, Italy
Mao A. Cheng	University of California, Berkeley, USA
Marc Plantevit	EPITA, France
Marc Tommasi	Lille University, France
Marcel Wever	Leibniz University Hannover, Germany
Marcilio de Souto	LIFO/Université d'Orleans, France
Marco Lippi	University of Florence, Italy
Marco Loog	Radboud University, Netherlands
Marco Mellia	Politecnico di Torino, Italy
Marco Podda	University of Pisa, Italy
Marco Polignano	Università di Bari, Italy
Marco Viviani	Università degli Studi di Milano Bicocca, Italy
Maria Vasconcelos	Fraunhofer Portugal AICOS, Portugal
Maria Sofia Bucarelli	Sapienza University of Rome, Italy

Mariana Oliveira	Universidade do Porto, Portugal
Mariana Vargas Vieyra	MostlyAI, Austria
Marielle Malfante	CEA, France
Marina Litvak	Shamoon College of Engineering, Israel
Mario Antunes	Universidade de Aveiro, Portugal
Mario Andres Munoz	University of Melbourne, Australia
Marius Koppel	Johannes Gutenberg University Mainz, Germany
Mark Junjie Li	Shenzhen University, China
Marko Robnik-Sikonja	University of Ljubljana, Slovenia
Marta Soare	Université d'Orleans, France
Martin Holena	Czech Academy of Sciences, Czech Republic
Martin Pilat	Charles University, Czech Republic
Martino Ciaperoni	Aalto University, Finland
Marwan Hassani	TU Eindhoven, Netherlands
Masahiro Suzuki	University of Tokyo, Japan
Massimo Guarascio	ICAR-CNR, Italy
Matej Mihelcic	University of Zagreb, Croatia
Mathias Verbeke	KU Leuven, Belgium
Mathieu Lefort	Université de Lyon, France
Matteo Francobaldi	University of Bologna, Italy
Matteo Riondato	Amherst College, USA
Matteo Salis	University of Turin, Italy
Matthew B. Middlehurst	University of Southampton, UK
Matthia Sabatelli	University of Groningen, Netherlands
Mattia Cerrato	JGU Mainz, Germany
Mattia Setzu	University of Pisa, Italy
Mattis Hartwig	German Research Center for Artificial Intelligence, Germany
Matyas Bohacek	Stanford University, USA
Maximilian T. Fischer	University of Konstanz, Germany
Maximilian Münch	University of Applied Sciences, Würzburg-Schweinfurt, Germany
Maximilian Stubbemann	University of Hildesheim, Germany
Maximilian Thiessen	TU Wien, Austria
Maximilian von Zastrow	Southern Denmark University, Denmark
Megha Khosla	TU Delft, Netherlands
Meiyun Zuo	Renmin University of China, China
Meng Liu	National University of Defense Technology, China
Mengying Zhu	Zhejiang University, China
Michael Granitzer	University of Passau, Germany
Michael B. Ito	University of Michigan, USA

Michael G. Madden	National University of Ireland, Galway, Ireland
Michal Wozniak	Wroclaw University of Science and Technology, Poland
Michele Fontana	Università di Pisa, Italy
Michiel Stock	Ghent University, Belgium
Miguel Rocha	University of Minho, Portugal
Miguel Silva	INESC TEC, Portugal
Mike Holenderski	Eindhoven University of Technology, Netherlands
Milos Savic	University of Novi Sad, Serbia
Mina Rezaei	LMU Munich, Germany
Minh P. Nguyen	University of Texas, Austin, USA
Minyoung Choe	Korea Advanced Institute of Science and Technology, South Korea
Minyu Chen	Shanghai Jiaotong University, China
Miquel Perello-Nieto	University of Bristol, UK
Mira Kristin Jurgens	Ghent University, Belgium
Miriam Santos	University of Porto, Portugal
Mirko Bunse	TU Dortmund, Germany
Mirko Polato	University of Turin, Italy
Mitra Baratchi	LIACS, University of Leiden, Netherlands
Mohammed Elbamby	Telefonica Scientific Research, Spain
Moises Rocha dos Santos	University of Porto, Portugal
Monowar Bhuyan	Umeå University, Sweden
Morteza Rakhshaninejad	Ghent University, Belgium
Mounim A. El Yacoubi	Télécom SudParis, France
Muhammad Rajabinasab	University of Southern Denmark, Denmark
Muhao Guo	Arizona State University, USA
Mustapha Lebbah	Paris Saclay University-Versailles, France
Nabeel Hussain Syed	Rheinland-Pfälzische Technische Universität, Kaiserslautern-Landau, Germany
Nandyala Hemachandra	Indian Institute of Technology Bombay, India
Nannan Wu	Tianjin University, China
Nanqing Dong	Shanghai Artificial Intelligence Laboratory, China
Naresh Manwani	International Institute of Information Technology, Hyderabad, India
Natan Tourne	Ghent University, Belgium
Nate Veldt	Texas A&M, USA
Nathalie Japkowicz	American University, USA
Natthawut Kertkeidkachorn	Japan Advanced Institute of Science and Technology (JAIST), Japan
Ngoc-Son Vu	ENSEA, France
Nhat-Tan Bui	University of Arkansas, USA

Nian Li	Tsinghua University, China
Nick Lim	University of Waikato, New Zealand
Nico Piatkowski	Fraunhofer IAIS, Germany
Nicolas Roque dos Santos	University of São Paulo, Brazil
Niklas A. Strauss	LMU Munich, Germany
Nikolaj Tatti	Helsinki University, Finland
Nikolaos Nikolaou	University College London, UK
Nikolaos Stylianou	Information Technologies Institute, Greece
Nikos Kanakaris	University of Southern California, USA
Ning Xu	Southeast University, China
Nripsuta Saxena	University of Southern California, USA
Nuwan Gunasekara	Halmstad University, Sweden
Olga Kurasova	Vilnius University, Lithuania
Olga Slizovskaia	AstraZeneca, UK
Olivier Teste	IRIT, University of Toulouse, France
Oswald C.	NIT Trichy, India
Oswaldo Solarte-Pabon	Universidad del Valle, Colombia
Ozge Alacam	University of Bielefeld, Germany
P. S. Sastry	Indian Institute of Science, India
Pablo Olmos	Universidad Carlos III de Madrid, Spain
Panagiotis Karras	University of Copenhagen, Denmark
Panagiotis Symeonidis	University of the Aegean, Greece
Pance Panov	Jožef Stefan Institute, Slovenia
Paolo Bonetti	Politecnico di Milano, Italy
Paolo Merialdo	Università degli Studi Roma Tre, Italy
Paolo Mignone	University of Bari Aldo Moro, Italy
Pascal Welke	TU Wien, Austria
Patrick Y. Wu	American University, USA
Paul Caillon	LAMSADE Université Paris Dauphine - PSL, France
Paul Davidsson	Malmo University, Sweden
Paul Prasse	University of Potsdam, Germany
Paulo J. Azevedo	Universidade do Minho, Portugal
Pawel Teisseyre	Warsaw University of Technology, Poland
Pawel Zyblewski	Wroclaw University of Science and Technology, Poland
Pedro G. Ferreira	University of Porto, Portugal
Pedro Larrañaga	Technical University of Madrid, Spain
Pedro Ribeiro	University of Porto, Portugal
Pedro H. Abreu	CISUC, Portugal
Peijie Sun	Tsinghua University, China
Peng Wu	Shanghai Jiao Tong University, China

Pengpeng Qiao	Institute of Science Tokyo, Japan
Peter Karsmakers	KU Leuven, Belgium
Peter Schneider-Kamp	SDU, Denmark
Peter van der Putten	Leiden University, Netherlands
Petia Georgieva	University of Aveiro, Portugal
Philipp Vaeth	Technical University of Applied Sciences Würzburg-Schweinfurt and Universität Bielefeld, Germany
Philippe Preux	Inria, France
Phung Lai	SUNY-Albany, USA
Pierre Geurts	Montefiore Institute, University of Liège, Belgium
Pierre Monnin	Université Côte d'Azur, Inria, CNRS, I3S, France
Pierre Schaus	UC Louvain, Belgium
Pierre Wolinski	Paris Dauphine University - PSL, France
Pieter Robberechts	KU Leuven, Belgium
Pietro Sabatino	ICAR-CNR, Italy
Pingchuan Ma	HKUST, China
Piotr Habas	Amazon, USA
Piotr Lipinski	University of Wroclaw, Poland
Piotr Porwik	University of Silesia, Katowice, Poland
Prithwish Chakraborty	IBM Corporation, USA
Lucie Flek	Marburg University, Germany
Przemyslaw Biecek	Warsaw University of Technology, Poland
Qiang Sheng	Institute of Computing Technology, Chinese Academy of Sciences, China
Qiang Zhou	Nanjing University of Aeronautics and Astronautics, China
Rafet Sifa	Fraunhofer IAIS, Germany
Raha Moraffah	Arizona State University, USA
Raivydas Simanas	Vilnius University, Lithuania
Rajeev Rastogi	Amazon, USA
Ranya Almohsen	Baylor College of Medicine, USA
Raphael Romero	Ghent University, Belgium
Raquel Sebastiao	ESTGV-IPV & IEETA-UA, Portugal
Ravi Kolla	Sony Research India, India
Raza Ul Mustafa	Loyola University, USA
Remy Cazabet	Université de Lyon 1, France
Renhe Jiang	University of Tokyo, Japan
Reza Akbarinia	Inria, France
Ricardo P. M. Cruz	University of Porto (FEUP), Portugal
Ricardo B. Prudencio	Universidade Federal de Pernambuco, Brazil
Ricardo Rios	Federal University of Bahia, Brazil

Ricardo Santos	Fraunhofer Portugal AICOS, Portugal
Riccardo Guidotti	University of Pisa, Italy
Robertas Damasevicius	Vytautas Magnus University, Lithuania
Roberto Corizzo	American University, USA
Roberto Interdonato	CIRAD, France
Rocio Chongtay	University of Southern Denmark, Denmark
Rohit Babbar	University of Bath, UK and Aalto University, Finland
Romain Tavenard	Université de Rennes, LETG/IRISA, France
Rosana Veroneze	LBiC, Italy
Ruggero G. Pensa	University of Turin, Italy
Rui Meng	BNU-HKBU United International College, USA
Rui Yu	University of Louisville, USA
Ruixuan Liu	Emory University, USA
Runqun Xiong	Southeast University, China
Runxue Bao	University of Pittsburgh, USA
Ruochun Jin	National University of Defense Technology, China
Ruta Juozaitiene	Vytautas Magnus University, Lithuania
Rytis Maskeliunas	PolsI, Poland
Salvatore Ruggieri	University of Pisa, Italy
Sam Verboven	Vrije Universiteit Brussel, Belgium
Sangkyun Lee	Korea University, South Korea
Sara Abdali	University of California, Riverside, USA
Sarah Masud	LCS2, IIIT-D, India
Sarwan Ali	Georgia State University, USA
Satoru Koda	Fujitsu Limited, Japan
Sebastian Buschjager	Lamarr Institute for ML and AI, Germany
Sebastian Jimenez	Ghent University, Belgium
Sebastian Meznar	Jožef Stefan Institute, Ljubljana, Slovenia
Sebastian Ventura Soto	University of Cordoba, Spain
Sebastien Razakarivony	Safran, France
Selpi Selpi	Chalmers University of Technology, Sweden
Sergio Greco	University of Calabria, Italy
Sergio Jesus	Feedzai, Portugal
Sha Lu	University of South Australia, Australia
Shalini Priya	Indian Institute of Technology Patna, India
Shanqing Guo	Shandong University, China
Shaofu Yang	Southeast University, China
Shazia Tabassum	INESCTEC, Portugal
Shengxiang Gao	Kunming University of Science and Technology, China

Shichao Pei	University of Massachusetts, Boston, USA
Shin Matsushima	University of Tokyo, Japan
Shin-ichi Maeda	Preferred Networks, Japan
Shiwen Ni	Chinese Academy of Sciences, China
Shiyou Qian	Shanghai Jiao Tong University, China
Shu Zhao	Anhui University, China
Shuai Li	University of Cambridge, UK and University of Tokyo, Japan, Tsinghua University, China
Shuang Cheng	Institute of Computing Technology, Chinese Academy of Sciences, China
Shubhranshu Shekhar	Brandeis University, USA
Shurui Cao	Carnegie Mellon University, USA
Shuteng Niu	Mayo Clinic, USA
Siamak Ghodsi	Leibniz University of Hannover, Germany
Sihai Zhang	University of Science and Technology of China, China
Silvia Chiusano	Politecnico di Torino, Italy
Silviu Maniu	Université de Grenoble Alpes, France
Simon Gottschalk	L3S Research Center, Leibniz Universität Hannover, Germany
Simona Nistico	University of Calabria, Italy
Simone Angarano	Politecnico di Torino, Italy
Sinong Zhao	Nankai University, China
Siwei Wang	Intelligent Game and Decision Lab, China
Sofoklis Kitharidis	LIACS, Netherlands
Songlin Du	University of Melbourne, Australia
Songlin Du	Southeast University, China
Soumyajit Chatterjee	Nokia Bell Labs, USA
Sourav Dutta	Huawei Research Centre, China
Stefan Duffner	University of Lyon, France
Stefan Heindorf	Paderborn University, Germany
Stefan Kesselheim	Forschungszentrum Jülich, Germany
Stefano Bortoli	Huawei Research Center, China
Stefanos Vrochidis	Information Technologies Institute, CERTH, Greece
Steffen Thoma	FZI Research Center for Information Technology, Germany
Stephan Doerfel	Kiel University of Applied Sciences, Germany
Steven D. Prestwich	University College Cork, Ireland
Suman Banerjee	IIT Jammu, India
Sunil Aryal	Deakin University, Australia
Surabhi Adhikari	Columbia University, USA

Susan McKeever	TU Dublin, Ireland
Swati Swati	Universität der Bundeswehr München, Germany
Szymon Wojciechowski	Wroclaw University of Science and Technology, Poland
Talip Ucar	AstraZeneca, UK
Taro Tezuka	University of Tsukuba, Japan
Tatiana Passali	Aristotle University of Thessaloniki, Greece
Tatiane Nogueira Rios	UFBA, Brazil
Telmo M. Silva Filho	University of Bristol, UK
Teng Lin	Hong Kong University of Technology (Guangzhou), China
Teng Zhang	Huazhong University of Science and Technology, China
Thach Le Nguyen	Insight Centre, Ireland
Thang Duy Dang	Fujitsu Limited, Japan
Thanh-Son Nguyen	A*STAR, Singapore
Theresa Eimer	Leibniz University Hannover, Germany
Thiago Andrade	INESC TEC & University of Porto, Portugal
Thomas Bonald	Telecom Paris, France
Thomas Guyet	Inria, Centre de Lyon, France
Thomas Lampert	University of Strasbourg, France
Thomas L. Lee	University of Edinburgh, UK
Thomas Mortier	Ghent University, Belgium
Tianyi Chen	Boston University, USA
Tie Luo	University of Kentucky, USA
Tiehang Duan	Mayo Clinic, USA
Tijl De Bie	Ghent University, Belgium
Timilehin B. Aderinola	University College Dublin, Ireland
Timo Bertram	Johannes-Kepler Universität, Germany
Timo Ropinski	Ulm University, Germany
Tobias A. Hille	University of Kassel, Germany
Tom Hanika	University of Hildesheim, Germany
Tomas Kliegr	University of Economics, Prague, Czech Republic
Tomasz Michalak	University of Warsaw and Ideas NCBiR, Poland
Tomasz Walkowiak	Wroclaw University of Science and Technology, Poland
Tommaso Zoppi	University of Florence, Italy
Tong Li	Hong Kong University of Technology, China
Tong Mo	Peking University, China
Tongya Zheng	Hangzhou City University, China
Tonio Weidler	Maastricht University, Netherlands
Tony Lindgren	Stockholm University, Sweden

Tsunenori Mine	Kyushu University, Japan
Tuan Le	New Mexico State University, USA
Tuwe Lofstrom	Jönköping University, Sweden
Ulf Johansson	Jönköping University, Sweden
Vadim Ermolayev	Ukrainian Catholic University, Ukraine
Vahan Martirosyan	CentraleSupélec, Belgium
Vana Kalogeraki	Athens University of Economics and Business, Greece
Vanessa Gomez-Verdejo	Universidad Carlos III de Madrid, Spain
Vasileios Iosifidis	SCHUFA Holding, Germany
Vasilis Gkolemis	ATHENA RC, Greece
Victor Charpenay	Mines Saint-Etienne, France
Vincent Derkinderen	KU Leuven, Belgium
Vincent Lemaire	Orange Research, France
Vincenzo Pasquadibisceglie	University of Bari, Aldo Moro, Italy
Virginijus Marcinkevicius	Vilnius University, Lithuania
Vitor Cerqueira	University of Porto, Portugal
Vivek Kumar	Universität der Bundeswehr München, Germany
Vivek Srikumar	University of Utah, USA
Wagner Meira Jr.	UFMG, Brazil
Wei Wu	Ben Gurion University of the Negev, Israel
Weichen Li	RPTU Kaiserslautern-Landau, Germany
Weifeng Xu	Independent Researcher, China
Weike Pan	Shenzhen University, China
Weiwei Jiang	Beijing University of Posts and Telecommunications, China
Weiwei Sun	Carnegie Mellon University, USA
Weiwei Yuan	Nanjing University of Aeronautics and Astronautics, China
Weixiong Rao	Tongji University, China
Wen-Bo Xie	Southwest Petroleum University, China
Wenhao Li	Tongji University, China
Wenhao Zheng	Shopee, Singapore
Wenjie Feng	National University of Singapore, Singapore
Wenjie Xi	George Mason University, USA
Wenshui Luo	Nanjing University of Science and Technology, China
Wentao Yu	Nanjing University of Science and Technology, China
Wenzhe Yi	Wuhan University, China
Wenzhong Li	Nanjing University, China
Wojciech Rejchel	Nicolaus Copernicus University, Torun, Poland

Xi Jiang	Southern University of Science and Technology, China
Xiang Li	East China Normal University, China
Xiang Lian	Kent State University, USA
Xiao Ma	Beijing University of Posts and Telecommunications, China
Xiao Zhang	Shandong University, China
Xiaobing Zhou	Yunnan University, China
Xiaofeng Cao	University of Technology Sydney, Australia
Xiaofeng Gao	Shanghai Jiaotong University, China
Xiaojun Chen	Institute of Information Engineering, Chinese Academy of Sciences, China
Xiao-Jun Zeng	University of Manchester, UK
Xiaoming Zhang	Beihang University, China
Xiaoting Zhao	Etsy, USA
Xiaowei Mao	Beijing Jiaotong University, China
Xiaoyu Shi	Chinese Academy of Sciences, China
Xin Du	University of Edinburgh, UK
Xin Qin	California State University, Long Beach, USA
Xing Tang	Tencent, China
Xing Xing	Tongji University, China
Xinning Zhu	Beijing University of Posts and Telecommunications, China
Xinpeng Lv	National University of Defense Technology, China
Xintao Wu	University of Arkansas, USA
Xinyang Zhang	University of Illinois at Urbana-Champaign, USA
Xinyu Guan	Xi'an Jiaotong University, China
Xixun Lin	Chinese Academy of Sciences, China
Xiyue Zhang	University of Bristol, UK
Xuan-Hong Dang	IBM T.J. Watson Research Center, USA
Xue Li	University of Queensland, Australia
Xue Yan	Institute of Automation, Chinese Academy of Sciences, China
Xuefeng Chen	Chongqing University, China
Xuemin Wang	Guilin University of Electronic Technology, China
Yachuan Zhang	East China University of Science and Technology, China
Yan Zhang	Peking University, China
Yang Li	University of North Carolina at Chapel Hill, USA
Yang Shu	East China Normal University, China
Yang Wei	Nanjing University of Science and Technology, China

Yanhao Wang	East China Normal University, China
Yanmin Zhu	Shanghai Jiao Tong University, China
Yansong Y. L. Li	University of Ottawa, Canada
Yao-Xiang Ding	Nanjing University, China
Yaqi Xie	Carnegie Mellon University, USA
Yasutoshi Ida	NTT, Japan
Yaying Zhang	Tongji University, China
Ye Zhu	Deakin University, Australia
Yeon-Chang Lee	Ulsan National Institute of Science and Technology, South Korea
Yexiang Xue	Purdue University, USA
Yi Wang	Xinjiang Technical Institute of Physics and Chemistry, Chinese Academy of Sciences, China
Yifeng Gao	University of Texas, Rio Grande Valley, USA
Yilun Jin	Hong Kong University of Science and Technology, China
Yin Zhang	University of Electronic Science and Technology of China, China
Ying Chen	RMIT University, Australia
Yinsheng Li	Fudan University, China
Yong Li	Huawei European Research Center, China
Yongyu Wang	JD Logistics, China
Youhei Akimoto	University of Tsukuba/RIKEN AIP, Japan
You-Wei Luo	Sun Yat-sen University and Jiaying University, China
Yuchen Li	Baidu, China
Yuchen Yang	Harbin Institute of Technology, China
Yudi Zhang	Eindhoven University of Technology, Netherlands
Yuhao Li	University of Melbourne, Australia
Yuheng Jia	Southeast University, China
Yujia Zheng	CMU, USA
Yulong Pei	TU Eindhoven, Netherlands
Yuncheng Jiang	South China Normal University, China
Yuntao Shou	Xi'an Jiaotong University, China
Yunyun Wang	Nanjing University of Posts and Telecommunications, China
Yutong Ye	East China Normal University, China
Yuzhou Chen	University of California, Riverside, USA
Zahraa Abdallah	University of Bristol, UK
Zaineb Chelly Dagdia	UVSQ, Paris-Saclay, France
Zehua Cheng	University of Oxford, UK
Zeyu Chen	University of Auckland, New Zealand

Zhaocheng Ge	Huazhong University of Science and Technology, China
Zhe Yang	Soochow University, China
Zhen Liu	Guangdong University of Foreign Studies, China
Zheng Chen	Osaka University, Japan
Zhenghao Liu	Northeastern University, China
Zhenyu Yang	Macquarie University, Australia
Zhi Li	Tsinghua University, China
Zhichao Han	ETHZ, Switzerland
Zhihui Wang	Fudan University, China
Zhilong Shan	South China Normal University, China
Zhipeng Yin	Florida International University, USA
Zhipeng Zou	Nanjing University of Science and Technology, China
Zhiwen Xiao	Southwest Jiaotong University, China
Zhiwen Zhang	LocationMind, Japan
Zhixin Li	Guangxi Normal University, China
Zhiyong Cheng	Shandong Academy of Sciences, China
Zhong Chen	Southern Illinois University, USA
Zhong Li	Leiden University, Netherlands
Zhong Zhang	Tsinghua University, China
Zhongjing Yu	Peking University, China
Zhuang Liu	Dongbei University of Finance and Economics, China
Zhuo Cao	Forschungszentrum Jülich, Germany
Zhuoming Xie	Guangdong University of Technology, China
Zhuoqun Li	Louisiana State University, USA
Zicheng Zhao	Nanjing University of Science and Technology, China
Zichong Wang	Florida International University, USA
Zifeng Ding	University of Cambridge, UK
Ziheng Chen	Walmart, USA
Zijie J. Wang	Georgia Tech, USA
Zirui Zhuang	Beijing University of Posts and Telecommunications, China
Zixing Song	Chinese University of Hong Kong, China
Ziyu Wang	University of Tokyo, Japan
Ziyue Li	University of Cologne, Germany
Zongxia Xie	Tianjin University, China
Zongyue Li	LMU Munich, Germany
Zuojin Tang	Zhejiang University, China

List of Editors

Bernhard Pfahringer	University of Waikato, New Zealand
Nathalie Japkowicz	American University, USA
Pedro Larrañaga	Technical University of Madrid, Spain
Rita P. Ribeiro	University of Porto, Portugal
Alípio M. Jorge	University of Porto, Portugal
Carlos Soares	University of Porto, Portugal
João Gama	University of Porto, Portugal
Pedro H. Abreu	University of Coimbra, Portugal

Program Committee – Applied Data Science Track

Nasrullah Sheikh	IBM Research, USA
Aakarsh Malhotra	MasterCard, USA
Aakash Goel	Amazon, USA
Abdoulaye Sakho	Artefact, France
Abhijeet Pendyala	Ruhr-Universität Bochum, Germany
Abu Shad Ahammed	University of Siegen, Germany
Adi Lin	Didi, China
Aditya Gautam	Meta, USA
Ahmed K. Mohamed	Meta, USA
Akihiro Yoshida	Kyushu University, Japan
Akshay Sethi	MasterCard, USA
Alejandro Kuratomi	Stockholm University, Sweden
Alessandro Gambetti	Nova School of Business and Economics, Portugal
Alessandro Leite	INSA Rouen, Inria, France
Alessio Russo	Politecnico di Milano, Italy
Alex Beeson	University of Warwick, UK
Alexander Galozy	Halmstad University, Sweden
Alexander Karlsson	University of Skovde, Sweden
Alexander Kovalenko	Czech Technical University in Prague, Czech Republic
Alexey Zaytsev	Skoltech, Russia
Alina Bazarova	Forschungszentrum Jülich, Germany
Alix Lheritier	Amadeus SAS, France
Allan Tucker	Brunel University London, UK
Alvaro Figueira	CRACS and Universidade do Porto, Portugal
Aman Gulati	Amazon, USA
Amira Soliman	Halmstad University, Sweden

Ana Gjorgjevikj — Jožef Stefan Institute, Slovenia
Anders Holst — RISE SICS, Sweden
André C. P. L. F. de Carvalho — University of São Paulo, Brazil
Andrea Seveso — University of Milan-Bicocca, Italy
Andreas Bender — LMU Munich, Germany
Andreas Henelius — Independent Researcher, Finland
Andreas Holzinger — University of Natural Resources and Life Sciences, Vienna, Austria
Andrei Shelopugin — Independent Researcher, Brazil
Angelo Impedovo — Niuma, Italy
Aniket Chakrabarti — Amazon, USA
Animesh Prasad — Roku, USA
Anisio Lacerda — UFMG, Brazil
Anli Ji — Georgia State University, USA
Antoine Doucet — La Rochelle Université, France
Anton Borg — Blekinge Institute of Technology, Sweden
Antonio Bevilacqua — Meetecho, Italy
Antonis Klironomos — University of Mannheim, Germany
Aron Henriksson — Stockholm University, Sweden
Artur Chudzik — Polish-Japanese Academy of Information Technology, Poland
Arun Venkitaraman — EPFL, Switzerland
Arunabha Choudhury — ASML, Netherlands
Asem Omari — Higher Colleges of Technology, UAE
Ashman Mehra — Birla Institute of Technology and Science, India
Ashwani Rao — Amazon, USA
Asier Rodriguez — BBVA, Spain
Asma Atamna — Ruhr-Universität Bochum, Germany
Atiye Sadat Hashemi — Halmstad University, Sweden
Atul Anand Gopalakrishnan — SUNY Buffalo, USA
Avani Wildani — Emory University, USA
Aviv Rovshitz — Ben-Gurion University of the Negev, Israel
Axel Brando — Barcelona Supercomputing Center (BSC) and Universitat de Barcelona (UB), Spain
Azadeh Alavi — RMIT University, Australia
Beihong Jin — Institute of Software, China
Benoit Frenay — University of Namur, Belgium
Berkay Aydin — Georgia State University, USA
Bijaya Adhikari — University of Iowa, USA
Bin Li — Alibaba Group, China
Bo Pang — University of Auckland, New Zealand
Bogdan Ruszczak — Opole University of Technology, Poland

Bohao Qu	Agency for Science, China
Bruno Veloso	INESC TEC, FEP-UP, Portugal
Buyue Qian	Xi'an Jiaotong University, China
Camille Kurtz	Université Paris Cité, France
Cangbai Li	Guangdong University of Technology, China
Carlo Metta	ISTI CNR, Italy
Carlos N. Silla	Pontifical Catholic University of Paraná (PUCPR), Brazil
Cecile Bothorel	IMT Atlantique, France
Cesar Ferri	Universitat Politècnica Valencia, Spain
Chang Li	Apple, USA
Chang-Dong Wang	Sun Yat-sen University, China
Chaofan Li	Karlsruhe Institute of Technology, Germany
Chaoyuan Zuo	Nankai University, China
Chen Gao	Tsinghua University, China
Chen Li	Computer Network Information Center, China
Chen Zhao	Baylor University, USA
Chen-Wei Chang	Virginia Tech, USA
Chenxi Xue	Nanjing Normal University, China
Chongke Bi	Tianjin University, China
Christian M. Adriano	Hasso-Plattner Institute, Germany
Christophe Rodrigues	DVRC Pôle universitaire Léonard de Vinci, France
Chuan Li	Sorbonne University, LIPADE, France
Chunhui Zhang	Dartmouth College, USA
Cristina Soguero Ruiz	Rey Juan Carlos University, Spain
Daheng Wang	Amazon, USA
Daifeng Li	Sun Yat-sen University, China
Damien Fay	HPE Labs, Ireland
Dania Herzalla	Technology Innovation Institute, UAE
Daniel Lemire	University of Quebec (TELUQ), Canada
Daniel Trejo Banos	SDSC, USA
Daochen Zha	Rice University, USA
Dawei Cheng	Tongji University, China
Dayne Freitag	SRI International, USA
Di Yao	Institute of Computing Technology, China
Dimitris Nick Dimitriadis	Aristotle University of Thessaloniki, Greece
Diogo F. Soares	Universidade de Lisboa, Portugal
Dirk Pflueger	University of Stuttgart, Germany
Doheon Han	University of Notre Dame, USA
Dongxiang Zhang	Zhejiang University, China
Dongxiao Yu	Shandong University, China

Dugang Liu	Guangdong Laboratory of Artificial Intelligence and Digital Economy (Shenzen), China
Ece Calikus	Uppsala University, Sweden
Edwyn Brient	Thales LAS/Mines Paris PSL, France
Efstathios Stamatatos	University of the Aegean, Greece
Elaine Faria	UFU, Brazil
Elio Masciari	University of Naples, Italy
Emilie Devijver	Université Grenoble Alpes, Inria, CNRS, Grenoble INP, LIG, France
Emmanuelle Claeys	IRIT, France
Enayat Rajabi	Halmstad University, Sweden
Enda Barrett	University of Galway, Ireland
Enyan Dai	Hong Kong University of Science and Technology (Guangzhou), China
Eric Peukert	ScaDS.AI, Germany
Eric Sanjuan	Avignon University, France
Erik Frisk	Linköping University, Sweden
Eui-Hong (Sam) Han	The Washington Post, USA
Eunil Park	Sungkyunkwan University, South Korea
Fabio Carrara	CNR-ISTI, Italy
Fabiola Pereira	Federal University of Uberlandia, Brazil
Fan Yang	Rice University, USA
Fangzhao Wu	MSRA, China
Fangzhou Shi	Didi Chuxing, China
Fathima Nuzla Ismail	State University of New York, USA
Flavio Bertini	University of Parma, Italy
Francesco Dente	EURECOM, France
Francesco Guerra	University of Modena e Reggio Emilia, Italy
Francesco Scala	CNR-ICAR, Italy
Francesco Spinnato	University of Pisa, Italy
Francesco Paolo Nerini	Sapienza University of Rome, Italy
Francisco P. Romero	UCLM, Spain
Franco Maria Nardini	ISTI-CNR, Italy
Francois Schwarzentruber	ENS Lyon, France
Fudong Lin	University of Delaware, USA
Gabriel Augusto Pinheiro	UNIFESP, Brazil
Gan Sun	South China University of Technology, China
Gargi Srivastava	Rajiv Gandhi Institute of Petroleum Technology Jais, India
Giacomo Boracchi	Politecnico di Milano, Italy
Giuseppe Garofalo	DistriNet, KU Leuven, Belgium
Giuseppina Andresini	University of Bari Aldo Moro, Italy

Goran Falkman	University of Skovde, Sweden
Grzegorz Nalepa	Jagiellonian University, Poland
Guanggang Geng	Jinan University, China
Guojun Liang	Halmstad University, Sweden
Haifang Li	Baidu, China
Haina Tang	University of Chinese Academy of Sciences, China
Hancheng Ge	Amazon, USA
Hao Li	National University of Defense Technology, China
Haohui Chen	CSIRO, Australia
Haomin Yu	Aalborg University, Denmark
Haoyi Xiong	Baidu, China
Hiba Najjar	DFKI, Germany
Hillol Kargupta	Agnik, USA
Hong Zhou	Meta, USA
Hongbin Pei	Xi'an Jiao Tong University, China
Hou-Wan Long	Chinese University of Hong Kong, China
Hua Wei	Arizona State University, USA
Huaiyuan Yao	Xi'an Jiaotong University, China
Huan Song	Amazon, USA
Hubert Baniecki	University of Warsaw, Poland
Hyunsung Kim	KAIST, Fitogether, South Korea
Ibtihal El Mimouni	Inria, France
Ildar Baimuratov	L3S Research Center, Germany
Ilir Jusufi	Blekinge Institute of Technology, Sweden
Inaam Ashraf	Bielefeld University, Germany
Ines Sousa	Fraunhofer AICOS, Portugal
Iris Heerlien	Saxion, Netherlands
Isak Samsten	Stockholm University, Sweden
Ishan Verma	TCS Research, India
Ismail Hakki Toroslu	METU, Turkey
Ivan Carrera	EPN, Ecuador
Jaakko Hollmen	Stockholm University, Sweden
Jairo Cugliari	Laboratoire ERIC, France
Jakub Nalepa	Silesian University of Technology, Poland
Jelica Vasiljević	Hoffmann-La Roche, Switzerland
Jens Lundstrom	Halmstad University, Sweden
Jesse Davis	KU Leuven, Belgium
Jiahui Bai	Meta, USA
Jiajun Gu	Carnegie Mellon University, USA
Jiali Pan	Department of Information Management, USA

Jian Yu	Auckland University of Technology, New Zealand
Jiangbin Zheng	Westlake University, China
Jianhua Yin	Shandong University, China
Jingbo Zhou	Baidu, China
Jingjing Liu	MD Anderson Cancer Center, USA
Jingwen Shi	Michigan State University, USA
Jingxuan Wei	University of Chinese Academy of Sciences, China
Jinyoung Han	Sungkyunkwan University, South Korea
Jiue-An Yang	City of Hope Beckman Research Institute, USA
Joao R. Campos	University of Coimbra, Portugal
Jochen De Weerdt	KU Leuven, Belgium
Joe Tekli	Lebanese American University, Lebanon
Joel Ky	University of Lorraine, CNRS, Inria, France
John McCall	Robert Gordon University, UK
John Mitros	University College Dublin, Ireland
Jonas Fischer	Ruhr-Universität Bochum, Germany
Jonas Nordqvist	Linnaeus University, Sweden
Joydeep Chandra	Indian Institute of Technology Patna, India
Julian Martin Rodemann	LMU Munich, Germany
Jun Shen	University of Wollongong, Australia
Junichi Tatemura	Google, USA
Junxuan Li	Microsoft, USA
Jyun-Yu Jiang	Amazon Science, USA
Kai Wang	Shanghai Jiao Tong University, China
Kaiping Zheng	National University of Singapore, Singapore
Kaiwen Dong	University of Notre Dame, USA
Katarzyna Bozek	University of Cologne, Germany
Katerina Schindlerova	UniVie, Austria
Katharina Dost	Jožef Stefan Institute, Slovenia
Katsiaryna Mirylenka	Zalando SE, Germany
Keith Burghardt	ISI, Germany
Klaus Brinker	Hamm-Lippstadt University of Applied Sciences, Germany
Koki Kawabata	Osaka University, Japan
Korbinian Randl	Stockholm University, Sweden
Krzysztof Krawiec	Poznań University of Technology, Poland
Krzysztof Kutt	Jagiellonian University, Poland
Kwan Hui Lim	Singapore University of Technology and Design, Singapore
Lamija Lemes	University of Zenica, Bosnia & Herzegovina
Le Nguyen	University of Oulu, Finland

Lei Li	Hong Kong University of Science and Technology (Guangzhou), China
Lei Liu	York University, Canada
Li Liu	Chongqing University, China
Li Zhang	University College London, UK
Liang Tang	Google, USA
Liang Tong	NEC Labs America, USA
Liang Wang	Alibaba Group, China
Lina Yao	University of New South Wales, Australia
Lingxiao Li	Michigan State University, USA
Lingyang Chu	McMaster University, Canada
Lixin Zou	Wuhan University, China
Lluis Garcia-Pueyo	Meta, USA
Lou Salaun	Nokia Bell Labs, USA
Luca Corbucci	University of Pisa, Italy
Luca Pappalardo	ISTI, Italy
Luca Romeo	University of Macerata, Italy
Luis Ferreira	Olympus Medical Products Portugal, Portugal
Luis Miguel Matos	ALGORITMI Centre, Portugal
Lukas Grasmann	TU Wien, Austria
Lukas Pensel	Johannes Gutenberg University Mainz, Germany
Maciej Grzenda	Warsaw University of Technology, Poland
Maciej Piernik	Poznań University of Technology, Poland
Madiraju Srilakshmi	Dream Sports, India
Mads C. Hansen	A.P. Moller-Maersk, Denmark
Mahardhika Pratama	University of South Australia, Australia
Mahmoud Rahat	Halmstad University, Sweden
Man Tianxing	Jilin University, China
Manish Gupta	Microsoft, USA
Manos Papagelis	York University, Canada
Manuel Lopes	Instituto Tecnico Superior, Portugal
Manuel Portela	Universitat Pompeu Fabra, Spain
Marc Tommasi	Lille University, France
Marco Fisichella	Leibniz Universität, Hannover, Germany
Maria Riveiro	Jonkoping University, Sweden
Maria Ulan	RISE Research Institutes of Sweden, Sweden
Marian Scuturici	LIRIS, France
Marianne Clausel	IECL, France
Mario Doller	University of Applied Sciences, Kufstein, Austria
Marius Schwammle	DLR/BT, Germany
Markus Gotz	Karlsruhe Institute of Technology (KIT), Germany

Markus Leyser	Technische Universität Dresden, Germany
Martin Boldt	Blekinge Institute of Technology, Sweden
Martin Mladenov	Google, USA
Martin Vita	Institute of Physics, Czech Academy of Sciences, Czech Republic
Matthias Demant	Fraunhofer ISE, Germany
Matthias Galipaud	SDSC, Switzerland
Matthias Petri	Amazon, USA
Matthieu Latapy	CNRS, France
Maurice Van Keulen	University of Twente, Netherlands
Maxime Cordy	University of Luxembourg, Luxembourg
Maxwell J. Jacobson	Purdue University, USA
Md Nahid Hasan	Miami University, USA
Md Zia Ullah	Edinburgh Napier University, UK
Mehtab Alam Syed	CIRAD, France
Melanie Neubauer	University of Leoben, Austria
Meng Chen	Shandong University, China
Mengxuan Zhang	Australian National University, Australia
Miao Fan	NavInfo, China
Michael Bain	University of New South Wales, Australia
Michele Bernardini	Uni eCampus.It, Italy
Michiel Dhont	EluciDATA Lab of Sirris, Belgium
Mickael Coustaty	L3i Laboratory, France
Miguel Couceiro	LORIA, France
Mihaela Mitici	Utrecht University, Netherlands
Min Lee	Singapore Management University, Singapore
Min Hun Lee	Singapore Management University, Singapore
Mina Rezaei	LMU Munich, Germany
Ming Ma	Inner Mongolia University, China
Minghao Chen	Tencent, China
Mirco Nanni	CNR-ISTI Pisa, Italy
Mirjam Wattenhofer	Google, USA
Mirko Marras	University of Cagliari, Italy
Mitra Heidari	University of Melbourne, Australia
Modesto Castrillon-Santana	Universidad de Las Palmas de Gran Canaria, Spain
Mohammadmehdi Saberioon	German Research Centre for Geosciences, Germany
Mohammed Amer	Fujitsu Research of Europe, Germany
Mohammed Ghaith Altarabichi	Halmstad University, Sweden
Mojgan Kouhounestani	University of Melbourne, Australia
Moonki Hong	Sogang University, South Korea

Munira Syed	Procter & Gamble, USA
Nan Li	Microsoft, USA
Narendhar Gugulothu	TCS Research, India
Nedra Mellouli	LIASD, Portugal
Ngoc Son Le	University of Hildesheim, Germany
Niklas Lavesson	Blekinge Institute of Technology, Sweden
Niraj Kumar	Fujitsu, Japan
Nitish Kumar	MasterCard, USA
Nuno Cruz Garcia	FCUL, Portugal
Nuno R. P. S. Guimaraes	INESC TEC, University of Porto, Portugal
Nuwan Gunasekara	Halmstad University, Sweden
Pablo Picazo-Sanchez	Halmstad University, Sweden
Pablo Torrijos Arenas	Universidad de Castilla-La Mancha, Spain
Pablo Jose Del Moral Pastor	Ekkono.ai, Finland
Pan He	Auburn University, USA
Panagiotis Kanellopoulos	University of Essex, UK
Panagiotis Papadakos	FORTH-ICS, Greece
Pandey Shourya Prasad	International Institute of Information Technology, Bangalore, India
Panpan Xu	Amazon AWS, USA
Paola Velardi	Sapienza University of Rome, Italy
Paolo Cintia	Kode, Italy
Pascal Plettenberg	Intelligent Embedded Systems, Italy
Paul Boniol	Inria, France
Pavel Blinov	Sber AI Lab, Russia
Pawel Parczyk	Wroclaw University of Science and Technology, Poland
Pedro M. Ferreira	University of Lisbon, Portugal
Pedro Seber	MIT, USA
Peng Qiao	NUDT, China
Pengyuan Wang	University of Georgia, USA
Petr Olegovich Sokerin	Skoltech, Russia
Philipp Bach	University of Hamburg, Germany
Philipp Froehlich	TU Darmstadt, Germany
Philipp Schmidt	Amazon Research, USA
Philipp Zech	University of Innsbruck, Austria
Pinar Karagoz	Middle East Technical University (METU), Turkey
Ping Luo	Chinese Academy of Sciences, China
Po Yang	University of Sheffield, UK
Pop Petrica	Technical University of Cluj-Napoca, Romania
Prathap Manohar Joshi R	Zoho Corporation, India

Praveen Borra	Florida Atlantic University, USA
Praveen Paruchuri	IIIT Hyderabad, India
Qian Li	Curtin University, Australia
Qihang Yao	Georgia Institute of Technology, USA
Qiwei Han	Nova School of Business and Economics, Portugal
Quentin Duchemin	Université Gustave Eiffel, France
Radu Tudor Ionescu	University of Bucharest, Romania
Rafal Kucharski	Jagiellonian University, Poland
Rafet Sifa	Fraunhofer IAIS & University of Bonn, Germany
Ramasamy Savitha	I2R A*STAR, Singapore
Ran Yu	DSIS Research Group, Singapore
Ranga Raju Vatsavai	North Carolina State University, USA
Raphael Couturier	University of Bourgogne Franche-Comte (UBFC), France
Renato M. Assuncao	ESRI, USA
Renaud Lambiotte	University of Oxford, UK
Reuben Kshitiz Borrison	ABB, Switzerland
Reza Shirvany	Zalando SE, Germany
Ricardo R. Pereira	Feedzai, Portugal
Riccardo Rosati	Università Politecnica delle Marche, Ancona, Italy
Richard Allmendinger	University of Manchester, UK
Richard Nordsieck	XITASO GmbH IT and Software Solutions, Germany
Richi Nayak	Queensland University of Technology, Australia
Roberto Trasarti	CNR, Italy
Rogerio Luis de C. Costa	Polytechnic of Leiria, Portugal
Romain Ilbert	Huawei Paris Research Center, France
Roy Ka-Wei Lee	Singapore University of Technology and Design, Singapore
Ruilin Wang	University of Aberdeen, UK
Sabrina Gaito	Università degli Studi di Milano, Italy
Sai Karthikeya Vemuri	Computer Vision Group Jena, Italy
Saisubramaniam Gopalakrishnan	Quantiphi, USA
Sajjad Shumaly	Max-Planck-Institut for Polymer Research, Germany
Salvatore Rinzivillo	KDD Lab, ISTI, CNR, Italy
Samaneh Shafee	LASIGE, Portugal
Sandra Wissing	Fachhochschule Münster, Germany
Sarwan Ali	Georgia State University, USA
Sebastian Becker	Fraunhofer ISST, Germany

Sebastian Honel	Linnaeus University, Sweden
Selin Colakhasanoglu	Saxion University of Applied Sciences, Netherlands
Senzhang Wang	Central South University, China
Sepideh Nahali	York University, Canada
Shahrooz Abghari	Blekinge Institute of Technology, Sweden
Shahroz Tariq	CSIRO, Australia
Shang Yanlei	BUPT, China
Shen Liang	Paris Cité University, France
Shengheng Liu	Southeast University, China
Shereen Elsayed	University of Hildesheim, Germany
Shi-ting Wen	NingboTech University, China
Shiv Krishna Jaiswal	Walmart Global Tech, USA
Shoujin Wang	Macquarie University, Australia
Shuai Li	University of Cambridge, UK and University of Tokyo, UK
Shuchu Han	Capital One Financial Group, Japan
Simon F. Weinberger	EssilorLuxottica, France
Siyuan Chen	Guangzhou University, China
Snehanshu Saha	BITS Pilani Goa Campus, India
Souhaib Ben Taieb	University of Mons, Abu Dhabi
Sriparna Saha	IIT Patna, India
Stefan Rueping	Fraunhofer IAIS, Germany
Stephane Chretien	Université Lyon 2, France
Sunil Aryal	Deakin University, Australia
Susana Ladra	University of A Coruña, Spain
Szymon Bobek	Jagiellonian University, Poland
Szymon Jaroszewicz	Institute of Computer Science, Poland
Szymon Wilk	Poznań University of Technology, Poland
Tanel Tammet	Tallinn University of Technology, Estonia
Thanh Thi Nguyen	Monash University, Australia
Thiago Zangato	Université Sorbonne Paris Nord, France
Theodora Tsikrika	Information Technologies Institute, Greece
Thibault Girardin	Université Jean Monnet, France
Thomas Czernichow	Darwinlabs, Portugal
Thorsteinn Rognvaldsson	Halmstad University, Sweden
Tiago Mendes-Neves	FEUP/INESC TEC, Portugal
Tianshu Yu	Chinese University of Hong Kong (Shenzhen), China
Ting Su	Imperial College London, UK
Tingrui Qiao	University of Auckland, New Zealand
Tobias Glasmachers	Ruhr-Universität Bochum, Germany

Tomas Olsson	RISE SICS, Sweden
Tome Eftimov	Jožef Stefan Institute, Slovenia
Topon Paul	Toshiba Corporation, Japan
Tsuyoshi Okita	Kyushu Institute of Technology, Japan
Unmesh Padalkar	Dream Sports, India
Vahid Shahrivari Joghan	Utrecht University, Netherlands
Valerio Bonsignori	Unipisa, Italy
Vanessa Borst	University of Würzburg, Germany
Venkata Sai Prakash Mukkamala	Quantiphi Analytics, USA
Veselka Boeva	Blekinge Institute of Technology, Sweden
Viacheslav Komisarenko	University of Tartu, Estonia
Vikas Gupta	HPCL, India
Vinayak Gupta	University of Washington, Seattle, USA
Vincent Auriau	Artefact Research Center, France
Vincenzo Pasquadibisceglie	University of Bari, Aldo Moro, Italy
Vincenzo Scotti	KASTEL, Germany
Vinothkumar Kolluru	Stevens Institute of Technology, USA
Vladimir Mic	Aarhus University, Denmark
Wang-Zhou Dai	Nanjing University, China
Wee Siong Ng	Institute for Infocomm Research, Singapore
Wei Cheng	NEC Laboratories America, USA
Wei Li	Harbin Engineering University, China
Wei Wang	Tsinghua University, China
Wei-Peng Chen	Fujitsu Research of America, USA
Wentao Wang	Michigan State University, USA
Wentao Wu	Microsoft Research, USA
Wray Buntine	VinUniversity, Vietnam
Xianchao Wu	Nvidia, USA
Xiang Lian	Kent State University, USA
Xianli Zhang	Xi'an Jiaotong University, China
Xiaobo Jin	Xi'an Jiaotong-Liverpool University, China
Xiaofei Zhou	University of Chinese Academy of Sciences, China
Xiaofeng Gao	Shanghai Jiaotong University, China
Xiaolin Han	Northwestern Polytechnical University, China
Xin Huang	Hong Kong Baptist University, China
Xin Liu	East China Normal University, China
Xing Tang	Tencent, China
Xiuqiang He	Tencent, China
Xiuyuan Hu	Tsinghua University, China
Xueping Peng	University of Technology Sydney, Australia
Yanchang Zhao	CSIRO, Australia

Yang Guo	Xidian University Hangzhou Institute of Technology, China
Yang Song	Apple, USA
Yijun Zhao	Fordham University, USA
Yinghui Wu	Case Western Reserve University, USA
Yingzhen Lin	Harbin Institute of Technology (Shenzhen), China
Yintao Yu	University of Illinois at Urbana-Champaign, USA
Yixiang Fang	Chinese University of Hong Kong, China
Yixuan Cao	Institute of Computing Technology, China
Yizheng Huang	York University, Canada
Yongchao Liu	Ant Group, China
Yu Huang	Indiana University, USA
Yu Wang	University of Oregon, USA
Yuantao Fan	Halmstad University, Sweden
Yucheng Zhou	University of Macau, China
Yue Shi	Meta, USA
Yueyuan Zheng	Beihang University, China
Yunchuan Shi	University of Sydney, Australia
Yunjun Gao	Zhejiang University, China
Yuting Ding	Southeast University, China
Yuzhuo Li	University of Auckland, New Zealand
Zahra Kharazian	Stockholm University, Sweden
Zahra Taghiyarrenani	Halmstad University, Sweden
Zahraa Abdallah	University of Bristol, UK
Zeyi Wen	Hong Kong University of Science and Technology (Guangzhou), China
Zeyu Zhu	National University of Defense Technology, China
Zhanyu Liu	Shanghai Jiao Tong University, China
Zhaogeng Liu	Jilin University, China
Zhaohui Liang	National Library of Medicine, USA
Zhen Zhang	Shandong University, China
Zhendong Chu	Squirrel Ai Learning, China
Zheng Zhang	University of California, USA
Zhengze Li	University of Göttingen, Germany
Zhibin Gu	Hebei Normal University, China
Zhuang Liu	Dongbei University of Finance and Economics, China
Ziyu Guan	Xidian University, China
Zoltan Miklos	Université de Rennes, France
Zunlei Feng	Zhejiang University, China

Program Committee – Demo Track

Andrzej Wójtowicz	Adam Mickiewicz University, Poznań, Poland
Anna Sokol	University of Notre Dame, USA
Arian Pasquali	Faktion AI, Belgium
Bruno Veloso	INESC TEC - FEP-UP, Portugal
Chongsheng Zhang	Henan University, China
Christos Doulkeridis	University of Piraeus, Greece
Danqing Zhang	PathOnAI.org, USA
Fátima Rodrigues	INESC TEC, Portugal
Grigorii Khvatskii	University of Notre Dame, USA
Joe Germino	University of Notre Dame, USA
Jungwon Seo	University of Stavanger, Norway
Ke Li	University of Exeter, England
Manfred Jaeger	Aalborg University, Denmark
Marcin Luckner	Warsaw University of Technology, Poland
Mehwish Alam	Institut Polytechnique de Paris, France
Nuno Moniz	University of Notre Dame, USA
Tânia Carvalho	FCUP, Portugal
Vitor Cerqueira	FEUP, Portugal
Wei-Wei Du	National Yang Ming Chiao Tung University, Taiwan

Additional Reviewers

Andrea D'Angelo	Antonia Hain
Patrick Altmeyer	Md Athikul Islam
Guiseppina Adresini	Michael Ito
Vedangi Bengali	Philipp Jahn
Michele Bernardini	Rahul Kumar
Zhi Cao	Bishal Lakha
Louis Carpentier	Yuwen Liu
Alessio Cascione	Jerry Lonlac
Lilia Chebbah	Shijie Luo
Meng Ding	Francesca Naretto
Roberto Esposito	Navid Nobani
Alina Fastowski	Diego Coello de Portugal
Roger Ferrod	Joana Santos
Michele Fontana	Francesco Scala
Chang Gong	Richard Serrano
Michal Grzejdziak-Zdziarski	Nuno Silva
Paul Hahn	Francesco Spinnato

Pedro C. Vieira
Xiao Wang
Yunyun Wang
Qi Wen
Jianye Xie

Huaiyuan Yao
Yutong Ye
Obaidullah Zaland
Efstratios Zaradoukas
Nan Zhang

Sponsors

Diamond

Platinum

liv   Organization

Gold

Silver

Bronze

Other Sponsors

Partners

Keynotes

Many Good Models Leads to …

Cynthia Rudin

Duke University, USA

Abstract. As it turns out, many good models leads to amazing things! The Rashomon Effect, coined by Leo Breiman, describes the phenomenon that there exist many equally good predictive models for the same dataset.

This phenomenon happens for many real datasets, and when it does it sparks both magic and consternation, but mostly magic. In light of the Rashomon Effect, my collaborators and I propose to reshape the way we think about machine learning, particularly for tabular data problems in the nondeterministic (noisy) setting. I'll address how the Rashomon Effect impacts (1) the existence of simple-yet-accurate models, (2) flexibility to address user preferences, such as fairness and monotonicity, without losing performance, (3) uncertainty in predictions, fairness, and explanations, (4) reliable variable importance, (5) algorithm choice, specifically, providing advanced knowledge of which algorithms might be suitable for a given problem, and (6) public policy. I'll also discuss a theory of when the Rashomon Effect occurs and why: interestingly, noise in data leads to a large Rashomon Effect. My goal is to illustrate how the Rashomon Effect can have a massive impact on the use of machine learning for complex problems in society.

Towards Causal Artificial Intelligence

Elias Bareinboim

Columbia University, USA

Abstract. While a significant portion of AI scientists and engineers believe we are on the verge of achieving highly general forms of AI, I offer a critical appraisal of this view through a causal lens. In particular, building on foundational developments in the field, I will present my perspective on the relationship between intelligence and causality – and the central role of the latter in building intelligent systems and advancing credible data science.

I frame this discussion in terms of five core capabilities that we should expect from an intelligent AI system: performing causal reasoning and articulating explanations; making precise, surgical, and sample-efficient decisions; generalizing across changing conditions and environments; generating and simulating in a causally consistent manner; and learning causal structures and variables.

In this talk, I will elaborate on this perspective and share current progress toward building causally intelligent AI systems. A more detailed discussion of this thesis is provided in my forthcoming textbook, a draft of which is available here: https://causalai-book.net/.

Not Just a Trend: Institutionalizing XAI for Responsible and Compliant AI Systems

Francisco Herrera

Granada University, Spain

Abstract. As artificial intelligence (AI) systems increasingly mediate decisions in high-stakes domains – from healthcare and finance to public policy – the demand for explainable AI (XAI) has grown rapidly. Yet many current XAI approaches remain disconnected from the practical needs of stakeholders and the requirements of emerging regulatory frameworks. This talk argues that XAI must not be treated as a passing trend or optional technical add-on, but as a foundational principle in the design and deployment of AI systems. We critically examine the state of the field, exposing the gap between model-centric explainability and stakeholder-centric accountability. In response, we propose a framework that aligns explainability with legal, ethical, and social responsibilities, emphasizing co-design with affected users, sensitivity to institutional contexts, and governance over opacity. Our goal is to advance XAI from superficial compliance toward deeply integrated transparency that fosters trust, accountability, and responsible innovation.

Compositional Intelligence: Coordinating Multiple LLMs for Complex Tasks

Mirella Lapata

University of Edinburgh, UK

Abstract. Recent years have witnessed the rise of increasingly larger and more sophisticated language models (LMs) capable of performing every task imaginable, sometimes at (super)human level. In this talk, I will argue that in many realistic scenarios, solely relying on a single general-purpose LLM is suboptimal. A single LLM is likely to underrepresent real-world data distributions, heterogeneous skills, and task-specific requirements. Instead, I will discuss multi-LLM collaboration as an alternative to monolithic generative modeling. By orchestrating multiple LLMs, each with distinct roles, perspectives, or competencies, we can achieve more effective problem-solving while being more inclusive and explainable. I will illustrate this approach through two case studies: narrative story generation and visual question answering, showing how a society of agents can collectively tackle complex tasks while pursuing complementary subgoals. Additionally, I will explore how these agent societies leverage reasoning to improve performance.

Towards a Fairer World: Uncovering and Addressing Human and Algorithmic Biases

Nuria Oliver

ELLIS Alicante Foundation, Spain

Abstract. In my talk, I will first briefly present ELLIS Alicante1, the only ELLIS unit that has been created from scratch as a non-profit research foundation devoted to responsible AI for Social Good. Next, I will provide an overview of AI with a focus on the ethical implications and limitations of today's AI systems, including algorithmic discrimination and bias. On this topic, I will present a few examples of our work on uncovering and mitigating both human and algorithmic biases with AI.

On the human front, I will present the body of work that we have carried out in the context of AI-based beauty filters that are so popular on social media. On the algorithmic front, I will explain the main approaches to address algorithmic discrimination and I will present three novel methods to achieve fairer decisions.

Tensor Logic: A Simple Unification of Neural and Symbolic AI

Pedro Domingos

University of Washington, USA

Abstract. Deep learning has achieved remarkable successes in language generation and other tasks, but is extremely opaque and notoriously unreliable. Both of these problems can be overcome by combining it with the sound reasoning and transparent knowledge representation capabilities of symbolic AI. Tensor logic accomplishes this by unifying tensor algebra and logic programming, the formal languages underlying respectively deep learning and symbolic AI. Tensor logic is based on the observation that predicates are compactly represented Boolean tensors, and can be straightforwardly extended to compactly represent numeric ones. The two key constructs in tensor logic are tensor join and project, numeric operations that generalize database join and project. A tensor logic program is a set of tensor equations, each expressing a tensor as a series of tensor joins, a tensor project, and a univariate nonlinearity applied elementwise. Tensor logic programs can succinctly encode most deep architectures and symbolic AI systems, and many new combinations.

In this talk I will describe the foundations and main features of tensor logic, and present efficient inference and learning algorithms for it. A system based on tensor logic achieves state-of-the-art results on a suite of language and reasoning tasks. How tensor logic will fare on trillion-token corpora and associated tasks remains an open question.

Artificial Intelligence for Science

Sašo Džeroski

Jožef Stefan Institute, Slovenia

Abstract. Artificial intelligence is already transforming science, with its future impact expected to be even greater. Realizing this potential requires addressing key scientific challenges, such as ensuring explainability (of models and their predictions), learning effectively from limited data, and integrating data with prior domain knowledge. It also requires the provision of support for open and reproducible science through formalizing and sharing scientific knowledge.

I will present an overview of my research on the development of AI methods suitable for use in science. These include methods for explainable machine learning – including multi-target prediction and relational learning – that deliver accurate yet interpretable models suitable for complex scientific domains. These methods have been applied in environmental science, life science and materials science. Learning from limited data is critical in science. I will discuss two complementary approaches: semi-supervised learning, which leverages unlabeled data directly, together with labeled data, and foundation models, which use representations learned from vast unlabeled data to support downstream tasks with minimal supervision, i.e., limited amounts of labeled data. Both paradigms expand AI's reach into data-scarce scientific problems.

I will then present our work on automated scientific modeling, where we learn interpretable models of dynamical systems – such as process-based models and differential equations – from time series data and domain knowledge. Finally, I will highlight the role of ontologies and semantic technologies in experimental computer science, including machine learning and optimization. In these areas, we have developed ontologies for the representation and annotation of both data and other artefacts produced by science, such as algorithms, models, and results of experiments.

Contents – Part VII

Robustness and Uncertainty

Present and Future Generalization of Synthetic Image Detectors 3
    Pablo Bernabeu-Pérez, Enrique Lopez-Cuena, and Dario Garcia-Gasulla

ECD: Efficient Contrastive Decoding with Probabilistic Hallucination
Detection 21
    *Laura Fieback, Nishilkumar Balar, Jakob Spiegelberg,
    and Hanno Gottschalk*

Lattice Climber Attack: Adversarial Attacks for Randomized Mixtures
of Classifiers 39
    Lucas Gnecco Heredia, Benjamin Negrevergne, and Yann Chevaleyre

Inconsistent Reasoning Attacks to Identify Weaknesses in Automatic
Scientific Claim Verification Tools 56
    Md Athikul Islam, Noel Ellison, Bishal Lakha, and Edoardo Serra

On Training Survival Models with Scoring Rules 74
    *Philipp Kopper, David Rügamer, Raphael Sonabend, Bernd Bischl,
    and Andreas Bender*

Towards Interpretable Adversarial Examples via Sparse Adversarial Attack 92
    Fudong Lin, Jiadong Lou, Hao Wang, Brian Jalaian, and Xu Yuan

Scaling Multi-label Conformal Prediction with Label Interactions
for a Large Number of Labels 111
    Ghassan Najjar, Céline Berthou, and Héléna Vorobieva

Understanding the Trade-Offs in Accuracy and Uncertainty Quantification:
Architecture and Inference Choices in Bayesian Neural Networks 129
    Alisa Sheinkman and Sara Wade

Variance-Aware Noisy Training: Hardening DNNs Against Unstable
Analog Computations 147
    Xiao Wang, Hendrik Borras, Bernhard Klein, and Holger Fröning

PAR-AdvGAN: Improving Adversarial Attack Capability with Progressive
Auto-regression AdvGAN 164
    *Jiayu Zhang, Zhiyu Zhu, Xinyi Wang, Silin Liao, Zhibo Jin,
Flora Salim, and Huaming Chen*

Sequence Models

AdvKT: An Adversarial Multi-step Training Framework for Knowledge
Tracing 183
    *Lingyue Fu, Ting Long, Jianghao Lin, Wei Xia, Xinyi Dai,
Ruiming Tang, Yasheng Wang, Weinan Zhang, and Yong Yu*

Leveraging Student Profiles and the Mamba Framework to Enhance
Knowledge Tracing 201
    *Mingxing Shao, Tiancheng Zhang, Minghe Yu, Zhenghao Liu,
Yifang Yin, Hengyu Liu, and Ge Yu*

Learning Submodular Sequencing from Samples 219
    Jing Yuan, Qi Cai, Xin Gao, and Shaojie Tang

Revisiting Applicable and Comprehensive Knowledge Tracing
in Large-Scale Data 235
    Yiyun Zhou, Wenkang Han, and Jingyuan Chen

Breaking Free: Decoupling Forced Systems with Laplace Neural Networks 252
    *Bernd Zimmering, Cecília Coelho, Vaibhav Gupta, Maria Maleshkova,
and Oliver Niggemann*

Streaming and Spatiotemporal Data

Self-balancing, Memory Efficient, Dynamic Metric Space Data
Maintenance, for Rapid Multi-kernel Estimation 273
    Aditya S. Ellendula and Chandrajit Bajaj

Merging Embedded Topics with Optimal Transport for Online Topic
Modeling on Data Streams 290
    *Federica Granese, Benjamin Navet, Serena Villata,
and Charles Bouveyron*

Going Offline: An Evaluation of the Offline Phase in Stream Clustering 308
    Philipp Jahn, Walid Durani, Collin Leiber, Anna Beer, and Thomas Seidl

Adaptive Options for Decision Trees in Evolving Data Stream Classification ... 327
    Daniel Nowak Assis, Jean Paul Barddal, and Fabrício Enembreck

ST-LoRA: Low-Rank Adaptation for Spatio-Temporal Forecasting 345
    Weilin Ruan, Wei Chen, Xilin Dang, Jianxiang Zhou, Weichuang Li,
    Xu Liu, and Yuxuan Liang

Identifiable Autoregressive Variational Autoencoders for Nonlinear
and Nonstationary Spatio-Temporal Blind Source Separation 362
    Mika Sipilä, Klaus Nordhausen, and Sara Taskinen

Text and Natural Language Processing

PromptDSI: Prompt-Based Rehearsal-Free Continual Learning
for Document Retrieval 383
    Tuan-Luc Huynh, Thuy-Trang Vu, Weiqing Wang, Yinwei Wei, Trung Le,
    Dragan Gasevic, Yuan-Fang Li, and Thanh-Toan Do

A Scalable Model for Frequency Distribution of Low Occurrence
Multi-words Towards Handling Very Large Spectrum of Text *Corpora* Sizes . . . 402
    Joaquim F. Silva and Jose C. Cunha

FinCPRG: A Bidirectional Generation Pipeline for Hierarchical Queries
and Rich Relevance in Financial Chinese Passage Retrieval 419
    Xuan Xu, Beilin Chu, Qinhong Lin, Yixiao Zhong, Fufang Wen,
    Jiaqi Liu, Binjie Fei, Yu Li, Zhongliang Yang, and Linna Zhou

Speech-to-Visualization: Toward End-to-End Speech-Driven Data
Visualization Generation from Natural Language Questions 437
    Haodi Zhang, Xinhe Zhang, Jihua Zhou, Kaishun Wu, Yuanfeng Song,
    and Raymond Chi-Wing Wong

Text-Guided Dual Interaction for Multimodal Relation Extraction in Social
Media 454
    Yachuan Zhang and Yi Guo

Time Series

MotiPlus and MotiSet: Discovering the Best Set of Motiflets in Time Series 473
    Len Feremans, Patrick Schäfer, and Wannes Meert

Right on Time: Revising Time Series Models by Constraining Their
Explanations 490
    Maurice Kraus, David Steinmann, Antonia Wüst, Andre Kokozinski,
    and Kristian Kersting

C^3DE: Causal-Aware Collaborative Neural Controlled Differential Equation for Long-Term Urban Crowd Flow Prediction 508
  Yuting Liu, Qiang Zhou, Hanzhe Li, Chenqi Gong, and Jingjing Gu

Bridging Neural Networks and Dynamic Time Warping for Adaptive Time Series Classification 526
  Jintao Qu, Zichong Wang, Chenhao Wu, Wenbin Zhang, and Dongmei Li

Author Index 543

Robustness and Uncertainty

Present and Future Generalization of Synthetic Image Detectors

Pablo Bernabeu-Pérez[✉], Enrique Lopez-Cuena, and Dario Garcia-Gasulla

Barcelona Supercomputing Center (BSC), Barcelona, Spain
pablo.bernabeu@estudiantat.upc.edu, {enrique.lopez,dario.garcia}@bsc.es

Abstract. The continued release of increasingly realistic image generation models creates a demand for synthetic image detectors. To build effective detectors, we must first understand how factors like data source diversity, training methodologies and image alterations affect their generalization capabilities. This work conducts a systematic analysis and uses its insights to develop practical guidelines for training robust synthetic image detectors. Model generalization capabilities are evaluated across different setups (*e.g.,* scale, sources, transformations), including real-world deployment conditions. Through extensive benchmarking of state-of-the-art detectors across diverse and recent datasets, we show that while current approaches excel in specific scenarios, no single detector achieves universal effectiveness. Critical flaws are identified in detectors and workarounds are proposed to enable practical applications that enhance accuracy, reliability and robustness beyond current limitations.

Keywords: synthetic image detection · ai-generated images · diffusion models · model generalization · detector robustness

1 Introduction

Synthetic image generation presents challenges regarding visual information integrity, misinformation mitigation and trust in digital environments. Due to these concerns, correctly attributing synthetic content has become a social demand and a top scientific priority. Recent legislation aligns with this context, mandating the identification and notification of synthetic digital content [39].

To address these needs, synthetic image *detection* (SID) has become locked in a race with synthetic image *generation* (SIG) [25]. SID aspires to win by developing universal detectors [8,32], but their generalization capacity remains uncertain. Meanwhile, new SIG models join the race every month, advancing in realism and posing new challenges. This work studies the SIG-SID relationship by analyzing the impact of training conditions on SID generalization (Sect. 4). The lessons learned are applied to train a baseline for evaluating generalization

Supplementary Information The online version contains supplementary material available at https://doi.org/10.1007/978-3-032-06109-6_1.

under deployment conditions, including variations in data and model sources and scaling factors (Sect. 5). Our final experiments (Sect. 6) benchmark recent detectors using synthetic data from the latest generators under optimized image scaling policies. Finally, ethical considerations related to SID research, including when and how detectors should be publicly released, are discussed (Sect. 7).

Our findings indicate that current methods are insufficient for reliable SID, as no tested model generalizes universally. Factors like rescaling play a major role in detector performance, exposing a vector of attack for malicious actors. While some models suffer major degradations, others benefit from resized inputs, emphasizing the importance of appropriate preprocessing techniques. Lastly, detectors perform much worse on private models, like `DALLE` and `Midjourney`, compared to open models, highlighting the crucial role of open science in synthetic attribution. This work illustrates how, as of today, generalization should never be assumed in the field of SID. In summary, our contributions include:

- A systematic analysis of training conditions affecting detector generalization, showing improved robustness when trained on newer generators and highlighting vulnerabilities to common image alterations.
- Development and release of `SuSy`, a multi-class detector trained with optimized augmentations, accompanied by practical deployment guidelines including optimal patch aggregation and standardized rescaling.
- Comprehensive benchmarking of state-of-the-art detectors across diverse datasets, identifying critical vulnerabilities related to image rescaling.

2 Related Work

Previous work on SID has primarily focused on GAN-generated content [18, 40,48], due to its historical prevalence and relative speed. However, recent studies show that GAN-focused detectors often fail to identify content from modern diffusion models [30,41]. While several recent works address the detection of diffusion-based content [3,19,23,28,32,46,50,51], which now produce the most perceptually convincing synthetic images, their generalization ability under diverse conditions remains largely untested.

Deep learning architectures such as CNNs [9,37] and Visual Transformers (ViTs) [3,28] have been used to learn hierarchical synthetic patterns, with CLIP-based methods enhancing detection through semantic [32] and intermediate feature analysis [23]. Models combining textual and visual features have also been adopted; [7] uses prompt tuning to detect deepfakes as a visual question-answering problem, while [44] applies contrastive learning guided by text. Hybrid models combine multiple detection signals, such as dual-stream networks analyzing texture and frequency artifacts [45] or CLIP features fused with low-level image statistics [35]. Across detection methods, frequency domain-based approaches are commonly used to reveal generation artifacts [10]. Some leverage Fast Fourier Transform analysis to capture characteristic patterns [5,36], while others explore wavelet-based features specifically for diffusion outputs [14].

In addition, local feature analysis examines texture contrast patterns [49] and intrinsic dimensionality properties [30] for complementary signals.

AI-generated image detectors are typically trained using data from a single source and evaluated across multiple sources to assess generalization [6,8,19,23,32,33,50,51]. Among various bias sources examined, image format and resolution stand out as key factors. In [23], authors highlight the impact of resizing operations, a common practice to adjust images to network input resolution. The study in [19] demonstrates biases associated with *JPEG* compression and image size, with detectors generally performing better on natural images that differ significantly from generated training images. This observation aligns with findings in [12], where dataset choice significantly impacts detection performance.

Recent efforts, such as the SIDBench framework [34], have performed SID evaluation across diverse datasets, including an analysis of resolution effects. Part of our work builds on the SIDBench framework but differs in scope and contribution. Firstly, we provide an analysis of resolution effects by examining a range of scaling factors, while SIDBench focuses on cropping versus resizing. We also investigate additional generalization factors, including generator family, model release date and dataset source, including both open and private models, as well as multiple sources for the same generators. Furthermore, we incorporate more authentic datasets and newer synthetic image generators. Lastly, we evaluate optimal scaling settings for individual detectors and benchmark their performance under real-world conditions, uncovering new insights.

3 Methods

To examine detector biases arising from training methodology, we employ a fixed architecture (see Sect. 3.1), train it using six image datasets (see Sect. 3.2) and evaluate it with fifteen additional datasets (see Sect. 3.3). To enable full reproducibility of our work, our codebase[1], training datasets[2] and model weights[3] for our best-performing detector are publicly released.

3.1 Architecture

For our experimentation, we use a ResNet [22] trained as a direct classifier, chosen for its robust performance [6,19,51] and lightweight design suitable for large-scale evaluation. Specifically, we adopt the staircase design from [31], which combines CNN-based feature extraction with MLP classification in a staircase design shown in Fig. 1 (see Appendix A for a detailed explanation of the architecture).

Detectors are commonly trained on image patches or downsampled images, as processing entire high-resolution images is computationally intensive and the most discriminating features are typically low-level. For each image, we select

---

[1] https://github.com/HPAI-BSC/SuSy.
[2] https://huggingface.co/datasets/HPAI-BSC/SuSy-Dataset.
[3] https://huggingface.co/HPAI-BSC/SuSy.

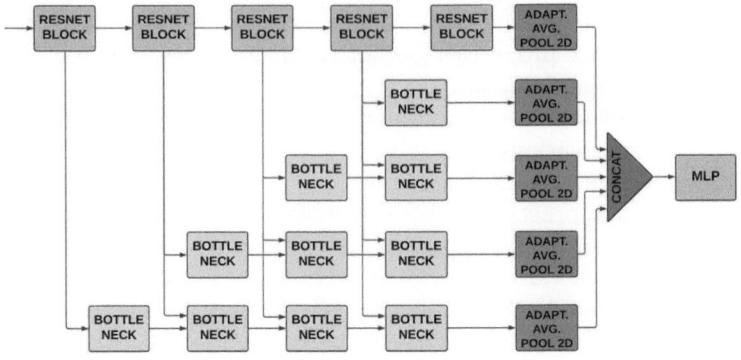

Fig. 1. Detector architecture used, based on a ResNet-18 from [31], including ResNet blocks (blue), bottlenecks (red), adaptative average pooling 2D (orange), concatenation (yellow) and an MLP (green). (Color figure online)

the five 224 × 224 patches exhibiting the highest contrast in their grey-level co-occurrence matrix [21]. These patches are processed individually through the network, producing per-patch predictions that are aggregated to yield image-level decisions. The impact of different aggregation strategies on detection performance is analyzed in Sect. 5.2.

For performance metrics, recall is used for single-dataset evaluations (authentic or synthetic), focusing solely on the model's ability to identify the target class. For multi-dataset classification scenarios, macro accuracy is employed to provide an unweighted mean of per-class accuracy, ensuring fair evaluation across all classes regardless of sample size.

3.2 Train Datasets

The training experiments detailed in Sect. 4 utilize two types of datasets: *authentic* real-world images sourced from COCO [27] and *synthetic* AI-generated images from DALLE3 [16], SD1.X [42], SDXL [15], MJ 1/2 [38] and MJ 5/6 [17]. These datasets represent different versions of three popular image generators: DALLE, StableDiffusion and Midjourney. To ensure balanced class representation, COCO and SD1.X are undersampled to a maximum of 5,435 images. Pre-existing train, validation and test splits are respected, defaulting to a standard 60%-20%-20% random split when such partitions are unavailable. For SDXL, the *realistic-2.2* split is used for training and validation, while the *realistic-1* split is reserved for testing. Further details are provided in Appendix C (Table 1).

3.3 Benchmarking Datasets

To evaluate SID models, we use fifteen datasets: eleven produced and gathered by others, two produced by others but gathered by us and two produced by us.

Table 1. Datasets with generative models, release date, image format, type and sample counts.

Dataset	Model	Year	Format	Type	Train	Val	Test
COCO	-	2017	JPG	Auth	2,967	1,234	1,234
dalle3-images	DALLE3	2023	JPG	Synth	987	330	330
diffusiondb	SD1.X	2022	PNG	Synth	2,967	1,234	1,234
SDXL	realisticSDXL	2023	PNG	Synth	2,967	1,234	1,234
mj-tti	MJ 1/2	2022	PNG	Synth	2,718	906	906
mj-images	MJ 5/6	2023	JPG	Synth	1,845	617	617
Evaluation Datasets							
Flickr30k	-	2014	JPEG	Auth	-	-	31,655
GLDv2	-	2020	JPEG	Auth	-	-	5,000
In-the-wild	-	2024	Mix	Auth	-	-	121
Synthbuster	Multiple	2024	PNG	Synth	-	-	9,000
SD3	SD 3	2024	PNG	Synth	-	-	8,192
FLUX.1	FLUX.1	2024	PNG	Synth	-	-	8,192
In-the-wild	?	2024	PNG	Synth	-	-	99

Image resolution distributions and visual samples are detailed in Appendices G and H, respectively.

The externally produced datasets include two subsets of 5,000 randomly selected authentic images: scenes depicting people from Flickr30k [47] and natural and human-made landmarks from GLDv2 [43]. Additionally, nine synthetic datasets from the Synthbuster superset [5] provide 1,000 images each, generated using common prompts across both models included in our training (*e.g.*, SDXL, DALLE3) and models outside our training set (*e.g.*, DALLE2, Firefly).

The In-the-wild dataset contains images gathered from online sources by the authors. The authentic split includes 121 manually curated images from sources like *Reddit* communities prohibiting AI content and *Flickr* uploads prior to 2020. The synthetic split consists of 99 photorealistic AI-generated images sourced from *Civitai* and *Reddit*'s synthetic content communities. Despite careful manual curation and community moderation, we acknowledge a residual risk of contamination due to possible mislabeling or oversight (Fig. 2).

Fig. 2. Examples of the In-the-wild dataset.

Finally, we generate two synthetic datasets containing 8,192 images each: `SD3`, created using Stable Diffusion 3-Medium [4], an MMDiT text-to-image model; and `FLUX.1`, generated with `FLUX.1-dev` [24], a 12B parameter model combining MMDiT and DiT architectures [26]. Additional details are in Appendix D.

4 Train Experiments

This section examines how different training strategies affect model generalization. For consistent experimental comparison, all models share identical architecture (Sect. 3.1) and hardware setup (see Appendix B for scaling details). Concretely, all experiments were conducted on the MareNostrum 5 supercomputer, hosted at the Barcelona Supercomputing Center (BSC). We utilize an Intel Xeon Platinum 8460Y processor and one NVIDIA Hopper H100 64 GB GPU. Training is capped at 20 epochs with a 2-epoch patience early stopping based on validation accuracy. The datasets described in Sect. 3.2 are augmented using horizontal flips with 50% probability, while additional transformations are analyzed in Sect. 4.3.

4.1 Single-Class Models

We evaluate relationships between SIG models by training binary classifiers, using each synthetic dataset in Sect. 3.2 as a positive class and `COCO` as the negative class. These single-class detectors are then tested on the remaining datasets to assess cross-model generalization (see Table 2).

Table 2. Patch-level recall (%) of single-class models for synthetic datasets. In bold, performance on the training dataset.

Training Dataset	Year	Evaluation Dataset					Avg.
		DALLE3	SD1.X	SDXL	MJ 1/2	MJ 5/6	
DALLE3	2023	**97.70**	27.59	70.19	50.73	97.02	68.64
SD1.X	2022	49.76	**98.30**	68.23	39.65	40.36	59.26
SDXL	2023	51.27	33.45	**97.57**	59.14	67.97	61.88
MJ 1/2	2022	31.39	17.63	73.14	**99.07**	51.51	54.55
MJ 5/6	2023	91.76	26.13	64.75	62.69	**99.25**	68.92
Avg.		64.38	40.62	74.78	62.26	71.22	

While single-class detectors achieve excellent recall (over 97%) on their target class, performance drops substantially when tested on other datasets. SIG model age emerges as the dominant factor affecting generalization. When evaluating newer detectors on older generators, we observe severe performance degradation, as shown in the last row of Table 2, where detectors trained on SD1.X and MJ 1/2 (both from 2022) show the lowest average values. This pattern likely stems from older generators producing more pronounced artifacts, which newer detectors struggle to identify without specific training. Conversely, detectors trained on recent datasets show better cross-SIG generalization, as evidenced by the higher average values for DALLE3, SDXL and MJ 5/6 in the last column. Paradoxically, this suggests that more realistic generators enhance the robustness and reduce the bias of detectors. In contrast, SIG family has a weak effect on generalization - the detector trained on SDXL is below average when tested on SD1.X and the SID model trained on MJ 1/2 is not particularly accurate on MJ 5/6. The effect of image format is also inconclusive.

4.2 Multi-class Models

Multi-class detectors offer richer decision boundaries compared to single-class detectors, which tend to collapse [13] *i.e.*, defaulting to predicting only one class. To explore the effects of this distinction on generalization, we train a binary classifier merging all synthetic data sources from Sect. 3.2 into a single synthetic class, including 14,323 synthetic images and an analogous amount drawn from COCO to compose the authentic class. We also train a six-class recognition model using the original splits defined in Sect. 3.2. To obtain binary classifications from the six-class model, we take *argmax* of the output probabilities, where all samples labeled as belonging to a synthetic class are considered equal predictions of the synthetic class. An alternative threshold mechanism was explored, with minimal impact on performance, and its results are reported in Appendix E.

Table 3. Patch level recall for *Single*: five models trained on each synthetic dataset (*i.e.*, Table 2 diagonal), *Binary*: model trained with all synthetic datasets merged, *6 Class*: multi-class model trained for the recognition task. Best in bold.

Model	Evaluation Alteration					
	Auth.	DALLE3	SD1.X	SDXL	MJ 1/2	MJ 5/6
Single	-	97.70	98.30	97.57	99.07	99.25
Binary	94.85	99.64	**98.98**	99.22	99.60	99.74
6 Class	**97.39**	**99.76**	97.89	**99.30**	**99.91**	**99.97**

Results in Table 3 show good performance from both the binary and the six-way classifiers on all synthetic datasets, better than single models, which means visual features of synthetic detectors are mutually beneficial for SID. In general, the six-way classifier outperforms all, with the only exception of one of the oldest and most distinct datasets (*i.e.*, SD1.X) (lowest generalization in Table 2).

4.3 Image Alteration Methods

Image transformations, while essential for storage optimization and transmission cost reduction, can significantly alter images and may be exploited by malicious actors to mask synthetic content. If SID models are not robust to these transformations, their utility in real-world scenarios becomes minimal. To evaluate this robustness, we test the six-class model from the previous section under common transformations from the Albumentations library [1]: blur (*AdvancedBlur* and *GaussianBlur*), brightness and gamma alterations (*RandomBrightnessContrast* and *RandomGamma*) and *JPEG compression*, all using default parameters.

For a complete assessment, we train five multi-class models, each with a different transformation applied to its training set, and evaluate these alongside our original six-class model across all transformations and unaltered images. The results are presented in Table 4 using multi-class macro accuracy, where any misclassification between synthetic classes is counted as an error. This metric was selected instead of the previously used binary metrics, as binary classification consistently achieved over 99% accuracy, limiting its ability to distinguish model performance in a multi-class context.

Table 4. Patch-level accuracy (%) of six-class recognition models when trained on one alteration method and evaluated on all. In bold, performance on the alteration used for training. Last column: model average across all transformations. Bottom row: average performance of all models for each transformation.

Training Alteration	Evaluation Alteration						Avg.
	None	Bright	γ	JPEG	ABlur	GBlur	
None	**90.90**	86.66	90.60	90.19	81.56	54.73	82.44
Bright	91.28	**89.68**	91.13	90.10	84.61	63.55	85.06
γ	91.52	87.51	**91.30**	90.02	85.57	65.22	85.19
JPEG	87.82	83.15	87.79	**86.21**	78.42	55.29	79.78
ABlur	90.13	86.23	90.12	88.15	**88.04**	81.54	87.37
GBlur	88.94	84.02	88.65	87.37	86.78	**81.88**	86.27
Avg.	90.10	86.21	89.93	88.67	84.16	67.04	

Table 4 shows blur is the transformation that most impacts detector performance. *GaussianBlur*, which causes drops in accuracy of over 7 points, is also the hardest transformation in training, showing the lowest diagonal score. However, both blur-trained models achieve the highest cross-transformation accuracies, demonstrating effective generalization and making blur a valuable addition to the training process.

5 Deployment Experiments

To study the impact of deployment factors on generalization, we use SuSy, a multi-class model trained with the setup described in Sect. 4. Training data from Sect. 3.2 is augmented with all transformations from Sect. 4.3, each applied with a 20% chance. We explore generalization to new data sources (Sect. 5.1),

5.1 Generalization to Source

The `SuSy` *(Patch)* column of Table 5 shows evaluation results under disjoint sets of data (see Sect. 3.3). For authentic datasets, the model generalizes well to `Flickr30k` (91.81%), moderately to `GLDv2` (68.37%) and poorly to `In-the-wild` images (30.91%). Robust performance across these diverse datasets suggests minimal impact from potential content biases introduced in the training data.

Table 5. Recall at patch level and five-patch majority voting at image level for `SuSy`. Best in bold. [†]Generators seen during training. [‡]Generators unseen during training.

Type	Data Source	SIG Model	Year	SuSy (Patch)	SuSy (Image)
Authentic	Flickr30k	None	2014	91.81	**94.48**
Authentic	GLDv2	None	2020	68.37	**71.80**
Authentic	In-the-wild	None	2024	**30.91**	27.27
Synthetic[†]	Synthbuster	SD 1.3	2022	88.56	**91.80**
Synthetic[†]	Synthbuster	SD 1.4	2022	88.50	**91.80**
Synthetic[†]	Synthbuster	MJ V5	2023	74.22	**78.40**
Synthetic[†]	Synthbuster	SD XL	2023	79.22	**83.80**
Synthetic[†]	Synthbuster	DALLE-3	2023	87.02	**92.50**
Synthetic[‡]	Synthbuster	Glide	2021	52.78	**53.20**
Synthetic[‡]	Synthbuster	SD 2	2022	68.32	**70.40**
Synthetic[‡]	Synthbuster	DALLE-2	2022	**24.50**	19.70
Synthetic[‡]	Synthbuster	Firefly	2023	53.04	**53.50**
Synthetic[‡]	Authors	SD 3	2024	91.51	**95.23**
Synthetic[‡]	Authors	FLUX.1	2024	94.37	**97.05**
Synthetic[‡]	In-the-wild	Unknown		90.51	**91.92**

The middle section of Table 5 shows datasets from generators seen during training but generated by different users. Although possible variations in SIG configurations, prompts and post-processing may introduce significant biases, `SuSy` achieves 74–88% recall across all cases.

For datasets from models unseen during training (bottom of Table 5), performance varies widely (24–94%). Model family inconsistently affects generalization: `SuSy` performs excellently on `SD3`, adequately on `SD2`, but poorly on `DALLE2`, despite training on versions of both generator families.

5.2 Image Decision Boundary

While SID models operate on image patches, real-world applications typically require whole-image predictions. To address this gap, we analyze the top five patches selected based on texture complexity (as described in Sect. 3.1).

We tested two aggregation strategies: majority voting of patch predictions and averaging patch logits before classification. Both improved over single-patch performance, with majority voting consistently outperforming across datasets (results in the last column of Table 5). This approach further improved recall for high-performing datasets while providing minimal gains for poorly performing ones, revealing both advantages and limitations of decision boundary tuning.

5.3 Scale Generalization

Image resizing is a widespread image alteration that can alter or eliminate frequency artifacts that SID models rely on, potentially decreasing their performance. To assess the extent of this factor, we evaluate SuSy using images scaled at six different sizes (224 to 1440px). First, if the image is not already square, equal padding is added to the shorter dimension to center it. Then, the squared image is resized to the specified dimensions using bilinear interpolation, from which the evaluated patches are extracted. Using the evaluation datasets described in Sect. 3.3, which follow a diverse distribution of sizes (see Appendix G), we compute recall separately for authentic and synthetic classes at each scale. This approach allows us to monitor both accuracy and balance in detection across different resolutions. This experiment is reproduced in the benchmarking analysis of Sect. 6 for comparison with other SID models.

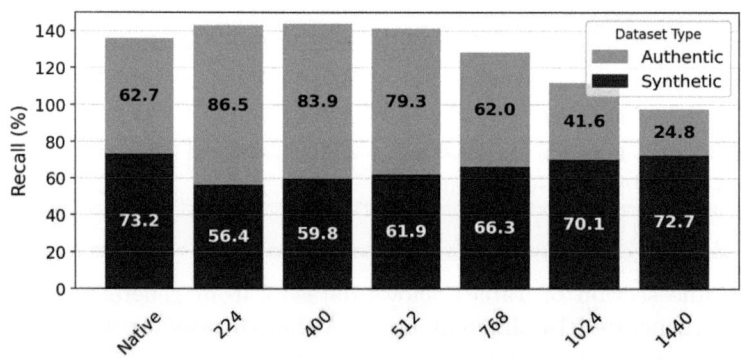

Fig. 3. Recall of SuSy under different scaling factors.

Figure 3 shows SuSy maintains stable performance at lower resolutions (224–512px). As resolution increases, predictions become increasingly biased toward the synthetic class. For consistent real-world performance, where images may have undergone prior resizing, we recommend including standardized rescaling in preprocessing pipelines.

5.4 Human Evaluators

To benchmark against human perception, we asked 10 social media users (aged 22-30) likely to be exposed to AI-generated content, to classify the In-the-wild dataset. Images were presented in random order on identical IPS LCD displays under controlled lighting conditions. Participants were not informed about the class distribution. On average, volunteers took 15 min to classify all 210 images under no time constraints. Using our optimal setup from previous sections, SuSy outperformed the average human evaluator by 1.5%.

6 Benchmarking Experiments

To complete this study, we test the performance of ten different SID models (most available through SIDBench [34]). Table 6 showcases the six best-performing models (exceeding 140 combined recall points): LGrad [37], GramNet [29] and DIMD [23], which use CNNs as feature extractors, along with transformer-based models Rine [23], DeFake [11] and FatFormer [28]. Appendix F provides architectural details and results for the remaining tested detectors: CNNDetect [40], Dire [41], FreqDetect [18] and UnivFD [32].

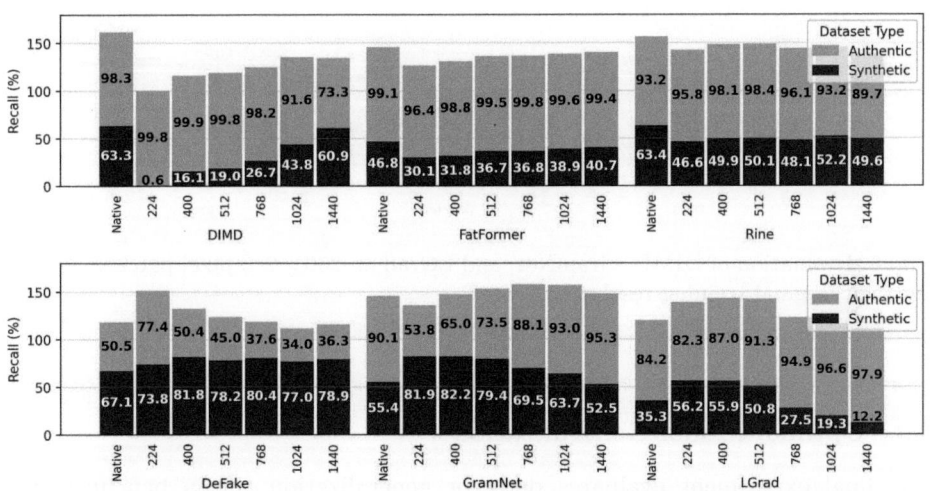

Fig. 4. Recall of state-of-the-art SID models under different scaling factors.

6.1 Rescaling

Given the crucial role of image scaling, detector performance is first assessed using the methodology from Sect. 5.3, providing insights on generalization under scale changes. Although DIMD, GramNet and LGrad were originally trained at

256×256, we standardize all evaluations at 224×224 patches across models to ensure consistency in processed information. To confirm the fairness of this approach, we performed a preliminary evaluation of these models at their native 256×256 resolution. The results, presented in Fig. 5, show that the change in resolution does not fundamentally alter their performance characteristics.

The models in the top row of Fig. 4 are highly sensitive to *any* scale modifications, with performance consistently deteriorating after rescaling (*i.e.*, optimal performance without resizing). This sensitivity creates a security vulnerability that malicious actors could exploit. Additionally, these models show bias toward the authentic class, with suboptimal synthetic image recall (63% for two models, while the third performs below random chance).

In contrast, detectors in the bottom row demonstrate resilience to *some* scale variations (*i.e.*, optimal performance includes resizing). DeFake and LGrad perform optimally at lower resolutions (224–512px), similar to SuSy, while GramNet excels at higher resolutions (768–1024px). Their optimal input resolution enhances resilience and enables deployment pipeline optimization. However, these models differ in prediction balance: DeFake excels in synthetic class detection, LGrad in authentic class identification, while GramNet and SuSy achieve more balanced performance across both categories.

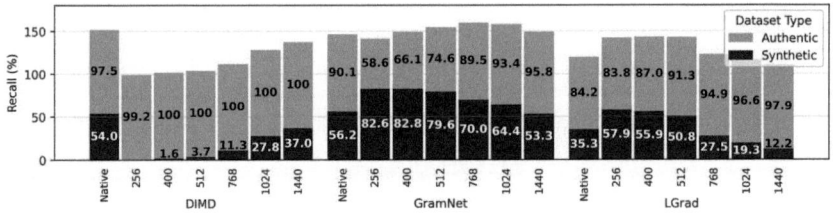

Fig. 5. Evaluation of DIMD, GramNet, and LGrad on 256×256 pixel patches, matching their original training resolution.

6.2 Optimal Model Generalization

The final experiment evaluates detector generalization across benchmarking datasets at optimal input scales. Results in Table 6 reveal a critical limitation: all detectors achieve less than 50% recall on at least four datasets, demonstrating that no universal detector exists. Performance metrics consistently favor the authentic class over synthetic, partly from optimal resolution selection and partly reflecting the more diverse and challenging synthetic distribution. A clear trade-off emerges: DeFake is simultaneously the best synthetic detector and worst authentic detector, while FatFormer shows the opposite pattern.

While DeFake leads in synthetic detection overall and DIMD excels in 8 of 17 synthetic datasets (including 6 of 7 StableDiffusion variants), both are

Table 6. Center-patch recall of detector models evaluated with their optimal input resize resolution (*Native* denotes no alteration). Best recall in bold and recalls below 50% underlined. Entries denoted by (−) for `SuSy` indicate training datasets excluded from evaluation.

SIG		Year	DIMD	FatFormer	Rine	DeFake	LGrad	SuSy	GramNet	Avg.
Resolution			Nat.	Nat.	Nat.	224	400	400	768	
Authentic Data										
`Flickr30k`	-	'14	99.92	**100.0**	99.54	93.62	99.82	94.76	99.94	**98.23**
`COCO`	-	'17	**100.0**	99.60	**100.0**	91.33	77.63	-	87.12	92.61
`GLDv2`	-	'20	96.54	99.92	77.42	78.32	98.66	82.62	**100.0**	90.50
`In-the-wild`	-	'24	96.69	**96.77**	95.87	<u>46.28</u>	71.90	74.38	65.29	78.17
Avg. Authentic			98.29	**99.07**	93.21	77.39	87.00	83.92	88.09	
Synthetic Data Sources										
`Synthbuster` Glide		'21	<u>6.10</u>	68.10	83.60	**86.50**	53.50	53.30	68.80	59.99
`mj-tti` MJ V1/V2		'22	<u>2.87</u>	55.29	<u>14.57</u>	**75.83**	<u>42.60</u>	-	63.58	<u>42.46</u>
`Synthbuster` SD 1.3		'22	**100.0**	88.20	99.90	86.20	81.10	87.00	90.00	90.34
`Synthbuster` SD 1.4		'22	**100.0**	88.00	99.60	87.20	81.30	87.10	90.70	**90.56**
`diffusiondb` SD 1.X		'22	**99.92**	86.33	96.03	76.01	52.11	-	93.52	83.99
`Synthbuster` SD 2		'22	**97.10**	<u>47.20</u>	85.80	<u>39.80</u>	53.80	<u>42.30</u>	75.50	63.07
`Synthbuster` DALLE-2		'22	<u>0.40</u>	<u>45.80</u>	70.80	<u>47.30</u>	76.00	<u>20.70</u>	**93.10**	50.59
`Synthbuster` MJ V5		'23	**98.10**	<u>30.60</u>	87.00	<u>49.90</u>	83.60	<u>36.50</u>	88.50	67.74
`mj-images` MJ V5/V6		'23	**90.11**	<u>5.16</u>	<u>31.28</u>	75.85	<u>8.27</u>	-	<u>15.56</u>	<u>37.71</u>
`Synthbuster` SDXL		'23	94.40	79.80	**97.60**	53.60	86.20	<u>45.90</u>	97.20	79.24
`real.SDXL` SDXL		'23	**97.65**	<u>28.64</u>	82.17	91.82	69.77	-	75.61	74.28
`Synthbuster` Firefly		'23	<u>18.10</u>	81.40	<u>43.30</u>	54.00	66.40	<u>24.50</u>	**83.00**	52.96
`Synthbuster` DALLE-3		'23	<u>0.00</u>	<u>0.00</u>	<u>2.00</u>	**93.60**	<u>35.00</u>	84.30	<u>30.40</u>	<u>35.04</u>
`dalle3-imgs` DALLE-3		'23	61.82	<u>3.92</u>	<u>28.79</u>	**81.21**	<u>3.03</u>	-	<u>1.52</u>	<u>30.05</u>
∗ `SD3` SD 3		'24	**99.24**	59.02	85.05	89.42	70.74	78.44	89.03	81.56
∗ `FLUX.1` Flux.1-dev		'24	62.89	<u>23.08</u>	54.72	81.43	63.92	85.40	**92.99**	66.35
`In-the-wild` Unknown			47.47	<u>5.00</u>	<u>16.16</u>	**84.85**	<u>22.22</u>	71.72	<u>32.32</u>	<u>39.96</u>
Avg. Synthetic			63.30	<u>46.80</u>	63.43	**73.80**	55.86	59.76	69.49	

highly sensitive to rescaling, making them unsuitable for deployment with uncontrolled inputs. DIMD's consistent performance across StableDiffusion models is exceptional, as detectors generally lack consistency across model families. Even when datasets use the same generative model, performance varies significantly—average recall differences between DALLE3 versions is 27.63% across detectors, while SDXL variations average 24.35%. While detectors may generalize to source changes under specific conditions (see Sect. 5.1), this is not universal. Even in controlled scenarios like Synthbuster, where identical prompts are used, detection performance exhibits substantial variability.

Private models (DALLE, Midjourney, Firefly) present particular challenges, with detectors achieving only 45.22% average recall on closed SIG models compared to 76.60% on open ones. Even the *best*-performing closed dataset achieves only 7.75% better recall than the *worst* open one, stressing the importance of open science in advancing the field of SID.

The In-the-wild dataset, serving as a proxy for real-world conditions, reveals additional limitations. No tested detector exceeds 50% recall for *both* authentic and synthetic versions across all input resolutions. Only SuSy demonstrates robust performance with over 70% recall in both subsets, but specifically when operating at its optimal input resolution.

7 Conclusions

In a race equilibrium paradox, better generative models appear regularly, making the task harder for humans, while detectors trained on these newer generators are more reliable (see Sect. 4.1), keeping the race close.

The demand for detectors grows as society seeks to preserve social trust and digital rights while combating disinformation. Yet, these detectors must improve their generalization capabilities to be truly effective. In that regard, the main lesson from this work is: *never* assume generalization in SID. Results in Table 6 indicate even within datasets produced by the same generative model, detection performance may largely vary, as a result of software and hardware setups and user bias. Similarly, generalization should not be assumed on synthetic images produced by older, less realistic generators either, even if these synthetic samples seem more obvious to the human eye. As shown in Table 2, samples from these models are hard to generalize to (but *not* to train for) due to their stronger biases and distinct artifacts. In fact, even simple post-processing methods, like blur, can significantly reduce detector performance (see Table 4).

Image scale can dramatically affect the performance of most detectors, as well as the balance of their performance (*i.e.*, *authentic* vs *synthetic*). Some detectors are highly sensitive to rescaling operations (see Fig. 4), exposing a vulnerability to malicious inputs. At the same time, other SID models work optimally when applied to data that has been scaled to a certain size (see Fig. 4). This can be used to tune data for its detection, boosting performance on deployment settings (see Table 6).

The final contribution of this work, beyond the released SuSy, code and datasets, is a list of policies for the SID field as a whole, including an ethical risk assessment. Our work emphasizes the importance of openness in generative AI. Results from Table 6 indicate open generative models can be more easily detected

(+20% combined recall points on average). While we are far from a universal detector (all detectors perform below random in some of our benchmarks), models trained for specific targets may be as good as humans at identifying synthetic content (see Sect. 5.4).

7.1 Ethical Risks

Image detection systems pose significant ethical concerns, primarily due to their inherent fallibility. These systems produce both false positives and negatives (see Table 6), potentially misidentifying authentic images as synthetic and vice versa. Such errors could infringe on digital rights and enable censorship. Therefore, human expert oversight is crucial when these systems are used in contexts affecting individual rights and their outputs should never serve as definitive evidence.

Additionally, model bias remains a critical challenge. Training datasets often contain inherent biases that can skew detection results (*e.g.,* rural landscapes could be tagged as synthetic more often than urban images). Thorough evaluation across all relevant demographic and contextual factors is essential before deployment. Furthermore, the datasets used for training may include samples with personal data. COCO contains images of real people and synthetic datasets used could include realistic depictions of specific individuals. However, given the training objective and parameter size of SuSy, it is highly unlikely that any such information could be encoded within the weights released in this work.

A final risk of releasing a SID model is dual use, as it can be used as a training objective for generative models (*e.g.,* adversarial training). To mitigate that, we add a specific clause in the terms of use of the model prohibiting such practice. Notice SuSy is not trained to be the best possible detector (not trained on all data) and should not be used *as is* in practice. We recommend any SID model produced for final use to be kept private, as long as its public release holds no special academic or social value.

7.2 Future Work

The results of this work point towards four research directions that could improve SID robustness and adaptability. The complementary strengths of different detector models indicate potential benefits from ensemble methods. Exploring training data scaling laws could reveal further insights into data requirements and generalization capabilities. Given the impact of input resolution, developing multi-resolution architectures could provide inherent resilience against scaling-based evasion attempts. Lastly, extending detection capabilities to video content is crucial to address the increasing quality of video generation models. These advancements are critical to ensure SID keeps pace in the ongoing race with SIG.

References

1. Buslaev, A., et al.: Albumentations: fast and flexible image augmentations. arXiv e-prints (2018)
2. Agency, E.E.: Greenhouse gas emission intensity of electricity generation in Europe (2024). https://www.eea.europa.eu/en/analysis/indicators/greenhouse-gas-emission-intensity-of-1
3. Aghasanli, A., Kangin, D., Angelov, P.: Interpretable-through-prototypes deepfake detection for diffusion models. In: Proceedings of IEEE/CVF International Conference on Computer Vision, pp. 467–474 (2023)
4. Stable diffusion 3 medium (2024). https://huggingface.co/stabilityai/stable-diffusion-3-medium
5. Bammey, Q.: Synthbuster: towards detection of diffusion model generated images. IEEE Open J. Signal Process. (2023)
6. Cazenavette, G., Sud, A., Leung, T., Usman, B.: Fakeinversion: learning to detect images from unseen text-to-image models by inverting stable diffusion. In: Proceedings of the IEEE/CVF Conference on Computer Vision and Pattern Recognition, pp. 10759–10769 (2024)
7. Chang, Y.M., Yeh, C., Chiu, W.C., Yu, N.: Antifakeprompt: prompt-tuned vision-language models are fake image detectors. arXiv preprint arXiv:2310.17419 (2023)
8. Chen, B., Zeng, J., Yang, J., Yang, R.: DRCT: diffusion reconstruction contrastive training towards universal detection of diffusion generated images. In: Forty-First International Conference on Machine Learning (2024)
9. Coccomini, D.A., Esuli, A., Falchi, F., Gennaro, C., Amato, G.: Detecting images generated by diffusers. PeerJ Comput. Sci. **10**, e2127 (2024)
10. Corvi, R., Cozzolino, D., Poggi, G., Nagano, K., Verdoliva, L.: Intriguing properties of synthetic images: from generative adversarial networks to diffusion models. In: Proceedings of the IEEE/CVF Conference on Computer Vision and Pattern Recognition, pp. 973–982 (2023)
11. Sha, Z., Li, Z., Yu, N., Zhang, Y.: DE-FAKE: detection and attribution of fake images generated by text-to-image generation models. arXiv preprint arXiv:2210.06998 (2023)
12. Cozzolino, D., Poggi, G., Corvi, R., Nießner, M., Verdoliva, L.: Raising the bar of AI-generated image detection with clip. In: Proceedings of the IEEE/CVF Conference on Computer Vision and Pattern Recognition, pp. 4356–4366 (2024)
13. Del Moral, P., Nowaczyk, S., Pashami, S.: Why is multiclass classification hard? IEEE Access **10**, 80448–80462 (2022)
14. Deng, Y., Deng, X., Duan, Y., Xu, M.: Diffusion-generated fake face detection by exploring wavelet domain forgery clues. In: 2023 International Conference on Wireless Communications and Signal Processing (WCSP), pp. 1–6. IEEE (2023)
15. DucHaiten: realisticsdxl (2023). https://huggingface.co/datasets/DucHaiten/DucHaiten-realistic-SDXL
16. ehristoforu: dalle-3-images (2024). https://huggingface.co/datasets/ehristoforu/dalle-3-images
17. ehristoforu: midjourney-images (2024). https://huggingface.co/datasets/ehristoforu/midjourney-images
18. Frank, J., Eisenhofer, T., Schönherr, L., Fischer, A., Kolossa, D., Holz, T.: Leveraging frequency analysis for deep fake image recognition. In: International Conference on Machine Learning, pp. 3247–3258. PMLR (2020)

19. Grommelt, P., Weiss, L., Pfreundt, F.J., Keuper, J.: Fake or jpeg? Revealing common biases in generated image detection datasets. arXiv preprint arXiv:2403.17608 (2024)
20. Gustavosta: Stable-diffusion-prompts (2023). https://huggingface.co/datasets/Gustavosta/Stable-Diffusion-Prompts
21. Haralick, R.M., Shanmugam, K., Dinstein, I.H.: Textural features for image classification. IEEE Trans. Syst. Man Cybern. **6**, 610–621 (1973)
22. He, K., Zhang, X., Ren, S., Sun, J.: Deep residual learning for image recognition. In: Proceedings of the IEEE Conference on Computer Vision and Pattern Recognition, pp. 770–778 (2016)
23. Koutlis, C., Papadopoulos, S.: On the detection of synthetic images generated by diffusion models. arXiv preprint arXiv:2402.19091 (2024)
24. Labs, B.F.: Flux.1-dev (2024). https://huggingface.co/black-forest-labs/FLUX.1-dev
25. Laurier, L., Giulietta, A., Octavia, A., Cleti, M.: The cat and mouse game: the ongoing arms race between diffusion models and detection methods. arXiv preprint arXiv:2410.18866 (2024)
26. Li, J., Xu, Y., Lv, T., Cui, L., Zhang, C., Wei, F.: DIT: self-supervised pre-training for document image transformer. In: Proceedings of the 30th ACM International Conference on Multimedia, pp. 3530–3539 (2022)
27. Lin, T.Y., et al.: Microsoft coco: common objects in context (2015)
28. Liu, H., Tan, Z., Tan, C., Wei, Y., Wang, J., Zhao, Y.: Forgery-aware adaptive transformer for generalizable synthetic image detection. In: Proceedings of the IEEE/CVF Conference on Computer Vision and Pattern Recognition, pp. 10770–10780 (2024)
29. Liu, Z., Qi, X., Torr, P.H.: Global texture enhancement for fake face detection in the wild. In: Proceedings of the IEEE/CVF Conference on Computer Vision and Pattern Recognition, pp. 8060–8069 (2020)
30. Lorenz, P., Durall, R.L., Keuper, J.: Detecting images generated by deep diffusion models using their local intrinsic dimensionality. In: Proceedings of the IEEE/CVF International Conference on Computer Vision, pp. 448–459 (2023)
31. López Cuena, E.: Super-resolution assessment and detection (2023). http://hdl.handle.net/2117/395959
32. Ojha, U., Li, Y., Lee, Y.J.: Towards universal fake image detectors that generalize across generative models. In: Proceedings of the IEEE/CVF Conference on Computer Vision and Pattern Recognition, pp. 24480–24489 (2023)
33. Ricker, J., Damm, S., Holz, T., Fischer, A.: Towards the detection of diffusion model deepfakes. arXiv preprint arXiv:2210.14571 (2022)
34. Schinas, M., Papadopoulos, S.: Sidbench: a python framework for reliably assessing synthetic image detection methods. arXiv preprint arXiv:2404.18552 (2024)
35. Song, J., Ye, D., Zhang, Y.: Trinity detector: text-assisted and attention mechanisms based spectral fusion for diffusion generation image detection. arXiv preprint arXiv:2404.17254 (2024)
36. Tan, C., Zhao, Y., Wei, S., Gu, G., Liu, P., Wei, Y.: Frequency-aware deepfake detection: improving generalizability through frequency space learning. arXiv preprint arXiv:2403.07240 (2024)
37. Tan, C., Zhao, Y., Wei, S., Gu, G., Wei, Y.: Learning on gradients: generalized artifacts representation for GAN-generated images detection. In: Proceedings of the IEEE/CVF Conference on Computer Vision and Pattern Recognition, pp. 12105–12114 (2023)

38. Turc, I., Nemade, G.: Midjourney user prompts & generated images (250k) (2022). https://doi.org/10.34740/KAGGLE/DS/2349267. https://www.kaggle.com/ds/2349267
39. Proposal for a regulation of the European parliament and of the council laying down harmonised rules on artificial intelligence (artificial intelligence act) and amending certain union legislative acts (2024). https://artificialintelligenceact.eu/
40. Wang, S.Y., Wang, O., Zhang, R., Owens, A., Efros, A.A.: CNN-generated images are surprisingly easy to spot... for now. In: Proceedings of the IEEE/CVF Conference on Computer Vision and Pattern Recognition, pp. 8695–8704 (2020)
41. Wang, Z., et al.: Dire for diffusion-generated image detection. In: Proceedings of the IEEE/CVF International Conference on Computer Vision, pp. 22445–22455 (2023)
42. Wang, Z.J., Montoya, E., Munechika, D., Yang, H., Hoover, B., Chau, D.H.: DiffusionDB: a large-scale prompt gallery dataset for text-to-image generative models. arXiv:2210.14896 (2022). https://arxiv.org/abs/2210.14896
43. Weyand, T., Araujo, A., Cao, B., Sim, J.: Google landmarks dataset V2-a large-scale benchmark for instance-level recognition and retrieval. In: Proceedings of the IEEE/CVF Conference on Computer Vision and Pattern Recognition, pp. 2575–2584 (2020)
44. Wu, H., Zhou, J., Zhang, S.: Generalizable synthetic image detection via language-guided contrastive learning. arXiv preprint arXiv:2305.13800 (2023)
45. Xi, Z., Huang, W., Wei, K., Luo, W., Zheng, P.: AI-generated image detection using a cross-attention enhanced dual-stream network. In: 2023 Asia Pacific Signal and Information Processing Association Annual Summit and Conference (APSIPA ASC), pp. 1463–1470. IEEE (2023)
46. Xu, Q., Wang, H., Meng, L., Mi, Z., Yuan, J., Yan, H.: Exposing fake images generated by text-to-image diffusion models. Pattern Recogn. Lett. **176**, 76–82 (2023)
47. Young, P., Lai, A., Hodosh, M., Hockenmaier, J.: From image descriptions to visual denotations: new similarity metrics for semantic inference over event descriptions. Trans. Assoc. Comput. Linguist. **2**, 67–78 (2014)
48. Zhang, X., Karaman, S., Chang, S.F.: Detecting and simulating artifacts in GAN fake images. In: 2019 IEEE International Workshop on Information Forensics and Security (WIFS), pp. 1–6. IEEE (2019)
49. Zhong, N., Xu, Y., Li, S., Qian, Z., Zhang, X.: Patchcraft: exploring texture patch for efficient AI-generated image detection. arXiv preprint arXiv:2311.12397, pp. 1–18 (2024)
50. Zhu, M., et al.: Gendet: towards good generalizations for AI-generated image detection. arXiv preprint arXiv:2312.08880 (2023)
51. Zhu, M., et al.: Genimage: a million-scale benchmark for detecting AI-generated image. In: Advances in Neural Information Processing Systems, vol. 36 (2024)

ECD: Efficient Contrastive Decoding with Probabilistic Hallucination Detection

Laura Fieback[1,2](✉), Nishilkumar Balar[1], Jakob Spiegelberg[1], and Hanno Gottschalk[2]

[1] Volkswagen AG, Berliner Ring 2, 38440 Wolfsburg, Germany
{laura.fieback,nishilkumar.balar,jakob.spiegelberg}@volkswagen.de
[2] TU Berlin, Straße des 17. Juni 136, 10623 Berlin, Germany
gottschalk@math.tu-berlin.de

Abstract. Despite recent advances in Large Vision Language Models (LVLMs), these models still suffer from generating hallucinatory responses that do not align with the visual input provided. To mitigate such hallucinations, we introduce Efficient Contrastive Decoding (ECD), a simple method that leverages probabilistic hallucination detection to shift the output distribution towards contextually accurate answers at inference time. By contrasting token probabilities and hallucination scores, ECD subtracts hallucinated concepts from the original distribution, effectively suppressing hallucinations. Notably, our proposed method can be applied to any open-source LVLM and does not require additional LVLM training. We evaluate our method on several benchmark datasets and across different LVLMs. Our experiments show that ECD effectively mitigates hallucinations, outperforming state-of-the-art methods with respect to performance on LVLM benchmarks and computation time.

Keywords: Multimodal large language models · Contrastive decoding · Hallucination mitigation · Hallucination detection · Meta classification

1 Introduction

By aligning textual and visual features, LVLMs have shown an impressive vision-language understanding across various multimodal tasks like visual question answering (VQA) or image captioning [5,8,31]. However, inconsistencies between the generated response and the visual input, a phenomenon called hallucinations [28,35], diminish the applicability of LVLMs in safety-critical applications such

---

Supplementary Information The online version contains supplementary material available at https://doi.org/10.1007/978-3-032-06109-6_2.

as autonomous driving [13,45] or medicine [18,26]. Motivated by recent findings [15,20] that identified overreliance of LVLMs on language priors as one of the main reasons for hallucinations, new hallucinatory datasets and fine-tuning strategies have been proposed to mitigate hallucinations [11,12,17]. Contrastive Decoding (CD) strategies [25,43] emerged as a training-free alternative, addressing concerns about computational costs and human effort required for data labeling. The idea of CD is to intervene in the decoding process of LVLMs by amplifying the language prior through distorted inputs and contrasting the output distribution with the distribution derived from original inputs. While this approach effectively mitigates hallucinations and computational overhead, it still increases the inference time by calculating two output distributions.

In this work, we investigate the potential of probabilistic hallucination detection for Efficient Contrastive Decoding (ECD). During the decoding process, token scores are contrasted with hallucination scores to suppress hallucinations. We employ the idea of meta classification [6,24] to train a lightweight detector to estimate hallucination scores based on hallucination features derived from the model output. By investigating features from intermediate LVLM layers, we achieve area under precision recall curve values [7] of up to 74.05%. In contrast to existing CD methods, our approach requires only one forward pass of the LVLM followed by the lightweight hallucination detection, effectively reducing the inference time. Moreover, instead of amplifying hallucinations through input uncertainty, we directly learn hallucinated concepts from internal LVLM calculations, outperforming recent CD methods across several state-of-the-art LVLMs and benchmarks. In detail, ECD mitigates the hallucination rate by up to 5.74pp, i.e., 32% in open-ended tasks and improves F1 Scores by 23.02pp, i.e., 33% in discriminative VQA benchmarks, while adding only minor computational overhead to the decoding process. Our main contributions are as follows:

- We propose new hallucination features to train a powerful lightweight hallucination detector.
- Based on this detector, we introduce ECD, a lightweight and training-free decoding method that effectively mitigates hallucinations in LVLMs by penalizing mendacious tokens through hallucination scores.
- Through extensive experiments, we show the effectiveness of our approach outperforming state-of-the-art methods on various benchmarks and in computational time.

2 Related Work

2.1 Hallucination Mitigation for LVLMs

The research area of vision-language pre-trained models has made substantial progress by incorporating Large Language Models (LLMs) building the powerful Large Vision Language Models (LVLMs). In general, LVLMs consist of (i) a vision encoder to extract vision features from the input image, (ii) a cross-modal alignment module, which aligns the visual and language features, and (iii) an

LLM, which generates the text response. Despite remarkable zero-shot capabilities in multimodal tasks, LVLMs suffer from hallucinations, i.e., they generate answers that do not align with the input image. Several hallucination mitigation methods have been proposed comprising new instruction tuning datasets for LVLM retraining [11,12,17], leveraging expert models for post hoc hallucination correction [41,46], or incorporating object grounding features [4,23,30]. However, these methods require extensive data collection and annotation, LVLM retraining or architecture changes, which can be time-consuming and computationally costly. To cope with this problem, simple contrastive decoding strategies have been introduced, which contrast the output distributions with original and distorted inputs during inference. Based on the observation that hallucinations often occur due to the overreliance of LVLMs on language priors [35], the authors of Visual Contrastive Decoding (VCD) [25] propose to contrast the original output distribution with the distribution derived from noisy input images to subtract the language bias from the original distribution. Similarly, Instruction Contrastive Decoding (ICD) [43] adds prefixes to the text input to increase multimodal alignment uncertainty and finally contrasts the resulting distribution with the original output. Although these methods successfully mitigate hallucinations, they increase the inference time by performing one forward pass with original inputs and one with distorted inputs. Instead, we propose to contrast the output distribution with hallucination scores derived from internal LVLM calculations using meta classification, which effectively reduces computational costs during contrastive decoding.

2.2 Meta Classification for Hallucination Detection

In order to judge the reliability of LVLM responses, different hallucination detection methods have been introduced. These methods either apply a pipeline of stacked LLMs and LVLMs [19,44] to detect hallucinations as a post hoc method or train L(V)LM-based classifiers [12,20] using hand-crafted hallucination datasets. Since these methods are computationally costly, the authors of MetaToken [24] introduced a lightweight and simple hallucination detection method based on meta classification [6]. In general, meta classification refers to the classification of true and false predictions based on uncertainty features derived from the model output. This idea has been applied to various fields like image classification [3], semantic segmentation [9,32,36], video instance segmentation [33], and object detection [22,38]. In [24] new input features for the hallucination detection problem have been proposed that outperform classical uncertainty-based features and can be derived from internal LVLM calculations.

3 Method

3.1 LVLM Decoding

In general, LVLMs generate text responses in an autoregressive way by predicting the probability distribution over the dictionary $\mathcal{V}$ based on the input image v, the

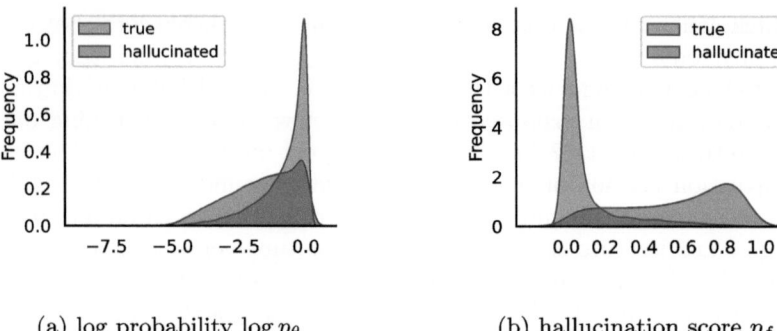

(a) log probability $\log p_\theta$ (b) hallucination score p_f

Fig. 1. Visualization of (a) log probability values and (b) hallucination scores for true and hallucinated tokens according to the MSCOCO CHAIR evaluation (see Sect. 4.2).

input query q, and the sequence already generated. In generation step t, the next token $y_t \in \mathcal{V}$ is generated by sampling from this distribution. Mathematically, this process can be formulated as

$$y_t \sim p_\theta(y_t|v, q, y_{<t}), \tag{1}$$

where θ denote the LVLM parameters and $y_{<t} = (y_0, \ldots, y_{t-1})$ the generated sequence up to generation step $t-1$. Note that a perfect model should assign high probabilities to true tokens and low probabilities to hallucinations. During this decoding mechanism, hallucinations might be generated when tokens with low probabilities are sampled from $p_\theta(y_t|v, q, y_{<t})$. However, as we can see in Fig. 1a, the phenomenon of hallucinations often occurs, as the model assigns high probability values to hallucinated tokens. Our approach corrects this undesired behavior by shifting the final distribution towards true tokens, reducing the probability assigned to hallucinations.

3.2 Probabilistic Hallucination Detection

As we have seen in the previous section, the probability distribution calculated during LVLM decoding does not properly distinguish between true and hallucinated tokens. The idea of meta classification is to learn this classification from hallucination features, which are derived from internal LVLM calculations. By learning from interactions and coherences of these features, the classifier can successfully distinguish between true tokens and hallucinations (see Fig. 1b).

To train our classifier, we build on the work of [24] and extend the set of input features to enhance the hallucination detection capabilities. While the features from [24] are based on the last LLM layer, we integrate further information from the preceding layers into our classifier. This idea is motivated by findings from the LLM literature [1,47] indicating that the middle layers contain information about the reliability of the generated response. To this end, let N denote the number of LLM transformer layers, let $v_0, \ldots, v_u$ denote the image tokens derived from the vision encoder and alignment module, and $q_0, \ldots, q_{w+t}$ the textual tokens representing the input query q and the sequence $y_{<t}$. The concatenated sequence of visual and textual tokens is fed into the LLM and successively processed by each layer i calculating the hidden states $\{h_0^i, \ldots, h_{u+(w+1)+t}^i\}$ with $i = 1, \ldots, N$. Finally, the vocabulary head $\phi(\cdot)$ predicts the probability distribution for the next token as

$$p_\theta(y_t | v, q, y_{<t}) = \text{softmax}\big[\phi(h_{u+(w+1)+t}^N)\big]_{y_t}, \quad y_t \in \mathcal{V}. \tag{2}$$

In order to extract information from the preceding layers, the early exit method [34, 39, 42] applies the language head to the hidden states of the earlier layers:

$$p_\theta^i(y_t | v, q, y_{<t}) = \text{softmax}\big[\phi(h_{u+(w+1)+t}^i)\big]_{y_t}, \quad i \in \{1, \ldots, N\}. \tag{3}$$

For a shorter notation, we write p_θ^i. Moreover, let $\text{Att}_{y_t}^{i,g}(j)$ denote the attention on token j in generation step t for layer i and attention head g with $g = 1, \ldots, G$. With this notation, we introduce new features based on intermediate layers:

- the negative log-likelihood for all layers

$$B^i(y_t) = -\log p_\theta^i, \quad i = 1, \ldots, N \tag{4}$$

- the KullbackLeibler (KL) [37] divergence between the preceding layers and the last layer

$$K^i(y_t) = \text{KL}(p_\theta^N \| p_\theta^i) := p_\theta^N \log \frac{p_\theta^N}{p_\theta^i}, \quad i = 1, \ldots, N-1 \tag{5}$$

- for each attention head, the entropy of the image attention over the layers

$$E_{v_k,g}^{\text{layer}}(y_t) = -\frac{1}{N} \sum_{i=1}^{N} \text{Att}_{y_t}^{i,g}(v_k) \log \text{Att}_{y_t}^{i,g}(v_k), \quad g = 1, \ldots, G \tag{6}$$

averaged over the image tokens with

$$E_g^{\text{layer}}(y_t) = \frac{1}{u+1} \sum_{k=0}^{u} E_{v_k,g}^{\text{layer}}(y_t) \tag{7}$$

- for each layer, the entropy of the image attention over the attention heads

$$E_{v_k,i}^{\text{head}}(y_t) = -\frac{1}{G} \sum_{g=1}^{G} \text{Att}_{y_t}^{i,g}(v_k) \log \text{Att}_{y_t}^{i,g}(v_k), \quad i = 1, \ldots, N \tag{8}$$

averaged over the image tokens with

$$E_i^{\text{head}}(y_t) = \frac{1}{u+1} \sum_{k=0}^{u} E_{v_k,i}^{\text{head}}(y_t). \tag{9}$$

We aggregate the features from [24] (see supplementary material A) and our proposed inputs to train the classifier. Let $\mathcal{M}$ denote the set of hallucination features and m_{y_l} the corresponding vector for a generated token $y_l \in \mathcal{V}$. The meta classifier can be defined as

$$f : \mathbb{R}^{|\mathcal{M}|} \to \{0, 1\}. \tag{10}$$

Following [24], we use the CHAIR evaluation [35] to extract true ($z_l = 0$) and hallucinated ($z_l = 1$) tokens from LVLM responses to build our training and validation data with standardized inputs m_{y_l} and corresponding labels z_l as

$$\{(m_{y_l}, z_l) \mid l = 1, \ldots, L\}. \tag{11}$$

Once the classifier is trained, we can detect hallucinations during the LVLM generation process by computing the proposed features and applying the classifier afterwards as

$$f(m_{y_t}) = \begin{cases} 1, & p_f(y_t|v, q, y_{<t}) \geq \tau \\ 0, & p_f(y_t|v, q, y_{<t}) < \tau \end{cases} \tag{12}$$

with the estimated probability $p_f(y_t|v, q, y_{<t})$ for tokens to be hallucinated, referred to as hallucination scores, and the threshold τ controlling the precision-recall ratio. Note that the input vector m_{y_t} can be calculated in an automated manner based on internal LVLM calculations only, without any knowledge of the ground truth data.

3.3 Efficient Contrastive Decoding

By directly learning hallucinated concepts, we suppress the generation of hallucinations during the decoding process without an additional LVLM forward pass. In contrast to existing methods, which model the language bias of LVLMs by generating a second output distribution with distorted inputs, we apply a lightweight classifier on the LVLM output to obtain hallucination scores $p_f(y_t|v, q, y_{<t})$, adding only minor computational overhead to the decoding process. At generation step t, the contrastive distribution is computed by subtracting the hallucination scores from the log probabilities $\log p_\theta(y_t|v, q, y_{<t})$ to penalize hallucinations while maintaining high probabilities for true tokens:

$$p_{ecd}(y_t|v, q, y_{<t}) = \text{softmax}\big[(1 + \alpha) \log p_\theta(y_t|v, q, y_{<t}) \\ - \alpha \log p_f(y_t|v, q, y_{<t})\big], \tag{13}$$

where α controls the magnitude of hallucination correction. Note that for $\alpha = 0$, p_{ecd} is equal to the initial LVLM distribution. Moreover, our proposed efficient contrastive decoding can be integrated into various decoding strategies such as the standard greedy search, beam search [10], and nucleus sampling [14].

3.4 Adaptive Plausibility Constraint

We follow the implementation of VCD [25] and ICD [43] and incorporate an adaptive plausibility constraint (APC) [27] based on the confidence level of the LVLM distribution to maintain high probabilities for semantically trivial tokens. By refining the final contrastive distribution, APC effectively prevents the generation of implausible tokens, and thus preserves the semantic accuracy of the response. This leads to the final formulation of our proposed decoding strategy:

$$y_t \sim p_{ecd}(y_t|v,q,y_{<t}), \quad \text{subject to}$$
$$y_t \in \mathcal{V}_{\text{head}} = \{y_t \in \mathcal{V} \mid p_\theta(y_t|v,q,y_{<t}) \geq \beta \max_\omega p_\theta(\omega|v,q,y_{<t})\} \quad (14)$$

with truncation parameter $\beta \in [0,1]$, where $\beta = 1$ implements the standard greedy search algorithm.

4 Experimental Setup

4.1 Hallucination Detection

We evaluate the information content of our proposed input features ($|\mathcal{M}| = 169$) to learn the differentiation between true and hallucinated answers. First, we sample 5,000 images from the MSCOCO [29] validation set and apply the prompt

"Describe all objects in the image."

to generate training and validation data for the probabilistic classifier. This results in approximately 30.000 data points depending on the number of objects generated by the respective LVLM (see [24]). As in [24], we employ a logistic regression (LR) and gradient boosting (GB) classifier, which have shown superior performance compared to small neural networks in previous studies [33], and use the features from [24] as our baseline. In detail, we use the LR[1] classifier with saga solver and the GB[2] classifier both with max_iter = 1000 and scikit-learn version 1.5.2. The detection results are evaluated in terms of accuracy (ACC), area under receiver operator characteristic curve (AUROC) and area under precision recall curve (AUPRC) [7]. We average our results over ten randomly sampled training-validation splits using a ratio of 80% training data and 20% validation data.

---

[1] https://scikit-learn.org/stable/modules/generated/sklearn.linear_model.LogisticRegression.html.
[2] https://scikit-learn.org/stable/modules/generated/sklearn.ensemble.HistGradientBoostingClassifier.html.

4.2 Datasets and Evaluation Metrics

CHAIR: The Caption Hallucination Assessment with Image Relevance (CHAIR) [35] metric is widely used in open-ended image captioning tasks and measures the hallucination and coverage rate of LVLMs by checking extracted objects from the generated response against MSCOCO ground-truth labels. CHAIR is defined on the instance level CHAIR_i and sentence level CHAIR_s as

$$\text{CHAIR}_i = \frac{|\{\text{hallucinated objects}\}|}{|\{\text{all objects mentioned}\}|}, \text{Coverage} = \frac{|\{\text{mentioned objects}\}|}{|\{\text{labeled objects}\}|}, \tag{15}$$

$$\text{and} \quad \text{CHAIR}_s = \frac{|\{\text{captions with hallucinated objects}\}|}{|\{\text{all captions}\}|}. \tag{16}$$

For the evaluation of our proposed contrastive decoding method, we sample additional 500 images from the MSCOCO validation set, which do not overlap with the hallucination detection training and validation data.

AMBER: An LLM-free Multi-dimensional Benchmark (AMBER) [21]. Since our probabilistic classifier was trained on the MSCOCO dataset, which might lead to biased results in the preceding evaluation, we additionally evaluate our method on the AMBER dataset, which covers a more diverse range of object categories. In detail, AMBER covers 337 objects compared to 80 categories for the MSCOCO dataset. The open-ended image captions are again evaluated using CHAIR_i, CHAIR_s, and Coverage metrics.

POPE: The Polling-based Object Probing Evaluation (POPE) [28] is a discriminative VQA benchmark to assess the quality of LVLMs with respect to object hallucinations. In detail, POPE uses the template

"Is there a {object} in the image?"

and applies three different sampling strategies to generate negative prompts, which refer to non-existent objects. The *random* (rand.) sampling chooses the probing objects randomly, *popular* (pop.) samples from high-frequency objects and *adversarial* (adv.) samples among objects, which frequently co-occur with the ground-truth objects. Positive prompts are generated on the basis of ground-truth data. The POPE benchmark covers three datasets, MSCOCO [29], A-OKVQA [40], and GQA [16]. For each dataset, POPE samples 500 images from the validation sets and formulates 6 probing questions (3 positive and 3 negative prompts) for each image and sampling strategy, yielding a total of 27,000 question-answer pairs. The results are evaluated in terms of Accuracy and F1 Score.

MME: The Multimodal LLM Evaluation (MME) benchmark [2] is another discriminative VQA benchmark, which measures perception and cognition abilities of LVLMs on 14 subtasks comprising 1,193 images. For each image, there is one positive and one negative question. The evaluation metric is a combined score of the accuracy over all questions and the accuracy+, which is based on each image, that is, both questions need to be answered correctly. Following [25], we average the results over five runs. The standard deviations are given in parentheses.

4.3 Baselines and Implementation Details

We evaluate our proposed ECD method on three state-of-the-art LVLMs, LLaVA 1.5 [31], InstructBLIP [5], and MiniGPT-4 [8] with Vicuna-7B LLM decoder, using nucleus sampling [14] with top_p $= 0.9$. The detailed configuration settings applied in our experiments are summarized in Table 1. We compare our approach against regular decoding (denoted as "regular" in our tables) and the contrastive decoding methods VCD [25] and ICD [43]. Throughout our experiments, we use $\alpha = 1$ unless explicitly stated otherwise. All experiments are performed on a single A100 GPU.

5 Results

5.1 Hallucination Detection Results

In this section, we evaluate the information content of our proposed input features (see Sect. 3.2) for probabilistic hallucination detection. The focus of our evaluation is on the AUPRC values as we observe highly imbalanced datasets, i.e., low hallucination rates. The results for the LR and GB classifier are stated in Table 2. Our new input features outperform the baseline features in all settings

Table 1. LVLM Generation Configurations. The generation configurations applied in our experiments for nucleus sampling [14] and greedy search.

parameter	nucleus sampling	greedy search
do_sample	True	False
top_p	0.9	1
temperature	1	1
num_beams	1	1
max_length	256	256
min_length	1	1
repetition_penalty	1	1
length_penalty	1	1

Table 2. Detection Results. Detection results for the LVLMs LLaVA 1.5 (LV), InstructBLIP (IB), and MiniGPT-4 (MG) with respective hallucination rates CHAIR$_i$ (C_i). The best results in each block are in bold face. The standard deviations are given in parentheses.

LVLM (C_i in %)	Set	ACC ↑		AUROC ↑		AUPRC ↑	
		LR	GB	LR	GB	LR	GB
LV	[24]	87.1$^{(\pm 0.2)}$	87.7$^{(\pm 0.3)}$	89.9$^{(\pm 0.4)}$	90.8$^{(\pm 0.4)}$	68.9$^{(\pm 1.1)}$	71.5$^{(\pm 0.9)}$
(18.61)	Ours	87.9$^{(\pm 0.2)}$	**88.3**$^{(\pm 0.3)}$	91.3$^{(\pm 0.3)}$	**91.9**$^{(\pm 0.4)}$	72.1$^{(\pm 1.2)}$	**74.1**$^{(\pm 1.0)}$
IB	[24]	91.8$^{(\pm 0.1)}$	91.9$^{(\pm 0.2)}$	90.2$^{(\pm 1.2)}$	90.4$^{(\pm 1.1)}$	56.7$^{(\pm 5.1)}$	56.7$^{(\pm 4.3)}$
(10.13)	Ours	**92.5**$^{(\pm 0.1)}$	92.3$^{(\pm 0.1)}$	**91.8**$^{(\pm 1.0)}$	91.5$^{(\pm 0.8)}$	**61.4**$^{(\pm 4.4)}$	60.1$^{(\pm 4.4)}$
MG	[24]	89.6$^{(\pm 0.3)}$	89.7$^{(\pm 0.3)}$	88.6$^{(\pm 1.8)}$	88.8$^{(\pm 1.4)}$	56.6$^{(\pm 6.5)}$	56.6$^{(\pm 5.9)}$
(13.05)	Ours	90.4$^{(\pm 0.2)}$	**90.5**$^{(\pm 0.3)}$	90.8$^{(\pm 1.6)}$	**90.9**$^{(\pm 1.2)}$	**62.5**$^{(\pm 8.8)}$	62.2$^{(\pm 5.5)}$

by up to 5.89pp in AUPRC values. While the LR and GB classifiers show equal performance on InstructBLIP and MiniGPT-4, we observe superiority of the GB model for LLaVA 1.5 with an improvement of 1.96pp in terms of AUPRC. Thus, we employ the GB model in the following experiments.

5.2 Discriminative Results

POPE: Table 3 summarizes our results on the POPE dataset in terms of accuracy (Acc) and F1 Scores. Our proposed ECD method is superior to the baselines in almost all settings while maintaining low computation costs, improving the F1 Score by up to 23.02pp, i.e., 33%. Note that although the probabilistic hallucination detection was trained on the MSCOCO dataset, our results demonstrate a consistent performance improvement across all datasets (MSCOCO, A-OKVQA, and GQA) underlining the ability of the meta classifier to judge hallucinations on new data. Furthermore, we observe consistent performance across all sampling strategies (random, popular, and adversarial) showing that the meta classifier effectively learned hallucinatory concepts beyond the language bias induced by the LVLM training [35]. For a detailed analysis of the precision and recall values, we refer to supplementary material B, unveiling the outstanding ability of our method to accurately negate negative prompts, which contain hallucinations.

MME: The MME benchmark evaluates hallucinations beyond the object level and measures general perception and cognition abilities. Table 4 presents our results. For LLaVA 1.5 and MiniGPT-4, our method not only improves the perception ability, but also enhances the performance in cognition and reasoning tasks compared to the baseline methods. Moreover, the detailed evaluation of the 14 subtasks and computational time in supplementary material B shows that

Table 3. Discriminative Results on POPE. Experimental results on the POPE benchmark in terms of accuracy (Acc.), F1 Score and the average inference time per question (time). The best results in each block are in bold face.

			LLaVA 1.5			InstructBLIP			MiniGPT-4		
			time ↓	Acc. ↑	F1 ↑	time ↓	Acc. ↑	F1 ↑	time ↓	Acc. ↑	F1 ↑
MSCOCO		regular	**0.7**	87.57	87.90	**0.5**	83.90	84.01	**1.3**	54.77	52.67
		VCD	1.3	88.10	88.49	1.0	86.00	85.92	2.6	55.63	51.33
		ICD	1.2	87.70	87.79	0.8	86.67	85.43	1.6	57.57	59.60
	rand.	Ours	**0.7**	**89.00**	**89.28**	0.7	**89.00**	**88.69**	1.4	**69.07**	**72.43**
		regular	**0.6**	83.50	84.57	**0.5**	77.63	79.18	**1.3**	48.60	49.31
		VCD	1.2	85.03	85.87	1.0	78.10	79.46	2.6	50.30	48.50
		ICD	1.2	85.93	86.46	0.8	79.47	78.93	1.6	52.70	57.68
	pop.	Ours	0.7	**86.97**	**87.60**	0.7	**82.57**	**83.23**	1.4	**58.63**	**66.27**
		regular	**0.6**	77.93	80.38	**0.5**	73.90	76.52	**1.3**	47.87	48.96
		VCD	1.2	78.23	80.62	1.0	75.10	77.36	2.5	48.83	47.77
		ICD	1.3	**80.07**	81.53	0.8	77.77	77.77	1.7	52.63	57.90
	adv.	Ours	0.7	79.37	**81.58**	0.7	**78.33**	**79.93**	1.4	**57.27**	**65.54**
A-OKVQA		regular	**0.6**	84.77	86.22	**0.5**	82.03	82.98	**1.3**	49.40	47.40
		VCD	1.2	84.30	85.92	1.0	82.70	83.42	2.6	52.13	48.49
		ICD	1.2	85.20	86.50	0.8	85.57	84.80	1.6	54.83	58.14
	rand.	Ours	0.8	**86.50**	**87.83**	0.7	**87.87**	**88.16**	1.4	**65.70**	**70.42**
		regular	**0.6**	78.17	81.47	**0.5**	75.83	78.35	**1.3**	46.37	47.50
		VCD	1.2	78.50	81.73	1.0	76.83	78.93	2.6	47.00	44.87
		ICD	1.2	**80.20**	82.69	0.8	79.33	79.39	1.6	49.10	55.13
	pop.	Ours	0.8	80.03	**82.96**	0.7	**80.23**	**82.13**	1.4	**58.13**	**66.11**
		regular	**0.6**	68.80	75.25	**0.5**	70.60	74.87	**1.3**	43.90	46.11
		VCD	1.1	69.20	75.65	1.0	70.47	74.69	2.6	45.77	45.31
		ICD	1.2	**71.63**	**76.98**	0.8	72.03	73.90	1.6	45.77	52.74
	adv.	Ours	0.8	69.07	75.80	0.7	**72.40**	**76.72**	1.4	**53.70**	**63.57**
GQA		regular	**0.6**	84.07	85.74	**0.6**	79.97	80.95	**1.3**	50.93	50.10
		VCD	1.2	84.80	86.36	1.0	81.53	82.33	2.5	53.80	53.58
		ICD	1.2	**86.53**	87.65	0.8	83.03	81.84	1.6	55.10	59.05
	rand.	Ours	0.8	86.43	**87.78**	0.7	**86.07**	**86.33**	1.4	**64.10**	**69.70**
		regular	**0.6**	74.60	78.99	**0.6**	73.57	76.34	**1.3**	45.43	47.45
		VCD	1.2	73.40	78.16	1.0	74.13	76.88	2.5	49.33	51.28
		ICD	1.1	**75.73**	**79.72**	0.8	75.93	76.22	1.6	47.83	55.20
	pop.	Ours	0.8	74.63	79.14	0.7	**77.63**	**79.77**	1.4	**55.50**	**64.99**
		regular	**0.6**	69.10	75.50	**0.6**	68.73	73.18	**1.3**	43.97	47.42
		VCD	1.2	69.73	**75.94**	1.0	70.57	74.43	2.6	46.97	49.06
		ICD	1.1	**70.03**	75.89	0.8	71.47	72.84	1.6	47.23	54.91
	adv.	Ours	0.8	69.10	75.89	0.7	**72.03**	**76.12**	1.4	**52.80**	**63.80**

Table 4. Discriminative Results on MME. Experimental results on the MME benchmark in terms of Perception and Cognition scores [2]. The best results in each block are in bold face.

	LLaVA 1.5		InstructBLIP		MiniGPT-4	
	Perception ↑	Cognition ↑	Perception ↑	Cognition ↑	Perception ↑	Cognition ↑
regular	1291.1$^{(\pm33.1)}$	317.4$^{(\pm21.0)}$	1117.5$^{(\pm23.6)}$	**322.1**$^{(\pm33.3)}$	409.9$^{(\pm20.2)}$	163.6$^{(\pm13.0)}$
VCD	1288.6$^{(\pm33.4)}$	338.9$^{(\pm16.9)}$	1155.2$^{(\pm29.9)}$	291.1$^{(\pm16.4)}$	355.9$^{(\pm22.2)}$	140.1$^{(\pm19.5)}$
ICD	1314.4$^{(\pm27.3)}$	318.9$^{(\pm22.4)}$	**1258.6**$^{(\pm19.7)}$	295.4$^{(\pm35.4)}$	**514.2**$^{(\pm29.4)}$	137.8$^{(\pm13.1)}$
Ours	**1400.3**$^{(\pm13.9)}$	**346.3**$^{(\pm19.2)}$	1105.2$^{(\pm17.4)}$	282.3$^{(\pm13.5)}$	502.8$^{(\pm17.1)}$	**176.4**$^{(\pm25.1)}$

Table 5. Generative Results. Experimental results on the CHAIR benchmark for the open-ended captioning tasks using the MSCOCO and AMBER datasets. The results are stated in terms of average inference time per image caption (time), CHAIR$_i$ (C_i), CHAIR$_s$ (C_s), and Coverage (Cov.). The best results in each block are in bold face.

	MSCOCO [29]											
	LLaVA 1.5				InstructBLIP				MiniGPT-4			
	time ↓	C_i ↓	C_s ↓	Cov. ↑	time ↓	C_i ↓	C_s ↓	Cov. ↑	time ↓	C_i ↓	C_s ↓	Cov. ↑
regular	**2.7**	17.86	55.00	82.14	**3.5**	9.26	30.80	90.74	**10.1**	11.60	**27.47**	88.40
VCD	5.3	16.32	53.80	83.68	6.3	8.45	30.80	91.55	18.9	10.58	28.60	89.42
ICD	4.5	14.27	45.40	85.73	5.8	10.92	37.80	89.08	15.4	10.51	28.20	89.49
Ours	3.6	**12.12**	**43.40**	**87.88**	4.6	**7.28**	**26.60**	**92.72**	12.8	**9.25**	31.66	**90.75**
	AMBER [21]											
	LLaVA 1.5				InstructBLIP				MiniGPT-4			
	time ↓	C_i ↓	C_s ↓	Cov. ↑	time ↓	C_i ↓	C_s ↓	Cov. ↑	time ↓	C_i ↓	C_s ↓	Cov. ↑
regular	**2.2**	9.99	45.56	**51.97**	**2.9**	8.74	39.38	**51.56**	**9.4**	16.68	61.78	57.71
VCD	4.1	8.16	38.42	51.63	5.4	7.73	34.36	50.50	17.4	14.18	**53.09**	58.23
ICD	3.5	8.46	36.87	49.98	5.3	8.11	35.71	49.02	15.3	16.83	58.11	55.35
Ours	2.8	**7.04**	**33.20**	51.21	4.2	**6.00**	**26.45**	50.39	12.4	**13.14**	61.58	**61.03**

ECD outperforms the baselines on most of these individual tasks and demonstrates the superior performance-cost trade-off, that is, ECD outperforms the baselines with respect to performance and inference time. Note that although the averaged ECD perception and cognition scores for InstructBLIP are below the baseline scores, our analysis of the subtasks shows that ECD outperforms the baselines on individual tasks while maintaining low computational costs.

5.3 Generative Results

MSCOCO: In addition to the discriminative results, we also evaluate our method on the open-ended captioning task. Note that for MiniGPT-4, we apply the parameter $\alpha = 6$ (see Sect. 5.4 for an ablation study for α). The results are summarized in Table 5. ECD distinctly reduces the hallucination rate both at the instance and sentence level, while simultaneously increasing the detailedness of the generated response in terms of Coverage. In all experiments, ECD is superior to the baseline methods VCD and ICD with respect to performance and computational time. Only in the case of MiniGPT-4, ECD increases the sentence level hallucination rate CHAIR$_s$ while still decreasing the total number of hallucinations CHAIR$_i$ and simultaneously increasing the Coverage. Compared to regular decoding, ECD reduces the instance level hallucination rate by up to 5.74pp, i.e., 32% while at the same time increasing the Coverage by 5.74pp, i.e., 7% while maintaining low computational costs.

Table 6. Ablation: Decoding Configuration. Ablation results on the discriminative POPE benchmark [28] for nucleus sampling [14] decoding with top_p = 1 and greedy decoding. The best results in each block are in bold face.

		LLaVA 1.5			InstructBLIP			MiniGPT-4		
		time ↓	Acc. ↑	F1 ↑	time ↓	Acc. ↑	F1 ↑	time ↓	Acc. ↑	F1 ↑
$p = 1$	regular	**0.6**	82.47	83.55	**0.5**	74.53	75.97	**1.3**	45.37	44.87
	VCD	1.2	84.13	85.13	1.0	77.53	79.13	2.6	48.33	46.40
	ICD	1.2	85.70	86.22	0.8	79.80	79.37	1.7	52.57	57.07
	Ours	0.8	**86.20**	**86.85**	0.6	**82.07**	**82.87**	1.4	**58.07**	**66.26**
greedy	regular	**0.6**	87.70	88.21	**0.5**	82.40	83.36	**1.3**	**71.20**	**73.35**
	VCD	1.2	87.70	88.21	0.9	81.03	81.99	2.6	68.60	68.11
	ICD	1.2	**88.10**	**88.31**	0.8	81.87	81.10	1.7	65.80	70.55
	Ours	0.8	87.60	88.13	0.7	**83.27**	**83.83**	1.4	60.17	69.98

AMBER: Since the ECD meta classifier was trained on the MSCOCO dataset, we investigate the potential of our classifier on new concepts. The results in Table 5 underline our findings from the discriminative results (Sect. 5.2). Again, ECD successfully suppresses hallucinations due to the classifier's ability to judge hallucinations on new data. More precisely, we reduce the instance level hallucination rate by 2.95pp, i.e., 30% while maintaining the detailedness of the generated response and low computational costs. While we see a minor decrease in Coverage for LLaVA 1.5 and InstructBLIP, ECD effectively reduces the hallucination rate in terms of both, CHAIR$_i$ and CHAIR$_s$. In the case of MiniGPT-4, we again observe an increase in CHAIR$_s$ while effectively improving the instance level hallucination rate CHAIR$_i$ as well as the Coverage.

5.4 Ablations

LVLM Decoding Configuration: We conduct additional experiments for the POPE MSCOCO popular setting using nucleus sampling with top_p = 1 and greedy search decoding. The results are summarized in Table 6. While the results

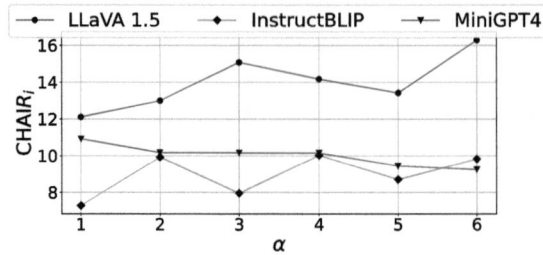

Fig. 2. Ablation study for hyperparameter α.

for regular nucleus sampling with top_p = 1 are below the top_p = 0.9 results from Table 3, all contrastive decoding strategies maintain the performance in the top_p = 1 setting. Again, our method outperforms VCD [25] and ICD [43] with respect to performance and computational time. Note that for the greedy search setting, the contrastive decoding methods achieve a minor performance increase only, where for MiniGPT-4 regular decoding performs best.

ECD Hyperparameter: Moreover, we investigate the influence of the hyperparameter α in our method on the CHAIR open-ended text generation task. Figure 2 depicts the results. While for LLaVA 1.5 and InstructBLIP the best results are achieved applying $\alpha = 1$, for MiniGPT-4 the best performance is achieved with $\alpha = 6$, i.e., a higher magnitude of hallucination correction. However, note that for MiniGPT-4 different α values result in minor performance changes in terms of the hallucination rate $CHAIR_i$ only.

6 Limitations

The focus of our paper is on visual hallucinations of LVLMs, where contextual hallucinations in LLMs might have different origins, which need to be studied to ensure a successful transfer of our method to the unimodal domain. However, note that many hallucination features are specifically designed for the transformer architecture, which can be directly transferred to LLMs, further broadening the impact of this work. Moreover, recent advances in video LVLMs motivate the investigation of temporal hallucinations, a problem we will tackle in future work.

7 Conclusion

In this paper, we investigate the power of probabilistic hallucination detection for contrastive decoding. We introduce Efficient Contrastive Decoding (ECD), a lightweight and training-free method, which shifts the LVLM output distribution towards accurate responses during decoding by penalizing hallucinations. Extensive experimental results demonstrate the efficacy of our proposed method, which outperforms state-of-the-art methods on various LVLM baselines. Our experiments show that ECD not only mitigates hallucinations but also enhances the perception capabilities of LVLMs. Moreover, in contrast to existing methods, our lightweight approach is computationally efficient, adding only minor computational overhead to the decoding process.

Ethics Considerations. Our work addresses the hallucination issue in state-of-the-art LVLMs enhancing the reliability and integrity of LVLMs in real-world scenarios, especially in safety-critical applications such as autonomous driving or medicine. Moreover, our work does not include any personal data, human subjects or sensitive data.

Disclaimer. The results, opinions and conclusions expressed in this publication are not necessarily those of Volkswagen Aktiengesellschaft.

Disclosure of Interests. The authors have no competing interests to declare that are relevant to the content of this article.

References

1. Azaria, A., Mitchell, T.: The internal state of an LLM knows when it is lying. In: Findings of the Association for Computational Linguistics: EMNLP 2023, pp. 967–976 (2023)
2. Fu, C., et al.: MME: a comprehensive evaluation benchmark for multimodal large language models. arXiv preprint arXiv:2306.13394 (2024)
3. Chen, T., Navratil, J., Iyengar, V., Shanmugam, K.: Confidence scoring using whitebox meta-models with linear classifier probes. In: Proceedings of the Twenty-Second International Conference on Artificial Intelligence and Statistics, pp. 1467–1475 (2019)
4. Chen, Z., Zhao, Z., Luo, H., Yao, H., Li, B., Zhou, J.: HALC: object hallucination reduction via adaptive focal-contrast decoding. In: Proceedings of the 41st International Conference on Machine Learning (2024)
5. Dai, W., et al.: InstructBLIP: towards general-purpose vision-language models with instruction tuning. In: Proceedings of the 37th International Conference on Neural Information Processing Systems (2023)
6. Hendrycks, D., Gimpel, K.: A baseline for detecting misclassified and out-of-distribution examples in neural networks. In: International Conference on Learning Representations (2017)
7. Davis, J., Goadrich, M.: The relationship between precision-recall and roc curves. In: Proceedings of the 23rd International Conference on Machine Learning, pp. 233–240 (2006)
8. Zhu, D., Chen, J., Shen, X., Li, X., Elhoseiny, M.: MiniGPT-4: enhancing vision-language understanding with advanced large language models. In: The Twelfth International Conference on Learning Representations (2024)
9. Fieback, L., Dash, B., Spiegelberg, J., Gottschalk, H.: Temporal performance prediction for deep convolutional long short-term memory networks. In: Advanced Analytics and Learning on Temporal Data, pp. 145–158 (2023)

10. Freitag, M., Al-Onaizan, Y.: Beam search strategies for neural machine translation. In: Proceedings of the First Workshop on Neural Machine Translation (2017)
11. Liu, F., Lin, K., Li, L., Wang, J., Yacoob, Y., Wang, L.: Mitigating hallucination in large multi-modal models via robust instruction tuning. In: The Twelfth International Conference on Learning Representations (2024)
12. Gunjal, A., Yin, J., Bas, E.: Detecting and preventing hallucinations in large vision language models. In: Proceedings of the AAAI Conference on Artificial Intelligence, pp. 18135–18143 (2024)
13. Gao, H., Wang, Z., Li, Y., Long, K., Yang, M., Shen, Y.: A survey for foundation models in autonomous driving. arXiv preprint arXiv:2402.01105 (2024)
14. Holtzman, A., Buys, J., Du, L., Forbes, M., Choi, Y.: The curious case of neural text degeneration. In: International Conference on Learning Representations (2020)
15. Yan, H., Liu, L., Feng, X., Huang, Q.: Overcoming language priors with self-contrastive learning for visual question answering. In: Multimedia Tools and Applications, pp. 16343–16358 (2023)
16. Hudson, D.A., Manning, C.D.: GQA: a new dataset for real-world visual reasoning and compositional question answering. In: 2019 IEEE/CVF Conference on Computer Vision and Pattern Recognition (CVPR), pp. 6693–6702 (2019)
17. Jiang, C., et al.: Hallucination augmented contrastive learning for multimodal large language model. In: 2024 IEEE/CVF Conference on Computer Vision and Pattern Recognition (CVPR), pp. 27026–27036 (2024)
18. Jiang, Y., et al.: Evaluating general vision-language models for clinical medicine. medRxiv (2024)
19. Jing, L., Li, R., Chen, Y., Du, X.: Faithscore: fine-grained evaluations of hallucinations in large vision-language models. In: Findings of the Association for Computational Linguistics: EMNLP 2024, pp. 5042–5063 (2024)
20. Wang, J., et al.: Evaluation and analysis of hallucination in large vision-language models. arXiv preprint arXiv:2308.15126 (2023)
21. Wang, J., et al.: Amber: an LLM-free multi-dimensional benchmark for mllms hallucination evaluation. arXiv preprint arXiv:2311.07397 (2024)
22. Kowol, K., Rottmann, M., Bracke, S., Gottschalk, H.: Yodar: uncertainty-based sensor fusion for vehicle detection with camera and radar sensors. In: Proceedings of the 13th International Conference on Agents and Artificial Intelligence, pp. 177–186 (2021)
23. Kim, M., Kim, M., Bae, J., Choi, S., Kim, S., Chang, B.: Exploiting semantic reconstruction to mitigate hallucinations in vision-language models. In: Computer Vision – ECCV 2024, pp. 236–252 (2025)
24. Fieback, L., Spiegelberg, J., Gottschalk, H.: Metatoken: detecting hallucination in image descriptions by meta classification. In: Proceedings of the 20th International Joint Conference on Computer Vision, Imaging and Computer Graphics Theory and Applications, pp. 126–137 (2025)
25. Leng, S., et al.: Mitigating object hallucinations in large vision-language models through visual contrastive decoding. In: Proceedings of the IEEE/CVF Conference on Computer Vision and Pattern Recognition (CVPR), pp. 13872–13882 (2024)
26. Li, C., et al.: Llava-med: training a large language-and-vision assistant for biomedicine in one day. In: Proceedings of the 37th International Conference on Neural Information Processing Systems (2023)
27. Li, X.L., et al.: Contrastive decoding: open-ended text generation as optimization. In: Proceedings of the 61st Annual Meeting of the Association for Computational Linguistics, pp. 12286–12312 (2023)

28. Li, Y., Du, Y., Zhou, K., Wang, J., Zhao, X., Wen, J.R.: Evaluating object hallucination in large vision-language models. In: Proceedings of the 2023 Conference on Empirical Methods in Natural Language Processing, pp. 292–305 (2023)
29. Lin, T.-Y., et al.: Microsoft COCO: common objects in context. In: Fleet, D., Pajdla, T., Schiele, B., Tuytelaars, T. (eds.) ECCV 2014. LNCS, vol. 8693, pp. 740–755. Springer, Cham (2014). https://doi.org/10.1007/978-3-319-10602-1_48
30. Zhao, L., Deng, Y., Zhang, W., Gu, Q.: Mitigating object hallucination in large vision-language models via classifier-free guidance. arXiv preprint arXiv:2402.08680 (2024)
31. Liu, H., Li, C., Wu, Q., Lee, Y.J.: Visual instruction tuning. In: Proceedings of the 37th International Conference on Neural Information Processing Systems (2023)
32. Maag, K., Rottmann, M., Gottschalk, H.: Time-dynamic estimates of the reliability of deep semantic segmentation networks. In: 2020 IEEE 32nd International Conference on Tools with Artificial Intelligence (ICTAI), pp. 502–509 (2020)
33. Maag, K., Rottmann, M., Varghese, S., Hüger, F., Schlicht, P., Gottschalk, H.: Improving video instance segmentation by light-weight temporal uncertainty estimates. In: 2021 International Joint Conference on Neural Networks (IJCNN), pp. 1–8 (2021)
34. Elbayad, M., Gu, J., Grave, E., Auli, M.: Depth-adaptive transformer. In: International Conference on Learning Representations (2020)
35. Rohrbach, A., Hendricks, L.A., Burns, K., Darrell, T., Saenko, K.: Object hallucination in image captioning. In: Proceedings of the 2018 Conference on Empirical Methods in Natural Language Processing, pp. 4035–4045 (2018)
36. Rottmann, M., et al.: Prediction error meta classification in semantic segmentation: detection via aggregated dispersion measures of softmax probabilities. In: 2020 International Joint Conference on Neural Networks (IJCNN), pp. 1–9 (2020)
37. Kullback, S., Leibler, R.A.: On information and sufficiency. Ann. Math. Stat. **22**(1), 79–86 (1951)
38. Schubert, M., Kahl, K., Rottmann, M.: Metadetect: uncertainty quantification and prediction quality estimates for object detection. In: 2021 International Joint Conference on Neural Networks (IJCNN), pp. 1–10 (2021)
39. Schuster, T., et al.: Confident adaptive language modeling. In: Proceedings of the 36th International Conference on Neural Information Processing Systems (2022)
40. Schwenk, D., Khandelwal, A., Clark, C., Marino, K., Mottaghi, R.: A-okvqa: a benchmark for visual question answering using world knowledge. In: Computer Vision – ECCV 2022, pp. 146–162 (2022)
41. Yin, S., et al.: Woodpecker: hallucination correction for multimodal large language models. Sci. China Inf. Sci. **67**, 220105 (2024)
42. Teerapittayanon, S., McDanel, B., Kung, H.T.: Branchynet: fast inference via early exiting from deep neural networks. In: 2016 23rd International Conference on Pattern Recognition (ICPR), pp. 2464–2469 (2016)
43. Wang, X., Pan, J., Ding, L., Biemann, C.: Mitigating hallucinations in large vision-language models with instruction contrastive decoding. In: Findings of the Association for Computational Linguistics: ACL 2024, pp. 15840–15853 (2024)
44. Wu, J., et al.: Logical closed loop: uncovering object hallucinations in large vision-language models. In: Findings of the Association for Computational Linguistics: ACL 2024, pp. 6944–6962 (2024)
45. Tian, X., et al.: DriveVLM: the convergence of autonomous driving and large vision-language models. In: 8th Annual Conference on Robot Learning (2024)

46. Zhou, Y., et al.: Analyzing and mitigating object hallucination in large vision-language models. In: The Twelfth International Conference on Learning Representations (2024)
47. Chuang, Y.-S., Xie, Y., Luo, H., Kim, Y., Glass, J., He, P.: Dola: decoding by contrasting layers improves factuality in large language models. In: The Twelfth International Conference on Learning Representations (2024)

Lattice Climber Attack: Adversarial Attacks for Randomized Mixtures of Classifiers

Lucas Gnecco Heredia[(✉)], Benjamin Negrevergne, and Yann Chevaleyre

LAMSADE, CNRS, Université Paris Dauphine - PSL, Paris, France
lucas.gnecco-heredia@dauphine.psl.eu

Abstract. Finite mixtures of classifiers (a.k.a. randomized ensembles) have been proposed as a way to improve robustness against adversarial attacks. However, existing attacks have been shown to not suit this kind of classifier. In this paper, we discuss the problem of attacking a mixture in a principled way and introduce two desirable properties of attacks based on a geometrical analysis of the problem (effectiveness and maximality). We then show that existing attacks do not meet both of these properties. Finally, we introduce a new attack called *lattice climber attack* with theoretical guarantees in the binary linear setting, and demonstrate its performance by conducting experiments on synthetic and real datasets.

Keywords: adversarial robustness · adversarial attacks · randomized classifiers · mixtures

1 Introduction

Deep neural networks have been shown to be vulnerable to adversarial attacks [10], i.e. small perturbations that, although imperceptible to humans, manage to drastically change the predictions of the model. This observation has led to numerous efforts to understand this phenomenon [4] and started a series of publications introducing various techniques to train robust models [14] as well as new algorithms to attack them [22].

One research direction that has been explored is the use of *randomized classifiers*, which include a source of randomness in their predictions. Examples of such classifiers include stochastic pruning [9,17], noise injection classifiers [12], classifiers with random input transformations [20,23], finite mixtures [15,19], among others. Unfortunately, the robustness of these randomized classifiers is not well understood, and most of them have been shown to be less robust than originally claimed under the white-box threat model. The classifier based on random input transformations by Xie et al. [23], which won the 2017 Neurips *Adversarial Attacks and Defences* Competition, was broken by Athalye et al. [2], together with stochastic pruning [9]. The defense by Panousis et al. [17] was debated on a Github issue[1] by the authors of Robustbench [6], who found that the classifier was not robust using a simple adaptation of AutoAttack [6]. The defense *Barrage of random transforms* by Raff et al. [20], which had impressive robustness results on Imagenet, was broken three years later by Sitawarin et al. [21], and Dbouk et al. [7] debate the robustness of finite mixtures.

In addition to showing that the real robustness of randomized classifiers is not yet fully understood, these results also highlight the lack of adaptive attacks for randomized models. The attacks used to evaluate the robustness of these models are often not suitable for the task, leading to an overestimation of their robustness, a phenomenon that is well known nowadays [2,22]. The lack of strong adaptive attacks for randomized classifiers has undermined research on this family of classifiers and limited its practical applications. As an example, one of the criteria used by the Robustbench benchmark to filter out defenses is the use of randomness in the forward pass, because such defenses often "only make gradient-based attacks harder but do not substantially improve robustness" [6].

Arguably, finite mixtures of classifiers [15,19] are one of the simplest kind of randomized classifiers, and yet they are not trivial to attack. Dbouk et al. [7] showed that the adaptations of projected gradient descent (PGD) [14] used by Pinot et al. [19] or Meunier et al. [15] were weak, thus overestimating the robustness of finite mixtures. They design ARC, the current state-of-the-art attack for finite mixtures of classifiers, and their evaluation shows a considerable drop in robustness with respect to the results reported by Pinot et al. [19].

In this work, we take a principled approach to understand adversarial attacks for finite mixtures of classifiers using a set-theoretic perspective and the concept of *vulnerability regions*. We show that the problem of attacking a finite mixture can be seen as the problem of climbing a lattice. Using this perspective, we identify a series of desirable properties and limitations of existing attacks. Afterward, we leverage the lattice reformulation to devise a new attack with better theoretical guarantees in binary classification with linear classifiers. More specifically, we make the following 3 contributions: First in Sect. 3 we model the problem of attacking a mixture using a semi-lattice, which allows us to better characterize the limitations of existing attacks like adaptations of PGD [14] and ARC [7]. Second, we propose in Sect. 4 a new attack algorithm called *lattice climber* that has strong guarantees in the binary linear setting compared to existing attacks. We then generalize to multiclass differentiable classifiers like neural networks. Finally, we provide extensive experimental results showing that our proposed attack is better at simultaneously attacking a finite mixture compared to existing attacks. Our code is available in https://github.com/lucasgneccoh/lattice_climber_attack, which also contains a reference to the extended version of this article that includes supplementary material.

---

[1] Available at https://github.com/fra31/auto-attack/issues/58.

2 Preliminaries

Notations. For a predicate C, we denote by $\mathbb{1}\{C\}$ the function that returns 1 if the predicate C is true and 0 otherwise. For an integer m, we use the notation $[m] = \{1, \cdots, m\}$. For a vector $u \in \mathbb{R}^d$, we denote by $u^{(j)}$ the j-th component of u. We denote by Δ^n the probability simplex in $\mathbb{R}^n$. For a probability vector $p \in \Delta^n$, we denote $\mathrm{Cat}(p)$ the categorical distribution on n elements, where $p^{(i)}$ is the probability of sampling element i. To alleviate the notation, when z is a random variable following the distribution $\mathrm{Cat}(p)$, we write $z \sim p$.

Problem Setting. Given a d–dimensional input space $\mathcal{X} \subset \mathbb{R}^d$ and a set $\mathcal{Y} = [K]$ of K class labels, a *deterministic* classifier $h : \mathcal{X} \to \mathcal{Y}$ is a function that maps each input point x to a predicted label $h(x)$. To measure the quality of the prediction of h at a point $(x, y) \in \mathcal{X} \times \mathcal{Y}$, we use the zero-one loss :

$$\mathcal{L}^{0-1}(h, x, y) = \mathbb{1}\{h(x) \neq y\} \tag{1}$$

In this paper, we consider finite mixtures of classifiers [15,19], which are a type of randomized classifier inspired by mixed strategies in game theory. Given a base set of deterministic classifiers $\mathbf{h} = \{h_1, \ldots, h_m\}$ and a probability distribution over them $\mathbf{q} \in \Delta^m$, the mixture classifier $\mathbf{h_q}$ will map any input x by first sampling a classifier $i \sim \mathbf{q}$, and then returning $h_i(x)$. Note that, unlike classical deterministic classifiers, mixtures may predict different labels for the same input x over repeated calls, thus the prediction $\mathbf{h_q}(x)$ is a random variable $\hat{y}$ over $\mathcal{Y}$, and the zero-one loss needs to be adapted to measure the expected error:

$$\mathcal{L}^{0-1}(\mathbf{h_q}, x, y) = \underset{i \sim \mathbf{q}}{\mathbb{E}}\left[\mathcal{L}^{0-1}(h_i, x, y)\right] = \sum_{i=1}^{m} \mathbf{q}^{(i)} \cdot \mathcal{L}^{0-1}(h_i, x, y). \tag{2}$$

In other words, the zero-one loss of a mixture represents the *probability* of predicting an incorrect label for input x.

Adversarial Attacks on Classifiers and Mixtures. Given an input point $x \in \mathcal{X}$ and its true label y, attacking a classifier h (deterministic or randomized) consists of crafting a norm bounded perturbation $\delta \in \mathbb{R}^d$ (with $\|\delta\| \leq \epsilon$) that increases the $0-1$ loss at (x, y). Various norms can be used to measure the magnitude of the perturbation δ, the most common being ℓ_p norms with $p = 2$ or $p = \infty$. For a given p-norm, we denote $B_p(x, \epsilon)$ the ball centered at x with radius ϵ i.e. $B_p(x, \epsilon) = \{x + \delta \in \mathcal{X} \text{ s.t. } \|\delta\| \leq \epsilon\}$. The adversarial zero-one loss $\mathcal{L}^{0-1}_\epsilon$ is defined as the zero-one loss under attack by an *optimal adversary*:

$$\mathcal{L}^{0-1}_{\epsilon,p}(h, x, y) = \sup_{x' \in B_p(x,\epsilon)} \mathcal{L}^{0-1}(h, x', y) \tag{3}$$

3 Failures of Existing Attacks

We start by analyzing of the limitations of existing attacks such as Expectation Over Transformation (EOT) [3] and ARC [7].

3.1 Attacks Based on Expectation Over Transformation (EOT)

Expectation Over Transformation (EOT) was initially developed by Athalye et al. [3], in order to craft attacks that are robust to real world perturbations. EOT introduces a set of transformations T that may be applied to the input, and optimizes the expected loss $\mathcal{L}$ over T:

$$\mathbb{E}_{t \sim T} \left[\mathcal{L}(h, t(x'), y) \right]. \tag{4}$$

The EOT principle was later adapted to attack finite mixture of classifiers by Pinot et al. [19]. Instead of considering random transformations, the idea is to account for the sampling of the classifier as the source of randomness. To attack the mixture $\mathbf{h_q}$, our objective function becomes the *Expectation Of the Loss* (EOL), as follows:

$$\mathbb{E}_{i \sim \mathbf{q}} \left[\mathcal{L}(h_i, x, y) \right] = \sum_{i=1}^{m} \mathbf{q}^{(i)} \, \mathcal{L}(h_i, x, y), \tag{5}$$

Note that if we choose $\mathcal{L}$ to be the zero-one loss, then maximizing the objective in Eq. (5) directly corresponds to maximizing the classification error of the mixture in Eq. (2). Therefore, *maximizing the EOL with the zero-one loss is the correct objective for attacking a finite mixture*. However, as we will demonstrate, this stops being true if we replace the zero-one loss with a surrogate loss function such as the cross-entropy loss.

Practical Adaptations for Attacking Finite Mixtures. To generate an adversarial example in practice, one can directly maximize the EOL objective in Eq. (5) (as in Eq. (6)), or maximize the loss computed on the expected output of the mixture (Eq. (7)) [19,22].

$$\sup_{x' \in B_p(x, \epsilon)} \sum_{i=1}^{m} \mathbf{q}^{(i)} \, \mathcal{L}(h_i, x', y). \tag{6}$$

$$\sup_{x' \in B_p(x, \epsilon)} \mathcal{L}\left(z \mapsto \sum_{i=1}^{m} \mathbf{q}^{(i)} \, h_i(z), x', y \right). \tag{7}$$

In practice, both of these problems are solved using first-order optimization methods like PGD. We refer to these attacks as EOL-PGD and LOE-PGD, respectively. The problem in doing so is that there is an underlying assumption that all classifiers can be attacked simultaneously and that their vulnerabilities are *aligned*, a concept we illustrate in Fig. 1. This is because the gradient of either objective can be rewritten as a linear combination of the gradients of the loss of the individual classifiers with positive coefficients. Thus, using first-order methods to solve problems Eqs. (6) or (7) is intuitively trying to attack all classifiers simultaneously, and the success of such attack relies on the assumption that this linear combination is a good attack direction. This can be effective in a scenario like the one depicted in Fig. 1 (left), in which all classifiers are vulnerable and their vulnerabilities are aligned, but fail when the vulnerabilities lie outside the set of admissible perturbations, as demonstrated in Fig. 1 (right).

This issue with EOL-PGD and LOE-PGD is the starting point for the development of ARC [7], a stronger attack against mixtures of classifiers, which we will discuss in the following section.

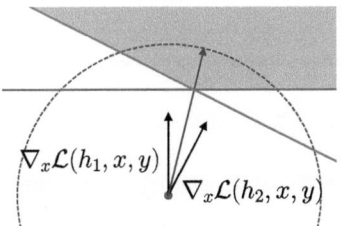 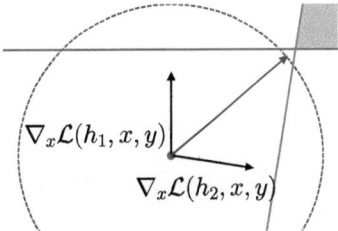

Fig. 1. Example of two linear classifiers with high (left) and low (right) alignment. The red arrow represents the gradient of the loss of the mixture, while the black arrows represent the gradient of the loss of individual classifiers. The red region in the top-right corner represents the points that are adversarial for both classifiers simultaneously. In the case of high alignment (left), the linear combination of the individual gradients is a successful attack direction, while in the case of low alignment (right), it is *not* an effective attack direction as it leads to a non-adversarial perturbation, even though adversarial perturbations do exist. (Color figure online)

3.2 ARC Attack and Its Limitations

Dbouk et al. [7] criticize EOL-PGD and LOE-PGD because of their lack of *consistency*[2] [7, Theorem 5.1], meaning that even if there exist adversarial attacks that increase the error of the mixture, EOL-PGD or LOE-PGD can miss them (*i.e.* Fig. 1 (right)). This motivates the authors to create *Attacking Randomized ensembles of Classifiers* (ARC) [7], an attack against finite mixtures of classifiers that is guaranteed to be consistent in binary classification against linear classifiers. In the rest of this section, we will compare ARC to EOL-PGD and discuss the limitations of ARC. We omit the discussion of LOE-PGD, but our analysis applies to it as well.

The key difference between ARC and EOL-PGD is that ARC attacks the classifiers one by one, instead of trying to attack all of them simultaneously. At each iteration, ARC follows the direction that attacks the one classifier at hand, and at the end of the iteration, the new perturbation will be kept only if the error of the whole mixture was strictly increased (see [7, Algorithm 1] for full details). The greedy approach of ARC makes it provably consistent when attacking binary

---

[2] This is the term used by authors in the original work. We rather use the term *effectiveness*. See Sect. 3.3.

linear classifiers (see [7, Theorem 5.1]). In Fig. 2 (left) we revisit a situation akin to Fig. 1 (right), and we can see that ARC is able to attack one of the classifiers successfully, while EOL-PGD fails to find an adversarial perturbation.

Dbouk et al. [7] train mixtures of two classifiers using the method proposed in [19] and find that when attacked with ARC[3], the robustness of these mixtures drops significantly compared to when they are attacked with EOL-PGD or LOE-PGD, which were the attacks used by Pinot et al. [19] for their evaluation. This behavior remains consistent across neural network architectures, datasets, and norms considered. Thus, ARC has proven to be a much stronger attack than EOL-PGD and LOE-PGD and remains, to this day, the state-of-the-art attack against finite mixtures of classifiers.

Although ARC resolves the main issue with EOL-PGD, it does so at the cost of losing the ability to attack multiple classifiers simultaneously in situations of medium alignment. Experimentally, one can verify that even for two linear classifiers in $\mathbb{R}^2$, ARC may fail to find a perturbation that is misclassified by both classifiers simultaneously when the region of common vulnerabilities within the ϵ-ball is very small. An example of such scenario is shown in Fig. 2 (right).

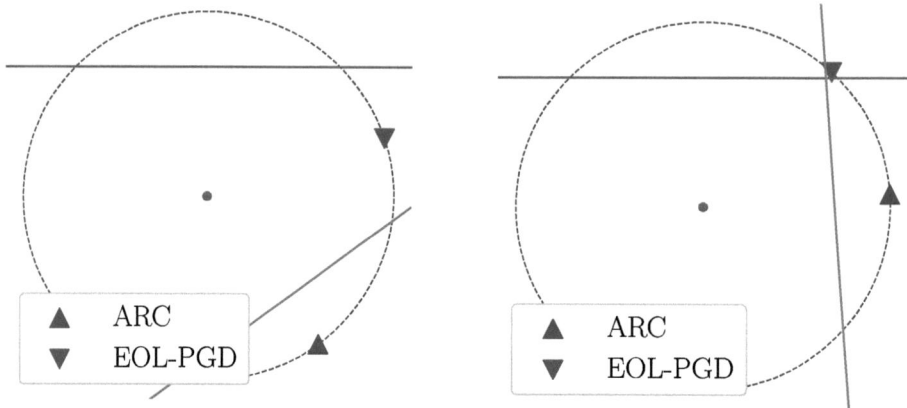

Fig. 2. Comparison between the perturbation proposed by EOL-PGD and ARC on a mixture of two linear classifiers with low to medium alignment.

To further demonstrate this issue, we test both EOL-PGD and ARC in situations that range from high to low alignment by changing the angle between the normal vectors of the linear classifiers from 0° (perfect alignment) to 180° (opposite normal vectors, low alignment). In Fig. 3, we plot the error induced by the perturbations found by both EOL-PGD and ARC and compare it to the optimal error, which is determined by checking if the intersection of the

---

[3] ARC is born from an analysis in the binary linear case, but it is generalized to the case of multiclass differentiable classifiers like neural networks. In their experiments comparing to the results in Pinot et al. [19], they used the latter.

two linear classifiers lies within the ϵ-ball or not. It can be seen that no attack dominates the other and that each outperforms the other in some regime that depends on the alignment of the decision boundaries.

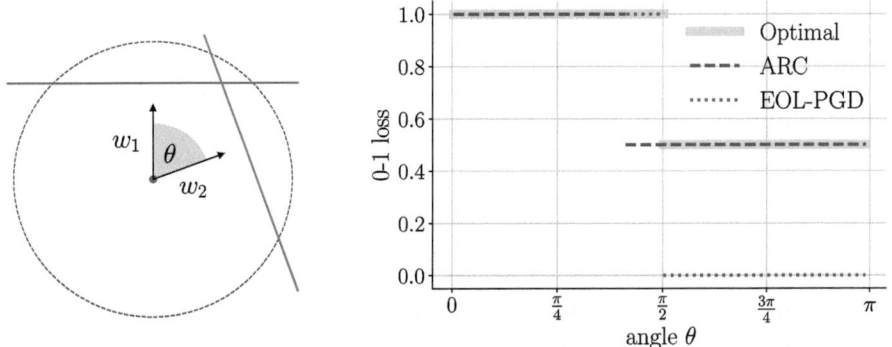

Fig. 3. Comparison between EOL-PGD and ARC w.r.t the level of alignment of the linear classifiers. On the left figure, a schema of the experiment that we run for a fixed angle θ. On the right figure, the error of the perturbations found by EOL-PGD and ARC compared to the optimal error w.r.t. θ.

We end this section with a comparison of ARC, EOL-PGD and LOE-PGD through the lens of the directions used to craft the perturbation at each iteration of the attack. Recall that the gradient directions used by EOL-PGD and LOE-PGD were linear combinations of the gradients of the loss of individual classifiers with non-zero coefficients for *all* of them. In the case of ARC, these coefficients are all zero except for one, which corresponds to the classifier being considered at the current step (see [7, Algorithm 2] for full details).

3.3 Desirable Properties of an Attack for Mixtures

In this section we will formalize the problem of attacking a mixture of classifiers as a combinatorial optimization problem, specifically as the problem of enumerating maximal elements of a lattice. Using this formalism, we will discuss the desirable properties for attack algorithm. This will allow us to identify a new property unsatisfied by existing algorithms: *maximality*.

Formalizing the Problem of Attacking a Finite Mixture. Note that a deterministic classifier h partitions the input space into at most K non-overlapping regions $h^{-1}(j) \subseteq \mathcal{X}$, $j \in [K]$, where each region corresponds to a class. Moreover, an optimal untargeted attacker only cares about forcing a prediction *different* from the true label y inside the set of admissible perturbations $B_p(x, \epsilon)$. In that sense, each classifier h induces a partition of the set of admissible perturbation

$B_p(x, \epsilon)$ into two disjoint regions of interest:

$$B_p(x, \epsilon) = \underbrace{B_p(x, \epsilon) \cap h^{-1}(y)}_{\text{non-adversarial}} \sqcup \underbrace{B_p(x, \epsilon) \cap \bigcup_{j \neq y} h^{-1}(j)}_{\text{Vulnerability region V}(h)}. \tag{8}$$

We call *vulnerability region* of h the set $B_p(x, \epsilon) \cap \bigcup_{j \neq y} h^{-1}(j)$, and denote it as V($h$). With the definition of vulnerability region, attacking h is equivalent to finding a point $x' \in V(h)$, so the error under attack of $\mathbf{h_q}$ at (x, y) becomes:

$$\mathcal{L}_{\epsilon, p}^{0-1}(\mathbf{h_q}, x, y) = \sup_{x' \in B_p(x, \epsilon)} \sum_{i=1}^{m} \mathbf{q}^{(i)} \, \mathbb{1}\{x' \in V(h_i)\}. \tag{9}$$

With Eq. (9) it is clear that the optimal attack belongs to the intersection of the vulnerability regions of the classifiers that maximizes the total mass according to $\mathbf{q}$. Let us define the *common vulnerability region* of a subset of classifiers $\mathbf{h}' \subseteq \mathbf{h}$ as $CV(\mathbf{h}') = \bigcap_{h \in \mathbf{h}'} V(h) \setminus \bigcup_{h \notin \mathbf{h}'} V(h)$. In simple terms, $CV(\mathbf{h}')$ is the set of points that are adversarial for exactly the classifiers in $\mathbf{h}'$, and thus, if $x' \in CV(\mathbf{h}')$, then $\mathcal{L}^{0-1}(\mathbf{h_q}, x', y) = \sum_{i \text{ s.t. } h_i \in \mathbf{h}'} \mathbf{q}^{(i)}$, and if $\mathbf{h}_1 \subseteq \mathbf{h}_2$ and $CV(\mathbf{h}_2) \neq \emptyset$, then the following holds:

$$\forall x_1 \in CV(\mathbf{h}_2), \, \forall x_2 \in CV(\mathbf{h}_1), \, \mathcal{L}^{0-1}(\mathbf{h_q}, x_2, y) \leq \mathcal{L}^{0-1}(\mathbf{h_q}, x_1, y), \tag{10}$$

which means that an attacker prefers to attack in the common vulnerability region of a larger set of classifiers whenever it is not empty.

Equation (10) suggests that the subsets of classifiers can be ordered by their preference for the attacker. Formally speaking, we can define the partial order

$$\mathbf{h}_1 \preceq \mathbf{h}_2 \iff \mathbf{h}_1 \subseteq \mathbf{h}_2 \text{ and } CV(\mathbf{h}_2) \neq \emptyset. \tag{11}$$

The order relation in Eq. (11) induces a *lower semilattice structure* in the family of subsets $\mathcal{S} = \{\mathbf{h}' \subseteq \mathbf{h} \mid CV(\mathbf{h}') \neq \emptyset\} \cup \{\emptyset\}$. For simplicity, we refer to it as *adversarial lattice* of $\mathbf{h_q}$ at (x, y).

The lattice object allows us to discuss desirable properties of an attack algorithm that faces mixtures of classifiers. The first has already been discussed under the name of consistency [7], but we redefine it as effectiveness:

Definition 1. (Effectiveness property). *An attack algorithm is effective if for any finite mixture $\mathbf{h_q}$ and point (x, y), it can generate an adversarial example increasing the error of the mixture whenever such a point exists.*

Definition 2. (Maximality property). *An attack algorithm is maximal if for any finite mixture $\mathbf{h_q}$ and any point (x, y), it can generate an adversarial example for a maximal subset of classifiers of the adversarial lattice.*

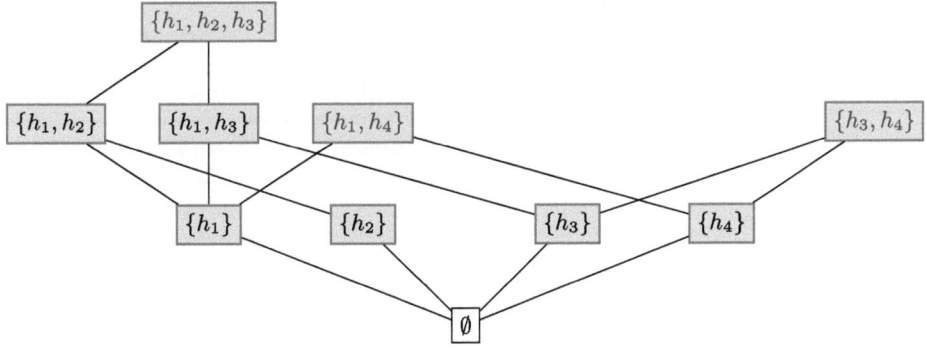

Fig. 4. Example of an adversarial lattice for a mixture of four classifiers.

Neither EOL-PGD nor ARC is maximal for binary linear classifiers, as counterexamples can be constructed where they fail to find a maximal subset of classifiers to attack (Fig. 2). Figure 4 illustrates an example of an adversarial lattice for a mixture of four classifiers. An *effective* attack is ensured to produce an adversarial attack x' that corresponds to *some* of the nodes highlighted with a blue rectangle. This property is a defining characteristic of ARC for binary linear classifiers –one that EOL-PGD lacks. However, there is no guarantee regarding the level of the lattice that is reached, and the effectiveness guarantee becomes less meaningful as the size of the lattice increases. The nodes with red font represent the maximal nodes, illustrating that the maximality guarantee is a stronger property than effectiveness.

The most desirable property of an attack for mixtures is be *optimality*:

Definition 3. (Optimality property). *An attack algorithm is optimal if for any finite mixture over $\mathbf{h_q}$ and any point (x, y), it can generate an adversarial example that achieves the highest possible 0–1 loss.*

The optimal attack corresponds to a *subset* of the maximal elements of the adversarial lattice, depending on the weights of the mixture. Unfortunately, no polynomial-time algorithm is guaranteed to achieve optimality, even when using linear classifiers in binary classification, due to the following result:

Theorem 1. (Hardness of attacking linear classifiers). *Consider a binary classification setting, ℓ_p norm with $p > 1$ and ϵ to be defined. Given a labeled point (x, y), a set of m linear classifiers $x \mapsto \mathbb{1}\{\theta_i^\top x + b_i \geq 0\}$ where $(\theta_i, b_i) \in \mathbb{R}^{d+1}$, a uniform mixture $\mathbf{h_q}$ composed of these linear classifiers and a value $\beta > 0$, there exists a noise budget $\epsilon > 0$ such that the problem of checking if there exists $x' \in B_p(x, \epsilon)$ such that $\mathcal{L}^{0-1}(\mathbf{h_q}, x', y) \geq \beta$ is NP-hard.*

As a consequence of Theorem 1, the attack algorithm that we will propose will prioritize *maximality* over optimality, which can be guaranteed in the case of binary linear classifiers and provides effectiveness for free.

4 Lattice Climber Attack

In this section, we introduce a new attack called Lattice Climber Attack (LCA). We first present a version of our attack that has maximality guarantees against mixtures of binary linear classifiers under mild assumptions, and then extend it to multiclass differentiable classifiers. Afterwards, we will present experimental results that compare LCA with EOL-PGD and ARC on synthetic and real-world datasets.

The idea behind LCA is to arrive at a maximal element of the lattice by climbing one level at a time. Similar problems have been studied under the name of *most specific sentences* or *maximal frequent itemsets* in the domain of data mining and knowledge discovery, where algorithms like AllMSS [11] have been proposed. Our approach is similar to A_Random_MSS in [11].

4.1 Binary Linear Classifiers

In this section and for simplicity, we consider class labels $y \in \{-1, 1\}$ and classifiers $h : \mathbb{R}^d \to \{-1, 1\}$ of the form $h(x) = \text{sign}(f(x))$ for some linear function $f : \mathbb{R}^d \to \mathbb{R}$. In this setting, h correctly classifies the data point (x, y) if $yf(x) > 0$. Therefore, attacking h translates to minimizing $yf(x)$. The optimal attack direction and margin to the decision boundary of a single linear classifier are known for all ℓ_p norm with $p \geq 1$ [7, Appendix A].

The first component of our attack algorithm is a procedure to attack a subset of classifiers $\mathbf{h}'$ and find $x + \delta \in \text{CV}(\mathbf{h}')$ whenever $\text{CV}(\mathbf{h}') \neq \emptyset$. Similar to [18], we consider the *reverse hinge loss* $\mathcal{L}^{rev}(yf(x)) = \max(yf(x), 0)$ as an objective to *minimize* in order to attack *one* binary linear classifier. Attacking a binary linear classifier with the traditional hinge loss would imply maximizing a convex function, for which there is no guarantee of convergence to a global optimum using algorithms like PGD. On the other hand, using the reverse hinge loss is equivalent to *minimizing* a bounded convex function, for which PGD is guaranteed to converge to a global optimum.

Another useful property of the reverse hinge loss is that the expected reverse hinge loss over a finite mixture of classifiers is convex and equal to zero if and only if all the classifiers in the mixture misclassify x. Then, in order to attack a set of classifiers $\mathbf{h}'$, we can minimize the *sum of reverse hinge losses* [18]

$$\text{SRH}(\mathbf{h}', x, y) = \frac{1}{|\mathbf{h}'|} \sum_{h \in \mathbf{h}'} \mathcal{L}^{rev}(yf(x)). \tag{12}$$

If there exists x' such that $\text{SRH}(\mathbf{h}', x', y) = 0$, then PGD with an appropriately chosen step size and sufficient number of iterations will converge to some x'' that is misclassified by all classifiers in $\mathbf{h}'$ (see [18, Theorem 3] for details).

The second component of our attack algorithm is a way to navigate the adversarial lattice. We propose a bottom-up navigation mechanism to climb a branch of the adversarial lattice that consists of keeping a pool of fooled classifiers, attempting to add each classifier in a fixed order. A classifier joins the pool

---
Algorithm 1: LCA for binary linear classifiers

Require: Set **h** of m binary linear classifiers in some order $(h_1, \ldots, h_m)$, starting point $(x, y) \in \mathbb{R}^d \times \{-1, 1\}$. T number of iterations and η step size for PGD.
1: Initialize pool $\mathbf{h}_{\text{pool}} = \emptyset$, $\delta = 0_d$
2: **for** $i = 1, 2 \cdots, m$ **do**
3:     $\mathbf{h}_{\text{pool}} = \mathbf{h}_{\text{pool}} \cup \{h_i\}$ {Add h_i to the pool}
4:     Attack $\text{SRH}(\mathbf{h}_{\text{pool}}, \cdot, y)$ starting at $x + \delta$ with PGD (T, η) to find new perturbation $\hat{\delta}$
5:     **if** $\text{SRH}(\mathbf{h}_{\text{pool}}, x + \hat{\delta}, y) = 0$ *i.e.* succeeded **then**
6:         $\delta = \hat{\delta}$ {Update current attack, keep h_i in pool}
7:     **else**
8:         $\mathbf{h}_{\text{pool}} = \mathbf{h}_{\text{pool}} \setminus \{h_i\}$ {Reset pool to last state}
9: **return** Adversarial example $x + \delta$
---

only if it can be fooled alongside all current members; otherwise, it is discarded. The algorithm terminates after evaluating all classifiers.

The order in which classifiers are considered is a parameter of the algorithm, and similarly to [7], we find that considering them in decreasing order of their associated weight yields good performance in general. For example, in the case $m = 2$, and with suitable parameters for the internal PGD, it ensures that LCA is optimal. Another reasonable option is to use a random permutation of the classifiers, which Dbouk et al. [8] found to be useful for ARC. The pseudocode of LCA in the binary linear setting is shown in Algorithm 1.

Recall that the step used by EOL-PGD can be expressed as linear combinations of the gradients of the loss of individual classifiers. For LCA, similar to ARC, the coefficients of this linear combination will be sparse: only the models within the pool $\mathbf{h}_{\text{pool}}$ will have non-zero coefficients. This behavior positions LCA as an intermediate approach between EOL-PGD and ARC: in LCA, the coefficients initially resemble those in ARC, but as the pool grows, they transition to resemble the denser pattern of EOL-PGD. This behavior makes it possible to adapt to different types of adversarial lattice: when classifiers are not simultaneously vulnerable, LCA will behave like ARC, which was created to ensure *effectiveness* for binary linear classifiers, and when they are simultaneously vulnerable, it will behave like EOL-PGD which attacks all classifiers simultaneously.

Maximality of LCA in the Binary Linear Setting. In the binary linear classifier setting, $\text{PGD}(T, \eta)$ is guaranteed to minimize the function $\text{SRH}(\mathbf{h}_{\text{pool}}, \cdot, y)$ because it is a convex optimization problem [18]. Thus, line 4 of Algorithm 1 ensures that we will find an adversarial attack $x + \hat{\delta} \in \text{CV}(\mathbf{h}_{\text{pool}})$ if $\text{CV}(\mathbf{h}_{\text{pool}}) \neq \emptyset$. This enables climbing to the top of the adversarial lattice along a branch determined by the classifier order. This is formalized in the following lemma:

Lemma 1. *Consider a set of m binary linear classifiers* **h**. *Fix $\epsilon > 0$ the attack budget and a point (x, y). If there exists a point $x' \in B_p(x, \epsilon)$ such that*

$SRH(\mathbf{h}, x', y) = 0$, then there exist parameters T and η such that minimizing $SRH(\mathbf{h}, x, y)$ w.r.t. x with $PGD(T, \eta)$ will return x'' such that $SRH(\mathbf{h}, x'', y) = 0$.

Lemma 1 allows us to prove that LCA is maximal for the set of binary linear classifiers:

Theorem 2. (LCA is maximal in the binary linear setting). *Let $\mathbf{h}$ be a finite set of binary linear classifiers and $\mathbf{h_q}$ a mixture over $\mathbf{h}$. Fix $\epsilon > 0$ the attack budget and a p-norm with $p > 1$. For any $(x, y) \in \mathbb{R}^d \times \{-1, 1\}$, there exist parameters T and η for the inner PGD such that Algorithm 1 returns an adversarial example $x + \delta \in CV(\mathbf{h}')$, where $\mathbf{h}'$ is a maximal element of the adversarial lattice of $\mathbf{h_q}$ at (x, y).*

4.2 Multiclass Differentiable Classifiers

The ideas developed in Sect. 4.1 for binary linear classifiers need to be adapted to the multiclass case with general differentiable classifiers, like neural networks, because we cannot have the guarantees provided by Lemma 1 and Theorem 2. Moreover, the reverse hinge loss was defined for binary classifiers and not for multiclass classifiers.

In order to attack a classifier h that predicts the class with the highest score according to the score function $f : \mathcal{X} \to \mathbb{R}^K$ at an arbitrary point (x, y), we choose the target label $y_{\text{adv}} \in [K] \setminus \{y\}$ with the largest score according to $f(x)$ and minimize the reverse hinge loss of the margin between $f(x)^{(y)}$ and $f(x)^{(y_{\text{adv}})}$, i.e. $\mathcal{L}^{rev}(f(x)^{(y)} - f(x)^{(y_{\text{adv}})})$. This is a common choice that has been used by Perdomo et al. [18] and also by Carlini et al. [5], who found it to perform well as an objective function for crafting adversarial attacks. As there is no guarantee on the convergence of the attack to $SRH(\mathbf{h}_{\text{pool}}, \cdot, y)$, we change the criteria to update the pool of classifiers: each time we find a perturbation δ with a higher error for the mixture, we keep it and update the pool to be the classifiers that misclassify the current adversarial example $x + \delta$.

5 Experiments

In this section, we show the experimental results that support the theoretical guarantees of LCA in the binary linear setting. We also compare the performance of LCA with ARC and EOL-PGD in the multiclass differentiable setting, in which guarantees are not provided, and show that LCA generally performs better than existing state-of-the-art attacks.

5.1 Synthetic Data: Linear Classifiers

Binary Linear Classifiers in High Dimension. In this experiment, we assess how the performance of EOL-PGD, ARC and LCA scale with the number of classifiers m in a higher dimension d. For each value m and a fixed value of $\epsilon = 1$, we repeat the following experiment 1000 times: we fix our point $(x, y) = (0_d, -1)$ and sample m i.i.d linear classifiers (w_i, b_i) where w_i is uniformly sampled from the unit sphere in $\mathbb{R}^d$ and $b_i \sim -|\mathcal{N}(\alpha, \beta)|$ follows a folded Gaussian distribution, and we test the three attacks against the sampled mixture. The hyperparameter α controls the expected distance from x to the decision boundary of the classifiers, and β the variance of such distance.

Figure 5 shows that the average performance of all attacks deteriorates as the number of models increases, but LCA remains superior for all m. Note that depending on the difficulty of the configurations (α and β), the performance of the attacks can change drastically. Nevertheless, LCA remained superior in all configurations, regardless of the dimension.

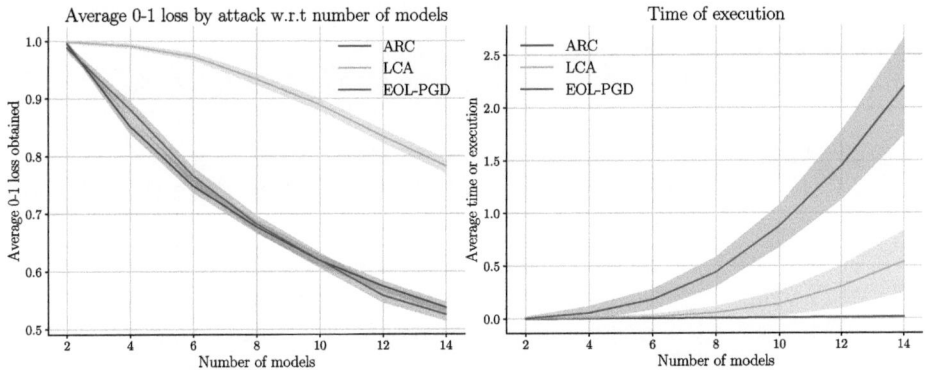

Fig. 5. On the left figure, the average error obtained by the attacks in $\mathbb{R}^{128}$ as a function of the number of classifiers in the mixture with 99% confidence intervals. The right figure shows the average time in seconds that each attack took to generate an adversarial example as a function of the number of classifiers with one standard deviation intervals. For each number of models, the experiment was repeated 1000 times. Note that the y-axis limits have been adapted for visualization purposes. In this case, $\alpha = 0.25$, $\beta = 0.2$.

5.2 CIFAR-10

Experimental Setup. To test our attack against differentiable multiclass classifiers, we measure the accuracy of mixtures built using models trained with different ensemble diversity techniques. To have a wide variety of models and training methods, we take the pre-trained models from the DVERGE [24] repository[4], which compares baseline models trained without any defense (BASE) against ensemble diversity defenses such as ADP [16], GAL [13], plain adversarial training (AT) [14] and DVERGE (DV) [24]. The authors made available 3 independent runs of each method (except for BASE), and we report the average

---

[4] https://github.com/zjysteven/DVERGE/tree/main.

Table 1. Expected accuracy of mixtures against EOL-PGD, ARC and LCA under the ℓ_∞ threat model. Attacker wants to minimize accuracy, so lower is better. All models use ResNet20 as the base architecture, except † which uses ResNet18.

Model		Nat	$\epsilon = 0.01$			$\epsilon = 0.03$		
			EOL	ARC	LCA	EOL	ARC	LCA
BASE/3		91.8%	15.0%	4.3%	**1.7%**	0.1%	0.2%	**0.0%**
BASE/5		91.9%	12.3%	6.1%	**2.7%**	0.0%	0.2%	0.1%
BASE/8		91.8%	10.6%	7.9%	**4.6%**	0.0%	0.2%	0.1%
ADP/3		89.4%	15.7%	**14.6%**	15.1%	0.4%	5.2%	1.8%
ADP/5	[16]	88.8%	15.4%	16.1%	**13.9%**	0.2%	2.5%	1.5%
ADP/8		88.5%	**15.2%**	18.4%	15.4%	0.3%	4.2%	3.3%
GAL/3		87.1%	43.0%	18.0%	**14.3%**	14.5%	5.8%	**0.9%**
GAL/5	[13]	88.7%	46.2%	45.1%	**36.0%**	11.5%	9.4%	**7.1%**
GAL/8		89.7%	**44.5%**	52.4%	50.2%	**3.9%**	11.7%	15.9%
AT/3		77.3%	68.6%	68.3%	**65.3%**	47.2%	47.7%	**42.4%**
AT/5	[14]	77.9%	69.0%	69.1%	**65.2%**	47.2%	49.2%	**42.7%**
AT/8		77.8%	69.0%	69.0%	**64.9%**	47.5%	50.3%	**44.3%**
DV/3		89.8%	52.6%	44.4%	**31.2%**	39.2%	5.8%	**1.9%**
DV/5	[24]	89.9%	59.0%	55.1%	**42.1%**	35.3%	10.1%	**6.0%**
DV/8		88.6%	62.1%	63.2%	**52.8%**	31.7%	18.4%	**15.0%**
DV+AT/3		81.7%	71.4%	71.3%	**69.0%**	44.4%	45.2%	**41.0%**
DV+AT/5	[24]	84.0%	72.8%	73.1%	**70.2%**	42.2%	44.6%	**39.9%**
DV+AT/8		84.0%	73.2%	73.4%	**70.9%**	44.3%	46.5%	**42.5%**
BARRE/5	[8]	76.3%	68.9%	69.4%	**66.2%**	50.6%	49.9%	**46.1%**
MR/5	[25]	73.7%	65.7%	66.4%	**62.3%**	46.3%	46.7%	**41.5%**
MR/5†		81.3%	72.7%	74.1%	**70.2%**	47.1%	51.4%	**46.5%**

accuracy over these 3 independent runs. We also trained a mixture of 5 models using the MRBoost [25] framework, using the ResNet20 and the ResNet18 architectures. All these methods are designed to promote ensemble diversity and reduce the joint adversarial vulnerability of the sub-models, so we consider them appropriate to evaluate the performance of attacks against mixtures. We also take pre-trained models from the BARRE [8] repository[5], in which authors propose a boosting algorithm to specifically train robust mixtures. All these models use the ResNet20 architecture as the base classifiers, except for MRBoost with ResNet18. We use the ℓ_∞ threat model with $\epsilon = 0.03$ as in standard practice, and also the $\epsilon = 0.01$ setting to compare with [24].

To provide a fair comparison, we adjusted the number of iterations T for each attack to ensure that LCA was not given any advantage. Note that the

---

[5] https://github.com/hsndbk4/BARRE/tree/main.

number of gradient computations is $T \cdot m$ for EOL-PGD, at most $4\, T \cdot m$ for ARC [7], and at most $T \cdot \frac{m(m+1)}{2}$ for LCA. In our case $m \in \{3, 5, 8\}$. Taking this into account, we set the number of iterations to 50 for LCA, and gave ARC and EOL-PGD up to 200 and 500 iterations respectively. We also tested ARC and EOL-PGD with fewer iterations, and report only the best result. We further give more advantage to EOL-PGD by allowing it to perform random initialization and 5 restarts. In contrast, ARC and LCA do not use random initialization or restarts.

Results. Table 1 shows the results of our evaluation. First, we can confirm the observations made in [7]: EOL-PGD, even with the advantage given, tends to overestimate the robustness of mixtures, and it is more notorious for BASE models with $\epsilon = 0.01$ and DV models. In these cases, ARC dramatically outperforms EOL-PGD (as was seen in [7]), and *LCA outperforms both ARC and EOL-PGD*. Note however that EOL-PGD is better than both ARC and LCA when models are simultaneously vulnerable and the individual gradients used for the attack are highly aligned [7,13], which seems to be the case for ADP models. This could be explained by the fact that ADP, contrary to methods like GAL, does not explicitly reduce gradient alignment during training.

GAL models show a peculiar behavior: robustness against EOL-PGD tends to *decrease* as the number of models increases, suggesting that the models become more aligned. A similar behavior was also reported in [24], suggesting that this method does not scale well with the number of models. However, robustness against ARC or LCA increases with the number of models. This contrast might suggest that GAL models are indeed more diverse locally, but still simultaneously vulnerable inside the ϵ-ball so that EOL-PGD is able to exploit this vulnerability by naively attacking all classifiers enough times.

For the more robust models (AT, DV+AT, BARRE and MR), LCA shows a clear improvement in performance when compared to both ARC and EOL-PGD. The average gap between LCA and ARC in the $\epsilon = 0.03$ setting is 4.9%, with a minimum gap of 3.8%.

6 Conclusions and Future Work

In this paper, we explore the properties of attacks for randomized mixtures and introduce the LCA algorithm that is *maximal* in the binary linear setting and demonstrates good empirical performances against multiclass differentiable classifiers. Despite employing state-of-the-art diversity inducing techniques, our robustness evaluation confirms that the robustness of mixtures largely depends on the robustness of individual models, often matching that of a single model (the robustness of a 5-ResNet20 mixture in [8] is similar to the robustness of a single ResNet20 reported in [7] by the same authors), limiting the practical impact of mixtures. This discrepancy between the theoretical advantages of mixtures and their practical robustness underscores the persistent challenge of training robust mixtures. Moreover, adversarial training has limited effectiveness for mixtures, as training with stronger adaptive attacks does not produce more robust models. New theoretical and practical approaches are needed to improve the training of robust mixtures and fully leverage their potential, a direction that has been started in [8].

Acknowledgments. This work was carried out using HPC resources from GENCI IDRIS (AD011014207 and AD011014207R1), and funded by the French National Research Agency (DELCO ANR-19-CE23-0016). Thanks to the reviewers for the valuable feedback.

Disclosure of Interests. The authors have no competing interests to declare that are relevant to the content of this article.

References

1. Amaldi, E., Kann, V.: The complexity and approximability of finding maximum feasible subsystems of linear relations. Theor. Comput. Sci. **147**(1–2), 181–210 (1995)
2. Athalye, A., Carlini, N., Wagner, D.: Obfuscated gradients give a false sense of security: circumventing defenses to adversarial examples. In: ICML, pp. 274–283. PMLR (2018)
3. Athalye, A., Engstrom, L., Ilyas, A., Kwok, K.: Synthesizing robust adversarial examples. In: ICML, pp. 284–293. PMLR (2018)
4. Bubeck, S., Lee, Y.T., Price, E., Razenshteyn, I.: Adversarial examples from computational constraints. In: ICML, pp. 831–840. PMLR (2019)
5. Carlini, N., Wagner, D.A.: Towards evaluating the robustness of neural networks. In: Symposium on Security and Privacy, pp. 39–57. IEEE Computer Society (2017)
6. Croce, F., et al.: Robustbench: a standardized adversarial robustness benchmark. arXiv preprint arXiv:2010.09670 (2020)
7. Dbouk, H., Shanbhag, N.: Adversarial vulnerability of randomized ensembles. In: ICML, pp. 4890–4917. PMLR (2022)
8. Dbouk, H., Shanbhag, N.R.: On the robustness of randomized ensembles to adversarial perturbations. arXiv preprint arXiv:2302.01375 (2023)
9. Dhillon, G.S., et al.: Stochastic activation pruning for robust adversarial defense. arXiv preprint arXiv:1803.01442 (2018)
10. Goodfellow, I.J., Shlens, J., Szegedy, C.: Explaining and harnessing adversarial examples. arXiv preprint arXiv:1412.6572 (2014)
11. Gunopulos, D., Mannila, H., Saluja, S.: Discovering all most specific sentences by randomized algorithms extended abstract. In: International Conference on Database Theory, pp. 215–229. Springer (1997)
12. He, Z., Rakin, A.S., Fan, D.: Parametric noise injection: trainable randomness to improve deep neural network robustness against adversarial attack. In: CCVPR, pp. 588–597 (2019)
13. Kariyappa, S., Qureshi, M.K.: Improving adversarial robustness of ensembles with diversity training. arXiv preprint arXiv:1901.09981 (2019)
14. Madry, A., Makelov, A., Schmidt, L., Tsipras, D., Vladu, A.: Towards deep learning models resistant to adversarial attacks. arXiv preprint arXiv:1706.06083 (2017)

15. Meunier, L., Scetbon, M., Pinot, R.B., Atif, J., Chevaleyre, Y.: Mixed nash equilibria in the adversarial examples game. In: ICML, pp. 7677–7687. PMLR (2021)
16. Pang, T., Xu, K., Du, C., Chen, N., Zhu, J.: Improving adversarial robustness via promoting ensemble diversity. In: ICML, pp. 4970–4979. PMLR (2019)
17. Panousis, K.P., Chatzis, S., Theodoridis, S.: Stochastic local winner-takes-all networks enable profound adversarial robustness. arXiv preprint arXiv:2112.02671 (2021)
18. Perdomo, J.C., Singer, Y.: Robust attacks against multiple classifiers. arXiv preprint arXiv:1906.02816 (2019)
19. Pinot, R., Ettedgui, R., Rizk, G., Chevaleyre, Y., Atif, J.: Randomization matters how to defend against strong adversarial attacks. In: ICML, pp. 7717–7727. PMLR (2020)
20. Raff, E., Sylvester, J., Forsyth, S., McLean, M.: Barrage of random transforms for adversarially robust defense. In: CCVPR, pp. 6528–6537 (2019)
21. Sitawarin, C., Golan-Strieb, Z.J., Wagner, D.: Demystifying the adversarial robustness of random transformation defenses. In: ICML, pp. 20232–20252. PMLR (2022)
22. Tramer, F., Carlini, N., Brendel, W., Madry, A.: On adaptive attacks to adversarial example defenses. Neurips **33**, 1633–1645 (2020)
23. Xie, C., Wang, J., Zhang, Z., Ren, Z., Yuille, A.L.: Mitigating adversarial effects through randomization. In: ICLR (2018)
24. Yang, H., et al.: DVERGE: diversifying vulnerabilities for enhanced robust generation of ensembles. Neurips **33**, 5505–5515 (2020)
25. Zhang, D., Zhang, H., Courville, A., Bengio, Y., Ravikumar, P., Suggala, A.S.: Building robust ensembles via margin boosting. In: ICML, vol. 162, pp. 26669–26692. PMLR (2022)

Inconsistent Reasoning Attacks to Identify Weaknesses in Automatic Scientific Claim Verification Tools

Md Athikul Islam(✉)[ID], Noel Ellison[ID], Bishal Lakha[ID], and Edoardo Serra[ID]

Boise State University, Boise, ID, USA
{mdathikulislam,noelellison,bishallakha}@u.boisestate.edu,
edoardoserra@boisestate.edu

Abstract. Scientific Claim Verification (SCV) tools are essential for evaluating the validity of scientific assertions, particularly within autonomous science. However, they often struggle to interpret complex scientific language and detect reasoning flaws, leading to potential misclassification. Adversarial attacks, particularly paraphrase attacks, reveal these weaknesses by rewording claims while maintaining their meaning. Paraphrase attacks are not the only way to identify weaknesses in SCV tools, but other existing methods often fail to preserve semantic equivalence, requiring extensive human filtering.

To address this, we define inconsistent reasoning attacks, a broader class of adversarial attack strategies that expose logical weaknesses in SCV systems. Using an evolutionary algorithm and large language models, this approach iteratively modifies claims to trigger misclassifications while maintaining logical inconsistencies. This method improves semantic accuracy and attack effectiveness, particularly for paraphrase-based attacks. Evaluation against a leading SCV system (MultiVerS) confirms persistent vulnerabilities, even though a retrieval-augmented generation (RAG) system with an Attack-Reflection mechanism shows potential in mitigating these issues. The findings emphasize the susceptibility of SCV systems to reasoning inconsistencies with a larger attack success rate than other attack techniques and highlight the Attack-Reflection mechanism as a promising defense.

Keywords: Automatic Scientific Claim · Verification Tools · Adversarial Attacks · Robustness · Large Language Models

1 Introduction

Scientific Claim Verification (SCV) tools are essential for assessing the validity of scientific claims, particularly in the emerging field of autonomous science or discovery [2,16] and the fast-evolving landscape of social media [21]. However, these tools face significant challenges due to the complexity of scientific

---

Supplementary Information The online version contains supplementary material available at https://doi.org/10.1007/978-3-032-06109-6_4.

language, which requires access to up-to-date research and a deep understanding of claims for accurate verification [23,27]. MultiVerS [26], one of the most advanced SCV models, leverages multitask loss for rationale selection and label prediction using long-document transformers. Despite these advancements, SCV tools remain vulnerable to reasoning errors, leading to incorrect or inconsistent claim classifications.

Standard NLP adversarial attacks [6,10,18] can be used to evaluate the robustness of SCV tools by altering text while attempting to preserve its meaning. However, in the context of SCV, these approaches often fail because the semantics of scientific claims are highly sensitive to small changes. For instance, replacing "Nonsteroidal anti-inflammatory drugs are ineffective as cancer treatments" with "Nonsteroidal anti-inflammatory drugs are indispensable as cancer treatments" drastically alters the meaning despite a minor word substitution. While these methods may work well in general NLP tasks, they do not adequately capture the strict semantic precision required for scientific claims, leading to misclassifications by SCV tools. To address these limitations, *paraphrase attacks* have been proposed as a more targeted adversarial strategy [12]. These attacks attempt to generate reworded claims that maintain semantic equivalence, thereby exposing SCV systems' weaknesses when semantically identical claims receive different truthfulness classifications. However, despite their improvements over standard NLP adversarial attacks, existing paraphrase attack methods still struggle to preserve meaning fully. Many generated paraphrases subtly alter the scientific validity of a claim, necessitating human intervention to filter out invalid attacks. This reliance on manual validation reduces the scalability of paraphrase attacks and limits their application in automated adversarial testing.

While paraphrase attacks provide a valuable means of identifying SCV vulnerabilities, they are not the only way to reveal inconsistencies in reasoning. Beyond lexical or syntactic changes, SCV tools can also be challenged by logical inconsistencies that do not rely solely on paraphrasing. To better capture these weaknesses, we introduce a broader taxonomy of adversarial attacks, which we term *inconsistent reasoning attacks*. These attacks systematically expose flaws in SCV decision-making by manipulating claim logic rather than just altering surface-level text. In addition to paraphrase attacks, inconsistent reasoning attacks also include specific-to-general attacks, which broaden a claim's scope by making it more general or vague (e.g., replacing "car" with "vehicle" or "strongly related" with "related"), and general-to-specific attacks, which instead refine broad claims by replacing general terms with more precise ones (e.g., replacing "vehicle" with "car").

Another type of inconsistent reasoning attack is negation manipulation, where the logical structure of a claim is altered by introducing double negatives or modifying negation patterns, like adding "does not fail to" into an affirmative statement. Union attacks are another form of inconsistent reasoning attacks that merge multiple claims into a single statement, introducing logical complexity that can mislead SCV systems and result in misclassified claims. By challenging SCV tools through these various logical inconsistencies, rather than just surface-level linguistic modifications, inconsistent reasoning attacks provide a more comprehensive framework for evaluating system vulnerabilities. Additionally, one of the key contributions of our approach is the ability to merge multiple types of reasoning attacks, compounding their effects to create stronger adversarial examples. This capability allows for more effective stress-testing of SCV tools by generating claims that simultaneously exploit multiple logical inconsistencies.

To generate these attacks, we develop a genetic algorithm leveraging large language models that iteratively evolve claims through mutation and crossover operations. This method ensures that inconsistencies in SCV classifications are systematically identified while minimizing invalid transformations. Unlike paraphrase-based approaches, our framework provides a more robust assessment of SCV weaknesses by uncovering reasoning errors rather than focusing solely on linguistic variation.

We evaluate these attacks against MultiVerS and a retrieval-augmented generation (RAG) system with Attack-Reflection mechanisms. Our findings indicate that MultiVerS, despite being one of the most robust SCV models, remains highly susceptible to inconsistent reasoning attacks. However, the RAG system with Attack-Reflection demonstrates promising potential in mitigating these vulnerabilities in zero-shot learning tasks, suggesting that integrating Attack-Reflection mechanisms could enhance SCV robustness against adversarial manipulations.

More specifically, this work presents the following key contributions:

- Beyond Paraphrase Attacks: We introduce *inconsistent reasoning attacks*, exposing logical inconsistencies in SCV decision-making beyond standard NLP adversarial techniques and paraphrase attacks.
- Evolutionary Attack Generation: We develop a *genetic algorithm* leveraging LLMs to iteratively craft adversarial claims that reveal reasoning failures in SCV tools. The main novelties include distinct attack strategies for each type of inconsistent reasoning attack and an LLM-based crossover operation.
- Multi-Type Inconsistency Attacks: Our method improves attack success rates, minimizes invalid transformations, and enables *attack merging* to create more challenging adversarial cases.
- SCV Tool Vulnerability Analysis: We assess MultiVerS, demonstrating its susceptibility to inconsistent reasoning attacks and exposing weaknesses.
- Mitigation via RAG with an Attack-Reflection Mechanism: We explore self-reflective mechanisms over attacks in RAG-based SCV models to address logical inconsistencies and enhance resilience against attacks.

2 Related Works

Scientific Claim Verification (SCV) tools aim to assess the truthfulness of claims by retrieving relevant research abstracts and analyzing supporting or refuting evidence. MultiVerS [26] is considered one of the most advanced and most effective SCV tools. MultiVerS retrieves relevant abstracts, selects rationale statements, and classifies the claim as SUPPORT or REFUTE. MultiVerS enhances prior methods by incorporating full abstracts using a long-document transformer

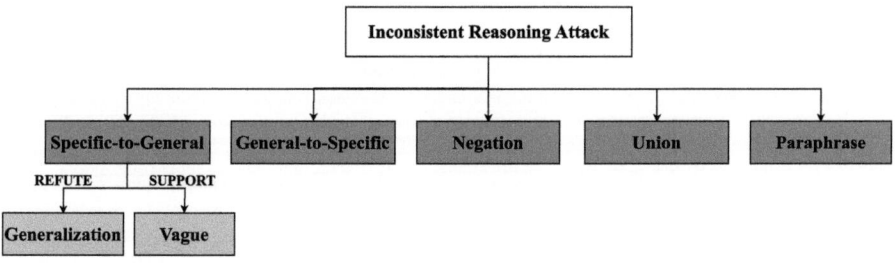

Fig. 1. Display of categories and subcategories of inconsistent reasoning attacks.

trained on the Semantic Scholar Open Research Corpus (S2ORC) [1], employing a multitask loss for rationale selection and label prediction.

The retrieval mechanism in SCV tools parallels Retrieval-Augmented Generation (RAG) [13], which enhances large language models (LLMs) by retrieving relevant document excerpts to improve factual grounding [5]. This mitigates hallucinations [8] and improves claim verification accuracy [3,11,22]. Unlike traditional SCV systems that rely on selecting static evidence, RAG-based approaches dynamically generate responses based on retrieved information [4], making them particularly suited for knowledge-intensive tasks such as scientific fact-checking [7,25]. Despite advancements in SCV, adversarial attacks on NLP models reveal vulnerabilities in automated fact-checking. TextFooler [10] perturbs claims by replacing important words with synonyms based on word embeddings, but this often leads to semantic drift, particularly in scientific contexts. PWWS (Probabilistic Word Replacement Strategy) [18] prioritizes impactful word substitutions using WordNet yet struggles with specialized terminology. BAE (BERT-based Adversarial Examples) [6] introduces token insertions, deletions, and replacements using pre-trained transformers, improving fluency but still failing to preserve domain-specific meaning.

As highlighted in [12], these adversarial methods are inadequate for SCV due to their simplistic word-replacement strategies that fail to maintain the technical integrity of claims. While [12] proposed a paraphrase-based attack generation approach to enhance semantic fidelity, it still requires manual filtering, limiting scalability and application in real-world scenarios. While standard NLP attacks report higher success rates than those in [12], a qualitative analysis reveals that [12] produces a greater number of valid attacks that preserve semantics compared to standard NLP attacks. However, the evolutionary attack algorithm in [12] lacks crossover operations with only mutations, which reduces its overall effectiveness in searching the space of possible attacks.

Our approach advances beyond existing methods by employing a full-stack evolutionary attack model with crossover and diverse mutation techniques implemented through LLMs. The inclusion of the crossover enables better attack generation by combining different adversarial strategies, leading to more effective and automated adversarial testing for SCV tools. The semantic and logical consistency of our proposed attacks is ensured through the use of LLMs and a self-

Table 1. Inconsistent Reasoning Attacks definitions and examples.

Category	Definition	Example
Generalization	Replace specific terms in the original claim with broader categories. Only considered when the original claim is refuted.	~~White Blood cells~~ **Blood cells** are NOT an important part of your immune system, which are positively correlated with detection and healing.
Vague	Substitute precise terms with more ambiguous language. Only considered when the original claim is supported.	White blood cells are an important part of your immune system, which are ~~positively~~ correlated with detection and healing.
General-to-Specific	Replace general terms with more specific ones.	~~White blood cells~~ **Neutrophils** are an important part of your immune system, which are positively correlated with detection and healing.
Negation	Introduce double negatives or reverse relational terms.	White blood cells are an important part of your immune system, which are ~~positively~~ **not negatively** correlated with detection and healing.
Union	Combine multiple claims into a single statement. Only considered when one claim is supported and the other is refuted.	White blood cells are an important part of your immune system **and neutrophils are not a type of red blood cell**.
Paraphrase	Rephrase the original claim while preserving its meaning.	White blood cells are an important part of your immune system, which are ~~positively correlated with detection and~~ good for healing.

reflection process. Moreover, our experimental results demonstrate a significantly higher attack success rate compared to standard NLP attacks. Consequently, our approach outperforms the method proposed in [12], as our approach achieves a higher attack success rate than standard NLP attacks, whereas [12] does not. Additionally, in Sect. 5.7, we follow the same qualitative analysis conducted in [12], and our results indicate superior performance.

3 Description of Inconsistent Reasoning Attacks

This section introduces the types of inconsistent reasoning attacks, illustrated in Fig. 1. Building on the concept of paraphrasing attacks defined in [12], we generalize to encompass a broader category of adversarial attacks. *An **inconsistent reasoning attack** occurs when an SCV tool assigns a label to an altered claim that is logically inconsistent with the label it assigned to the original claim.* A paraphrasing attack falls under this category since it involves a semantic rewording of the original claim that should not affect its label, yet the SCV tool assigns a different label. This discrepancy reveals an inconsistency in reasoning, as a change in label is unjustified when the meaning remains the same. In machine learning, traditional adversarial attacks introduce small perturbations in order to alter labels. In contrast, paraphrasing attacks implement perturbations that can be substantial while still maintaining semantic equivalence. Some inconsistent reasoning attacks extend beyond semantic equivalence, increasing the level of perturbation even further. The types of inconsistent reasoning attacks depicted in Fig. 1 comprise five attack types: specific-to-general, general-to-specific, negation, union, and paraphrase. These categories are not intended to be exhaustive and we anticipate that this research will inspire further categories of inconsistent reasoning attacks. Table 1 provides definitions and examples for each attack type.

Specific-to-general attacks involve replacing specific terms in the claim with more generic terminology. Generalization attacks, a subset of specific-to-general attacks, replace specific terms in the original claim with broader categories. This approach leverages the hierarchical structure inherent in many scientific claims, where concepts are organized from broader groups into narrower categories. For example, replacing "car" with "vehicle" since vehicle is the broader, higher-level group encompassing "cars" in addition to other vehicle types. Similar to the generalization example in Table 1 where "white blood cells" was replaced with "blood cells." These attacks succeed only when the original claim is refuted, as a refuted claim about a specific subset remains refuted at the broader level, as it is refuted for at least one subset. However, a supported statement for a specific subset may not be supported for all subsets encompassed by the broader level.

Another subset of specific-to-general attacks involves vague generalization, where precise terms are substituted with more ambiguous language. For example, removing the word "positively" from the phrase "positively correlated" in the vague example in Table 1. Unlike generalization attacks, vague generalization is only effective when the original claim is supported, as the broader wording still encompasses the specific case.

In contrast, general-to-specific attacks move in the opposite direction, replacing general terms with more specific ones. For instance, substituting "vehicle" with "car" makes the claim more precise. Similar to the general-to-specific example in Table 1 where "white blood cells" was replaced with "neutrophils", which is a specific type of white blood cell. These attacks are effective when the original claim is supported, as a statement supported at a general level remains valid for its specific subcategories. However, a refuted general claim may not necessarily apply to all its subgroups.

Negation attacks manipulate the logical structure of claims by introducing double negatives or reversing relational terms. Scientific statements often describe relationships between concepts, using paired terms such as increase/decrease, positive/negative, or rise/fall. A negation attack alters these relationships by replacing a term with its opposite and introducing negation, such as changing "increases" to "does not decrease". For example, when the negation attack in Table 1 replaces "positively" with the double negative of "not negatively". Some variants make the claim more ambiguous by removing directional indicators entirely, effectively converting it into a vague attack rather than a strict negation. Another common transformation involves adding phrases like "does not fail to", which modifies the logical interpretation of the statement.

Union attacks merge a refuted original claim with a supported claim (retrieved from the training set) into a single statement. The resulting union claim should still be classified as refuted. These attacks are considered successful only if the final claim is misclassified as supported. The union of two supported claims resulting in a refuted classification would be evidence of a hallucination

Algorithm 1. Inconsistent Reasoning Attacks

Input: SCV model m, LLM llm, Iterations R, Population size N_{pop}, Dataset DB
1: **function** generateAttack(*claim*, *label*)
2:    $Pop_{list} \leftarrow \{(claim, label)\}$
3:    $mutationPrompts = [paraphrase, union, negation, generalToSpecific, generalization, vague]$
4:    $crossOverPrompt = crossOver$
5:    **Filter** *mutationPrompts* based on the *label*'s value.
6:    **for** $iter = 1$ to R **do**
7:       $mutatedClaims \leftarrow mutatePop(mutationPrompts, Pop_{list})$
8:       $crossedClaims \leftarrow crossOverPop(crossOverPrompt, Pop_{list})$
9:       **Add** *mutatedClaims* and *crossedClaims* to Pop_{list}
10:      $Pop_{list} \leftarrow selection(Pop_{list})$
11:    **end for**
12: **end function**
13: **function** mutatePop(*mutationPrompts*, Pop_{list})
14:    $mutatedClaims \leftarrow \{\}$
15:    **for** $pop = 1$ to N_{pop} **do**
16:       $mutationPrompt \leftarrow$ Random selection from *mutationPrompts*
17:       $(claim, label) \leftarrow$ Random selection from Pop_{list}
18:       **if** $prompt = union$ **then**
19:          **Extend** *claim* by a neighbor claim from the DB
20:       **end if**
21:       **Pre-process** *mutationPrompt* using *claim*
22:       $invokeLLM(mutatedClaims, mutationPrompt, label)$
23:    **end for**
24:    **Return** *mutatedClaims*
25: **end function**
26: **function** crossOverPop(*crossOverPrompt*, Pop_{list})
27:    $crossedClaims \leftarrow \{\}$
28:    **for** $pop = 1$ to N_{pop} **do**
29:       $(claim1, label1) \leftarrow$ Random selection from Pop_{list}
30:       $(claim2, label2) \leftarrow$ Random selection from Pop_{list}
31:       **Pre-process** *crossOverPrompt* using *claim1* and *claim2*
32:       $invokeLLM(crossedClaims, crossOverPrompt, label)$
33:    **end for**
34:    **Return** *crossedClaims*
35: **end function**
36: **function** invokeLLM(*claimList*, *prompt*, *label*)
37:    $newClaim \leftarrow llm(prompt)$
38:    $newLabel \leftarrow m.predict(newClaim)$
39:    **if** $newLabel \neq label$ **then**
40:       $attackSuccess \leftarrow$ **True**
41:       **Exit function.**
42:    **end if**
43:    **Add** $(newClaim, newLabel)$ to *claimList*
44: **end function**
45: **function** selection(Pop_{list})
46:    **Score** Pop_{list} using m.score(Pop_{list})
47:    **Sort** Pop_{list} by the scores (descending)
48:    **Return** $Pop_{list} \leftarrow Pop_{list}[: N_{pop}]$
49: **end function**

(likely resulting from linking two supported claims in an improper way), which would be considered an unsuccessful attack. Combining two refuted statements such that an SCV tool would classify the union as supported would be a difficult task and was therefore not considered as it would result in minimal, if any, successful attacks. An example of a union attack can be found in Table 1, where the supported claim "White blood cells are an important part of your immune system" is combined with the refuted claim "Neutrophils are not a type of red blood cell".

Paraphrase attacks rephrase a claim while preserving its meaning. For example, in Table 1, the claim "White blood cells are an important part of your immune system, which are positively correlated with detection and good for healing" is paraphrased by removing "...positively correlated with detection and...". While negation and paraphrasing attacks retain semantic equivalence, double negation can be seen as a form of paraphrasing attack. However, we classify negation separately due to its distinct nature [12].

4 Inconsistent Reasoning AttacksGenerator

Inspired by genetic algorithms, the Inconsistent Reasoning Attacks (IRA) generator iteratively challenges the Scientific Claim Verification (SCV) target model, m, by generating adversarial claims. The attack operates over multiple **global iterations**, denoted as R, during which a population of claims undergoes systematic perturbations. Each iteration consists of two primary operations: **mutation** and **crossover**. These operations leverage an LLM to generate diverse claim variations that can mislead m. To ensure meaningful perturbations, a **self-reflection mechanism** refines the generated claims, evaluating their alignment with attack objectives. The generator continues iteratively until a perturbed claim successfully alters m's classification or the maximum number of iterations is reached. Algorithm 1 provides a step-by-step breakdown of this process. All prompts used in this paper are provided in Prompts.pdf (additional material).

4.1 Mutation Operation

The **mutation operation** introduces localized changes to an input claim, altering its structure or semantics while retaining its contextual essence. This step leverages a predefined set of mutation strategies, including paraphrasing, generalization, negation, and others, to generate adversarial claims.

Mutation Prompts: A predefined list of mutation strategies guides the LLM in generating new claims. Simple attacks such as paraphrasing require minimal modifications, while more complex mutations integrate additional contextual information through supplementary examples in the LLM prompt. Figure 2 illustrates an example prompt design for generalization attacks.

Process: A mutation strategy is randomly applied to a claim from the population. The LLM generates a new claim, which is evaluated against m. If the

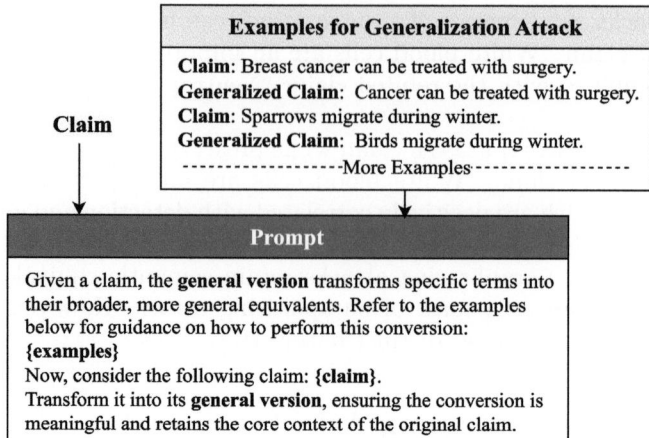

Fig. 2. Prompt design for generalization attacks.

model's prediction changes, the attack is successful. This iterative process refines adversarial claims through self-reflection to maximize their impact.

Self-Reflection of LLM: To enhance adversarial claim generation, Inconsistent Reasoning Attacks employs a **self-reflection mechanism**, inspired by its effectiveness in problem-solving [19,20] and reducing hallucinations [9]. The LLM-Reflector evaluates each mutated claim, refining it iteratively until it reaches a meaningful deviation or a maximum number of iterations, R_{sr}. Figure 3 illustrates this workflow, where the LLM-Generator perturbs claims and the LLM-Reflector evaluates and refines them.

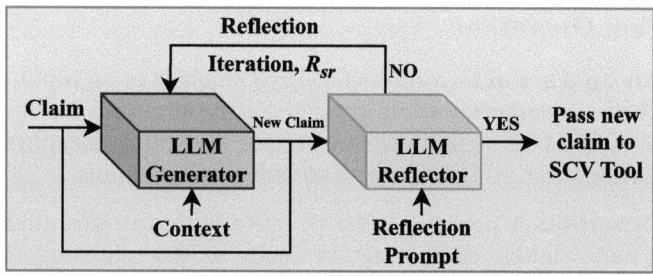

Fig. 3. Self-reflection of LLM.

4.2 Crossover Operation

The **crossover operation** merges two claims to create a hybrid adversarial claim, introducing novel perturbations that increase the likelihood of altering m's classification. The crossover mechanism is structured as follows:

Crossover Prompt. A specialized prompt directs the LLM to combine semantic components from two distinct claims into a single hybrid claim.

Process. Two claims are selected from the population, and the LLM synthesizes a new claim by integrating relevant aspects of both. The generated claim is then tested against m, and if its prediction is altered, the attack is deemed successful.

Like mutation, the crossover process benefits from **self-reflection**, refining the hybrid claim through iterative assessment and modification. The crossover's impact is further strengthened by the population selection mechanism, ensuring only the most effective claims persist across iterations.

4.3 Population Selection

The **Population Selection** mechanism manages the evolving set of adversarial claims throughout the attack process. It maintains an optimal population of claims by evaluating and ranking them based on their success in misleading m.

Each claim undergoes evaluation based on m's classification confidence and perturbation effectiveness. The claims are ranked in descending order of their impact, with only the top N_{pop} claims retained for subsequent iterations (Algorithm 1, lines 46–48). An attack iteration is considered successful if at least one perturbed claim generates a different label from m compared to the original claim. This signifies that the adversarial modification effectively misled the classification process. At each iteration, newly generated claims are evaluated and ranked, ensuring that only the most potent adversarial examples persist. The attack continues until either a successful perturbation is achieved or the maximum global iterations, R, are reached.

Through this iterative process of mutation, crossover, self-reflection, and population selection, Inconsistent Reasoning Attacks systematically generates robust adversarial claims that challenge m's decision boundary, demonstrating the efficacy of genetic-inspired attack mechanisms in adversarial NLP research.

5 Experiment

This section evaluates *IRA* against three state-of-the-art NLP attacks on two datasets and three victim models. We detail the datasets, baselines, victim models, implementation, evaluation metrics, analyses, ablation studies, and hyperparameters.

5.1 Datasets

We use two well-known datasets for scientific claim verification, summarized in Table 2:

SciFact [25] is a curated dataset of scientific claims annotated with abstracts. Claims are labeled as SUPPORT, REFUTE, or NOINFO. For SUPPORT and

Table 2. Dataset Splits with Class Distribution

Dataset	Train		Val		Test	
	Support	Refute	Support	Refute	Support	Refute
SciFact	332	173	124	64	100	100
HealthVer	3782	2411	533	391	671	425

REFUTE labels, rationales and key statistics, such as the number of sentences per rationale and evidence abstracts per claim, are provided.

HealthVer [17] is a COVID-19-focused dataset for fact-checking health claims. It contains manually annotated claim-evidence pairs extracted from web snippets and verified against scientific literature. Each pair is categorized as SUPPORT, REFUTE, or NEUTRAL.

5.2 NLP Attack Methods and Victim Models

We compare *IRA* against the following three attack methods.[1]:

PWWS [18] uses WordNet[2] to generate synonym-based substitutions and prioritizes word replacements based on model probability shifts and word significance.

TextFooler [10] ranks word importance by measuring the cumulative probability change before and after its removal.

BAE-Attack [6] is a black-box attack that generates adversarial examples by applying contextual perturbations using a BERT-masked language model. BAE-Attack modifies text by masking tokens and replacing or inserting alternatives suggested by BERT-MLM.

For adversarial attacks, we evaluate the following SCV tools as victim models:

MultiVerS uses a Longformer encoder for claim verification at both abstract and sentence levels [26]. It selects rationales via three-way classification, discarding Not Enough Information (NEI) labels and retaining SUPPORT and REFUTE. Abstract retrieval involves gathering candidates and refining predictions with a neural re-ranking mechanism.

Retrieval-Augmented Generation (RAG) operates by indexing the entire corpus of abstracts [13]. For each fact-checking instance, the search query embedding is matched against the indexed corpus. The top-K documents retrieved are then provided, along with the query, to the LLM for final classification.

Attack-Reflection-RAG extends RAG by integrating additional information about potential attacks, thereby improving its adversarial robustness. This approach first processes the claim and queries the LLM for possible perturbations

---

[1] As explained in Sect. 2, we do not include a comparison with [12], as it underperforms based on the metrics defined in Sect. 5.3 for the considered NLP attacks.

[2] https://wordnet.princeton.edu/.

introduced by an attack. If the LLM detects a potential adversarial modification, it supplies this information as additional context to the RAG model during inference, helping it make more informed predictions. The prompts used and further details are in Prompts.pdf in the additional material.

5.3 Metrics

To assess the effectiveness of *IRA* against the victim models, we use three metrics:
Clean Accuracy (Clean%) represents the classification accuracy on the clean test dataset. This metric evaluates the performance of the victim model when it is not exposed to any adversarial attacks. A higher Clean% indicates that the model generalizes well to unseen data and can accurately classify clean instances.

Accuracy Under Attack (Aua%) measures the model's accuracy in adversarial settings [14,15,28]. A higher Aua% indicates greater resilience to adversarial attacks, making it a crucial metric in adversarial robustness research.

Attack Success Rate (Suc%) represents the proportion of successfully altered texts out of the total attempted examples [14,15,28]. A lower Suc% indicates greater model robustness.

5.4 Implementation Settings

We generate the adversarial examples using NVIDIA GeForce RTX 4090. We employ the LLM LLaMA-3.1, accessed via the open-source library Ollama[3], for both retrieval-augmented generation (RAG) and adversarial generation. The clean accuracy (Clean%) is calculated across the entire test dataset. We reproduce all victim models using their respective open-source implementations and predefined hyperparameters. Our GitHub repository for reproducibility is available at[4].

Table 3. Experimental results of *IRA* compared to three state-of-the-art textual attacks against MultiVerS and RAG-based SCV tools on two datasets, SciFact and HealthVer. The best performance is highlighted in bold.

Model	Dataset	Clean%	PWWS		TextFooler		BAE-Attack		IRA	
			Aua%	Suc%	Aua%	Suc%	Aua%	Suc%	Aua%	Suc%
MultiVerS	SciFact	90.43	55.85	38.24	58.51	35.29	82.45	8.82	**29.26**	**67.65**
	HealthVer	74.73	32.41	56.61	35.16	52.94	67.58	9.56	**22.52**	**69.85**
RAG	SciFact	79.26	30.85	61.07	33.51	57.72	69.15	12.75	**18.09**	**77.18**
	HealthVer	71.98	24.18	66.41	26.37	63.36	59.89	16.69	**15.38**	**78.63**
Attack-Reflection-RAG	SciFact	76.06	40.43	46.85	43.09	43.35	70.21	7.69	**28.19**	**62.94**
	HealthVer	70.33	37.91	46.09	42.86	39.06	62.63	10.93	**27.47**	**60.94**

---

[3] https://ollama.com/.
[4] https://github.com/atikbappy/inconsistency-reasoning.

5.5 Main Results

Table 3 presents the experimental results of *IRA* compared to state-of-the-art attacks PWWS, TextFooler, and BAE-Attack on MultiVerS and RAG-based SCV tools across two datasets, SciFact and HealthVer. Since the test set for SciFact is private [24], we report results on its development set, while for HealthVer, we use the test set. Across all models and datasets, *IRA* consistently achieves the highest Suc%, demonstrating its superior ability to degrade model performance. Specifically, for MultiVerS, *IRA* reduces Aua% to 29.26 on SciFact and 22.52 on HealthVer, surpassing PWWS, TextFooler, and BAE-Attack while maintaining a significantly higher Suc% (67.65 and 69.85). Similar trends hold for RAG, where *IRA* lowers accuracy to 18.09 on SciFact and 15.38 on HealthVer, with an Suc% of 77.18 and 78.63, respectively. For the Attack-Reflection-RAG model, *IRA* continues to demonstrate effectiveness. On SciFact, *IRA* reduces Aua% to 28.19 with an Suc% of 62.94. On HealthVer, it lowers Aua% to 27.47 with an Suc% of 60.94, outperforming baselines. Notably, on HealthVer, where baseline attacks have success rates below 47%, *IRA* is the only method with a dominant impact. Overall, *IRA* improves Suc% by +35.17 on MultiVerS, +31.58 on RAG, and +29.61 on Attack-Reflection-RAG, confirming its superiority over prior attacks in degrading scientific claim verification models.

Table 4. Ablation study results showing both Aua% and Suc% for SciFact and HealthVer. "Excluded" means the attack was excluded, "Used" means only that attack was applied. The row "All" corresponds to the overall performance when all attacks are applied (or equivalently, when no attack is excluded).

Attack Type	SciFact				HealthVer			
	Excluded		Used		Excluded		Used	
	Aua%	Suc%	Aua%	Suc%	Aua%	Suc%	Aua%	Suc%
Paraphrase	55.32	38.82	53.72	41.17	40.11	46.33	40.11	46.32
Negation	37.77	58.23	78.19	14.11	26.37	64.71	67.58	10.29
General-to-Specific	29.79	67.06	87.23	3.52	29.67	60.29	60.44	19.11
Generalization	33.51	62.94	83.51	8.23	28.02	62.50	66.48	11.03
Vague	33.51	62.94	88.30	2.35	25.82	65.44	66.68	8.08
Union	41.49	54.12	83.51	7.64	31.32	58.09	57.69	22.79
All	**29.26**	**67.65**	**29.26**	**67.65**	**22.52**	**69.85**	**22.52**	**69.85**

Attack-Reflection-RAG is highly resilient to attacks, except for MultiVerS outperforming it on SciFact–likely due to parameter estimation on the same test set. This anomaly aside, attack reflection warrants further investigation as a mitigation strategy.

5.6 Ablation Study

We perform an ablation study to assess the impact of individual attacks on IRA. Two experiments were conducted: excluding a specific attack to evaluate overall performance and isolating a single attack to analyze its contribution. Table 4 presents the excluded and isolated attacks, along with their attack success rate (Suc%) and accuracy under attack (Aua%) for SciFact and HealthVer.

IRA is most effective when all attacks are combined, achieving the lowest Aua% (29.26% for SciFact, 22.52% for HealthVer) and the highest Suc% (67.65% and 69.85%, respectively), as shown in Table 4. This underscores the strength of a diversified attack strategy.

Among individual attacks, excluding *Paraphrase* causes the largest Aua% increase (around 26% for SciFact, 18% for HealthVer), emphasizing its crucial role. Its standalone effectiveness is further confirmed by achieving the highest Aua% and Suc%.

5.7 Qualitative Analysis

For the qualitative analysis, we analyze 54 paraphrasing attacks that had been deemed successful by the model and show an example of a single attack that combined multiple inconsistent reasoning attacks in one.

Table 5. Results of the qualitative analysis to show the success of attacks and evaluate quality.

Quality Metric	Count (%)
Rejected Attacks	12 (22.2%)
Successful Attacks	42 (77.8%)
Quality of Successful Attacks	
High	28 (66.7%)
Medium	13 (31.0%)
Low	1 (2.4%)

Among the 54 paraphrasing attacks that were reviewed, we identified any successful attacks that were truly unsuccessful, that is, an attack where the logic of the original claim had not been maintained, and the classification from the SCV tool was correct in reversing its original label.

Attacks that were truly successful were evaluated, and the quality of the attack was ranked: high/medium/low. Table 5 presents the results of the qualitative analysis. Most of the attacks were truly successful (77.8%), and all but one was of high or medium quality.

Of the 54 paraphrasing attacks that were reviewed, 12 (22.2%) were rejected and deemed unsuccessful. The attacks were rejected for one of three reasons: 1) changed meaning, 2) hallucination, or 3) nonsensical statement.

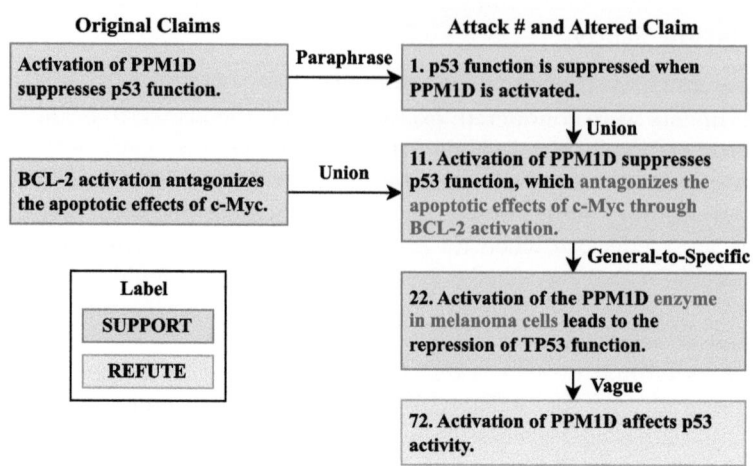

Fig. 4. Example of a generated combined inconsistent reasoning attacks

An attack "changed meaning" if the meaning from the original claim had been altered or reversed in the attack. A "hallucination" occurred when the attack added new information that was contrary to the original claim. A "nonsensical statement" was an attack that contained nonsensical grammar, facts, or science. Of the 12 rejections, 7 were hallucinations (58.3%), 4 changed meaning (33.3%), and 1 was a nonsensical statement (8.3%). Hallucinations were expected due to the greedy nature of inconsistent reasoning attacks, which optimize for modification of an original claim that reverses the classification of the SCV tool.

The single attack that combined multiple inconsistent reasoning attacks that were reviewed went through 72 iterations, applying an inconsistent reasoning attack at each iteration. Figure 4 displays 4 of the 72 intermediate states (the 1st, 11th, 22nd, and 72nd states).

These 4 intermediate states include paraphrasing, union, general-to-specific, and vague inconsistent reasoning attacks. When possible, added or updated text is colored red. This figure shows how two original claims were joined (union), rephrased (paraphrase), made more specific (general-to-specific), and made more vague in order to form an attack claim that reversed the classification of the SCV tool from SUPPORT to REFUTE making this a successful attack.

5.8 Hyperparameter Analysis

Figure 5 illustrates the impact of key hyperparameters - Number of iterations (R), Number of Population (N_{pop}) and Number of Self-Reflection Iterations (R_{sr}) - on the performance of IRA, as measured by Aua%

Number of Iterations. Increasing the number of iterations reduces the Aua% consistently, as shown in subfigure 5a. This shows that longer iterative processes allow the algorithm to explore more potential attack strategies, resulting

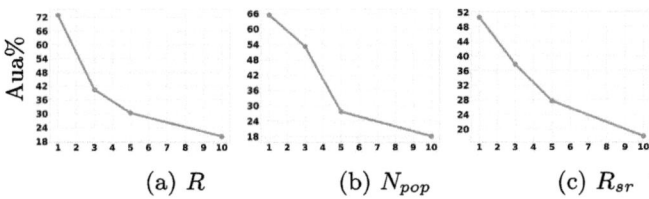

(a) R (b) N_{pop} (c) R_{sr}

Fig. 5. Hyperparameter Analysis for *IRA*. 50 random samples from SciFact dataset were used to compute Aua% for given hyperparameters.

in better performance. However, balancing performance improvement with the increased computational costs is crucial when choosing R.

Number of Population. Subfigure 5b demonstrates that a larger population contributes to a steady decline in Aua%, indicating that a diverse candidate pool during optimization improves the overall outcome of *IRA*. While higher N_{pop} values lead to better results, they demand additional computational resources and can slow down the process.

Number of Self Reflection Iterations. Subfigure 5c highlights a negative correlation between R_{sr} and Aua%. With more self-reflection iterations, LLMs can increasingly refine its strategies, leading to more effective attacks. Nonetheless, higher R_{sr} requires higher computational resources, so choosing a good trade-off is necessary.

6 Conclusion

Scientific Claim Verification (SCV) tools play a crucial role in assessing the validity of scientific claims; however, they remain vulnerable to logical inconsistencies. Adversarial attacks provide a powerful approach for identifying these vulnerabilities and enhancing SCV systems. In this study, we introduce inconsistent reasoning attacks, a broader class of adversarial manipulations encompassing five types: specific-to-general, general-to-specific, negation, union, and paraphrase. To detect and test these weaknesses, we develop an evolutionary algorithm that leverages large language models to generate effective adversarial attacks targeting logical inconsistencies.

Evaluation against MultiVerS reveals persistent vulnerabilities, while a retrieval-augmented generation (RAG) system with an Attack-Reflection mechanism shows promise in mitigating these issues. Strengthening SCV systems against such attacks is essential for ensuring their reliability. Future research should integrate self-reflection and adversarial robustness to improve SCV effectiveness.

References

1. Beltagy, I., Peters, M.E., Cohan, A.: Longformer: the long-document transformer (2020)
2. Coley, C.W., Eyke, N.S., Jensen, K.F.: Autonomous discovery in the chemical sciences part i: progress. Angew. Chem. Int. Ed. **59**(51), 22858–22893 (2020)
3. Dey, A.U., Llabrés, A., Valveny, E., Karatzas, D.: Retrieval augmented verification: Unveiling disinformation with structured representations for zero-shot fact-checking of multi-modal social media posts. arXiv preprint arXiv:2404.10702 (2024)
4. Dmonte, A., Oruche, R., Zampieri, M., Calyam, P., Augenstein, I.: Claim verification in the age of large language models: a survey. arXiv preprint arXiv:2408.14317 (2024)
5. Gao, Y., et al.: Retrieval-augmented generation for large language models: a survey (2024)
6. Garg, S., Ramakrishnan, G.: BAE: BERT-based adversarial examples for text classification. In: Proceedings of EMNLP 2020, pp. 6174–6181. ACL (2020)
7. Guan, J., Dodge, J., Wadden, D., Huang, M., Peng, H.: Language models hallucinate, but may excel at fact verification. arXiv preprint arXiv:2310.14564 (2023)
8. Huang, L., Yu, W., Ma, W., Zhong, W., et al.: A survey on hallucination in large language models: principles, taxonomy, challenges, and open questions. ACM Trans. Inf. Syst. (2024)
9. Ji, Z., Yu, T., Xu, Y., Lee, N., Ishii, E., Fung, P.: Towards mitigating LLM hallucination via self reflection. In: Findings of ACL: EMNLP 2023, pp. 1827–1843. ACL, Singapore (2023)
10. Jin, D., Jin, Z., Zhou, J.T., Szolovits, P.: Is BERT really robust? A strong baseline for NLP attack on text classification and entailment. In: Proceedings of AAAI, vol. 34, pp. 8018–8025 (2020)
11. Khaliq, M.A., Chang, P., Ma, M., Pflugfelder, B., Miletić, F.: Ragar, your falsehood radar: Rag-augmented reasoning for political fact-checking using multimodal LLMs. arXiv preprint arXiv:2404.12065 (2024)
12. Layne, J., Ratul, Q.E.A., Serra, E., Jajodia, S.: Analyzing robustness of automatic scientific claim verification tools against adversarial rephrasing attacks. ACM Trans. Intell. Syst. Technol. **15**(5) (2024)
13. Lewis, P., et al.: Retrieval-augmented generation for knowledge-intensive NLP tasks. Adv. Neural. Inf. Process. Syst. **33**, 9459–9474 (2020)
14. Li, Z., et al.: Searching for an effective defender: benchmarking defense against adversarial word substitution. In: Proceedings of 2021 Conference on Empirical Methods in NLP, pp. 3137–3147. ACL, Online and Punta Cana, Dominican Republic (2021)
15. Liu, Q., et al.: Flooding-X: improving BERT's resistance to adversarial attacks via loss-restricted fine-tuning. In: Proceedings of 60th Annual Meeting of the Association for Computational Linguistics (Vol. 1: Long Papers), pp. 5634–5644. ACL, Dublin, Ireland (2022)
16. Maffettone, P.M., et al.: What is missing in autonomous discovery: open challenges for the community. Digital Discov. **2**(6), 1644–1659 (2023)
17. Mourad Sarrouti, Asma Ben Abacha, Y.M., Demner-Fushman, D.: Evidence-based fact-checking of health-related claims. In: EMNLP (2021)
18. Ren, S., Deng, Y., He, K., Che, W.: Generating natural language adversarial examples through probability weighted word saliency. In: Proceedings of the 57th Annual Meeting of the Association for Computational Linguistics, pp. 1085–1097 (2019)

19. Renze, M., Guven, E.: Self-reflection in LLM agents: effects on problem-solving performance (2024)
20. Salehi, S.: Improving problem-solving through reflection. Stanford University (2018)
21. Sarrouti, M., Abacha, A.B., M'rabet, Y., Demner-Fushman, D.: Evidence-based fact-checking of health-related claims. In: Findings of the Association for Computational Linguistics: EMNLP 2021, pp. 3499–3512 (2021)
22. Singhal, R., Patwa, P., Patwa, P., Chadha, A., Das, A.: Evidence-backed fact checking using rag and few-shot in-context learning with LLMs. arXiv preprint arXiv:2408.12060 (2024)
23. Tan, N.Ö., Tandon, N., Wadden, D., Tafjord, O., Gahegan, M., Witbrock, M.: Faithful reasoning over scientific claims. In: Proceedings of the AAAI Symposium Series, vol. 3, pp. 263–272 (2024)
24. Wadden, D.: The multivers model: Source code (2023). https://github.com/dwadden/multivers. Code associated with the MultiVerS paper. Accessed 10 Feb 2025
25. Wadden, D., et al.: Fact or fiction: verifying scientific claims. In: Proceedings of EMNLP 2020, pp. 7534–7550. ACL, Online (2020)
26. Wadden, D., Lo, K., Wang, L.L., Cohan, A., Beltagy, I., Hajishirzi, H.: MultiVerS: improving scientific claim verification with weak supervision and full-document context. In: Findings of ACL: NAACL 2022, pp. 61–76. ACL, Seattle, United States (2022)
27. Wang, L.: Using machine learning to verify scientific claims. Artif. Intell. Sci. 120 (2023)
28. Wang, Z., Liu, Z., Zheng, X., Su, Q., Wang, J.: RMLM: a flexible defense framework for mitigating word-level adversarial attacks. In: Proceedings of the 61st Annual Meeting of ACL (Vol. 1: Long Papers), pp. 2757–2774. ACL, Toronto, Canada (2023)

On Training Survival Models with Scoring Rules

Philipp Kopper[1,2], David Rügamer[1,2], Raphael Sonabend[3], Bernd Bischl[1,2], and Andreas Bender[1,2(✉)]

[1] Department of Statistics, LMU Munich, 80539 Munich, Germany
{philipp.kopper,david.ruegamer,bernd.bischl}@stat.uni-muenchen.de
[2] Munich Center for Machine Learning (MCML), LMU Munich, 80539 Munich, Germany
andreas.bender@stat.uni-muenchen.de
[3] OSPO Now, London, UK

Abstract. Scoring rules are an established way to compare predictive performance between model classes. In the context of survival analysis, they require adaptation in order to accommodate censoring and other aspects specific to survival tasks. This work investigates the use of scoring rules for model training rather than evaluation. Doing so, we establish a general framework for training survival models that is model-agnostic and can learn event time distributions parametrically or non-parametrically. In addition, our framework is not restricted to any specific scoring rule. Although we focus on neural network-based implementations, we also provide proof-of-concept implementations using gradient boosting, generalized additive models, and trees. Empirical comparisons on synthetic and real-world data indicate that scoring rules can be successfully incorporated into model training and yield competitive predictive performance with established time-to-event models.

Keywords: Proper Scoring Rules · Survival Analysis · Neural Networks

1 Introduction

Survival analysis (SA) is an important branch of statistics and machine learning that deals with time-to-event data analysis. Let $Y > 0$ be a random variable representing a time-to-event of interest (e.g., time-to-death after operation) and y its realization. In many studies, Y cannot be observed in all cases due to censoring $C > 0$. Thus, in the presence of right-censoring, we can only observe realizations of $T := \min(Y, C)$ and status indicator $D := I(Y \leq C)$. Observed data is then given by tuples $(t_i, d_i, \mathbf{x}_i), i = 1, \ldots, n$, where t_i is an observed event or censoring time, d_i the status indicator and $\mathbf{x}_i^\top = (x_{i1}, \ldots, x_{ip})$ a p-dimensional feature vector.

Notably, while we are interested in inference about Y, we only have realizations of (T, Δ). Therefore, the usual metrics for evaluating predictive performance based on the difference in the true and observed value $(y_i - \hat{y}_i)$ cannot be calculated for the censored data from time to event. For the same reason, most survival models do not generate predictions $\hat{y}$, but rather probabilistic predictions $\hat{F}_Y(\tau) = \mathbb{P}(Y \leq \tau), \tau \in \mathbb{R}_0^+$, or equivalently the survival function $\hat{S}_Y(\tau) = 1 - \hat{F}_Y(\tau)$. At the estimation stage, censoring must be accounted for to obtain unbiased estimates of $S_Y(\tau)$. Common approaches include parametric models that assume a specific distribution for the event times with a censoring-adjusted likelihood (e.g., accelerated failure time models) as well as non- and semi-parametric approaches that partition the follow-up into intervals and estimate the (baseline) hazard rate within each interval (e.g., Kaplan-Meier, Cox, discrete-time approaches).

For predictive modeling, dedicated evaluation metrics that consider the data's survival nature have been proposed in the literature (see [26] for an overview). Such metrics are often model-agnostic to allow comparison of predictive performances across model classes. While concordance-based metrics [e.g. Harrell's C, 14] are popular in practice, they only allow for evaluating how well the model ranks the risk for an event. On the other hand, (strictly proper) scoring rules have been proposed as suitable tools to evaluate probabilistic (distribution) predictions [12]. As these scores often only rely on point-wise survival probability predictions (without requiring a density estimate, for example), scores can be compared across different model classes. One such scoring rule is the continuous rank probability score or integrated brier score [12]. [13] adapted it to the survival setting by weighting the scores concerning the individuals' probabilities of being censored (IPCW). This work refers to it as integrated survival brier score (ISBS). While ubiquitous in practice, recent work suggests that the ISBS is not proper [24,26,32], and proper alternatives have been proposed. As scoring rules in survival analysis are established in the context of model evaluation and comparison, so far only few attempts have been made to use them as a loss function for model training.

Our Contributions. In this work, we investigate the use of censoring-adapted scoring rules for model training rather than evaluation. The developed framework uses gradient-based optimization of the scoring rule of choice, evaluated at discrete partitions of the follow-up. In contrast to previous contributions, it is scoring-rule agnostic, allows parametric and non-parametric estimation of the event time distribution, and extends scoring rule-based estimation to the important case of competing risks. Additionally, while our main implementation is based on neural networks, we also show that our framework is applicable to other model classes, such as gradient boosting, trees, and generalized additive modeling. We empirically evaluate the approach on synthetic and real-world data, showing competitive predictive performance compared to established state-of-the-art survival models.

2 Related Literature

Scoring Rules. Scoring rules are established tools for model evaluation and comparison, particularly in the context of probabilistic predictions. A comprehensive summary is given in [12], who also investigate the role of scoring rules in estimation. Adaptations of scoring rules for survival analysis (see Table 1 for an overview of selected scores) have been pioneered by [13], who defined the ISBS, which weights the integrated brier score by an estimate of the censoring distribution $\hat{G}$, usually using the Kaplan-Meier estimator. Other adaptations are discussed in [9,24,26,32]. [24] propose the right-censored log-likelihood (RCLL) and claim to prove its properness, but its calculation requires an estimate of the density f_Y, which is not readily available for non- and semi-parametric methods that often only return survival probability predictions. The score proposed by [32] is also claimed to be proper but relies on an oracle parameter that is not known in practice. [26] suggest a class of re-weighted scoring rules (Eq. (1)), including the re-weighted ISBS (RISBS) and re-weighted integrated survival log-loss (RISLL):

$$\mathrm{SR}_{R,i}(\tau) = \frac{d_i}{\hat{G}(t_i)} \mathrm{SR}_i(\tau), \tag{1}$$

with d_i being the status indicator, $\mathrm{SR}_i(\tau)$ is a suitable point-wise scoring rule (e.g. the IBS) of observation i at time τ and $\hat{G}(t_i)$ an estimate of the censoring distribution at time t_i, which is estimated beforehand. SR is computed up to a $\tau^* < \tau^{max}$, the largest observed survival time, and [26] recommend to consider all fully observed i still at risk at τ^* with $d_i = 1$.

Survival Models. Most of the existing methods model the hazard function non- or semi-parametrically (i.e. without (strong) distributional assumptions) based on prior partitioning or discretization of the follow-up (for example, Cox regression [7], (extensions of) piece-wise exponential models [5,10] and discrete-time approaches [28]), or use specific distributional assumptions with dedicated loss functions for censored data [e.g., 30]. More recently, adaptations of these approaches based on machine and deep learning have been suggested [cf. 29,31, forrespectivereviews]. According to the latter, most deep learning models are adaptations of the Cox model, followed by discrete-time approaches. The latter are popular as they allow for transforming a survival task to a classification task and don't require strong distributional assumptions. Concretely, the follow-up is partitioned into J intervals $(\tau_{j-1}, \tau_j), j = 1, \ldots, J$; $\tau_0 := 0$ and new status indicators are defined for each interval $d_{ij} = I(t_i \in (\tau_{j-1}, \tau_j] \wedge d_i = 1)$. Assuming a Bernoulli distribution for these new event indicators, discrete time methods that optimize the resulting Binomial log-likelihood. Popular methods within this class include DeepHit [23] and *nnet-survival* [11]. Another stream of models that reduces the survival problem to a (Poisson) regression problem through discretization are methods based on piece-wise exponential models. State-of-the-art examples include [3,20,21]. While this reduction idea relates to our approach, we do not further review this model class in this contribution, as there are too many disjunctions.

In the context of SA, only a few have suggested using scoring rules at the estimation or training rather than the evaluation step. A notable exception is [2], who use a survival-adapted continuous rank probability score (SCRPS). Additionally, [24] illustrate how RCLL can be used for training and evaluating survival models. While [2] evaluate the SCRPS to estimate the parameters of a log-normal distribution, the approach by [24] is distribution-free, but requires an estimate of the density f_Y which usually needs to be approximated. The two approaches suggested in this work differ from previous endeavors. In contrast to other methods, our non-parametric approach learns increments of a function for event probabilities (i.e., survival or cumulative incidence) based on a scoring rule, whereas others use a specific likelihood. Our parametric approach is similar to [2] but not restricted to SCRPS or the log-normal distribution. Importantly, we extend the scoring rule-based estimation to the important case of competing risks and illustrate how the proposed estimation routine can be incorporated in various modeling approaches (deep learning, boosting, trees, and additive models).

3 Training with Scoring Rules

We aim to learn F_Y by discretely evaluating an associated scoring rule. While our approach is scoring rule agnostic, we focus on the rules in Table 1. The ISBS is of great historical significance and is a popular evaluation metric in the majority of benchmark experiments for SA. The alternatives in Table 1 have been suggested only recently and therefore have not been applied often in practice. The SCRPS, as implemented in [2], is the ISBS but without weighting contributions by inverse probability of censoring weights. The weighting factor in RISBS and RISLL means that contributions of censored observations are always set to zero. Non-censored observations are weighted by the probability of not being censored until the observed event time.

In order to use scoring rules for training, we partition the follow-up into J equidistant intervals $(\tau_{j-1}, \tau_j], j = 1, \ldots, J$, with $\tau_0 = 0$ and τ_J the largest observed event time. We then minimize the objective O that evaluates scoring rule $\text{SR}_i(\tau_j|\hat{G})$ for observation i at time τ_j, given censoring distribution $\hat{G}$:

$$O = \frac{1}{N} \sum_{i=1}^{N} \frac{1}{J} \sum_{j=1}^{J} \text{SR}_i(\tau_j|\hat{G}). \qquad (2)$$

To do so, we need J point-wise estimates of $S(\tau_j|\mathbf{x}_i) = 1 - F(\tau_j|\mathbf{x}_i)$. These can be generated in two ways:

1) *Parametric Learning*: Estimation of the parameters of an assumed distribution;
2) *Distribution-free Approach*: Direct estimation of the survival function without distributional assumption.

Table 1. Selected model-agnostic scoring rules. Here, $F_i(\tau) := F(\tau|\mathbf{x}_i)$; S_i, f_i equivalently. RCLL is only evaluated at the observed time t_i, while all other rules are evaluated over $[0, \tau^*]$.

Abbreviation (Source)	Definition
ISBS [13]	$\int_0^{t_i} \frac{F_i(\tau)^2}{\hat{G}(\tau)} d\tau + \int_{t_i}^{\tau^*} \frac{d_i S_i(\tau)^2}{\hat{G}(t_i)} d\tau$
SCRPS [2]	$\int_0^{t_i} F_i(\tau)^2 d\tau + \int_{t_i}^{\tau^*} S_i(\tau)^2 d\tau$
RISBS [26]	$\int_0^{t_i} \frac{d_i F_i(\tau)^2}{\hat{G}(t_i)} d\tau + \int_{t_i}^{\tau^*} \frac{d_i S_i(\tau)^2}{\hat{G}(t_i)}$
RISLL [26]	$-\frac{d_i}{\hat{G}(t_i)}\left(\int_0^{t_i} \log(F_i(\tau)) + \int_{t_i}^{\tau^*} \log(S_i(\tau)) d\tau\right)$
RCLL [24]	$-\log(d_i f_i(t_i) + (1-d_i) S_i(t_i))$

In both cases, the data transformation is identical as depicted in Fig. 1. The shown transformation contains all sufficient information for all scoring rules and model classes discussed in this work. However, for some scoring rules, the computation of the weights (w_j) varies or is not necessary, or only a limited number of intervals is needed. Also, the features do not necessarily need to be transformed as well if the model class can facilitate such mapping internally. For example, neural networks can do this by reshaping.

3.1 Modeling Approaches

Both approaches 1) and 2) share the same objective function (2) and only differ in the way the predictions $\hat{S}(\tau_j|\mathbf{x}_j)$ are obtained. Both variants ensure that $\hat{S}$ is monotonically decreasing. Details are given below.

Parametric Learning. One way to obtain estimates for $S(\tau|\mathbf{x}_j)$ is by assuming a parametric distribution of event times and learning the distribution's parameters. Let $F(\tau|\boldsymbol{\theta})$ be a distribution suitable to represent event times $Y > 0$, with parameters $\boldsymbol{\theta} \in \mathbb{R}^m$ depending on the input features, i.e., $\boldsymbol{\theta}(\mathbf{x}) = (\theta_1(\mathbf{x}), \theta_2(\mathbf{x}), \ldots, \theta_m(\mathbf{x}))^\top$. Some popular parametric survival distributions include the Weibull, log-logistic, and log-normal distribution. Given parameter estimates $\hat{\boldsymbol{\theta}}(\mathbf{x})$, all quantities of the distribution, including the survival function $\hat{S}(\tau|\hat{\boldsymbol{\theta}}(\mathbf{x})) = 1 - \hat{F}(\tau|\hat{\boldsymbol{\theta}}(\mathbf{x}))$, are fully specified and thus prediction can be obtained at any time point τ. Depending on the distribution, parameters may have restrictions, e.g. for the log-normal distribution $\boldsymbol{\theta}(\mathbf{x}) = (\mu(\mathbf{x}), \sigma(\mathbf{x}))^\top$ with $\mu \in \mathbb{R}$ and $\sigma \in \mathbb{R}_+$. The distribution parameters $\boldsymbol{\theta}$ are learned by minimizing Eq. (2) w.r.t. the model parameters.

Distribution-free Approach. Instead of obtaining an estimate of the survival function by learning the parameters of an assumed distribution, we can also learn the survival function by estimating the increments $\alpha_{i,j} := \alpha_{i,j}(\mathbf{x}_i)$ between the survival functions at subsequent discrete time points/intervals τ_{j-1}, τ_j. We require the following properties to obtain a correctly specified survival function:

id	status	time	x
1	0	3.1	2.3
2	1	1.4	2.4
3	0	1.2	-1.3

⟹

id	d_j	τ_j	w_j	x
1	0	0.5	1.70	2.3
1	0	1.5	1.70	2.3
1	0	2.5	1.70	2.3
...	...	...	...	...
2	0	0.5	1.23	2.4
2	1	1.5	1.23	2.4
2	1	2.5	1.23	2.4
...	...	...	...	...
3	0	0.5	0.00	-1.3
3	0	1.5	0.00	-1.3
3	0	2.5	0.00	-1.3
...	...	...	...	...

Fig. 1. Example of the transformation of original survival data into a discretized data set with $\tau_j \in \{0.5, 1.5, 2.5, ...\}$. (Time-constant) Features (x) are simply repeated. The survival indicator d_j switches from 0 to 1 when a failure is observed and remains 1 for the remaining intervals. The weights are computed for the RISBS scoring rule. For other scoring rules, weights can be time-varying. As the first observation is fully observed (censored after $\tau_{max} = 2.9$) it has positive weights ($w_{1j} = \frac{1}{\hat{G}(t=2.9)}$) while the third observation has zero-weights not being fully observed.

(a) $S(\tau_j|\mathbf{x}_i)$ needs to be monotonically decreasing, i.e. $\alpha_{i,j} \leq 0$;
(b) $S(\tau_j|\mathbf{x}_i) \in [0, 1]$;
(c) $\alpha_{i,j} \in [-1, 0]$.

In order to learn the increments $\alpha_{i,j}$, we require appropriate activation functions $\gamma_u(x) \in [0, 1], u \in \{1, 2\}$, such as the sigmoid or truncated ReLU function $f(\cdot) = \min(1, \max(0, \cdot))$, and a model g_l (e.g., a neural network) for the lth interval. By defining

$$\hat{S}(\tau_j|\mathbf{x}_i) = \gamma_2 \left(\sum_{l=1}^{j} (-\gamma_1(g_l(\mathbf{x}_i))) \right)$$

through increments $\hat{\alpha}_{i,l} := -\gamma_1(\hat{g}_l(\mathbf{x}_i)) \in [-1, 0]$, we obtain a monotonically decreasing survival function $\hat{S}(\tau_j|\mathbf{x}_i) = \gamma_2(\sum_{l=1}^{j} \hat{\alpha}_{i,l}) \in [0, 1]$ for each time interval τ_j with $\tau_0 = 0$ and $\hat{S}(\tau_0|\mathbf{x}_i) = 1$. In contrast to the parametric learning approach, this approach initially only produces discrete survival probabilities $\hat{S}(\tau_j|\mathbf{x})$. However, simple interpolation or smoothing can be applied to obtain meaningful predictions at time points between initial interval points τ_j.

3.2 Competing Risks

In the competing risks setting, we are interested in the time until the first of K competing events is observed. Let $E \in \{1, ..., K\}$ be a random variable representing the possible event types with realizations e. In this setting, we are typically interested in estimating $P(Y \leq \tau, E = e|\mathbf{x})$, i.e., the probability of observing an event of type e before time τ given feature set $\mathbf{x}$. This quantity is usually referred to as cumulative incidence function (CIF) and denoted by $\text{CIF}_k(\tau|\mathbf{x}), k = 1, ..., K$.

In the case of our parametric framework, we either learn the set of parameters for each competing risk k with separate sub-models for distribution parameters $\boldsymbol{\theta}_k$ or train a single joint model for all parameters $\boldsymbol{\Theta} = \{\boldsymbol{\theta}\}_{k=1}^{K}$.

The CIF in the non-parametric case is modeled via

$$\widehat{\text{CIF}}_k(\tau_j|\mathbf{x}_i) = \gamma_2\left(\sum_{l=1}^{j}(\gamma_1(g_{l,k}(\mathbf{x}_i)))\right), \tag{3}$$

where $g_{l,k}$ are now interval- and risk-specific models.

To evaluate competing risk models, we can use the single-risk scoring rules, but need to define a cause-specific status indicator

$$d_{i,k} = d_i \mathbb{1}(e_i = k) \in \{0, \ldots, K\}, \tag{4}$$

where e_i is the cause observed for subject i. We further constrain

$$\sum_{k=1}^{K}\hat{F}_k(\tau_j|\mathbf{x}_i) \leq 1.$$

This can be achieved through the network architecture (by directly constraining the sum of the outputs) or by reweighting the resulting CIFs using their increments. Putting everything together, we optimize the competing risks objective

$$O^{\text{CR}} = \sum_{k=1}^{K}\frac{1}{N}\sum_{i=1}^{N}\frac{1}{J}\sum_{j=1}^{J}\text{SR}_{i,k}(\tau_j|\hat{G}), \tag{5}$$

where $\text{SR}_{i,k}$ is a single-event scoring rule (e.g. Table 1) with the status indicator d_i replaced by the competing risks indicator from Eq. (4). Predictions can be directly obtained from the model or internally reweighted depending on the scoring rule.

3.3 Optimization and Implementation

Gradient-Based Optimization. For all scoring rules discussed in this paper, first derivatives with respect to an arbitrary weight vector ω of

$$S(\tau|\mathbf{x}_i, \omega) \text{ or } F(\tau|\mathbf{x}_i, \omega)$$

exist. For example, for RISBS and a single observed individual i and interval j

$$\frac{\partial}{\partial \omega}\text{SR}(\tau; \hat{G}) \propto F(\tau|\mathbf{x}_i, \omega)\frac{\partial}{\partial \omega}F(\tau|\mathbf{x}_i, \omega)$$

if $\hat{G}(t_i)$ is considered constant, which is usually the case if it is determined *a priori*. If $\hat{S}(\tau|\mathbf{x}_i)$ is differentiable itself, which is typically the case for neural networks, the model itself is differentiable.

Implementation. Our framework can be easily implemented in a neural network. The network trunk can have an arbitrary shape whereas the output layer contains $J \times K$ units for both the parametric and non-parametric variant. The final layer of the parametric variant is a deterministic distributional layer that automatically enforces monotonicity by implementing the cumulative distribution or survival function of a parametric distribution. By the chain rule, backpropagation is given by the derivative of the SR w.r.t. the parameters $\boldsymbol{\theta}_k$ of the chosen survival distribution for each risk k times the gradients of $\boldsymbol{\theta}_k$ w.r.t. the network's weights. For the non-parametric version, the output layer is specified as in Eq. (3). The selected architectures must reflect the general modeling flow shown in Fig. 2. Example architectures are depicted in Fig. 3.

Overfitting can, e.g., be addressed by dropout layers throughout the network architectures and L2 regularization on the ultimate layer's weights. The parametric framework produces smooth, continuous estimates, the non-parametric one interpolates step-functions, as shown in Fig. 3. In many cases, it is reasonable not to choose $\tau^* = \tau^{max}$ but slightly smaller (e.g. the 80th or 90th percentile) as late events have outlier character in small data sets [26].

Alternative Implementations. While neural networks achieve the most versatile implementation, the idea can be generalized to arbitrary machine learning models. Particularly, the parametric framework with RISLL or ISLL as a loss function applies to some established machine learning models without further modification. For an assumed lognormal or log-logistic distribution with location μ and scale σ, we only need to model the linear predictor $\log(\tau)/\sigma - \mu/\sigma$, apply a logit (for an assumed log-logistic distribution) or probit (for an assumed lognormal distribution) link, and optimize a weighted binary cross-entropy loss with the weights being determined by the scoring rule used. As $\sigma > 0$ by definition, monotonicity must be enforced on the estimation of $\gamma = \frac{1}{\sigma}$ where γ is the linear coefficient for $\log(\tau)$ (the natural logarithm of the discretized follow-up time). For generalized linear models, linear estimates guarantee (weak) monotonicity. While technically, negative estimates are possible for γ, this doesn't occur in practice in our experience when estimated with maximum likelihood optimization. In boosting applications, monotonicity can be explicitly enforced through constraints on the estimation of the feature $\log(\tau)$. Essentially, we can fit a GLM using the discretized data with the following form:

$$P(d_{ij} = 1|\mathbf{x}_i, \tau) = g^{-1}(\gamma \log \tau + \mathbf{x}_{ij}\nu),$$

where τ is part of the feature matrix, γ is a scalar coefficient, ν is a vector of coefficients and $g()$ is the respective link function. Survival predictions can be directly made from the model. Location and scale parameters can be obtained indirectly via γ. Furthermore, we can use distributional regression software to generate predictions for any model class, e.g. trees, independent of their optimization.

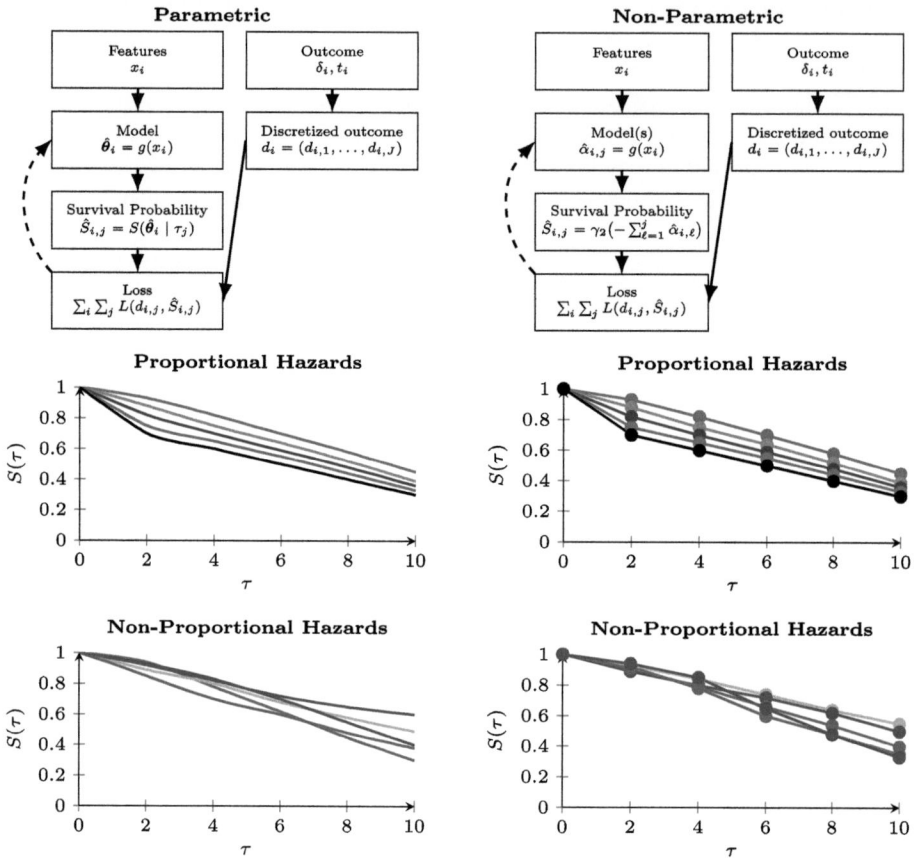

Fig. 2. Schematic model flow graphs (top) for parametric (left) and non-parametric (right) variants with schematic survival predictions (bottom). Features are used to learn model weights, optimized with respect to discretized outcomes and a loss function or **scoring rule**. Some models may require feature transformations (not depicted). In the parametric model, these weights determine a parameter vector ($\boldsymbol{\theta}_i$) for each individual (e.g., location and scale). In the non-parametric approach, survival increments $\alpha_{i,j}$ are estimated directly. The parameters $\boldsymbol{\theta}_i$ generate a continuous prediction of survival probabilities, resulting in smooth predictions (left bottom panels). For optimization, only the subset $\tilde{\mathcal{S}} = \{S_{i,j} \forall j \in 1, ..., J\}$ is needed. In the non-parametric case, this subset is available by construction, leading to point-wise predictions that are linearly interpolated (right bottom panels). Models are said to assume proportional hazards when survival functions do not intersect (upper panel of bottom graph).

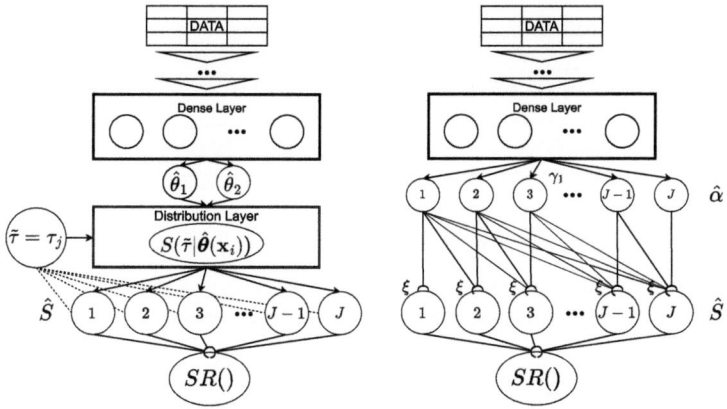

Fig. 3. Examples for architectures of our proposed method in the single risk case. Top: Parametric approach. We pass the data through a fully connected neural network to estimate the parameters (here θ_1 and θ_2) of a survival distribution. We generate predictions for each $\tilde{\tau} = \tau_j$ using the parameterized F. Bottom: Non-parametric approach. We pass the data through a fully-connected neural network to estimate the survival increments α_j and use them to generate survival predictions for each τ_j, where $\xi(\cdot) := \gamma_2(-\sum(\cdot))$.

4 Numerical Experiments

In the following sections, we evaluate our framework empirically. First, we test our approach with simulated data. While our proposed method can represent arbitrarily complex associations, our goal is to show that the proposed method can estimate parametric and semi-parametric SA methods that traditionally optimize likelihoods: Accelerated Failure Time models (AFT) and the Cox proportional hazard model (CPH). Furthermore, we explore how well our framework performs on benchmark data sets commonly used in SA for both single and competing risks. We benchmark our neural network implementation against other deep learning algorithms for a meaningful comparison. However, we also include the oblique random survival forest [ORSF; 18], which has been shown to yield good predictive performance in SA tasks. Last, we illustrate that the framework also applies to learners different from neural networks.

Evaluation and Tuning. In all experiments, we make use of repeated subsampling. For all benchmark data sets, we repeat the subsampling 25 times, and, except for KKBox, use 80% of the data for training and 20% for evaluation. Repeated subsampling is preferred over cross-validation as the test set needs to be sufficiently large to estimate the censoring probability for all evaluation metrics. The number of subsamples depends on the complexity of the underlying experiments. For KKBox, 2% of the data (ca. 1,000 events) is sufficient for model evaluation. If tuning is necessary, we use a random search with a budget of 25 configurations. The inner loop of the nested resampling is a five-fold cross-validation. Early stopping is performed when necessary based on the validation error. In all experiments, models are evaluated using the RISBS as our primary evaluation metric at different quantiles (25, 50, and 75%) of the follow-up.

4.1 Comparison to Maximum Likelihood Estimation

We first empirically check whether our approach can recover the parameters of a known event time distribution without explicitly using its likelihood for estimation. We compare the goodness of approximation with the true parameters and those estimated through maximum likelihood. To do so, we simulate event times from an AFT model via

$$\log(T_i) = \beta_0 + \beta_1 x_1 + \beta_2 x_2 + \beta_3 x_3 + \theta_2 \epsilon_i \tag{6}$$

with $\boldsymbol{\beta}^\top = (2, 0.5, 0.2, 0)$ and let ϵ follow the (i) Logistic, (ii) Normal, and (iii) Extreme value distribution, implying event times $T \sim F(\theta_1(x_1, x_2, x_3), \theta_2)$ that follow a (i) Loglogistc, (ii) Log-normal and (iii) Weibull distribution, respectively. We only let one parameter of the distribution depend on features, i.e. $\theta_1(x_1, x_2, x_3) = \beta_0 + \beta_1 x_1 + \beta_2 x_2 + \beta_3 x_3$ and set $\theta_2 = \sigma = 0.4$.

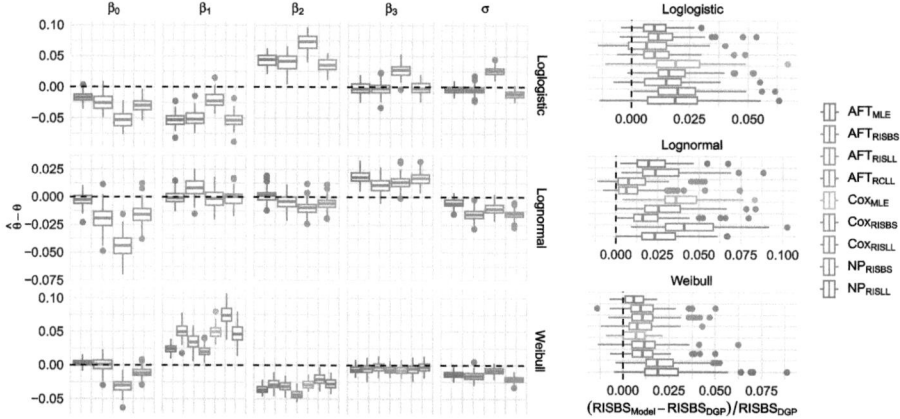

Fig. 4. Results of the comparison to ML estimation. **Left**: difference of estimated parameter $\hat{\theta}$ to oracle parameters θ. Parameter comparison for Cox PH models is limited to the coefficients β_1, β_2 and β_3, and the Weibull distribution. **Right**: Relative difference in the predictive performance w.r.t. the data generating process (DGP). Optimal performance is given by $\text{RISBS}_{\text{DGP}}$, obtained by using true parameters in the correctly specified model.

For the simulation, we draw $n = 1500$ event times from each distribution based on Eq. (6) and introduce censoring assuming a uniform distribution over the follow-up, resulting in approximately 28% censoring. We repeat this $B = 100$

times, each time splitting the data into train (80%) and test (20%) data. In each iteration, we calculate

$$\beta_j - \hat{\beta}_{j,m};\ j = 0,\ldots,3;$$
$$m \in \{\text{AFT}_{\text{MLE}}, \text{Cox}_{\text{MLE}}, \text{AFT}_{\text{SR}}, \text{Cox}_{\text{SR}}\},$$

where we either optimize the respective correctly specified AFT models and Cox PH models via maximum likelihood estimation (MLE) or one of the scoring rules (SR) based approaches as proposed in Sect. 3. Additionally, we consider the difference between the estimated and true scale $\hat{\sigma} - \sigma$. In addition to recovering coefficients, we report the aggregated predictive performance of all models in terms of the RISBS, RISLL, and ISBS. For predictive performance evaluation, we also fit the non-parametric variant of our framework, NP_{SR} with SR $\in$ {RISBS, RISLL}. The AFT model estimated within our framework with RCLL provides a direct comparison to AFT_{MLE}. This results in a total of 4 AFT models (3 SR and 1 MLE), 2 Cox PH models (2 SR and 1 MLE), and 2 non-parametric models (both SR) for the main analysis.

The experimental results are presented in Fig. 4. The methods specified within our framework recover the true coefficients well, with, however, a little approximation error. This approximation error is negligibly small when considering the predictive performance in the right panel. This finding holds for both, AFT and Cox PH model. When considering the model performances, we also see that a simple, untuned, yet regularized, non-parametric scoring-rule-based method performs comparably to the other (correctly specified) methods. In contrast to other deep AFT (e.g. [2]) approaches, our method allows the estimation of a variety of distributions using the parametric framework, including the Weibull distribution, which has repeatedly been reported to suffer from poor computational conditioning [e.g., 2].

4.2 Benchmark Study

In this section, we evaluate the models' predictive performance on synthetic and real-world data for both single (Table 2) and competing risks (Table 3) settings.

Single Risk. We compare our framework to other popular deep learning models for survival analysis, namely nnet-survival [11], DeepHit [23], and DeepSurv [19], as well as the Countdown model (with an assumed log-normal distribution) as proposed in [2] ($\text{AFT}^{\text{deep}}_{\text{SCRPS}}$). For our framework we fit both, a non-parametric version NP_{RISBS} and a deep parametric variant $\text{AFT}^{\text{deep}}_{\text{RISBS}}$. Furthermore, we compare with baselines (KM and CPH) and Oblique Random Survival Forests (ORSF). All methods have been tuned over 50 configurations (10 for KKBox)

Table 2. Predictive performance of different learning algorithms for different data sets for a single event using the RISBS (smaller is better). We report the mean and standard deviation (in brackets) from 25 distinct train-test splits and highlight the best method in **bold**. The AFT models are also tuned with respect to the distribution family.

		KM	Cox PH	ORSF	DeepSurv	nnet	DeepHit	$\text{AFT}^{\text{deep}}_{\text{SCRPS}}$	$\text{AFT}^{\text{deep}}_{\text{RISBS}}$	NP_{RISBS}
tumor	Q25	7.4 (1.58)	6.6 (1.43)	6.5 (1.23)	6.6 (1.52)	6.5 (2.03)	6.7 (1.80)	**6.4 (1.30)**	6.5 (1.37)	6.6 (1.30)
$n=776$	Q50	13.0 (1.46)	11.7 (1.46)	11.8 (1.40)	11.6 (1.51)	11.5 (1.84)	11.6 (1.91)	11.4 (1.21)	**11.3 (1.24)**	11.3 (1.32)
$p=7$	Q75	17.8 (1.17)	16.3 (1.47)	16.4 (1.40)	16.3 (1.40)	16.2 (1.37)	16.2 (1.67)	16.2 (1.29)	**16.1 (1.30)**	16.1 (1.39)
gbsg2	Q25	4.9 (0.80)	4.7 (0.75)	**4.6 (0.73)**	4.7 (0.80)	4.9 (1.03)	**4.6 (1.01)**	4.7 (0.75)	4.7 (0.69)	**4.6 (0.80)**
$n=2232$	Q50	10.1 (0.80)	9.3 (0.69)	9.2 (0.73)	9.3 (0.82)	9.2 (0.95)	9.5 (0.83)	**9.1 (0.69)**	9.4 (0.68)	**9.1 (0.79)**
$p=7$	Q75	15.4 (0.56)	13.9 (0.47)	13.6 (0.60)	13.7 (0.62)	13.6 (0.82)	13.4 (0.71)	13.4 (0.61)	13.3 (0.54)	**13.2 (0.61)**
metabric	Q25	5.1 (0.64)	5.0 (0.61)	5.1 (0.56)	5.0 (0.60)	5.5 (0.51)	5.2 (0.55)	**4.9 (0.61)**	**4.9 (0.56)**	5.0 (0.65)
$n=1904$	Q50	11.4 (0.80)	10.8 (0.78)	10.9 (0.67)	10.7 (0.60)	10.9 (0.58)	10.9 (0.70)	**10.4 (0.73)**	**10.4 (0.72)**	10.4 (0.79)
$p=9$	Q75	16.5 (0.61)	15.2 (0.60)	15.8 (0.66)	15.1 (0.55)	15.1 (0.46)	15.4 (0.52)	15.0 (0.61)	**14.8 (0.55)**	14.8 (0.59)
breast	Q25	2.2 (1.14)	2.2 (1.14)	2.1 (1.11)	2.3 (1.13)	2.2 (1.01)	2.2 (1.02)	**2.0 (0.86)**	2.1 (0.97)	2.4 (1.12)
$n=614$	Q50	4.6 (1.51)	4.6 (1.51)	**4.3 (1.44)**	4.8 (1.59)	4.4 (1.35)	4.5 (1.42)	4.4 (1.18)	4.4 (1.26)	4.4 (1.54)
$p=1690$	Q75	7.8 (1.62)	7.8 (1.62)	**7.0 (1.61)**	7.6 (1.71)	7.2 (1.60)	7.3 (1.64)	7.2 (1.50)	7.3 (1.52)	7.3 (1.75)
KKBox	Q25	1.02 (0.05)	0.92 (0.04)	–	0.87 (0.05)	0.95 (0.07)	0.93 (0.06)	**0.85 (0.06)**	0.86 (0.05)	0.90 (0.07)
$n=865\,K$	Q50	1.66 (0.06)	1.41 (0.05)	–	1.25 (0.05)	1.31 (0.06)	1.35 (0.06)	1.27 (0.05)	1.21 (0.05)	**1.20 (0.07)**
$p=6$	Q75	2.72 (0.09)	2.19 (0.07)	–	**1.89 (0.06)**	2.00 (0.05)	2.01 (0.06)	1.94 (0.06)	1.92 (0.06)	**1.89 (0.06)**
synthetic	Q25	6.7 (0.70)	4.7 (0.51)	4.2 (0.66)	3.5 (0.63)	4.4 (0.66)	3.9 (0.61)	**3.3 (0.48)**	3.4 (0.40)	3.5 (0.56)
$n=1500$	Q50	13.9 (0.78)	9.2 (0.53)	8.8 (0.81)	6.7 (0.78)	8.5 (0.71)	8.0 (0.69)	**6.4 (0.36)**	**6.4 (0.38)**	**6.4 (0.51)**
$p=4$	Q75	19.7 (0.26)	12.8 (0.56)	10.0 (1.01)	9.2 (0.76)	9.6 (0.83)	9.5 (0.67)	8.6 (0.45)	**8.3 (0.46)**	8.4 (0.50)

except for the KM and CPH baselines. $\text{AFT}^{\text{deep}}_{\text{SCRPS}}$ approximates the model proposed in [2] (log-normal distribution, SCRPS as scoring rule). The model by [2] itself suffered from computational issues and did not result in adequate predictive performance. While not being perfectly identical to [2] $\text{AFT}^{\text{deep}}_{\text{SCRPS}}$ adapts their idea.

We selected common data sets in the survival analysis literature primarily related to various medical conditions with observations in the high hundreds or low thousands and a large churn data set: tumor [4], gbsgs2 [25], metabric [8], breast [27], and mgus2 [22]. KKBox [17] is a large churn data set obtained from Kaggle that we processed for SA. For KKBox, ORSF evaluations, however, failed due to the size of the data set. For similar computational reasons, Cox PH only uses one feature for *breast*, where the other methods use all $p > n$ features.

Results. In summary, the results indicate that our proposed methods provide good predictive performance, competitive with established methods. We observe that for the AFT model, both scoring rules (SCRPS and RISBS) have very similar performances. This finding is in line with [26], who empirically study differences between proper and improper scoring rules and report only small differences. NP tends to perform worst on early quantiles, indicating potential overfitting for the early cut points.

Competing Risks. For competing risk, we compare our approach against the baseline methods Aalen-Johannsen estimator [AJ; 1] and competing risks piece-

Table 3. Prediction accuracy of different methods (columns) for different competing risks data sets (rows) evaluated using the ISBS (smaller is better). We report the mean and standard deviation (in brackets) from 25 distinct train-test splits and highlight the best method in **bold**.

		AJ	CR PAMM	DeepHit	$\text{AFT}^{\text{deep}}_{\text{ISBS}}$
mgus2	Q25	**1.1** (0.39)	**1.1** (0.39)	**1.1** (0.42)	1.2 (0.58)
(cause 1)	Q50	2.1 (0.59)	**2.0** (0.57)	2.2 (0.59)	2.2 (0.58)
$n = 1384$	Q75	3.2 (0.84)	3.2 (0.80)	**3.1** (0.85)	3.3 (0.79)
mgus2	Q25	9.1 (1.18)	**8.6** (1.16)	8.7 (1.04)	8.7 (1.10)
(cause 2)	Q50	14.3 (1.03)	13.2 (1.17)	**12.9** (1.20)	13.0 (1.34)
$p = 6$	Q75	18.2 (0.74)	15.8 (0.99)	**15.6** (1.07)	15.7 (1.22)
synthetic	Q25	5.4 (0.66)	3.7 (0.49)	3.2 (0.56)	**3.1** (0.45)
(cause 1)	Q50	10.9 (0.96)	7.3 (0.67)	**5.7** (0.69)	**5.7** (0.60)
$n = 1500$	Q75	16.9 (0.83)	11.5 (0.55)	**8.3** (0.77)	8.4 (0.65)
synthetic	Q25	2.2 (0.72)	**2.0** (0.59)	**2.0** (0.62)	2.1 (0.53)
(cause 2)	Q50	5.8 (0.97)	**4.7** (0.78)	5.0 (0.79)	4.9 (0.73)
$p = 4$	Q75	9.7 (1.06)	7.9 (0.94)	7.9 (1.00)	**7.8** (0.79)

wise exponential additive model [CR PAMM; 15] as well as DeepHit, which is typically considered when dealing with competing risks. Next, the real-world data set *mgus2*, we also consider a synthetic data set with a risk with complex (cause 1) and simple (cause 2) feature associations.

Results. DeepHit and our method perform similarly well in estimating survival probabilities in a competing risk setting. In some cases, both methods cannot outperform a CR PAMM that assumes linear effects on the log hazards. However, this is most likely due to the differences between the empirical incidence of the two causes (only 12% of observed events in *mgus2* are due to cause 1) and by construction (cause 2 of *synthetic* assumes only linear associations).

Alternative Implementations. To test alternative implementations of our framework, we use two datasets: *simple* is the simulation introduced in Sect. 4.1 and reflects linear effects only, while *complex* uses four features that partially exhibit non-linearities and interactions. Both settings assume a log-normal distribution. As learners, we include KM and Cox PH for baseline comparisons and prototype implementations for an XGBoost [6], generalized additive model (GAM; [16]), and soft regression tree. Performance is reported quantile-wise and estimated with 25 times repeated subsampling (80-20). Methods are not tuned; our goal is only to show that these alternatives work in principle. We find that all methods perform better than the baseline (KM). However, a single tree does not outperform a Cox PH model. In the simple setting, GAM performs best. This is because the Cox PH model is slightly misspecified in the presence of

Table 4. Comparison of predictive performances of different learners (columns) for different datasets (rows). We report the mean (top) and standard deviation (below in brackets) from 25 distinct train-test splits. The best method is highlighted in **bold**.

		KM	Cox PH	$\text{AFT}_{\text{RISLL}}^{\text{GAM}}$	$\text{AFT}_{\text{RISBS}}^{\text{tree}}$	$\text{AFT}_{\text{RISLL}}^{\text{XGB}}$
simple	Q25	5.1	3.2	**3.0**	4.5	3.2
		(0.46)	(0.46)	(0.43)	(0.87)	(0.42)
$n = 1500$	Q50	10.7	6.3	**6.1**	8.9	6.3
		(0.87)	(0.43)	(0.40)	(0.69)	(0.43)
$p = 3$	Q75	15.5	8.7	**8.5**	13.3	8.9
		(0.42)	(0.51)	(0.44)	(0.60)	(0.51)
complex	Q25	6.7	4.7	3.8	6.2	**3.6**
		(0.71)	(0.52)	(0.54)	(0.59)	(0.47)
$n = 1500$	Q50	13.9	9.2	7.2	12.7	**6.6**
		(0.78)	(0.53)	(0.59)	(0.62)	(0.44)
$p = 4$	Q75	19.7	12.8	9.6	18.2	**8.6**
		(0.26)	(0.56)	(0.51)	(0.51)	(0.40)

Table 5. Predictive performance of the ablation study. For two data sets from the benchmark study, we changed the training scoring rule to RISLL, RCLL, and ISBS, respectively. For RISLL and ISBS we only consider the 75% percentile for τ^*. We also evaluate using the same scoring rules. RCLL is reported as -RCLL.

		$\text{AFT}_{\text{RISBS}}^{\text{deep}}$	$\text{AFT}_{\text{RISLL}}^{\text{deep}}$	$\text{AFT}_{\text{RCLL}}^{\text{deep}}$	$\text{AFT}_{\text{ISBS}}^{\text{deep}}$
gbsg2	RISBS	13.6 (0.54)	**13.4** (0.59)	13.5 (0.58)	13.6 (0.56)
	RISLL	40.8 (1.39)	**40.7** (1.35)	40.8 (1.47)	41.2 (1.55)
$n = 2232$	RCLL	2.67 (0.76)	2.65 (0.72)	**2.60** (0.70)	2.69 (0.79)
$p = 7$	ISBS	13.1 (0.53)	13.1 (0.59)	**13.0** (0.62)	13.2 (0.63)
synthetic	RISBS	**8.3** (0.46)	**8.3** (0.50)	8.4 (0.45)	8.6 (0.63)
	RISLL	26.7 (1.18)	**26.5** (1.17)	26.6 (1.28)	26.9 (1.20)
$n = 1500$	RCLL	1.58 (0.06)	**1.57** (0.06)	1.59 (0.06)	1.60 (0.07)
$p = 4$	ISBS	**8.5** (0.38)	**8.5** (0.35)	8.6 (0.34)	8.6 (0.58)

log-normally distributed survival times. Unsurprisingly, the (untuned) XGBoost model overfits in this simple regime. For the complex setting, we allowed the GAM to capture non-linearities, yet no interactions. While this significantly boosts performance over Cox PH, the XGBoost approach achieves very good generalization despite being untuned. All in all, this suggests that the methods work as intended and provide reasonable results (Table 4).

4.3 Ablation: Altering the Scoring Rule

As discussed in Sect. 3, our framework is scoring-rule agnostic. While we mainly focused on RISBS in the experiments, we also implemented all other scoring rules from Table 1. To investigate their influence, we study how the results from the benchmarking study qualitatively change when the optimized scoring rule is changed for the parametric sub-framework.

Results. In Table 5, we observe that using different scoring rules only leads to minor changes for both training and evaluation. Choosing ISBS as the evaluation metric seems to give a slight advantage to the model, which is also trained on an ISBS loss. Among the proper scoring rules, we do not observe a similar pattern.

5 Discussion and Conclusion

We proposed a new method for estimating event time distributions from censored data, including competing risks, using scoring rules as a loss function. Our framework can be seamlessly integrated into neural networks, but also into tree-based models, generalized additive models, and gradient boosting. Empirical results demonstrate that the proposed integration of scoring rules yields good predictive performance, and the proposed framework is on par with other state-of-the-art approaches. We particularly highlight the results from the recovery and ablation study in sections Sect. 4.1 and Sect. 4.3 that confirm that the framework can be used in a variety of settings and configurations. This validates theoretical propositions and claims and provides proof-of-concept evidence for the entire framework.

The use of scoring rules in survival model training can be viewed as another method for reducing survival problems into classification or regression problems through discretization. By extending the framework to any arbitrary model class, this work makes an important taxonomic contribution. We show that this specific discretization (in combination with a suitable scoring rule) is generally applicable (e.g. in single event and competing risks settings), similar to piecewise exponential models or discrete hazard models. This finding goes beyond previous attempts that assessed scoring-rule-based model training. In contrast to them, this work provides a rigorous separation of a learner into a loss (scoring rule in combination with discretization), a hypothesis space (model classes), and an optimization (dependent on model class). This point of view allows a very agnostic application of the framework and makes it easy to extend.

Limitations and Future Work. While our approach works for right-censored data and competing risks, other SA use cases, such as interval-censored data, multistate modeling, or recurrent events, are contemporary challenges that could be an interesting extension of our proposal for future research. The choice of a specific scoring rule and respective advantages and disadvantages for model optimization could also be explored further in the future.

Disclosure of Interests. The authors have no competing interests to declare that are relevant to the content of this article.

References

1. Aalen, O.: Nonparametric inference for a family of counting processes. Ann. Stat. 701–726 (1978)
2. Avati, A., Duan, T., Zhou, S., Jung, K., Shah, N.H., Ng, A.Y.: Countdown regression: sharp and calibrated survival predictions. In: Uncertainty in Artificial Intelligence, pp. 145–155. PMLR (2020)
3. Bender, A., Rügamer, D., Scheipl, F., Bischl, B.: A general machine learning framework for survival analysis. In: Joint European Conference on Machine Learning and Knowledge Discovery in Databases, pp. 158–173. Springer (2020)
4. Bender, A., Scheipl, F.: pammtools: piece-wise exponential Additive Mixed Modeling tools. arXiv:1806.01042 (2018)
5. Bender, A., Scheipl, F., Hartl, W., Day, A.G., Küchenhoff, H.: Penalized estimation of complex, non-linear exposure-lag-response associations. Biostatistics **20**(2), 315–331 (2019)
6. Chen, T., Guestrin, C.: Xgboost: a scalable tree boosting system. In: Proceedings of the 22nd ACM SIGKDD International Conference on Knowledge Discovery and Data Mining, pp. 785–794 (2016)
7. Cox, D.R.: Regression models and life-tables. J. Roy. Stat. Soc. Ser. B (Methodol.) **34**(2), 187–220 (1972)
8. Curtis, C., Shah, S.P., Chin, S.F., Turashvili, G., Rueda, O.M., et al.: The genomic and transcriptomic architecture of 2,000 breast tumours reveals novel subgroups. Nature **486**(7403), 346–352 (2012)
9. Dawid, A.P., Musio, M.: Theory and applications of proper scoring rules. Metron **72**(2), 169–183 (2014). https://doi.org/10.1007/s40300-014-0039-y
10. Friedman, M.: Piecewise exponential models for survival data with covariates. Ann. Stat. **10**(1), 101–113 (1982)
11. Gensheimer, M.F., Narasimhan, B.: A scalable discrete-time survival model for neural networks. PeerJ **7**, e6257 (2019)
12. Gneiting, T., Raftery, A.E.: Strictly proper scoring rules, prediction, and estimation. J. Am. Stat. Assoc. **102**(477), 359–378 (2007)
13. Graf, E., Schmoor, C., Sauerbrei, W., Schumacher, M.: Assessment and comparison of prognostic classification schemes for survival data. Stat. Med. **18**, 2529–2545 (1999)
14. Harrell, F.E., Califf, R.M., Pryor, D.B., Lee, K.L., Rosati, R.A.: Evaluating the yield of medical tests. JAMA **247**(18), 2543–2546 (1982)
15. Hartl, W.H., et al.: Protein intake and outcome of critically ill patients: analysis of a large international database using piece-wise exponential additive mixed models. Crit. Care **26**(1), 1–12 (2022)
16. Hastie, T., Tibshirani, R.: Generalized additive models. Stat. Sci. **1**(3), 297–310 (1986)
17. Howard, A., Chiu, A., McDonald, M., Kan, W., Yianchen: WSDM - KKBox's music recommendation challenge (2017)
18. Jaeger, B.C., et al.: Oblique random survival forests. Ann. Appl. Stat. **13**(3), 1847–1883 (2019)

19. Katzman, J., Shaham, U., Cloninger, A., Bates, J., et al.: Deepsurv: personalized treatment recommender system using a cox proportional hazards deep neural network. BMC Med. Res. Methodol. **18**(1), 1–12 (2018)
20. Kopper, P., Wiegrebe, S., Bischl, B., Bender, A., Rügamer, D.: DeepPAMM: deep piecewise exponential additive mixed models for complex hazard structures in survival analysis. In: Pacific-Asia Conference on Knowledge Discovery and Data Mining, pp. 249–261 (2022)
21. Kvamme, H., Borgan, Ø.: Continuous and discrete-time survival prediction with neural networks. Lifetime Data Anal. **27**(4), 710–736 (2021). https://doi.org/10.1007/s10985-021-09532-6
22. Kyle, R.A., et al.: A long-term study of prognosis in monoclonal gammopathy of undetermined significance. N. Engl. J. Med. **346**(8), 564–569 (2002)
23. Lee, C., Zame, W.R., Yoon, J., van der Schaar, M.: DeepHit: a deep learning approach to survival analysis with competing risks. In: 23nd AAAI Conference on Artificial Intelligence (2018)
24. Rindt, D., Hu, R., Steinsaltz, D., Sejdinovic, D.: Survival regression with proper scoring rules and monotonic neural networks. In: International Conference on Artificial Intelligence and Statistics, pp. 1190–1205. PMLR (2022)
25. Schumacher, M., Bastert, G., Bojar, H., Hübner, K., Olschewski, M., et al.: Randomized 2 × 2 trial evaluating hormonal treatment and the duration of chemotherapy in node-positive breast cancer patients. J. Clin. Oncol. **12**(10), 2086–2093 (1994)
26. Sonabend, R., Zobolas, J., De Bin, R., Kopper, P., Burk, L., Bender, A.: Examining properness in the external validation of survival models with squared and logarithmic losses. arXiv preprint arXiv:2212.05260 (2022)
27. Ternes, N., Rotolo, F., Heinze, G., Michiels, S.: Identification of biomarker-by-treatment interactions in randomized clinical trials with survival outcomes and high-dimensional spaces. Biom. J. **59**(4), 685–701 (2017)
28. Tutz, G., Schmid, M.: Modeling Discrete Time-to-Event Data. Springer Series in Statistics. Springer, Cham (2016)
29. Wang, P., Li, Y., Reddy, C.K.: Machine learning for survival analysis: a survey. ACM Comput. Surv. (CSUR) **51**(6), 1–36 (2019)
30. Wei, L.J.: The accelerated failure time model: a useful alternative to the cox regression model in survival analysis. Stat. Med. **11**(14–15), 1871–1879 (1992)
31. Wiegrebe, S., Kopper, P., Sonabend, R., Bischl, B., Bender, A.: Deep learning for survival analysis: a review. Artif. Intell. Rev. **57**(3), 65 (2024)
32. Yanagisawa, H.: Proper scoring rules for survival analysis. In: International Conference on Machine Learning, pp. 39165–39182. PMLR (2023)

Towards Interpretable Adversarial Examples via Sparse Adversarial Attack

Fudong Lin[1], Jiadong Lou[1], Hao Wang[2], Brian Jalaian[3], and Xu Yuan[1(✉)]

[1] University of Delaware, Newark, DE 19716, USA
{fudong,loujd,xyuan}@udel.edu
[2] Stevens Institute of Technology, Hoboken, NJ 07030, USA
hwang9@stevens.edu
[3] University of West Florida, Pensacola, FL 32514, USA
bjalaian@uwf.edu

Abstract. Sparse attacks are to optimize the magnitude of adversarial perturbations for fooling deep neural networks (DNNs) involving only a few perturbed pixels (*i.e.*, under the l_0 constraint), suitable for interpreting the vulnerability of DNNs. However, existing solutions fail to yield interpretable adversarial examples due to their poor sparsity. Worse still, they often struggle with heavy computational overhead, poor transferability, and weak attack strength. In this paper, we aim to develop a sparse attack for understanding the vulnerability of DNNs by minimizing the magnitude of initial perturbations under the l_0 constraint, to overcome the existing drawbacks while achieving a fast, transferable, and strong attack to DNNs. In particular, a novel and *theoretical sound* parameterization technique is introduced to approximate the NP-hard l_0 optimization problem, making directly optimizing sparse perturbations computationally feasible. Besides, a novel loss function is designed to augment initial perturbations by maximizing the adversary property and minimizing the number of perturbed pixels simultaneously. Extensive experiments are conducted to demonstrate that our approach, with theoretical performance guarantees, outperforms state-of-the-art sparse attacks in terms of computational overhead, transferability, and attack strength, expecting to serve as a benchmark for evaluating the robustness of DNNs. In addition, theoretical and empirical results validate that our approach yields sparser adversarial examples, empowering us to discover two categories of noises, *i.e.*, "obscuring noise" and "leading noise", which will help interpret how adversarial perturbation misleads the classifiers into incorrect predictions. Our code is available at https://github.com/fudong03/SparseAttack.

Keywords: Sparse Attack · Adversarial Attack · Interpretability

---

Supplementary Information The online version contains supplementary material available at https://doi.org/10.1007/978-3-032-06109-6_6.

© The Author(s), under exclusive license to Springer Nature Switzerland AG 2026
R. P. Ribeiro et al. (Eds.): ECML PKDD 2025, LNAI 16019, pp. 92–110, 2026.
https://doi.org/10.1007/978-3-032-06109-6_6

1 Introduction

Deep neural networks (DNNs) have demonstrated impressive performance on a range of challenging tasks, including image classification [12,16,21,42], natural language processing [8,48], and various other domains [1,5,17,18,24,26,28, 31,39,55]. However, recent studies [15,45] have revealed a critical vulnerability: DNNs can be easily fooled by adversarial examples. These examples are generated by adding small, human-imperceptible perturbations to natural images, causing the models to make incorrect predictions with high confidence. This vulnerability leads to severe security threats on DNNs, *e.g.*, a prior study [13] reported that adding human-imperceptible perturbation to a *Stop* sign made state-of-the-art classifiers misclassify it as a Speed Limit 45, thereby hindering DNNs' wide applicability to such security-critical domains as face recognition [22,46], autonomous driving [13,19], *etc.*.

The mainstream attack strategy targeting DNNs is to optimize the magnitude of adversarial perturbations. In general, a perturbation is constrained by l_p norm, with $p = 0, 1, 2$, or ∞, and can be categorized into two clusters, *i.e.*, dense attack and sparse attack. The former needs to modify almost all pixels under the l_2 or l_∞ constraint [9], while the latter perturbs a few pixels under the l_0 (or sometimes l_1) constraint [57].

To date, Fast Gradient Sign Method (FGSM)-based approaches [10,11,15, 22,53] are known to be prominent dense attacks, because they arrive at fast and highly transferable adversarial attacks by optimizing adversarial perturbations under the l_∞ constraint. However, they tend to perturb almost all pixels, making them hard to interpret adversarial attacks due to their overly perturbed adversarial examples. In sharp contrast, sparse attacks [6,9,14,34,35,38,43,49,51,57] minimize the l_0 distance between natural images and adversarial examples, for attacking DNNs with only a few perturbed pixels. Hence, sparse attacks usually provide additional insights into adversarial attacks, able to better interpret the vulnerability of DNNs [14]. However, optimizing the magnitude of perturbations under the l_0 constraint falls into the NP-hard problem, so previous solutions often get trapped in local optima [35,57], making the resulted attacks possess an insufficient adversary property. As such, existing sparse attacks suffer from the drawbacks of heavy computational overhead [9], poor transferability, and weak attack intensity. Worse still, their resultant adversarial examples suffer from poor sparsity, making them unsuitable for interpreting the vulnerability of DNNs.

In this work, we focus on the sparse attack, aiming to develop a new solution that yields interpretable adversarial examples, allowing us to have a deep understanding in the vulnerability of DNNs. To achieve our goal, we introduce a novel and *theoretically solid* reparameterization technique to effectively approximate the NP-hard l_0 optimization problem, making direct optimization of sparse perturbations computationally tractable. In addition, a novel loss function is proposed to augment initial perturbations through maximizing the adversary property and minimizing the number of perturbed pixels simultaneously. As such, our approach, underpinned by theoretical performance guarantees, can yield a fast, transferable, and powerful adversarial attack while unveiling the mystery underlying adversarial perturbations. Extensive experimental results demonstrate that our approach outperforms state-of-the-art sparse attacks in terms of computational complexity, transferability, and attack strength. Meanwhile, we theoretically and empirically validate that our approach yields much sparser adversarial examples, suitable for interpreting the vulnerability of DNNs. Through analyzing the minimal perturbed adversarial examples, we discover two categories of adversarial perturbations to help understand how adversarial perturbations mislead the classifiers, resulted directly from "obscuring noise" and "leading noise", where the former obscures the classifiers from identifying true classes, while the latter misleads the classifiers into targeted predictions.

2 Related Work

The state-of-the-art solutions for adversarial attacks can be grouped into two categories, *i.e.*, dense attack and sparse attack. We shall discuss how our work relates to, and differs from, prior solutions.

Dense attacks optimize the magnitude of adversarial perturbations under the l_2 or l_∞ constriant. Popularized by Fast Gradient Sign Method (FGSM) [15], FGSM-based methods are the most prominent dense attacks, where adversarial examples (under the l_∞ constraint) are effectively produced by adding the gradients of the classification loss to natural images. Subsequent work includes I-FGSM [22] which applies FGSM in multiple rounds, R-FGSM [47] which augments FGSM with random initialization, PGD [32] which extends I-FGSM with multiple random restarts, MI-FGSM [10] which boosts I-FGSM with momentum, and DI-FGSM [53] and TI-FGSM [11] which improve transferability respectively with random resizing and translation operations. Other dense attacks include [2–4,27,33,36,45], which perform effective dense attacks by minimizing the l_2 (or l_∞) distance between natural images and adversarial examples. However, this category of solutions requires modification of almost all pixels, infeasible to be used for interpreting the vulnerability of DNNs. Our solution, by contrast, perturbs only a few pixels, able to provide additional insights about adversarial vulnerability.

Sparse attacks minimize the magnitude of perturbations under the l_0 (or sometimes l_1) constraint. Previous sparse attacks include C&W L_0 attack [2] which iteratively fixes less important pixels, OnePixel [43] which applies an evolutionary algorithm, SparseFool [35] which converts the l_0 optimization problem to the l_1 constraint one, GreedyFool [9] which uses a two-stage greedy strategy, Homotopy attack [57] which utilizes a homotopy algorithm to jointly optimize the sparsity and the perturbation bound, among many others [6,7,14,34,37,38,49,51,54]. Unfortunately, prior sparse attacks suffer from considerable computational overhead, poor transferability, and weak attack intensity. In contrast, we propose a theoretical sound reparameterization technique to approximate the NP-hard l_0 optimization problem and a novel loss function to augment initial perturbations. As such, our approach advances existing sparse attacks in terms of computational efficiency, transferability, and attack strength. In addition, we theoretically and empirically validate that our approach yields much sparser adversarial examples, empowering us to interpret the vulnerability of DNNs.

3 Preliminary

Given a well-trained classifier f_θ, the cross-entropy loss function J, and a natural image x with the ground-truth label y_{true}, the adversary aims to mislead the classifier f_θ into an incorrect prediction via adding certain perturbation δ (under the constraint ϵ) into the natural image, mathematically expressed as follows:

$$f_\theta(x + \delta) = y_{\text{adv}} \quad \text{s.t.} \quad \|\delta\|_p \leq \epsilon \quad \text{and} \quad x + \delta \in [0, 1]^d, \tag{1}$$

where y_{adv} represents the adversarial label and is different from y_{true}, $\|\cdot\|_p$ denotes the l_p norm (with $p = 0, 1, 2,$ or ∞), and manipulating a natural image should yield one valid image. Note here the pixel values are normalized over $[0, 1]$ to simplify the calculation.

FGSM (Fast Gradient Sign Method) [15] aims to mislead classifiers to predict incorrectly through adding gradients to natural images. The sign function is leveraged to ensure the perturbation δ under the l_∞ constraint of ϵ, i.e.,

$$\delta = \epsilon \cdot \text{sign}(\nabla_x J(x, y_{\text{true}})) \quad \text{s.t.} \quad f_\theta(x + \delta) = y_{\text{adv}} \quad \text{and} \quad x + \delta \in [0, 1]^d. \tag{2}$$

FGSM is deemed as the fastest attack algorithm [10]. Subsequent solutions [11, 22, 32, 53] have been proposed, yielding fast and highly transferable dense attacks. **I-FGSM** (Iterative Fast Gradient Sign Method) [22] augments FGSM to have a stronger white-box attack by applying a small step length α to FGSM iteratively:

$$x_0^{\text{adv}} = x, \quad x_{N+1}^{\text{adv}} = x_N^{\text{adv}} + \alpha \cdot \text{sign}(\nabla_x J(x, y_{\text{true}})). \tag{3}$$

We can simply set $\alpha = \epsilon/T$ (T is the number of iterations) to satisfy the l_∞ constraint ϵ. Note that Eq. (3) performs a non-target attack by adding positive gradients to natural images x for maximizing the classification loss. To perform a targeted attack, we can maximize the logical probability of y_{adv} on natural image x (i.e., $\log p(y_{\text{adv}}|x)$) by iteratively moving towards the direction of $\text{sign}\{\nabla_x \log p(y_{\text{adv}}|x)\}$:

$$x_0^{\text{adv}} = x, \quad x_{N+1}^{\text{adv}} = x_N^{\text{adv}} - \alpha \cdot \text{sign}(\nabla_x J(x, y_{\text{adv}})). \tag{4}$$

The intuition behind Eq. (4) is that adding negative gradients to the natural image x can make the prediction of classifier f_θ iteratively move towards the adversarial class y_{adv}. Notably, both Eq. (3) and Eq. (4) must also satisfy the constraint $x_{N+1}^{\text{adv}} \in [0, 1]^d$ to ensure that the resulting adversarial examples remain valid input images.

4 Our Approach

4.1 Problem Statement

Sparse attacks optimize the magnitude of perturbations under the l_0 constraint, aiming to achieve successful attacks with a small number of perturbed pixels, as formulated below:

$$\text{minimize } \|\boldsymbol{\delta}\|_0 \quad \text{s.t.} \quad f_{\boldsymbol{\theta}}(\boldsymbol{x}+\boldsymbol{\delta}) = y_{\text{adv}} \text{ and } \boldsymbol{x}+\boldsymbol{\delta} \in [0,1]^d. \qquad (5)$$

Unfortunately, Eq. (5) is an NP-hard problem. When solving it, prior sparse attacks often got trapped in local optima [7,57], causing the resulting attacks to suffer from poor sparsity, unable to be used for interpreting the vulnerability of DNNs. To address this limitation, we develop a sparse attack that yields highly sparse adversarial examples, suitable for understanding the vulnerability of DNNs.

4.2 Challenges

Several challenges are to be addressed, as elaborated below.
Box Constraint. "Box constraint" is fundamental to adversarial attacks. It ensures that manipulating natural images should yield valid images (*i.e.*, $\boldsymbol{x}+\boldsymbol{\delta} \in [0,1]^d$). Two strategies exist to meet the box constraint for sparse attacks: i) *clipping invalid pixels* which exceed the valid range and ii) *changing the optimization direction* to make resulting adversarial examples valid. However, the former results in a severe reduction in the fooling rate, while the latter incurs a large computational burden. So far, how to effectively handle the "box constraint" with desired properties remains challenging.
Computational Efficiency. Optimizing the magnitude of perturbations under the l_0 constraint is NP-hard. Prior sparse attacks attempt different approximation algorithms to reduce the computational burden, *e.g.*, BruSLeAttack [49]. Yet, considerable computational overhead still incurs (see Fig. 1d, where 36.9 s are taken). Hence, how to efficiently minimize the number of perturbed pixels remains open.
Transferability and Attack Strength. Prior sparse attacks often suffer from poor transferability and weak attack intensity. For example, as shown in Fig. 1b, BruSLeAttack fails to perform a black-box attack, *i.e.*, the adversarial example generated by VGG-16 fails to fool VGG-19. It is challenging to develop a transferable and powerful sparse attack with only a small amount of perturbed pixels.

4.3 Our Idea

To overcome the aforementioned challenges, we aim to develop a novel sparse attack by optimizing the magnitudes of initial perturbations generated by I-FGSM under the l_0 constraint. In particular, a novel loss function is introduced to augment initial perturbations through maximizing the adversary property and

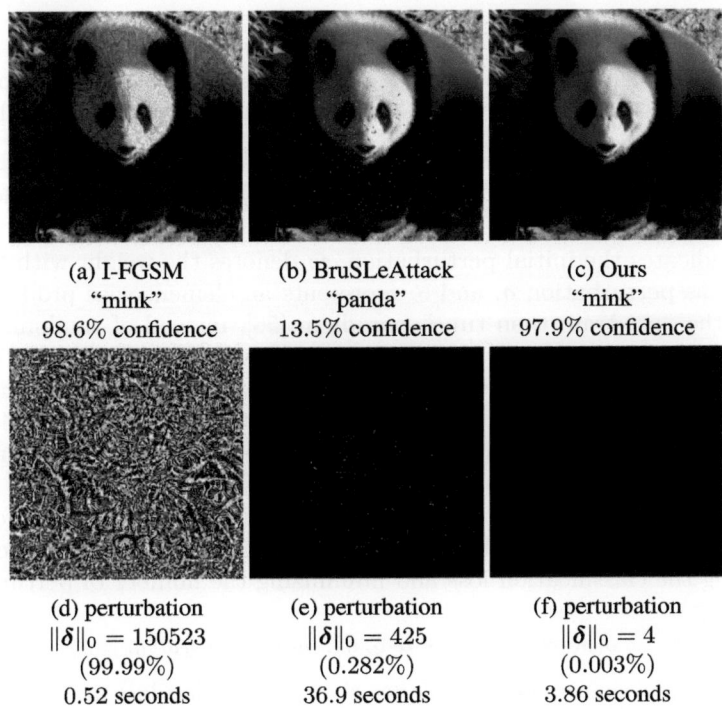

Fig. 1. Illustration of adversarial examples (AEs) computed by different attack algorithms. (a), (b), and (c) show AEs computed by I-FGSM, BruSLeAttack, and our approach, respectively, dependent on the classifier VGG-16. (d), (e), and (f) exhibit the adversarial perturbation with respect to (a), (b), and (c). The classification results, *i.e.*, "mink", "panda", "mink" (below (a), (b), and (c), respectively) and classification confidence levels, are reported by VGG-19. The number of ($\|\delta\|_0$) and the percentage of perturbed pixels, as well as the computation time, are all listed below (d), (e), and (f).

minimizing the number of perturbed pixels simultaneously. Two observations motivate this idea. *First*, a prior study [29] reported that different models tend to learn similar decision boundaries. Hence, starting from initial perturbations generated by dense attacks accelerates convergence and makes our approach more likely to reach the global optima [44]. *Second*, I-FGSM results in overly perturbed adversarial examples, and thereby reducing the number of perturbed pixels may not negatively affect its adversary property. For example, as depicted in Fig. 1a (I-FGSM) and Fig. 1c (Our Approach), both I-FGSM and our approach mislead VGG-19 into the same incorrect prediction (*i.e.*, "mink"). Therefore, it is feasible to optimize the magnitude of perturbations produced by I-FGSM under the l_0 constraint without sacrificing its transferability. Furthermore, a new box constraint strategy is designed to make our solution always yield valid adversarial examples.

4.4 Our Proposed Approach

Objective. To achieve our goal, we propose a novel sparse attack by optimizing the magnitude of initial perturbations under the l_0 constraint. Our problem can be formulated as follows:

$$\text{minimize } \|\boldsymbol{w}\|_0 \quad \text{s.t.} \quad f_{\boldsymbol{\theta}}(\boldsymbol{x} + \boldsymbol{w} \odot \boldsymbol{\delta}) = y_{\text{adv}} \text{ and } \boldsymbol{x} + \boldsymbol{w} \odot \boldsymbol{\delta} \in [0, 1]^d, \quad (6)$$

where $\boldsymbol{\delta}$ indicates the initial perturbation, $\boldsymbol{w}$ denotes the weight with the same dimension as perturbation $\boldsymbol{\delta}$, and $\odot$ represents an element-wise product. Motivated by the "pre-train then tune" paradigm [56], instead of randomly initializing the perturbation $\boldsymbol{\delta}$, we pre-compute it by using *Iterative Fast Gradient Sign Method* (I-FGSM) [22], which in turn accelerates convergence and makes the resulting perturbation more likely to reach the global optima [44]. Note that solving the problem formulated by Eq. (6) yields near-optimal solutions for Eq. (5), i.e., with the fewest perturbed pixels.

To augment initial perturbations, we follow prior work [2,29] to reformulate our problem of Eq. (6) via the Lagrangian relaxation formulation for concurrently maximizing the classification loss and minimizing the number of perturbed pixels, yielding:

$$J_{\text{adv}} = J(f_{\boldsymbol{\theta}}(\boldsymbol{x} + \boldsymbol{w} \odot \boldsymbol{\delta}), y_{\text{adv}}) + \lambda \|\boldsymbol{w}\|_0, \quad (7)$$

where λ is a hyperparameter to balance the classification loss and the degree of perturbation. As negative elements in $\boldsymbol{w}$ indicate that the corresponding perturbations in $\boldsymbol{\delta}$ negatively affect the adversary property, a simple but effective way to augment Eq. (7) is via applying the ReLU function to drop negative values in $\boldsymbol{w}$, i.e.,

$$J_{\text{adv}} = J(f_{\boldsymbol{\theta}}(\boldsymbol{x} + \pi(\boldsymbol{w}) \odot \boldsymbol{\delta}), y_{\text{adv}}) + \lambda \|\pi(\boldsymbol{w})\|_0, \quad (8)$$

where $\pi(\cdot)$ represents the ReLU function.

Reparameterization Technique. However, as indicated by [30], the l_0 norm of $\pi(\boldsymbol{w})$ is non-differentiable, so directly optimizing Eq. (8) is computationally intractable. To address this intractability, let $H(\cdot)$ be the Heaviside step function and consider a simple re-parametrization technique:

$$\|\pi(\boldsymbol{w})\|_0 = \sum_{j=1}^{d} H(\pi(w_j)), \text{ with } H(x) = \begin{cases} 1, & x > 0 \\ 0, & x \leq 0 \end{cases}. \quad (9)$$

As such, we can reformulate Eq. (8) as follows,

$$J_{\text{adv}} = J(f_{\boldsymbol{\theta}}(\boldsymbol{x} + \pi(\boldsymbol{w}) \odot \boldsymbol{\delta}), y_{\text{adv}}) + \lambda \sum_{j=1}^{d} H(\pi(w_j)). \quad (10)$$

Obviously, penalizing the second term of Eq. (10) is equivalent to penalize the l_0 norm of $\pi(\boldsymbol{w})$. However, it is impractical to directly optimize Eq. (10) because the distributional derivative of the Heaviside step function, i.e., the Dirac delta function, equals to zero almost everywhere [50]. The Dirac delta function, by definition, can be simply regarded as a function that is zero everywhere except at the origin, where it is infinite, *i.e.*,

$$p(x) \simeq \begin{cases} \infty, & x = 0 \\ 0, & x \neq 0 \end{cases}. \quad (11)$$

To make the Heaviside step function differentiable, we devise a novel reparametrization technique to approximate the Dirac delta function, resorting to the zero-centered normal distribution presented as follows:

$$q_a(x) = \frac{1}{|a|\sqrt{\pi}} \exp^{-(x/a)^2}. \quad (12)$$

Here, the variance of $q_a(x)$ is determined by the hyperparameter a. When the hyperparameter a approaches zero, the function $q_a(x)$ converges to the Dirac delta function $p(x)$, as stated next.

Theorem 1. *(Convergence) Let $p(x)$ denote the Dirac delta function. Consider $q_a(x)$ defined as $q_a(x) = \frac{1}{|a|\sqrt{\pi}} \exp^{-(x/a)^2}$, which represents a zero-centered normal distribution with variance dependent on the hyperparameter a. Then, in the distributional sense, we have:*

$$\lim_{a \to 0} q_a(x) = p(x). \quad (13)$$

Proof. First, consider the case when $x = 0$, we always have:

$$\lim_{a \to 0} q_a(x) = \lim_{a \to 0} \frac{1}{|a|\sqrt{\pi}} \exp^{-(0/a)^2} = \lim_{a \to 0} \frac{1}{|a|\sqrt{\pi}} = \infty. \quad (14)$$

Second, when $x \neq 0$, we need to consider both the positive and negative directions of a, *i.e.*, $\lim_{a \to 0+}$ and $\lim_{a \to 0-}$. Starting with the positive direction, let $t = \frac{1}{a}$, we have

$$\lim_{a \to 0+} q_a(x) = \lim_{a \to 0} \frac{1}{a\sqrt{\pi}} \exp^{-(x/a)^2} = \lim_{t \to \infty} \sqrt{\pi} t \cdot \exp^{-x^2 t^2} = \lim_{t \to \infty} \frac{\sqrt{\pi} t}{\exp^{x^2 t^2}}$$

$$= \lim_{t \to \infty} \frac{\sqrt{\pi}}{2x^2 t \cdot \exp^{x^2 t^2}} \text{ (L'Hopital's rule)} = \frac{\sqrt{\pi}}{\infty} = 0. \quad (15)$$

Similarly, for the negative direction of a, we have:

$$\lim_{a \to 0-} q_a(x) = \lim_{a \to 0} -\frac{1}{a\sqrt{\pi}} \exp^{-(x/a)^2} = \lim_{t \to \infty} -\sqrt{\pi} t \cdot \exp^{-x^2 t^2}$$

$$= \lim_{t \to \infty} -\frac{\sqrt{\pi} t}{\exp^{x^2 t^2}} = \lim_{t \to \infty} -\frac{\sqrt{\pi}}{2x^2 t \cdot \exp^{x^2 t^2}} = -\frac{\sqrt{\pi}}{\infty} = 0. \quad (16)$$

Based on the above discussion, we have:

$$\lim_{a \to 0} q_a(x) = \begin{cases} \infty, & x = 0 \\ 0, & x \neq 0 \end{cases} = p(x). \quad (17)$$

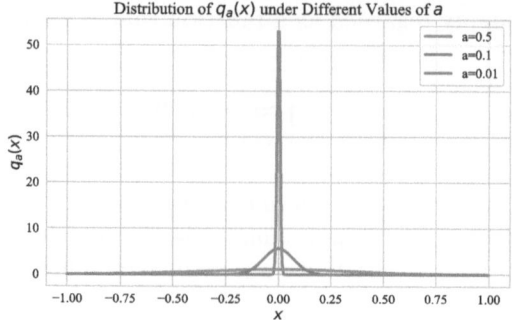

Fig. 2. Distribution of $q_a(x)$ under different values of a. As a approaches to 0, $q_a(x)$ increasingly resembles the Dirac delta function.

Figure 2 presents the distribution of $q_a(x)$ for various values of a. It is clear that as a approaches zero, the shape of $q_a(x)$ more closely resembles the Dirac delta function, a crucial aspect in estimating the derivative of the Heaviside step function. This estimation is significant as it allows for the differentiability of Eq. (10), demonstrated by:

$$\frac{dH}{dx} \approx \frac{1}{|a|\sqrt{\pi}} \exp^{-(x/a)^2}. \tag{18}$$

Here, the hyperparameter a modulates the balance between optimization smoothness and approximation accuracy.

Performance Guarantees. A simple trick to increase the sparsity for convergence acceleration is to tailor the ReLU function as follows:

$$\pi'(\boldsymbol{w}) = \pi(\boldsymbol{w} - \frac{\tau}{\epsilon}), \tag{19}$$

where ϵ is the l_∞ constraint for I-FGSM and τ is used to simplify hyperparameter tuning. By using our tailored ReLU function $\pi'(\cdot)$, we can re-write the loss function given below:

$$J_{\text{adv}} = J(f_\theta(\boldsymbol{x} + \pi(\boldsymbol{w} - \frac{\tau}{\epsilon}) \odot \boldsymbol{\delta}), y_{\text{adv}}) + \lambda \sum_{j=1}^{d} H\left(\pi(w_j - \frac{\tau}{\epsilon})\right). \tag{20}$$

By employing Eq. (20), our approach yields much sparser adversarial examples, as stated below.

Proposition 1. *(Sparsity) Given an initial perturbation $\boldsymbol{\delta} \in [-\epsilon, \epsilon]^d$ under some l_∞ constraint ϵ ($\epsilon > 0$), let $\boldsymbol{w} \in \mathbb{R}^d$ be the weight matrix used in our study, and $\pi(\cdot)$ be the ReLU function, in terms of the l_0 norm, we have:*

$$\|\pi(\boldsymbol{w} - \frac{\tau}{\epsilon}) \odot \boldsymbol{\delta}\|_0 \leq \|\pi(\boldsymbol{w}) \odot \boldsymbol{\delta}\|_0 \leq \|\boldsymbol{w} \odot \boldsymbol{\delta}\|_0. \tag{21}$$

The proof of Proposition 1 is deferred to Appendix A.1 for conserving sparse.

Although Eq. (20) can yield more sparse adversarial examples, it cannot guarantee valid pixel values, i.e., $\exists\, w_j \in \boldsymbol{w}, x_j + \pi(w_j - \frac{\tau}{\epsilon}) \odot \delta_j \notin [0,1]$. To remedy this, we devise a new strategy to satisfy the box constraint:

$$\boldsymbol{w}' = \boldsymbol{\Omega} \odot H\left(\pi(\boldsymbol{w} - \frac{\tau}{\epsilon})\right), \tag{22}$$

where $\boldsymbol{\Omega}$ serves to impose a tight bound on the resulting perturbation. Following this step, we are able to obtain valid adversarial examples, as stated next.

Proposition 2. *(Box constraint) Let $\boldsymbol{x} \in [0,1]^d$ be a natural image, $\boldsymbol{\delta} \in [-\epsilon,\epsilon]^d$ be the initial perturbation under a l_∞ constraint ϵ ($\epsilon > 0$), and $\boldsymbol{w}'$ be the output of Eq. (22). If $\boldsymbol{\Omega} = \min(\frac{\boldsymbol{x}}{\epsilon}, \frac{1-\boldsymbol{x}}{\epsilon})$, the resulting adversarial example is valid, i.e.,*

$$\boldsymbol{x} + \boldsymbol{w}' \odot \boldsymbol{\delta} \in [0,1]^d. \tag{23}$$

The proof of Proposition 2 is deferred to Appendix A.2. Note that such a box constraint strategy can automatically yield valid pixels, making adversarial attacks escape from local optima, as stated in the prior study [2]. Details of our algorithm flow are deferred to Appendix B.

5 Experiments and Results

5.1 Experimental Settings

Datasets. We experimentally benchmark our approach on three widely used image datasets: i) 70,000 greyscale examples of **MNIST** [25]; ii) 60,000 RGB examples of **CIFAR-10** [20]; iii) 10,000 RGB examples randomly selected from the **ImageNet** [40] validation set.

Compared Methods. We compare our approach to ten sparse attack counterparts, i.e., **C&W L_0** [2], **OnePixel** [43], **SparseFool** [35], **GreedyFool** [9], **FMN** [38], **Homotopy** [57], **Sparse-RS** [6], **SA-MOO** [51], **EGS-TSSA** [34] and **BruSLeAttack** [49]. Hyperparameters for compared methods, if not specified, are set as mentioned in their respective articles. All comparative results represent the average of 5 trials.

Parameter Settings. Four pre-trained models, VGG-16 [42], VGG-19, ResNet-101 [16], and ResNet-152, are exploited to evaluate the adversarial perturbation under ImageNet. The hyperparameters for I-FGSM, unless specified otherwise, are set as $\epsilon = 4/255$, $\alpha = 1/255$, and the number of iterations equal to 10. We optimize the weight in our approach by using SGD with a momentum of 0.9 and a learning rate of $1e-2$. A mini-batch of 256 is used for MNIST and CIFAR-10, and of 64 for ImageNet. We set $\lambda = 1e-2$ for MNIST and CIFAR-10, and $\lambda = 1e-3$ for ImageNet. We grid-search a (and τ) and empirically set them to 0.1 (and 0.30) for all three datasets. The number of iterations for our approach is set to 100, 100, and 200 for MNIST, CIFAR-10, and ImageNet, respectively. For the targeted attack, we follow prior studies [22,23] by setting the least-likely class as the targeted label. All experiments were conducted on a workstation equipped with an RTX 4090 GPU.

5.2 Evaluation on Sparsity

We compare our approach to sparse attacks listed in Sect. 5.1 in terms of sparsity (*i.e.*, l_0 norm of perturbation) under the non-targeted and targeted attack scenarios. ResNet-18 and VGG-16 are used to generate adversarial examples and report the classification results for CIFAR-10 and ImageNet, respectively. For all methods (except for OnePixel), we report the averagely required amount of perturbed pixels for achieving a fooling rate of 100% in both scenarios. Note that OnePixel cannot achieve such a fooling rate because its perturbations are limited to an extreme case. Table 1 presents the experimental results. Under the non-targeted attack scenario, we observe that except for OnePixel, our approach achieves the minimal magnitude of perturbations, with the averaged number of 44 (1.45% pixels) and of 57 (0.04% pixels) for CIFAR-10 and ImageNet, respectively. Although OnePixel outperforms our approach in terms of sparsity, it suffers from an extremely poor fooling rate, substantially inferior to our approach. Similarly, under the targeted attack scenario, our approach achieves the best sparsity of 69 (2.27% pixels) and of 136 (0.09% pixels) for CIFAR-10 and ImageNet, respectively, significantly outperforming all its counterparts. Notably, OnePixel and SpareFool cannot perform effective targeted attacks, so their results are unavailable.

Table 1. Comparative results of sparsity under CIFAR-10 and ImageNet, with the minimum amounts of perturbed pixels required to achieve the fooling rate (FR) of 100% for non-targeted and targeted attacks reported

Method	Non-targeted Attack				Targeted Attack			
	CIFAR-10		ImageNet		CIFAR-10		ImageNet	
	FR	Sparsity	FR	Sparsity	FR	Sparsity	FR	Sparsity
C&W L_0	100%	52	100%	424	100%	102	100%	5132
OnePixel	35.2%	1	20.5%	3	-	-	-	-
SparseFool	100%	76	100%	234	-	-	-	-
FMN	100%	106	100%	632	100%	183	100%	1087
Sparse-RS	100%	167	100%	758	100%	244	100%	1293
SA-MOO	100%	173	100%	1392	100%	305	100%	2896
EGS-TSSA	100%	105	100%	549	100%	218	100%	1054
BruSLeAttack	100%	93	100%	164	100%	148	100%	678
Ours	100%	44	100%	57	100%	69	100%	136

Next, we conduct qualitative experiments to evaluate the sparsity under the targeted attack scenario. Figure 3 shows the visualized results, where our approach modifies only 123, 107, and 218 pixels, respectively, with its adversarial examples able to mislead the classifier into targeted mispredictions. In contrast, C&W L_0, GreedyFool, and Homotopy have to perturb 3555, 1070, and

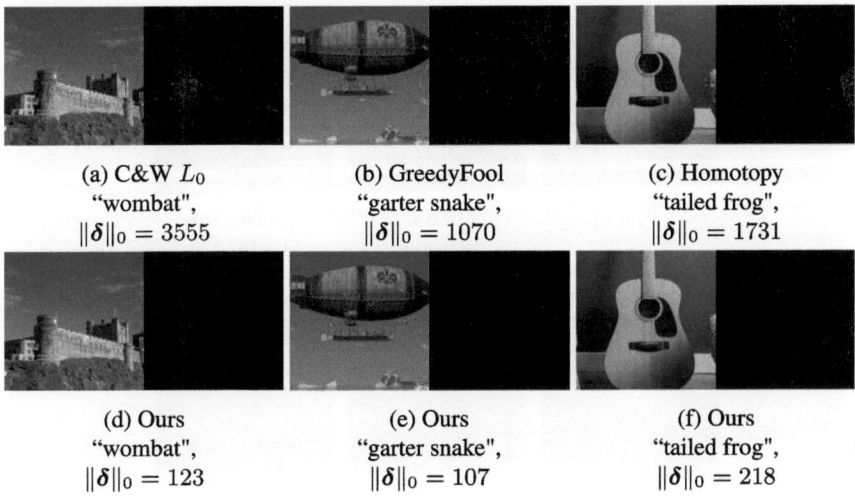

Fig. 3. Illustration of targeted attacks by sparse attack counterparts (Top) and our approach (Bottom). From left to right, the ground-truth classes are "castle", "airship", and "guitar", respectively. The incorrect predictions and the sparsity (*i.e.*, $\|\delta\|_0$) are listed under each image.

1731 pixels, respectively, to perform effective targeted attacks. These qualitative results demonstrate the effectiveness of our approach on sparsity. We also conduct qualitative comparison under the non-targeted attack scenario, with the results deferred to Appendix C.1 of supplementary materials.

5.3 Interpreting the Adversarial Perturbation

Despite extensive attention to sparse attacks, limited work has ever clearly explained how adversarial perturbations mislead DNNs into incorrect predictions. This is due to the mediocre performance results of prior sparse attacks on sparsity, as discussed in Sect. 5.2. We aim to fill this gap by unveiling the mystery underlying the proposed adversarial perturbation, resorting to Grad-CAM and Guided Grad-CAM visualizations [41]. Specifically, we let the prediction made by a well-trained VGG-16 as the decision of interest for Grad-CAM and Guided Grad-CAM visualizations. As such, we can interpret adversarial perturbations by comparing visualizations on clean images with those on their corresponding adversarial examples.

Figure 4 exhibits the experimental results, where our generated perturbations mislead VGG-16 to mispredict "toilet tissue" on an image as "candle". In particular, Figs. 4a, 4b and 4c show visualizations on the clean image. We observed that the "candle wick" is the critical region for making a correct prediction on the "candle". By contrast, Figs. 4d, 4e and 4f depict visualizations of the adversarial example generated by our approach. From Fig. 4d, we observe that the adversarial perturbation can be divided into two categories, namely, "obscuring

Fig. 4. Illustration of how adversarial perturbations computed by our approach mislead VGG-16 to predict the label of "candle" to "toilet tissue". **Left:** clean image and adversarial example with their predicted labels. **Middle:** Grad-CAM visualization. **Right:** Guided Grad-CAM visualization.

noise" (*i.e.*, perturbations within the red box) and "leading noise" (*i.e.*, perturbations within the green box). The former prevents the classifier from identifying the true label by covering essential features of the true class, *i.e.*, obscuring the feature of "candle wick", whereas the latter leads the classifier to mispredict the adversarial example by adding the essential features of the targeted class, *i.e.*, adding noise within the shape of "toilet tissue"; see Figs. 4b versus 4e and Figs. 4c versus 4f.

We also conduct experiments to show how the two types of perturbations mislead ResNet-50 to make an incorrect prediction as "wing" on an image of "canoe", with the results deferred to Appendix C.2 of the supplementary materials. To the best of our knowledge, we are the first to interpret how adversarial perturbations mislead DNNs into incorrect predictions, by discovering the "obscuring noise" and "leading noise".

5.4 Attacking Robust Models

We next compare our approach to sparse attacks in terms of attack strength, *i.e.*, the fooling rate on robust models trained adversarially by PGD Adversarial Training (PGD-AT) [32] or Fast Adversarial Training (Fast-AT) [52]. We set $\epsilon = 0.3$, $\epsilon = 8/255$, $\epsilon = 2/255$ for MNIST, CIFAR-10, and ImageNet, respectively. Table 2 presents the experimental results.

Table 2. The fooling rates (%) on different robust models trained adversarially by PGD-AT and Fast-AT, respectively, with the best results are shown in bold

Method	PGD-AT		Fast-AT		
	MNIST	CIFAR-10	MNIST	CIFAR-10	ImageNet
C&W L_0	11.8	52.8	12.1	62.3	67.8
GreedyFool	3.6	26.8	4.9	23.5	24.9
FMN	7.9	55.0	9.8	52.9	54.1
Homotopy	8.5	51.9	7.2	53.2	58.7
Sparse-RS	10.3	54.6	10.9	57.1	56.3
SA-MOO	11.5	56.9	7.8	58.9	62.8
EGS-TSSA	10.7	57.8	8.4	61.6	63.8
BruSLeAttack	11.2	61.2	9.6	58.9	65.1
Ours	**13.8**	**62.5**	**14.6**	**66.4**	**72.1**

From Table 2, we observe that our approach achieves the most powerful attacks under all scenarios, with the best fooling rate of 14.6%, 66.4%, and 72.1% on MNIST, CIFAR-10, and ImageNet, respectively. The reason is that i) our novel loss function (*i.e.*, Eq. (20)) significantly augments the adversary property; and ii) the proposed theoretically sound box constraint strategy yields valid adversarial examples without the need of clipping invalid pixels, empowering our approach to generate more optimized solutions. Meanwhile, all sparse attacks, including our approach, achieve smaller fooling rates on MNIST than those on CIFAR-10 and ImageNet. This is because adversarial training can significantly improve the model's robustness on the simple dataset. But, for CIFAR-10 (or ImageNet), our approach can achieve the averaged fooling rate of 62.5% and of 66.4% (or 72.1%), respectively, on PGD-AT and Fast-AT.

5.5 Comparison on Transferability

We take two models, *i.e.*, VGG-19 and ResNet-101, to generate adversarial examples, which are then employed to attack four different classifiers, *i.e.*, VGG-16, VGG-19, ResNet-101, and ResNet-152. Table 3 presents the comparative results of our approach and sparse attack counterparts in terms of transferability. Notably, the adversarial examples generated via VGG-19 (or ResNet-101) to attack VGG-19 (or ResNet-101) are considered as white-box attacks, while all others are black-box attacks. We observe that compared to other sparse attacks, our approach achieves the best performance under all scenarios, with the largest fooling rate of 99.1% (or 99.9%) under the black-box (or white-box) attack. This demonstrates that modifying a few pixels is sufficient to make our approach enjoy high transferability.

Table 3. Comparison of transferability (*i.e.*, Mean Fooling Rate (%)) under ImageNet. The first column denotes the models where adversarial samples are generated while the first row indicates the target models for attacking, with the best results shown in bold and * indicating white-box attacks

Model	Method	VGG-16	VGG-19	ResNet-101	ResNet-152
VGG-19	C&W L_0	84.6	96.2*	55.6	47.5
	GreedyFool	10.6	19.2*	8.2	9.0
	FMN	83.4	91.8*	43.0	46.8
	Homotopy	65.8	87.6*	24.0	9.8
	Sparse-RS	85.2	96.0*	46.8	48.2
	SA-MOO	86.2	92.8*	44.5	49.2
	EGS-TSSA	87.7	93.2*	51.3	51.2
	BruSLeAttack	89.4	94.4*	56.7	51.8
	Ours	**99.1**	**99.9***	**63.3**	**55.1**
ResNet-101	C&W L_0	82.6	81.9	91.2*	50.5
	GreedyFool	11.4	13.4	9.4*	8.4
	FMN	82.6	81.8	60.1*	41.6
	Homotopy	63.6	63.6	72.0*	46.2
	Sparse-RS	85.2	76.8	89.4*	65.6
	SA-MOO	86.6	84.3	91.1*	61.3
	EGS-TSSA	86.1	83.8	91.5*	62.6
	BruSLeAttack	86.8	84.2	92.6*	67.8
	Ours	**87.6**	**86.3**	**99.9***	**89.9**

5.6 Comparison on Computational Complexity

We conduct the white-box attacks under ImageNet to show the superior computational efficiency of our approach for high-dimensional data. Four classifiers, *i.e.*, VGG-16, VGG-19, ResNet-101, and ResNet-152, are taken into account. Table 4 lists the experimental results. Clearly, our approach runs much faster than all sparse attack counterparts (*i.e.*, C&W L_0, Homotopy, Sparse-RS, SA-MOO, EGS-TSSA, and BruSLeAttack) for all examined classifiers, enjoying 3.0x, 62.8x, 4.6x, 64.0x, 8.0x, and 13.0x, and computational speedups on average. Specifically, our approach takes only 4.6s, 5.3s, 18.7s, and 27.5s, on VGG-16, VGG-19, ResNet-101, and ResNet-152, respectively. This is because our reparameterization technique (*i.e.*, Eq. (18)) can efficiently approximate the NP-hard l_0 optimization problem and hence substantially accelerate the convergence.

We also conducted ablation studies to exhibit the hyperparameter sensitivity of a, λ, and τ respectively in Eq. (18), Eq. (19), and Eq. (20), with their details deferred to Section C.3 of supplementary materials.

Table 4. Comparing various sparse attacks in terms of computational complexity under different models, with the best results shown in bold

Method	Time Cost (s)			
	VGG-16	VGG-19	ResNet-101	ResNet-152
C&W L_0	20.8	23.4	28.7	43.6
Homotopy	519.4	531.5	1011.9	1462.2
Sparse-RS	69.0	76.4	71.6	99.7
SA-MOO	537.4	628.1	1123.8	1379.1
EGS-TSSA	71.8	79.5	120.9	175.9
BruSLeAttack	87.2	93.7	142.2	212.3
Ours	**4.6**	**5.3**	**18.7**	**27.5**

6 Conclusion

This paper has addressed a sparse attack that yields interpretable adversarial examples, thanks to their superb sparsity. Meanwhile, our approach enjoys fast convergence, high transferability, and powerful attack strength. The key idea is to approximate the NP-hard l_0 optimization problem via a theoretical sound reparameterization technique, making direct optimization of sparse perturbations computationally tractable. Besides, a novel loss function and a theoretically sound box constraint strategy have been proposed to make our solution generate superior adversarial examples, yielding fast, transferable, and powerful sparse adversarial attacks. Experimental results demonstrate that our approach clearly outperforms state-of-the-art sparse attacks in terms of computational efficiency, transferability, and attack intensity. In addition, theoretical and empirical results verify that our approach yields sparser adversarial examples, empowering us to experimentally interpret how adversarial examples mislead state-of-the-art DNNs into incorrect predictions. Our work is expected to i) serve as the benchmark for evaluating the robustness of DNNs, and ii) shed light on future work about interpreting the vulnerability of DNNs.

Acknowledgments. This work was supported in part by NSF under Grants 2019511, 2315613, 2325564, 2438898, 2523997, 2534286, 2315612, and 2332638. Any opinions and findings expressed in the paper are those of the authors and do not necessarily reflect the views of funding agencies.

References

1. Ali, A., et al.: Enabling scalable and adaptive machine learning training via serverless computing on public cloud. Perform. Eval. **167**, 102451 (2025)
2. Carlini, N., Wagner, D.A.: Towards evaluating the robustness of neural networks. In: IEEE Symposium on Security and Privacy (2017)

3. Chen, J., Jordan, M.I., Wainwright, M.J.: Hopskipjumpattack: a query-efficient decision-based attack. In: IEEE Symposium on Security and Privacy, 2020 (2020)
4. Chen, L., Min, Y., Zhang, M., Karbasi, A.: More data can expand the generalization gap between adversarially robust and standard models. In: International Conference on Machine Learning (ICML) (2020)
5. Chu, T., et al.: Bonemet: an open large-scale multi-modal murine dataset for breast cancer bone metastasis diagnosis and prognosis. In: The Thirteenth International Conference on Learning Representations (ICLR) (2025)
6. Croce, F., Andriushchenko, M., Singh, N.D., Flammarion, N., Hein, M.: A versatile framework for query-efficient sparse black-box adversarial attacks. In: AAAI, Sparse-rs (2022)
7. Croce, F., Hein, M.: Sparse and imperceivable adversarial attacks. In: ICCV (2019)
8. Devlin, J., Chang, M.-W., Lee, K., Toutanova, K.: BERT: pre-training of deep bidirectional transformers for language understanding. In: Conference of the North American Chapter of the Association for Computational Linguistics: Human Language Technologies (NAACL-HLT) (2019)
9. Dong, X., et al.: Distortion-aware sparse adversarial attack. In: NeurIPS, Greedyfool (2020)
10. Dong, Y., et al.: Boosting adversarial attacks with momentum. In: Conference on Computer Vision and Pattern Recognition (CVPR) (2018)
11. Dong, Y., Pang, T., Su, H., Zhu, J.: Evading defenses to transferable adversarial examples by translation-invariant attacks. In: Conference on Computer Vision and Pattern Recognition (CVPR) (2019)
12. Dosovitskiy, A., et al.: An image is worth 16×16 words: transformers for image recognition at scale. In: ICLR (2021)
13. Eykholt, K., et al.: Robust physical-world attacks on deep learning visual classification. In: CVPR (2018)
14. Fan, Y., et al.: Sparse adversarial attack via perturbation factorization. In: ECCV (2020)
15. Goodfellow, I.J., Shlens, J., Szegedy, C.: Explaining and harnessing adversarial examples. In: International Conference on Learning Representations (ICLR) (2015)
16. He, K., Zhang, X., Ren, S., Sun, J.: Deep residual learning for image recognition. In: IEEE Conference on Computer Vision and Pattern Recognition (CVPR) (2016)
17. He, Y., Lin, F., Yuan, X., Tzeng, N.-F.: Interpretable minority synthesis for imbalanced classification. In: Proceedings of the Thirtieth International Joint Conference on Artificial Intelligence (IJCAI), pp. 2542–2548 (2021)
18. Jumper, J., et al.: Highly accurate protein structure prediction with alphafold. Nature **596**(7873), 583–589 (2021)
19. Kong, Z., Guo, J., Li, A., Liu, C.: Physgan: generating physical-world-resilient adversarial examples for autonomous driving. In: IEEE Conference on Computer Vision and Pattern Recognition (CVPR) (2020)
20. Krizhevsky, A., Hinton, G., et al.: Learning multiple layers of features from tiny images. Technical Report, University of Toronto (2009)
21. Krizhevsky, A., Sutskever, I., Hinton, G.E.: Imagenet classification with deep convolutional neural networks. In: Advances in Neural Information Processing Systems (NIPS) (2012)
22. Kurakin, A., Goodfellow, I.J., Bengio, S.: Adversarial examples in the physical world. In: International Conference on Learning Representations (ICLR) (2017)
23. Kurakin, A., Goodfellow, I.J., Bengio, S.: Adversarial machine learning at scale. In: 5th International Conference on Learning Representations (ICLR) (2017)

24. Lan, G., et al.: Contextual integrity in LLMs via reasoning and reinforcement learning. arXiv preprint arXiv:2506.04245 (2025)
25. LeCun, Y., Cortes, C.: MNIST handwritten digit database (2010)
26. Lin, F., Crawford, S., Guillot, K., Zhang, Y., Chen, Y., Yuan, X., et al.: Mmstvit: climate change-aware crop yield prediction via multi-modal spatial-temporal vision transformer. In: IEEE/CVF International Conference on Computer Vision (ICCV), pp. 5751–5761 (2023)
27. Lin, F., Lou, J., Yuan, X., Tzeng, N.-F.: Towards robust vision transformer via masked adaptive ensemble. In: Proceedings of the 33rd ACM International Conference on Information and Knowledge Management (CIKM), pp. 1389–1399 (2024)
28. Lin, F., et al.: Comprehensive transformer-based model architecture for real-world storm prediction. In: Joint European Conference on Machine Learning and Knowledge Discovery in Databases (ECML-PKDD), pp. 54–71 (2023)
29. Liu, Y., Chen, X., Liu, C., Song, D.: Delving into transferable adversarial examples and black-box attacks. In: ICLR (2017)
30. Louizos, C., Welling, M., Kingma, D.P.: Learning sparse neural networks through L_0 regularization. In: ICLR (2018)
31. Ma, X., et al.: Malletrain: deep neural networks training on unfillable supercomputer nodes. In: Proceedings of the 15th ACM/SPEC International Conference on Performance Engineering, pp. 190–200 (2024)
32. Madry, A., Makelov, A., Schmidt, L., Tsipras, D., Vladu, A.: Towards deep learning models resistant to adversarial attacks. In: International Conference on Learning Representations (ICLR) (2018)
33. Min, Y., Chen, L., Karbasi, A.: The curious case of adversarially robust models: more data can help, double descend, or hurt generalization. In: Uncertainty in Artificial Intelligence (2021)
34. Ming, D., Ren, P., Wang, Y., Feng, X.: Transferable structural sparse adversarial attack via exact group sparsity training. In: Computer Vision and Pattern Recognition (CVPR), pp. 24696–24705 (2024)
35. Modas, A., Moosavi-Dezfooli, S.-M., Frossard, P.: Sparsefool: a few pixels make a big difference. In: IEEE Conference on Computer Vision and Pattern Recognition (CVPR) (2019)
36. Moosavi-Dezfooli, S.-M., Fawzi, A., Frossard, P.: Deepfool: a simple and accurate method to fool deep neural networks. In: Conference on Computer Vision and Pattern Recognition (CVPR) (2016)
37. Papernot, N., et al.: The limitations of deep learning in adversarial settings. In: European Symposium on Security and Privacy (EuroS&P) (2016)
38. Pintor, M., Roli, F., Brendel, W., Biggio, B.: Fast minimum-norm adversarial attacks through adaptive norm constraints. In: Neural Information Processing Systems (NeurIPS), pp. 20052–20062 (2021)
39. Rives, A., et al.: Biological structure and function emerge from scaling unsupervised learning to 250 million protein sequences. Proceedings of the National Academy of Sciences 118(15) (2021)
40. Russakovsky, O., et al.: ImageNet Large Scale Visual Recognition Challenge. Int. J. Comput. Vis. (IJCV) (2015)
41. Ramprasaath, R., et al.: Visual explanations from deep networks via gradient-based localization. In: ICCV, Grad-cam (2017)
42. Simonyan, K., Zisserman, A.: Very deep convolutional networks for large-scale image recognition. In: International Conference on Learning Representations (ICLR) (2015)

43. Su, J., Vargas, D.V., Sakurai, K.: One pixel attack for fooling deep neural networks. IEEE Trans. Evol, Comput (2019)
44. Suya, F., Chi, J., Evans, D., Tian, Y.: Finding black-box adversarial examples with limited queries. In: USENIX, Hybrid batch attacks (2020)
45. Szegedy, C., et al.: Intriguing properties of neural networks. In: International Conference on Learning Representations (ICLR) (2014)
46. Thys, S., Van Ranst, W., Goedemé, T.: Fooling automated surveillance cameras: Adversarial patches to attack person detection. In: IEEE Conference on Computer Vision and Pattern Recognition Workshops (CVPRW) (2019)
47. Tramèr, F., Kurakin, A., Papernot, N., Goodfellow, I.J., Boneh, D., McDaniel, P.D.: Ensemble adversarial training: attacks and defenses. In: International Conference on Learning Representations (ICLR) (2018)
48. Vaswani, A., et al.: Attention is all you need. In: Advances in Neural Information Processing Systems (NIPS) (2017)
49. Vo, V.Q., Abbasnejad, E., Ranasinghe, D.: Brusleattack: a query-efficient score-based black-box sparse adversarial attack. In: International Conference on Learning Representations (ICLR) (2024)
50. Wikipedia. Heaviside step function (2024). Accessed 01 Jan 2024
51. Williams, P.N., Li, K.: Black-box sparse adversarial attack via multi-objective optimisation. In: Computer Vision and Pattern Recognition (CVPR) (2023)
52. Wong, E., Rice, L., Zico Kolter, J.: Fast is better than free: Revisiting adversarial training. In: International Conference on Learning Representations (ICLR) (2020)
53. Xie, C., et al.: Improving transferability of adversarial examples with input diversity. In: IEEE Conference on Computer Vision and Pattern Recognition (CVPR) (2019)
54. Kaidi, X., et al.: Towards general implementation and better interpretability. In: ICLR, Structured adversarial attack (2019)
55. Zawad, S., et al.: Fedcust: offloading hyperparameter customization for federated learning. Perform. Eval. **167**, 102450 (2025)
56. Zeiler, M.D., Fergus, R.: Visualizing and understanding convolutional networks. In: European Conference on Computer Vision (2014)
57. Zhu, M., Chen, T., Wang, Z.: Sparse and imperceptible adversarial attack via a homotopy algorithm. In: ICML (202)1

Scaling Multi-label Conformal Prediction with Label Interactions for a Large Number of Labels

Ghassan Najjar[✉], Céline Berthou, and Héléna Vorobieva

Safran Tech, Rue des Jeunes Bois, Châteaufort, 78114 Magny-Les-Hameaux, France
{ghassan.najjar,celine.berthou,helena.vorobieva}@safrangroup.com

Abstract. Multi-label classification is the task where a single instance may belong to multiple classes simultaneously. The Label Powerset approach (LP) allows to apply Inductive Conformal Prediction (ICP) on multi-label classification tasks, by considering each label set as a single class and by assigning a non-conformity score to each of them. The construction of the prediction set $\mathcal{C}$ requires selecting all the label sets –represented as binary vectors– that satisfy a given conformity criterion. Since the number of possible outputs is exponentially growing with the number of classes, constructing $\mathcal{C}$ by testing the conformity criterion on all cases is unaffordable. We propose an algorithm that efficiently computes $\mathcal{C}$, even in the difficult case where the non-conformity score involves label interactions. It is based on a customized partial order relation on the set of binary vectors coupled with a monotone lower bound of the non-conformity score. Our tests confirm the algorithm's efficiency, even with a high class count.

Keywords: Multi-label Classification · Inductive Conformal Prediction · Label Powerset · Computational Efficiency · Trees

1 Introduction

In the realm of machine learning, multi-label classification is a complex and challenging problem, where a single data instance can belong to multiple classes simultaneously. This scenario is ubiquitous in various real-world applications, such as text classification and medical diagnosis. For instance, in medical diagnosis, the patient may suffer from multiple diseases at the same time. In the case of multi-label classification with c classes, given an input, the classifier predicts a set of classes, instead of predicting one single class.

In high-sensitivity tasks and applications requiring certification such as in the aeronautical or health industries, it is valuable to provide statistically valid

Supplementary Information The online version contains supplementary material available at https://doi.org/10.1007/978-3-032-06109-6_7.

uncertainty quantification. Conformal Prediction [9] tackles this challenge by extending traditional classification outputs, providing a set of multiple possible outputs with explicit guarantees under the assumption of data exchangeability. Within the family of conformal prediction methods, several techniques have been proposed for multi-label classification, such as Binary Relevance Conformal Prediction (BRCP) [2] and the Label-Powerset Conformal Prediction (LPCP) [5]. BRCP transforms the problem into a binary classification task for each class, but does not natively account for dependencies between different classes: for a given $\alpha > 0$, it applies Conformal Prediction (CP) independently with a significance level of $\frac{\alpha}{c}$ for each label, applying then the union bound gives a significance level of α for the whole prediction. This method is not adapted for large values of c because of the $\frac{\alpha}{c}$ fraction. Another approach [8] employs a hierarchical tree and uses the technique of multiple hypothesis testing to address multi-label conformal prediction. However, this method requires to construct a tree with more than 2^c nodes, which is infeasible for very large c.

LPCP modifies the problem into a multi-class mono-label one by treating each label set as a unique class, and applies classical CP methods for mono-label problems. LPCP has the advantage of enabling the use of non-conformity scores that account for label dependencies. We therefore chose to follow the LPCP method and model each label set as a vector $y \in \{0,1\}^c$: a 1 coordinate at position i corresponding to the presence of class i.

By calibration for a chosen threshold $\alpha > 0$, under exchangeability assumption of data, ICP [6] returns prediction regions with marginal coverage guarantee of at least $1 - \alpha$. This method needs a preliminary definition of a non-conformity score, which assigns a real number to each label set. The non-conformity score introduced in [5] accounts for interactions between labels by penalizing combinations that never simultaneously appeared in the data. This allows to significantly reduce the size of the conformal prediction sets, as shown in [5] and [4].

The main disadvantage of LPCP is its high computational complexity. The work [3] solves this problem in the case of a large number of labels (tested up to $c = 90$ labels), with an L^p non-conformity score, which does not account for label interactions.

The present work aims to reduce the computational complexity in the case of non-conformity scores that account for label interactions, as in [5] and [4]. We aim to find an algorithm that constructs the prediction set efficiently in the challenging case of label-interacting non-conformity scores.

For the purpose of certification, it is essential to compute the prediction set exactly, ensuring that no elements are omitted. The following section recalls the ICP framework and states the problem. Section 3 gives a first algorithmic solution (ECP) of the problem of prediction set construction and an optimized variant (CAECP). In Sect. 4, we present an even more optimized algorithm (PBECP) based on CAECP.

2 Problem Statement

2.1 Preliminaries

ICP assumes we have a calibration set denoted as $(X_i, Y_i)_{i \leq n}$, where X_i and Y_i are inputs and outputs. The X_i and Y_i are considered here as random variables in $\mathcal{X} \times \{0,1\}^c$ with $\mathcal{X}$ the input space, c, the number of classes and n the number of data. Let (X_{test}, Y_{test}), denote a test point such that the dataset $((X_i, Y_i)_{i \leq n}, (X_{test}, Y_{test}))$ is exchangeable.

Assume we have a pre-trained model $\hat{f}$ trained on the set $\mathcal{D}_{pre-trained}$ assumed independent of the calibration data and test point. The output of $\hat{f}$ can be seen as scores assigned to each class:

$$\hat{f}: \mathcal{X} \to [0,1]^c$$

Then ICP can use this underlying model through a *non-conformity* score, which is allowed to depend on $\mathcal{D}_{pre-trained}$:

$$s: [0,1]^c \times \{0,1\}^c \to \mathbb{R}$$

$s(\hat{f}(x), y)$ is a measure of dissimilarity between the model prediction $\hat{f}(x)$ and the candidate output y. For each input X_i, we denote by $\hat{Y}_i := \hat{f}(X_i) \in [0,1]^c$.

Let $\alpha > 0$ and let q, be the empirical quantile of order $\frac{(n+1)(1-\alpha)}{n}$ of the calibration scores $s(\hat{Y}_i, Y_i)$. This quantile is used to form a prediction set for the new input X_{test}:

$$C(X_{test}) = \{y \in \{0,1\}^c \mid s(\hat{Y}_{test}, y) \leq q\} \quad (1)$$

Under exchangeability assumption of all the $n+1$ samples, the marginal coverage guarantee holds:

$$\mathbb{P}(Y_{test} \in C(X_{test})) \geq 1 - \alpha \quad (2)$$

where the probability is taken over both the calibration data and the test point. During inference, for a given sample x_{test}, which is a realization of X_{test}, the prediction set $C(x_{test})$ is useful in practice only if $\text{Card}(C(x_{test}))$ is low. It is crucial to thoughtfully design the s function to achieve this goal. Thus, we opted for a non-conformity score that considers label interactions. This approach allows us to incorporate practical prior knowledge, such as: "if two labels have never appeared simultaneously in the training data, then it is unlikely that they to co-occur in the future". The non-conformity score introduced in [5] addresses the two mentioned requirements:

$$\forall \hat{y} \in [0,1]^c, \forall y \in \{0,1\}^c, s_\mu(\hat{y}, y) = \sum_{i=1}^{c} |\hat{y}_i - y_i|^\phi + \lambda \sum_{1 \leq i \leq j \leq c} \mu_{i,j} y_i y_j \quad (3)$$

where $\lambda \geq 0$, $\phi > 0$, $\mu_{i,j} = 0$ if labels i and j have been simultaneously observed in the training set, and $\mu_{i,j} = 1$ otherwise. This non-conformity score allows the reduction of the cardinality of the prediction set $C(x_{n+1})$. However, constructing $C(x_{n+1})$ is computationally very demanding: a naive approach would require generating the 2^c vectors y to test whether $s(\hat{y}_{n+1}, y) \leq q$.

2.2 Main Contribution and General Setting of the Problem

Our work proposes an efficient way to compute exactly the prediction set $C(x_{n+1})$ for the non-conformity score (3) and even for a more general one:

$$s_\mu(\hat{y}, y) = \sum_{i=1}^{c} \varphi(|\hat{y}_i - y_i|) + \sum_{1 \leq i \leq j \leq c} \mu_{i,j} y_i y_j \qquad (4)$$

where the parameters $(\mu_{i,j})_{1 \leq i \leq j \leq c}$ are arbitrary elements of $\mathbb{R}^+$ and $\varphi : \mathbb{R}^+ \to \mathbb{R}^+$ is an arbitrary increasing function. $(\mu_{i,j})_{1 \leq i \leq j \leq c}$ can be chosen *a priori* or can be the result of a data-based optimization on $\mathcal{D}_{pre-trained}$.

In order to compute the prediction set, we make the following assumptions. Firstly, we assume that q has been calibrated and that we are at inference stage. Given a new input x -or more precisely the underlying classifier's raw predictions $\hat{y}$- we want to compute:

$$C_{\mu,q}(\hat{y}) = \{y \in \{0,1\}^c | s_\mu(\hat{y}, y) \leq q\} \qquad (5)$$

Fixing $\hat{y}$ for the rest of the paper, we can simplify the notation and write:

$$s(y) := s_\mu(\hat{y}, y) \qquad (6)$$

Secondly, we assume from now on that the coordinates of the vector $\hat{y} \in [0,1]^c$ are in **decreasing order**. To achieve that, one can apply a permutation $\sigma \in \mathfrak{S}_c$ such that the coordinates of $\hat{y}^\sigma := (\hat{y}_{\sigma(i)})_i$ are in decreasing order. If we consider the permuted vector $y^\sigma := (y_{\sigma(i)})_i$ and the new family $(\mu^\sigma_{i,j})_{i \leq j}$ defined by

$$\mu^\sigma_{i,j} = \begin{cases} \mu_{\sigma(i),\sigma(j)} & \text{if } \sigma(i) \leq \sigma(j) \\ \mu_{\sigma(j),\sigma(i)} & \text{else} \end{cases} \qquad (7)$$

Then we have this permutation invariance property:

Proposition 1.

$$s_{\mu^\sigma}(\hat{y}^\sigma, y^\sigma) = s_\mu(\hat{y}, y) \qquad (8)$$

See proof in appendix.[1]

Using σ is not constraining: if the coordinates of $\hat{y}$ are not in a decreasing order, we solve first the problem with μ^σ and $\hat{y}^\sigma$. From the solution $C_{\mu^\sigma,q}(\hat{y}^\sigma)$ we then get the solution of the initial problem $C_{\mu,q}(\hat{y})$ applying the permutation σ^{-1} to each vector of $C_{\mu^\sigma,q}(\hat{y}^\sigma)$.

3 (Children-Anticipating) Efficient Conformal Prediction: An Efficient Computation of the Prediction Set Based on Single-Root Candidate Generation

3.1 Definition of an Exploration Tree of $\{0,1\}^c$

Our goal is to construct a tree $\mathcal{T}$ whose nodes are the elements of $\{0,1\}^c$. This tree explores these elements in an order which enables pruning and saves time.

---

[1] The key proofs of the paper are presented in the main document, while less critical proofs are included in the appendix: https://github.com/Ghassan01/appendix_icp/.

Definition 1. *The max-1-position of a binary vector $y \in \{0,1\}^c$, denoted as $l(y)$ is defined the following way:*

$$l(y) = \begin{cases} max\{i \in [\![1;c]\!] | y_i = 1\} & \text{if } \{i \in [\![1;c]\!] | y_i = 1\} \neq \emptyset \\ 0 & \text{else} \end{cases} \quad (9)$$

It is the last index of 1-coordinate in y if there exists at least one.

Definition 2. *We denote by l_0 the max-1-position of the vector $(1_{\hat{y}_i > 0.5})_i$.*

From the decreasing order assumption of $\hat{y}$, l_0 is also the number of coordinates of $\hat{y}$ that are above 0.5.

Definition 3. *We define the binary relation $\leq$ on $\{0,1\}^c$ the following way:*

$$\forall y, z \in \{0,1\}^c, \quad y \leq z \Leftrightarrow (y_i)_{i \leq l(y)} = (z_i)_{i \leq l(y)} \quad (10)$$

Meaning $y \leq z$ and $y \neq z$ if and only if z is obtained by replacing at least one of the right zeros (the zeros at a position greater than $l(y)$) of y by a 1. We clearly observe that:

Proposition 2. *The binary relation $\leq$ on $\{0,1\}^c$ is a partial order relation.*

We can now construct the tree $\mathcal{T}$ whose nodes are the elements of $\{0,1\}^c$, rooted at the null vector $0 \in \{0,1\}^c$, such that $y \in \{0,1\}^c$ is an ascendant of $z \in \{0,1\}^c$ if and only if $y \leq z$. Figure 1 shows $\mathcal{T}$ in the case $c = 4$. The partial order relation provides a natural and beneficial order of exploration of the elements of $\{0,1\}^c$ following this tree. It is clear that:

Proposition 3. *The depth l of tree $\mathcal{T}$ is composed of binary vectors containing exactly a number l of 1 coordinates*

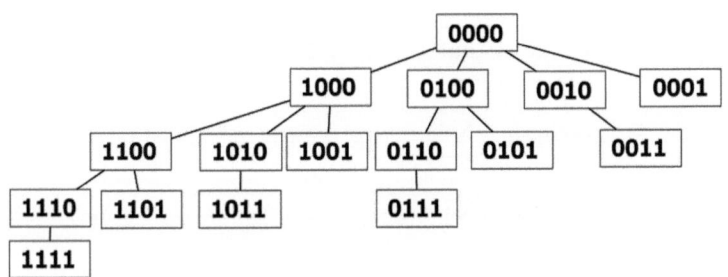

Fig. 1. $\mathcal{T}$ in the case $c = 4$

Next, we explore the nodes of the tree in a depth-first-search manner to construct $C_{\mu,q}(\hat{y})$ efficiently. At each node y, we choose whether to include it in $C_{\mu,q}(\hat{y})$, and in the next section, we establish a criterion to test whether we can prune all the descendants of y to exclude them from the search process.

3.2 Lower Bound of the Non-conformity Score

Definition 4. *We define the function m defined on $\{0,1\}^c$, the following way:*

$$m(y) = \sum_{i=1}^{l(y)} \varphi(|\hat{y}_i - y_i|) + \sum_{i=l(y)+1}^{c} \varphi(|\hat{y}_i - 1_{\hat{y}_i > 0.5}|) + \sum_{1 \leq i \leq j \leq c} \mu_{i,j} y_i y_j \quad (11)$$

Proposition 4. *m is a lower bound of s.*

Proof. $s(y) - m(y) = \sum_{i=l(y)+1}^{c} \varphi(|\hat{y}_i - y_i|) - \varphi(|\hat{y}_i - 1_{\hat{y}_i > 0.5}|)$.
Since the y_i are in $\{0,1\}$, it is clear that $\forall i \in [\![1;c]\!]$, $|\hat{y}_i - 1_{\hat{y}_i > 0.5}| \leq |\hat{y}_i - y_i|$.
We conclude using the increasing property of φ. $\square$

Remark 1. Given that the higher $l(y)$ is, the closer $m(y)$ is to $s(y)$, we remark that m is a relatively close lower bound of s. If l_0 is the max-1-position of the vector $(1_{\hat{y}_i > 0.5})_{1 \leq i \leq c}$, the Proposition 5 gives a bound of the minoration gap.

Proposition 5.

$$\forall y \in \{0,1\}^c, \quad 0 \leq s(y) - m(y) \leq (l_0 - l(y))^+ ||\varphi||_\infty$$

With the convention $0 \times \infty = 0$ *if* $(l_0 - l(y))^+ = 0$ *and* $||\varphi||_\infty = \infty$.

Remark 2. $(.)^+$ denotes the positive part function. In particular, if y contains a 1 coordinate at a position higher than l_0, then we have the strong equality $s(y) = m(y)$. As l_0 is often expected to be low in practice, m is a high-quality lower bound.

The introduced partial order on $\{0,1\}^c$ and the lower bound m are particularly significant as m is monotonic:

Proposition 6. *The lower bound m is increasing for "$\leq$".*

Proof. Let $y, z \in \{0,1\}^c$ such that $y \leq z$. Hence, $l(y) \leq l(z)$ and we obtain

$$m(z) - m(y) = \sum_{i=l(y)+1}^{l(z)} \varphi(|\hat{y}_i - z_i|) - \varphi(|\hat{y}_i - 1_{\hat{y}_i > 0.5}|)$$
$$+ \sum_{1 \leq i \leq j \leq c} \mu_{i,j}((z_i - y_i)z_j + (z_j - y_j)y_i)$$

The terms $\varphi(|\hat{y}_i - z_i|) - \varphi(|\hat{y}_i - 1_{\hat{y}_i > 0.5}|)$ are non-negative since φ is increasing. The terms $\mu_{i,j}((z_i - y_i)z_j + (z_j - y_j)y_i)$ are also non-negative because $l(y) \leq l(z)$ implies that $\forall i \in [\![1;c]\!]$, $y_i \leq z_i$. $\square$

This monotonicity implies in $\mathcal{T}$ higher values of m for the descendants than for the father: then, excluding a node y following the criterion $m(y) > q$ allows to exclude the whole descendance of y.

3.3 A First Candidate Generation Algorithm

In this section, we present Algorithm 1, Efficient Conformal Prediction (ECP), which generates a reasonable amount of candidates for the prediction set through a clever node exploration of the tree $\mathcal{T}$. The cornerstone results from:

Proposition 7. *If $y \in \{0,1\}^c$ and $m(y) > q$, then*

$$\forall z \in \{0,1\}^c, \quad z \geq y \implies z \notin C_{\mu,q}(\hat{y})$$

Proof. This follows directly from: 1) m is a lower bound of s, 2) the elements of $C_{\mu,q}(\hat{y})$ satisfy $s(y) \leq q$, 3) m is an increasing function. □

Definition 5. *We denote by $M(r)$, the descendance of r in the tree, i.e.*

$$M(r) = \{y \in \{0,1\}^c | r \leq y\} \tag{12}$$

Remark 3. If $m(y) > q$, then neither y nor elements of $M(y)$ are in $C_{\mu,q}(\hat{y})$.

ECP performs a tree traversal, pruning great parts as it progresses. Importantly, constructing the entire tree is unnecessary (generating all the 2^c nodes is impractical for large c values). Instead, only the direct children of the current node are generated, when beneficial, and explored recursively. Using Proposition 7, ECP efficiently avoids generating many unnecessary nodes.

Algorithm 1. Efficient Conformal Prediction (ECP)

Input: $r, \hat{y}, \mu, q$
Output: $C_{\mu,q}(\hat{y}) \cap M(r)$
1: $C \leftarrow \emptyset$
2: $E \leftarrow \{r\}$ ▷ Nodes to explore
3: **while** $E \neq \emptyset$ **do**
4:     Let $p \in E$
5:     $E \leftarrow E - \{p\}$
6:     **if** $m(p) \leq q$ **then**
7:         Generate F, set of children of p
8:         $E \leftarrow E \cup F$
9:         **if** $s_\mu(\hat{y}, p) \leq q$ **then** $C \leftarrow C \cup \{p\}$
10: **return** C

ECP algorithm iteratively performs pruning at line 6 and generates children at line 7

Algorithm 1 returns $C_{\mu,q}(\hat{y}) \cap M(r)$, given r as input, that is to mean all the elements of $C_{\mu,q}(\hat{y})$ in the descendance of a given node r.

Remark 4. $M((0)_{1 \leq i \leq c}) = \{0,1\}^c$, which implies the Proposition 8.

Proposition 8. *Algorithm 1, applied with $r = 0$ solves the problem of constructing $C_{\mu,q}(\hat{y})$.*

ECP hence provides a first solution to our problem.

3.4 CAECP: An Optimized ECP Based on Children Anticipation

In Algorithm 1, a node is generated if its parent p has been generated and satisfies $m(p) \leq q$. Here we propose an optimization of ECP, which consists in adding a supplementary condition on p to generate its children. In this section, we introduce Algorithm 2, Children-Anticipating Efficient Conformal Prediction (CAECP), which may stop exploring a branch one step earlier than ECP.

Definition 6. *Assume that $l(p) \neq c$, meaning p has a non empty set of children, then we define $Q(p)$ as:*

$$Q(p) = \left(\sum_{i=1}^{l(p)} \varphi(|\hat{y}_i - p_i|)\right) + \varphi(|\hat{y}_{l(p)+1} - 1|) + \sum_{i=l(p)+2}^{c} \varphi(|\hat{y}_i - 1_{\hat{y}_i > 0.5}|)$$
$$+ \sum_{1 \leq i \leq j \leq c} \mu_{i,j} p_i p_j$$

Proposition 9. *If y is a direct child of p, then $m(y) \geq Q(p)$.*

Corollary 1. $\forall\, p \in \{0,1\}^c : l(p) \neq c, \quad Q(p) > q \implies (\forall\, y > p,\ y \notin C_{\mu,q}(\hat{y}))$

Proof. This follows from: if $y > p$, then there exists a direct child y' of p such that $y \geq y'$. □

The correctness of CAECP is a direct consequence of Corollary 1. Next proposition shows that the condition $Q(p) \leq q$ is stronger than $m(p) \leq q$, which proves that CAECP is an optimization of ECP, generating less useless vectors.

Algorithm 2. Children-Anticipating Efficient Conformal Prediction (CAECP)

Input: root r, $\hat{y}$, μ, q
Output: $C_{\mu,q}(\hat{y}) \cap M(r)$
1: $C \leftarrow \emptyset$
2: $E \leftarrow \{r\}$ ▷ Nodes to explore
3: **while** $E \neq \emptyset$ **do**
4:    Let $p \in E$
5:    $E \leftarrow E - \{p\}$
6:    **if** $s_\mu(\hat{y}, p) \leq q$ **then** $C \leftarrow C \cup \{p\}$
7:    **if** $l(p) \neq c$ **then**
8:      **if** $Q(p) \leq q$ **then** ▷ Stronger condition than $m(p) \leq q$
9:        Generate F, set of children of p
10:        $E \leftarrow E \cup F$
11: **return** C

CAECP behaves as ECP, with a stronger condition for children generation (line 8)

Proposition 10. *The condition $Q(p) \leq q$ is stronger than $m(p) \leq q$ since:*

$$\forall\, p \in \{0,1\}^c \text{ such that } l(p) \neq c, \quad m(p) \leq Q(p)$$

Remark 5. The proof of this result (cf. appendix) shows that the introduction of $Q(p)$ is useful only for those p that satisfy $l(p) \geq l_0$. Otherwise, $Q(p) = m(p)$.

ECP is conceptually simpler and is sufficient in most cases in practice. Since CAECP is an optimization of ECP, and takes the same input and returns the same output, we only mention CAECP until the end of the paper.

4 Prefix-Based ECP (PBECP): An Optimized Algorithm Based on Multi-root Candidate Generation

Given any root vector r, CAECP returns $C_{\mu,q}(\hat{y}) \cap M(r)$. To construct $C_{\mu,q}(\hat{y})$ one just needs to apply CAECP with $r = 0$. Here we expose a new algorithm which is useful when the parameters $(\mu_{i,j})_{1 \leq i \leq j \leq c}$ have many zero values.

Preliminary Example. Let $c = 100$ and $l_0 = 15$ (ie. $\forall i \in [\![1;15]\!]$, $\hat{y}_i > 0.5$ since the $(\hat{y}_i)_i$ are in decreasing order). In that case, the binary vectors composing $C_{\mu,q}(\hat{y})$ are likely to contain many 1 coordinates (approximately 15, for small q). According to Proposition 3, those vectors are at depth around 15 in $\mathcal{T}$. Let $y \in C_{\mu,q}(\hat{y})$, if we apply directly CAECP with root $r=(0)$, all vectors on the path between (0) and y in $\mathcal{T}$ are generated.

We understand on this example that we could have an optimized version if instead of executing CAECP with root $r = (0)$, we execute CAECP with more 1-containing roots such as $(1,1,1,1,1,0,...,0)$. The difficulty is to ensure that we do not forget any of the smaller binary vectors. In this section, to select roots without exploring all of them, we use a differently built tree with another goal.

4.1 Definitions

Definition 7. *Assuming that* $\{k \in [\![1;l_0]\!] | \sum_{1 \leq i \leq j \leq k} \mu_{i,j} = 0\} \neq \emptyset$, *we define*

$$l_1 := max\{k \in [\![1;l_0]\!] | \sum_{1 \leq i \leq j \leq k} \mu_{i,j} = 0\} \quad (13)$$

This is the maximum integer l_1 such that $y := (1_{i \leq l_1})_{i \leq c}$ has no penalization $\sum_{1 \leq i \leq j \leq k} \mu_{i,j} y_i y_j$. We suppose from now on that $l_1 \geq 2$.

Definition 8. *The set of l_1-prefixes is defined as*

$$Pref_{l_1} := \{y \in \{0,1\}^c | (y_i)_{i > l_1} = (0)\} \subset \{0,1\}^c \quad (14)$$

Definition 9. *We define the l_1-completion of a prefix $p \in Pref_{l_1}$ as:*

$$Compl_{l_1}(p) := \{z \in \{0,1\}^c | (z_i)_{i \leq l_1} = (p_i)_{i \leq l_1}\} \subset \{0,1\}^c \quad (15)$$

Remark 6. For a prefix $p \in Pref_{l_1}$, $Compl_{l_1}(p) \subset M(p)$ but we do not have mutual inclusion, because we do not necessarily have $l_1 = l(p)$.

Remark 7. $\bigcup_{p \in Pref_{l_1}} Compl_{l_1}(p) = \{0,1\}^c$ and the union is disjoint.

4.2 Construction of a Tree on $Pref_{l_1}$

We start by defining a tree on $Pref_{l_1}$, to establish a prefix exploration order.

Definition 10. *We define the tree $\mathcal{T}_{pref}$ rooted on $r = (1_{i \leq l_1})_{i \leq c}$: the only child of r is $(1_{i \leq l_1 - 1})_{i \leq c}$ and given a node $p \neq r$ of $\mathcal{T}_{pref}$, let's denote by i_{first0} the smallest index of a zero coordinate of $(p_i)_{i \leq l_1}$.*

1. *If $i_{first0} > 1$ then its left child $p^{(left)}$ is obtained from p by exchanging $p_{i_{first0}}$ and $p_{i_{first0}-1}$ and the right child $p^{(right)}$, by imposing $p^{(right)}_{i_{first0}-1} = 0$.*
2. *If $i_{first0} = 1$ (that is to mean p starts by a 0), then p has no child.*

Figure 2 shows $\mathcal{T}_{pref}$ in the case $c = 6$ and $l_1 = 4$.

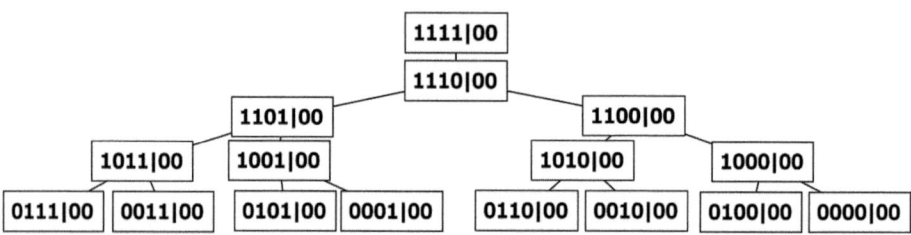

Fig. 2. $\mathcal{T}_{pref}$ for $c = 6$ and $l_1 = 4$. The bar — delimits pre-l_1 from post-l_1 coordinates

Proposition 11. *The set of nodes of $\mathcal{T}_{pref}$ is the whole set $Pref_{l_1}$.*

Hence we do not forget any element of $Pref_{l_1}$ by exploring $\mathcal{T}_{pref}$.

Proposition 12. *$\mathcal{T}_{pref}$ naturally defines a partial order relation $\leq_{pre}$ on its nodes $Pref_{l_1}$ ($p_1 \leq_{pre} p_2 \iff p_1$ is an ascendant of p_2), and the quantity:*

$$g(p) = \sum_{i=1}^{l_1} \varphi(|\hat{y}_i - p_i|) + \sum_{i=l_1+1}^{c} \varphi(|\hat{y}_i - 1_{\hat{y}_i > 0.5}|) \tag{16}$$

is an increasing function of p for $\leq_{pre}$ and is a lower bound of s. In addition, for any node p having two children, $g(p^{(left)}) \leq g(p^{(right)})$.

Proof. The lower bound property and $\leq_{pre}$ defining a partial order are clear. The monotonicity of g for $\leq_{pre}$, and the comparison between both children follow from $l_1 \leq l_0$ and the decreasing order assumption of $\hat{y}_i$. □

Definition 11. *We define the set of selected prefixes $SelPref_{l_1}$ as:*

$$SelPref_{l_1} := \{p \in Pref_{l_1} | g(p) \leq q\} \tag{17}$$

Remark 8. The non-conformity score s also increases on this tree, but to uphold Proposition 13, s cannot replace g to construct $SelPref_{l_1}$, unless l_1 is maximal (cf. Proposition 15). $SelPref_{l_1}$ is smaller than $Pref_{l_1}$: this filtering narrows down the subparts of $\mathcal{T}$ on which to apply CAECP. Proposition 13 guarantees that this approach suffices to fully construct $C_{\mu,q}(\hat{y})$.

We use Proposition 12 to design Algorithm 3: "Efficient Prefix Selection" (EPS). EPS returns $SelPref_{l_1}$ efficiently, following the same pruning strategy than the ECP algorithm, replacing the function m by the function g. Furthermore, we use the supplementary optimization of generating $p^{(right)}$ only if $g(p^{(left)}) \leq q$.

Algorithm 3. Efficient Prefix Selection (EPS)

Input: $\hat{y}, \mu, q$
Output: $SelPref_{l_1}$
1: Compute l_1 (function of $\hat{y}$ and μ)
2: $r = (1_{i \leq l_1})_{i \leq c}$
3: $P \leftarrow \emptyset$
4: $E \leftarrow \emptyset$ ▷ Nodes that are already in P and whose children are to be explored
5: **if** $g(r) \leq q$ **then** $E \leftarrow \{r\}, P \leftarrow \{r\}$
6: **while** $E \neq \emptyset$ **do**
7:     Let $p \in E$
8:     $E \leftarrow E - \{p\}$
9:     **if** p is the root node and is not a leaf **then**
10:         Generate p', the only child of p in $\mathcal{T}_{pref}$
11:         **if** $g(p') \leq q$ **then** $E \leftarrow E \cup \{p'\}, P \leftarrow P \cup \{p'\}$
12:     **if** p is not the root node and is not a leaf **then**
13:         Generate $p^{(left)}$
14:         **if** $g(p^{(left)}) \leq q$ **then**
15:             $E \leftarrow E \cup \{p^{(left)}\}, P \leftarrow P \cup \{p^{(left)}\}$
16:         Generate $p^{(right)}$
17:         **if** $g(p^{(right)}) \leq q$ **then** $E \leftarrow E \cup \{p^{(right)}\}, P \leftarrow P \cup \{p^{(right)}\}$
18: **return** P

EPS pre-selects relevant prefixes for CAECP algorithm. Like ECP, EPS applies a pruning framework but limited to prefixes, with another increasing lower bound g and on another tree $\mathcal{T}_{pref}$. In addition, we first compute g on the left child before computing g on the right one.

4.3 PBECP Algorithm

In this section, we present the Prefix-Based Efficient Conformal Prediction algorithm (PBECP), using EPS as an upstream component.

Definition 12. *We define the first-stage-l_1-completion of a prefix $p \in Pref_{l_1}$:*

$$FSC_{l_1}(p) := \{z \in \{0,1\}^c | (z_i)_{i \leq l_1} = (p_i)_{i \leq l_1} \text{ and } \exists! j > l_1, \ z_j = 1\} \quad (18)$$

We use this concept in Proposition 13 which states that the computation of $C_{\mu,q}(\hat{y})$ reduces to multiple calls of CAECP.

Proposition 13. *The set $C_{\mu,q}(\hat{y})$ is decomposable into a **disjoint union** of simpler sets:*

$$C_{\mu,q}(\hat{y}) = \bigcup_{p \in SelPref_{l_1}} \left((C_{\mu,q}(\hat{y}) \cap \{p\}) \cup \bigcup_{p' \in FSC_{l_1}(p)} C_{\mu,q}(\hat{y}) \cap M(p') \right)$$

The terms $C_{\mu,q}(\hat{y}) \cap M(p')$ of Proposition 13 can be computed by calling CAECP with $r = p'$, and since the unions are all disjoint, PBECP does not explore the same parts of $\mathcal{T}$ twice. We always have $SelPref_{l_1} \subset Pref_{l_1}$, and our goal is for $SelPref_{l_1}$ to be a very smaller subset. This would ensure that PBECP explores only a fraction of the tree $\mathcal{T}$ compared to CAECP, which is the cornerstone of its efficiency.

The Prefix-Based Efficient Conformal Prediction Algorithm (PBECP). Using Proposition 13, we propose Algorithm 4 (PBECP), which first performs prefix selection and then calls CAECP on judiciously chosen roots.

Algorithm 4. Prefix-Based Efficient Conformal Prediction (PBECP)

Input: $\hat{y}, \mu, q$
Output: $C_{\mu,q}(\hat{y})$
1: Compute l_1 (function of $\hat{y}$ and μ)
2: Execute EPS: $SelPref_{l_1} = EPS(l_1, \hat{y}, \mu, q)$
3: $SP \leftarrow SelPref_{l_1}$
4: $C \leftarrow \emptyset$
5: **while** $SP \neq \emptyset$ **do**
6:     Let $p \in SP$
7:     $SP \leftarrow SP - \{p\}$
8:     **if** $s_\mu(\hat{y}, p) \leq q$ **then** $C \leftarrow C \cup \{p\}$
9:     **for** $p' \in FSC_{l_1}(p)$ **do**
10:        $C \leftarrow C \cup CAECP(r = p')$ ▷ Calls of CAECP with different roots
11: **return** C

PBECP is an alternative to directly calling CAECP(r=0), it rather calls CAECP(r) for multiple judiciously chosen r. At line 10, we call CAECP(r) for r varying in the first-stage completions of the elements of SP.

Commentary on the Optimization. For computational efficiency, we must ensure that the multiple calls of CAECP($r = p'$) in Algorithm 4 do not lead to redundant computations.

Proposition 14. *In PBECP, we do not explore the same node of $\mathcal{T}$ twice. More precisely, for two different p'_1 and p'_2 appearing at line 10 of Algorithm 4 - corresponding to different stages of the execution- the respective calls $CAECP(r=p'_1)$ and $CAECP(r=p'_2)$ explore disjoint sets of vectors.*

In the frequent case where $l_1 = l_0$, the following proposition explains the optimality of lower bound functions used in PBECP in this case.

Proposition 15. *If l_1 is maximal (i.e. $l_1 = l_0$), then:*

1. *During the execution of EPS at line 2 of Algorithm 4, the lower bound g of the non-conformity score s is always equal to s.*
2. *During the execution of $CAECP(r = p')$ at line 10 of Algorithm 4, the lower bound m of the non-conformity score s is always equal to s.*

Optimal Case. If $l_1 = l_0$, then PBECP operates as if traversing a virtual tree $\mathcal{T}_{virtual}$ defined over all binary vectors. The non-conformity score is an increasing function on that tree and is directly used for the pruning of the descendants. $\mathcal{T}_{virtual}$ is obtained from $\mathcal{T}_{pref}$ with the following steps:

1. Start with $\mathcal{T}_{pref}$.
2. For each node p of $\mathcal{T}_{pref}$, let F be its set of children in $\mathcal{T}_{pref}$, then $F \leftarrow F \cup FSC_{l_1}(p)$. We obtain the tree $\mathcal{T}'$.
3. For each leaf y of $\mathcal{T}'$ element of a certain $FSC_{l_1}(p)$, we expand it into the subtree of $\mathcal{T}$ rooted at this y.
4. **We obtain a tree on the whole set $\{0,1\}^c$ on which the non-conformity score is increasing**.

This shows the optimality of PBECP in practical cases where l_1 is maximal, which appears when μ is defined as in [5] and where the labels predicted by $(1_{\hat{y}_i > 0.5})_i$ have been seen simultaneously pairwise in the training dataset (which is very common).

For computational complexity computation, we introduce the following:

Definition 13. *For a given algorithm A, we denote by $\mathcal{G}(A)$ the following set:*

$$\mathcal{G}(A) = \{y \in \{0,1\}^c |\ y \text{ is generated during execution of } A\}$$

Remark 9. The correctness of Algorithms 2, 3, and 4 implies that:

$$C_{\mu,q}(\hat{y}) \subset \mathcal{G}(CAECP(r=0)),\ SelPref_{l_1} \subset \mathcal{G}(EPS),\ C_{\mu,q}(\hat{y}) \subset \mathcal{G}(PBECP)$$

Remark 10. Card$(\mathcal{G}(A))$ is a measure of the complexity of algorithm A, and we aim to minimize this value. It is worth noting that, in any case, the naive method yields a complexity of Card$(\mathcal{G}(naive)) = 2^c$.

During execution, many binary vectors are generated, but they are not all kept in the result $C_{\mu,q}(\hat{y})$. Note that since A is an algorithm which computes $C_{\mu,q}(\hat{y})$, we at least generate Card$(C_{\mu,q}(\hat{y}))$ vectors: hence Card$(C_{\mu,q}(\hat{y})) \leq$ Card$(\mathcal{G}(A))$. So Card$(\mathcal{G}(A))$ strongly depends on Card$(C_{\mu,q}(\hat{y}))$. To better assess algorithmic efficiency, it is natural to consider not just the total number of generated vectors, but the proportion of them that are actually useful. This motivates Definition 14, introducing an inverse measure of complexity, called *usefulness ratio*, which we aim to maximize.

Definition 14. *The usefulness ratio for algorithm A executed on $(\hat{y}, q)$ inputs, is defined as:*
$$R(A, \hat{y}, q) = \frac{\text{Card}(C_{\mu,q}(\hat{y}))}{\text{Card}(\mathcal{G}(A(\hat{y}, q)))}$$

Remark 11. A usefulness ratio of 0.1 means that 10% of the generated vectors are useful, and such a value would typically indicate a high level of efficiency, especially when compared to the naive algorithm. Indeed, the usefulness ratio of the naive algorithm which generates all the 2^c vectors is $\frac{\text{Card}(C_{\mu,q}(\hat{y}))}{2^c} \sim \frac{1}{2^c}$ when $\text{Card}(C_{\mu,q}(\hat{y}))$ is low. For instance, for $c = 100$, and $\text{Card}(C_{\mu,q}(\hat{y})) = 1$ we have $R(\text{naive}, \hat{y}, q) \sim 10^{-30}$, and only a proportion of about 10^{-30} of the generated vectors is useful.

The following proposition states that in the optimal case where $l_1 = l_0$, the computational complexity of PBECP grows only linearly with c, in contrast to the exponential complexity of the naive approach.

Proposition 16. *If μ and $\hat{y}$ are such that l_1 is maximal (i.e. $l_1 = l_0$), then we can ensure that we do not generate too many vectors:*
$$\text{Card}(\mathcal{G}(PBECP)) \leq (c - l_0 + 3) \times \text{Card}(C_{\mu,q}(\hat{y})) + 1$$

Stated differently, if $C_{\mu,q}(\hat{y}) \neq \emptyset$, we give a lower bound of the usefulness ratio:
$$\forall\, q > 0, \quad \frac{1}{c - l_0 + 3 + \frac{1}{\text{Card}(C_{\mu,q}(\hat{y}))}} \leq R(PBECP, \hat{y}, q)$$

Remark 12. Hence, since $\text{Card}(C_{\mu,q}(\hat{y})) \geq 1$, we always have
$$R(\text{naive}, \hat{y}, q) \sim \frac{1}{2^c} \ll \frac{1}{(c - l_0 + 4)} \leq R(PBECP, \hat{y}, q) \tag{19}$$

5 Experiments

The primary goal of this article is to develop an algorithm capable of efficiently computing the set $C_{\mu,q}(\hat{y})$, given a specific quantile q and an operational vector $\hat{y}$. In this section, we evaluate whether the proposed algorithms can compute prediction sets within reasonable time frames, even as the number of labels increases. Additionally, we compare the computational complexities of these algorithms as a supplementary analysis.

To assess performance, we use the usefulness ratio as the main evaluation metric across various quantile values ($q \in [q_{min}, q_{max}]$), noting that a higher usefulness ratio indicates greater algorithmic efficiency. To conduct these experiments, we try to compute the set $C_{\mu,q}(\hat{y})$ for different values of $(\mu_{i,j})_{1 \leq i \leq j \leq c}$ (one for each dataset), for q varying in a range $[q_{min}, q_{max}]$ and for a fixed challenging vector $\hat{y}$ (one per dataset). To illustrate our algorithms in practical contexts, we select two real datasets: **arxiv_category** [7], **ASRS** [1], and one **dummy** dataset.

arxiv_category is composed of 203,961 titles and abstracts categorized into 130 different classes. We used 163,168 samples to construct μ.

ASRS (Aviation Safety Reporting System) database stands out as the most renowned incident reporting dataset. We used 96,986 incident reports of US flights from 2000 to 2022 categorized into 63 different classes to construct μ.

We construct a **dummy dataset** with a large number of classes to explore a more complicated case: $c = 150$. It contains $N = 65$ random training samples (elements of $\{0,1\}^c$) with a maximum of 28 simultaneously observed labels.

For all the experiments, we choose q_{min} so that $\text{Card}(C_{\mu,q_{min}}(\hat{y})) = 1$ and q_{max} so that $\text{Card}(C_{\mu,q_{max}}(\hat{y}))$ is very high and beyond any reasonably exploitable prediction set's cardinality. Being able to construct very big and concretely unexploitable prediction sets (corresponding to high q) indicates we are able to construct any exploitable prediction set (for lower q). We used $\varphi = (.)^2$ and constructed $(\mu_{i,j})_{i,j}$ following the methodology described in Preliminaries (see Appendix for visualization). We denote by $density(\mu)$ the proportion of ones in $(\mu_{i,j})_{1 \leq i \leq j \leq c}$ and gives an indication of $\text{Card}(C_{\mu,q}(\hat{y}))$.

Table 1 lists important properties of each experiment. One $\hat{y}$ is chosen so that its l_0 is maximal while its L^2-closest binary vector $(1_{\hat{y}_i > 0.5})_i$ is an element of dataset (to ensure that $l_1 = l_0$). This approach ensures that we focus on constructing the prediction set for a particularly challenging vector, one with numerous 1 entries (relatively deep in the tree $\mathcal{T}$). By doing so, we can restrict our experiments to a single $\hat{y}$ per dataset. Successfully handling such a difficult case gives us confidence that the algorithm will also be effective for other, less complex vectors. Note that having μ and $\hat{y}$ such that $l_1 = l_0$ is very frequent since in most cases we want to predict labels that already appeared pairwise simultaneously.

Table 1. Properties of Datasets and Experiments

	#classes c	$l_0 = \|\|(1_{\hat{y}_i > 0.5})_i\|\|_1$	$density(\mu)$	$[q_{min}, q_{max}]$	$\#C_{\mu,q_{max}}(\hat{y})$
dummy	150	28	51%	[0.4, 3.6]	4 320
arxiv_category	130	4	96%	[0.4, 7]	16 712
ASRS	63	13	37%	[0.4, 4]	39 254

Figure 3 shows our ability to construct the prediction sets across all experiments. The usefulness ratios indicate that PBECP outperforms CAECP in this context, and that CAECP remains superior to ECP as theoretically proven. Higher usefulness ratios for PBECP means that it generates less superfluous vectors, highlighting its efficiency, particularly when l_1 is maximal, as described in Proposition 15. The right-hand side of Fig. 3 presents the number of vectors generated by each algorithm (on a logarithmic scale), alongside the cardinal of the conformal prediction set. We observe that the algorithms do not generate

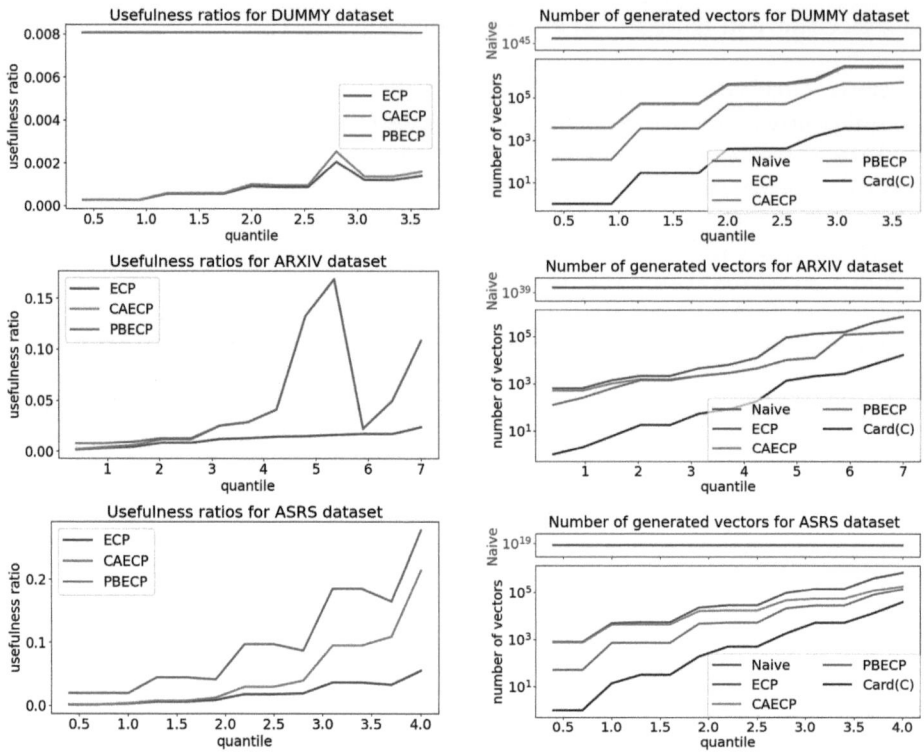

Fig. 3. Evolution of $R(A, \hat{y}, q)$ (left) and evolution of $\text{Card}(\mathcal{G}(A(\hat{y}, q)))$ and $\text{Card}\,(C_{\mu,q}(\hat{y}))$ (right) as functions of q.

too much superfluous vectors since their values of $\text{Card}(\mathcal{G}(A(\hat{y}, q)))$ are not too far from $\text{Card}\,(C_{\mu,q}(\hat{y}))$ (especially when compared with the naive algorithm).

Table 2 provides computation times and the associated cardinalities of the prediction sets for different values of q. While the specific q values are not listed –since the main interest lies in the actual cardinalities $\text{Card}\,(C_{\mu,q}(\hat{y}))$– the results offer practical insight into the scaling behavior. All measurements were obtained using a single core of an AMD EPYC 9534 with 16 GB of RAM. Reported computation times are averaged over 10 runs to account for potential variability. The higher cardinalities already represent quite large prediction sets in practice, suggesting that in typical operational contexts, the computation time would likely be shorter. Further evaluation in concrete applications would be necessary to confirm this hypothesis.

In another experiment not related here, we created a new dummy dataset with $c = 1000$. It is remarkable that the method remains tractable, producing sets of a few dozen elements within a few seconds. Nevertheless, practical limitations begin to emerge for higher dimensions: memory usage and computational demands for generating high-dimensional vectors become significant, rendering the approach infeasible for even larger problems.

Table 2. Computation times (in seconds) for constructing $\text{Card}(C_{\mu,q}(\hat{y}))$ with PBECP across datasets (left to right) and q values (top to bottom).

$\text{Card}(C_{\mu,q}(\hat{y}))$	$t(s)$	$\text{Card}(C_{\mu,q}(\hat{y}))$	$t(s)$	$\text{Card}(C_{\mu,q}(\hat{y}))$	$t(s)$
1	0.008	1	0.013	1	0.019
5	0.020	70	0.049	315	0.089
29	0.093	388	0.099	501	0.096
407	0.807	2280	0.482	851	0.256
1562	3.44	7358	2.21	4903	0.519
3683	7.45	16748	2.55	21254	1.945
Dummy		**Arxiv**		**ASRS**	

In operational settings, interpreting the prediction set can be challenging, as it consists of multiple combinations of labels rather than a single outcome. Nevertheless, it offers valuable insight by revealing the full range of plausible scenarios. Unlike a simple list of possible labels, the prediction set captures not only which labels may be present, but also how they can realistically co-occur, providing a more nuanced understanding of potential outcomes.

6 Conclusion

In this study, we propose an efficient computation of prediction sets for inductive conformal prediction on multi-label classification using the Label-Powerset approach with a generic non-conformity score accounting for label interactions.

To address the computational bottlenecks typically associated with the label-powerset strategy for prediction set generation, we developed ECP: a pruning algorithm based on a tailored exploration tree combined with a lower bound function of the non-conformity score.

We further introduced CAECP, an optimization of ECP that imposes an additional condition for child generation during tree exploration. Building on this, we presented PBECP, an even more efficient algorithm, which initiates with a careful selection of roots for CAECP and combines multiple but lighter calls to CAECP. The experiments demonstrated that we are able to compute $\text{Card}(C_{\mu,q}(\hat{y}))$ for problems involving a large number of labels.

However, our work is limited to the scope of inductive conformal prediction and thus inherits its assumptions and constraints. Additionally, while the label-powerset approach enables flexible modeling of label interactions, the sets of label vectors it produces may lack interpretability, which highlights the potential benefit of employing complementary methods to analyze or better understand them.

Acknowledgments. Thanks to Dong Quan Vu (Safran Tech, Rue des Jeunes Bois, Châteaufort, 78114 Magny-Les-Hameaux) for providing the preprocessed ASRS data.

Disclosure of Interests. The authors have no competing interests to declare that are relevant to the content of this article.

References

1. Billings, C.E., Reynard, W.D.: Human factors in aircraft incidents: results of a 7-year study. Aviat. Space Environ. Med. **55**(10), 960–965 (1984)
2. Lambrou, A., Papadopoulos, H.: Binary relevance multi-label conformal predictor. In: Conformal and Probabilistic Prediction with Applications: 5th International Symposium (COPA), Madrid, Spain, 20–22 April 2016, pp. 90–104. Springer (2016)
3. Maltoudoglou, L., Paisios, A., Lenc, L., Martínek, J., Král, P., Papadopoulos, H.: Well-calibrated confidence measures for multi-label text classification with a large number of labels. Pattern Recogn. **122**, 108271 (2022)
4. Paisios, A., Lenc, L., Martínek, J., Král, P., Papadopoulos, H.: A deep neural network conformal predictor for multi-label text classification. In: Proceedings of the 8th Symposium on Conformal and Probabilistic Prediction and Applications, pp. 228–245. PMLR (2019)
5. Papadopoulos, H.: A cross-conformal predictor for multi-label classification. In: 10th IFIP International Conference on Artificial Intelligence Applications and Innovations (AIAI), Rhodes, Greece, pp. 241–250 (2014)
6. Papadopoulos, H., Proedrou, K., Vovk, V., Gammerman, A.: Inductive confidence machines for regression. In: 13th European conference on machine learning (ECML), Helsinki, Finland, pp. 345–356. Springer (2002)
7. Schopf, T., Blatzheim, A., Machner, N., Matthes, F.: Efficient few-shot learning for multi-label classification of scientific documents with many classes. In: Proceedings of the 7th International Conference on Natural Language and Speech Processing (ICNLSP), pp. 186–198. Association for Computational Linguistics, Trento (2024)
8. Tyagi, C., Guo, W.: Multi-label classification under uncertainty: a tree-based conformal prediction approach. In: Conformal and Probabilistic Prediction with Applications, pp. 488–512. PMLR (2023)
9. Vovk, V., Gammerman, A., Shafer, G.: Algorithmic Learning in a Random World. Springer, Heidelberg (2005)

Understanding the Trade-Offs in Accuracy and Uncertainty Quantification: Architecture and Inference Choices in Bayesian Neural Networks

Alisa Sheinkman[(✉)] and Sara Wade

School of Mathematics and Maxwell Institute for Mathematical Sciences, University of Edinburgh, Edinburgh, UK
a.sheinkman@sms.ed.ac.uk, sara.wade@ed.ac.uk

Abstract. As modern neural networks get more complex, specifying a model with high predictive performance and sound uncertainty quantification becomes a more challenging task. Despite some promising theoretical results on the true posterior predictive distribution of Bayesian neural networks, the properties of even the most commonly used posterior approximations are often questioned. Computational burdens and intractable posteriors expose miscalibrated Bayesian neural networks to poor accuracy and unreliable uncertainty estimates. Approximate Bayesian inference aims to replace unknown and intractable posterior distributions with some simpler but feasible distributions. The dimensions of modern deep models, coupled with the lack of identifiability, make Markov chain Monte Carlo (MCMC) tremendously expensive and unable to fully explore the multimodal posterior. On the other hand, variational inference benefits from improved computational complexity but lacks the asymptotical guarantees of sampling-based inference and tends to concentrate around a single mode. The performance of both approaches heavily depends on architectural choices; this paper aims to shed some light on this, by considering the computational costs, accuracy and uncertainty quantification in different scenarios including large width and out-of-sample data. To improve posterior exploration, different model averaging and ensembling techniques are studied, along with their benefits on predictive performance. In our experiments, variational inference overall provided better uncertainty quantification than MCMC; further, stacking and ensembles of variational approximations provided comparable accuracy to MCMC at a much-reduced cost.

Keywords: Approximate Bayesian Inference · Bayesian Deep Learning · Ensembles · Out-of-Distribution · Uncertainty Quantification

---

Supplementary Information The online version contains supplementary material available at https://doi.org/10.1007/978-3-032-06109-6_8.

© The Author(s), under exclusive license to Springer Nature Switzerland AG 2026
R. P. Ribeiro et al. (Eds.): ECML PKDD 2025, LNAI 16019, pp. 129–146, 2026.
https://doi.org/10.1007/978-3-032-06109-6_8

1 Introduction

Despite the tremendous success of deep learning in areas such as natural language processing [45] and computer vision [8,27], often there is no clear understanding of why a particular model performs well [44,55]. Even though the universal approximation theorem guarantees that a wide enough feed-forward neural network with a single hidden layer can express any smooth function [24], in practice, constructing a model which is not only expressive but generalizes well is challenging. In contrast, the so-called no free lunch theorem [51] dictates that there is no panacea to solve every problem, and one should be careful when designing a model appropriate to the task. Many modern machine learning models are overparametrized and prone to overfitting, especially given the limited size of the dataset. Complex problems demand exploring bigger model spaces, and there is a danger of choosing an excessively over-parametrized model, which is going to overfit and have a high variance. Additionally, conventional deep models do not offer human-understandable explanations and lack interpretability [31]. By default, classical neural networks do not address the uncertainty associated with their parameters and whilst there exist proposals enabling neural networks (NNs) to provide some uncertainty estimates, they are often miscalibrated [17]. As a result, these models are typically overconfident, provide a low level of uncertainty even when data variations occur [38], and are easily fooled and are susceptible to adversarial attacks [35,44]. At the same time, reliable uncertainty quantification (UQ) is crucial for any decision-making process, and it is not enough to obtain a point estimate of the prediction.

The key distinguishing property of the Bayesian framework is that it incorporates domain expertise and deals with uncertainty quantification in a principled way: by marginalizing with respect to the posterior distribution of parameters. As a result, Bayesian models are more resistant to distribution shifts and can improve the accuracy and calibration of classical deep models [50]. Nevertheless, the reliability of uncertainty estimates and the gap between within-the-sample and out-of-sample performance still require improvement [11]. The posterior distributions arising in Bayesian neural networks (BNNs) are analytically unavailable and highly multimodal, and the core challenge lies in estimating the posterior [39]. One should not only find a model that matches the task but, as importantly, achieve the alignment between the model and the applied inference algorithm [15]; and the most theoretically grounded sampling methods and approximation techniques are limited by the computing budget, size of the dataset, and sheer number of parameters. We list several characteristics of classical and Bayesian neural networks in the Table 1.

Outline. In this work, we consider some of the challenges and nuances of Bayesian neural networks and evaluate the performance with different architectures and for different posterior inference algorithm choices. Specifically, we study the sensitivity of BNNs to the choice of width in Sect. 2.3, depth in Sect. 2.4, and investigate the performance of BNNs under the distribution shift in Sect. 2.5. Across all the experiments in Sect. 2, we observe that for different inference algorithms, one model can provide strikingly diverse performances. The

Table 1. Some of the challenges and properties of classical and Bayesian neural networks

Property	Classical NN	Bayesian NN
Interpretability	poor	improved ✓
Robustness to OOD	poor	improved ✓
Adversarial attacks	sensitive	less sensitive ✓
Overconfidence	typical	less typical ✓
Training outcome	point estimate	posterior distribution $\mathbb{P}$
Incorporate prior	no	yes
Require initialization	yes	yes

challenge of comparative model assessment is addressed in Sect. 3.1, where we introduce the estimated pointwise loglikelihood as a measure of model utility. While given some set of models, the Bayesian approach has the potential to deal with the model choice by comparing posterior model probabilities, such comparison tends to favour one candidate disproportionally strongly [36]. Thus, the classical Bayesian model averaging (BMA) based on model probabilities [22] is only optimal if the true model is among the comparison set. In response to the limitations of BMA, in Sects. 3.2 and 3.3 we consider ensembling, stacking and pseudo-BMA [54].

2 Empirical Study of Limiting Scenarios

2.1 Architecture Components

Whilst the dimensions of the input and the output are determined by the dimensionality of the data set, the dimension of the weight space plays an essential part in specifying neural networks and can be tuned to improve prediction performance. In the case of feed-forward neural networks, this amounts to finding optimal depth and width. While the universal approximation theorem advocates for single-layer neural networks [24], variants of the universal approximation theorem exist for deeper networks [19,32]. Further, deep neural networks gained popularity due to their expressiveness and tremendous success in real-world applications, allowed by the increase in available computing power [5]. At the same time, the more parameters one has, the more nuanced the choice of the model becomes. No matter what the prediction task is, overly complex models suffer from the curse of dimensionality which causes not only poor performance but also computational problems.

On a slightly different line, we recall the seminal result first obtained for neural networks with one hidden layer [34] and then extended to arbitrary depth [33] which states that under general conditions, as the width of a BNN tends to infinity, the distribution of the network's output induced by the prior converges to a Gaussian process (GP) with a neural network kernel, also known as the

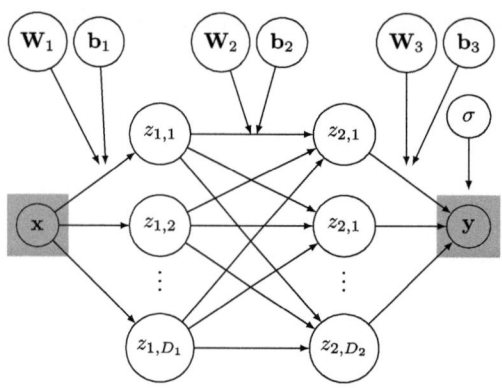
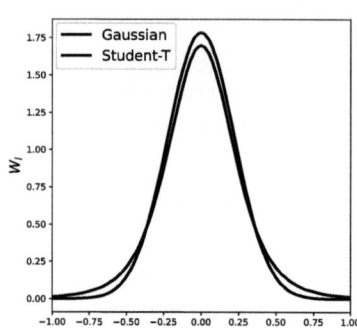

(a) Example of the DAG of the neural network when $L = 2$.

(b) Examples of priors of $\boldsymbol{W}_l$ for $l = 2, \ldots, L+1$ and $D_l = 20$.

Fig. 1. Examples of the directed acyclic graph (DAG) of the neural network and of the priors used in the experiments

neural network GP (NNGP); there is a similar correspondence relating GPs and distributions induced by the posterior [25]. When defining BNNs, choosing a prior and understanding how properties and prior beliefs on the weight space translate to the functions is a major challenge. Generally, we require priors which are: (1) interpretable, e.g. we want to be able to specify the hyperparameters of the prior based on the task at hand; (2) have large support, i.e. prior should not concentrate around a small subset of the parameter space; (3) lead to feasible inference and favour reasonable approximations of the posterior and predictive distributions.

Finally, to specify any neural network, one needs to choose the activation function, which (apart from being nonlinear) is required to be differentiable. In our experiments, we consider the widely-used rectified linear unit function (ReLU) defined as $\max(0, x)$, which switches the negative inputs off and leaves the positive ones unchanged, as well as the sigmoid activation function defined as $\sigma(x) = \exp(x)/(\exp(x) + 1)$.

2.2 Setup of the Experiments

In the experiments, we consider the following BNN, illustrated by the Fig. 1a

$$\begin{aligned} \boldsymbol{y} &\sim \mathrm{N}\left(\boldsymbol{b}_{L+1} + \boldsymbol{W}_{L+1}\boldsymbol{z}_L, \boldsymbol{\sigma}\right), \quad \boldsymbol{\sigma} \sim |\mathrm{N}(0, 0.001)| \\ \boldsymbol{z}_l &= g\left(\boldsymbol{b}_l + \boldsymbol{W}_l \boldsymbol{z}_{l-1}\right) \text{ for } l = 1, \ldots, L, \end{aligned} \quad (1)$$

where we consider two different choices of activations g, namely, the ReLU and the sigmoid; $|\mathrm{N}(,)|$ denotes a half-normal distribution; and $\boldsymbol{z}_0 = \boldsymbol{x}$. We consider two possible choices of priors on the weights (illustrated by Fig. 1b): (i) Gaussian priors as the most conventional choice [1,12]; (ii) Student-t priors, motivated by the observation that empirical weight distributions of SGD-trained networks are heavy-tailed [13,18]. We finish specifying the model by placing Gaussian priors on the biases, that is:

$$\boldsymbol{W}_1 \sim F\left(0, \frac{1}{4L}\right), \quad \boldsymbol{W}_l \sim F\left(0, \frac{4}{D_{l-1}}\right) \quad \text{for} \quad l = 2, \ldots, L+1,$$

$$\boldsymbol{b}_l \sim \mathrm{N}\left(0, \frac{1}{4L}\right) \quad \text{for} \quad l = 1, \ldots, L+1,$$

where the notation $F(\mu, \sigma^2)$ represents a distribution with mean μ and scale σ, and specifically, here is chosen as either Gaussian or Student-t with 5°C of freedom. To avoid divergence in wider networks and mitigate the damage caused by the nonlinear deformation [20], the weights' variance is scaled by the inverse of the preceding layer's width.

The BNN defined by Eq. 1 and trained with automatic differentiation variational inference (ADVI) [28], which assumes a mean-field (diagonal) Gaussian variational family, is referred to as mfVIR or mfVIS, depending on the choice of the activation: ReLU or sigmoid, respectively. The model trained with the Hamiltonian Monte Carlo (HMC), using the No U-Turn Sampler (NUTS) [23] is denoted as HMCR or HMCS. For simplicity, we often refer to one-layer neural networks of particular width D as to mfVIRD, mfVISD, HMCRD or HMCSD (e.g. one-layer BNN with 20 hidden units and ReLU activation trained with mean-field VI is called mfVIR20). All experiments are implemented with Numpyro [40], ArviZ [29], JAX [4] and Flax [21]. We record the run time of the approximate inference (TT), the root mean squared error RMSE and empirical coverage for the function and observations (EC). Note that we compute empirical coverage as a fraction of observations contained within the 95% confidence interval (CI), this means that in the ideal settings the computed EC should equal to 0.95. If EC > 0.95 then the confidence intervals are too wide; a worse scenario occurs when EC < 0.95 as it means that the CIs are too narrow and the model is overconfident in predictions. Details on the computed metrics and the corresponding formulas are discussed in the supplementary, where we provide further information on the initialization and parameters for the inference algorithms[1].

The absence of the test log-likelihood among the recorded metrics is motivated by the observation that the higher test log-likelihood does not necessarily correspond to a more accurate posterior approximation nor to lower predictive error (such as RMSE) [7].

2.3 Increasing the Width of the Network

We consider a simple synthetic dataset with one-dimensional input and output:

$$\boldsymbol{x} \sim \mathrm{Unif}([0, 2]), \quad \boldsymbol{y} = \sin(10\boldsymbol{x})\boldsymbol{x}^2 + \boldsymbol{\epsilon}, \quad \boldsymbol{\epsilon} \sim \mathrm{N}(0, 0.25).$$

---

[1] The code is available on GitHub.

The training data $\mathcal{D}$ consists of $N = 500$ observations and the new data for testing $\tilde{\mathcal{D}}$ consists of $\tilde{N} = 100$ observations. We first study the performances of mfVIR, mfVIS, HMCR and HMCS with 1 hidden layer and either Gaussian or Student-t priors as the width increases, and illustrate the metrics for $D_1 = 20, 200, 1000$ and 2000 hidden units by the Fig. 2a. The predictions of the four combinations of activation and inference algorithm with Gaussian priors when $D_1 = 2000$ are provided on the Fig. 2b; similar results were obtained when weights have Student-t distribution, the figures are presented in the supplementary. For either choice of priors, performance of the mfVIS dips with the increase in the dimension of the hidden layer; moreover, for $D_1 = 1000$ and $D_1 = 2000$ its posterior predictive distribution fails to capture the data, and, in fact, degenerates to the prior (Fig. 2b). An explanation of why such behaviour occurs was obtained via the correspondence of Gaussian processes and BNNs. While as the width increases the true posterior of a BNN converges to a NNGP posterior [25], any optimal mean-field Gaussian variational posterior of a BNN with odd (up to a constant offset) Lipschitz activation function converges to the prior predictive distribution of the NNGP [6]. In other words, the mean-field variational approximations of wide BNNs with sigmoid activations ignore the data. If one abandons the mean-field assumption and proposes a full-rank variational family, then using variational inference (VI) for wider networks would take at least a hundred times more time than using HMC, which undermines the benefits of using VI. Such degenerate behaviour is not observed with HMC (Figure 2b, but this comes at a significant increase in training time. For wider networks, the HMCR model exhibits a better performance than the HMCS both in terms of accuracy and uncertainty quantification. In terms of predictive accuracy, HMC is preferred over mfVI in all of the combinations of the activation function and width. However, in terms of uncertainty quantification, the HMC is inferior to mfVI (with one exception of a BNN with Student-t priors, sigmoid activation and 2000 hidden units). In our experiment, HMC underestimates the uncertainty of the signal much more than VI (Fig. 2a and 2b). Note that whilst variational inference is often cursed to underestimate the uncertainty [46], that is not always the case [3,14]. Markov chain Monte Carlo (MCMC) methods are known to struggle to effectively explore multimodal posteriors [26,39], and a lack of uncertainty could be a result of poor mixing of the chain.

General Summary. In wider networks, the ReLU is preferred over the sigmoid activation for both HMC and mfVI. Crucially, **when it comes to the mean-field VI the sigmoid activation should only be used when the limited width is suitable for the task at hand**. It is reasonable to suppose that the same could be said about any odd (up to adding a constant) activation function. Further, while the HMC was preferred over the mfVI when looking at accuracy alone, the required computational resources could be an obstacle. Moreover, uncertainty quantification is far from ideal for HMC (CIs are too narrow for the signal); instead, mfVI with the ReLU achieves a good balance between accuracy, UQ, and time, particularly for wider networks.

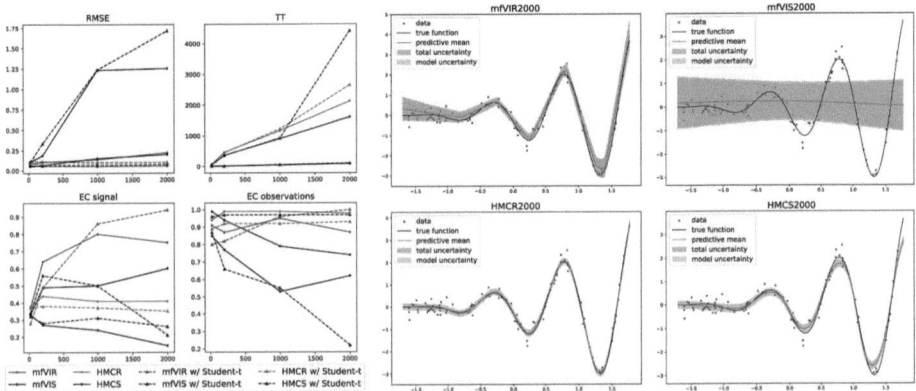

(a) Metrics of methods as the number of hidden units increases.

(b) Predictions and uncertainty estimates for each method with $D_1 = 2000$ and Gaussian priors.

Fig. 2. Predictive performance of BNNs as the width increases

2.4 Increasing the Depth of the Networks

Consider the data of Sect. 2.3 and neural networks defined by Eq. 1 with the number of layers L varying from 1 to 6 and a fixed number of hidden units in each layer $D_h = 20$. Figure 3a provides the recorded metrics, and Fig. 3b illustrates the predictions of the four combinations of activation and inference algorithm with $L = 6$ and Gaussian priors (analogous figures for Student-t priors are provided in the supplementary). First, observe that overall both RMSE and empirical coverage of mfVIR approximations improve with the increase of depth, with one exception of $L = 5$ and Student-t priors, when the prediction quality of the network drops drastically. The mfVIS follows a similar pattern, except for the case of $L = 5$ and Gaussian priors. Indeed, the approximate posteriors of deep neural networks obtained with the mean-field variational inference were shown to be as flexible as the much richer approximate posteriors of shallower BNNs [10]. We do not obtain the same improvement in the prediction quality of models trained with HMC: for either choice of priors, the performance of HMCR falls, whilst the HMCS does not improve as the depth increases. This undesirable behaviour could be a result of the multimodality of distributions in overparametrized models combined with the challenges of MCMC in exploring the high-dimensional space [26,39]. Compared to the findings of Sect. 2.3, we note that the deeper NNs are less sensitive to the choice of the activation function. It is needless to say that the HMC algorithm scales rather poorly, and as the number of layers changes from $L = 1$ to $L = 6$, the time needed to train HMCR and HMCS gets more than 15 and 30 times greater, respectively. We note that for models with more than one hidden layer, training of the network with sigmoid activations takes roughly twice as much time as the network with ReLU. The striking discrepancy in training times could arise due to the difference in the leapfrog integrator step sizes [2].

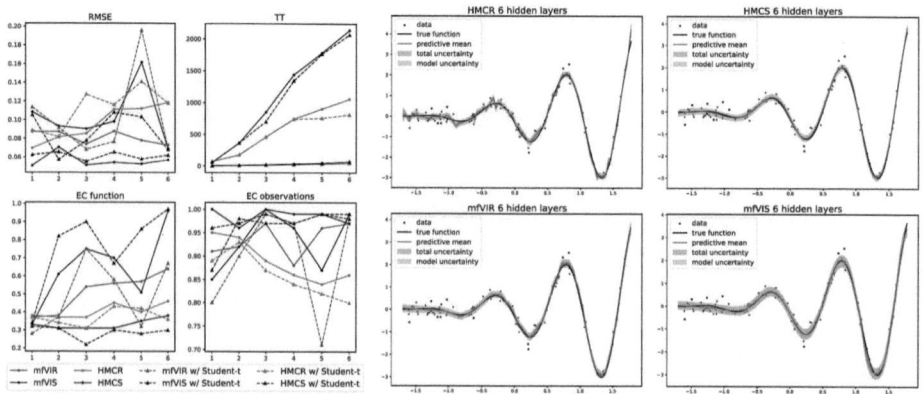

(a) Metrics of methods as the number of hidden layers increases.

(b) Predictions and uncertainty estimates for each method when $L = 6$ and Gaussian priors.

Fig. 3. Prediction performance of BNNs as the depth increases.

General Summary. In terms of the training time, HMC becomes less and less feasible with the increase in depth. With the need to explore high-dimensional parameter spaces, multimodality of the posteriors should be kept in mind as an arising challenge for both mfVI and HMC. **In terms of the balance between accuracy and UQ, the mean-field variational inference with ReLU activation function is able to outperform MCMC with the increase in depth.**

2.5 Out-of-Distribution Prediction

While it is not surprising that the accuracy and the quality of uncertainty quantification of any model decreases under a distribution shift, reliable uncertainty estimates that are robust to the out-of-distribution (OOD) data become exceptionally important in safety-critical applications. The challenge is especially intricate since better accuracy and lower calibration error of a certain model on the in-domain data do not imply better accuracy and lower calibration error in the OOD settings [38]. Here, we wish to validate the models' predictive abilities when the test data points come from previously unseen regions of data space. The kind of out-of-distribution data we consider could be described as 'complement-distributions', such data arises in open-set recognition or could be the result of an adversary [9]. Note that in Sect. 3.3 as well as in the supplementary, we consider a much milder example with 'related-distributions' data. We split the training data used in Sect. 2.3 and 2.4 into the train and test data covering complement regions of the function. Specifically, $\mathcal{D} = \mathcal{D}_c \sqcup \tilde{\mathcal{D}}_c$, the observed data $\mathcal{D}_c$ consists of $N = 370$, the new data $\tilde{\mathcal{D}}_c$ consists of $\tilde{N} = 130$

and the observed and the new data are disjoint (see Fig. 4):

$$\mathcal{D}_c = \{(x_n, y_n) \mid x_n \in [-1.7, 1.7]\},$$
$$\tilde{\mathcal{D}}_c = \{(x_n, y_n) \mid x_n \in [-2.8, -1.7) \cup (1.7, 1.9)]\}.$$

Strictly speaking, we do not expect any model to be robust to such an extreme case and, mainly, want to asses and better understand the quality of the uncertainty estimates. In this experiment, we are hoping that the relationship between the distributions of the observed and the new data makes this challenge somewhat tractable. On Fig. 4a we illustrate the metrics for $D_1 = 20, 200, 1000$ and 2000 hidden units; Fig. 4b compares non-OOD and OOD predictions obtained by the BNNs with ReLU activation, Gaussian priors and $D_1 = 200$. The poor performance of the mfVIS, especially for wider networks, is not surprising, however, we notice that for wide networks HMCS with Gaussian priors suffers from much higher RMSE than HMCS with Student-t priors and mfVIR and HMCR with either choice of priors. And while HMCR has a lower RMSE than any model trained with mean-field VI, the ability of HMC to capture the uncertainty deteriorates, and it becomes overconfident. Whilst HMCR200 and mfVIR200 do not show any of the expected increase in the uncertainty, on certain regions both methods are able to provide accurate predictive mean (see Fig. 4b for examples with Gaussian priors, the right-hand side region of the function, where $x > 1.5$). Finally, as the width of the network increases, mfVIR outperforms all of the methods.

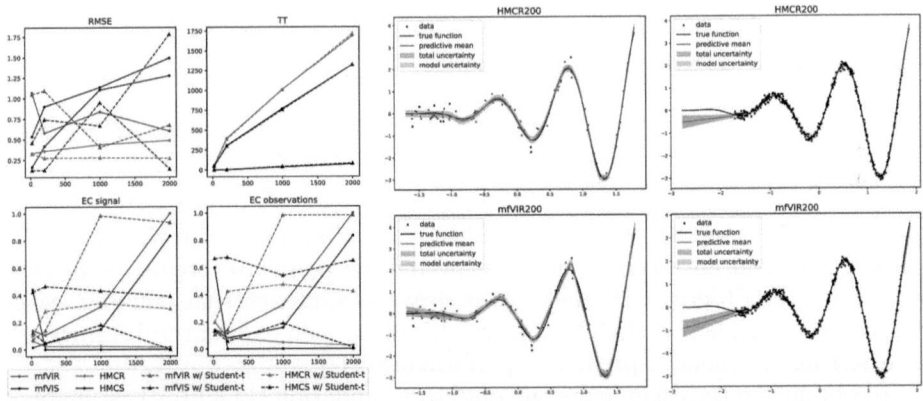

(a) Out-of-sample metrics of all the methods compared.

(b) Within-the sample (left) and out-of-sample (right) predictions and uncertainty estimates for $D_1 = 200$, ReLU activation and Gaussian priors.

Fig. 4. Out-of-distribution prediction for the 'complement-distributions' data

General Summary. In terms of the accuracy alone, the HMC with ReLU is more robust to the out-of-distribution data, however, that comes with the largest computational costs among all the models. We already saw in Sect. 2.3 that uncertainty quantification with HMC degrades with increasing width. In OOD settings, this becomes even more extreme, with very overconfident predictions that do not cover the truth (an empirical coverage of almost zero). **Finally, with the increase in depth, in the extreme OOD settings, the mfVI with ReLU becomes almost as accurate as HMC with ReLU and provides better UQ at a much lower cost.**

3 Bayesian Model Averaging and Stacking

3.1 Predictive Methods for Model Assessment

When considering synthetic datasets, we can choose a desired metric and sample any number of data points, so that evaluation of the models performance becomes trivial. For example, in Sect. 2.5 we have specifically created an extreme case when the training data $\mathcal{D}_c$ and the new data $\tilde{\mathcal{D}}_c$ were covering disjoint regions of the true function. In reality, the new previously unseen data is not available, and one can only estimate the expected out-of-sample predictive performance. Suppose that we only observe $\mathcal{D}$, the unseen observations $\tilde{\mathcal{D}}$ are generated by $p_t(\tilde{\mathcal{D}})$, and we wish to be able to assess the generalization ability of the model without having access to the test data. To keep the notation simple, we omit the dependency on x and $\tilde{x}$ when writing down the posteriors in this section. Given a new data point $\tilde{y}_n$, the log score $\log p(\tilde{y}_n|\mathcal{D})$ is one of the most common utility functions used in measuring the quality of the predictive distribution. The log score benefits from being a local and proper scoring rule [48]. Then, the expected log pointwise predictive density for a new dataset serves as a measure of the predictive accuracy of a given model:

$$\text{elpd} = \sum_{n=1}^{\tilde{N}} \int p_t(\tilde{D}_n) \log p(\tilde{y}_n|\mathcal{D}) d\tilde{D}_n,$$

where $p(\tilde{y}_n|\mathcal{D})$ is model's posterior predictive distribution. In the absence of $\tilde{\mathcal{D}}$, one might obtain an estimate of the expected log pointwise predictive density by re-using the observed $\mathcal{D}$. Here, we review the approach that employs leave-one-out cross-validation (LOO-CV), which can be seen as a natural framework for assessing the model's predictive performance [47].

To obtain the Bayesian leave-one-out cross-validation (LOO-CV) estimate of the expected utility $\widehat{\text{elpd}}_{\text{loo}}$ and avoid re-fitting the model N times, one could use importance sampling. However, the classical importance weights would have a large variance, and the obtained estimates would be noisy. Recently, the problem was solved with Pareto smoothed importance sampling (PSIS), which allows evaluating the LOO-CV expected utility in a reliable yet efficient way [47]:

$$\widehat{\text{elpd}}_{\text{loo}} = \sum_{n=1}^{N} p(y_n|x_n, \mathcal{D}_{-n}) = \sum_{n}^{N} \log \left(\frac{\sum_{s=1}^{S} r_i^s p(y_n|\boldsymbol{\theta}^s)}{\sum_{s=1}^{S} r_i^s} \right), \qquad (2)$$

where r_i^s are the smoothed importance weights, which benefit from smaller variance than the classical weights. We refer to the individual logarithms in the sum as $\widehat{\mathrm{elpd}}_{\mathrm{loo},n}$. The advantage of PSIS is that the estimated shape parameter of the Pareto distribution provides a diagnostic of the reliability of the resulting expected utility. Although methods of model selection which reuse the data can be vulnerable to overfitting when the size of the dataset is too small and/or the data is sparse, it is (relatively) safe to use cross-validation to compare a small number of models and given a large enough dataset [49]. In the supplementary material, we implement $\widehat{\mathrm{elpd}}_{\mathrm{loo}}$ in the empirical experiment, where we additionally consider posterior predictive checks (PPC) and an alternative to the LOO-CV approach of estimating the expected log pointwise utility.

3.2 Alternatives to Classical Bayesian Model Averaging

Let $\mathcal{M} = \{M_1, \ldots, M_K\}$ be a collection of models and denote the parameters of each of the M_k as $\boldsymbol{\theta}_k$. The assumptions one has on the prediction task and on $\mathcal{M}$ with respect to the true data-generating process can be categorized into three scenarios: $\mathcal{M}$-closed, $\mathcal{M}$-open and $\mathcal{M}$-complete. If $M_k \in \mathcal{M}$ for some k recovers the true data generating process, then we are in the $\mathcal{M}$-closed case. The task is $\mathcal{M}$-complete if there exists a true model but it is not included in $\mathcal{M}$ (e.g. for computational reasons). Finally, we are in the $\mathcal{M}$-open scenario when the true model is not in $\mathcal{M}$ and the data-generating mechanism cannot be conceptually formalized to provide an explicit model [48]. The Bayesian framework allows to define the probabilities over the model space, and for the $\mathcal{M}$-closed case, classical Bayesian Model Averaging (BMA) would give optimal performance. The BMA solution provides an averaged predictive posterior as [22]

$$p(\tilde{\boldsymbol{y}} \mid \boldsymbol{\mathcal{D}}) = \sum_{k=1}^{K} p(\tilde{\boldsymbol{y}} \mid \boldsymbol{\mathcal{D}}, M_k) p(M_k \mid \boldsymbol{\mathcal{D}}), \qquad (3)$$

$$\text{where } p(M_k \mid \boldsymbol{\mathcal{D}}) \propto p(\boldsymbol{\mathcal{D}} \mid M_k) p(M_k). \qquad (4)$$

However, in the $\mathcal{M}$-open and $\mathcal{M}$-complete prediction tasks, BMA is not appropriate as it gives a strong preference to a single model and so assumes that this particular model is the true one. Now, if we replace the weights $p(M_k|\boldsymbol{\mathcal{D}})$ with the products of Bayesian LOO-CV densities $\prod_{n=1}^{N} p(y_n \mid x_n, \boldsymbol{\mathcal{D}}_{-n}, M_k)$, we arrive at pseudo-Bayesian model averaging (pseudo-BMA). In other words, the weights w_k of pseudo-BMA are proportional to the estimated log pointwise predictive density $\exp(\widehat{\mathrm{elpd}}_{\mathrm{loo}}^k)$ introduced in Sect. 3.1. One could further correct each $\widehat{\text{elpd}}_{\text{loo}}$ estimate of Eqaution 2 by the standard errors and obtain

$$w_k = \frac{\exp(\widehat{\text{elpd}}_{\text{loo}}^{k,\text{reg}})}{\sum_{k=1}^{K} \exp(\widehat{\text{elpd}}_{\text{loo}}^{k,\text{reg}})},$$

$$\widehat{\text{elpd}}_{\text{loo}}^{k,\text{reg}} = \widehat{\text{elpd}}_{\text{loo}}^{k} - \frac{1}{2}\sqrt{\sum_{n=1}^{N}\left(\widehat{\text{elpd}}_{\text{loo},n}^{k} - \frac{\widehat{\text{elpd}}_{\text{loo}}^{k}}{N}\right)^2},$$

where for each model M_k we find $\widehat{\text{elpd}}_{\text{loo}}^{k,\text{reg}}$ by utilizing a log-normal approximation. Fortunately, we have already seen that these densities can be efficiently estimated with PSIS.

An alternative way to obtain the averaged predictive posterior given the set of $p(\tilde{y} \mid \mathcal{D}, M_k)$ is to employ the stacking approach [54]. Define the set $S^K = \{w \in [0,1]^K \mid \sum_{k}^{K} w_k = 1\}$, then the stacking weights are found as the optimal (according to the logarithmic score) solution of the following problem

$$w = \max_{w \in S^K} \frac{1}{N}\sum_{n=1}^{N}\log\sum_{k=1}^{K} w_k p(y_n \mid \mathcal{D}_{-n}, M_k),$$

$$= \max_{w \in S^K} \frac{1}{N}\sum_{n=1}^{N}\log\sum_{k=1}^{K} w_k \left(\frac{\sum_{s=1}^{S} r_i^s p(y_n \mid \boldsymbol{\theta}_k^s, M_k)}{\sum_{s=1}^{S} r_i^s}\right),$$

where a PSIS estimate of the predictive LOO-CV density is used, and r_i^s are the smoothed (truncated) importance weights.

Finally, we recall that deep ensembles of classical non-Bayesian NNs [30] behave similarly to Bayesian model averages, and both lead to solutions strongly favouring one single model [50]. In contrast, the ensembles of BNN posteriors in Eq. 3 with $p(M_k \mid \mathcal{D}) = K^{-1}$ can be seen as a trivial case of BMA, which combines models and does not give preference to a single solution. Alternatively, when implementing variational inference and combining BNNs, the analogy can be drawn with the simplified version of adaptive variational Bayes, which combines variational posteriors with certain weights and, under certain conditions, attains optimal contraction rates [37].

3.3 Ensembles and Averages

We compare three model averaging methodologies: deep ensembles of Bayesian neural networks, stacking and pseudo-BMA based on PSIS-LOO [54]. We do not consider the Bayesian Bootstrap (BB) [43] motivated by the recent observation that in the settings of modern neural networks deep ensembles of non-Bayesian NNs and BB are equivalent, and both are often misspecified [52]. Combining several estimates of BNNs can be effective not only when predictions are coming from different models, but also when dealing with several predictions obtained by the same model [37]. This is of particular use for multimodal posteriors arising in BNNs, where different modes could be explored by random initializations [54]. Additionally, recall that the ELBO, the objective of variational inference, is a non-convex function, so that the optimum is only local and depends on the starting point. We note that combining models trained with HMC and VI would be meaningless for several reasons. First of all, training a set of HMC models becomes rather expensive: for instance, training the HMCR20 once takes the same amount of time as 35 trainings of mfVIR20. Second, the estimates of the log pointwise predictive densities (provided in the supplementary) for HMC and VI have different scales and are not easily compared; in this case, the result of averaging HMC and VI would be equivalent to classical BMA.

Now consider the mfVIR20 model with Gaussian priors and the 'complement-distributions' data of Sect. 2.5. We choose 10 random initialization points, obtain 10 posterior predictive distributions and compute estimated expected log pointwise predictive densities. We then construct ensemble, pseudo-BMA and stacking approximations; the results are illustrated Fig. 5. Ensembling and stacking are superior to pseudo-BMA, which has worse accuracy and fails to capture any uncertainty. Similar results for the mfVIR20 model with Student-t priors are provided in the supplementary material. While here we focus only on models with 20 hidden units, it would be reasonable to assume that not only do the performance of individual models depend on architectural choices, but the model averaging techniques are themselves influenced by these modelling choices (for empirical justification of this claim, the reader is referred to the supplementary material, where we consider the data simulated when designing a novel rocket booster [16,42] and provide the results of ensembling and averaging for various architectures).

Given the nature of the test data we use, the predictions as well as the $\widehat{\text{elpd}}_{\text{loo}}$ estimates may be unreliable. Thus, we consider a simpler data-generating mechanism in which test data comes from a slightly broader region; such a scenario could be called an OOD task with 'related-distributions' [9]. Specifically, the data are generated as follows:

$$x \sim \text{Unif}([0,1]), \quad y = \sin(10x)x^2 + \epsilon, \quad \epsilon \sim 0.05 N(0,1).$$

The data for training $\mathcal{D}_r$ and the testing $\tilde{\mathcal{D}}_r$ consist of $N = 450$ and $\tilde{N} = 50$ observations, respectively, where $\tilde{\mathcal{D}}_r$ comes from the broader region than $\mathcal{D}_r$, i.e. $(\min_{n=1...N}(x_n), \max_{n=1...N}(x_n)) \subsetneq (\min_{n=1...\tilde{N}}(\tilde{x}_n), \max_{n=1...\tilde{N}}(\tilde{x}_n))$. For 10 posterior predictive distributions of mfVIR20 with Gaussian priors (results for Student-t priors are provided in the supplementary), we compare ensembling, pseudo-BMA and stacking in Fig. 5 (similar results with having Student-t priors are presented in the supplementary, where we additionally provide the results of ensembling and averaging in the deeper networks.). Whilst the total uncertainty estimates of pseudo-BMA are, somewhat, adequate, the model uncertainty is underestimated. Both stacking and deep ensembles lead to improved predictive performance and uncertainty quantification, with stacking showing some better gains compared to deep ensembles (see e.g. improved coverage of stacking on the right-hand side of Fig. 5).

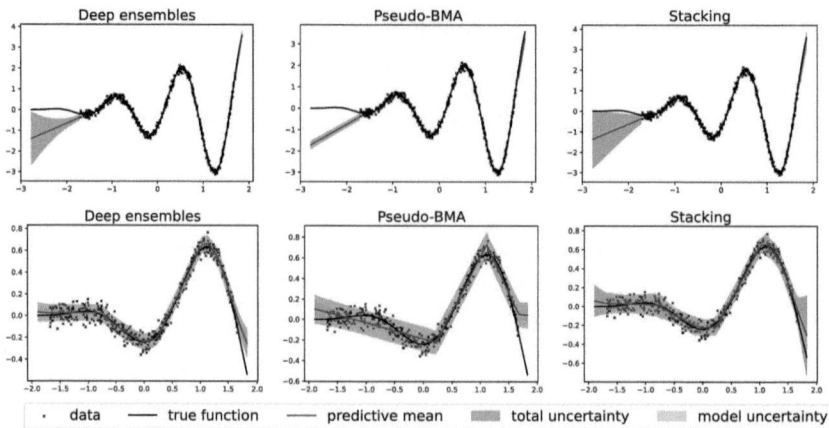

Fig. 5. Predictions obtained by ensembling, stacking and pseudo-BMA when applied to mfVIR20 with Gaussian priors in the 'complement-distributions' (top) and 'related-distributions' (bottom) OOD tasks. Pseudo-BMA is worse than the other methodologies, and stacking provides improvements over DE in uncertainty quantification

General Summary. We observe that, similar to BMA, the pseudo-BMA is not preferable in $\mathcal{M}$-open and $\mathcal{M}$-complete settings. Namely, in 'complement-distributions' and 'related-distributions' experiments, pseudo-BMA was confirmed to be inferior to stacking and ensembles of BNNs both in terms of the predictive accuracy and uncertainty quantification. **Stacking and ensembles of BNNs performed comparable to each other and provided an improvement, with modest gains for stacking, which is especially significant in terms of uncertainty quantification in the OOD setting.**

4 Discussion

The message of an optimist's conclusion could question the common belief that the mean-field variational approximations are generally overly restrictive and do not capture the true posterior and the uncertainty well. Even with increases in computing power, the computational costs of sampling algorithms suggest that it may not be feasible for most modern neural networks and datasets. Moreover, although HMC is often considered as a gold standard, we have seen this may not be the case for BNNs due to complexity and multimodality of the posterior. Indeed, in a variety of experiments considered in Sects. 2.3 to 2.4 to 2.5 and 3.3 **mfVI overall provided better uncertainty quantification than HMC,** and in out-of-distribution settings, the empirical coverage of the latter was close to zero. We note that **for single-layer neural networks, HMC outperformed mfVI only in terms of accuracy.** At the same time, for deeper networks and in out-of-distribution scenarios, the accuracy of mfVI was often comparable to HMC. Further, in Sect. 2.4 we confirmed that even for slightly deeper networks the time needed for HMC becomes a burden, which makes variational inference a very attractive alternative to sampling. Nevertheless, in Sect. 2.3 we observed that **the restrictions imposed by the factorized families can obstruct models from effectively learning from the data**. In real-life scenarios where one is required to evaluate the future predictive performance of the model before applying it to the unseen data, the estimate of the expected log pointwise predictive density can serve as a reliable diagnostic and thus, PSIS-LOO estimates can be beneficial for model assessment and combination. In Sect. 3.3, **stacking and ensembles of BNNs were shown to be a possible solution when dealing with multimodal posteriors, helping to both improve accuracy and uncertainty quantification even in the extreme OOD scenario.** We find that stacked or ensembled variational approximations are competitive to HMC at a much-reduced cost. Finally, we note that overall in our experiments, there was no considerable and systematic difference in the performance between the BNNs with Gaussian and Student-t priors.

This work highlights the model's sensitivity to architectural choices, namely, width, depth and activation function. Future work could study the performance of various more elaborate than Gaussian or Student-t choices of priors placed on the weights, including sparsity-inducing priors which have been shown to improve the accuracy and calibration [3,41]. Further, an important avenue for research is to consider the so-called structured variational inference with less restrictive variational families, and more generally, study the trade-off between the expressiveness of the variational family and scalability. Finally, given the multimodal nature of distributions arising in Bayesian neural networks, a promising avenue for research is to continue improving model combination techniques. This includes developing a better understanding of the number of models required for optimal performance with existing ensembling methods, as well as exploring more advanced approaches such as adaptive variational Bayes frameworks [37] or hierarchical stacking and pointwise model combination [53].

References

1. Arbel, J., Pitas, K., Vladimirova, M., Fortuin, V.: A primer on Bayesian neural networks: review and debates. arXiv preprint arXiv:2309.16314 (2023)
2. Betancourt, M.J., Byrne, S., Girolami, M.: Optimizing the integrator step size for Hamiltonian Monte Carlo (2015)
3. Blundell, C., Cornebise, J., Kavukcuoglu, K., Wierstra, D.: Weight uncertainty in neural network. In: Proceedings of the International Conference on Machine Learning, pp. 1613–1622. PMLR (2015)
4. Bradbury, J., et al.: JAX: composable transformations of Python+NumPy programs (2018). http://github.com/jax-ml/jax
5. Chatziafratis, V., Nagarajan, S.G., Panageas, I.: Better depth-width trade-offs for neural networks through the lens of dynamical systems. In: Proceedings of The International Conference on Machine Learning, pp. 1469–1478. PMLR (2020)

6. Coker, B., Bruinsma, W.P., Burt, D.R., Pan, W., Doshi-Velez, F.: Wide mean-field Bayesian neural networks ignore the data. In: International Conference on Artificial Intelligence and Statistics, pp. 5276–5333. PMLR (2022)
7. Deshpande, S.K., Ghosh, S., Nguyen, T.D., Broderick, T.: Are you using test log-likelihood correctly? Trans. Mach. Learn. Res. (2024)
8. Dosovitskiy, A., et al.: An image is worth 16×16 words: transformers for image recognition at scale. In: International Conference on Learning Representations (2020)
9. Farquhar, S., Gal, Y.: What 'out-of-distribution' is and is not. In: NeurIPS ML Safety Workshop (2022)
10. Farquhar, S., Smith, L., Gal, Y.: Liberty or depth: deep Bayesian neural nets do not need complex weight posterior approximations. Adv. Neural. Inf. Process. Syst. **33**, 4346–4357 (2020)
11. Foong, A., Burt, D., Li, Y., Turner, R.: On the expressiveness of approximate inference in Bayesian neural networks. Adv. Neural. Inf. Process. Syst. **33**, 15897–15908 (2020)
12. Fortuin, V.: Priors in Bayesian deep learning: a review. Int. Stat. Rev. **90**(3), 563–591 (2022)
13. Fortuin, V., et al.: Bayesian neural network priors revisited (2022)
14. Gal, Y., Ghahramani, Z.: Dropout as a Bayesian approximation: representing model uncertainty in deep learning. In: International Conference on Machine Learning, pp. 1050–1059. PMLR (2016)
15. Gelman, A., et al.: Bayesian workflow (2020)
16. Gramacy, R.B., Lee, H.K.H.: Bayesian treed Gaussian process models with an application to computer modeling. J. Am. Stat. Assoc. **103**(483), 1119–1130 (2008)
17. Guo, C., Pleiss, G., Sun, Y., Weinberger, K.Q.: On calibration of modern neural networks. In: Proceedings of The International Conference on Machine Learning. Proceedings of Machine Learning Research, vol. 70, pp. 1321–1330. PMLR (2017)
18. Gurbuzbalaban, M., Simsekli, U., Zhu, L.: The heavy-tail phenomenon in SGD. In: Proceedings of the 38th International Conference on Machine Learning. Proceedings of Machine Learning Research, vol. 139, pp. 3964–3975. PMLR (2021)
19. Hanin, B.: Universal function approximation by deep neural nets with bounded width and ReLU activations. Mathematics **7**(10), 992 (2019)
20. He, K., Zhang, X., Ren, S., Sun, J.: Delving deep into rectifiers: surpassing human-level performance on ImageNet classification. In: Proceedings of the IEEE International Conference on Computer Vision, pp. 1026–1034 (2015)
21. Heek, J., et al.: Flax: a neural network library and ecosystem for JAX (2024). http://github.com/google/flax
22. Hoeting, J.A., Madigan, D., Raftery, A.E., Volinsky, C.T.: Bayesian model averaging: a tutorial. Stat. Sci. **14**(4), 382–417 (1999)
23. Hoffman, M.D., Gelman, A.: The No-U-Turn sampler: adaptively setting path lengths in Hamiltonian Monte Carlo. J. Mach. Learn. Res. **15**(47), 1593–1623 (2014)
24. Hornik, K., Stinchcombe, M., White, H.: Multilayer feedforward networks are universal approximators. Neural Netw. **2**(5), 359–366 (1989)
25. Hron, J., Novak, R., Pennington, J., Sohl-Dickstein, J.: Wide Bayesian neural networks have a simple weight posterior: theory and accelerated sampling. In: Proceedings of the 39th International Conference on Machine Learning. Proceedings of Machine Learning Research, vol. 162, pp. 8926–8945. PMLR (2022)

26. Izmailov, P., Vikram, S., Hoffman, M.D., Wilson, A.G.G.: What are Bayesian neural network posteriors really like? In: Proceedings of the 38th International Conference on Machine Learning. Proceedings of Machine Learning Research, vol. 139, pp. 4629–4640. PMLR (2021)
27. Krizhevsky, A., Sutskever, I., Hinton, G.E.: ImageNet classification with deep convolutional neural networks. Commun. ACM **60**(6), 84–90 (2017)
28. Kucukelbir, A., Tran, D., Ranganath, R., Gelman, A., Blei, D.M.: Automatic differentiation variational inference. J. Mach. Learn. Res. **18**(14), 1–45 (2017)
29. Kumar, R., Carroll, C., Hartikainen, A., Martin, O.: Arviz a unified library for exploratory analysis of Bayesian models in python. J. Open Source Softw. **4**(33), 1143 (2019)
30. Lakshminarayanan, B., Pritzel, A., Blundell, C.: Simple and scalable predictive uncertainty estimation using deep ensembles. In: Advances in Neural Information Processing Systems, vol. 30. Curran Associates, Inc. (2017)
31. Lipton, Z.C.: The mythos of model interpretability: in machine learning, the concept of interpretability is both important and slippery. Queue **16**(3), 31–57 (2018)
32. Lu, Z., Pu, H., Wang, F., Hu, Z., Wang, L.: The expressive power of neural networks: a view from the width. In: Proceedings of the 31st International Conference on Neural Information Processing Systems, pp. 6232–6240 (2017)
33. Matthews, A.G., Hron, J., Rowland, M., Turner, R., Ghahramani, Z.: Gaussian process behaviour in wide deep neural networks. In: ICLR (2018)
34. Neal, R.: Bayesian learning for neural networks. Springer Science & Business Media, vol. 118 (1995)
35. Nguyen, A., Yosinski, J., Clune, J.: Deep neural networks are easily fooled: High confidence predictions for unrecognizable images. In: Proceedings of the IEEE Conference on Computer Vision and Pattern Recognition, pp. 427–436 (2015)
36. Oelrich, O., Ding, S., Magnusson, M., Vehtari, A., Villani, M.: When are Bayesian model probabilities overconfident? (2020)
37. Ohn, I., Lin, L.: Adaptive variational Bayes: optimality, computation and applications. Ann. Stat. **52**(1), 335–363 (2024)
38. Ovadia, Y., et al.: Can you trust your model's uncertainty? Evaluating predictive uncertainty under dataset shift. In: Advances in Neural Information Processing Systems, vol. 32 (2019)
39. Papamarkou, T., Hinkle, J., Young, M.T., Womble, D.: Challenges in Markov chain Monte Carlo for Bayesian neuralnetworks. Stat. Sci. **37**(3), 425–442 (2022)
40. Phan, D., Pradhan, N., Jankowiak, M.: Composable effects for flexible and accelerated probabilistic programming in NumPyro. In: Program Transformations for ML Workshop at NeurIPS (2019)
41. Polson, N.G., Ročková, V.: Posterior concentration for sparse deep learning. In: Advances in Neural Information Processing Systems, vol. 31 (2018)
42. Rogers, S., Aftosmis, M., Pandya, S., Chaderjian, N., Tejnil, E., Ahmad, J.: Automated CFD parameter studies on distributed parallel computers. In: 16th AIAA Computational Fluid Dynamics Conference, p. 4229 (2003)
43. Rubin, D.B.: The Bayesian bootstrap. Ann. Stat., 130–134 (1981)
44. Szegedy, C., et al.: Intriguing properties of neural networks. In: 2nd International Conference on Learning Representations, ICLR 2014 (2014)
45. Touvron, H., et al.: LLaMA: open and efficient foundation language models (2023)
46. Trippe, B., Turner, R.: Overpruning in variational Bayesian neural networks (2018)
47. Vehtari, A., Gelman, A., Gabry, J.: Practical Bayesian model evaluation using leave-one-out cross-validation and WAIC. Stat. Comput. **27**(5), 1413–1432 (2016)

48. Vehtari, A., Ojanen, J.: A survey of Bayesian predictive methods for model assessment, selection and comparison. Stat. Surv. **6**, 142–228 (2012). https://doi.org/10.1214/12-SS102
49. Vetari, A., Gabry, J., Magnusson, M., Yao, Y., Gelman, A.: Efficient leave-one-out cross-validation and WAIC for Bayesian models (2019). https://mc-stan.org/loo
50. Wilson, A.G., Izmailov, P.: Bayesian deep learning and a probabilistic perspective of generalization. Adv. Neural. Inf. Process. Syst. **33**, 4697–4708 (2020)
51. Wolpert, D.H.: The lack of a priori distinctions between learning algorithms. Neural Comput. **8**(7), 1341–1390 (1996)
52. Wu, L., Williamson, S.A.: Posterior uncertainty quantification in neural networks using data augmentation. In: Proceedings of The 27th International Conference on Artificial Intelligence and Statistics. Proceedings of Machine Learning Research, vol. 238, pp. 3376–3384. PMLR (2024)
53. Yao, Y., Vehtari, A., Gelman, A.: Stacking for non-mixing Bayesian computations: the curse and blessing of multimodal posteriors. J. Mach. Learn. Res. **23**(1), 3426–3471 (2022)
54. Yao, Y., Vehtari, A., Simpson, D., Gelman, A.: Using stacking to average Bayesian predictive distributions (with discussion). Bayesian Anal. **13**(3) (2018). https://doi.org/10.1214/17-ba1091
55. Zhang, C., Bengio, S., Hardt, M., Recht, B., Vinyals, O.: Understanding deep learning (still) requires rethinking generalization. Commun. ACM **64**(3), 107–115 (2021)

Variance-Aware Noisy Training: Hardening DNNs Against Unstable Analog Computations

Xiao Wang(✉), Hendrik Borras, Bernhard Klein, and Holger Fröning

Hardware and Artificial Intelligence Lab, Institute of Computer Engineering, Heidelberg University, Heidelberg, Germany
{xiao.wang,hendrik.borras,bernhard.klein, holger.froening}@ziti.uni-heidelberg.de

Abstract. The disparity between the computational demands of deep learning and the capabilities of compute hardware is expanding drastically. Although deep learning achieves remarkable performance in countless tasks, its escalating requirements for computational power and energy consumption surpass the sustainable limits of even specialized neural processing units, including the Apple Neural Engine and NVIDIA TensorCores. This challenge is intensified by the slowdown in CMOS scaling.

Analog computing presents a promising alternative, offering substantial improvements in energy efficiency by directly manipulating physical quantities such as current, voltage, charge, or photons. However, it is inherently vulnerable to manufacturing variations, nonlinearities, and noise, leading to degraded prediction accuracy. One of the most effective techniques for enhancing robustness, Noisy Training, introduces noise during the training phase to reinforce the model against disturbances encountered during inference. Although highly effective, its performance degrades in real-world environments where noise characteristics fluctuate due to external factors such as temperature variations and temporal drift.

This study underscores the necessity of Noisy Training while revealing its fundamental limitations in the presence of dynamic noise. To address these challenges, we propose Variance-Aware Noisy Training, a novel approach that mitigates performance degradation by incorporating noise schedules which emulate the evolving noise conditions encountered during inference. Our method substantially improves model robustness, without training overhead. Through experiments on image classification tasks in dynamic noise environments, we demonstrate a significant increase in robustness, from 79.3% with conventional Noisy Training to 97.6% with Variance-Aware Noisy Training on CIFAR-10 and from 32.4% to 99.7% on Tiny ImageNet.

Keywords: noisy training · noisy computations · analog computing · robustness · neural networks

1 Introduction

Deep neural networks (DNNs) have driven remarkable advancements in a wide array of machine learning applications, from computer vision and natural language, speech and signal processing. These breakthroughs are largely enabled by digital compute platforms, such as graphics processing units (GPUs) or specialized accelerators, which offer high throughput and flexibility. However, as DNNs grow in scale and are increasingly deployed in energy-constrained environments, the quest for more efficient hardware solutions becomes paramount. In addition, Complementary Metal-Oxide-Semiconductor (CMOS) technology scaling is stuttering, thus alternative approaches to maintain performance scaling have to be found. Analog computing architectures replace discrete quantities with continuous ones, leveraging the inherent properties of physical systems to perform computations efficiently. These architectures enhance computational efficiency, reduce data movement overhead, and enable highly parallel multiply-accumulate (MAC) operations, while their most significant advantage lies in superior energy efficiency [8,36].

Analog accelerators leverage the intrinsic physical properties of existing and emerging device technologiessuch as analog CMOS-based computing [34], photonic computing [11], resistive random-access memory (ReRAM), phase-change memory (PCM), and other non-volatile devicesto perform approximate MAC operations based on physical quantities such as charge, even directly in the memory array [41]. These architectures can significantly cut down power consumption and latency, surpassing many of their digital counterparts [1,6]. However, these advantages come at the cost of increased susceptibility to analog non-idealities and noise. Factors such as device variations, thermal fluctuations, mismatch, drift, and aging can degrade both the performance and reliability of analog DNN implementations [14,35,36].

From a machine learning perspective, various works have reported that adding small amounts of noise to the training data can improve generalization [2,15,22], thus acting as a form of data augmentation. Noise injection is often also referred to as "distortion" or "jitter", in particular in early works. Besides injecting such (usually Gaussian) noise to input variables, there are similar methods on adding noise to other parts of a neural architecture, including weights [15], gradients [32] and activations [18]. However, this applies only to small noise levels and is limited to training, while inference remains noise-free. Thus analog hardware noise has the potential to distort intermediate activations and weights, undermining the model's inference accuracy if left unmitigated. Consequently, there is substantial interest in techniques that preserve DNN accuracy under noise. One of the most widely studied methods is Noisy Training, where noise is intentionally injected during the training process to emulate the hardware imperfections encountered during inference [20,43]. Exposure to noise from the outset enables the model to adapt its parameters, enhancing robustness to real-world noise variations. From a broader perspective, there are adjacent works in multiple directions: on adversarial effects to improve the robustness of DNNs

[38], on Noisy Training to introduce sparsity in the activation space [4], as well as on using noise in physical computations as a source of stochasticity [5].

While Noisy Training has been shown to be successful in various use cases, it is important to note that its efficacy strongly depends on the fidelity with which one can replicate the true hardware noise characteristics during training. When there is a mismatch—e.g., in distribution (statistical shape), amplitude (magnitude), or temporal correlation (noise in real hardware sometimes changes over time)—between training noise and inference noise, DNNs often fail to generalize the learned robustness and may suffer a decrease in prediction quality. It is important to emphasize that in analog devices, maintaining a constant noise level is highly uncommon. Even under controlled laboratory conditions, stabilizing noise over time presents significant challenges. Environmental factors such as temperature fluctuations, electromagnetic induction, and various timing effects inherently influence noise characteristics. Given these dynamic influences, it is reasonable to assume that noise in analog hardware is not static but evolves over the device's operational lifetime. This variability underscores the necessity of considering time-dependent noise models when designing robust deep learning systems for analog accelerators. This observation raises an important research question: How precisely must one capture the analog hardware's noise characteristics during training to ensure robust inference? Addressing this question is non-trivial, given that the noise profiles in analog circuits can evolve over time due to changing environmental conditions, device aging, or even variations in operating modes.

A second challenge arises when perfectly matching the real hardware noise in training is either impractical or impossible. While techniques like hardware-in-the-loop training can provide more accurate noise profiles [33], they may be expensive or time-consuming to implement. In practical implementations, only approximations or partial knowledge of noise statistics may be available. This raises a key question: How can training algorithms ensure robustness when training noise only partially matches deployment conditions?

In response to these challenges, research has increasingly focused on rigorous noise modeling and robust training schemes that can handle real-world analog non-idealities [3,20,24,26,33,43]. Understanding how noise affects different DNN layers and accumulates through network depth is crucial for mitigating its impact. Sophisticated training techniquesranging from gradient-based noise modeling to Bayesian approacheshave been proposed to enhance model reliability under noisy conditions [43]. Ultimately, the goal is to facilitate a new generation of DNN accelerators that can achieve cutting-edge performance while maintaining a significantly lower energy footprint.

In this paper, we systematically explore the interplay between Noisy Training and real-world dynamic noise environments. Specifically:

- **Quantifying Noise Mismatch:** We study how varying degrees of mismatch between the noise injected during training and the real noise encountered in inference affect the final model accuracy.

- **Evaluation of Robustness Techniques:** We evaluate the effectiveness of robustness techniques, including Noisy Training, Quantization, and Perturbation on weights, in dynamic noise environments characteristic of analog hardware. Our results indicate that Noisy Training significantly outperforms the alternative methods, establishing it as the most reliable baseline for robustness in such settings.
- **Strategies for Imperfect Noise Knowledge:** We propose a novel training procedure designed to mitigate the adverse effects of partial or inaccurate noise assumptions: *Variance-Aware Noisy Training (VANT)*
- **Guidelines for Robust Analog DNN Training:** Drawing on our theoretical and experimental findings, we offer practical guidelines on how to tailor *VANT* to diverse analog hardware setups.

By addressing these facets, we contribute to the broader effort of understanding and optimizing DNNs for analog hardware deployment. Our results demonstrate that carefully designed Noisy Training enables robust energy-efficient inference, even under non-ideal and time-varying hardware noise. Ultimately, we aim to offer both theoretical and practical contributions that inform the design of next-generation hardening methods for DNNs on analog accelerators.

2 Related Work

Neural network robustness is a critical research area, addressing threats such as adversarial attacks, compression errors, and computational noise. Noise injection plays a central role both as an evaluation metric and a training technique to enhance resilience. This section overviews research on robustness, noise injection, and Noisy Training in analog computing.

Quantization and Robustness. Quantization, a prevalent technique in hardware-efficient deep learning, reduces numerical precision and thereby affects model robustness. Prior research has extensively examined its impact on adversarial resilience. For example, studies have demonstrated that adversarial robustness exhibits a non-monotonic relationship with bit-width, indicating that increased precision does not always enhance robustness [13]. Similarly, findings suggest that quantization can improve resilience against adversarial attacks while incurring minimal accuracy loss [10]. To mitigate error amplification that exacerbate adversarial perturbations, methods such as controlling the Lipschitz constant during quantization have been proposed [29]. Further analyses have investigated quantization effects across various neural architectures, revealing that highly complex models can recover from severe weight quantization through retraining, whereas smaller models experience greater performance degradation [37].

Perturbation and Robustness. By perturbing the weights of a DNN, SGD can find regions within the parameter space, which are more robust in general. Or inversely: When injecting noise into a DNN, its predictions are more likely to be correct if the DNN is trained towards a robust loss region. Motivated by the relationship between the loss landscape sharpness and generalization, SAM [12] seeks parameter values whose entire neighborhoods maintain consistently low training loss. Moreover, other research has incorporated pertutbation on both weights and inputs, improving the robustness against adversarial attacks [40].

Noise Injection for Robustness. Noise injection has long been recognized as an effective strategy to improve generalization in machine learning models [17,31]. Early works explored its utility in mitigating overparameterization, comparing it with techniques such as weight decay and early stopping [23]. With the rise of adversarial attacks, noise injection evolved into a robust defense mechanism alongside adversarial training [16]. Various approaches have been proposed, including globally injected additive Gaussian noise [21] and ensembles leveraging layer-wise noise injection [30]. However, they often assume static noise distributions, overlooking dynamic variations in real-world scenarios.

Noisy Training in Analog Computing. Unlike adversarial perturbations that affect input sensitivity, noisy analog hardware primarily introduces stochasticity into internal computations, particularly affecting neural network weights and dot product calculations. Studies have modeled non-volatile memory noise as an additive zero-mean i.i.d. Gaussian noise term on model weights, demonstrating the benefits of injecting similar noise during training and extending robustness via knowledge distillation [43]. Other research has incorporated memristor perturbation models to simulate drift in neural network weights, capturing long-term instability in analog devices and proposing architecture search and layer-specific dropout to increase robustness against drifts [42].

Dependent on the considered hardware implementation noise might be dominant in different parts of the accelerator and thus occur at different positions in the computations. Techniques have been developed to address noise from both weight readout [42,43] and subsequent computations, such as injecting noise at the output activation level [3]. Thereby, latter accounts for accumulated noise and extends further by introducing layer-specific noise to evaluate robustness and learning dynamics [3].

Additionally, Noisy Training approaches have been extended to exploit noise as an inherent feature of analog computing systems, enhancing adversarial robustness and supporting stochastic inference [5,7,39].

Despite their effectiveness, most Noisy Training strategies assume static noise characteristics. This limits real-world deployment, where noise fluctuates due to temperature changes, voltage instability, and device aging. Variance-Aware Noisy Training addresses this by integrating dynamic noise schedules that reflect realistic inference-time variations.

3 Neural Networks and Noisy Environments

We begin with an overview of the datasets and model architectures used in our work, followed by a comprehensive analysis of existing methods and their characteristics. Additionally, we describe the methodology for simulating a noisy analog environment and outline our approach to evaluating robustness.

Datasets, Models and Experimental Setup. In order to establish the effectiveness of our proposed method, experiments are performed for different networks and datasets. For the initial and comprehensive evaluation, we perform image classification on CIFAR-10 [25], CINIC-10 [9] and Tiny ImageNet [27]. For CIFAR-10, we evaluate two model architectures: LeNet-5 [28] and ResNet-18 [19]. While for Tiny ImageNet and CINIC-10, LeNet-5 is undersized and thus we focus on ResNet-18 and ResNet-50.

LeNet-5 and ResNet-18 use initial learning rates of 0.001 and 0.01 on CIFAR-10, respectively, while both ResNet-18 and ResNet-50 use a learning rate of 0.001 on Tiny ImageNet and CINIC-10. All models are trained with Adam and cosine learning rate decay, using a batch size of 128 for 400 epochs.[1]

3.1 Global Noise Injection and Noisy Training

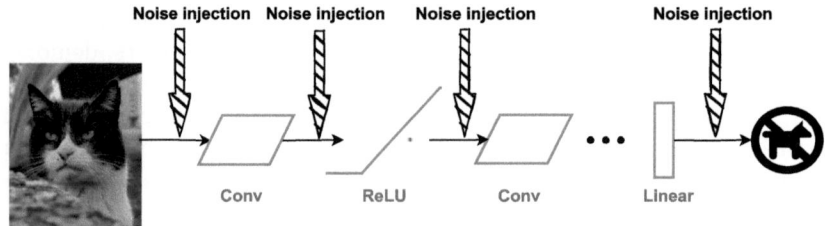

Fig. 1. Global noise injection in a DNN. Noise is applied to activations between layers

To simulate the noisy environment present in analog hardware, we inject noise at a global level during model computation. In this work, we follow the *Walking Noise* [3] methodology, which focuses on injecting noise at the activations. We consider additive Gaussian noise, due to its widespread occurrence in natural processes and its demonstrated effectiveness in previous works on noise injection [43]. To inject noise without bias, we sample with zero mean, i.e. $\mathcal{N}(0, \sigma)$, with σ being the standard deviation of the noise. A schematic of the noise injection is shown in Fig. 1. By varying the noise level σ during inference, we assess the model's robustness under noisy environments of different intensities.

Noise injection during training has been shown to significantly improve network accuracy under noisy computations [24, 43]. We also evaluate performance of standard Noisy Training by injecting noise in the forward pass during the training procedure. Figure 2 reveals the impact of noise injection to accuracy for models trained with and without noise injection. When a model is trained with

---
[1] The code is available at: https://github.com/HAWAIILAB/VANT.

the same noise level it encounters during inference, it typically achieves optimal accuracy. By connecting these optimal points, we obtain the dashed curve, which represents the best achievable performance using Noisy Training at each noise level. We assume the dashed curve thus to be the theoretical upper bound in terms of robustness and accuracy for any given noise level.

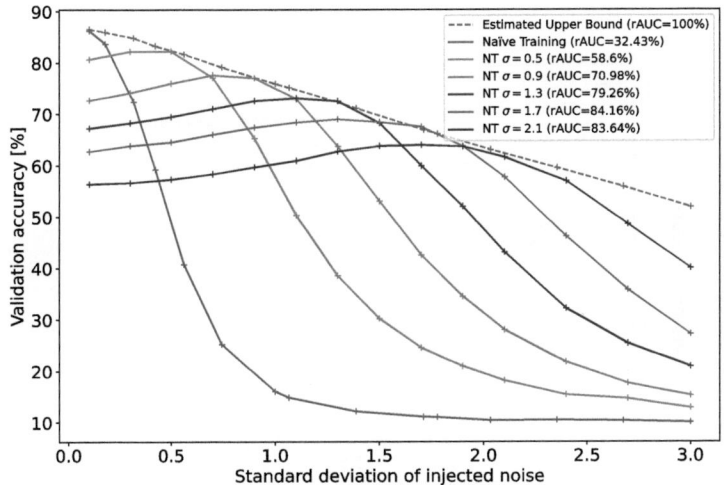

Fig. 2. Accuracy degradation under noise. NT: Models trained with Noisy Training (NT) at noise of σ. Dashed line indicates the upper bound, when using the same noise for training and inference. ResNet-18 on CIFAR-10

3.2 Evaluation: Quantifying Robustness Under Noise

The standard deviation of the noise σ under test is selected from the range $[0.1, 3.0]$. This selection is based on previous findings [24], which report noise levels on analog hardware to fall within this interval. This ensures that our robustness assessment is both relevant and practical for deployment scenarios involving noisy analog computations.

To quantify the robustness under noisy computation, we utilize the Area Under the Curve (AUC) as primary performance metric. However, directly comparing AUC values can be misleading, as accuracy is influenced by factors such as model complexity and dataset difficulty. Moreover, absolute AUC values do not directly indicate how close a method's performance is to the upper bound. To provide a fair comparison, we use the **relative AUC percentage (rAUC)**, defined as:

$$\text{rAUC} = \frac{\text{AUC of the method}}{\text{AUC of the upper bound curve}} [\%]$$

This metric directly indicates how close a method is to the best possible result.

4 Noisy Training: Strong but Not Flawless

As shown, training with noise injection significantly enhances robustness compared to a baseline model trained without noise. However, it is important to understand how other robustness-enhancing methods contribute to overall performance. In the following, we explore these methods as well as the limitations of Noisy Training.

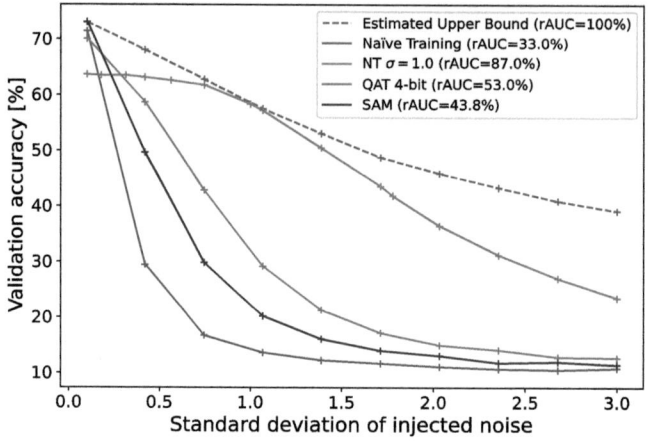

Fig. 3. Comparison of typical hardening methods for LeNet-5 on CIFAR-10

4.1 The Importance of Noisy Training

We begin with the assumption that we do not have prior knowledge of noise characteristics in analog hardware and explore how to mitigate its impact. We consider quantization and the generalization method Sharpness-Aware Minimization (SAM) [12] as potential countermeasures.

Intuitively, quantization introduces quantization error during computation, which may however increase the stability of DNNs when subjected to noise perturbations. To evaluate the impact of quantization techniques on the robustness of neural networks against computational noise, we test a quantized network in a noisy environment. For our evaluations we employ quantization-aware training (QAT)[2]. Figure 3 shows that a model quantized to 4-bit outperforms the baseline model. We further evaluate the impact of the perturbation method SAM, as described in Sect. 2. As shown in Fig. 3, while SAM offers improvements it remains less effective than quantization.

However, neither quantization nor SAM can match the performance of Noisy Training in enhancing robustness. This is largely due to the fundamental characteristics of noise in analog hardware: it is pervasive, affecting not only the input

---

[2] Our implementation is based on Brevitas (https://github.com/Xilinx/brevitas).

but also internal computations; its magnitude can be substantial; and, critically, it accumulates as signals propagate through the neural network. These factors highlight that an effective countermeasures must account for the specific noise properties of the hardware.

4.2 Limitations of Noisy Training

While Noisy Training is essential for robustness, a key challenge remains: the noise characteristics of analog hardware can fluctuate over time due to environmental factors such as temperature variations. Additionally, different hardware units usually exhibit notable variations in noise levels. We define the noise level present in a specific hardware instance at the time of measurement as σ_{train}.

This raises an important question: even if a model is trained under a specific noise level, how well does it generalize when the on-device noise deviates from the training conditions? To explore this, we train the model under a fixed noise level and then evaluate its performance across different noise strengths. The orange curve in Fig. 3 illustrates the performance of LeNet-5 trained with $\sigma_{\text{train}} = 1.0$. As expected, the model achieves optimal performance when the noise level matches the training condition. However, as the noise deviates from $\sigma_{\text{train}} = 1.0$, accuracy declines, highlighting sensitivity to mismatched noise levels.

This observation leads to a crucial conclusion: Noisy Training is only effective when the noise characteristics are precisely known. If the noise level during training does not align with the actual noise encountered during deployment, the model's robustness can be significantly compromised. This leads to the central research question of this work:

> How can we train models that remain robust across an entire fleet of devices, each potentially exhibiting different noise strengths over time?

5 Beating the Odds: Variance-Aware Noisy Training

In order to address the previously presented shortcomings of Noisy Training we present a novel training technique, *Variance-Aware Noisy Training (VANT)* which is more robust against unstable noise settings.

5.1 Methodology: Variance-Aware Noisy Training

The central assumption behind standard (stable) Noisy Training is that one can model the accelerator's noise perfectly, in particular, that it will remain constant over time and devices. This way gradient descent adjusts a given DNN to the characteristics of a given accelerator. Centrally missing however is any treatment of variation in the noise. We thus extend Noisy Training as follows:

$$\begin{aligned} x &\sim \mathcal{N}\left(0, \sigma_{\text{var}}\right), \\ \sigma_{\text{var}} &\sim \mathcal{N}\left(\alpha \cdot \sigma_{\text{train}}, \theta\right). \end{aligned} \quad (1)$$

Here σ_{train} is an extrinsic parameter, representing the known noise characteristic of a given hardware target. *VANT* additionally introduces two parameters: θ adjusts Noisy Training to the time variations of a given accelerator, while α is a calibration parameter for σ_{train}. Looking forward to Sects. 5.2 and 5.3, we note that *VANT* is rather insensitive to α, while θ strongly depends on the chosen σ_{train}.

During training σ_{var} is then sampled for each input image, while additively injected noise (x) is sampled for each activation. All sampling and thus noise injection only applies during the forward pass of gradient descent training.

5.2 Experiments on CIFAR-10

In order to evaluate how the parameters of *VANT* behave, we run initial evaluations on CIFAR-10. In a later step we then evaluate how well *VANT* transfers to a more complex dataset, when utilizing the same parameters obtained here.

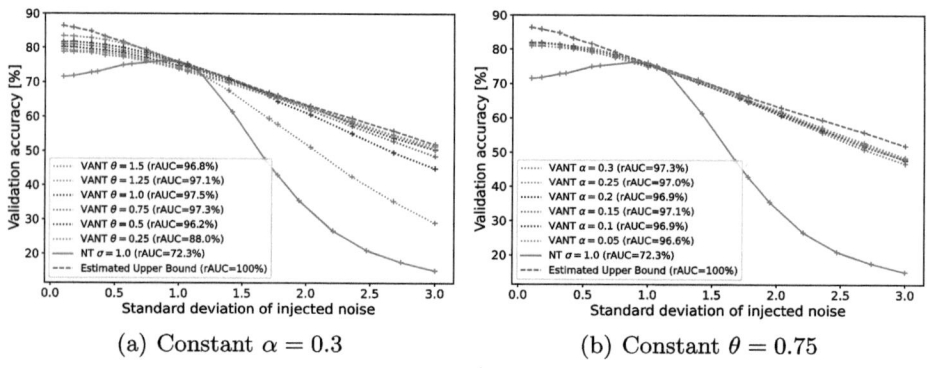

(a) Constant $\alpha = 0.3$ (b) Constant $\theta = 0.75$

Fig. 4. Exploration of *VANT* hyperparameters for ResNet-18 on CIFAR-10, when plotted over the injected noise. Here compared to Noisy Training (NT) at $\sigma_{\text{train}} = 1.0$

Initially we evaluate α and θ individually to explore their general behavior (Fig. 4). For any setting of α and θ, the robustness (rAUC) of *VANT* is significantly better compared to standard Noisy Training. And results are similar for LeNet-5. While variations in α appear to have little impact on the overall robustness as seen in Fig. 4b, θ plays a significant role in both the overall robustness and shape of the curve, see Fig. 4a. Furthermore, in Fig. 4a it also becomes apparent that the method does not necessarily preserve the peak accuracy of standard Noisy Training at σ_{train}. The variation of noise, θ, effectively increases the maximum noise observed, which shifts the point of optimal accuracy for *VANT*. Thus, during the evaluation of α and θ this influence needs to be considered. This is accomplished by measuring how close the accuracy at σ_{train} is to standard Noisy Training, since ideally *VANT* should preserve all advantages of Noisy Training. In order to quantify this behavior, a new metric is introduced:

Preserved Accuracy. It measures by how much the accuracy of *VANT* and standard Noisy Training differ at the noise injection point of σ_{train}. Ideally a setting of α and θ can be found, which keeps this metric at zero or higher, perfectly preserving the accuracy of standard Noisy Training.

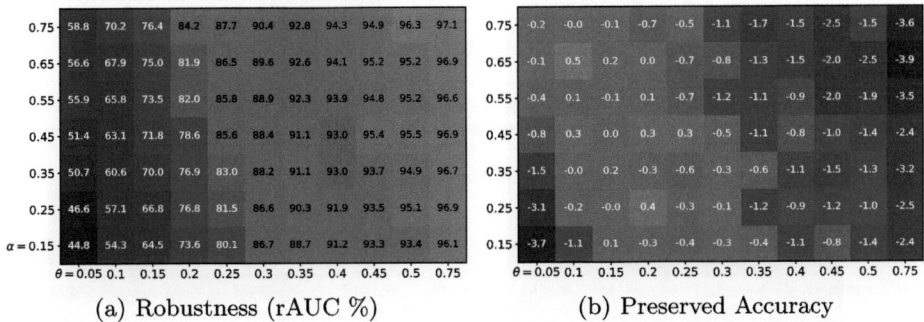

Fig. 5. Heatmap of quality metrics for *VANT* with ResNet-18 on CIFAR-10, when varying both hyperparameters of *VANT*, while keeping $\sigma_{\text{train}} = 0.4$ constant

To further identify the dependency of the robustness (rAUC) and preserved accuracy on α and θ, a grid scan for both parameters across a wide range is performed in Fig. 5. For the robustness we primarily observe that θ plays a strictly monotonic role in improving robustness. We further note that α similarly monotonically increases the robustness. While this effect appears to suggest that one should simply increase both α and θ, this is not the case. Instead the maximally achievable robustness is bounded by the preserved accuracy, as this value should stay at zero or larger in Fig. 5b. Notably a sweet spot becomes visible for finding an optimal set of parameters for *VANT*. While this sweet spot is well constrained in θ, it is relatively broad for α.

Selecting the best set of α and θ parameters is done as follows:

1. Select all sets of α and θ, for which the preserved accuracy is above 0, ensuring parity to Noisy Training.
2. Sub-select α and θ for which the robustness is maximized.

In the case of Fig. 5, we select $\alpha = 0.45$ and $\theta = 0.25$ as the optimal parameters.

Since different analog accelerators require different initial noise levels, we now explore how *VANT* behaves for different σ_{train}. As *VANT* is largely invariant to α we fix it to 0.45, as a middle ground for the sweet spot from Fig. 5b.

Similarly to Figs. 5 and 6 shows both robustness and preserved accuracy. However, in this case the x-axis denotes the change in σ_{train}, e.g. different hardware accelerators, and the y-axis explores the behavior of θ. Again, there is a trade-off to be made between the preserved accuracy and the robustness.

Notably, θ shows a broad optimum for the robustness. However, when following the procedure for selecting the best θ as stated in the steps above, then

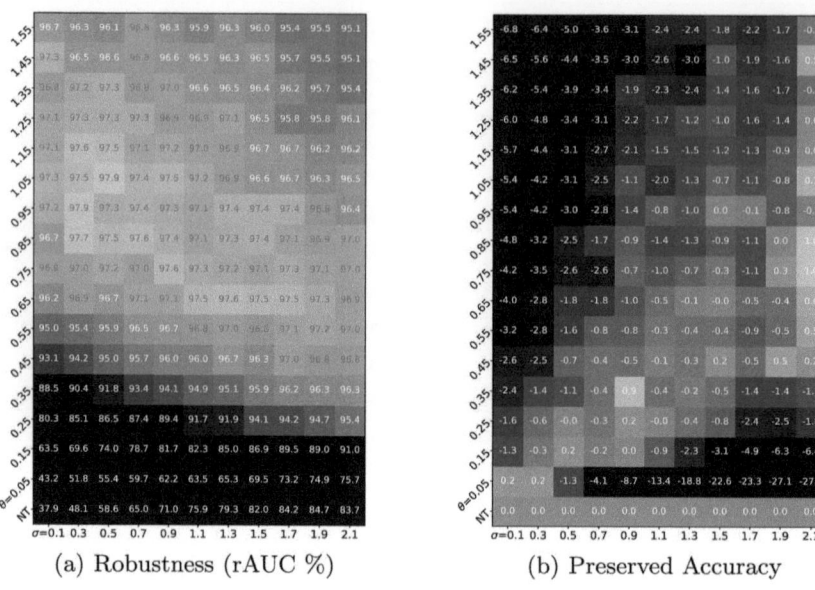

Fig. 6. Heatmap of quality metrics for *VANT* with ResNet-18 on CIFAR-10, when varying θ and the reference hardware noise σ_{train}. While keeping $\alpha = 0.45$ constant, as it is largely invariant. NT: Noisy Training as baseline at the bottom

θ is tightly confined by an approximately linear relationship between σ_{train} and θ, which is approximately: $\theta = 0.4 \cdot \sigma_{\text{train}}$

Table 1. Quality metrics for *VANT* with ResNet-18 on CIFAR-10 for the optimal θ and α, when varying the reference hardware noise σ_{train}

σ_{train}	0.1	0.3	0.5	0.7	0.9	1.1	1.3	1.5	1.7	1.9	2.1
θ	0.05	0.05	0.25	0.35	0.35	0.45	0.65	0.65	0.95	0.75	0.85
Preserved Accuracy	0.2	0.2	0	−0.4	0.9	−0.1	−0.1	0	−0.1	0.3	1.0
rAUC [%] NT	37.9	48.1	58.6	65.0	71.0	75.9	79.3	82.0	84.2	84.7	83.7
rAUC [%] VANT	43.2	51.8	86.5	93.4	94.1	96.0	**97.6**	97.5	97.5	97.1	97.0

However, for all following experiments, we choose θ as described with the steps above, as these are more accurate given the ground truth data available. These can be found in Table 1. All selected settings for *VANT* simultaneously preserves the accuracy of standard Noisy Training and strictly improve the robustness, as visible by comparing them to the bottom row in Fig. 6.

5.3 Generalizing to Complex Data: CINIC-10 and Tiny ImageNet

In the following we explicitly test for two properties of *VANT*: How well it transfers to more complex datasets and if the parameters of *VANT* additionally show stability across varying architectures. As such all settings for α and θ for the following experiments are chosen from the optimal results of the previous section, shown in Table 1.

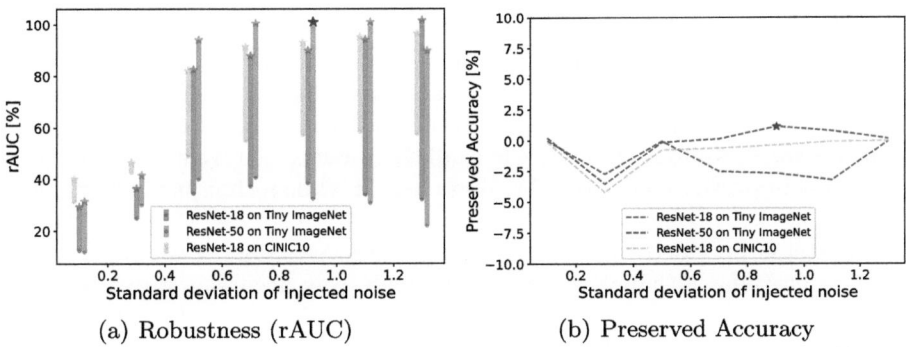

Fig. 7. Quality metrics for *VANT* with ResNet-18/50 on CINIC-10 and Tiny ImageNet at varying σ_{train}. For the robustness (rAUC): The dot at the bottom of the bars represents standard Noisy Training, while the star at the top of the bar represents *VANT*

As a naturally more complex architecture we investigate ResNet-50. On the dataset side we increase complexity in two steps: CINIC-10 and Tiny ImageNet.

Results for both quality metrics under consideration are shown in Fig. 7. Looking first at the preserved accuracy, one can observe that the accuracy is generally preserved across datasets and models. A notable exception is $\sigma = 0.3$, where the preserved accuracy drops across all experiments and increases in robustness are also low. We postulate that for this specific setting θ was ill-chosen. Further investigating the robustness in Fig. 7a, we observe that *VANT* improves the robustness for all models, datasets and strengths of injected noise. However the effect is not consistent across the whole range of injected noise. *VANT* provides less significant robustness improvements for noise strengths of $\sigma_{\text{train}} < 0.5$. The underlying reason is that in order to achieve high accuracy under low noise, regions of higher noise are less prominently sampled. This results in subpar performance for much of the investigated range by the rAUC metric. Notably this behavior is largely inherited from Noisy Training.

For $\sigma_{\text{train}} \geq 0.5$, however, *VANT* is considerably more robust. Interestingly the largest improvements can be found on Tiny ImageNet with ResNet-50, the most complex dataset and model investigated, where the rAUC increases dramatically from 32.4% to 99.7% at $\sigma_{\text{train}} = 0.9$. Nonetheless, significant improvements are also visible for ResNet-18 and CINIC-10.

Concluding we find, that *VANT* shows good generalization across both datasets and models. While the performance of a set of chosen hyper-parameters remains consistent at the same time.

6 Summary

The increasing computational demands of modern deep learning models pose significant challenges for conventional digital CMOS technology, which is approaching fundamental scaling limits. To address this bottleneck, alternative computing paradigms have gained attention, with analog computing emerging as a promising candidate. However, analog accelerators introduce new challenges, particularly due to inherent noise that can degrade model performance.

In this work, we first examine the challenges associated with training DNNs under these imperfect conditions. We observe that while techniques such as quantization and SAM contribute to improved model robustness, they fall short of the robustness provided by Noisy Training. However, Noisy Training itself has critical limitations: although it can achieve high peak accuracy, it exhibits poor generalization when subjected to variations in noise levels, as typically encountered in analog hardware. Specifically, standard Noisy Training tends to overfit to a particular noise configuration, leading to suboptimal performance when the noise characteristics shift due to factors such as temperature fluctuations and hardware aging common occurrences in analog accelerators.

To address this robustness gap, we propose *Variance-Aware Noisy Training (VANT)*, an extension of standard Noisy Training that explicitly accounts for temporal variations in noise. *VANT* incorporates an additional term which models the expected evolution of the noise environment over time. It thus enhances the generalization capabilities of DNNs under real-world deployment conditions, where noise characteristics are dynamic rather than fixed.

Empirical evaluations demonstrate the effectiveness of *VANT* in improving robustness across different noise regimes and dataset complexities. For instance, under typical analog noise conditions, *VANT* increases robustness from 79.3% to 97.6% on CIFAR-10. On the more challenging Tiny ImageNet dataset, VANT similarly yields significant gains, improving performance from 32.4% to 99.7%.

In summary, our findings highlight a crucial principle for deploying DNNs on noisy analog hardware: it is not sufficient to account solely for the immediate noise environment during training; rather, it is essential to model the temporal evolution of noise over time. By adopting a more comprehensive approach that considers the dynamic nature of hardware noise, *VANT* represents a significant step toward enabling robust deep learning models on fleets of analog accelerators.

Disclosure of Interests. The authors have no competing interests to declare that are relevant to the content of this article.

References

1. Ambrogio, S., et al.: Equivalent-accuracy accelerated neural-network training using analogue memory. Nature **558**(7708), 60–67 (2018). https://doi.org/10.1038/s41586-018-0180-5
2. Bishop, C.M.: Training with noise is equivalent to tikhonov regularization. Neural Comput. **7**(1), 108–116 (1995). https://doi.org/10.1162/neco.1995.7.1.108
3. Borras, H., Klein, B., Fröning, H.: Walking Noise: on layer-specific robustness of neural architectures against noisy computations and associated characteristic learning dynamics. In: European Conference on Machine Learning and Principles and Practice of Knowledge Discovery in Databases. ECML-PKDD (2024). https://doi.org/10.1007/978-3-031-70359-1_3
4. Bricken, T., Schaeffer, R., Olshausen, B., Kreiman, G.: Emergence of sparse representations from noise. In: International Conference on Machine Learning. Proceedings of Machine Learning Research, vol. 202, pp. 3148–3191. PMLR (2023). https://proceedings.mlr.press/v202/bricken23a.html
5. Brückerhoff-Plückelmann, F., et al.: Probabilistic photonic computing with chaotic light. Nat. Commun. **15**(1), 10445 (2024). https://doi.org/10.1038/s41467-024-54931-6
6. Burr, G.W., et al.: Neuromorphic computing using non-volatile memory. Adv. Phys. X **2**(1), 89–124 (2017). https://doi.org/10.1080/23746149.2016.1259585
7. Cappelli, A., Ohana, R., Launay, J., Meunier, L., Poli, I., Krzakala, F.: Adversarial robustness by design through analog computing and synthetic gradients. In: IEEE International Conference on Acoustics, Speech and Signal Processing (2022). https://doi.org/10.1109/ICASSP43922.2022.9746671
8. Chi, P., et al.: PRIME: a novel processing-in-memory architecture for neural network computation in ReRam-based main memory. In: International Symposium on Computer Architecture (ISCA) (2016). https://doi.org/10.1109/ISCA.2016.13
9. Darlow, L.N., Crowley, E.J., Antoniou, A., Storkey, A.J.: CINIC-10 is not ImageNet or CIFAR-10. CoRR abs/1810.03505 (2018). arXiv:1810.03505
10. Duncan, K., Komendantskaya, E., Stewart, R., Lones, M.: Relative robustness of quantized neural networks against adversarial attacks. In: International Joint Conference on Neural Networks. IJCNN, IEEE (2020). https://doi.org/10.1109/IJCNN48605.2020.9207596
11. Feldmann, J., et al.: Parallel convolutional processing using an integrated photonic tensor core. Nature **589**(7840), 52–58 (2021). https://doi.org/10.1038/s41586-020-03070-1
12. Foret, P., Kleiner, A., Mobahi, H., Neyshabur, B.: Sharpness-aware minimization for efficiently improving generalization. In: International Conference on Learning Representations (2021). https://openreview.net/forum?id=6TmlmposlrM
13. Giacobbe, M., Henzinger, T.A., Lechner, M.: How many bits does it take to quantize your neural network? In: Tools and Algorithms for the Construction and Analysis of Systems. TACAS (2020). https://doi.org/10.1007/978-3-030-45237-7_5
14. Gokmen, T., Vlasov, Y.: Acceleration of deep neural network training with resistive cross-point devices: design considerations. Front. Neurosci. **10**, 333 (2016). https://doi.org/10.3389/fnins.2016.00333
15. Goodfellow, I., Bengio, Y., Courville, A.: Deep learning. MIT press (2016)
16. Goodfellow, I.J., Shlens, J., Szegedy, C.: Explaining and harnessing adversarial examples. CoRR abs/1412.6572 (2014). arXiv:1412.6572

17. Grandvalet, Y., Canu, S., Boucheron, S.: Noise injection: theoretical prospects. Neural Comput. **9**(5) (1997). https://doi.org/10.1162/neco.1997.9.5.1093
18. Gulcehre, C., Moczulski, M., Denil, M., Bengio, Y.: Noisy activation functions. In: Balcan, M.F., Weinberger, K.Q. (eds.) International Conference on Machine Learning. Proceedings of Machine Learning Research, vol. 48, pp. 3059–3068. PMLR (2016). https://proceedings.mlr.press/v48/gulcehre16.html
19. He, K., Zhang, X., Ren, S., Sun, J.: Deep residual learning for image recognition. In: IEEE/CVF Conference on Computer Vision and Pattern Recognition. CVPR (2016). https://doi.org/10.1109/CVPR.2016.90
20. He, Z., Lin, J., Ewetz, R., Yuan, J.S., Fan, D.: Noise injection adaption: end-to-end ReRam crossbar non-ideal effect adaption for neural network mapping. In: Design Automation Conference. DAC, ACM (2019). https://doi.org/10.1145/3316781.3317870
21. He, Z., Rakin, A.S., Fan, D.: Parametric noise injection: Trainable randomness to improve deep neural network robustness against adversarial attack. In: IEEE/CVF Conference on Computer Vision and Pattern Recognition (2019), https://doi.org/10.1109/CVPR.2019.00068
22. Holmstrom, L., Koistinen, P.: Using additive noise in back-propagation training. IEEE Trans. Neural Networks **3**(1), 24–38 (1992). https://doi.org/10.1109/72.105415
23. Jiang, Y., Zur, R.M., Pesce, L.L., Drukker, K.: A study of the effect of noise injection on the training of artificial neural networks. In: International Joint Conference on Neural Networks (2009). https://doi.org/10.1109/IJCNN.2009.5178981
24. Klein, B., et al.: Towards addressing noise and static variations of analog computations using efficient retraining. In: ECML PKDD 2021 Workshops (2021). https://doi.org/10.1007/978-3-030-93736-2_32
25. Krizhevsky, A., Hinton, G.E.: Learning multiple layers of features from tiny images. Technical report, University of Toronto (2009)
26. Kuhn, L., Klein, B., Fröning, H.: On the non-associativity of analog computations, pp. 183–195 (2025). https://doi.org/10.1007/978-3-031-74643-7_15
27. Le, Y., Yang, X.S.: Tiny ImageNet visual recognition challenge (2015). https://api.semanticscholar.org/CorpusID:16664790
28. LeCun, Y., Bottou, L., Bengio, Y., Haffner, P.: Gradient-based learning applied to document recognition. Proc. IEEE **86** (1998). https://doi.org/10.1109/5.726791
29. Lin, J., Gan, C., Han, S.: Defensive quantization: when efficiency meets robustness. In: International Conference on Learning Representations. ICLR (2019). https://openreview.net/forum?id=ryetZ20ctX
30. Liu, X., Cheng, M., Zhang, H., Hsieh, C.J.: Towards robust neural networks via random self-ensemble. In: European Conference on Computer Vision (2018). https://doi.org/10.1007/978-3-030-01234-2_23
31. Murray, A., Edwards, P.: Enhanced MLP performance and fault tolerance resulting from synaptic weight noise during training. IEEE Trans. Neural Netw. **5**(5) (1994). https://doi.org/10.1109/72.317730
32. Neelakantan, A., et al.: Adding gradient noise improves learning for very deep networks. CoRR abs/1511.06807 (2015). arXiv:1511.06807
33. Neftci, E.O., Mostafa, H., Zenke, F.: Surrogate gradient learning in spiking neural networks. CoRR abs/1901.09948 (2019). arXiv:1901.09948
34. Schemmel, J., Billaudelle, S., Dauer, P., Weis, J.: Accelerated analog neuromorphic computing. CoRR abs/2003.11996 (2020). arXiv:2003.11996

35. Sebastian, A., Le Gallo, M., Khaddam-Aljameh, R., Eleftheriou, E.: Memory devices and applications for in-memory computing. Nat. Nanotechnol. **15**(7), 529–544 (2020). https://doi.org/10.1038/s41565-020-0655-z
36. Shafiee, A., et al.: ISAAC: A convolutional neural network accelerator with in-situ analog arithmetic in crossbars. In: International Symposium on Computer Architecture. ISCA (2016). https://doi.org/10.1109/ISCA.2016.12
37. Sung, W., Shin, S., Hwang, K.: Resiliency of deep neural networks under quantization. CoRR abs/1511.06488 (2015). arXiv:1511.06488
38. Tsipras, D., Santurkar, S., Engstrom, L., Turner, A., Madry, A.: Robustness may be at odds with accuracy. arXiv e-prints arXiv:1805.12152 (2018). https://doi.org/10.48550/arXiv.1805.12152
39. Wu, C., et al.: Harnessing optoelectronic noises in a photonic generative network. Sci. Adv. **8**(3) (2022). https://www.science.org/doi/abs/10.1126/sciadv.abm2956
40. Wu, D., Xia, S.T., Wang, Y.: Adversarial weight perturbation helps robust generalization. In: Advances in Neural Information Processing Systems, vol. 33 (2020). https://doi.org/10.5555/3495724.3495973
41. Yang, J.J., Strukov, D.B., Stewart, D.R.: Memristive devices for computing. Nature Nanotech **8**(1), 13–24 (2013). https://doi.org/10.1038/nnano.2012.240
42. Ye, N., et al.: Improving the robustness of analog deep neural networks through a bayes-optimized noise injection approach. Commun. Eng. **2** (2023). https://doi.org/10.1038/s44172-023-00074-3
43. Zhou, C., Kadambi, P., Mattina, M., Whatmough, P.N.: Noisy Machines: understanding noisy neural networks and enhancing robustness to analog hardware errors using distillation. CoRR abs/2001.04974 (2020). http://arxiv.org/abs/2001.04974

PAR-AdvGAN: Improving Adversarial Attack Capability with Progressive Auto-regression AdvGAN

Jiayu Zhang[1], Zhiyu Zhu[2], Xinyi Wang[3], Silin Liao[4], Zhibo Jin[2], Flora Salim[5], and Huaming Chen[6(✉)]

[1] Suzhou University of Technology, Suzhou, China
zjy@szut.edu.cn
[2] University of Technology Sydney, Ultimo, Australia
{zhiyu.zhu,zhibo.jin}@student.uts.edu.au
[3] University of Malaya, Kuala Lumpur, Malaysia
22103906@siswa.um.edu.my
[4] Nanning Normal University, Nanning, China
anivie@email.nnnu.edu.cn
[5] University of New South Wales, Kensington, Australia
flora.salim@unsw.edu.au
[6] The University of Sydney, Camperdown, Australia
huaming.chen@sydney.edu.au

Abstract. Deep neural networks have demonstrated remarkable performance across various domains. However, they are vulnerable to adversarial examples, which can lead to erroneous predictions. Generative Adversarial Networks (GANs) can leverage the generators and discriminators model to quickly produce high-quality adversarial examples. Since both modules train in a competitive and simultaneous manner, GAN-based algorithms like AdvGAN can generate adversarial examples with better transferability compared to traditional methods. However, the generation of perturbations is usually limited to a single iteration, preventing these examples from fully exploiting the potential of the methods. To tackle this issue, we introduce a novel approach named Progressive Auto-Regression AdvGAN (PAR-AdvGAN). It incorporates an auto-regressive iteration mechanism within a progressive generation network to craft adversarial examples with enhanced attack capability. We thoroughly evaluate our PAR-AdvGAN method with a large-scale experiment, demonstrating its superior performance over various state-of-the-art black-box adversarial attacks, as well as the original AdvGAN. Moreover, PAR-AdvGAN significantly accelerates the adversarial example generation, i.e., achieving the speeds of up to 335.5 frames per second on Inception-v3 model, outperforming the gradient-based transferable attack algorithms. Our code is available at: https://github.com/LMBTough/PAR.

Supplementary Information The online version contains supplementary material available at https://doi.org/10.1007/978-3-032-06109-6_10.

1 Introduction

Deep neural networks (DNNs) are widely used in different real-world applications, i.e., image classification [20], emotional analysis [29], and item recommendations [27]. DNNs demonstrate human-surpassed performance when properly trained. However, DNNs can be vulnerable to adversarial examples crafted by attackers [5,24,32], which is a concern in safety-critical scenarios. Thus, a practical approach is to develop effective attack algorithms that can assess the robustness of DNNs against adversarial attacks at an early stage, ultimately enhancing model safety.

Currently, both white-box and black-box attack algorithms, such as gradient-based methods like FGSM [10], NAA [38], SSA [23], and optimization-based approaches such as PGD [25] and C&W [1], require continuous computation of the model's gradient information throughout the attack process. However, they all require extensive running time. Generative Adversarial Networks (GANs) [9] have demonstrated promising results for realistic sample generation by leveraging both generator and discriminator for training [2,4,11,17]. While the generator constructs high-quality examples, a discriminator learn to distinguish the original and generated examples. Furthermore, once the generator is trained, there will be no additional gradient computation for input examples.

As an early GAN-based model, AdvGAN incorporates a perturbation, denoted as $G(x)$, into the original image instance x for attack [34]. AdvGAN aims to obtain the manipulated image $x + G(x)$ from the original instance x through the discriminator. To achieve high attack success rates in both white-box and black-box attacks, AdvGAN introduces an adversarial loss on top of GANs loss, ensuring the adversarial image is generated in a direction more effective for adversarial attacks. Additionally, it employs hinge loss to limit perturbation range, thereby preventing significant deviations between the adversarial and original images. Subsequently, AdvGAN++ [15] further enhances the attack success rate by utilizing latent features instead of input image instances x. It optimizes the latent features during adversarial examples generation.

However, GAN-based methods suffer from several challenges. Both AdvGAN and AdvGAN++ generate perturbations in a single iteration, which limits their control over these perturbations. We observe the reason may be the generator continuously increases the perturbations during the iterative process (as illustrated in the **Appendix 1.1**). This may not be effective against adversarial defenses and impacts the attack capability. It is critical since the goal is to maximize attack effectiveness with minimal perturbation. Furthermore, the transferability performance of such attacks is concerning, especially since internal model information is typically unavailable in real-world scenarios.

Inspired by recent works that utilise auto-regressive properties to generate realistic images or text [2,26,37], we propose a novel GAN-based algorithm, Progressive Auto-Regression AdvGAN (PAR-AdvGAN) to generate adversarial examples with enhanced transferability. PAR-AdvGAN employs a progressive, auto-regressive iterative method to effectively capture the specific structures of input examples. This process gradually generates more diverse and realistic adversarial examples. Specifically, at time step t, we combine the input examples x_{adv}^{t-1} from time step $t-1$ with the initial examples x_0 to generate the perturbation $G(x_{adv}^{t-1}, x_0)$ at time step t. Consequently, the manipulated examples shifts from $x + G(x)$ in the original AdvGAN to $x_{adv}^{t-1} + G(x_{adv}^{t-1}, x_0)$ in PAR-AdvGAN.

To achieve optimal performance with minimal perturbation, we propose L_p loss to limit the perturbation range during iteration, thereby ensuring that the adversarial examples remain imperceptible to human. Furthermore, to enhance the quality of adversarial examples and mitigate potential distortions and significant noise during the generation process, we introduce L_d loss, imposing a stringent constraint between the final adversarial examples x_t and initial examples x_0. Finally, by independently optimising the generator and discriminator during training, we fine-tune the parameters of PAR-AdvGAN for more effective adversarial examples. Notably, owing to the high stealth and robust generalization capabilities, non-targeted adversarial attacks subject models to more rigorous evaluations and reveal more subtle vulnerabilities. Thus, we primarily focus on non-targeted adversarial attacks. We summarise the contributions as follows:

- We empirically study the limited transferability of adversarial examples generated by existing GAN-based algorithms. To address this, we explore the use of progressive generator network to enhance transferability.
- We propose an auto-regression iterative method and provide theoretical analysis on formulating L_p and L_d loss to ensure minimal distortions in the adversarial samples.
- Extensive experiments demonstrate that our PAR-AdvGAN significantly outperforms other methods, achieving highest attack success rates. Moreover, it outperforms traditional gradient-based transferable attack algorithms in both transferability and attack speed. We release the code of PAR-AdvGAN for future research development.

2 Related Work

2.1 Adversarial Attacks

While numerous adversarial algorithms are dedicated to generating high-quality and robust adversarial samples, gradient-based attack algorithms constitute a main type. FGSM [10] was the first to utilise the model's gradients, which adds a small perturbation to the input data in the direction of the gradient, thereby maximising the loss function through gradient ascent to achieve optimal attack performance. MI-FGSM [6] incorporates a momentum factor in each iteration to mitigate the impact of local optima on the attack success rate. TI-FGSM [7] employs shifted images to calculate the input gradient, a process that involves convolving the original image's input gradient with a kernel matrix.

Other adversarial attack algorithms, such as PGD [25], project samples onto suitable attack directions and limit the size of perturbations to generate robust adversarial examples. C&W method minimises the attack's objective function to optimise the generation process [1]. AdvGAN [34] employs an adversarial training process between the generator and discriminator. This process bolsters the generator's ability to produce adversarial samples, making them challenging for the discriminator to distinguish from genuine data. Besides attack purpose, we also note some other iterative training methods for GANs, such as the Progressive GAN [16] which divides the Generator into several layers, with each layer undergoing individual training. In our approach, we consider an auto-regression methods, where each subsequent generation is based on the results of previous step. Although auto-regression GAN has been improved for continuous generation tasks, all we need is the attack result of the last state, so we need to redesign it for this situation.

2.2 Adversarial Defenses

Adversarial defense represents an effective approach to mitigate the impact of attacks on DNNs. Commonly used adversarial defense techniques include denoising and adversarial training. The denoising technique employs preprocessing mechanisms to filter out adversarial examples, thereby preventing the poisoning of training data and reducing the likelihood of subsequent attacks on the model. Other notable works include HRGD [21], R&P [35] and so on [3,8].

Adversarial training enhances model robustness by incorporating adversarial examples into the training process. Ensemble adversarial training [12] works by decoupling the target model from adversarial examples generated by other black-box models, thereby defending against transferable attacks. To enhance the robustness of our algorithm against adversarial defenses, we validated the attack effectiveness of PAR-AdvGAN on the target model subjected to ensemble adversarial training.

3 Methodology

In this section, we first provide the problem definition of adversarial attacks. Then, we discuss the issue of perturbation escalation in AdvGAN and propose three strategies to optimise the generator, aiming to generate highly transferable adversarial samples. Finally, we provide a detailed implementation for the proposed PAR-AdvGAN method.

3.1 Problem Definition of Adversarial Attacks

Consider a clean data distribution p_{data} in which benign samples are represented by $X \subseteq p_{data}$. In an untargeted attack, the network f is misled by the manipulated sample x_{adv}. For the original sample $x \in X$, with the original label denoted as m, the adversarial goal can be defined as:

$$f(x_{adv}) \neq m \tag{1}$$

$$\|x_{adv} - x\|_n \leq \epsilon \tag{2}$$

where $\|\cdot\|_n$ represents the n-order norm (e.g., L_2 norm), and ϵ denotes the maximum perturbation.

3.2 Perturbation Escalation in AdvGAN

AdvGAN adopts a non-repetitive iterative approach to improve attack performance. However, as iterations progress, the perturbation magnitude of the adversarial example increases rapidly. This issue arises because it treats each iterated example as an independent instance, neglecting its relation to the initial sample x_0. Additionally, AdvGAN fails to impose constraints on the distance between the generated samples and the initial samples. This suggests that the perturbations generated in each iteration will have significant magnitudes. To address this issue, we introduce three propositions:

Proposition 1. *The generator should obtain information about the original sample x_0.*

Proposition 2. *To train the generative model, the inputs to the generator should include a significant number of non-initial samples, particularly those encountered during the adversarial process.*

Proposition 3. *The generator should enforce constraints on the distance between adversarial samples and the initial sample x_0 throughout the iterative progress*

3.3 Progressive Auto-regression AdvGAN

In this section, we first introduce the solutions for three propositions, namely progressive generator network, auto-regression iterative method, and generator constraints. Next, we explain the training processes for both the discriminator and the generator. Finally, as shown in Algorithm. 1, we provided the pseudo-code for the PAR-AdvGAN approach.

Progressive Generator Network. For Proposition 1, we adjust the generator to include initial example x_0 as an input, resulting in a revised generator $G(x_{adv}^t, x_0)$. To do this, we expand the channel dimension of the generator's first layer, and employ a concat operator to merge x_{adv}^t and x_0 along the channel dimension. This design enables the generator to leverage information from both the current adversarial example x_{adv}^t and initial input x_0, thus facilitating the generation of incremental adversarial perturbations during the iterative process (refer to line 5 in Algorithm 1).

Auto-regression Iterative Method. In Proposition 2, during each training iteration, we utilise a hyperparameter T to regulate the number of interactions for x_{adv}^t instances (refer to line 4). We iteratively generate x_{adv}^t by adding perturbations $G(x_{adv}^{t-1}, x_0)$ to the preceding x_{adv}^{t-1} (see line 6), then use the resulting gradient progression to update and train the generator.

$$\nabla_\theta = \frac{\partial L_{adv}}{\partial x + G(x)} \cdot \underbrace{\frac{\partial x + G(x)}{\partial G(x)}}_{1} \cdot \frac{\partial G(x)}{\partial \theta} \qquad (3)$$

Algorithm 1. Progressive Auto-regression AdvGAN (PAR-AdvGAN)

Input: iteration number T, batch size n, progressive generator G, discriminator D, target network N, corresponding label m, learning rate η_1, η_2, weight hyper-parameter $\lambda_1, \lambda_2, \lambda_3$
Output: θ_D, θ_G
1: **for** i in (range) epoch **do**
2:     Sample a mini-batch of n examples $x = \{x(1), ..., x(n)\}$;
3:     $x_0 = x$
4:     **for** $t = 1, ..., T$ **do**
5:         $P_t = G(x_{adv}^{t-1}, x_0)$, here $x_{adv}^0 = x_0$
6:         $x_{adv}^t = clip(x_{adv}^{t-1} + P_t)$
7:         **for** $k = 1, ..., S_d$ **do**
8:             $g_{\theta_D} = \nabla_{\theta_D} L_D$
9:             Update the discriminator by descending its stochastic gradient S_d times:
10:            $\theta_D = \theta_D - \eta_1 \cdot g_{\theta_D}$
11:         **end for**
12:         **for** $k = 1, ..., S_g$ **do**
13:             $L_{adv} = -Cross\ Entropy(x_{adv}^t, m)$
14:             $L_p = \|P_t\|_2$
15:             $L_d = \|x_{adv}^t - x_0\|_2$
16:             $L_G = (1 - D(x_{adv}^t))^2$
17:             $g_{\theta_G} = \nabla_{\theta_G}(L_G + \lambda_1 L_p + \lambda_2 L_d + \lambda_3 L_{adv})$
18:             Update the generator by descending its stochastic gradient S_g times:
19:             $\theta_G = \theta_G - \eta_2 \cdot g_{\theta_G}$
20:         **end for**
21:     **end for**
22: **end for**
23: **return** θ_D, θ_G

To better understand the auto-regression iterative progress, we decompose ∇_θ in Eq. 3. Here, $\frac{\partial x + G(x)}{\partial G(x)}$ equals 1, so it can be omitted (See **Appendix 1.3** for detailed proof). Following this, we further explore the relationship between $\frac{\partial G(x)}{\partial \theta}$ and $\frac{\partial L_{adv}}{\partial x + G(x)}$. Thus, $\frac{\partial G(x)}{\partial \theta}$ represents the degree of change in $G(x)$ with respect to changing in θ. $\frac{\partial L_{adv}}{\partial x + G(x)}$ can be interpreted as the degree of change in L_{adv} when changing $x + G(x)$. Therefore, we can interpret the gradient ascent process of the parameter θ as a modification of θ to drive $x + G(x)$ able to obtain a better adversarial effect. At this point, to enable G to iteratively generate perturbations, we will replace x with x_{adv}^t. This transforms the first part of Eq. 3 into $\frac{\partial L_{adv}}{\partial x_{adv}^t + G(x_{adv}^t)}$, indicating that G continues to generate perturbations based on x_{adv}^t.

Given a network N that accurately maps image x sampled from the distribution p_{data} to its corresponding label m. The adversarial sample x_{adv}^t at time t can be expressed as:

$$P_t = G(x_{adv}^{t-1}, x_0) \tag{4}$$

$$x_{adv}^t = clip(x_{adv}^{t-1} + P_t) \tag{5}$$

such that
$$N(x_{adv}^t) \neq m \tag{6}$$

Here, P_t is the perturbation at time t, thus we have $x_{adv}^1 = x_0 + P_1$. And $G(\cdot, x_0)$ is the progressive generator network.

Training of the Discriminator. We train the discriminator to accurately distinguish adversarial samples generated by the progressive generator and actual samples from the data distribution p_{data}. Specifically, we fix the parameters related to the progressive generator and trained the discriminator S_d times (line 7). The loss function L_D can be written as:

$$L_D = (1 - D(x))^2 + D(x_{adv}^t)^2 \tag{7}$$

It is worth noting that we did not choose to calculate L_D in the form of $log(1 - D(x))$ as in AdvGAN. This is because we find that the gradient of $log(1 - D(x))$ for D will be very large and not smooth when $D(x)$ is close to 1, and gradient explosion will occur during iteration. We employ a squared form in the Eq. 10 to help mitigate this issue.

Hence, the gradient of the discriminator with respect to the parameters θ_D can be expressed using Eq. 8 (line 8):

$$g_{\theta_D} = \nabla_{\theta_D} L_D \tag{8}$$

By updating θ_D through gradient descent, we finally obtain the optimal parameters for the discriminator (line 9–10):

$$\theta_D = \theta_D - \eta_1 \cdot g_{\theta_D} \tag{9}$$

Here η_1 is the learning rate in discriminator training.

Constraints on the Generator. We propose the use of L_{adv} to measure whether the adversarial samples are generated in a direction more conducive to the attack (refer to line 13).

$$L_{adv} = -Cross\ Entropy\ (x_{adv}^t, m) \tag{10}$$

It is worth noting that, in untargeted attacks, a larger value of *cross entropy* (x_{adv}^t, m) indicates a more effective adversarial example. Consequently, to enhance the adversarial nature of x_{adv}^t during gradient descent on L_{adv}, we prepend a negative sign to *cross entropy*(x_{adv}^t, m). It is also feasible to replace *cross entropy* with the loss function used in C&W [1].

To prevent the issue of perturbation explosion in the auto-regression iterative process, we introduce L_p to constrain the magnitude of perturbation (refer to line 14), where $\|\cdot\|_2$ stands for the l_2 norm:

$$L_p = \|P_t\|_2 = \|G(x_{adv}^{t-1}, x_0)\|_2 \tag{11}$$

To fulfill Proposition 3, we introduce an additional loss function L_d that enforces the generated adversarial examples to remain close to the initial example. This constraint ensures that the iterative progress of generating adversarial perturbations does not deviate significantly from the original input, thus maintaining the adversarial samples' proximity to the initial data (see line 15).

$$L_d = \left\| x_{adv}^t - x_0 \right\|_2 \tag{12}$$

Training of the Progressive Generator. We train the progressive generator to generate adversarial samples with high transferability and low distortions from original samples while attacking the target neural network N. Specifically, we fixed the parameters related to the discriminator and trained the progressive generator S_g times (refer to line 12).

As shown in Eq. 14, we computed the gradient of the progressive generator with respect to the parameters θ_G (line 16):

$$L_G = (1 - D(x_{adv}^t))^2 \tag{13}$$

$$g_{\theta_G} = \nabla_{\theta_G}(L_G + \lambda_1 L_p + \lambda_2 L_d + \lambda_3 L_{adv}) \tag{14}$$

Note that L_G is the loss function to deceive the discriminator and $\lambda_1, \lambda_2, \lambda_3$ are the weight hyper-parameters that control the balance between loss functions. By updating θ_G through gradient descent, we ultimately obtain the optimal parameters for the progressive generator (line 17–18):

$$\theta_G = \theta_G - \eta_2 \cdot g_{\theta_G} \tag{15}$$

Here η_2 is the learning rate in discriminator training.

4 Experiments

In this section, we present the experiments conducted to evaluate the performance of our method. To guide the analysis, we address the following research questions.

- What is the attack success rate of PAR-AdvGAN compared to the baseline AdvGAN? (**RQ1**)
- How does PAR-AdvGAN's performance in attack transferability and attack speed compare to state-of-the-art methods in adversarial attacks? Is it effective? (**RQ2**)
- Why does PAR-AdvGAN work effectively? (**RQ3**)

4.1 Experiment Setup

Dataset and Models. We conducted the experiments on the ImageNet-compatible dataset consisting of 1000 images with a resolution of 299293 [28][1]. The dataset generation process follows the literature [6,7]

---
[1] https://github.com/cleverhans-lab/cleverhans/tree/master/cleverhans_v3.1.0/examples/nips17_adversarial_competition/dataset.

Here we refer to the typical and state-of-the-art transferable adversarial attack methods [6,7,22,34,36,38]. To ensure experiment fairness, we selected representative models from two types: normally-trained and defense-trained models. The normally trained models include Inceptionv3 (Inc-v3) [31], Inception-v4 (Inc-v4) [30], Inception-ResNet-v2 (IncRes-v2) [30], ResNet-v2-50 (Res-50) [13,14], ResNet-v2-101 (Res-101) [13,14], and ResNet-v2-152 (Res-152) [13,14]. As for the defense-trained models through ensemble adversarial training, we selected Inc-v3ens3 [33], Inc-v3ens4 [33], and IncResv2ens [33].

Baseline Methods. We employ the original AdvGAN [34] algorithm as our baseline to validate the transferability performance by incorporating self-regressive iteration in PAR-AdvGAN. Meanwhile, to evaluate our proposed PAR-AdvGAN, we selected seven state-of-the-art black-box adversarial attack methods as our competitive baselines, including FGSM [10], BIM [19], PGD [25], DI-FGSM [36], TI-FGSM [7], MI-FGSM [6], and SINI-FGSM [22].

Parameter Settings. All experiments in this study are conducted using the Nvidia RTX 6000 Ada 48GB. In all experiments, we set the following fixed parameters for each algorithm according to the settings in [18]. For AdvGAN and PAR-AdvGAN, the training epochs are set to 60. The initial learning rate for both the Generator and Discriminator is set to 0.001, which is then reduced to 0.0001 at the 50th epoch. For DI-FGSM, we set the decay to 0, the resize_rate to 0.9, and the diversity_prob to 0.5. For TI-FGSM, decay is set to 0, kernel_name is set to "gaussian", len_kernel is set to 15, resize_rate is set to 0.9, and the diversity_prob is set to 0.5. For MI-FGSM, decay is set to 1. For SINI-FGSM, decay is set to 1, and m is set to 5.

Metrics. Attack success rate (ASR) is a metric to evaluate the transferability of attacks. It quantifies the average proportion of mislabeled samples among all generated samples after the attack. Thus, a higher attack success rate signifies better transferability.

Additionally, we use Frames Per Second (FPS) to assess the attack speed. Another crucial measure, the perturbation rate, is utilised to ensure that the adversarial images do not largely diverge from the original images in visual perception. A low value of this rate suggests that the adversarial examples maintain close visual fidelity to their originals. Detailed formulas are in the **Appendix 1.4.**

4.2 RQ1: Attacking Performance

As shown in Table 1, we compare the attack success rates of the original AdvGAN and our proposed PAR-AdvGAN at three different perturbation rates of 8, 9, and 10. The comparisons are conducted using Inc-v3 and Inc-v4 as surrogate models and attacks are lunched on IncRes-v2. The results indicate that in most cases, our algorithm outperforms AdvGAN in terms of attack success rate.

Table 1. ASR (%) of AdvGAN and PAR-AdvGAN on IncRes-v2. The adversarial examples are crafted on Inc-v3 and Inc-v4

Model	Attack	IncRes-v2
Inc-v3	AdvGAN	13.9/38.9/43.2
	PAR-AdvGAN	**27.1/35.2/41.4**
Inc-v4	AdvGAN	6.1/9.6/15.9
	PAR-AdvGAN	**21.4/30.8/34.7**

Table 2. The attack success rates (%) on four undefended models and three adversarial trained models by various transferable adversarial attacks. The adversarial examples are crafted on Inc-v3 with different perturbations. The best results are in bold

Model	Attack	Perturbation	Inc-v4	Res-50	Res-101	Res-152	Inc-v3ens3	Inc-v3ens4	IncResv2ens	mASR
Inc-v3	AdvGAN	8.41/9.88/10.26	32.9/61.9/65.9	42.6/77.7/82.8	47.8/75.3/83.1	38.8/66.6/72.8	15.1/44.0/52.5	30.2/54.5/63.0	9.9/25.7/26.5	31.04/57.95/63.80
	PAR-AdvGAN	**8.29/9.27/9.95**	**53.7/63.1/68.4**	**74.8/85.0/89.8**	**79.3/86.2/89.5**	**68.2/78.0/82.5**	**39.4/53.5/63.8**	**45.7/60.8/69.4**	**28.0/39.0/46.5**	**55.58/66.51/72.84**
	FGSM	8.79/9.74/10.69	26.2/28.0/30.3	26.2/29.0/30.6	23.3/25.8/27.6	22.8/24.1/27.0	13.8/14.5/15.5	14.0/14.3/14.3	6.0/6.1/6.1	18.9/20.25/21.62
	BIM	8.46/9.50/9.96	47.6/52.2/56.6	42.1/45.8/48.5	36.7/40.6/42.9	35.6/39.2/39.3	14.4/16.0/15.8	14.1/14.6/14.5	8.5/8.1/8.4	28.42/30.92/32.28
	PGD	8.76/9.79/10.35	44.6/46.2/50.2	38.6/40.7/43.5	33.1/35.5/37.3	28.9/34.5/35.8	12.4/14.2/14.4	12.4/13.3/13.1	6.8/7.4/7.7	25.25/27.40/28.85
	DI-FGSM	8.51/9.56/10.02	66.0/70.0/70.9	54.0/60.0/61.4	50.7/55.1/55.2	49.3/53.7/52.7	19.1/19.6/20.0	18.4/20.4/19.1	10.5/11.0/11.0	38.28/41.40/41.47
	TI-FGSM	8.60/9.65/10.10	52.4/55.3/56.5	39.7/45.2/45.2	34.4/39.9/41.1	34.8/39.0/43.1	31.6/34.8/35.3	34.1/37.7/39.2	21.4/25.9/25.8	35.48/39.68/40.88
	MI-FGSM	8.98/9.77/10.55	44.5/47.9/51.4	39.9/41.7/45.1	36.5/38.8/41.0	34.3/37.8/38.9	16.3/17.1/16.8	15.6/14.9/16.2	6.5/7.7/7.4	27.65/29.41/30.97
	SINI-FGSM	8.99/9.77/10.55	56.0/59.7/64.2	53.8/58.0/62.5	47.2/51.1/55.2	45.6/50.7/53.8	24.6/24.4/26.4	23.9/23.8/25.9	11.0/12.0/12.6	37.44/39.95/42.94

We can see that compared to the most representative AdvGAN algorithm, PAR-AdvGAN has made significant improvements for attacking performance at a low perturbation rate. Specifically, similar to AdvGAN, PAR-AdvGAN, as a generative model, does not require additional gradient calculations based on different input data after training the generator. Compared to traditional gradient-based black-box transferable attack methods, it possesses faster attack speed. Therefore, we consider the PAR-AdvGAN algorithm feasible and suitable for attack scenarios that demand high transferability and fast generation of adversarial samples.

4.3 Effectiveness Experiment for RQ2: Transferability and Attack Speed

To validate the transferability and attack speed of PAR-AdvGAN compared to other SOTA methods, we conduct the experiments using various attack methods on Inc-v3, Inc-v4, and IncRes-v2 as source models to generate adversarial samples. We then conduct transferable attacks on different target models and use ASR and FPS as the main metrics, to validate the effectiveness of our algorithm.

Experiments on Inc-V3. As shown in Table 2, we conduct attacks using Inc-v3 as the source model with three different perturbation rates on target models of Inc-v4, Res-50, Res-101, Res-152, Inc-v3ens3, Inc-v3ens4, and IncRes-v2. We can see that our PAR-AdvGAN algorithm has achieved an average increase of 30.3% in attack success rate compared to other baselines. Moreover, despite DI-FGSM achieving better performance than PAR-AdvGAN on Inc-v4, which may

Table 3. The attack success rates (%) on four undefended models and three adversarial trained models by various transferable adversarial attacks. The adversarial examples are crafted on Inc-v4 with different perturbations. The best results are in bold

Model	Attack	Perturbation	Inc-v3	Res-50	Res-101	Res-152	Inc-v3ens3	Inc-v3ens4	IncResv2ens	mASR
Inc-v4	AdvGAN	9.64/11.67/12.11	55.6/75.9/59.1	48.6/77.5/70.6	54.4/74.8/69.5	40.4/67.0/58.4	13.4/26.5/24.4	20.3/54.6/43.0	16.0/25.7/21.1	35.52/57.42/49.44
	PAR-AdvGAN	**9.55/11.05/11.60**	**72.9/85.0/87.8**	**66.1/79.0/85.0**	**73.7/86.4/89.8**	**55.7/69.2/74.8**	13.0/17.4/20.2	**35.0/50.9/58.2**	15.7/25.6/30.2	**47.44/59.24/63.71**
	FGSM	9.74/11.64/12.58	28.4/31.9/32.9	23.7/26.3/28.4	21.1/24.2/25.4	20.6/24.3/25.6	13.1/13.2/13.4	10.9/11.7/12.3	5.9/6.6/6.8	17.67/19.74/20.68
	BIM	9.98/11.46/11.91	60.1/62.5/62.4	42.5/45.8/46.2	38.9/40.2/41.0	34.7/39.8/39.8	13.9/15.7/16.1	13.5/15.7/14.8	9.3/10.9/9.6	30.41/32.94/32.84
	PGD	9.78/11.35/11.88	49.8/55.6/58.8	35.7/38.8/40.7	28.2/36.4/36.2	28.6/32.7/34.1	12.4/14.9/14.5	12.7/13.8/14.1	7.8/7.8/8.3	25.02/28.57/29.52
	DI-FGSM	10.01/11.49/11.94	75.4/80.4/80.3	57.6/63.7/62.9	51.2/57.5/56.5	49.9/55.0/55.7	18.5/19.6/20.6	16.4/18.5/18.7	10.7/13.5/12.4	39.95/44.02/43.87
	TI-FGSM	9.61/11.08/12.00	61.5/67.5/68.4	41.6/50.0/52.4	37.0/44.0/48.0	38.6/44.7/49.3	**33.6/38.5/39.7**	34.8/39.3/40.3	**24.1/28.5/32.0**	38.74/44.64/47.15
	MI-FGSM	9.81/11.42/12.22	53.2/61.2/61.7	40.2/43.2/47.0	36.7/41.6/43.9	34.0/39.8/41.3	15.0/15.6/16.4	14.6/15.3/15.0	6.2/7.9/7.6	28.55/32.08/33.27
	SINI-FGSM	9.79/11.39/12.18	75.1/78.2/80.1	63.1/69.0/70.6	58.3/65.9/66.7	56.9/62.6/64.8	27.8/31.1/32.1	26.4/28.8/29.9	14.3/16.6/17.4	45.98/50.31/51.65

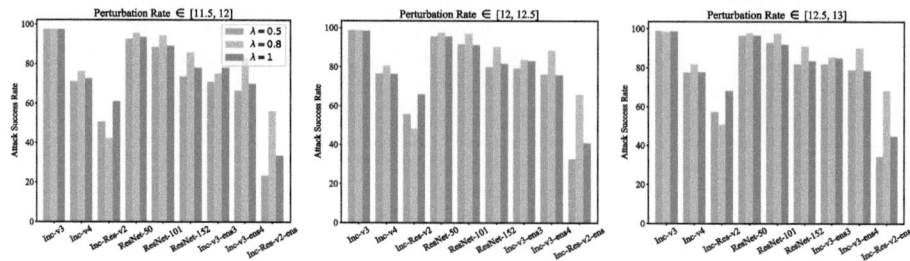

Fig. 1. The performance of PAR-AdvGAN at different high perturbation rate intervals

be attributed to the randomness in model training, a comprehensive comparison across all models reveals that the attack success rate of PAR-AdvGAN is elevated by 24.6% compared to the best-performing competing baseline, DI-FGSM.

Experiments on Inc-V4. As shown in Table 3, we conduct attacks using Inc-v4 as the source model with three different perturbation rates on target models of Inc-v3, Res-50, Res-101, Res-152, Inc-v3ens3, Inc-v3ens4, and IncRes-v2. We can see that our PAR-AdvGAN algorithm has achieved an average increase of 20.13% in attack success rate compared to other baselines. Furthermore, compared to the best performing SINI-FGSM among competitive baselines, PAR-AdvGAN achieved an increase of 7.48% in ASR.

Experiments on IncRes-V2. In this section, we conduct transferability tests on Inc-v3, Inc-v4, Res-50, Res-101, Res-152, Inc-v3ens3, Inc-v3ens4, and IncRes-v2 as target models with three different perturbation rates using IncRes-v2 as the source model. We have included the results in the Table 4. The results demonstrate that PAR-AdvGAN achieves an average increase of 14.96% in ASR compared to other baselines. We can see that although PAR-AdvGAN achieves a lower ASR of 0.02% than the best performing SINI-FGSM among competitive baselines, it outperforms AdvGAN by 6.31%.

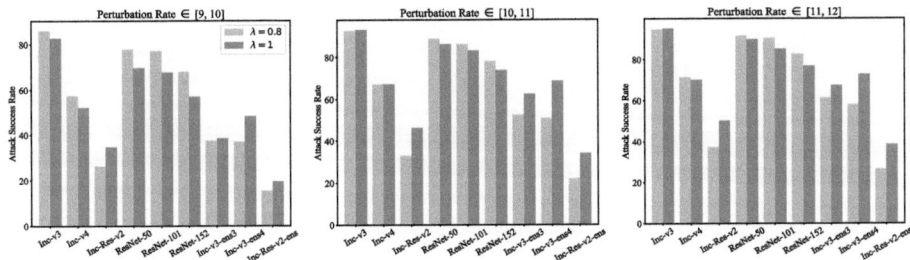

Fig. 2. The performance of PAR-AdvGAN at different low perturbation rate intervals

Table 4. The attack success rates (%) on four undefended models and three adversarial trained models by various transferable adversarial attacks. The adversarial examples are crafted on IncRes-v2. The best results are in bold

Model	Attack	Inc-v3	Inc-v4	Res-50	Res-101	Res-152	Inc-v3ens3	Inc-v3ens4	IncResv2ens	mASR
IncRes-v2	AdvGAN	55.6/66.6/88.3	48.9/55.7/87.4	48.8/57.8/93.4	42.2/49.8/91.9	35.8/45.2/90.8	12.0/17.4/52.5	14.0/15.4/45.2	5.6/7.4/40.3	32.86/39.41/73.72
	PAR-AdvGAN	66.8/70.3/71.9	**71.2/75.1/76.4**	**77.6/80.3/82.0**	63.2/67.4/69.5	**66.0/70.8/73.0**	31.1/33.7/35.8	25.3/27.8/29.9	16.5/18.7/19.2	52.21/55.51/57.21
	FGSM	23.3/26.2/27.4	17.5/18.6/19.4	20.5/21.7/23.2	18.1/19.1/20.5	18.5/19.7/20.1	11.3/11.4/11.3	10.4/10.9/11.1	6.1/6.3/6.1	15.71/16.73/17.38
	BIM	58.4/62.0/63.8	47.1/51.8/40.7	41.9/46.4/47.3	36.6/39.4/42.2	35.6/38.7/41.8	14.9/14.7/15.2	12.8/13.8/14.6	9.9/10.8/11.2	32.15/34.70/35.85
	PGD	51.7/55.9/55.2	40.6/42.2/44.9	35.4/38.0/39.3	31.3/34.0/34.2	29.3/31.4/31.8	14.4/14.2/13.2	12.2/13.1/14.2	7.7/8.4/9.3	27.82/29.65/30.26
	DI-FGSM	**79.5/79.0/79.3**	69.7/72.0/74.8	61.8/61.7/67.2	58.3/59.6/62.5	57.2/56.9/59.9	20.9/20.5/22.2	18.9/20.3/20.9	14.8/15.1/14.7	47.63/48.13/50.18
	TI-FGSM	66.6/69.3/69.1	63.6/65.1/65.1	53.1/55.7/57.7	50.5/50.3/53.4	47.6/51.7/51.6	**43.3/45.2/46.5**	**44.0/44.8/48.8**	**39.5/41.1/40.9**	51.02/52.90/54.13
	MI-FGSM	58.2/59.8/61.7	49.8/50.1/55.7	43.7/46.1/48.4	39.2/44.7/43.3	37.6/39.5/42.6	15.0/16.1/17.4	14.8/15.4/15.3	8.9/9.4/9.8	33.40/35.13/36.77
	SINI-FGSM	76.7/79.3/80.6	70.1/73.8/75.7	66.1/70.4/73.0	**63.8/66.7/71.0**	60.9/63.9/66.6	34.7/35.2/37.0	29.5/29.9/31.4	20.6/20.7/22.4	**52.80/54.98/57.21**

Table 5. The attack success rates (%) on four undefended models and three adversarial trained models by various transferable adversarial attacks. The adversarial examples are crafted on ResNet-50 with different perturbations. The best results are in bold

Model	Attack	Perturbation	Inc-v3	Inc-v4	Res-101	Res-152	Inc-v3ens3	Inc-v3ens4	IncResv2ens	mASR
ResNet-50	AdvGAN		8.32/9.15/10.40	28.2/38.5/27.5	31.7/33.5/21.6	30.3/34.5/26.9	29.4/32.4/19.7	14/23.9/7.3	16.7/19.9/12.8	9.5/10.9/5.3	22.83/27.66/17.3
	PAR-AdvGAN		**8.24/9.10/10.37**	**67.2/72.5/79.3**	43.7/48.8/55.1	**69.8/76.1/82.4**	52.7/61.9/69.6	**36.3/46.6/57.3**	**42.3/51.6/60.1**	**25.4/32/42.9**	**48.2/55.64/63.81**
	FGSM		8.79/9.74/10.69	27/29.6/31.6	22.4/24.5/26	24.9/27.3/29.4	24.7/27/28.6	11.9/12.9/13.6	12.3/12/12.2	5.7/5.9/6.3	18.41/19.89/21.1
	BIM		8.50/9.54/10.42	41.5/45.6/49.9	35.7/38.6/42.3	37/39.5/41.6	34/37.9/40.9	13.5/14/14.5	12/13.1/13.2	8.1/8/8.6	25.97/28.1/30.14
	PGD		8.34/9.37/10.46	30.8/35.6/39.2	26.4/30.3/33.1	26.9/32/32.5	24.5/27.9/31.5	11.6/11.6/13.1	10.4/11.8/12.6	6/6/7.5	19.51/21.74/24.21
	DI-FGSM		8.59/9.17/10.52	67.2/71.1/74.8	**65.5/68.8/73.1**	63.8/69.1/72.4	**62.2/64.9/70.6**	16.8/17/19	15/15.6/9	10.4/10.6/11.7	42.99/45.21/48.36
	TI-FGSM		8.45/9.46/10.38	51/54.9/60.1	48.9/54.9/58.2	44.9/47/52.2	42.7/45.8/51.1	34.4/36.5/38.2	35.4/39.1/41.2	24.7/28.1/31.3	40.29/43.76/47.47
	MI-FGSM		8.87/9.65/10.43	41.5/43.7/48.1	36.5/40/41.2	35.6/38.9/40.8	36.1/37.7/39.5	14.2/15/15.6	13.6/12.4/12.8	7.2/7.9/8	26.39/27.94/29.43
	SINI-FGSM		8.26/9.85/10.63	41.4/49.4/53.3	35.7/43.9/48.7	38.1/46.1/48.9	33.4/43.5/47.3	14.8/15.4/16.6	14.6/14/15.1	6.2/7.1/7.8	26.31/31.34/33.96

Experiments on ResNet-50. As shown in Table 5, we conduct attacks using ResNet-50 as the source model with three different perturbation rates on target models of Inc-v3, Inc-v4, Res-101, Res-152, Inc-v3ens3, Inc-v3ens4, and IncRes-v2. The experimental results demonstrate that PAR-AdvGAN consistently achieves superior performance across all target models compared to other baseline methods. Specifically, PAR-AdvGAN achieves the highest mASR of 48.2%, 55.64%, and 63.81% for the three perturbation rates, outperforming the best-performing baseline DI-FGSM by 5.21%, 10.43%, and 15.45%, respectively. Furthermore, PAR-AdvGAN shows significant improvements over AdvGAN, with an average increase in attack success rate of 25.37%. Although DI-FGSM achieves competitive performance on certain models such as Inc-v4 and Res-101, the overall effectiveness of PAR-AdvGAN across all models underscores its robustness and transferability.

Table 6. he attack success rates (%) on four undefended models and three adversarial trained models by various transferable adversarial attacks. The adversarial examples are crafted on ViT-B/16 with different perturbations. The best results are in bold

Model	Attack	Perturbation	Inc-v3	Inc-v4	Res-50	Res-101	Res-152	Inc-v3ens3	Inc-v3ens4	IncResv2ens	mASR
ViT-B/16	AdvGAN	10.59/11.30/12.25	75.6/72/80.3	70.3/60.5/70.2	72.5/75.7/84.3	70.8/75.2/84.9	68.9/71.8/77.1	61.2/74.9/83.4	61.8/69.5/79.1	53.8/50/60.5	66.86/68.7/77.46
	PAR-AdvGAN	**10.21/11.12/12.01**	**76.1/81.8/84.5**	63.6/67/70.9	**80.3/84.9/87.3**	**79.9/84.8/87.3**	**75.7/80.4/83**	**82.3/87.6/90.6**	**73.9/79.5/83.1**	**55.2/62.5/66.3**	**73.38/78.56/81.63**
	FGSM	10.76/11.71/12.65	35/36.3/38.6	31.9/34.6/36.4	33.6/35.1/37.6	32.2/34/36	31.9/34/36	27.9/30.1/31.7	29.9/30.3/31.5	23.8/25.3/26.5	30.78/32.46/34.29
	BIM	10.90/11.47/12.37	55.5/58.7/60.7	50.5/49.7/54.1	54.2/55.6/59.2	48.5/51.4/56.8	46.6/47.6/54.4	39.2/38.5/42.4	39.7/41/42.8	30.5/32.4/35.1	45.59/46.86/50.69
	PGD	10.73/11.23/12.24	46.6/48/53	40.7/42.3/44	44.2/47/49.6	40.3/42.7/45.7	37.9/39.6/42.4	28.2/29.7/31.7	31.8/31.5/33.9	21.8/22.9/25.2	36.44/37.96/40.69
	DI-FGSM	10.59/11.58/12.04	75.6/77.8/78.9	**70.3/74.1/75.1**	72.5/77/74.9	70.8/74.5/73.1	68.9/71.8/71.9	61.2/67.7/67.4	61.8/65.8/67.5	53.8/58.5/57.9	66.86/70.9/70.84
	TI-FGSM	10.77/11.21/12.23	60.5/61/65.4	54.1/56.2/59.9	53.1/55.4/60.2	52.6/54.6/58.3	50.7/54.8/59.3	56.4/58.6/61.2	59.4/62.4/63.6	52.1/53/57.7	54.86/57/60.7
	MI-FGSM	10.75/11.58/12.36	53.7/55.6/59.1	47.4/49/52.8	50.9/54.3/57.7	47.7/50.5/52.2	45.5/48.9/50.9	38.6/40.5/43.7	40.5/42.6/43.9	30.7/33.7/36.7	44.38/46.89/49.75
	SINI-FGSM	10.83/11.66/12.45	58.2/61.8/65.5	52.7/56.3/60.9	55.7/61.2/64.7	51.1/56.1/59.6	49.8/54.1/57.9	44.5/47.5/49.4	44.1/46.7/50.4	37.9/39.7/43.9	49.25/52.93/56.54

Experiments on ViT-B/16. In Table 6, we present the results of attacks using ViT-B/16 as the source model with three different perturbation rates on several target models, including Inc-v3, Inc-v4, Res-50, Res-101, Res-152, Inc-v3ens3, Inc-v3ens4, and IncRes-v2. Unlike traditional convolutional neural networks (CNNs), Vision Transformers (ViTs) adopt a fundamentally different architecture for image classification tasks. Our experimental findings show that the proposed PAR-AdvGAN algorithm performs exceptionally well when transferred to ViT-based models, achieving an average increase of 6.85% in attack success rate (ASR) compared to AdvGAN across all target models. Specifically, PAR-AdvGAN consistently delivers the highest mean ASR values of 73.38%, 78.56%, and 81.63% across the three perturbation rates, surpassing all baseline methods, including DI-FGSM, which was the best performer in certain cases. These results underscore the robustness and transferability of PAR-AdvGAN, demonstrating its ability to maintain high effectiveness not only with traditional CNNs but also with more recent transformer-based models like ViT, thus proving its versatility and reliability across different model architectures.

Attack Transferability Result Analysis. With the results from Tables 2, 3, 4, 5 and 6, it can be observed that in most cases, our adversarial attack algorithm shows significantly improved transferability compared to the original AdvGAN, especially at lower perturbation rates. Additionally, compared to other competitive baselines, PAR-AdvGAN exhibits the best transferability. Notably, to ensure the fairness of the experiments, our algorithm was consistently compared with other methods for a lowest perturbation rate. In instances where the perturbation rates were higher, some algorithms did not exhibit a proportional increase in attack transferability. However, the transferability is overall improved.

As shown in Table 7, we evaluated the computational efficiency of PAR-AdvGAN and seven competitive baselines using Inc-v3, Inc-v4, and IncRes-v2 as source models. We use FPS as the metric for measuring attack speed, representing the number of images that can be processed by the attack per second. It can be observed that across Inc-v3, Inc-v4, and IncRes-v2, PAR-AdvGAN exhibits speed improvements of 61, 88.3, and 158.5 times over the slowest-performing PGD algorithm among the competitive baselines. Furthermore, in comparison

Table 7. FPS comparison of PAR-AdvGAN with seven competitive baselines

Method	Inc-v3	Inc-v4	IncRes-v2
FGSM	176.5	116.7	76.1
BIM	10.6	6.5	4.1
PGD	5.5	3.3	2.1
DI-FGSM	10.8	6.6	4.1
TI-FGSM	10.6	6.5	4.2
MI-FGSM	42.7	26	16.4
SINI-FGSM	8.6	5.3	3.3
PAR-AdvGAN	**335.5**	**291.3**	**332.8**

to the fastest-performing FGSM algorithm among the competitive baselines, PAR-AdvGAN achieves speed enhancements of 1.9, 2.5, and 4.4 times, respectively. We assert that PAR-AdvGAN demonstrates significantly higher attack speed in comparison to traditional gradient-based transferable methods, while simultaneously achieving state-of-the-art transferability performance.

4.4 Ablation Experiment for RQ3

We investigate the effects of parameter λ on the attack transferability as it is an important parameter to control the perturbation range. Figure 1 shows the performance of PAR-AdvGAN with Inc-v3 as the source model, with a fixed ϵ of 20, and λ set to 0.5, 0.8, and 1 for different target models. At λ of 0.5, the specific perturbation rates are 11.75, 12.56, and 12.89. At λ of 0.8, the specific perturbation rates are 11.55, 12.59, and 12.90. At λ of 1, the specific perturbation rates are 11.66, 12.45, and 12.81. We can see that at higher perturbation rate intervals, setting λ to 0.8 achieves best transferability performance.

Figure 2 compares the results with fixed ϵ of 16 and λ set to 0.8 and 1. At λ of 0.8, the specific perturbation rates are 9.40, 10.60, and 11.20. At λ of 1, the corresponding perturbation rates are 8.95, 10.88, and 11.40. For lower perturbation rates, setting λ to 1 achieves the best transferability.

5 Conclusion

In this paper, we present a novel PAR-AdvGAN algorithm to boost adversarial attack capability through iterative perturbations. Specifically, to address the perturbation escalation issue in AdvGAN, we first adopt a progressive generator network to incorporate the initial sample x_0 in the perturbation generation process. An auto-regression iterative method is then proposed to include non-initial sample information in generator training. Furthermore, we constrain the distance between initial samples and subsequent samples. Our extensive experimental results exhibit the superior attack transferability of our method. Moreover, compared with the state-of-the-art gradient-based transferable attacks, our method achieves an accelerated attack efficiency.

References

1. Carlini, N., Wagner, D.: Towards evaluating the robustness of neural networks. In: 2017 IEEE Symposium on Security and Privacy (SP), pp. 39–57. IEEE (2017)
2. Chang, H., Zhang, H., Jiang, L., Liu, C., Freeman, W.T.: MaskGIT: masked generative image transformer. In: Proceedings of the IEEE/CVF Conference on Computer Vision and Pattern Recognition, pp. 11315–11325 (2022)
3. Cohen, J., Rosenfeld, E., Kolter, Z.: Certified adversarial robustness via randomized smoothing. In: International Conference on Machine Learning, pp. 1310–1320. PMLR (2019)
4. Croce, D., Castellucci, G., Basili, R.: GAN-BERT: generative adversarial learning for robust text classification with a bunch of labeled examples (2020)
5. Deng, Y., Zheng, X., Zhang, T., Chen, C., Lou, G., Kim, M.: An analysis of adversarial attacks and defenses on autonomous driving models. In: 2020 IEEE International Conference on Pervasive Computing and Communications (PerCom), pp. 1–10. IEEE (2020)
6. Dong, Y., Liao, F., Pang, T., Su, H., Zhu, J., Hu, X., Li, J.: Boosting adversarial attacks with momentum. In: Proceedings of the IEEE Conference on Computer Vision and Pattern Recognition, pp. 9185–9193 (2018)
7. Dong, Y., Pang, T., Su, H., Zhu, J.: Evading defenses to transferable adversarial examples by translation-invariant attacks. In: Proceedings of the IEEE/CVF Conference on Computer Vision and Pattern Recognition, pp. 4312–4321 (2019)
8. Dziugaite, G.K., Ghahramani, Z., Roy, D.M.: A study of the effect of jpg compression on adversarial images. arXiv preprint arXiv:1608.00853 (2016)
9. Goodfellow, I., et al.: Generative adversarial nets. In: Advances in Neural Information Processing Systems, vol. 27 (2014)
10. Goodfellow, I.J., Shlens, J., Szegedy, C.: Explaining and harnessing adversarial examples. arXiv preprint arXiv:1412.6572 (2014)
11. Haidar, M.A., Rezagholizadeh, M.: TextKD-GAN: text generation using knowledge distillation and generative adversarial networks. In: Advances in Artificial Intelligence: 32nd Canadian Conference on Artificial Intelligence, Canadian AI 2019, Kingston, ON, Canada, May 28–31, 2019, Proceedings 32, pp. 107–118. Springer (2019)
12. Hang, J., Han, K., Chen, H., Li, Y.: Ensemble adversarial black-box attacks against deep learning systems. Pattern Recogn. **101**, 107184 (2020)
13. He, K., Zhang, X., Ren, S., Sun, J.: Deep residual learning for image recognition. In: Proceedings of the IEEE Conference on Computer Vision and Pattern Recognition, pp. 770–778 (2016)
14. He, K., Zhang, X., Ren, S., Sun, J.: Identity mappings in deep residual networks. In: Leibe, B., Matas, J., Sebe, N., Welling, M. (eds.) ECCV 2016. LNCS, vol. 9908, pp. 630–645. Springer, Cham (2016). https://doi.org/10.1007/978-3-319-46493-0_38
15. Jandial, S., Mangla, P., Varshney, S., Balasubramanian, V.: AdvGAN++: harnessing latent layers for adversary generation. In: Proceedings of the IEEE/CVF International Conference on Computer Vision Workshops (2019)
16. Karras, T., Aila, T., Laine, S., Lehtinen, J.: Progressive growing of GANs for improved quality, stability, and variation. arXiv preprint arXiv:1710.10196 (2017)

17. Karras, T., et al.: Alias-free generative adversarial networks. Adv. Neural. Inf. Process. Syst. **34**, 852–863 (2021)
18. Kim, H.: TorchAttacks: a PyTorch repository for adversarial attacks. arXiv preprint arXiv:2010.01950 (2020)
19. Kurakin, A., Goodfellow, I.J., Bengio, S.: Adversarial examples in the physical world. In: Artificial Intelligence Safety and Security, pp. 99–112. Chapman and Hall/CRC (2018)
20. Li, X., Li, X., Pan, D., Zhu, D.: On the learning property of logistic and softmax losses for deep neural networks. In: Proceedings of the AAAI Conference on Artificial Intelligence, vol. 34, pp. 4739–4746 (2020)
21. Liao, F., Liang, M., Dong, Y., Pang, T., Hu, X., Zhu, J.: Defense against adversarial attacks using high-level representation guided denoiser. In: Proceedings of the IEEE Conference on Computer Vision and Pattern Recognition, pp. 1778–1787 (2018)
22. Lin, J., Song, C., He, K., Wang, L., Hopcroft, J.E.: NESTEROV accelerated gradient and scale invariance for adversarial attacks. arXiv preprint arXiv:1908.06281 (2019)
23. Long, Y., Zhang, Q., Zeng, B., Gao, L., Liu, X., Zhang, J., Song, J.: Frequency domain model augmentation for adversarial attack. In: Computer Vision–ECCV 2022: 17th European Conference, Tel Aviv, Israel, October 23–27, 2022, Proceedings, Part IV, pp. 549–566. Springer (2022)
24. Ma, X., et al.: Understanding adversarial attacks on deep learning based medical image analysis systems. Pattern Recogn. **110**, 107332 (2021)
25. Madry, A., Makelov, A., Schmidt, L., Tsipras, D., Vladu, A.: Towards deep learning models resistant to adversarial attacks. arXiv preprint arXiv:1706.06083 (2017)
26. Ni, H., Szpruch, L., Wiese, M., Liao, S., Xiao, B.: Conditional Sig-Wasserstein GANs for time series generation. arXiv preprint arXiv:2006.05421 (2020)
27. Pan, D., Li, X., Li, X., Zhu, D.: Explainable recommendation via interpretable feature mapping and evaluation of explainability. arXiv preprint arXiv:2007.06133 (2020)
28. Papernot, N., et al.: Technical report on the CleverHans v2.1.0 adversarial examples library. arXiv preprint arXiv:1610.00768 (2018)
29. Qiang, Y., Li, X., Zhu, D.: Toward tag-free aspect based sentiment analysis: a multiple attention network approach. In: 2020 International Joint Conference on Neural Networks (IJCNN), pp. 1–8. IEEE (2020)
30. Szegedy, C., Ioffe, S., Vanhoucke, V., Alemi, A.: Inception-v4, inception-ResNet and the impact of residual connections on learning. In: Proceedings of the AAAI Conference on Artificial Intelligence, vol. 31 (2017)
31. Szegedy, C., Vanhoucke, V., Ioffe, S., Shlens, J., Wojna, Z.: Rethinking the inception architecture for computer vision. In: Proceedings of the IEEE Conference on Computer Vision and Pattern Recognition, pp. 2818–2826 (2016)
32. Szegedy, C., et al.: Intriguing properties of neural networks. arXiv preprint arXiv:1312.6199 (2013)
33. Tramèr, F., Kurakin, A., Papernot, N., Goodfellow, I., Boneh, D., McDaniel, P.: Ensemble adversarial training: attacks and defenses. arXiv preprint arXiv:1705.07204 (2017)
34. Xiao, C., Li, B., Zhu, J.Y., He, W., Liu, M., Song, D.: Generating adversarial examples with adversarial networks. arXiv preprint arXiv:1801.02610 (2018)
35. Xie, C., Wang, J., Zhang, Z., Ren, Z., Yuille, A.: Mitigating adversarial effects through randomization. arXiv preprint arXiv:1711.01991 (2017)

36. Xie, C., et al.: Improving transferability of adversarial examples with input diversity. In: Proceedings of the IEEE/CVF Conference on Computer Vision and Pattern Recognition, pp. 2730–2739 (2019)
37. Yoon, J., Jarrett, D., Van der Schaar, M.: Time-series generative adversarial networks. In: Advances in Neural Information Processing Systems, vol. 32 (2019)
38. Zhang, J., et al.: Improving adversarial transferability via neuron attribution-based attacks. In: Proceedings of the IEEE/CVF Conference on Computer Vision and Pattern Recognition, pp. 14993–15002 (2022)

Sequence Models

AdvKT: An Adversarial Multi-step Training Framework for Knowledge Tracing

Lingyue Fu[1], Ting Long[2], Jianghao Lin[1], Wei Xia[3], Xinyi Dai[3], Ruiming Tang[3], Yasheng Wang[3], Weinan Zhang[1(✉)], and Yong Yu[1(✉)]

[1] Shanghai Jiao Tong University, Shanghai, China
{fulingyue,chiangel,wnzhang,yyu}@sjtu.edu.cn
[2] Jilin University, Changchun, China
longting@jlu.edu.cn
[3] Huawei Noah's Ark Lab, Montreal, Canada
{daixinyi5,tangruiming,wangyasheng}@huawei.com

Abstract. Knowledge Tracing (KT) monitors students' knowledge states and simulates their responses to question sequences. Existing KT models typically follow a single-step training paradigm, which leads to discrepancies with the multi-step inference process required in real-world simulations, resulting in significant error accumulation. This accumulation of error, coupled with the issue of data sparsity, can substantially degrade the performance of recommendation models in the intelligent tutoring systems. To address these challenges, we propose a novel Adversarial Multi-Step Training Framework for Knowledge Tracing (AdvKT), which, for the first time, focuses on the multi-step KT task. More specifically, AdvKT leverages adversarial learning paradigm involving a generator and a discriminator. The generator mimics high-reward responses, effectively reducing error accumulation across multiple steps, while the discriminator provides feedback to generate synthetic data. Additionally, we design specialized data augmentation techniques to enrich the training data with realistic variations, ensuring that the model generalizes well even in scenarios with sparse data. Experiments conducted on four real-world datasets demonstrate the superiority of AdvKT over existing KT models, showcasing its ability to address both error accumulation and data sparsity issues effectively.

Keywords: Knowledge Tracing · Educational Data Mining · Student Simulator

1 Introduction

Intelligent tutoring systems (ITS), such as Massive Online Open Courses (MOOCs), aim to help students learn more efficiently through learning path recommendation and question recommendation. Knowledge Tracing (KT) is a vital component of ITS, which estimates the knowledge state by predicting the student responses, i.e., whether a student can answer each question correctly or not. KT models are used in two ways: as monitors to provide human instructors with insights into students mastery levels, and as *student simulators* to supply reward signals for recommendation models.

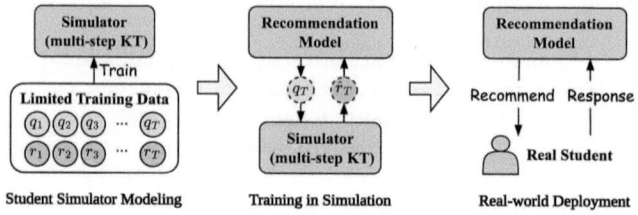

(a) Application of the student simulator.

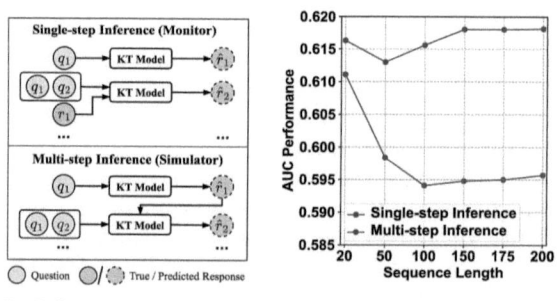

(b) Inference Comparison. (c) AUC Comparison.

Fig. 1. (a) Illustration of the students simulator's application and the comparison between single-step and multi-step inference KT. (b) Comparison of single-step inference and multi-step inference (simulator) and the primary application of the simulator. Input of single-step inference: historical question and ground-truth response. Input of multi-step inference: historical question and predicted response. (c) Performance comparison of the single-step inference and multi-step inference with a single-step training approach. With increased sequence length, errors accumulate gradually under the multi-step inference setting

Existing KT models [1,7,16,19,26] show promising performance as monitors of students learning progress. By taking students' real-time responses to various questions as input, these models estimate the knowledge states of students and make predictions for the next questions. The predictions can be a reference for human instructors, helping them identify areas where students may need additional support or challenge.

KT models are more frequently employed in ITS as *student simulators* for question recommendation models [8,15,18]. As illustrated in Fig. 1a, after the recommendation model generates a sequence of questions, the pre-trained simulator (KT model) provides simulated student responses, which serve as rewards to optimize the recommendation model. The objective of the recommendation model is to maximize the reward provided by the student simulator. In this setting, the accuracy of the simulation has a significant impact on the effectiveness of the recommendation model in the real-world deployment phase.

Despite their widespread use, existing KT models largely overlook their role as student simulators, leading to a gap between *single-step training* and *multistep inference*. Typically, these models follow a single-step training paradigm, where they are optimized to predict a students response for only the next question in a sequence, assuming the ground-truth response history is always accessible. In real-world simulations, however, the simulator must predict responses for an entire recommended question sequence at once. As illustrated in Fig. 1b, during multi-step inference, the simulator iteratively generates responses based on its previous predictions, as ground-truth history is unavailable.

The discrepancy between single-step training and multi-step inference results in significant *error accumulation* over longer sequences, adversely affecting the recommendation model's performance. As shown in Fig. 1c, we train EERNNA [29] using a single-step training approach and evaluate it under both single-step and multi-step inference settings. In the single-step setting, where ground-truth history is available, the model performs stably across varying sequence lengths, as input sequences remain error-free. In contrast, under the multi-step inference setting, prediction errors gradually accumulate as the sequence length increases, leading to a substantial degradation in performance. This discrepancy highlights the need for KT models that better align with the multi-step inference nature of real-world simulations.

Furthermore, current ITS suffer from the data sparsity problem. Existing KT models are generally supervised by optimizing the binary cross-entropy (BCE) loss and, therefore, minimizing the KL divergence between the model and data distributions, which casts heavy demands on the quantity of training data. However, in real-world ITS, the number of students in each class is typically limited, and each student exercises a finite number of questions. For example, in ASSIST09 dataset[1], there are only 2,661 students with 165,455 interactions, which contains 14,083 questions. The interactive data are sparse with respect to the whole space of question sequences, thus it is difficult for KT models to capture the students' learning patterns precisely.

To conquer the above challenges, we propose a novel Adversarial Multi-Step Training Framework for Knowledge Tracing, named **AdvKT**. To the best of our knowledge, this is the first work to formalize the multi-step KT task and the first to introduce adversarial learning to the KT task. AdvKT enables models to effectively handle the iterative nature of multi-step simulations by leveraging adversarial learning to diversify training sequences, thereby mitigating error propagation during inference. Additionally, we propose specialized data augmen-

---

[1] https://sites.google.com/site/assistmentsdata/home/2009-2010-assistment-data.

tation techniques to enrich training data with realistic variations, ensuring the model generalizes effectively even in sparse data scenarios.

To sum up, our contributions are summarized as follows:

- We propose a novel Adversarial Multi-Step Training Framework for the KT task (*i.e.*, **AdvKT**) to address the challenge of error accumulation in multi-step inference. To the best of our knowledge, this is the first work that focuses on the nature of multi-step prediction in the KT task.
- We design tailored data augmentation techniques specifically for KT tasks and incorporate them into AdvKT, thereby reducing the prediction bias caused by the data sparsity problem and uneven distributions.
- Extensive experiments on four real-world datasets demonstrate that AdvKT achieves state-of-the-art performance under the multi-step inference setting, as well as superior capabilities to tackle the data sparsity.

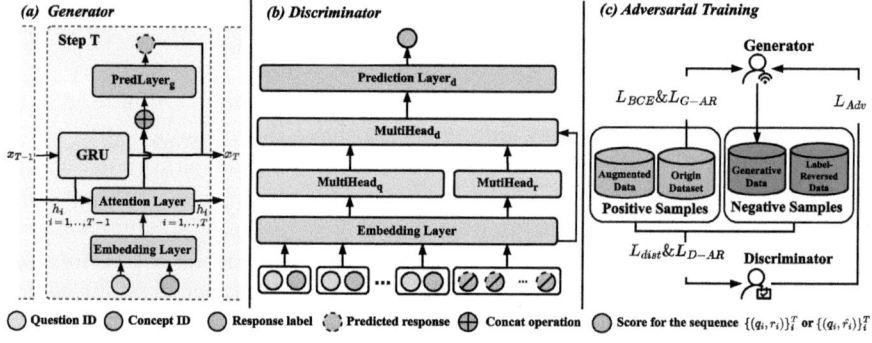

Fig. 2. The overview of the proposed AdvKT framework.

2 Problem Formulation

In ITS, let $\mathcal{S}$ represent the set of students, $\mathcal{Q}$ the set of questions, and $\mathcal{C}$ the set of concepts. Each question $q \in \mathcal{Q}$ is associated with a subset of concepts from the set $\mathcal{C}$, denoted as $\mathcal{C}^q = \{c_1^q, \ldots, c_k^q\} \subset \mathcal{C}$. The student's learning sequence is recorded as $s = [(q_i, r_i)]_{i=1}^T$, where $q_i \in \mathcal{Q}$ is the question, and $r_i \in 0, 1$ indicates whether the student answered question q_i correctly ($r_i = 1$ for correct, and $r_i = 0$ for incorrect).

Previous KT models typically follow a single-step training and inference paradigm, where the ground-truth responses to previous questions are used to predict the next response. The single-step prediction at step T can be formulated as:

$$\hat{r}_T = p\left(r_T = 1 | [(q_t, r_t)]_{t=1}^{T-1}, q_T\right). \tag{1}$$

In contrast to existing KT models, we focus on a multi-step prediction paradigm, which is more in line with real-world applications. Specifically, this approach involves predicting the student's response r_T using previously predicted responses $[\hat{r}_t]_{t=1}^{T-1}$, which can be expressed as:

$$\hat{r}_T = p\left(r_T = 1 | [(q_t, \hat{r}_t)]_{t=1}^{T-1}, q_T\right). \tag{2}$$

3 Methodology

In this section, we introduce the framework of AdvKT, as dipicted in Fig. 2. AdvKT consists of two main components: a generator that predicts the student's responses for a given question sequence, and a discriminator that distinguishes between real and fake data. We employ adversarial training over the generator and the discriminator with data augmentation.

3.1 Embedding Layer

To project discrete IDs to dense representations, we create a question embedding matrix $\mathbf{Emb}^Q \in \mathbb{R}^{|Q| \times d}$ and a concept embedding matrix $\mathbf{Emb}^C \in \mathbb{R}^{|C| \times d}$, where d denotes the embedding size. Let $\mathbf{e}_q = \mathbf{Emb}_q^Q \in \mathbb{R}^d$ and $\mathbf{e}_c = \mathbf{Emb}_c^C \in \mathbb{R}^d$ be the embedding vectors of question q and concept c, respectively. Following [31], we represent question q by concatenating the question embedding with the mean aggregation of its corresponding concept embeddings:

$$\mathbf{v}_{c,q} = \frac{1}{|C^q|} \sum_{i=1}^{|C^q|} \mathbf{e}_{c_i^q}, \quad \mathbf{v}_q = \mathbf{e}_q \oplus \mathbf{v}_{c,q}, \tag{3}$$

where $\oplus$ denotes the vector concatenation. Similarly, embedding vectors of position $o \in [1, T]$ and response $r \in \{0, 1\}$ are $\mathbf{e}_o = \mathbf{Emb}_o^O \in \mathbb{R}^d$ and $\mathbf{e}_r = \mathbf{Emb}_r^R \in \mathbb{R}^d$, respectively.

3.2 Generator

The generator $\mathcal{G}([(q_t, \hat{r}_t)]_{i=t}^{T-1}, q_T)$ predicts the student's response to question q_T based on historical questions with its own predicted responses. We utilize Gated Recurrent Unit (GRU) to represent students' learning states at step T

$$\mathbf{h}_T = \mathrm{GRU}_g(\mathbf{x}_T, \mathbf{h}_{T-1}), \tag{4}$$

where $\mathbf{x}_T$ is the student interaction vector in step T which would be introduce later. According to [29], the student's current state is a weighted sum aggregation of all the historical states. Hence, we assign different levels of importance to the historical states by applying an attention layer:

$$\mathbf{Q} = \mathbf{v}_{q_T}, \mathbf{K} = \{\mathbf{v}_{q_1}, \cdots, \mathbf{v}_{q_{T-1}}\}, \mathbf{V} = \{\mathbf{h}_1, \cdots, \mathbf{h}_{T-1}\},$$
$$\mathbf{a}_T = \mathrm{Attention}(\mathbf{Q}, \mathbf{K}, \mathbf{V}). \tag{5}$$

Next, we apply a prediction layer to calculate the probability of answering question q_T correctly:

$$\hat{r}_T = \text{Sigmoid}\left(\text{PredLayer}_g(\mathbf{v}_{q_T} \oplus \mathbf{h}_{T-1} \oplus \mathbf{a}_T)\right), \tag{6}$$

where PredLayer is a two-layer fully connected network.

Finally, according to the predicted student response $\hat{r}_T$, we concatenate the question representation $\mathbf{v}_{q_T}$ and weighted historical state $\mathbf{a}_T$ to form the student interaction vector $\mathbf{x}_T$, which serves as the recurrent input for the next GRU process:

$$\mathbf{x}_T = \begin{cases} \mathbf{v}_{q_T} \oplus \mathbf{a}_T \oplus \mathbf{0}_\mathbf{q} \oplus \mathbf{0}_\mathbf{a}, & \hat{r} \geq 0.5, \\ \mathbf{0}_\mathbf{q} \oplus \mathbf{0}_\mathbf{a} \oplus \mathbf{v}_{q_T} \oplus \mathbf{a}_T, & \hat{r} < 0.5, \end{cases} \tag{7}$$

where $\mathbf{0}_\mathbf{q}$ and $\mathbf{0}_\mathbf{a}$ are zero vectors with the same size as the vector $\mathbf{v}_{q_T}$ and $\mathbf{a}_T$, respectively.

3.3 Discriminator

The discriminator $\mathcal{D}\left([(q_t, r_t)]_{t=1}^T\right)$ distinguishes whether the sequence is derived from real data (*i.e.*, positive) or fake data (*i.e.*, negative). The responses in the input sequence can be either ground-truth responses r_i or generated ones $\hat{r}_i$. For simplicity, hereinafter, we use r_i to denote the input responses. We adopt the classical multi-head attention architecture to encode the sequence, which can be formulated as:

$$\begin{aligned} \text{MultiHead}(\mathbf{Q}, \mathbf{K}, \mathbf{V}) &= (\text{head}_1 \oplus \cdots \oplus \text{head}_h) \mathbf{W}^o, \\ \text{head}_i &= \text{Attention}\left(\mathbf{W}_i^q \mathbf{Q}, \mathbf{W}_i^k \mathbf{K}, \mathbf{W}_i^v \mathbf{V}\right), \end{aligned} \tag{8}$$

where the number of heads h is a hyperparameter, $\mathbf{W}_i^q, \mathbf{W}_i^k, \mathbf{W}_i^v$ and $\mathbf{W}^o$ represent the learnable parameters.

The discriminator takes the question sequence $[q_i]_{i=1}^T$, response sequence $[r_i]_{i=1}^T$, and positions $[o_i]_{i=1}^T$ as inputs. We define the question-position matrix $\mathbf{v}_q$ and response-position matrix $\mathbf{v}_r$ as:

$$\mathbf{V}_q = \begin{pmatrix} \mathbf{e}_{q_1} \oplus \mathbf{e}_{o_1} \\ \mathbf{e}_{q_2} \oplus \mathbf{e}_{o_2} \\ \cdots \\ \mathbf{e}_{q_T} \oplus \mathbf{e}_{o_T} \end{pmatrix}, \mathbf{V}_r = \begin{pmatrix} \mathbf{e}_{r_1} \oplus \mathbf{e}_{o_1} \\ \mathbf{e}_{r_2} \oplus \mathbf{e}_{o_2} \\ \cdots \\ \mathbf{e}_{r_T} \oplus \mathbf{e}_{o_T} \end{pmatrix}. \tag{9}$$

Then, we apply multi-head attention module to encode the sequence and finally output the estimated score of the sequence:

$$\begin{aligned} \mathbf{w}_q &= \text{MultiHead}_q(\mathbf{V}_q, \mathbf{V}_q, \mathbf{V}_q), \\ \mathbf{w}_r &= \text{MultiHead}_r(\mathbf{V}_r, \mathbf{V}_r, \mathbf{V}_r), \\ \mathbf{D}_o &= \text{MultiHead}_d(\mathbf{w}_q, \mathbf{w}_r, \mathbf{w}_q \oplus \mathbf{w}_r), \\ score &= \text{Sigmoid}(\text{PredLayer}_d(\mathbf{D}_o)). \end{aligned} \tag{10}$$

The structure of PredLayer_d is identical to PredLayer_g. The final output $score \in [0, 1]$ denotes the probability that the input sequence is a positive sample.

3.4 Adversarial Training

In AdvKT, the generator and the discriminator are alternately updated according to their respective loss functions until convergence. Meanwhile, data augmentation enriches training data to enhance the discriminator's robustness, enabling it to guide the generator in simulating realistic responses through adversarial training.

Generator Loss. We train the generator in a multi-step paradigm to minimize the gap between training and inference. The generator has three training goals: (1) aligning predictions with real-world data, (2) making the generated data indistinguishable to the discriminator, and (3) learning more robust and generalized question representations.

The binary cross-entropy (BCE) loss provides a supervised loss to align with the real-world data:

$$\mathcal{L}_{\text{BCE}} = -\sum_{t=1}^{T} \left(r_t \log(\hat{r}_t) + (1 - r_t) \log(1 - \hat{r}_t) \right). \tag{11}$$

After generating the responses, the generator obtains a score from the discriminator, and can be adversarially updated by policy gradient [30]:

$$\mathcal{L}_{\text{Adv}} = \frac{1}{T} \sum_{t=1}^{T} |\hat{r}_t - 0.5| \times R_t, \tag{12}$$

where $|\hat{r}_t - 0.5|$ is the confidence, and R_t represents the accumulative reward as follows:

$$R_t = -\log\left(1 - \mathcal{D}([(q_i, r_i)]_{i=1}^{t})\right) + \gamma R_{t+1}, \tag{13}$$

where $\gamma \in [0,1]$ is the decay factor. Moreover, inspired by [17], for more generalized question representations, we also introduce an additional autoregressive loss $\mathcal{L}_{AR}$ to predict the next question q_t based on the student interaction vector $\mathbf{x}_T$:

$$\hat{q}_t = \text{PredLayer}_{gq}(\mathbf{x}_T) \in \mathbb{R}^{|\mathcal{Q}|},$$
$$\mathcal{L}_{\text{G-AR}} = -\sum_{t=1}^{T} \sum_{i=1}^{|\mathcal{Q}|} \mathbb{I}(q_t = i) \log \hat{q}_t[i]. \tag{14}$$

Overall, the objective function of the generator is:

$$\mathcal{L}_G = \mathcal{L}_{\text{BCE}} + \lambda_1 * \mathcal{L}_{\text{Adv}} + \lambda_2 * \mathcal{L}_{\text{G-AR}}, \tag{15}$$

where λ_1 and λ_2 are hyperparameters.

Discriminator Loss. Due to the data sparsity, we artificially enrich the positive and negative samples based on the student learning pattern to improve the robustness of the discriminator.

Positive samples comprise the original dataset $\mathcal{R}$ and augmented data $\mathcal{T}$. The enrichment of positive samples includes four types: mask, crop, permute, and replace.

- **Mask**: Replace some questions in the origin sequences with a special token [MASK].
- **Crop**: Extract subsequences from the origin sequence.
- **Permute**: Randomly shuffle a subsequence.
- **Replace**: Calculate the difficulty of each question q by

$$\text{Difficulty}_q = \frac{\#\text{Correctly Answering } q}{\#\text{Answering } q},$$

and randomly replace questions that the student answers correctly or incorrectly with easier or more difficult ones.

These four augmentation methods generally follow the student learning patterns, ensuring the rationality of the augmented data.

Negative samples include generative data $\mathcal{E}$ and label-reversed data $\mathcal{V}$. The generative data refer to the sequences with responses generated by the generator instead of the ground-truth ones. In addition to the vanilla sequences in the original dataset, we design a heuristic method to generate synthetic sequences to be further labeled by the generator. Specifically, for each question pair (q_A, q_B), we calculate the probability of question q_B occurring after question q_A:

$$p(q_A, q_B) = \frac{\#(q_A, q_B)}{\sum_{q \in \mathcal{Q}} \#(q_A, q)}, \quad \forall q_A, q_B \in \mathcal{Q}. \tag{16}$$

We can sample the subsequent questions one by one based on the calculated probabilities above to generate more reasonable synthetic sequences. Furthermore, in addition to the generative data $\mathcal{E}$, we also selectively reverse the binary responses of the sequence in the original dataset $\mathcal{R}$ to create negative samples, denoted $\mathcal{V}$.

The training of the discriminator, based on the enriched positive and negative samples, aims to achieve two objectives: (1) to distinguish between positive and negative samples, and (2) to ensure the stability of the training process. For sequence discrimination, the goal is to maximize the difference between the scores of each positive and negative sample. This is achieved by optimizing the following loss term:

$$\mathcal{L}_{\text{dist}} = -\frac{1}{|\mathcal{R} \cup \mathcal{T}||\mathcal{G} \cup \mathcal{V}|} \sum_{i \in \mathcal{R} \cup \mathcal{T}} \sum_{j \in \mathcal{G} \cup \mathcal{V}} (score_i - score_j). \tag{17}$$

Moreover, to ensure the training stability, we introduce the Gradient Penalty proposed in [10] to restrict the gradient of the discriminator:

$$GP = \alpha \times (\|\nabla_{D_o} \mathcal{D}(q, r)\|_2 - 1)^2, \tag{18}$$

where α is a hyperparameter to balance the gradient penalty. In conclusion, the objective of the discriminator is:

$$\mathcal{L}_D = -\mathcal{L}_{\text{dist}} + GP. \tag{19}$$

Adversarial Learning. The general training algorithm is illustrated in Appendix A. We employ an alternating update strategy to iteratively update the discriminator and the generator. When updating the discriminator, we first generate four types of training data with rules, and compute the loss function in Eq. (19), through which the augmented discriminator learns gain robust capabilities. During the training of the generator, it receives rewards from the discriminator, guiding it to simulate more realistic responses, while also being trained by the additional losses in Eq. (15).

Note that the augmented data and label-reversed data are not directly used as the training corpus for the generator, as their sequence properties are highly similar to those in the training set. This similarity limits the effectiveness of GRU-based models. However, it could enhance the attention mechanism by introducing diverse local variations and encouraging more detailed learning of key sequence features, making it more suitable for improving the discriminator.

4 Experiment

4.1 Experimental Setup

Datasets. To evaluate the performance of our model, we conduct experiments on four real-world public datasets: ASSIST09, EdNet, Slepemapy and Junyi. Datasets in this paper are from sampling real students' learning logs of different subjects, indicating that the students exhibit different latent learning patterns. The detailed statistics of the datasets are shown in Table 1. The datasets possess varying levels of packing density and distribution, enabling us to test our method's robustness across different data characteristics. We retain students in the dataset who had more than 10 interactions with the platform and select the last 200 records for each student. In order to simulate the scenario with limited data, we randomly select 500 or 6000 students for training, while reserving 20% of the original datasets for testing.

Table 1. Dataset Statistics

Dataset	ASSIST09	EdNet	Slepemapy	Junyi
Subject	Math	English	Geography	Math
# Students	500	500	6,000	6,000
# Records	41,741	34,262	553,797	532,139
# Questions	15,003	13,170	4,332	2,164
# Concepts	122	190	1,332	40
Attempts per Q.	2.78	2.60	127.8	245.90
Attempts per C.	342.14	180.32	415.76	13,303.47

Baselines and Evaluation Metrics. To evaluate the effectiveness of our model, we compare AdvKT with 15 frequently used KT models. Models trained based on BCE loss include DKT [26], DFKT [23], SAINT [4], EERNNA [29], AKT [7], CKT [28], SAKT [25], GKT [24], DKVMN [34], SKVMN [1], LBKT [32], and simpleKT [19]. Models trained with other objectives include DHKT [31], IEKT [20] and CL4KT [14].

For a fair comparison, these baseline models are also trained under a multi-step setting, *i.e.*, the input of them are question sequences and historically predicted responses. We adopt Accuracy (ACC) and the Area Under Curve (AUC) as metrics. A higher AUC or ACC indicates better performance of the KT task.

Implementation Detail. The maximum length of each student's learning sequence is 200. The dimension of the hidden state of GRU is set to 64. The question embedding, concept embedding, response embedding and position embedding all have a dimension of 64. We utilize a 4-headed Transformer in the discriminator. The value of γ in Eq. (12) is chosen in $\{0.9, 0.93, 0.95, 0.98\}$. In Eq. (15), λ_1 is set to 1000, and λ_2 is chosen from $\{0, 1\}$. The optimizer used is Adam [35]. We update the discriminator every 2 epochs. The learning rate of the generator is 0.001, while the learning rate of the discriminator is 0.005. The memory overhead incurred during training by AdvKT is comparable to that of recent knowledge tracing models, with AdvKT requiring approximately 15,000 MiB, while LBKT [32] utilizes around 12,600 MiB. During inference stage, AdvKT only requires the use of the generator, thereby reducing GPU memory requirements by half. Our model is implemented on PyTorch and is available on Github[2].

4.2 Overall Performance

We compare AdvKT with all baselines under the multi-step training and inference setting. As shown in Table 2, we can obtain the following observations: (1) Baseline models have erratic performance across different datasets. Due to the complexity of student response behaviors, existing models struggle to generalize well when confronted with datasets that emphasize different learning patterns. As a result, each model could only capture specific learning patterns and data characteristics, suffering from multi-step error accumulation and data sparsity. (2) Baselines trained by BCE loss and other objectives show no significant differences compared to those trained with other objectives, because the effectiveness of alternative objectives depends on data distribution and can sometimes introduce noise. (3) AdvKT generally achieves significant performance improvements over the baseline models in both ACC and AUC. On average, our model outperforms the best baseline (AKT) by 1.79% on ACC and 3.98% on AUC. The performance validates the effectiveness of our proposed AdvKT. The adversarial learning paradigm not only help AdvKT acquire students' learning pattern under multi-step prediction scenarios, but also alleviate the data sparsity problem.

---

[2] Source code for AdvKT: https://github.com/fulingyue/AdvKT.

Table 2. Overall performance of AdvKT on four public datasets. The best performing and second-best models are denoted in bold and underlined. * indicates p-value < 0.05 in the significance test

Groups	Models	ASSIST09		EdNet		Slepemapy		Junyi		Average Performance	
		ACC	AUC	ACC	AUC	ACC	AUC	ACC	AUC	Avg. ACC	Avg. AUC
BCE Loss	AKT	0.6689	0.6178	0.6318	0.6515	0.7611	0.6520	<u>0.7532</u>	0.7547	<u>0.7037</u>	<u>0.6690</u>
	SAINT	0.6344	0.5272	0.6166	0.6384	0.7605	<u>0.6553</u>	0.7355	<u>0.7599</u>	0.6867	0.6452
	SAKT	0.6127	0.5513	0.6134	0.6333	0.7587	0.6393	0.7319	0.7525	0.6792	0.6441
	CKT	0.6813	0.6342	0.5976	0.5959	0.6884	0.5643	0.7082	0.6930	0.6689	0.6218
	DFKT	0.6426	0.6202	0.6331	0.6589	0.6959	0.5902	0.7291	0.7394	0.6751	0.6522
	DKT	0.6411	0.6188	0.6297	0.6525	0.7474	0.6171	0.7289	0.7360	0.6868	0.6561
	EERNNA	<u>0.6913</u>	0.6182	0.6340	0.6341	0.7535	0.6281	0.7076	0.7161	0.6966	0.6491
	SKVMN	0.6833	0.5515	0.6332	0.6289	0.7428	0.6063	0.7126	0.7334	0.6930	0.6300
	DKVMN	0.6823	0.5323	0.6293	0.6391	<u>0.7609</u>	0.6049	0.7229	0.7265	0.6988	0.6257
	GKT	0.6728	0.5861	0.6001	0.5819	0.6994	0.6039	0.6786	0.6228	0.6627	0.5986
	LBKT	0.6857	0.6249	0.5961	<u>0.6595</u>	0.7603	0.6021	0.6807	0.7108	0.6807	0.6493
	simpleKT	0.6741	<u>0.6402</u>	0.5925	0.6151	0.6976	0.5810	0.7079	0.7318	0.6680	0.6420
Other Objectives	DHKT	0.6898	0.6224	0.6310	0.6303	0.7393	0.6119	0.7167	0.7278	0.6942	0.6481
	IEKT	0.6821	0.6260	<u>0.6376</u>	0.6469	0.6908	0.5853	0.7188	0.7191	0.6823	0.6443
	CL4KT	0.6691	0.6061	0.6151	0.6268	0.7465	0.6295	0.7303	0.7578	0.6902	0.6550
Adv. Learning	AdvKT	**0.6993** *	**0.6529** *	**0.6464** *	**0.6710** *	**0.7642** *	**0.6724** *	**0.7552** *	**0.7863** *	**0.7163** *	**0.6956** *

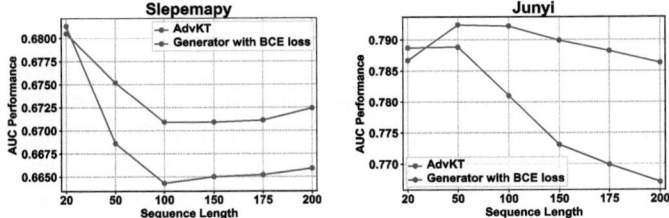

Fig. 3. Comparison results of the influence of learning sequence length of the generator with BCE loss and AdvKT

4.3 Mitigation of Error Accumulation

In the context of multi-step prediction, error accumulation is a prevalent issue. Typically, in the prediction of long sequences, errors from previous predictions tend to have a more significant impact on the current step. We compare the performance of the generator trained by BCE loss only and our proposed AdvKT under various learning sequence lengths, with AUC as the metric. As depicted in Fig. 3, our proposed AdvKT enjoys a relatively stable performance with different lengths of sequence, while the generator trained with BCE loss only suffers from severe error accumulation and meets a dramatic performance degeneration as the sequence length gradually increases. The comparison demonstrates the effectiveness of our proposed adversarial learning framework in AdvKT to tackle the error accumulation problem under real-world multi-step prediction scenarios. The generator does not only fit the one-step data distribution via BCE loss, but also expand its horizon upon the entire sequence by receiving sequence-wise reward guidance from the discriminator.

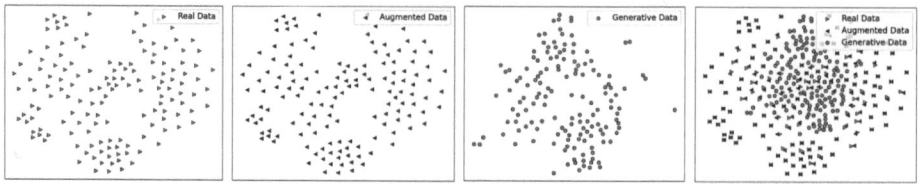

Fig. 4. Distribution of question-response pair visualized with two-dimensional t-SNE on ASSIST09. Green points are real data in dataset. Blue points correspond to data generated by positive data augmentation methods. Red points represent generative data (Color figure online)

4.4 Mitigation of Data Sparsity

In Fig. 4, we visualize the distribution of (q, r) pairs in (i) original data $\mathcal{R}$ in the dataset, (ii) augmented data $\mathcal{T}$ and (iii) generative data $\mathcal{E}$ on ASSIST09. Visualization of distribution on other datasets are demonstrated in Appendix B. Our discriminator encodes the entire sequence and obtains hidden state representations. These representation vectors are reduced to two dimensions using t-SNE [21].

The figure shows that the augmented data closely resembles the original data, validating the augmentation methods. However, there are noticeable gaps in both the original and augmented data, and the distribution boundaries are uneven. Although the augmented data increases the data size, it is insufficient to simply combine it with the original data for training a KT model. By generating new sequences, the generative data (red points) fills the gaps and boundary areas of the original data, ensuring a uniform distribution in the problem sequence subspace. Consequently, the discriminator can be trained more stably with the expanded dataset, providing better guidance for the generator to capture comprehensive student learning patterns.

4.5 Ablation Study

Ablation on Data Augmentation. To investigate the contribution of data augmentation, we conduct ablation studies on four datasets. We remove the following components to train the discriminator: (i) augmented data $\mathcal{T}$, (ii) label-reversed data $\mathcal{V}$, and (iii) both $\mathcal{T}$ and $\mathcal{V}$ simultaneously. Note that the generative data $\mathcal{G}$ cannot be removed due to the requirement of adversarial learning. The results, shown in Table 3, indicate that the performance of AdvKT decreases regardless of which type of data is removed. We attribute this to the fact that data augmentation provides more diverse data, enhancing the robustness of the discriminator and offering better reward guidance for the generator to capture student response patterns. Furthermore, augmented data contributes more significantly than label-reversed data, as it generates new sequences of questions.

Table 3. Performance comparison between AdvKT and its variants: (i) train discriminator without augmented data $\mathcal{T}$; (ii) train discriminator without reverse label data $\mathcal{V}$; (iii) train discriminator without $\mathcal{T}$ and $\mathcal{V}$. Note that generative data cannot be removed, which is required by adversarial training

Models	ASSIST09		EdNet		Slepemapy		Junyi	
	ACC	AUC	ACC	AUC	ACC	AUC	ACC	AUC
AdvKT	**0.6993**	**0.6529**	**0.6464**	**0.6710**	**0.7642**	**0.6724**	**0.7552**	**0.7863**
(i) w/o $\mathcal{T}$	0.6895	0.6486	0.6455	0.6693	0.7537	0.6664	0.7518	0.7836
(ii) w/o $\mathcal{V}$	0.6916	0.6501	0.6462	0.6699	0.7564	0.6645	0.7521	0.7843
(iii) w/o $\mathcal{V}$ & $\mathcal{T}$	0.6887	0.6488	0.6460	0.6687	0.7557	0.6610	0.7544	0.7833

Table 4. Ablation studies on different training loss: (i) Remove $\mathcal{L}_{\text{Adv}}$ and train the generator without reward guidance from the discriminator, *i.e.*, supervised learning; (ii) Remove $\mathcal{L}_{\text{BCE}}$ and train the generator only under the supervisions from the discriminator; (iii) Train the discriminator without gradient penalty; (iv) Replace $\mathcal{L}_{\text{dist}}$ for the discriminator with BCE loss.

Models	ASSIST09		EdNet		Slepemapy		Junyi	
	ACC	AUC	ACC	AUC	ACC	AUC	ACC	AUC
AdvKT	**0.6993**	**0.6529**	**0.6464**	**0.6710**	**0.7642**	**0.6724**	**0.7552**	**0.7863**
(i) w/o $\mathcal{L}_{\text{Adv}}$	0.6859	0.6451	0.6462	0.6672	0.7479	0.6659	0.7532	0.7671
(ii) w/o $\mathcal{L}_{\text{BCE}}$	0.5766	0.5299	0.5931	0.5575	0.7083	0.5661	0.7125	0.6588
(ii) w/o GP	0.6735	0.6342	0.6511	0.6683	0.7600	0.6284	0.7541	0.7842
(iv) $\mathcal{L}_{\text{dist}} \rightarrow \mathcal{L}_{\text{BCE}}^{\text{dist}}$	0.6908	0.6497	0.6434	0.6698	0.7545	0.6685	0.7463	0.7818

Ablation on Loss Functions. We investigate the impact of different loss functions designed for the generator $\mathcal{G}$ and the discriminator $\mathcal{D}$, with results presented in Table 4.

Firstly, we assess the contribution of loss functions for the generator. Removing either the adversarial loss $\mathcal{L}_{\text{Adv}}$ or the binary cross-entropy loss $\mathcal{L}_{\text{BCE}}$ significantly degrades AdvKT's performance. This suggests the necessity of balancing adversarial learning ($\mathcal{L}_{\text{Adv}}$) with supervised learning ($\mathcal{L}_{\text{BCE}}$) to effectively capture multi-step student response patterns.

Next, we perform an ablation study on the loss functions of the discriminator. We can observe that GP is crucial for maintaining the training stability of the discriminator, ensuring that the generator receives consistent and meaningful reward guidance for enhanced predictive performance. Moreover, replacing our custom-designed distance loss $\mathcal{L}_{\text{dist}}$ with a simple BCE loss $\mathcal{L}_{\text{BCE}}^{\text{dist}}$ results in a noticeable performance decline for AdvKT. The distance loss $\mathcal{L}_{\text{dist}}$ focuses more on the internal ranking of positive and negative samples, rather than merely achieving pointwise scores close to 0 or 1 as indicated by the BCE loss. Consequently, our distance loss assigns higher scores to positive samples than negative ones, ensuring more accurate reward guidance for the generator.

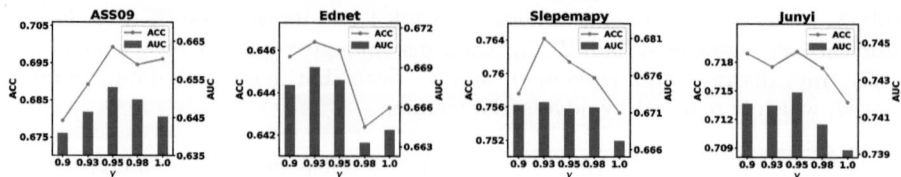

Fig. 5. Ablation study on the hyper-parameter γ on four datasets

Ablation on Discount Factor γ. To assess the sensitivity of our model, we evaluate the impact of discount factor γ. We test our method with $\gamma = \{0.9, 0.93, 0.95, 0.98, 1\}$ across four datasets, keeping other hyperparameters constant. As illustrated in Fig. 5, the performance fluctuates when tuning the discount factor. The discount factor γ determines the importance the generator places on future predictive performance and should be adjusted based on the specific dataset requirements.

4.6 Insight of Adversarial Learning

Generative data $\mathcal{G}$ plays a crucial role in training the generator alongside the real dataset. The quality and diversity of these synthetic sequences directly influence the supervision signal ($\mathcal{L}_{\text{adv}}$) obtained by the generator. In Fig. 6, we present a generated synthetic sequence along with its most similar learning sequences from the dataset. Four subsequences are found within the original sequences, highlighting a certain similarity between the generated and original sequences. However, each generated sequence remains distinct from any single original sequence.

This similarity ensures that the generated sequences maintain the logical consistency of the original data, such as presenting simpler questions before more challenging ones. Meanwhile, the diversity in the generated sequences helps AdvKT tackle data sparsity by enriching the dataset with varied examples. This diversity also enables the model to learn from accumulated errors across different sequences, further reducing the impact of error accumulation.

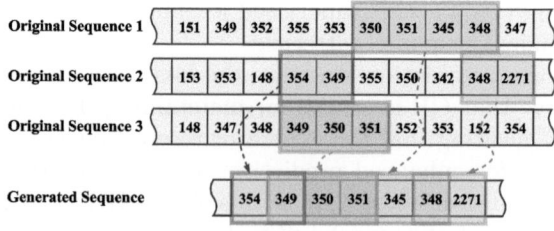

Fig. 6. Demonstration of generated question sequences and original question sequences

5 Related Work

5.1 Knowledge Tracing

To investigate students' learning patterns, numerous knowledge tracing models have been proposed under a single-step training paradigm.

Deep Knowledge Tracing (DKT) [26] pioneers using the deep learning-based knowledge tracing methods. It uses the hidden states of long short-term memory (LSTM) [13] networks to describe the students' knowledge states. After DKT, DHKT [31] and other variants of DKT introduce extra information like question-skill relations and additional regularization terms to improve the performance. Inspired by Key-Value Memory Network (KVMN) [22], several works [1,34] use key-matrix and value-matrix to represent concepts and student's mastery level. GKT randomly builds a similarity graph of skills, GIKT [33] applies the graph of skills and questions to obtain better representations of questions. After the transformer architecture was proposed, some works [4,29] tried to utilize the attention mechanism in KT tasks.

Recently, StableKT [16] highlighted the presence of error accumulation in single-step KT scenarios. All the aforementioned methods experience more severe error accumulation under multi-step inference. At the same time, they suffer significant performance degradation when training data is sparse. Although approaches [3,6,11] enhance learning from question text using large language models, educational datasets still face challenges at the ID level, with limited and uneven interaction data. AdvKT utilizes an adversarial learning paradigm, thereby improving both training paradigms and data utilization.

5.2 Adversarial Learning

In recent years, GAN [9] has been widely used for data augmentation in computer vision and Natural Language Processing. Combining the idea of GAN with Inverse Reinforcement Learning (IRL), researchers propose GAIL [12] framework to learn policy by imitating expert trajectories. Many previous work [2,5,27] adopt GAN and GAIL frameworks for user modeling. These work models and simulates users' behavior (clicking, buying) on the web search page or shopping websites.

Unlike user interest modeling, the KT task includes the change of users' state, *i.e.*, knowledge state transition. In AdvKT, we consider the students' learning patterns and generate logical question sequences to estimate the knowledge state of students.

6 Conclusion

In this work, we propose a novel adversarial multi-step training framework for knowledge tracing (AdvKT), which, for the first time, explicitly models real-world multi-step prediction by introducing the adversarial learning framework.

AdvKT adversarially trains a generator and a discriminator, aiming at alleviating error accumulation and data sparsity problem. The generator is designed to simulate students' learning process under the multi-step setting, *i.e.*, generating students' responses based on the question sequence and its previous predicted responses instead of the ground-truth ones. The discriminator, whose training data is augmented by well-designed rules, distinguishes whether the learning sequence is derived from real data or fake data, and therefore provides sequence-wise reward guidance for the generator to capture student response patterns. Extensive experiments on four real-world datasets demonstrate the superiority of AdvKT compared with existing baseline models, as well as its capabilities for mitigating the error accumulation and data sparsity problem.

Acknowledgments. The Shanghai Jiao Tong University team is partially supported by National Key R&D Program of China (2022ZD0114804), Shanghai Municipal Science and Technology Major Project (2021SHZDZX0102) and National Natural Science Foundation of China (62322603, 62177033).

Disclosure of Interests. The authors have no competing interests to declare that are relevant to the content of this article.

References

1. Abdelrahman, G., Wang, Q.: Knowledge tracing with sequential key-value memory networks (2019)
2. Bai, X., Guan, J., Wang, H.: Model-based reinforcement learning with adversarial training for online recommendation (2019)
3. Cao, Y., Zhang, W.: Mamba4KT:an efficient and effective mamba-based knowledge tracing model (2024)
4. Choi, Y., et al.: Towards an appropriate query, key, and value computation for knowledge tracing (2020)
5. Dai, X., et al.: An adversarial imitation click model for information retrieval (2021)
6. Fu, L., et al.: SINKT: a structure-aware inductive knowledge tracing model with large language model. In: Proceedings of the 33rd ACM International Conference on Information and Knowledge Management, pp. 632–642. CIKM '24, ACM (2024)
7. Ghosh, A., Heffernan, N., Lan, A.S.: Context-aware attentive knowledge tracing. In: Proceedings of the 26th ACM SIGKDD International Conference on Knowledge Discovery & Data Mining, pp. 2330–2339. KDD '20, Association for Computing Machinery, New York, NY, USA (2020)
8. Gong, J., Wang, S., Wang, J., Feng, W., Peng, H., Tang, J., Yu, P.S.: Attentional graph convolutional networks for knowledge concept recommendation in MOOCs in a heterogeneous view. In: Proceedings of the 43rd International ACM SIGIR Conference on Research and Development in Information Retrieval, pp. 79–88 (2020)
9. Goodfellow, I.J., et al.: Generative adversarial networks (2014)
10. Gulrajani, I., Ahmed, F., Arjovsky, M., Dumoulin, V., Courville, A.: Improved training of Wasserstein GANs. In: Proceedings of the 31st International Conference on Neural Information Processing Systems, pp. 5769–5779. NIPS'17, Curran Associates Inc., Red Hook, NY, USA (2017)

11. Guo, Y., et al.: Mitigating cold-start problems in knowledge tracing with large language models: an attribute-aware approach. In: Proceedings of the 33rd ACM International Conference on Information and Knowledge Management, pp. 727–736 (2024)
12. Ho, J., Ermon, S.: Generative adversarial imitation learning (2016)
13. Hochreiter, S., Schmidhuber, J.: Long short-term memory. Neural Comput. **9**, 1735–80 (1997)
14. Lee, W., Chun, J., Lee, Y., Park, K., Park, S.: Contrastive learning for knowledge tracing. In: Proceedings of the ACM Web Conference 2022, pp. 2330–2338. WWW '22, Association for Computing Machinery, New York, NY, USA (2022)
15. Li, Q., et al.: Graph enhanced hierarchical reinforcement learning for goal-oriented learning path recommendation. In: Proceedings of the 32nd ACM International Conference on Information and Knowledge Management, pp. 1318–1327 (2023)
16. Li, X., et al.: Enhancing length generalization for attention based knowledge tracing models with linear biases. In: Proceedings of the Thirty-Third International Joint Conference on Artificial Intelligence (IJCAI), pp. 5918–5926. International Joint Conferences on Artificial Intelligence (2024)
17. Liotet, P., Venneri, E., Restelli, M.: Learning a belief representation for delayed reinforcement learning. In: 2021 International Joint Conference on Neural Networks (IJCNN), pp. 1–8 (2021)
18. Liu, Q., Tong, S., Liu, C., Zhao, H., Chen, E., Ma, H., Wang, S.: Exploiting cognitive structure for adaptive learning. In: KDD '19: Proceedings of the 25th ACM SIGKDD International Conference on Knowledge Discovery & Data Mining, pp. 627–635 (2019)
19. Liu, Z., Liu, Q., Chen, J., Huang, S., Luo, W.: simpleKT: a simple but tough-to-beat baseline for knowledge tracing (2023)
20. Long, T., Liu, Y., Shen, J., Zhang, W., Yu, Y.: Tracing knowledge state with individual cognition and acquisition estimation. In: Proceedings of the 44th International ACM SIGIR Conference on Research and Development in Information Retrieval, pp. 173–182. SIGIR '21, Association for Computing Machinery, New York, NY, USA (2021)
21. Van der Maaten, L., Hinton, G.: Visualizing data using T-SNE. J. Mach. Learn. Res. **9**(11) (2008)
22. Miller, A., Fisch, A., Dodge, J., Karimi, A.H., Bordes, A., Weston, J.: Key-value memory networks for directly reading documents (2016)
23. Nagatani, K., Zhang, Q., Sato, M., Chen, Y.Y., Chen, F., Ohkuma, T.: Augmenting knowledge tracing by considering forgetting behavior. In: WWW '19: The World Wide Web Conference, pp. 3101–3107 (2019)
24. Nakagawa, H., Iwasawa, Y., Matsuo, Y.: Graph-based knowledge tracing: modeling student proficiency using graph neural network. In: IEEE/WIC/ACM International Conference on Web Intelligence, pp. 156–163. WI '19, Association for Computing Machinery, New York, NY, USA (2019)
25. Pandey, S., Karypis, G.: A self-attentive model for knowledge tracing (2019)
26. Piech, C., et al.: Deep knowledge tracing (2015)
27. Shi, J.C., Yu, Y., Da, Q., Chen, S.Y., Zeng, A.X.: Virtual-Taobao: virtualizing real-world online retail environment for reinforcement learning (2018)
28. Shuanghong, S., et al.: Convolutional knowledge tracing: modeling individualization in student learning process. In: SIGIR '20: Proceedings of the 43rd International ACM SIGIR Conference on Research and Development in Information Retrieval, pp. 1857–1860 (2020)

29. Su, Y., et al.: Exercise-enhanced sequential modeling for student performance prediction. In: Proceedings of the Thirty-Second AAAI Conference on Artificial Intelligence and Thirtieth Innovative Applications of Artificial Intelligence Conference and Eighth AAAI Symposium on Educational Advances in Artificial Intelligence. AAAI'18/IAAI'18/EAAI'18, AAAI Press (2018)
30. Sutton, R.S., McAllester, D.A., Singh, S.P., Mansour, Y.: Policy gradient methods for reinforcement learning with function approximation. Adv. Neural. Inf. Process. Syst. **12**, 1057–1063 (2000)
31. Wang, T., Ma, F., Gao, J.: Deep hierarchical knowledge tracing. In: Lynch, C., Merceron, A., Desmarais, M., Nkambou, R. (eds.) EDM 2019 - Proceedings of the 12th International Conference on Educational Data Mining, pp. 671–674. EDM 2019 - Proceedings of the 12th International Conference on Educational Data Mining, International Educational Data Mining Society (2019)
32. Xu, B., Huang, Z., Liu, J., Shen, S., Liu, Q., Chen, E., Wu, J., Wang, S.: Learning behavior-oriented knowledge tracing. In: Proceedings of the 29th ACM SIGKDD Conference on Knowledge Discovery and Data Mining, pp. 2789–2800. KDD '23, Association for Computing Machinery, New York, NY, USA (2023)
33. Yang, Y., et al.: GIKT: a graph-based interaction model for knowledge tracing (2020)
34. Zhang, J., Shi, X., King, I., Yeung, D.Y.: Dynamic key-value memory networks for knowledge tracing (2016)
35. Kingma, D.P., Ba, J.: Adam: a method for stochastic optimization (2014)

Leveraging Student Profiles and the Mamba Framework to Enhance Knowledge Tracing

Mingxing Shao[1], Tiancheng Zhang[1(✉)], Minghe Yu[2], Zhenghao Liu[1], Yifang Yin[3], Hengyu Liu[4], and Ge Yu[1]

[1] School of Computer Science and Engineering, Northeastern University, Shenyang, China
2301935@stu.neu.edu.cn, {tczhang,liuzhenghao,yuge}@mail.neu.edu.cn
[2] College of Software, Northeastern University, Shenyang, China
yuminghe@mail.neu.edu.cn
[3] Institute for Infocomm Research, A*STAR, Singapore, Singapore
yin_yifang@i2r.a-star.edu.sg
[4] Department of Computer Science, Aalborg University, Aalborg, Denmark
heli@cs.aau.dk

Abstract. Knowledge tracing (KT) predicts students' knowledge mastery based on their interaction history to forecast future performance. Although current KT methods have achieved good results, because of the lacking of students' information, these methods can only make sequence-level inference, assuming that students are independent and homogeneous. Additionally, due to the typically long student sequences in KT tasks, mainstream RNN-based student state modeling methods suffer from long-sequence forgetting, while attention-based models require manually set bias functions. To address these issues, this paper proposes a **D**ual-**G**raph **M**amba framework for **K**nowledge **T**racing (DGMKT), which models student profiles based on students' interaction sequence through a **D**ual-**G**raph **S**tudent-**P**rofile Aware **M**odule (DGSPM). Meanwhile, we model student mastery states based on Mamba, avoiding the long-sequence forgetting problem in RNN-based models and the need for bias functions in attention-based models for KT tasks. To the best of our knowledge, this is the first application of the Mamba architecture in KT tasks. We evaluate DGMKT on four datasets and compare it with ten baselines to demonstrate its superiority. Furthermore, we showcase its broad adaptability by integrating DGSPM with various KT models.

Keywords: Knowledge Tracing · Student Profile · Mamba Structure

---

Supplementary Information The online version contains supplementary material available at https://doi.org/10.1007/978-3-032-06109-6_12.

1 Introduction

With the rapid growth of computer science and cognitive diagnosis, online education platforms like MOOCs, EDX, and Coursera have become increasingly popular, generating vast amounts of student learning data daily. Using the data to evaluate students' knowledge and recommend appropriate exercises is a major challenge for these platforms.

Knowledge tracing (KT) addresses this by tracking students mastery of knowledge points to predict their future performance. Most knowledge tracing models are primarily based on Recurrent Neural Network and Self-Attention mechanism. Although some researchers have explored other neural networks such as [9,24], the mainstream research still focuses on the exploration of DNN (Deep Neural network) applied to knowledge tracing tasks.

However, most existing DNN-based studies lack a unique identifier for each student. These models only receive interaction sequence information and don't know the student-specific details corresponding to the sequence, so they can only make sequence-level inferences. As shown in Fig. 1, although the two students' sequences are the same before time step 6, as distinct individuals, they are likely to provide different answers at step 6. Existing models often assume that the two students will provide the same response at time step 6 in this case.

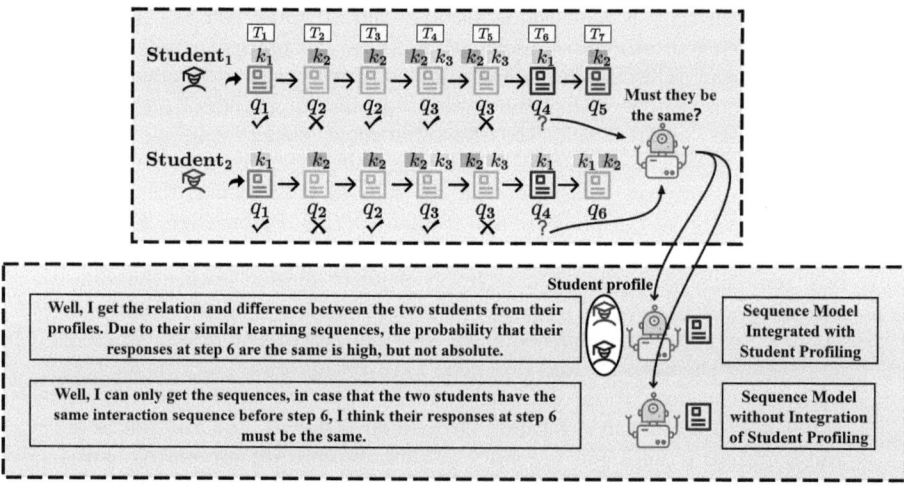

Fig. 1. An illustration comparing sequence modeling methods with and without the integration of student profiling

Therefore, we propose the definition of the student profile in the context of knowledge tracing tasks: **The student profile serves as a unique identifier for students, allowing for the distinction between different students**

while also enabling the aggregation of information across similar students. In contrast to recent studies that focus on generating high-quality embeddings for individual items or concepts, our proposed method can be understood as generating students' identifier based on the sequence and frequency of interactions with items by students. These identifiers are then used to guide the model in tracking the students' knowledge states throughout the entire process.

Another issue is that since the student interaction sequences in knowledge tracing tasks are usually quite long, knowledge tracing models based on RNN [15,16,22,26] and Self-Attention mechanism [2,6,13,18,19] inevitably suffer from performance issues due to inherent limitations in their architectures, such as the forgetting problem in RNN caused by vanishing gradients and the need for manually defined bias functions in Self-Attention-based architectures. In 2023, Gu et al. [3] proposed the Mamba architecture, which has been demonstrated to perform well in long-sequence tasks [28]. Due to the long-sequence issue in KT tasks, this characteristic makes Mamba particularly suitable for application in knowledge tracing tasks.

To address these issues, we propose the DGMKT framework, which consists of three components: the **D**ual-**G**raph **S**tudent **P**rofile Aware **M**odule (DGSPM) and the **M**amba **S**equence **M**odeling **M**odule (MSMM) and the Integration Module. The DGSPM generates two student profiles for each student through their interaction sequence. Specifically, the dual-graph in DGSPM includes a Student-Exercise Association Hypergraph (SEAHG) and an Exercise-Directed Transition Graph (EDTG). For students' interaction sequences, SEAHG is designed to capture what exercises students interact with, without considering the order of interactions. As a complement, EDTG is specifically designed to capture the sequential order in which students interact with the exercises. In SEAHG, Define a student as a node, an exercise as a hyperedge, since each student can interact with an exercise many times, so we allow a hyperedge to connect the same node many times. as shown in Fig. 2, given sequences of two students as in Fig. 2(a), Construct the SEAHG as in Fig. 2(b). In EDTG, an exercise is defined as a node, and a transition between two exercises is represented as a directed edge. Based on the sequence of $student_2$ in Fig. 2(a), the corresponding EDTG is constructed as shown in Fig. 2(c).

The Mamba Sequence Modeling Module consists of two components: the linear layer projects input features to the question embedding dimension, and the Mamba layer captures sequential dependencies to model students' states.

Finally, after obtaining the predictions of the two sets of linear-Mamba layers, In Integration Module, we integrate the two predictions through a method similar to the online knowledge distillation proposed by DGEKT [1].

In summary, our contributions are as follows:

- We propose the definition of student profiles and introduce a Dual-Graph Student Profile Aware Module (DGSPM) for modeling student profiles in Knowledge Tracing tasks through students' interaction sequences.

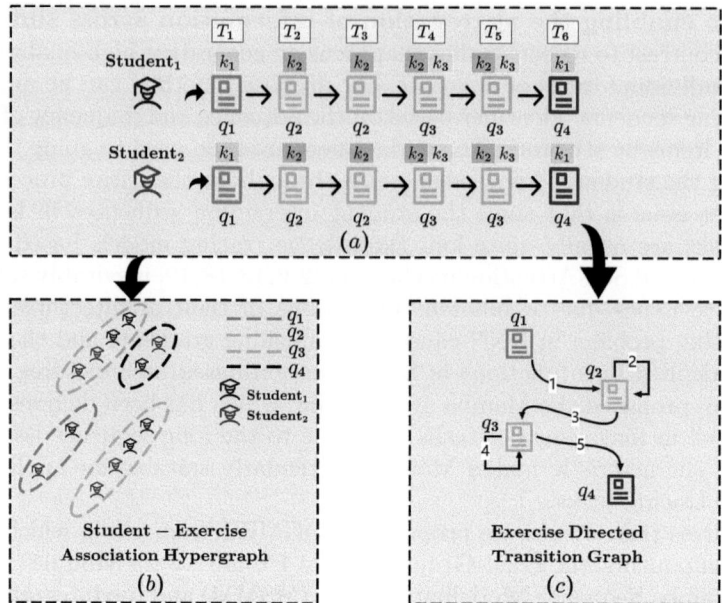

Fig. 2. The process of constructing SEAHG and EDTG through students' interaction sequence

- We propose Mamba Sequence Modeling Module (MSMM) to model students' knowledge states, adapting to the characteristics of long sequences in knowledge tracing tasks.
- We demonstrate the effectiveness and adaptability of the proposed DGSPM in modeling student profiles by integrating it with different knowledge tracing methods. Additionally, we showcase the superiority of the proposed MSMM in modeling students' mastery compared to mainstream RNN-based and Self-Attention-based modeling approaches.

2 Related Work

2.1 Knowledge Tracing

The development of knowledge tracing methods can be divided into two stages: the probabilistic graphical model-based stage and the Deep Neural Network-based stage. Among probabilistic models, Bayesian Knowledge Tracing (BKT) is one of the most representative models. BKT is a Hidden Markov Model that models a learner's latent knowledge state as a set of binary variables, where each variable represents whether a student has mastered a particular knowledge concept. Since BKT assumes the homogeneity of both students and problems, researchers have gradually incorporated personalized components into BKT to enhance its effectiveness [7,25]. Additionally, some researchers have made personalized improvements to BKT's skill-specific parameters [20,21] and student-specific parameters [29].

With the advent of DNN, the first DNN-based knowledge tracing model [22] made traditional models less competitive. Modern research focuses on RNN-based [16,22] and Self-Attention-based [2,18,19] KT models, as well as hybrid architectures [4,13,24]. However, beacause the length of sequence in KT tasks is long, RNN often suffer from forgetting issues [4], and Self-Attention models require manually designed bias functions, which affect performance [2,6,19].

To address these limitations, we model student mastery states using Mamba, which has been proven effective for long-sequence tasks [28] and does not require the setting of a bias function.

2.2 Student Profile

While student profiling is not commonly discussed in Knowledge Tracing tasks, it is frequently explored in areas like academic failure prediction. For example, Liang et al. [12] propose a student profiling method based on online learning behavior data. This method analyzes learning features, behavioral similarity, and learning attitudes to enhance the quality of student learning and the level of personalized services in E-Learning platforms through intelligent guidance. Khasanah et al. [8] employ a feature selection and classification algorithm approach, using selected features as the basis for student profiling to predict the likelihood of academic failure. Shen et al. [23] construct student profiles by combining labels that describe students' personal information and learning behaviors with the code they submitted, and used these profiles to predict their scores in programming tests.

Although effective, these methods often depend on personal information like age or economic status, which is unavailable in traditional Knowledge Tracing tasks that only provide interaction sequences. To address this issue, we propose a method capable of modeling student profiles based on their response sequences. The inspiration for this approach stems from the observation that students with similar response sequences often share analogous learning factors, such as learning pace and prior knowledge. Moreover, the correctness of their responses tends to be more similar.

2.3 Mamba

As a highly promising neural network architecture, Mamba is similar to RNN in its recursive information propagation. However, it avoids the forgetting issues commonly associated with RNN. Additionally, its parameterized input structure dynamically determines the importance of input components without the need for manually setting bias functions, as required by attention mechanism.

Mamba has demonstrated competitive performance and has even achieved state-of-the-art results in various tasks, such as biomedical image segmentation [14], pan-sharpening [5], computer vision [31], and natural language processing

[3]. Notably, Mamba's advantages become particularly evident in tasks involving long sequences. These achievements suggest that modeling the student mastery state in knowledge tracing task as a new application of Mamba could significantly improve the performance of knowledge tracing models.

3 Method

Given a student s_k's exercise sequence up to time $t-1$, denoted as $E_k = \{e_1, e_2, ..., e_{t-1} \mid i = 1, ..., t-1\}$, where $e_i \in \mathcal{E}$ represents the exercise attempted by the student at time i, and $\mathcal{E}$ denotes the set of all exercises with cardinality $|\mathcal{E}|$. The SEAHG and EDTG are constructed as shown in Fig. 2. With the two graphs, we will get two student profiles through the Hypergraph Convolution and the Directed Graph Convolution illustrated in Sect. 3.1. Then, given E_k and the corresponding response sequence $A_k = \{a_1, a_2, ..., a_{t-1} \mid i = 1, ..., t-1\}$ where a_i indicates the correctness of the response at time i: $a_i = 1$ denotes a correct response and $a_i = 0$ denotes an incorrect response, and the two student s_k's profiles, we will get s_k's two sets of knowledge mastery state at each time step through the Mamba Sequence Modeling Module illustrated in Sect. 3.2. Finally, we integrate the two sets of knowledge mastery state through the Integration Module illustrated in Sect. 3.3 and get the final predictions of time t: $P(a_t = 1 \mid I_k, e_t, s_k)$. The above process can be illustrated in Fig. 3.

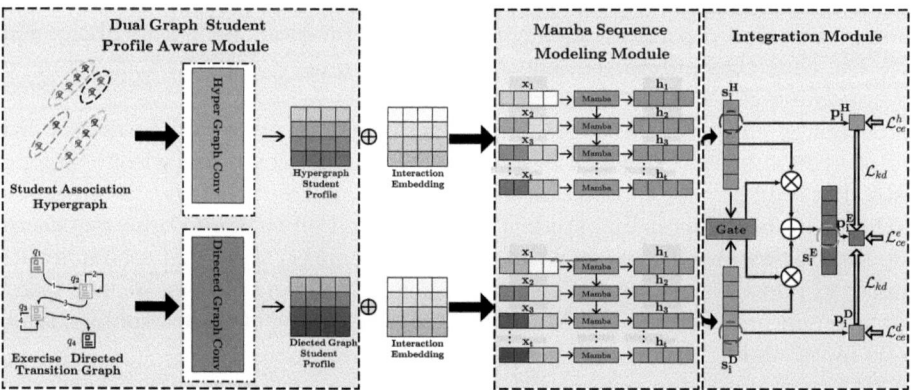

Fig. 3. The overall framework of proposed DGMKT. Student profiles (sp) are generated from DGSPM. After concatenating with interaction embeddings (ie), sp ⊕ i.e. is passed through the Mamba Sequence Model to generate predictions, which will be sent to the Integration Module

3.1 Dual-Graph Student-Profile Aware Module

Student-Exercise Association Hypergraph. In student association hypergraph, we consider the student set $\mathcal{S}$, with a sample student represented by s_i and $|\mathcal{S}| = n$. Similarly, we define an exercise set $\mathcal{E}$ with a sample exercise e_i and $|\mathcal{E}| = m$. To avoid confusion, each student in the hypergraph is represented by a node v_i, and each exercise by a hyperedge h_j. Since a student may complete the same exercise multiple times, we allow hyperedges to connect to the same nodes multiple times.

Based on this, let H_i denote the set of hyperedges connected to a node v_i, with $|H_i| \leq m$, and let h_i^o represent the number of times this node connects to each hyperedge h_o. The degree of a node can thus be defined as $d_v^i = \sum_{o=1} h_i^o$, representing the total number of exercises completed by student s_i.

Next, we define V_j as the set of nodes connected by hyperedge h_j, with $|V_j| \leq n$, and let v_j^k represent the number of times a particular node v_k is connected by the hyperedge. The degree of a hyperedge h_j is then given by $d_h^j = \sum_{k=1} v_j^k$, reflecting the total number of interactions with the exercise.

With these definitions, we employ an information propagation rule defined by hypergraph convolutional networks. The convolution operator in each layer aggregates information from v_i itself and from its local neighbors within each hyperedge to which v_i is connected, thereby updating x_i:

$$x_{i,H}^{(l)} = \sigma \left(\sum_{h_j \in H_i} \frac{1}{d_h^j} \sum_{v_k \in V_j} \frac{1}{\sqrt{d_v^k d_v^i}} \Theta^{l-1} x_{i,H}^{(l-1)} \right) \tag{1}$$

where $\Theta \in \mathbb{R}^{d_{model} \times d_{model}}$ is a learnable weight parameter, and σ is the ReLU activation function. $x_{i,H}^{(l-1)} \in \mathbb{R}^{1 \times d_{model}}$ and $x_{i,H}^{(l)} \in \mathbb{R}^{1 \times d_{model}}$ represent the input and output embeddings of node v_i in the l-th layer, respectively.

Thus, we obtain the profile $x_{i,H}$ for student s_i generated by the hypergraph, which primarily captures information on which exercises the student interacted with.

Exercise Directed Transition Graph. In Directed Graph, let the set of exercises be denoted as $\mathcal{E}$, where $|\mathcal{E}| = m$. For each student s_k, the interaction sequence $\mathcal{I}_k$ includes several tuples $(e_x, a_x) \in \mathcal{I}_k$, representing exercises and responses. From this, we obtain the students exercise sequence $E_k = \{e_1, e_2, e_3, \ldots, e_L\}$. This sequence can be broken down into a series of exercise pairs, such as $\bar{E}_k = \{(e_1, e_2), (e_2, e_3), \ldots, (e_{L-1}, e_L)\}$. In student s_k directed graph, we represent all exercises $\mathcal{E}$ as nodes $\mathcal{V}$ and each individual exercise pair in a students sequence $\bar{E}_k$ as directed edges $h_{i,j}$. A separate directed graph is constructed for each student, where $h_{i,j}$ represents that exercise e_i is immediately followed by e_j. We use $g_{i,j}$ to denote the number of times the pair (e_i, e_j) appears. The adjacency matrix A of this directed graph is defined as follows:

$$A_{i,j} = \begin{cases} 1 \times g_{i,j} & \text{if } h_{i,j} \text{ exists}, \\ 0 & \text{otherwise}. \end{cases} \tag{2}$$

Next, we add self-loops to the adjacency matrix by setting $\hat{A}_{i,i} = A_{i,i}+1$, thereby constructing the matrix $\hat{A}$. In $\hat{A} \in \mathbb{R}^{m \times m}$, we treat $\hat{A}$ as an adjacency graph where the degree of node $v_i \in \mathcal{V}$ is defined as $d_v^i = \sum_{j=1}^{m} A_{i,j}$. From matrix $\hat{A}$, we obtain the degree matrix $\hat{D} \in \mathbb{R}^{m \times m}$ and apply the following formula for graph convolution:

$$\mathbf{x}_{k,D}^{(l)} = \sigma \left(\hat{\mathbf{D}}^{-\frac{1}{2}} \hat{\mathbf{A}} \hat{\mathbf{D}}^{-\frac{1}{2}} \mathbf{x}_{k,D}^{(l-1)} \mathbf{W}^{(l-1)} \right), \tag{3}$$

where $W^{(l)} \in \mathbb{R}^{d_{model} \times d_{model}}$ denote a learnable weight matrix, and let σ represent the ReLU activation function. Specifically, $x_{k,D}^{l-1}$ and $x_{k,D}^{l} \in \mathbb{R}^{m \times d_{model}}$ are the input and output embeddings of node set $\mathcal{V}$, respectively.

Using the students exercise sequence E_k, we index these embeddings to retrieve the convolutional representations of the exercises $\hat{x}_{k,D} \in \mathbb{R}^{L \times d_{model}}$ in the sequence:

$$\hat{x}_{k,D} = E_k \rightarrow x_{k,D}. \tag{4}$$

For a student s_k with an interaction sequence length of L, we introduce a set of learnable weights $A = \{\alpha_1, \alpha_2, \ldots, \alpha_L\}$, $A \in \mathbb{R}^L$ as the weighting parameters. After applying the softmax function, these weights are multiplied by the obtained sequence embeddings $\hat{x}_{k,D}$ to get the student profile of directed graph:

$$\hat{A} = \text{softmax}(\mathbf{A}) = \left[\hat{\alpha}_1 = \frac{\exp(\alpha_1)}{\sum_{i=1}^{L} \exp(\alpha_i)}, \ldots, \hat{\alpha}_L = \frac{\exp(\alpha_L)}{\sum_{i=1}^{L} \exp(\alpha_i)} \right], \tag{5}$$

$$\tilde{x}_{k,D} = \sum_{o=1}^{L} \hat{\alpha}_o \cdot \hat{x}_{k,D}^o. \tag{6}$$

Thus, we derive the representation $\tilde{x}_{k,D} \in \mathbb{R}^{d_{model}}$ for student s_k, generated from the directed graph, which captures the ordering of exercises completed by the student.

3.2 Mamba Sequence Modeling Module

At this stage, we have obtained the hyper graph student profile $x_{i,H}$ and directed graph student profile $\tilde{x}_{i,D}$ for student s_i. Next, we concatenate $x_{i,H}$ and $\tilde{x}_{i,D}$ respectively with the interactive embedding x_i for further analysis:

$$\begin{aligned} x_{input,i}^{H} &= x_{i,H} \oplus x_i, \\ x_{input,i}^{D} &= \hat{x}_{i,D} \oplus x_i. \end{aligned} \tag{7}$$

The interactive embedding x_i is derived from the exercise sequence $E_i = \{e_1, e_2, \ldots, e_L\}$ completed by student s_i and the corresponding response sequence $A_i = \{a_1, a_2, \ldots, a_L\}$, which are processed through an embedding layer to obtain x_i^e and x_i^a. These are then concatenated as described below:

$$x_i = \begin{cases} x_i^e \oplus x_i^a, & \text{if } a_i = 1, \\ x_i^a \oplus x_i^e, & \text{if } a_i = 0, \end{cases} \tag{8}$$

where the embeddings $x^H_{input,i} \in \mathbb{R}^{3d_{model}}$ and $x^D_{input,i} \in \mathbb{R}^{3d_{model}}$ are each passed through a linear layer and a Mamba layer to obtain the knowledge mastery state of the student at each time step, denoted as $h^H_i \in \mathbb{R}^{L \times d_{model}}$ and $h^D_i \in \mathbb{R}^{L \times d_{model}}$:

$$h^H_i = Mamba_1(Linear_1(x^H_{input,i})), \\ h^D_i = Mamba_2(Linear_2(x^D_{input,i})), \tag{9}$$

where Mamba1 and Mamba2 represent two distinct Mamba layers, while Linear1 and Linear2 are two different linear layers with weight matrices shaped as $\mathbb{R}^{3d_{model} \times d_{model}}$. The execution process of the Mamba block is illustrated in Fig. 4.

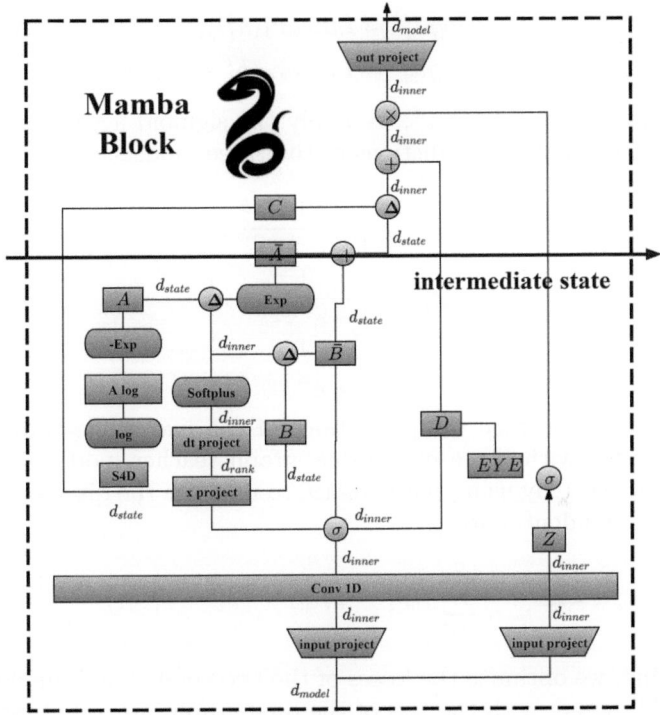

Fig. 4. The detail of Mamba Layer, Where **xx project** represents a simple linear layer, **Conv 1D** refers to a one-dimensional convolution. **S4D** stands for "shape for dimension," indicating a one-dimensional tensor to be expanded. The σ function corresponds to the SiLU activation function, while Δ and $\times$ denote matrix multiplication, and $+$ represents matrix addition. Finally, **EYE** is used to initialize a tensor with ones

3.3 Integration Module

To further integrate the results produced by the two graphs, we employ the online knowledge distillation integration method proposed in DGEKT. Through a gating mechanism, h_i^H and h_i^D are combined into h_i^E:

$$h_i^E = g \odot h_i^H + (1-g) \odot h_i^D, \tag{10}$$

$$g = \sigma\left((W_H h_i^H + b_H) + (W_D h_i^D + b_D)\right), \tag{11}$$

where $W_H, W_D \in \mathbb{R}^{d_{model} \times d_{model}}$, $b_H, b_D \in \mathbb{R}^{d_{model}}$ are learnable parameters, σ is a *sigmoid* function, $\odot$ is a simple multiplication.

These combined representations are then mapped to the problem dimension through three linear layers with weight matrices shaped as $\mathbb{R}^{d_{model} \times d_c}$, yielding $logitD$, $logitH$, and $logitE \in \mathbb{R}^{L \times d_c}$:

$$\begin{aligned} logit_i^H &= Linear_3(h_i^H), \\ logit_i^D &= Linear_4(h_i^D), \\ logit_i^E &= Linear_5(h_i^E). \end{aligned} \tag{12}$$

Given $logit_i^D$, $logit_i^H$, and $logit_i^E$, we apply the sigmoid activation function to each, resulting in the final predictions of the three models: p_i^d, p_i^h, and p_i^e. The equations are as follows:

$$\begin{aligned} p_i^D &= \frac{1}{1+e^{-logit_i^D}}, \\ p_i^H &= \frac{1}{1+e^{-logit_i^H}}, \\ p_i^E &= \frac{1}{1+e^{-logit_i^E}}. \end{aligned} \tag{13}$$

Subsequently, to encourage the predictions of the two single-graph models to align more closely with those of the dual-graph teacher model, we follow the approach in DGEKT by using the L_1-norm to measure the discrepancy between the teacher and student models:

$$\mathcal{L}_{kd} = \frac{1}{n} \sum_{i=1}^{n} \left(\|p_i^E - p_i^H\|_1 + \|p_i^E - p_i^D\|_1 \right). \tag{14}$$

During training, we optimize the losses of the two single-graph models, denoted as $\mathcal{L}_{ce}^h$ and $\mathcal{L}_{ce}^d$, along with the loss of the dual-graph integrated model $\mathcal{L}_{ce}^e$, as well as a distillation loss controlled by a constant λ. Unlike in DGEKT, here λ is fixed as 1/(batchsize × seqlen), where seqlen is the length of the students response sequence. During testing, we use the average of the predictions from the three models as the final result, instead of using only the teacher model as the final result in DGEKT [1]:

$$\mathcal{L} = \mathcal{L}_{ce}^h + \mathcal{L}_{ce}^d + \mathcal{L}_{ce}^e + \lambda \mathcal{L}_{kd}, \tag{15}$$

$$p_i = \frac{(p_i^E + p_i^D + p_i^H)}{3}. \tag{16}$$

Notably, in this paper, $\mathcal{L}_{ce}$ represents the cross-entropy loss function, which can be calculated as:

$$\mathcal{L}_{ce} = -\frac{1}{L}\sum_{l=1}^{L}(y_i^l \log(p_i^l) + (1-y_i^l)\log(1-p_i^l)), \quad (17)$$

where y_i^l represents the correctness of student s_i's actual response at time step l, and p_i^l denotes the model's prediction of the correctness of student s_i's response at time step l. L denotes the length of student s_i's interaction sequence.

4 Experiments

4.1 Experimental Setting

Benchmark Datasets. In the experiment, we used four datasets to evaluate our model and the proposed methods. The descriptions of the four datasets are as follows:

Statics2011[1]: The Statics2011 dataset was collected from a collegelevel engineering course on statics containing 189,927 responses with 1223 KSs from 333 students

Kddcup2010[2]: This dataset was originally used for the 2010 kdd cup competition. It has 868,410 responses with 660KSs from 690 students.

Assist2017[3]: This dataset is gathered from the ASSISTments online tutoring platform, which contains 525,637 responses with 110 KSs from 4151 students.

Assist2009[4]: This dataset is also from the same platform as Assist2009. It has 942,816 responses with 102 KSs from 1709 students.

The detailed information for each dataset is provided in Table 1. We use the preprocessed versions of these four datasets provided by the literature on AKT [2] and DKT [22] for fair comparison.

Table 1. Statistics of the four benchmark datasets

Dataset Name	Students	KSs	Responses	Res.per.stu
Kddcup2010	690	660	868,410	1,258.56
Statics2011	333	1,223	189,297	568.45
Assist2009	5,151	110	325,637	63.21
Assist2017	1,709	102	942,816	551.67

---

[1] https://pslcdatashop.web.cmu.edu/DatasetInfo?datasetId=507.
[2] https://pslcdatashop.web.cmu.edu/KDDCup.
[3] https://sites.google.com/view/assistmentsdatamining.
[4] https://sites.google.com/site/assistmentsdata/home/2009-2010-assistment-data.

Baseline Methods and Evaluation Metric. We compared the proposed model with the following ten state-of-art models:

DKT [22]: The first work to apply deep neural networks (DNN) for knowledge tracing, using RNN to model students' knowledge states.

DKVMN [30]: Utilizing a key-value memory network, where the key matrix stores static knowledge concepts and the value matrix tracks the students mastery level, providing a degree of interpretability.

SAKT [18]: The first model to use an attention network for knowledge tracing, predicting mastery by identifying relevant parts of the students past interactions associated with the current knowledge concept.

AKT [2]: An attention-based method proposes a monotonic attention mechanism to capture the connections between a student's current and previous interactions.

KQN [9]: Modeling knowledge interaction as the dot product of the knowledge state and skill vectors, with neural networks encoding student responses and skills into vectors of equal dimensions.

GKT [17]: Using graph convolutional networks on a graph of knowledge concepts, constructed through statistical or learning-based methods, to model students' proficiency in each concept.

FoLiBiKT [6]: Building on attention networks with a linear bias to model student forgetting behaviors.

DTransformer [27]: Proposing a stable and truly effective framework for tracking students' knowledge status.

StableKT [10]: Proposing StableKT to enhance length generalization in knowledge tracing tasks. It captures the relationships between questions and knowledge components through a multi-head aggregation module.

ExtraKT [11]: Proposing a framework, which improves length extrapolation capability by negatively biasing attention scores.

These methods provide a strong baseline for evaluating the DGMKT model. Following standard metrics in knowledge tracing, we use AUC and ACC to measure prediction performance.

Implementation Details. We conducted 5-fold cross-validation on all datasets with a 3:1:1 split for training, validation, and test sets. For fairness, we compared the baserline variant that uses knowledge skill (KS) information, as our model and all baselines rely exclusively on KS information.

In the experiments, we set exercise and response embedding dimensions to 512 and used four Mamba layers. Sequences longer than 500 were truncated. Training used a batch size of 24 across all datasets, the Adam optimizer with an initial learning rate of 0.001 and a decay factor of 0.5, for up to 500 epochs. Early stopping was applied if validation loss did not improve for five epochs. All experiments were implemented in PyTorch on two NVIDIA GeForce RTX 3080 GPUs.

4.2 Comparison with Baselines

In Table 2, we present the prediction performance of various methods, showing the averages and standard deviations across five test folds. It is evident that the proposed DGMKT consistently outperforms all other methods across all datasets.

Table 2. Performance comparison across different models and datasets. The best AUC value in each dataset is highlighted in **bold**, and the second-best in *italic*

Dataset	Statics2011		ASSIST2009		ASSIST2017		kddcup2010	
Model	AUC	ACC	AUC	ACC	AUC	ACC	AUC	ACC
DKT	0.8106	0.7965	0.8023	0.7609	0.7052	0.6807	0.7874	0.8341
DKVMN	0.7966	0.7951	0.7314	0.7185	0.6704	0.6691	0.7823	0.8355
SAKT	0.8022	0.7975	0.7361	0.7205	0.6492	0.6607	0.7736	0.8272
AKT	*0.8251*	0.8045	0.8053	0.7675	0.6918	0.6821	0.7898	0.8318
FoLiBiKT	0.8232	0.8044	0.8004	0.7643	0.6882	0.6783	0.7917	0.8283
GKT	0.7997	0.7982	0.7708	0.7472	0.6773	0.6720	0.7737	0.8316
KQN	0.8245	0.8041	*0.8107*	*0.7688*	*0.7200*	*0.6889*	*0.7956*	*0.8390*
DTrans	0.8202	0.8044	0.7865	0.7538	0.6859	0.6774	0.7867	0.8323
StableKT	0.8250	*0.8052*	0.8059	0.7658	0.6963	0.6805	0.7943	0.8320
ExtraKT	0.8215	0.7977	0.8090	0.7670	0.7006	0.6814	0.7947	0.8316
DGMKT	**0.8261**	**0.8058**	**0.8180**	**0.7722**	**0.7339**	**0.6966**	**0.7986**	**0.8391**

4.3 Adaptability Study of DGSPM in Different Architecture

To validate the Adaptability of our proposed student profiling method, we integrated the DGSPM into Self-Attention-based knowledge tracing models as well as the RNN-based model. We then compared the AUC performance with dual-graph (model with DGSPM) and no-graph (model) configurations under identical parameter settings. The results are shown in Table 3. It can be observed

Table 3. The performance of proposed DGSPM in RNN-Based method (DKT) and Attention-Based method (SAKT)

Dataset	statics2011		Assist2009		Assist2017		kddcup2010	
Model	AUC	ACC	AUC	ACC	AUC	ACC	AUC	ACC
DKT	0.8106	0.7965	0.8023	0.7609	0.7052	0.6807	0.7874	0.8341
DKT^{DGSPM}	**0.8209**	**0.8028**	**0.8102**	**0.7661**	**0.7183**	**0.6878**	**0.7960**	**0.8378**
SAKT	0.8022	0.7975	0.7361	0.7205	0.6492	0.6607	0.7736	0.8272
SAKT^{DGSPM}	**0.8108**	**0.8024**	**0.7453**	**0.7246**	**0.6561**	**0.6646**	**0.7852**	**0.8307**

that SAKT and DKT with DGSPM acheive better performance in all of four datasets than their original versions.

4.4 Ablation Study of DGSPM and MSMM

Dual-Graph Student Profile Aware Module. We validate the effectiveness of the proposed component Dual-Graph Student Profile Aware Module (DGSPM) by comparing its different variants.

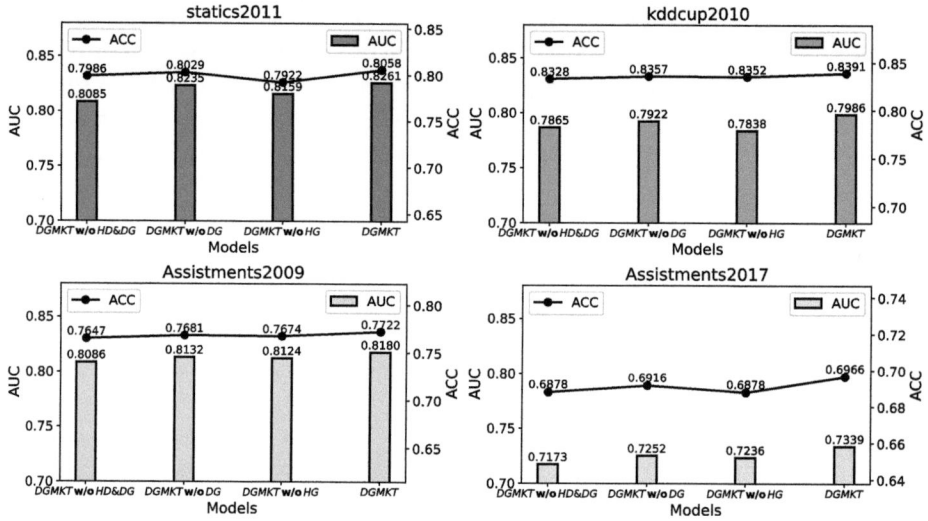

Fig. 5. Different variants of DGSPM are proposed to examine the effectness of DGSPM. Retaining only the SEAHG in DGSPM (DGMKT w/o DG), only the EDTG in DGSPM (DGMKT w/o HG), or removing both of the two graphs in DGSPM (DGMKT w/o HG&DG), as well as the complete proposed approach (DGSPM), while keeping other parameters constant.

The results presented in Fig. 5 demonstrate that the model with the complete proposed method outperforms all ablation models, thereby validating the effectiveness of the proposed DGSPM.

Mamba Sequence Modeling Module. To validate the effectiveness of the proposed component Mamba Sequence Modeling Module (MSMM), we compare Mamba sequence modeling method with RNN-based and Self-Attention-based sequence modeling method. Similarly, we keep other parameters constant, and compare three kinds of methods (Mamba-based, RNN-based, Self-Attention-based) with and without DGSPM. The results in Fig. 6 demonstrates that Mamba as an approach for modeling student learning states, demonstrates superior performance compared to the mainstream RNN and Self-Attention methods.

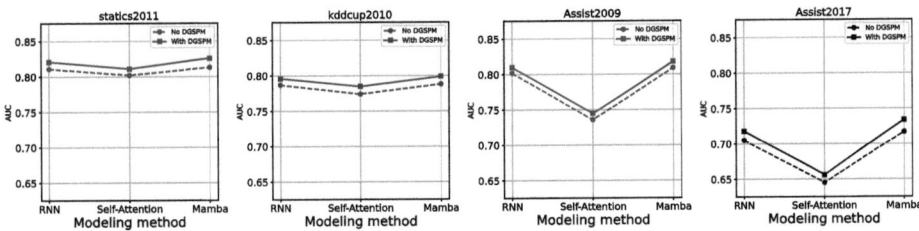

Fig. 6. The performance of the proposed Mamba Sequence Modeling Module compared with RNN-based and Self-Attention based sequence modeling method

4.5 Computational Efficiency Analysis of DGSPM

To rigorously evaluate the computational resource demands of the proposed DGSPM, we report the resouce consumption profiles of various DGMKT variants on Assist2017 dataset, as detailed in Table 4. To facilitate computational efficiency and ensure comparability, we configure the number of Mamba layers to a single layer (n_layer = 1), while maintaining the embedding dimension at 512, consistent with prior experimental settings.

It can be observed that, in terms of training time, the variant incorporating only directed graphs exhibits training durations comparable to the comprehensive method, both significantly exceeding that of the variant employing hypergraphs. This disparity arises because the Graph Convolutional Network (GCN) necessitates the generation of a distinct directed graph for each student. The sequential processing of individual students decomposes batch operations into serial computations, thereby constraining the parallel computing capabilities of the GPU.

Regarding memory consumption, the variant utilizing solely hypergraphs incurs substantially higher GPU memory usage compared to the variant with directed graphs. This is attributed to the representation of students as nodes and exercises as hyperedges, which requires the construction of a hypergraph structure. Such a structure may encompass millions of connections, forming a complex hypergraph. The hypergraph convolution process involves aggregating information across all connected nodes and hyperedges, resulting in significant GPU memory demands.

Table 4. Computational resource requirements of the four DGMKT variants

Model	Parameter	GPU Usage	Training Time
DGMKT	26.75 MB	3919 MB	2458.2 s
DGMKT w/o DG	12.14 MB	2515 MB	271.4 s
DGMKT w/o HG	9.17 MB	1571 MB	1803.4 s
DGMKT w/o HG&DG	9.13 MB	1473 MB	107.7 s

Although the dual-graph structure entails additional computational resources, it is noteworthy that the computational overhead of the dual-graph approach remains within a reasonable range.

4.6 Model Visualization

To evaluate the performance of the proposed DGMKT model in knowledge tracing, we visualize a student's mastery of various knowledge skills (KS) during 36 exercises, as shown in Fig. 7. The top section records the student's performance, with different colors representing the KSs involved in each exercise. The middle heatmap shows the mastery levels of each knowledge point (KS) over time, where darker colors indicate higher mastery levels.

Initially, all KS mastery levels are updated after each exercise. Correct answers increase the mastery level of relevant KSs, while incorrect answers decrease it. For example, after correctly answering exercises related to "finding-percents" at step 11, the mastery level for this KS increases in the heatmap. Changes in other rows highlight potential connections between KSs, where mastering one skill can influence others. More model visualization experiments can be found in Appendix A.

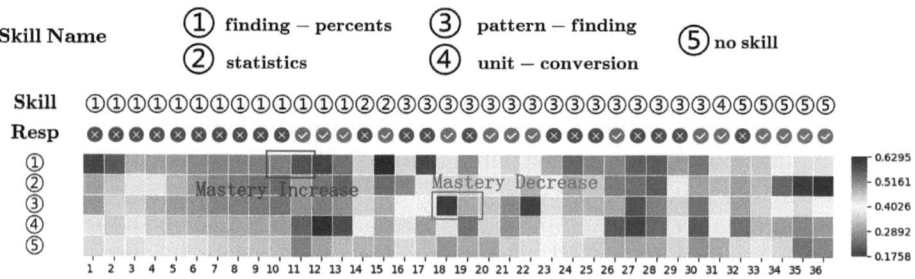

Fig. 7. A students knowledge state evolution over 36 time steps

5 Conclusion

We propose a novel method for modeling student profiles and long-term knowledge states, called DGMKT which contains two main Modules (DGSPM, MSMM) and an Integration Module. The DGSPM models student profiles from two perspectives: the exercises the student has interacted with and the sequence in which these exercises were interacted with, through the student association hypergraph and the exercise transition directed graph. Experimental results show that this student profiling method not only enhances the performance of knowledge tracing models but also demonstrates strong adaptability, making it suitable for various knowledge tracing model architectures. More importantly, we introduce MSMM, the first application of the Mamba structure to knowledge tracing tasks, which avoids the forgetting issue in RNN-based models and the need for manually setting bias functions in Self-Attention-based models, enabling long-term modeling of student knowledge states. The source code and datasets are publicly available at https://github.com/collegestu1231/DGMKT/tree/master.

Acknowledgments. This research was supported by the National Natural Science Foundation of China under Grant (Nos. 62137001, 62272093, 62372097).

Disclosure of Interests. The authors have no competing interests to declare that are relevant to the content of this article.

References

1. Cui, C., et al.: DGEKT: a dual graph ensemble learning method for knowledge tracing. ACM Trans. Inf. Syst. **42**(3), 1–24 (2024)
2. Ghosh, A., Heffernan, N., Lan, A.S.: Context-aware attentive knowledge tracing. In: SIGKDD, pp. 2330–2339 (2020)
3. Gu, A., Dao, T.: Mamba: linear-time sequence modeling with selective state spaces (2023)
4. Guo, X., Huang, Z., Gao, J., Shang, M., Shu, M., Sun, J.: Enhancing knowledge tracing via adversarial training. In: Proceedings of the 29th ACM International Conference on Multimedia, pp. 367–375 (2021)
5. He, X., et al.: Pan-Mamba: effective pan-sharpening with state space model. Inf. Fus., 102779 (2024)
6. Im, Y., Choi, E., Kook, H., Lee, J.: Forgetting-aware linear bias for attentive knowledge tracing. In: CIKM, pp. 3958–3962 (2023)
7. Khajah, M.M., Huang, Y., González-Brenes, J.P., Mozer, M.C., Brusilovsky, P.: Integrating knowledge tracing and item response theory: a tale of two frameworks. In: CEUR Workshop Proceedings, vol. 1181, pp. 7–15. University of Pittsburgh (2014)
8. Khasanah, A.U., et al.: A comparative study to predict student's performance using educational data mining techniques. In: IOP Conference Series: Materials Science and Engineering, vol. 215, p. 012036. IOP Publishing (2017)
9. Lee, J., Yeung, D.Y.: Knowledge query network for knowledge tracing: how knowledge interacts with skills. In: Proceedings of the 9th International Conference on Learning Analytics & Knowledge, pp. 491–500 (2019)
10. Li, X., et al.: Enhancing length generalization for attention based knowledge tracing models with linear biases. In: IJCAI, pp. 5918–5926 (2024)
11. Li, X., et al.: Extending context window of attention based knowledge tracing models via length extrapolation. In: ECAI, pp. 1479–1486. IOS Press (2024)
12. Liang, K., Zhang, Y., He, Y., Zhou, Y., Tan, W., Li, X.: Online behavior analysis-based student profile for intelligent e-learning. J. Electr. Comput. Eng. **2017**(1), 9720396 (2017)
13. Long, T., et al.: Improving knowledge tracing with collaborative information. In: WSDM, pp. 599–607 (2022)
14. Ma, J., Li, F., Wang, B.: U-Mamba: enhancing long-range dependency for biomedical image segmentation (2024)

15. Minn, S., Yu, Y., Desmarais, M.C., Zhu, F., Vie, J.J.: Deep knowledge tracing and dynamic student classification for knowledge tracing. In: 2018 IEEE International Conference on Data Mining (ICDM), pp. 1182–1187. IEEE (2018)
16. Nagatani, K., Zhang, Q., Sato, M., Chen, Y.Y., Chen, F., Ohkuma, T.: Augmenting knowledge tracing by considering forgetting behavior. In: WWW, pp. 3101–3107 (2019)
17. Nakagawa, H., Iwasawa, Y., Matsuo, Y.: Graph-based knowledge tracing: Modeling student proficiency using graph neural network. In: IEEE/WIC/ACM International Conference on Web Intelligence, pp. 156–163 (2019)
18. Pandey, S., Karypis, G.: A self-attentive model for knowledge tracing (2019)
19. Pandey, S., Srivastava, J.: RKT: relation-aware self-attention for knowledge tracing. In: CIKM, pp. 1205–1214 (2020)
20. Pardos, Z.A., Heffernan, N.T.: Modeling individualization in a Bayesian networks implementation of knowledge tracing. In: De Bra, P., Kobsa, A., Chin, D. (eds.) UMAP 2010. LNCS, vol. 6075, pp. 255–266. Springer, Heidelberg (2010). https://doi.org/10.1007/978-3-642-13470-8_24
21. Pardos, Z.A., Heffernan, N.T.: KT-IDEM: introducing item difficulty to the knowledge tracing model. In: Konstan, J.A., Conejo, R., Marzo, J.L., Oliver, N. (eds.) UMAP 2011. LNCS, vol. 6787, pp. 243–254. Springer, Heidelberg (2011). https://doi.org/10.1007/978-3-642-22362-4_21
22. Piech, C., et al.: Deep knowledge tracing. In: Advances in Neural Information Processing Systems, vol. 28 (2015)
23. Shen, G., Yang, S., Huang, Z., Yu, Y., Li, X.: The prediction of programming performance using student profiles. Educ. Inf. Technol. **28**(1), 725–740 (2023)
24. Wang, F., et al.: Neural cognitive diagnosis for intelligent education systems. In: AAAI, vol. 34, pp. 6153–6161 (2020)
25. Wilson, K.H., Karklin, Y., Han, B., Ekanadham, C.: Back to the basics: Bayesian extensions of IRT outperform neural networks for proficiency estimation (2016)
26. Yeung, C.K., Yeung, D.Y.: Addressing two problems in deep knowledge tracing via prediction-consistent regularization. In: Proceedings of the Fifth Annual ACM Conference on Learning at Scale, pp. 1–10 (2018)
27. Yin, Y., et al.: Tracing knowledge instead of patterns: Stable knowledge tracing with diagnostic transformer. In: WWW, pp. 855–864 (2023)
28. Yu, W., Wang, X.: MambaOut: do we really need Mamba for vision? (2024)
29. Yudelson, M.V., Koedinger, K.R., Gordon, G.J.: Individualized Bayesian knowledge tracing models. In: Lane, H.C., Yacef, K., Mostow, J., Pavlik, P. (eds.) AIED 2013. LNCS (LNAI), vol. 7926, pp. 171–180. Springer, Heidelberg (2013). https://doi.org/10.1007/978-3-642-39112-5_18
30. Zhang, J., Shi, X., King, I., Yeung, D.Y.: Dynamic key-value memory networks for knowledge tracing. In: WWW, pp. 765–774 (2017)
31. Zhu, L., Liao, B., Zhang, Q., Wang, X., Liu, W., Wang, X.: Vision Mamba: efficient visual representation learning with bidirectional state space model (2024)

Learning Submodular Sequencing from Samples

Jing Yuan[1], Qi Cai[1], Xin Gao[1], and Shaojie Tang[2](✉)

[1] Department of Computer Science and Engineering, University of North Texas, Denton, USA
[2] Center for AI Business Innovation, Department of Management Science and Systems, University at Buffalo, Buffalo, USA
shaojiet@buffalo.edu

Abstract. This paper addresses the problem of sequential submodular maximization: selecting and ranking items in a sequence to optimize some composite submodular function. In contrast to most of the previous works, which assume complete knowledge of the utility function, we assume that we are given only a set of samples. Each sample includes a random sequence of items and its associated utility. We present an algorithm that, given polynomially many samples drawn from a two-stage uniform distribution, achieves an approximation ratio dependent on the curvature of individual submodular functions. Our results apply to a wide variety of real-world scenarios, such as ranking products in online retail platforms, where complete knowledge of the utility function is often impossible to obtain. Our algorithm gives an empirically useful solution in such contexts, thus proving that limited data can be of great use in sequencing tasks. From a technical perspective, our results extend prior work on "optimization from samples" by generalizing from optimizing a set function to a sequence-dependent function.

Keywords: Optimization from samples · Submodular sequencing · Approximation algorithms

1 Introduction

Submodular optimization is one of the most important problems in machine learning, with applications in sparse reconstruction [10], data summarization [14], active learning [13,19], and viral marketing [17]. Most of the existing work deals with the problem of selecting a subset of items that maximizes some submodular function. However, many real applications require not only the selection of items, but also their ranking in a certain order [3,18,21]. This paper focuses on one such problem, termed *sequential submodular maximization* [2,20,22]. The problem's input consists of a ground set Ω and k submodular functions, denoted as $f_1, \cdots, f_k : 2^\Omega \to \mathbb{R}^+$. Our objective is to select a sequence of k items, denoted as $\pi = \{\pi_1, \cdots, \pi_k\}$, from Ω, in order to maximize $F(\pi) \stackrel{\text{def}}{=} \sum_{t \in [k]} f_t(\pi_{[t]})$. Here,

$\pi_{[t]} \stackrel{\text{def}}{=} \{\pi_1, \cdots, \pi_t\}$ represents the first t items of π. Notably, each function f_t takes the first t items from the ranking sequence π as its input.

This problem captures the position bias in item selection, finding applications in sequential active learning and recommendation systems [22]. One illustrative example would be product ranking in any of the online retail platforms, like Amazon [2]. Consider Amazon's daily task of selecting and sequencing a list of products, possibly in vertical order, for display to its customers. Customers browse through this list, reaching a certain position, and may proceed to make purchases from the products they view. Then one of the primary objectives of most platforms is to optimize selection and ranking of products to maximize the chance of a purchase. It turns out that this application can be framed as a sequential submodular maximization problem. In this context, parameters of $F(\pi)$ can be interpreted as follows: Let Ω be the set of products and let k be the window size of displayed products. Given a sequence of products π of length k, for each $t \in \{1, 2, \cdots, k\}$, $f_t(\pi_{[t]})$ is the probability of purchase by customers with patience level t, where a customer with a patience level of t would consider viewing the first t products, $\pi_{[t]}$. Typically, f_t is modeled as a submodular function. In this case, $F(\pi)$ captures the expected purchase probability given that a customer is shown the sequence of products π.

While sequential submodular maximization has been extensively explored in the literature [2,20,22], existing studies typically assume complete knowledge of $f_1, \cdots, f_k : 2^\Omega \to \mathbb{R}^+$ and consequently F. However, this assumption is often unrealistic. For instance, in the aforementioned context of recommendation systems, accurately estimating the purchase probability for every product set is often extremely challenging, if not impossible. Instead, a more realistic scenario involves the platform gathering a potentially extensive dataset comprising browsing histories. Each record (a.k.a. sample) within this dataset includes the sequence of displayed products along with customer feedback. For instance, a record could look like this: {*Sequence*: Product A, Product B; *Feedback*: B was purchased}. Consequently, the platform aims to identify the best sequence of products based on the samples drawn from some distribution. This problem is highly non-trivial since the platform does not have direct access to the original utility function F, making the existing result on submodular sequencing inapplicable. It has been demonstrated that optimizing a set function from samples is generally impossible, even if the set function is a coverage function [7]. Our challenge is compounded by the fact that our function F is defined over a sequence, rather than a set, of items.

Fortunately, in practice, we often encounter submodular functions that may demonstrate more favorable behavior. To this end, we introduce a notation called *curvature* [6]. Intuitively, curvature measures the deviation of a given function from a modular function. Specifically, we say a submodular function f has curvature $c \in [0, 1]$ if $f(i \mid S) \geq (1-c)f(\{i\})$ for any $S \subseteq \Omega$ and $i \notin S$. Here $f(i \mid S) \stackrel{\text{def}}{=} f(S \cup \{i\}) - f(S)$ denotes the marginal utility of an item $i \in \Omega$ on top of a set of items $S \subseteq \Omega$. Hence, if f is a modular function, it has a curvature of 0. In general, the complexity of optimizing a submodular function often hinges on the curvature of the focal function. That is, the instances of submodular optimization become challenging typically only when the curvature is unbounded, i.e., c close to 1. In this paper, we study how to optimize a function $F(\pi) = \sum_{t \in [k]} f_t(\pi_{[t]})$ from samples when the curvature of each individual function f_t is bounded. Our contribution is the development of an approximation algorithm that draws polynomially-many samples from a natural two-stage uniform distribution over feasible sequences and achieves an approximation ratio dependent on the curvature.

2 Related Work

While submodular maximization has been extensively studied in the literature [15], most existing studies assume that the submodular function to be optimized is known. Recently, there has been a line of research focused on learning a submodular function from samples [4,5,11,12], aiming to construct a function that approximates those from which the samples were collected. It has been shown that monotone submodular functions can be approximately learned from samples drawn from a specific distribution [5]. However, it has also been demonstrated that even if an objective function is learnable from samples, optimization for such a function might still be impossible [7]. Despite these negative results, there exists a series of studies [6,8,9] that develop effective algorithms to optimize submodular functions from samples.

In our paper, we focus on an important variant of submodular optimization known as sequential submodular maximization. The objective of sequential submodular maximization is more general than simply selecting a subset of items: it involves jointly selecting and sequencing items. [2] studied this problem with monotone and submodular functions. [20] extended this study to the non-monotone setting. However, all these studies assume a known utility function. Our research builds on and extends these studies by expanding the "learning-from-samples" framework [6] from set functions to sequence functions. Moreover, we identify a gap in the analysis presented in existing studies; more details are provided in Sect. 5.1.

3 Preliminaries and Problem Formulation

Throughout the remainder of this paper, let $[m] = \{0, 1, 2, \ldots, m\}$ for any positive integer m. Given a function f, let $f(i \mid S) \stackrel{\text{def}}{=} f(S \cup \{i\}) - f(S)$ denote the marginal utility of an item $i \in \Omega$ on top of a set of items $S \subseteq \Omega$. We say a function f is submodular if and only if for any two sets X and Y such that $X \subseteq Y$ and any item $i \notin Y$, $f(i \mid X) \geq f(i \mid Y)$. Moreover, we say a submodular function f has curvature $c \in [0, 1]$ if $f(i \mid S) \geq (1 - c)f(\{i\})$ for any $S \subseteq \Omega$ and $i \notin S$.

3.1 Utility Function

Now we are ready to introduce our research problem. Given k submodular functions $f_1, \cdots, f_k : 2^\Omega \to \mathbb{R}^+$, the sequential submodular maximization problem aims to find a sequence $\pi = \{\pi_1, \cdots, \pi_k\}$ from a ground set Ω that maximizes the value of $F(\pi)$. Here,

$$F(\pi) \stackrel{\text{def}}{=} \sum_{t \in [k]} f_t(\pi_{[t]}), \qquad (1)$$

where $\pi_{[t]} \stackrel{\text{def}}{=} \{\pi_1, \cdots, \pi_t\}$ represents the first t items of π. That is, each function f_t takes the first t items from π as its input. Throughout this paper, we use the notation π to denote both a sequence of items and the set of items in that sequence.

Existing studies on sequential submodular maximization all assume that $f_1, \cdots, f_k$ are known in advance, however, in our setting, we do not have direct access to those functions. Instead, we rely on a dataset comprising observations $(\pi, \phi(\pi))$, where in each sample $(\pi, \phi(\pi))$, π denotes a feasible sequence and $\phi(\pi)$ denotes the observed utility of π. It is important to note that the observed utility of a sequence π may be subject to randomness, rendering $\phi(\pi)$ a realization of this stochastic variable. Take, for instance, the product sequencing example outlined in the introduction: $F(\pi)$ denotes the likelihood of purchase from a product sequence π. Here, the observed utility $\phi(\pi)$ of π is a binary variable, with $\phi(\pi) = 1$ denoting a purchase and $\phi(\pi) = 0$ denoting a non-purchase. In this example, randomness stems from two sources: the user's type, characterized by their patience level (i.e., a random function f_t is sampled from $\{f_1, \cdots, f_k\}$), and the probabilistic decision-making process of whether the user will purchase a product from π (note that f_t represents only the *aggregated* likelihood of purchase).

3.2 Problem Formulation

Our objective is to compute a sequence $\pi = \{\pi_1, \cdots, \pi_k\}$ that maximizes the value of $F(\pi)$ based on the samples drawn from a distribution $\mathcal{D}$. We say this problem is γ-optimizable with respect to a distribution $\mathcal{D}$, if there exists an algorithm which, given polynomially many samples drawn from $\mathcal{D}$, returns with high probability a sequence π of size at most k such that $F(\pi) \geq \gamma F(\pi^*)$ where π^* denotes the optimal solution of this problem.

As with the standard PMAC-learning framework, we fix a distribution called *two-stage uniform sampling* and assume that samples are drawn i.i.d. from this distribution. In particular, two-stage uniform sampling works in two stages: In the first stage, a length t is randomly selected from the set $\{1, \cdots, k\}$ with uniform probability. Subsequently, a sequence of length t is randomly chosen, and its realized utility is observed. We would like to clarify that in the first stage, we randomly select the sequence length displayed to the user. However, we do not assume that the attention span of different users (e.g., the actual number

Algorithm 1. Sequencing-from-Samples (SeqSamp)
1: Solve **P.1** to obtain π^s
2: **if** $(1-c)^2 \geq \alpha \cdot \frac{1-c}{1+c-c^2}$ **then**
3: $\quad \pi^\circ \leftarrow \pi^s$
4: **else if** $(1-c)\sum_{t \in \{1,\cdots,k\}} \widetilde{\Delta}(\pi_t^s, t-1) \geq \text{avg}(\Phi_k)$ **then**
5: $\quad \pi^\circ \leftarrow \pi^s$
6: **else**
7: $\quad \pi^\circ \leftarrow$ a random sequence of length k
8: **return** π°;

of items they browse) follows a uniformly random distribution. In the following, we present an approximation algorithm with respect to this distribution.

4 Algorithm Design

Our algorithm first estimates the expected marginal contribution $\Delta(i,t)$ of each item $i \in \Omega$ to a uniformly random sequence of size t, that does not contain i, for every item $i \in \Omega$ and every size $t \in [k-1]$. A formal definition of $\Delta(i,t)$ is given by:

$$\Delta(i,t) = \mathbb{E}_{\Pi_{t+1,i}}[F(\Pi_{t+1,i})] - \mathbb{E}_{\Pi_{t,-i}}[F(\Pi_{t,-i})] \qquad (2)$$

where $\Pi_{t+1,i}$ denotes a random sequence of length $t+1$ with i being placed at the last slot and $\Pi_{t,-i}$ denotes a random sequence of length t that does not contain i. Unfortunately, one can not access the value of either $\mathbb{E}_{\Pi_{t+1,i}}[F(\Pi_{t+1,i})]$ or $\mathbb{E}_{\Pi_{t,-i}}[F(\Pi_{t,-i})]$ directly. To estimate these values, we draw inspiration from a technique proposed in [6], estimating the value of $\mathbb{E}_{\Pi_{t+1,i}}[F(\Pi_{t+1,i})]$ and $\mathbb{E}_{\Pi_{t,-i}}[F(\Pi_{t,-i})]$ using $\text{avg}(\Phi_{t+1,i})$ and $\text{avg}(\Phi_{t,-i})$ respectively. Here, $\text{avg}(\Phi_{t+1,i})$ represents the average (observed) utility of all samples where the length is $t+1$ and i is placed at the last slot, while $\text{avg}(\Phi_{t,-i})$ denotes the average (observed) utility of all samples with length t that do not contain i. Then we use

$$\widetilde{\Delta}(i,t) = \text{avg}(\Phi_{t+1,i}) - \text{avg}(\Phi_{t,-i}) \qquad (3)$$

as an estimation of $\Delta(i,t)$ for all $i \in \Omega$ and $t \in [k-1]$.

In the following, we treat $\widetilde{\Delta}(i,t)$ as the weight of placing i at position $t+1$. As a subroutine of our algorithm, we aim to find a feasible sequence that maximizes the total weight. This objective can be reframed as a *maximum weight matching problem*. Specifically, we introduce a set of item-position pairs $\Psi = \{(i,t) \mid i \in \Omega, t \in \{1,2,\cdots,k\}\}$, where selecting a pair (i,t) indicates assigning item i to position t. Consequently, the task of identifying a feasible sequence maximizing the total weight is transformed into the following maximum weight matching problem.

> **P.1** $\max_{\psi \subseteq \Psi : |\psi| \leq k} \sum_{(i,t) \in \psi} \widetilde{\Delta}(i, t-1)$
> **subject to** $|\psi \cap \Psi_i| \leq 1$ for all $i \in \Omega$; $|\psi \cap \Psi_t| = 1$ for all $t \in [k-1]$.

Here $\Psi_i = \{(i,t) \mid t \in \{1, 2, \cdots, k\}\}$ denote the set of all item-position pairs involving item i, and $\Psi_t = \{(i,t) \mid i \in \Omega\}$ denote the set of all item-position pairs involving position t. The condition "$|\psi \cap \Psi_i| \leq 1$ for all $i \in \Omega$" ensures that each item appears at most once in a sequence, while "$|\psi \cap \Psi_t| = 1$ for all $t \in [k-1]$" ensures that each position contains exactly one item. It is straightforward to confirm the existence of a one-to-one correspondence between feasible sequences and feasible solutions of **P.1**. That is, given a feasible solution ψ of **P.1**, one can construct a feasible sequence such that for each $i \in \Omega$ and $t \in \{1, 2, \cdots, k\}$, item i is placed in position t if and only if $(i,t) \in \psi$.

Because **P.1** is a classic maximum weighted matching problem, it can be solved efficiently in polynomial time [16]. Now we are ready to present our final algorithm SeqSamp (as listed in Algorithm 1). Assume all individual functions $f_1, \cdots, f_k$ have curvature c, that is, for all $t \in [k]$, we have $f_t(i \mid S) \geq (1-c)f_t(\{i\})$ for any $S \subseteq \Omega$ and $i \notin S$. First, we solve **P.1** optimally, and let π^s denote the sequence corresponding to this solution. Then, we compute the final sequence as follows: If $(1-c)^2 \geq \alpha \cdot \frac{1-c}{1+c-c^2}$, where $\alpha = \frac{n-k}{n} \cdot \frac{n-k-1}{n-1} \cdots \cdot \frac{n-2k+1}{n-k+1}$, then our algorithm returns π^s as the final solution. Otherwise, if $(1-c)^2 < \alpha \cdot \frac{1-c}{1+c-c^2}$ and $(1-c)\sum_{t \in \{1, \cdots, k\}} \widetilde{\Delta}(\pi_t^s, t-1) \geq \text{avg}(\Phi_k)$, then our algorithm still returns π^s as the final solution. Here, $\text{avg}(\Phi_k)$ denotes the average utility of all samples with a sequence length of k. Otherwise, our algorithm returns a random sequence of length k as the final solution. We note that the overall design-randomly selecting between a carefully crafted solution and a randomly generated one-is inspired by the framework developed in [6].

4.1 Remark

While our algorithm assumes the curvature of all individual functions is known, this assumption can be relaxed. Specifically, if its exact value is unknown, any upper bound on this value can be used as a surrogate for the curvature without affecting the algorithm's analysis. In the extreme case where the curvature is entirely unknown, one can simply adopt π^s, which yields an approximation ratio of $(1-c)^2$ (an immediate corollary of Lemma 1).

5 Performance Analysis

Let $\pi^\diamond$ be the sequence returned from Algorithm 1, we next analyze the approximation ratio of $\pi^\diamond$, assuming f_t is a monotone submodular function with curvature c for all $t \in \{1, 2, \cdots, k\}$. We first present two technical lemmas. The first lemma derives an approximation ratio for the case when $(1-c)^2 \geq \alpha \cdot \frac{1-c}{1+c-c^2}$, while the second lemma derives an approximation ratio for the remaining cases. The final approximation ratio is the better of these values.

Lemma 1. *Assume f_t is a monotone submodular function with curvature c for all $t \in \{1, 2, \cdots, k\}$, for the case when $(1-c)^2 \geq \alpha \cdot \frac{1-c}{1+c-c^2}$, we have that, with a sufficiently large polynomial number of samples, $F(\pi^\circ) \geq ((1-c)^2 - o(1))F(\pi^*)$ where $\alpha = \frac{n-k}{n} \cdot \frac{n-k-1}{n-1} \cdot \ldots \cdot \frac{n-2k+1}{n-k+1}$.*

Proof. According to Line 2 in Algorithm 1, when $(1-c)^2 \geq \alpha \cdot \frac{1-c}{1+c-c^2}$, it returns π^s as π°. Here π^s denotes the sequence corresponding to the optimal solution of **P.1**. To prove this lemma, it suffices to show that $F(\pi^s) \geq ((1-c)^2 - o(1))F(\pi^*)$.

Let $\pi^s = \{e_1, e_2, \cdots, e_k\}$ and $\pi^s_{[t]} = \{e_1, e_2, \cdots, e_t\}$, it follows that

$$F(\pi^s) = \sum_{t \in [k-1]} F(\pi^s_{[t+1]}) - F(\pi^s_{[t]}) = \sum_{t \in [k-1]} \sum_{j \in \{t+1, \cdots, k\}} f_j(e_{t+1} \mid \pi^s_{[t]})$$

$$\geq (1-c) \sum_{t \in [k-1]} \sum_{j \in \{t+1, \cdots, k\}} f_j(e_{t+1})$$

$$\geq (1-c) \sum_{t \in [k-1]} \sum_{j \in \{t+1, \cdots, k\}} \mathbb{E}_{R_{t,-e_{t+1}}} [f_j(e_{t+1} \mid R_{t,-e_{t+1}})]$$

$$= (1-c) \sum_{t \in [k-1]} \left(\mathbb{E}_{\Pi_{t+1, e_{t+1}}} [F(\Pi_{t+1, e_{t+1}})] - \mathbb{E}_{\Pi_{t,-e_{t+1}}} [F(\Pi_{t,-e_{t+1}})] \right)$$

$$= (1-c) \sum_{t \in [k-1]} \Delta(e_{t+1}, t)$$

where $R_{t,-e_{t+1}}$ denotes a random set of size t that excludes item e_{t+1}. The first inequality is by the curvature of f_t and fact that $e_{t+1} \notin \pi^s_{[t]}$ for all $t \in [t-1]$, and the second inequality is by the assumption that f_t is submodular for all $t \in \{1, 2, \cdots, k\}$.

Recall that $\Delta(i, t) = \mathbb{E}_{\Pi_{t+1, i}}[F(\Pi_{t+1, i})] - \mathbb{E}_{\Pi_{t,-i}}[F(\Pi_{t,-i})]$ and $\widetilde{\Delta}(i, t) = \text{avg}(\Phi_{t+1,i}) - \text{avg}(\Phi_{t,-i})$ is an estimation of $\Delta(i, t)$. In the appendix (Lemma 3), we show that with a sufficiently large polynomial number of samples, the estimation $\widetilde{\Delta}(i, t)$ is n^2-close to $\Delta(i, t)$ for all $i \in \Omega$ and $t \in [k-1]$, with high probability, i.e.,

$$\Delta(i,t) + \frac{\delta}{n^2} \geq \widetilde{\Delta}(i,t) \geq \Delta(i,t) - \frac{\delta}{n^2}. \tag{4}$$

where $\delta = \max_{\pi: |\pi| \leq k} \phi(\pi)$ denotes the maximum realized value of any sequence with a length of at most k. Recall that in the example of product sequencing, $\phi(\pi) = 1$ indicates a purchase, while $\phi(\pi) = 0$ indicates a non-purchase. Therefore, in this example, $\delta = 1$.

This, together with the previous inequality, implies that

$$F(\pi^s) \geq (1-c) \sum_{t \in [k-1]} \Delta(e_{t+1}, t) \geq (1-c) \sum_{t \in [k-1]} \widetilde{\Delta}(e_{t+1}, t) - \frac{\delta}{n}. \tag{5}$$

Recall that $\pi^s = \{e_1, e_2, \cdots, e_k\}$ is the sequence corresponding to the optimal solution of **P.1**, we have

$$\sum_{t \in [k-1]} \tilde{\Delta}(e_{t+1}, t) \geq \sum_{t \in [k-1]} \tilde{\Delta}(e^*_{t+1}, t) \geq \sum_{t \in [k-1]} \Delta(e^*_{t+1}, t) - \frac{\delta}{n}. \quad (6)$$

Here the second inequality is derived using inequality (4).

In addition, observe that

$$\sum_{t \in [k-1]} \Delta(e^*_{t+1}, t)$$

$$= \sum_{t \in [k-1]} \left(\mathbb{E}_{\Pi_{t+1, e^*_{t+1}}} [F(\Pi_{t+1, e^*_{t+1}})] - \mathbb{E}_{\Pi_{t, -e^*_{t+1}}} [F(\Pi_{t, -e^*_{t+1}})] \right)$$

$$= \sum_{t \in [k-1]} \sum_{j \in \{t+1, \cdots, k\}} \mathbb{E}_{R_{t, -e^*_{t+1}}} [f_j(e^*_{t+1} \mid R_{t, -e^*_{t+1}})]$$

$$\geq \sum_{t \in [k-1]} \sum_{j \in \{t+1, \cdots, k\}} \mathbb{E}_{R_{t, -e^*_{t+1}}} [(1-c) f_j(e^*_{t+1})]$$

$$= (1-c) \sum_{t \in [k-1]} \sum_{j \in \{t+1, \cdots, k\}} f_j(e^*_{t+1}) \geq (1-c) F(\pi^*)$$

where the first inequality is by the curvature of f_t and fact that $e^*_{t+1} \notin R_{t, -e^*_{t+1}}$ for all $t \in [k-1]$, and the second inequality is by the assumption that f_t is submodular for all $t \in \{1, 2, \cdots, k\}$.

This, together with inequality (6), implies that

$$\sum_{t \in [k-1]} \tilde{\Delta}(e_{t+1}, t) \geq \sum_{t \in [k-1]} \Delta(e^*_{t+1}, t) - \frac{\delta}{n} \geq (1-c) F(\pi^*) - \frac{\delta}{n}. \quad (7)$$

Inequalities (5) and (7) imply that

$$F(\pi^s) \geq ((1-c)^2 - o(1)) F(\pi^*). \quad (8)$$

□

We proceed to providing the second technical lemma.

Lemma 2. *Assume f_t is a monotone submodular function with curvature c for all $t \in \{1, 2, \cdots, k\}$, for the case when $(1-c)^2 < \alpha \cdot \frac{1-c}{1+c-c^2}$, we have that, with a sufficiently large polynomial number of samples,*

$$F(\pi^\diamond) \geq \alpha \cdot \left(\frac{1-c}{1+c-c^2} - o(1) \right) F(\pi^*) \quad (9)$$

where $\alpha = \frac{n-k}{n} \cdot \frac{n-k-1}{n-1} \cdots \cdot \frac{n-2k+1}{n-k+1}$.

Proof. Let us define a function $F(\pi \uplus \pi^*)$ for a sequence π of length k and an optimal solution π^* as follows:

$$F(\pi \uplus \pi^*) = \sum_{t \in [k]} f_t(\pi_{[t]} \cup \pi^*_{[t]}) \tag{10}$$

Here, $\pi_{[t]}$ (and $\pi^*_{[t]}$) represent all items from π (and π^*) respectively, that are placed up to position t. That is, $\pi \uplus \pi^*$ can be envisioned as a virtual sequence where both π_t and π^*_t are placed at position t for all $t \in \{1, 2, \cdots, k\}$.

Let Π' denote a random sequence of length k that is sampled over items from $\Omega \setminus \pi^*$, and $\Pi'_{[t]}$ denotes the first t items from Π', observe that,

$$\mathbb{E}_{\Pi'}\left[F(\Pi' \uplus \pi^*) - F(\pi^*)\right] = \mathbb{E}_{\Pi'}\Big[\sum_{t \in \{1,2,\cdots,k\}} f_t(\Pi'_{[t]} \cup \pi^*_{[t]}) - \sum_{t \in \{1,2,\cdots,k\}} f_t(\pi^*_{[t]})\Big]$$

$$= \mathbb{E}_{\Pi'}\Big[\sum_{t \in \{1,2,\cdots,k\}} (f_t(\Pi'_{[t]} \cup \pi^*_{[t]}) - f_t(\pi^*_{[t]}))\Big] = \mathbb{E}_{\Pi'}\Big[\sum_{t \in \{1,2,\cdots,k\}} f_t(\Pi'_{[t]} \mid \pi^*_{[t]})\Big]$$

$$= \sum_{t \in \{1,2,\cdots,k\}} \mathbb{E}_{\Pi'}\left[f_t(\Pi'_{[t]} \mid \pi^*_{[t]})\right] \geq \sum_{t \in \{1,2,\cdots,k\}} (1-c)\mathbb{E}_{\Pi'}[f_t(\Pi'_{[t]})]$$

$$\geq (1-c)\mathbb{E}_{\Pi'}\Big[\sum_{t \in \{1,2,\cdots,k\}} f_t(\Pi'_{[t]})\Big] = (1-c)\mathbb{E}_{\Pi'}[F(\Pi')].$$

To establish the first inequality, we utilize the fact that $\Pi'_{[t]}$ is a random set of size t and $\Pi'_{[t]} \subseteq \Omega \setminus \pi^*_{[t]}$. Consequently, this inequality can be derived by substituting $R = \Pi'_{[t]}$ and $S = \pi^*_{[t]}$ into Lemma 4 which is presented in the appendix.

In addition, observe that

$$F(\pi^*) + \mathbb{E}_{\Pi'}[F(\Pi' \uplus \pi^*)] - F(\pi^*)$$
$$= \mathbb{E}_{\Pi'}[F(\Pi')] + \mathbb{E}_{\Pi'}[F(\Pi' \uplus \pi^*)] - \mathbb{E}_{\Pi'}[F(\Pi')]$$

and $\sum_{t \in [k-1]} \Delta(e^*_{t+1}, t) \geq \alpha \cdot \mathbb{E}_{\Pi'}\left[F(\Pi' \uplus \pi^*) - F(\Pi')\right]$ where $\alpha = \frac{n-k}{n} \cdot \frac{n-k-1}{n-1} \cdots \cdot \frac{n-2k+1}{n-k+1}$ (by Lemma 5 in the appendix). We have

$$F(\pi^*) + \mathbb{E}_{\Pi'}[F(\Pi' \uplus \pi^*)] - F(\pi^*) \leq \mathbb{E}_{\Pi'}[F(\Pi')] + \frac{1}{\alpha}\sum_{t \in [k-1]} \Delta(e^*_{t+1}, t).$$

This, together with the previous observation that $\mathbb{E}_{\Pi'}[F(\Pi' \uplus \pi^*)] - F(\pi^*) \geq (1-c)\mathbb{E}_{\Pi'}[F(\Pi')]$, implies that $F(\pi^*) + (1-c)\mathbb{E}_{\Pi'}[F(\Pi')] \leq \mathbb{E}_{\Pi'}[F(\Pi')] + \frac{1}{\alpha}\sum_{t \in [k-1]} \Delta(e^*_{t+1}, t)$. It follows that

$$\sum_{t \in [k-1]} \Delta(e^*_{t+1}, t) \geq \alpha \left(1 - c\frac{\mathbb{E}_{\Pi'}[F(\Pi')]}{F(\pi^*)}\right) F(\pi^*). \tag{11}$$

This, together with inequality (7), implies that

$$(1-c)\sum_{t\in[k-1]}\widetilde{\Delta}(e_{t+1},t) \geq (1-o(1))(1-c)\sum_{t\in[k-1]}\Delta(e^*_{t+1},t)$$
$$\geq (1-o(1))(1-c)\alpha\left(1-c\frac{\mathbb{E}_{\Pi'}[F(\Pi')]}{F(\pi^*)}\right)F(\pi^*). \qquad(12)$$

According to Line 4 of Algorithm 1 and inequality (5), when $(1-c)^2 < \alpha \cdot \frac{1-c}{1+c-c^2}$, π° achieves an utility of at least $\max\{(1-o(1))\mathbb{E}_\Pi[F(\Pi)], (1-o(1))(1-c)\sum_{t\in[k-1]}\widetilde{\Delta}(e_{t+1},t)\}$ where Π denotes a random sequence of length k that is sampled over items from Ω. Hence, the approximation ratio of our algorithm is at least $\max\{(1-o(1))\frac{\mathbb{E}_\Pi[F(\Pi)]}{F(\pi^*)}, (1-o(1))\frac{(1-c)\sum_{t\in[k-1]}\widetilde{\Delta}(e_{t+1},t)}{F(\pi^*)}\}$. According to inequality (12), $\frac{(1-c)\sum_{t\in[k-1]}\widetilde{\Delta}(e_{t+1},t)}{F(\pi^*)} \geq (1-o(1))\alpha(1-c)(1-c\frac{\mathbb{E}_{\Pi'}[F(\Pi')]}{F(\pi^*)})$. It follows that the approximation ratio of our algorithm is at least $\max\{(1-o(1))\frac{\mathbb{E}_\Pi[F(\Pi)]}{F(\pi^*)}, (1-o(1))\alpha(1-c)(1-c\frac{\mathbb{E}_{\Pi'}[F(\Pi')]}{F(\pi^*)})\} = (1-o(1))\max\{\frac{\mathbb{E}_\Pi[F(\Pi)]}{F(\pi^*)}, \alpha(1-c)(1-c\frac{\mathbb{E}_{\Pi'}[F(\Pi')]}{F(\pi^*)})\} \geq (1-o(1))\max\{\frac{\alpha\mathbb{E}_{\Pi'}[F(\Pi')]}{F(\pi^*)}, \alpha(1-c)(1-c\frac{\mathbb{E}_{\Pi'}[F(\Pi')]}{F(\pi^*)})\} = (1-o(1))\alpha\max\{\frac{\mathbb{E}_{\Pi'}[F(\Pi')]}{F(\pi^*)}, (1-c)(1-c\frac{\mathbb{E}_{\Pi'}[F(\Pi')]}{F(\pi^*)})\}$ where the inequality is by the observation that the probability that Π is sampled from $\Omega \setminus \pi^*$ is at least $\alpha = \frac{n-k}{n} \cdot \frac{n-k-1}{n-1} \cdot \ldots \cdot \frac{n-2k+1}{n-k+1}$. Observe that $\max\{\frac{\mathbb{E}_{\Pi'}[F(\Pi')]}{F(\pi^*)}, (1-c)(1-c\frac{\mathbb{E}_{\Pi'}[F(\Pi')]}{F(\pi^*)})\}$ is at least $\frac{1-c}{1+c-c^2}$, hence, the approximation of π° is at least $\alpha \cdot \frac{1-c}{1+c-c^2} - o(1)$. □

Combining Lemma 1 and Lemma 2, we have the following theorem.

Theorem 1. *Let π° be the sequence returned from Algorithm 1, assuming f_t is a monotone submodular function with curvature c for all $t \in \{1, 2, \cdots, k\}$, we have that, with a sufficiently large polynomial number of samples,*

$$F(\pi^\circ) \geq \max\{(1-c)^2 - o(1), \alpha \cdot \frac{1-c}{1+c-c^2} - o(1)\}F(\pi^*) \qquad(13)$$

where $\alpha = \frac{n-k}{n} \cdot \frac{n-k-1}{n-1} \cdot \ldots \cdot \frac{n-2k+1}{n-k+1}$.

5.1 Remark

While our study builds on the work of [6] by extending the "learning-from-samples" approach from set functions to sequence functions, there is a potential gap in their original analysis. Specifically, their proof of Lemma 1 relies on the assumption that $f(R \mid S^*) \geq (1-c)f(R)$, where S^* is an optimal set solution, R is a uniformly random set of size $k-1$ (with k being the size constraint of the final solution) and c is the curvature of function f. This assumption is, unfortunately, not generally valid; according to the definition of the curvature c, this assumption holds only if $R \cap S^* = \emptyset$. Our study addresses this issue by introducing the notion of α and further extends their research to a more complex sequence function.

6 Performance Evaluation

We evaluate the performance of the proposed sequential submodular maximization algorithm in the context of assortment optimization, where a sequence of items are selected for display to the users with the goal of maximizing the purchase probability. Given the dynamic nature of user purchase behavior, there is always a challenge to accurately capture the probability of a user purchasing one product from the sequence that is displayed to her. In this case, it is essential to relax the assumption that there is a known function that captures the purchase behavior of each individual user type. To obtain a high quality sequence of items for display, our algorithms merely require a small collection of samples each comprises a random sequence of displayed items and its corresponding realized outcome (purchase or no purchase). Our results demonstrate the superiority of our algorithm that lies in its comparable performance to the upper bound. The performance is evaluated in terms of the expected utility with respect to changes in number of samples, user patience level, and item preference distribution.

Experimental Setup. We exploit the widely used Multinomial Logit (MNL) model [1] to capture the underlying user behavior. Our individual function is defined as $f_t(\pi_{[t]}) = \lambda_t * (\sum_{i \in [t]} v_{u,i})/(1 + \sum_{i \in [t]} v_{u,i})$, where $v_{u,i}$ denotes the user u's preference towards item i. Given a sequence π, $f_t(\pi_{[t]})$ captures the purchase probability of a user with a specific patience level t who is willing to browse the first t items $\pi_{[t]}$. Note that our algorithms do not have direct access to this model, which is only used as an underlying model for generating samples and calculating the utility of a solution.

Algorithms. We compare our proposed Sequencing-from-Samples algorithm (labeled as SeqSamp) against two benchmarks, namely, GKF and BestSamp, under various parameter settings. GKF *has access to the underlying choice model* and operates greedily, iteratively selecting the item with the largest marginal gain with respect to $F(\pi)$ in each iteration. BestSamp is a sampling-based algorithm that selects the single best sample with the largest utility. Like SeqSamp, BestSamp does not have access to the choice model, when multiple samples with the same largest value exist, it randomly picks one to break the tie. We use the solu-

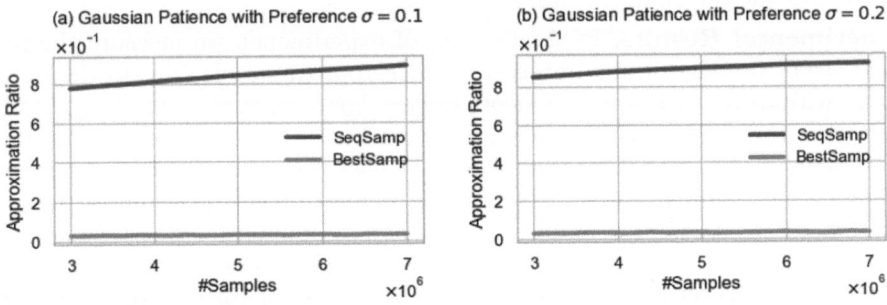

Fig. 1. SeqSamp achieves superior approximation ratio under normal distributed user preferences

tion returned by GKF as an upper bound. We obtain the approximation ratio of the expected utility of the sampling-based algorithms to the upper bound.

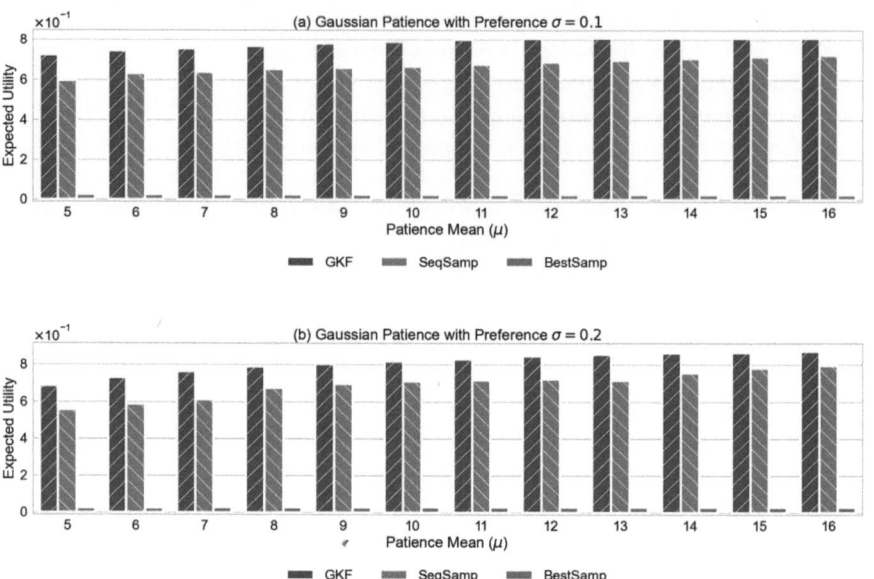

Fig. 2. SeqSamp achieves superior expected utility with respect to varying user patience levels

Parameter Settings. Note that choice models can vary among individuals. We test different user preference distributions to capture this phenomena. Specifically, we follow a normal distribution $\mathcal{N}(\mu, \sigma^2)$ to sample the values for λ_t. We explore the impact of user preference distribution on the performance of the algorithms by varying the value of μ and σ. We also evaluate the impact of user type (patience level t) distribution. Our experiments are run on AMD Ryzen Threadripper PRO Processor with 128 GB RAM. We run each set of experiments 100 rounds and the average results are reported below. Complete source code is provided in supplementary materials.

Experimental Results. In the first set of experiments, we measure the performance of the algorithms in terms of their approximation ratio to the upper bound with respect to various sizes of samples. For each item i, we set $v_{u,i}$, users' preference towards i, to follow a normal distribution with μ ranging from 0.01 to 0.5 with $\sigma = 0.1$ and 0.2, respectively. We vary the value of σ to test the reliability of our algorithm when different users' have diverse preferences towards the same item. A larger σ indicates more diverse opinions. We set the number of items to be $n = 10^4$ and number of user types to be $k = 20$. The average user's patience is set to be 15. As shown in Fig. 1(a), for the case of $\sigma = 0.1$, we observe that with 3.5×10^6 samples, SeqSamp already achieves a 80% approximation ratio to the upper bound. With 7×10^6 samples, SeqSamp achieves a

88.6% approximation ratio. As shown in Fig. 1(b), when users' preferences are more diverse, SeqSamp achieves a 91.95% approximation ratio with 7×10^6 samples. All of our experiments have the solutions returned within one minute. Note that for our main theoretical result to hold (i.e., Lemma 3), a sample size on the order of n^8 (i.e., 10^{32}) is required. This highlights that, in practice, our approach requires significantly fewer samples than our analysis suggests.

In the second set of experiments, we measure the performance of the algorithms in terms of their expected utility with respect to various user patience levels, ranging from 5 to 16. We follow the parameter settings as above. Figure 2 shows the results for SepSamp and BestSamp based on 7×10^6 samples, compared to the upper bound (GKF). We observe that as users are willing to browse more items on the average, the expected utility tends to increase with a diminishing marginal gain. SeqSamp achieves a comparable performance to the upper bound and significantly outperforms BestSamp, both for $\sigma = 0.1$ (Fig. 2(a)) and $\sigma = 0.2$ (Fig. 2(b)). This again demonstrates the superiority of our sequencing-from-sampling approach that it yields an outstanding utility with a small collection of samples and is reliable under various user purchase behaviors.

7 Conclusion

In this paper, we build on the framework of "optimization from samples" by extending the focus from optimizing set functions to sequence-dependent functions. Our objective is to determine an optimal ordering of items that maximizes an unknown utility function, given only a set of i.i.d. samples drawn from a specific distribution. We propose an approximation algorithm, with its performance guarantee depending on the curvature of the underlying functions. In future work, we aim to apply our findings to other real-world applications and further extend our results to encompass broader classes of sample distributions.

Acknowledgement. This work was supported in part by CAHSI-Google institutional Research Program.

A Appendix

Lemma 3. *With a sufficiently large polynomial number of samples, the estimation $\widetilde{\Delta}(i,t)$ is n^2-close to $\Delta(i,t)$ for all $i \in \Omega$ and $t \in [k-1]$, with high probability, i.e., $\Delta(i,t) + \frac{\delta}{n^2} \geq \widetilde{\Delta}(i,t) \geq \Delta(i,t) - \frac{\delta}{n^2}$ where $\delta = \max_{\pi:|\pi| \leq k} \phi(\pi)$ denotes the maximum realized value of any sequence with a length of at most k.*

Proof. Our proof is inspired by the one presented in [6] (Appendix A) and extends their analysis from set functions to sequence functions. Consider an arbitrary pair of $i \in \Omega$ and $t \in [k-1]$.

Observation 1: The probability of sampling a sequence of length t is no less than $1/k$, whose value is at least $1/n$. Note that the case when $t = 0$ is trivial because the value of an empty sequence is known to be zero. Furthermore, given that the sampled sequence has a length of t, the probability of it not containing item i is at least $1 - t/n \geq 1/n$. Hence, the probability of sampling a sequence of length t without i is at least $1/n^2$.

Observation 2: The probability of sampling a sequence of length $t+1$ is no less than $1/k$, where $1/k$ is at least $1/n$. Additionally, given that the sampled sequence has a length of $t+1$, the likelihood of the last item being i is at least $1/n$. Consequently, the probability of sampling a sequence of length $t+1$ with i at position $t+1$ is at least $1/n^2$.

The above two observations, together with Chernoff bounds, imply that gathering a minimum of n^5 samples of length t that do not contain i, and at least n^5 samples of length $t+1$ wherein i resides at position $t+1$, can be accomplished with high probability by obtaining n^8 samples.

By Hoeffding's inequality and the fact that δ is the largest possible value observed from any sequence of size at most k, we have

$$\Pr[|\text{avg}(\pi_{t,-i}) - \mathbb{E}_{\Pi_{t,-i}}[F(\Pi_{t,-i})]| \geq \frac{\delta}{2n^2}] \leq 2e^{-2n^5(\delta/2n^2)^2/\delta^2} \leq 2e^{-n/2},$$

and

$$\Pr[|\text{avg}(\pi_{t+1,i}) - \mathbb{E}_{\Pi_{t+1,i}}[F(\Pi_{t+1,i})]| \geq \frac{\delta}{2n^2}] \leq 2e^{-n/2}.$$

Given that $\Delta(i,t) = \mathbb{E}_{\Pi_{t+1,i}}[F(\Pi_{t+1,i})] - \mathbb{E}_{\Pi_{t,-i}}[F(\Pi_{t,-i})]$ and $\widetilde{\Delta}(i,t) = \text{avg}(\pi_{t+1,i}) - \text{avg}(\pi_{t,-i})$, we can deduce that, with a sample size of n^8, the following inequalities hold for all $i \in \Omega$ and $t \in [k-1]$, with high probability: $\Delta(i,t) + \frac{\delta}{n^2} \geq \widetilde{\Delta}(i,t) \geq \Delta(i,t) - \frac{\delta}{n^2}$. □

Lemma 4. *Let $f : 2^\Omega \to \mathbb{R}_{\geq 0}$ be a monotone and submodular function, given any subset of items $S \subseteq \Omega$ such that $|S| \leq k$, let R be a set of size t that is randomly sampled from $\Omega \setminus S$, for any $t \leq \min\{k, |\Omega \setminus S|\}$, $\mathbb{E}_R[f(R \mid S)] \geq (1-c)\mathbb{E}_R[f(R)]$.*

Proof. Assuming R is obtained by sequentially sampling t items without replacement, let $R = \{r_1, \cdots, r_t\}$, where r_j represents the j-th sampled item. Let $R_{[j]} = \{r_1, \cdots, r_j\}$ denote the first j sampled items,

$$\mathbb{E}_R[f(R \mid S)] = \sum_{j \in [t-1]} \mathbb{E}_R[f(r_{j+1} \mid R_{[j]} \cup S)]. \tag{14}$$

Consider any given sample R, because $r_{j+1} \notin R_{[j]}$ and $r_{j+1} \notin S$ (by the assumption that $R \subseteq \Omega \setminus S$), then by the curvature of f, $f(r_{j+1} \mid R_{[j]} \cup S) \geq (1-c)f(r_{j+1})$. It follows that $\mathbb{E}_R[f(R \mid S)] = \mathbb{E}_R[\sum_{j \in [t-1]} f(r_{j+1} \mid R_{[j]} \cup S)] = \sum_{j \in [t-1]} \mathbb{E}_R[f(r_{j+1} \mid R_{[j]} \cup S)] \geq \sum_{j \in [t-1]}(1-c)\mathbb{E}_R[f(r_{j+1})] = (1-c)\mathbb{E}_R[\sum_{j \in [t-1]} f(r_{j+1})] \geq (1-c)\mathbb{E}_R[f(R)]$ where the first inequality is by the observation that $f(r_{j+1} \mid R_{[j]} \cup S) \geq (1-c)f(r_{j+1})$ for any R and the last inequality is by the assumption that f is a submodular function. □

Lemma 5. Let Π' denote a random sequence of length k that is sampled over items from $\Omega \setminus \pi^*$ where $\pi^* = \{e_1^*, \cdots, e_k^*\}$ denotes the optimal solution, we have $\sum_{t \in [k-1]} \Delta(e_{t+1}^*, t) \geq \alpha \cdot \mathbb{E}_{\Pi'}[F(\Pi' \uplus \pi^*) - F(\Pi')]$ where $\alpha = \frac{n-k}{n} \cdot \frac{n-k-1}{n-1} \cdot \ldots \cdot \frac{n-2k+1}{n-k+1}$.

Proof. Let Π denote a random sequence of length k that is sampled over items from Ω. Hence, the probability that the first t items $\Pi_{[t]}$ is sampled from $\Omega \setminus \pi^*$ is at least $\alpha = \frac{n-k}{n} \cdot \frac{n-k-1}{n-1} \cdot \ldots \cdot \frac{n-2k+1}{n-k+1}$ for any $t \in \{1, \cdots, k\}$. Recall that Π' denotes a random sequence of length k that is sampled over items from $\Omega \setminus \pi^*$. It follows that $\mathbb{E}_\Pi[f_t(i \mid \Pi_{[t]})] \geq \alpha \mathbb{E}_{\Pi'}[f_t(i \mid \Pi'_{[t]})]$ for all $t \in \{1, \cdots, k\}$ and any item $i \in \Omega$.

Observe that $\sum_{t \in [k-1]} \Delta(e_{t+1}^*, t)$

$$= \sum_{t \in [k-1]} \mathbb{E}_{\Pi_{t+1,e_{t+1}^*}}[F(\Pi_{t+1,e_{t+1}^*})] - \mathbb{E}_{\Pi_{t,-e_{t+1}^*}}[F(\Pi_{t,-e_{t+1}^*})]$$

$$= \sum_{t \in [k-1]} \mathbb{E}_{\Pi_{t,-e_{t+1}^*}}\left[\sum_{z \in \{t+1,\cdots,k\}} f_z(e_{t+1}^* \mid \Pi_{t,-e_{t+1}^*})\right]$$

$$\geq \sum_{t \in [k-1]} \mathbb{E}_\Pi\left[\sum_{z \in \{t+1,\cdots,k\}} f_z(e_{t+1}^* \mid \Pi_{[t]})\right]$$

$$\geq \sum_{t \in [k-1]} \mathbb{E}_\Pi\left[\sum_{z \in \{t+1,\cdots,k\}} f_z(e_{t+1}^* \mid \Pi_{[z]})\right]$$

$$= \sum_{t \in [k-1]} \sum_{z \in \{t+1,\cdots,k\}} \mathbb{E}_\Pi[f_z(e_{t+1}^* \mid \Pi_{[z]})]$$

$$\geq \sum_{t \in [k-1]} \sum_{z \in \{t+1,\cdots,k\}} \alpha \mathbb{E}_{\Pi'}[f_z(e_{t+1}^* \mid \Pi'_{[z]})]$$

$$= \alpha \mathbb{E}_{\Pi'}\left[\sum_{t \in [k-1]} \sum_{z \in \{t+1,\cdots,k\}} f_z(e_{t+1}^* \mid \Pi'_{[z]})\right]$$

$$\geq \alpha \mathbb{E}_{\Pi'}[F(\Pi' \uplus \pi^*) - F(\Pi')]$$

where the forth inequality is by the previous observation that $\mathbb{E}_\Pi[f_t(i \mid \Pi_{[t]})] \geq \alpha \mathbb{E}_{\Pi'}[f_t(i \mid \Pi'_{[t]})]$ for all $t \in \{1, \cdots, k\}$. □

References

1. Anderson, S.P., De Palma, A., Thisse, J.F.: Discrete Choice Theory of Product Differentiation. MIT press (1992)
2. Asadpour, A., Niazadeh, R., Saberi, A., Shameli, A.: Sequential submodular maximization and applications to ranking an assortment of products. Oper. Res. **71**(4), 1154–1170 (2022)
3. Azar, Y., Gamzu, I.: Ranking with submodular valuations. In: Proceedings of the Twenty-Second Annual ACM-SIAM Symposium on Discrete Algorithms, pp. 1070–1079. SIAM (2011)

4. Balcan, M.F., Constantin, F., Iwata, S., Wang, L.: Learning valuation functions. In: Conference on Learning Theory, pp. 4–1. JMLR Workshop and Conference Proceedings (2012)
5. Balcan, M.F., Harvey, N.J.: Learning submodular functions. In: Proceedings of the Forty-Third Annual ACM Symposium on Theory of Computing, pp. 793–802 (2011)
6. Balkanski, E., Rubinstein, A., Singer, Y.: The power of optimization from samples. In: Advances in Neural Information Processing Systems, vol. 29 (2016)
7. Balkanski, E., Rubinstein, A., Singer, Y.: The limitations of optimization from samples. In: Proceedings of the 49th Annual ACM SIGACT Symposium on Theory of Computing, pp. 1016–1027 (2017)
8. Chen, W., Sun, X., Zhang, J., Zhang, Z.: Optimization from structured samples for coverage functions. In: International Conference on Machine Learning, pp. 1715–1724. PMLR (2020)
9. Chen, W., Sun, X., Zhang, J., Zhang, Z.: Network inference and influence maximization from samples. In: International Conference on Machine Learning, pp. 1707–1716. PMLR (2021)
10. Das, A., Kempe, D.: Submodular meets spectral: greedy algorithms for subset selection, sparse approximation and dictionary selection. In: Proceedings of the 28th International Conference on International Conference on Machine Learning, pp. 1057–1064 (2011)
11. Feldman, V., Kothari, P.: Learning coverage functions and private release of marginals. In: Conference on Learning Theory, pp. 679–702. PMLR (2014)
12. Feldman, V., Kothari, P., Vondrák, J.: Representation, approximation and learning of submodular functions using low-rank decision trees. In: Conference on Learning Theory, pp. 711–740. PMLR (2013)
13. Golovin, D., Krause, A.: Adaptive submodularity: theory and applications in active learning and stochastic optimization. J. Artif. Intell. Res. **42**, 427–486 (2011)
14. Lin, H., Bilmes, J.: A class of submodular functions for document summarization. In: Proceedings of the 49th Annual Meeting of the Association for Computational Linguistics: Human Language Technologies, pp. 510–520 (2011)
15. Nemhauser, G.L., Wolsey, L.A., Fisher, M.L.: An analysis of approximations for maximizing submodular set functions-i. Math. Program. **14**(1), 265–294 (1978)
16. Schrijver, A., et al.: Combinatorial Optimization: Polyhedra and Efficiency, vol. 24. Springer (2003)
17. Tang, S., Yuan, J.: Influence maximization with partial feedback. Oper. Res. Lett. **48**(1), 24–28 (2020)
18. Tang, S., Yuan, J.: Cascade submodular maximization: question selection and sequencing in online personality quiz. Prod. Oper. Manag. **30**(7), 2143–2161 (2021)
19. Tang, S., Yuan, J.: Optimal sampling gaps for adaptive submodular maximization. In: AAAI (2022)
20. Tang, S., Yuan, J.: Non-monotone sequential submodular maximization. In: Proceedings of the AAAI Conference on Artificial Intelligence, vol. 38, pp. 15284–15291 (2024)
21. Tschiatschek, S., Singla, A., Krause, A.: Selecting sequences of items via submodular maximization. In: Thirty-First AAAI Conference on Artificial Intelligence (2017)
22. Zhang, G., Tatti, N., Gionis, A.: Ranking with submodular functions on a budget. Data Min. Knowl. Disc. **36**(3), 1197–1218 (2022)

Revisiting Applicable and Comprehensive Knowledge Tracing in Large-Scale Data

Yiyun Zhou, Wenkang Han, and Jingyuan Chen[✉]

Zhejiang University, Hangzhou, China
{yiyunzhou,wenkangh,jingyuanchen}@zju.edu.cn

Abstract. Knowledge Tracing (KT) is a fundamental component of Intelligent Tutoring Systems (ITS), enabling the modeling of students' knowledge states to predict future performance. The introduction of Deep Knowledge Tracing (DKT), the first deep learning-based KT (DLKT) model, has brought significant advantages in terms of applicability and comprehensiveness. However, recent DLKT models, such as Attentive Knowledge Tracing (AKT), have often prioritized predictive performance at the expense of these benefits. While deep sequential models like DKT have shown potential, they face challenges related to parallel computing, storage decision modification, and limited storage capacity. To address these limitations, we propose DKT2, a novel KT model that leverages the recently developed xLSTM architecture. DKT2 enhances applicable input representation using the Rasch model and incorporates Item Response Theory (IRT) for output interpretability, allowing for the decomposition of learned knowledge into familiar and unfamiliar knowledge. By integrating this knowledge with predicted questions, DKT2 generates comprehensive knowledge states. Extensive experiments conducted across three large-scale datasets demonstrate that DKT2 consistently outperforms 18 baseline models in various prediction tasks, underscoring its potential for real-world educational applications. This work bridges the gap between theoretical advancements and practical implementation in KT. Our code, datasets and Appendix are fully available at https://github.com/zyy-2001/DKT2.

Keywords: Knowledge Tracing · Information Interaction

1 Introduction

The rapid expansion of educational data within Intelligent Tutoring Systems (ITS) [26] (e.g., AutoTutor [29]) has exposed significant limitations in traditional machine learning approaches [4]. In contrast, the advent of deep learning has introduced novel opportunities for addressing these challenges [18, 36]. A critical

---

Supplementary Information The online version contains supplementary material available at https://doi.org/10.1007/978-3-032-06109-6_14.

component of ITS is Knowledge Tracing (KT), which models students' knowledge states and predicts future performance by analyzing their interaction data. Deep learning, with its advanced feature learning paradigm, offers enhanced modeling power and predictive accuracy in this context.

Deep Knowledge Tracing (DKT) [31] represents the first significant application of deep learning to KT, employing Long Short-Term Memory (LSTM) networks [13] to capture the complexity of students' learning processes. As a pioneering deep learning-based KT (DLKT) model, DKT has demonstrated superior predictive performance compared to traditional machine learning-based KT models (*e.g.*, Bayesian Knowledge Tracing (BKT) [7]), offering notable advantages in applicability and comprehensiveness.

DKT encodes students' **historical** interactions to generate a comprehensive representation of their knowledge states (*i.e.*, proficiency scores[1] for **each concept** at each time step) and predicts future performance. **However, recent DLKT models, such as the Attentive Knowledge Tracing (AKT)** [10]**, while excelling in predictive accuracy** [15,16,23,40,42]**, present limitations in applicability and comprehensiveness (the related details are in Sect. 3.2)**. Specifically, AKT requires both historical and future interactions as input, complicating its practical application since future responses are typically unavailable. Additionally, unlike DKT, AKT directly predicts scores on future questions without generating a comprehensive knowledge state, potentially weakening the correlations between different concepts and narrowing the definition of knowledge states in KT. Our review of 60 KT-model-related papers published in top AI/ML conferences and journals over the past decade (see Appendix A.1) reveals a trend where evaluation performance has been prioritized at the expense of practical applicability, risking a disconnect between theoretical advancements and real-world implementation.

Deep sequential models like DKT have intrinsic limitations that may prevent them from achieving optimal performance. LSTM networks, for instance, face challenges in dynamically updating stored information and exhibit limited storage capacity due to their scalar cell state design. Moreover, their inherent sequential processing nature hinders parallelization, limiting their scalability to large datasets. The recently proposed xLSTM [3], however, addresses these challenges by introducing two new variants: sLSTM, which improves LSTM's storage decision by incorporating an exponential activation function, and mLSTM, which replaces scalar cell states with matrix memory for increased storage capacity and improved retrieval efficiency, while achieving full parallelization by abandoning memory mixing. Building on the strengths of xLSTM, we introduce DKT2, an enhanced DLKT model designed for greater applicability and comprehensiveness. DKT2 integrates the Rasch model [32] from educational psychology to process historical interactions, using xLSTM for knowledge learning. DKT2 then incorporates Item Response Theory (IRT) [25,37] to interpret the learned knowledge, differentiating between familiar and unfamiliar knowledge, and ultimately

---

[1] Proficiency scores range from 0 to 1, with higher values indicating greater knowledge and skill level.

integrates this knowledge with predicted questions to generate comprehensive knowledge states.

Our primary contributions are as follows:

- We provide a systematic analysis of input and output settings in KT, proposing DLKT models optimized for real-world applicability and comprehensiveness.
- We introduce DKT2, a model built on xLSTM, adhering to rigorous applicable input and comprehensive output settings, and incorporating both the Rasch model for input and an interpretable IRT-based output module.
- We conduct extensive experiments, including one-step prediction, multi-step prediction, and predictions with varying history lengths, across three large-scale datasets. Our findings demonstrate that DKT2 consistently outperforms 18 baseline models, with additional analysis on the impact of input settings and multi-concept output predictions on KT performance.

2 Related Work

Since DKT [31] first applied deep learning methods to the KT task a decade ago, deep learning techniques have flourished in KT. Current DLKT models can be categorized into the following 8 types:

- **Deep sequential models** use recurrent structures to encode students' chronologically ordered interactions, e.g., DKT uses LSTM to model complex student cognitive processes. Two variants of DKT have emerged in subsequent research. DKT+ [39] introduces two regularization terms to improve the consistency of KT predictions, while DKT-F [27] enhances KT by considering forgetting behavior.
- **Attention-based models** capture long-term dependencies between interactions through attention mechanisms, e.g., SAKT [30] is the first to use attention mechanisms to capture correlations between concepts and interactions. AKT [10] employs a novel monotonic attention to represent the time distance between questions and students' historical interactions. Due to AKT's outstanding predictive performance, numerous powerful KT models are subsequently derived, such as simpleKT [23], FoLiBiKT [16], sparseKT [15], DTransformer [40], and stableKT [20].
- **Mamba-based models** are strong competitors to Transformer models. The recently proposed Mamba4KT [5] is the first KT model to explore evaluation efficiency and resource utilization.
- **Graph-based models** use graph structures to characterize the relationships between questions, concepts, or interactions, e.g., GKT [28] uses a graph to model the intrinsic relationships between concepts.
- **Memory-augmented models** capture latent relationships between concepts through memory networks, e.g., DKVMN [41] uses a static key matrix to store relationships between different concepts and updates students' knowledge states through a dynamic value matrix. SKVMN [1], a variant of DKVMN, also integrates the advantages of LSTM in recurrent modeling.

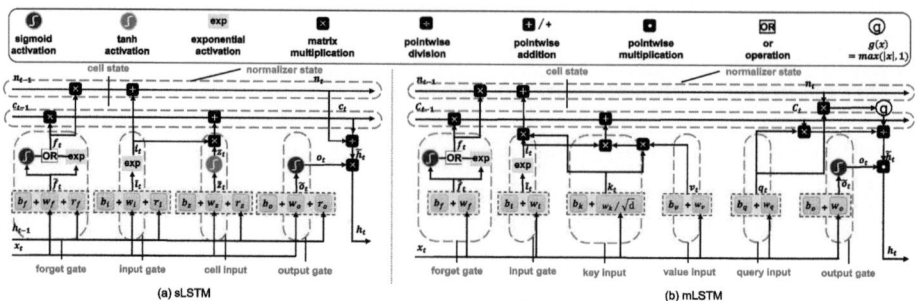

Fig. 1. Architecture of xLSTM.

- **Adversarial-based models** use adversarial techniques to enhance the model's generalization ability, *e.g.*, ATKT [11] mitigates overfitting and improves generalization by adding perturbations to student interactions during training.
- **Contrastive learning-based models** use contrastive learning to learn rich representations of student interactions, *e.g.*, CL4KT leverages contrastive learning to strengthen representation learning by distinguishing between similar and dissimilar learning histories.
- **Other representative models** include interpretable models and models with auxiliary tasks, *e.g.*, Deep-IRT [38] introduces item response theory [25] based on DKVMN to make deep learning-based KT explainable. AT-DKT [22] enhances KT by introducing two auxiliary learning tasks: question tagging prediction and individualized prior knowledge prediction.

Our proposed DKT2, by breaking the parallelization limitations of deep sequential models, can be classified as a new type of deep sequential models (**Deep sequential models***).

3 Methodology

3.1 Problem Statement

In the KT task, formally, let $\mathcal{S}$, $\mathcal{Q}$, and $\mathcal{C}$ represent the sets of students, questions, and concepts respectively. For each student $s \in \mathcal{S}$, there exists a sequence of k time steps $X_k = \{(q_1, c_1, r_1, t_1), (q_2, c_2, r_2, t_2), \ldots, (q_k, c_k, r_k, t_k)\}$, where $q_i \in \mathcal{Q}, c_i \subset \mathcal{C}, r_i \in \{0,1\}$, and t_i represent the question attempted by the student, the concepts related to question q_i, whether the student responded correctly (0 for incorrect, 1 for correct), and the timestamp of the response, respectively. At time step $k+1$, DKT2 predicts $\hat{r}_{k+1}$ based on the student's interaction sequence X_k:

$$\hat{r}_{k+1} = \text{DKT2}(X_k, q_{k+1}, c_{k+1}, t_{k+1} \mid \theta), \tag{1}$$

where θ represents the parameters learned during training.

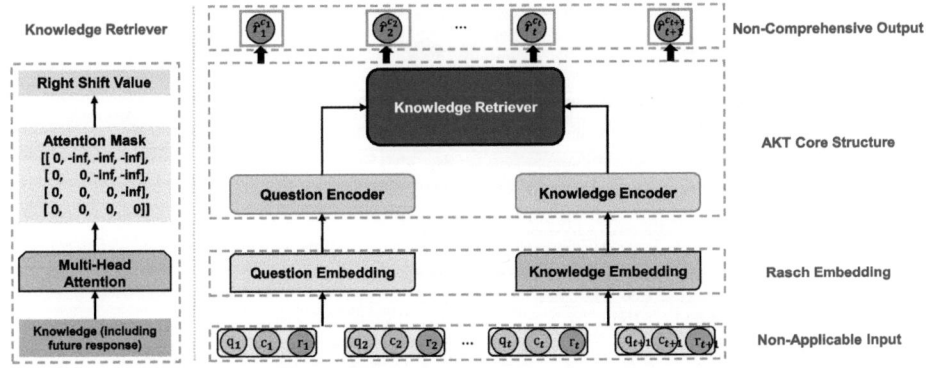

Fig. 2. Structural sketch of AKT.

3.2 Preliminaries

LSTM and the Extended LSTM. LSTM[2] is one of the earliest popular deep learning methods applied to NLP, but it has been overshadowed for a period by the success of Transformers [34,43]. However, the architecture is recently regaining attention and undergoing significant improvements. The improved LSTM is called extended Long Short-Term Memory (xLSTM) [3], which mainly addresses three limitations in traditional LSTM: (1) inability to revise storage decisions, (2) limited storage capacities, and (3) lack of parallelizability. xLSTM introduces two new members to the LSTM family to overcome these limitations: sLSTM and mLSTM, as described in Fig. 1. **Since our work does not focus on the architecture of xLSTM, we have placed the detailed introduction of xLSTM in A.3.**

Weakly Applicable Input and Comprehensive Output Settings in DLKT Models. We use AKT [10] as an example to describe the common weakly applicable input and comprehensive output settings in DLKT models. Figure 2 shows a structural sketch of AKT. Clearly, AKT takes both historical interactions and future interactions as input during training and inference, ignoring future information through attention masking while representing knowledge learned up to the current time step through offset (right-shifting values in attention), and directly predicts questions at each time step. From this, we can see that although AKT's setup is reasonable and does not lead to future information leakage, this input setting, while convenient, also **causes complications in engineering implementation** (engineering often requires cumbersome representation of future information as a padding value, and this common processing method does not seem suitable for KT, as KT tasks typically involve predicting future questions $2 \sim t+1$ based on historical interactions $1 \sim t$). Moreover, AKT only outputs the response for the current time step's question, without considering the student's proficiency in different dimensions, which **contradicts the**

---

[2] Refer to Appendix A.2 for details on LSTM.

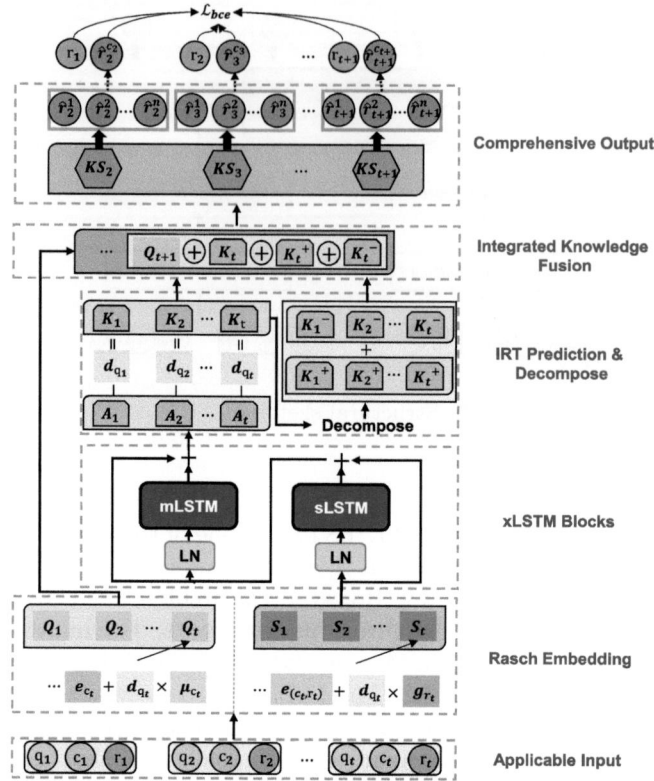

Fig. 3. Architecture of DKT2.

multidimensional nature of real-world student knowledge and narrows the definition of KT.

3.3 DKT2

Figure 3 illustrates the architecture of our proposed DKT2, as described below.

Rasch Embedding. We use the classic Rasch model [32] from educational psychology to construct embeddings of questions and student skills. This model explicitly uses scalars to represent the degree of deviation between questions and the concepts they cover. Additionally, we choose to use question-specific difficulty vectors to capture differences among various questions within the same concept. DKT2 takes **applicable interactions (*i.e.*, inputs not involving the future response r_{t+1}, distinguishing it from models like AKT)** as input, denoted as $\{q_i, c_i, r_i\}_{i=1}^{t}$, and at time step t, the embeddings of questions and student skills, Q_t and S_t respectively, are represented as:

$$Q_t = e_{c_t} + d_{q_t} \cdot \mu_{c_t}, S_t = e_{(c_t, r_t)} + d_{q_t} \cdot g_{r_t}, e_{(c_t, r_t)} = e_{c_t} + e_{r_t}, \qquad (2)$$

where $e_{c_t} \in \mathbb{R}^d$ and $e_{r_t} \in \mathbb{R}^d$ are the embeddings of concept c_t and response r_t, respectively. $d_{q_t} \in \mathbb{R}$ is a difficulty scalar and $\mu_{c_t} \in \mathbb{R}^d$ summarizes the variation of questions containing concept c_t. $e_{(c_t, r_t)} \in \mathbb{R}^d$ is the interaction representation of the concept and student response, $g_{r_t} \in \mathbb{R}^d$ is the variant embedding of the response. d is the dimension of the embeddings.

xLSTM Blocks. DKT2 further learns the student's ability representation $A_{1:t}$ at time step t through two xLSTM blocks (sLSTM and mLSTM) based on the original representation of student ability $S_{1:t}$:

$$A_{1:t} = \text{Res}\left(\text{LN}\left(\text{mLSTM}\left(\text{Res}\left(\text{LN}\left(\text{sLSTM}(S_{1:t})\right)\right)\right)\right)\right), \tag{3}$$

where LN and Res refer to layer normalization [2] and residual connection [12], respectively.

IRT Prediction and Decompose. The core idea of IRT (Item Response Theory) lies in the interactive relationship between student ability and question difficulty [37]. Specifically, **if a student's ability is far above the question's difficulty, the probability of the student responding to the question correctly is very high, and vice versa.** This is also why IRT is often used for interpretable predictions in KT [33,38] (**our work focuses not on the interpretability of KT models but on evaluating their applicability and comprehensive setup**). Therefore, the knowledge acquired by a student, denoted as $K_{1:t}$, can be represented as:

$$K_{1:t} = A_{1:t} - d_{q_{1:t}}, \tag{4}$$

where $d_{q_{1:t}}$ is the sequence representation of d_{q_t} from Eq. 2 up to time step t.

Further, DKT2 roughly distinguishes between the familiar and unfamiliar knowledge $K_{1:t}^+$ and $K_{1:t}^-$ based on correct and incorrect responses:

$$K_{1:t}^+ = \exp(r_{1:t}, d) \circ K_{1:t},\ K_{1:t}^- = \exp(\mathbf{one} - r_{1:t}, d) \circ K_{1:t}, \tag{5}$$

where $\exp(\cdot, d)$ denotes expanding the last dimension of the tensor to d dimensions. $\circ$ denotes element-wise multiplication. $\mathbf{one} \in \mathbb{R}^t$ is a vector of all ones.

Integrated Knowledge Fusion. DKT2 estimates the student's knowledge $X_{2:t+1}$ based on the knowledge $K_{1:t}$ and the questions $Q_{2:t+1}$ that need to be predicted:

$$X_{2:t+1} = Q_{2:t+1} \oplus K_{1:t} \oplus K_{1:t}^+ \oplus K_{1:t}^-, \tag{6}$$

where $\oplus$ denotes the concatenation operation. In addition to integrating the questions and the student's current knowledge, DKT2 also includes the student's familiar and unfamiliar knowledge $K_{1:t}^+$ and $K_{1:t}^-$. This is because, intuitively, **if the knowledge required to respond to a question is familiar to the student, the predicted score tends to be higher, and conversely, lower if unfamiliar.**

Finally, DKT2 predicts the student's comprehensive knowledge states $KS_{2:t+1}$:

$$KS_{2:t+1} = \sigma(\text{ReLU}(X_{2:t+1}W_1 + b_1)W_2 + b_2), \tag{7}$$

where $W_1 \in \mathbb{R}^{4d \times 2d}, W_2 \in \mathbb{R}^{2d \times n}, b_1 \in \mathbb{R}^{2d}, b_2 \in \mathbb{R}^n$ are learnable parameters in the MLP. $\sigma(\cdot)$ is the Sigmoid function and $\text{ReLU}(\cdot)$ is the activation function. n is the number of concepts (due to data sparsity, KT often predicts the concepts corresponding to questions).

Equation 7 can be further represented as:

$$KS_i = (\hat{r}_i^1, \hat{r}_i^2, \ldots, \hat{r}_i^n), 2 \leq i \leq t+1, \tag{8}$$

where $\hat{r}_i^j$ represents the prediction score of DKT2 for concept j at time step i. **The comprehensive output of DKT2 enables the prediction of multiple concepts at the same time step, whereas models like AKT can only predict $\hat{r}_i^{c_i}$ at time step** i. We will analyze the multi-concept prediction scenario in detail in Sect. 4.3, where some unexpected results have been discovered.

Model Training. The loss of DKT2 is defined as the binary cross-entropy loss between the prediction $\hat{r}_t$ and the actual response r_t, calculated as follows:

$$\mathcal{L}_{\text{DKT2}} = -\sum_{i=2}^{t+1} r_i \log(\hat{r}_i) + (1-r_i)\log(1-\hat{r}_i). \tag{9}$$

Conversion of Input and Output Settings. We attempt to convert the weakly applicable input and comprehensive output settings in DLKT models into strongly applicable input and comprehensive output settings. Similarly, using AKT as an example, like DKT2, as shown in Fig. 3, the transformed AKT only takes the historical interactions $\{(q_i, c_i, r_i)\}_{i=1}^{t}$ as input, with everything else remaining unchanged (note that the right-shift operation still needs to be retained because the attention does not mask the knowledge of the current time step). Before outputting the predicted score $\hat{r}_i^{c_i}$, it first concretizes knowledge into the knowledge of each concept (by converting the original dimensions into the number of concepts through an MLP) and then the comprehensive knowledge state is obtained through a Sigmoid function.

4 Experiments

Our goal is to answer the following research questions:

- **RQ1**: How does DKT2 perform compared to 18 baselines from 8 different categories under applicable input and comprehensive output settings?
- **RQ2**: How do different input settings for KT models with weak applicability and comprehensiveness and multi-concept prediction of various KT models affect their performance?
- **RQ3**: What are the impacts of the components (*e.g.*, the Rasch embedding and IRT prediction) on DKT2?

4.1 Experimental Setup

Datasets. We conduct extensive experiments on three of the latest large-scale benchmark datasets from different platforms: Assist17 [9], EdNet [6], and Comp [14]. Details of the datasets are provided in Appendix A.4.

Baselines. To comprehensively and systematically evaluate the performance of DKT2 and analyze the impact of input-output settings on KT models, we compare DKT2 with 18 DLKT baselines from 8 categories, as mentioned in Sect. 2. Detailed descriptions of the aforementioned DLKT baselines can be found in Appendix A.5.

Implementation. Similar to CL4KT [19], we employ five-fold cross-validation, with folds divided by students. 10% of the training set is used for model evaluation and also for the early stopping strategy: if the AUC does not improve within 10 epochs during the 300 epochs, the training will be stopped. The averages across five test folds are reported. We focus on the most recent 100 interactions (history length) for each student, as this latest information is crucial for future predictions. During training, all models are trained using the Adam optimizer [17] with the following settings: batch size is fixed at 512, learning rate is 0.001, dropout rate is 0.05, and embedding dimension is 64. The seed is set to 12405 to reproduce experimental results. Similar to existing DLKT research, our evaluation metrics include two classification metrics, Area Under the ROC Curve (AUC) and Accuracy (ACC), and one regression metric, Root Mean Square Error (RMSE). Note that our experimental parameter configuration is consistent with CL4KT.

4.2 Applicable and Comprehensive Performance Comparison (RQ1)

Under applicable input and comprehensive output settings, we evaluate three common prediction tasks in KT [24]: 1) one-step prediction, 2) multi-step prediction, and 3) prediction with varying history lengths.

One-Step Prediction. KT's one-step prediction can provide immediate feedback for ITS and be used for short-term adjustments of personalized learning paths [7]. Table 1 shows the one-step prediction performance of DKT2 and 18 baselines from 8 different categories in three large-scale datasets. Overall, in this fair large-scale data competition, our DKT2 has emerged as the final winner by a narrow margin. We observe:

- Compared to previous research [10], under the input-output settings, attention-based models like AKT still generally outperform deep sequential models like DKT, **suggesting that attention-based models like AKT may be less affected by these settings.**

Table 1. One-step prediction performance of DKT2 and 18 baselines from different categories. The **best result** is in bold, the second best is underlined. ✓ indicates strong applicability and comprehensiveness, ✗ indicates weak applicability and comprehensiveness, † indicates strong applicability but weak comprehensiveness. - indicates the model fails to be applied to such a large-scale dataset, resulting in a program crash.

Category	Model	Assist17			EdNet			Comp		
		AUC↑	ACC↑	RMSE↓	AUC↑	ACC↑	RMSE↓	AUC↑	ACC↑	RMSE↓
Deep sequential	DKT✓	0.6621	0.6370	0.4731	0.6834	0.6451	0.4687	0.7585	0.8129	0.3681
	DKT+✓	0.6668	0.6415	0.4711	0.6884	0.6483	0.4673	0.7593	0.8129	0.3679
	DKT-F✓	0.6633	0.6429	0.4724	<u>0.6917</u>	<u>0.6503</u>	<u>0.4668</u>	0.7615	0.8138	0.3672
Attention-based	SAKT†	0.6211	0.6108	0.4828	0.6773	0.6415	0.4708	0.7560	0.8123	0.3690
	AKT✗	0.6789	0.6464	0.4723	0.6855	0.6440	0.4686	0.7601	0.8119	0.3686
	simpleKT✗	0.6709	0.6441	0.4746	0.6865	0.6444	0.4686	0.7633	0.8135	0.3672
	FoLiBiKT✗	0.6771	0.6444	0.4750	0.6849	0.6432	0.4687	0.7599	0.8120	0.3685
	sparseKT✗	0.6674	0.6424	0.4740	0.6856	0.6430	0.4701	**0.7690**	**0.8178**	**0.3604**
	DTransformer✗	0.6480	0.6305	0.4770	0.6727	0.6355	0.4722	0.7551	0.8106	0.3699
	stableKT✗	0.6781	0.6455	0.4751	0.6841	0.6411	0.4695	0.7591	0.8126	0.3683
Mamba-based	Mamba4KT✓	<u>0.7001</u>	<u>0.6555</u>	<u>0.4701</u>	0.6667	0.6351	0.4764	0.7575	0.8121	0.3687
Graph-based	GKT✓	0.6408	0.6185	0.4802	0.6841	0.6361	0.4724	0.7390	0.8055	0.3766
Memory-augmented	DKVMN✗	0.6505	0.6308	0.4774	0.6778	0.6410	0.4705	0.7534	0.8113	0.3697
	SKVMN✗	0.6350	0.6184	0.4809	0.6800	0.6427	0.4696	0.7220	0.8040	0.3790
Adversarial-based	ATKT✓	0.6453	0.6313	0.4821	0.6780	0.6403	0.4714	0.7560	0.8123	0.3688
Contrastive learning-based	CL4KT✗	0.6540	0.6319	0.4783	-	-	-	0.7645	0.8146	0.3669
Other representative	Deep-IRT✗	0.6448	0.6268	0.4814	0.6661	0.6317	0.4769	0.7517	0.8108	0.3703
	AT-DKT✓	0.6720	0.6433	0.4708	0.6888	0.6494	0.4673	0.7655	0.8141	0.3663
Deep sequential*	**DKT2✓**	**0.7042**	**0.6594**	**0.4630**	**0.6929**	**0.6504**	**0.4660**	<u>0.7679</u>	<u>0.8165</u>	<u>0.3652</u>

- The recently proposed Mamba4KT performs well on Assist17, but underperforms compared to DKT on larger-scale datasets like EdNet and Comp. This may be due to mamba's poorer performance in context learning in large-scale experiments, which is consistent with previous research findings [35].
- DLKT models based on graph, memory augmentation, adversarial, or contrastive learning do not show significant performance improvements. We believe this is because large-scale data contains more noise and diversity, making it challenging for complex models (*e.g.*, graph-based and memory-augmented models) to effectively extract useful information during training. Moreover, large-scale data usually covers various student learning behaviors and knowledge states, meaning that basic models might already be sufficient for effective knowledge tracing, thus the advantages of adversarial-based and contrastive learning-based models are not pronounced.
- Our proposed DKT2 performs almost the best on all metrics across all datasets. This performance improvement can be attributed to the superiority of DKT2, which includes the exponential activation function in sLSTM that helps improve memory and forgetting processes, and the matrix memory introduced in mLSTM that gives DKT2 advantages in large-scale applications and long sequence processing.

Table 2. Multi-step prediction performance of DKT2 and several representative baselines on Assist17. The results for EdNet and Comp can be found in Appendix A.6.

Step	5			10			15			20		
Metric	AUC↑	ACC↑	RMSE↓	AUC↑	ACC↑	RMSE↓	AUC↑	ACC↑	RMSE↓	AUC↑	ACC↑	RMSE↓
DKT	0.6244	0.6104	0.4831	0.6048	0.5978	0.4868	0.5962	0.5960	0.4874	0.5902	0.5918	0.4890
SAKT	0.6103	0.6010	0.4860	0.6013	0.5966	0.4860	0.5989	0.5983	0.4860	0.5961	0.5960	0.4869
AKT	0.6486	0.6285	**0.4763**	0.6321	0.6213	**0.4798**	0.6231	0.6140	**0.4819**	0.6189	0.6134	**0.4827**
Mamba4KT	0.6222	0.6077	0.4869	0.5909	0.5938	0.4876	0.5875	0.5911	0.4880	0.5858	0.5907	0.4884
DKVMN	0.6205	0.6096	0.4851	0.6008	0.5958	0.4880	0.5905	0.5923	0.4879	0.5830	0.5856	0.4893
ATKT	0.6246	0.6186	0.4831	0.6176	0.6139	0.4847	0.6125	0.6118	0.4855	0.6094	0.6090	0.4865
CL4KT	0.6347	0.6186	0.4832	0.6128	0.6037	0.4882	0.6043	0.5987	0.4896	0.5991	0.5971	0.4890
Deep-IRT	0.6100	0.6020	0.4959	0.5867	0.5834	0.5022	0.5737	0.5713	0.5072	0.5652	0.5666	0.5049
AT-DKT	0.6424	0.6260	0.4782	0.6271	0.6154	0.4820	0.6206	0.6115	0.4832	0.6170	0.6082	0.4849
DKT2	**0.6496**	**0.6313**	**0.4763**	**0.6335**	**0.6221**	0.4802	**0.6246**	**0.6160**	0.4822	**0.6199**	**0.6148**	0.4828

Multi-step Prediction. KT's accurate multi-step prediction not only provides valuable feedback for selecting and constructing personalized learning materials, but also assists ITS in flexibly adjusting future curriculum based on student needs [23]. Table 2 and Table 7 in Appendix A.6 show the multi-step (step = 5, 10, 15, 20) prediction performance of DKT2 and several representative baselines from different categories. The main observations are as follows: (1) As the prediction steps increase, the performance of all models consistently decreases. This is due to error accumulation, meaning that small errors in one-step prediction can accumulate over multiple steps, leading to a decrease in multi-step prediction performance. (2) Compared to one-step prediction, attention-based models perform well in multi-step prediction. This is because the attention mechanism can capture long-distance dependencies, making its advantages more apparent. In contrast, Mamba4KT performs poorly, as mamba-based models are highly dependent on context [21] and are more susceptible to error accumulation. (3) Our DKT2 generally outperforms all models in multi-step prediction. We can similarly attribute this to the exponential activation function introduced in sLSTM of DKT2, which can mitigate error accumulation by modifying storage decisions, as it allows the model to update its internal state at each step, while the matrix memory introduced in mLSTM provides support for large-capacity storage space.

Varying-History-Length Prediction. Analyzing the impact of different history lengths can help ITS better understand students' knowledge acquisition and forgetting processes, thereby improving teaching strategies. Figure 4, Fig. 7 and Fig. 8 in Appendix A.6 show the prediction performance of DKT2 and several representative baselines with different history lengths. From these, we can observe: 1) As the history length increases, the prediction performance of almost all models generally improves, as longer sequences provide more historical information. Surprisingly, Mamba4KT's performance consistently decreases. A pos-

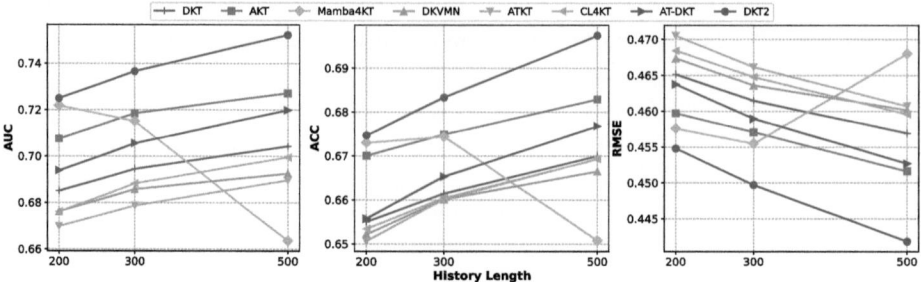

Fig. 4. The prediction performance of DKT2 and several representative baselines on Assist17 with different history lengths. The results for EdNet and Comp are in Appendix A.6.

Table 3. The prediction performance of KT models with weak applicability and comprehensiveness in the last 5 steps on Assist17 under three different input settings. The △ setting represents masking all interaction information (including questions, concepts and responses) for the last 5 steps, the ○ setting represents masking the responses for the last 5 steps, without masking questions and concepts, and the ● setting represents no masking, i.e., predicting the responses under the regular setting. The results for EdNet and Comp can be found in Appendix A.6.

Setting	Metric	AKT	simpleKT	FoLiBiKT	sparseKT	DTransformer	stableKT	DKVMN	CL4KT	Deep-IRT
△	AUC↑	0.6554	0.6507	0.6545	0.6405	0.5995	0.6490	0.6228	0.5941	0.6234
	ACC↑	0.6154	0.6129	0.6117	0.6120	0.5755	0.6159	0.5899	0.5696	0.5915
	RMSE↓	0.4822	0.4840	0.4835	0.4865	0.5040	0.4837	0.4890	0.5090	0.4892
○	AUC↑	0.6505	0.6675	0.6471	0.6574	0.5989	0.6329	0.6203	0.6293	0.6182
	ACC↑	0.6202	0.6240	0.6226	0.6210	0.5625	0.6045	0.5862	0.6016	0.5884
	RMSE↓	0.4853	0.4866	0.4842	0.4836	0.5206	0.4908	0.5010	0.5037	0.5015
●	AUC↑	0.6320	0.6508	0.6192	0.6474	0.5994	0.6533	0.6087	0.6195	0.6001
	ACC↑	0.6066	0.6153	0.5980	0.6060	0.5770	0.6223	0.5787	0.5933	0.5728
	RMSE↓	0.4881	0.4999	0.4944	0.4944	0.4981	0.4833	0.5074	0.5083	0.5012

sible reason is that mamba-based models are better at capturing local temporal dependencies but may struggle to effectively capture long-distance dependencies within longer sequences. 2) Notably, DKT, using only one LSTM, can maintain a strong ranking position across different history lengths, further encouraging KT researchers to design simple yet effective models [23]. 3) Our DKT2 maintains optimal performance across different history lengths, with more significant performance improvements as the history length increases. This is not only due to the increased storage capacity of mLSTM but also related to sLSTM providing a broader output range as the sequence length increases.

4.3 In-Depth Analysis (RQ2 and RQ3)

Analysis of Different Input Settings. We analyze three different input settings for the KT models with weak applicability and comprehensiveness. In

Table 4. Multi-concept prediction performance of DKT2 and several representative baselines.

Dataset	Assist17			EdNet			Comp		
Metric	AUC↑	ACC↑	RMSE↓	AUC↑	ACC↑	RMSE↓	AUC↑	ACC↑	RMSE↓
DKT	0.5841	0.5787	0.4913	0.6600	0.6225	0.4775	0.7091	0.8045	0.3806
SAKT	0.5596	0.5534	0.5048	0.6546	0.6198	0.4788	0.6994	0.8037	0.3824
AKT	0.6185	0.6040	0.4862	0.6649	0.6241	**0.4765**	0.7054	0.8039	0.3815
Mamba4KT	0.5660	0.5660	0.4956	0.6531	0.6192	0.4796	0.7054	0.8043	0.3813
DKVMN	0.5730	0.5701	0.4964	0.6572	0.6205	0.4781	0.7050	0.8034	0.3817
ATKT	0.6205	0.6077	0.4836	0.6639	0.6229	0.4768	0.7111	0.8049	0.3802
CL4KT	0.5892	0.5911	0.4890	-	-	-	0.7044	0.8032	0.3820
Deep-IRT	**0.6445**	**0.6263**	**0.4808**	**0.6664**	**0.6321**	0.4767	**0.7515**	**0.8107**	**0.3704**
AT-DKT	0.6087	0.5962	0.4882	0.6644	0.6245	0.4766	0.7093	0.8046	0.3805
DKT2	0.6174	0.6041	0.4872	0.6646	0.6243	0.4768	0.7064	0.8047	0.3810

Table 3 and Table 8 in Appendix A.6, we present the prediction performance of these models in the last 5 steps. From these, we have the following findings: (i) The performance differences among these three settings are more pronounced on EdNet and Comp, as larger-scale data can provide richer information for more accurate prediction. (ii) The models under guessing △ setting seems to perform well on Assist17, which may be because the models remember the answer bias [8] and make predictions directly, while the models under the ○ and ● settings achieve comparable performance, indicating that **the applicable ○ setting does not significantly reduce the model's performance.** This confirms the hypothesis proposed in the Sect. 4.2 (One-step Prediction).

Multi-concept Prediction. Comprehensive KT can be used for multi-concept prediction. Multi-concept prediction can provide a more comprehensive learning assessment, explore relationships between concepts, and create precise personalized learning plans for students. Due to the lack of datasets for multi-concept prediction (to our knowledge, existing datasets do not include students' proficiency scores for all concepts at different learning stages), our experiments are conducted under a weak assumption: the change in a student's knowledge state is a gradual process and is unlikely to experience sudden shifts over the long term. In our experiments, we use the knowledge state at the intermediate time step to predict subsequent questions. Table 4 shows the multi-concept prediction performance of DKT2 and several representative baselines. From this, we discover an unexpected phenomenon: Deep-IRT and ATKT, which are generally not advantageous in previous performance comparisons, achieve impressive results, while our DKT2 can only rank in the top four. These results might make us question the validity of the weak assumption, but the empirical evidence of

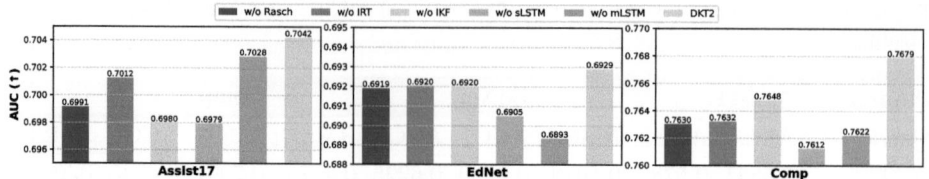

Fig. 5. Ablation study on AUC.

the almost consistent performance rankings of Deep-IRT and ATKT across the three datasets dispels our doubts. This interesting phenomenon makes us ponder: is it necessary to excessively pursue prediction accuracy while neglecting the assessment of multiple concepts in practice? We will explore this important topic in depth in future KT research.

Ablation Study. Figure 5 and Fig. 9 in Appendix A.6 illustrate the impact of different components on DKT2. "w/o. Rasch" indicates the removal of Rasch embedding from DKT2 (setting d_{q_t} to 0 in Eq. 2), "w/o. IRT" represents the removal of the IRT module, "w/o. IKF" means DKT2 ignores the integrated knowledge fusion, while "w/o. sLSTM" and "w/o. mLSTM" denote the removal of sLSTM block and mLSTM block, respectively. The results show that DKT2 achieves the highest AUC scores across all datasets compared to other variants, demonstrating the importance of each component on DKT2. Notably, "w/o. mLSTM" generally outperforms DKT2 on ACC and RMSE scores on Assist17, which is due to mLSTM's inability to demonstrate significant advantages in small-scale data, as evidenced by its poorer performance on larger datasets, EdNet and Comp.

5 Conclusion

This paper introduces DKT2, an applicable and comprehensive DLKT model that addresses key limitations of deep sequential models like DKT. By leveraging xLSTM, the Rasch model, and Item Response Theory (IRT), DKT2 effectively balances predictive performance with practical applicability. Our extensive experiments across three large-scale datasets demonstrate DKT2's superiority over 18 baseline models in various prediction tasks, highlighting its robustness and potential for real-world educational applications.

6 Limitations

Our work represents an attempt to apply xLSTM in the KT domain on large-scale data with fair input and output settings. In our experiments, we observe that as the number of students increases, DKT2 gradually demonstrates a performance advantage that widens the gap with other DLKT models. Additionally, in our multi-concept prediction experiments, we find that Deep-IRT exhibits a leading, dataset-independent advantage, the reasons for which give us pause for reflection. Therefore, our future research directions include: 1) further exploration of deeper knowledge tracing methodologies based on xLSTM, particularly in the context of ultra-large-scale data, and 2) enhancing multi-concept predictive analysis by collecting and analyzing students' proficiency scores across different concepts at various learning stages.

Acknowledgments. This research was supported by grants from the "Pioneer" and "Leading Goose" R&D Program of Zhejiang (2025C02022), National Natural Science Foundation of China (No.62307032), and Shanghai Rising-Star Program (23QA1409000).

References

1. Abdelrahman, G., Wang, Q.: Knowledge tracing with sequential key-value memory networks. In: Proceedings of the 42nd International ACM SIGIR Conference on Research and Development in Information Retrieval, pp. 175–184 (2019)
2. Ba, J.L., Kiros, J.R., Hinton, G.E.: Layer normalization (2016)
3. Beck, M., et al.: XLSTM: extended long short-term memory. arXiv preprint arXiv:2405.04517 (2024)
4. Bengio, Y., Courville, A., Vincent, P.: Representation learning: a review and new perspectives. IEEE Trans. Pattern Anal. Mach. Intell. **35**(8), 1798–1828 (2013)
5. Cao, Y., Zhang, W.: MAMBA4KT: an efficient and effective mamba-based knowledge tracing model. arXiv preprint arXiv:2405.16542 (2024)
6. Choi, Y., et al.: EDNet: a large-scale hierarchical dataset in education. In: Bittencourt, I.I., Cukurova, M., Muldner, K., Luckin, R., Millán, E. (eds.) AIED 2020. LNCS (LNAI), vol. 12164, pp. 69–73. Springer, Cham (2020). https://doi.org/10.1007/978-3-030-52240-7_13
7. Corbett, A.T., Anderson, J.R.: Knowledge tracing: modeling the acquisition of procedural knowledge. User Model. User-Adap. Inter. **4**, 253–278 (1994)
8. Cui, C., et al.: Do we fully understand students' knowledge states? Identifying and mitigating answer bias in knowledge tracing. arXiv preprint arXiv:2308.07779 (2023)
9. Feng, M., Heffernan, N., Koedinger, K.: Addressing the assessment challenge with an online system that tutors as it assesses. User Model. User-Adap. Inter. **19**, 243–266 (2009)
10. Ghosh, A., Heffernan, N., Lan, A.S.: Context-aware attentive knowledge tracing. In: Proceedings of the 26th ACM SIGKDD International Conference on Knowledge Discovery & Data Mining, pp. 2330–2339 (2020)
11. Guo, X., Huang, Z., Gao, J., Shang, M., Shu, M., Sun, J.: Enhancing knowledge tracing via adversarial training. In: Proceedings of the 29th ACM International Conference on Multimedia, pp. 367–375 (2021)
12. He, K., Zhang, X., Ren, S., Sun, J.: Deep residual learning for image recognition. arXiv preprint arXiv:1512.03385 (2015)
13. Hochreiter, S., Schmidhuber, J.: Long short-term memory. Neural Comput. **9**(8), 1735–1780 (1997)

14. Hu, L., et al.: PTADISC: a cross-course dataset supporting personalized learning in cold-start scenarios. In: Thirty-seventh Conference on Neural Information Processing Systems Datasets and Benchmarks Track (2023)
15. Huang, S., Liu, Z., Zhao, X., Luo, W., Weng, J.: Towards robust knowledge tracing models via k-sparse attention. In: Proceedings of the 46th International ACM SIGIR Conference on Research and Development in Information Retrieval, pp. 2441–2445 (2023)
16. Im, Y., Choi, E., Kook, H., Lee, J.: Forgetting-aware linear bias for attentive knowledge tracing. In: Proceedings of the 32nd ACM International Conference on Information and Knowledge Management, pp. 3958–3962 (2023)
17. Kingma, D.P., Ba, J.: Adam: a method for stochastic optimization (2017)
18. LeCun, Y., Bengio, Y., Hinton, G.: Deep learning. Nature **521**(7553), 436–444 (2015)
19. Lee, W., Chun, J., Lee, Y., Park, K., Park, S.: Contrastive learning for knowledge tracing. In: Proceedings of the ACM Web Conference 2022, pp. 2330–2338 (2022)
20. Li, X., et al.: Enhancing length generalization for attention based knowledge tracing models with linear biases
21. Lieber, O., et al.: Jamba: a hybrid transformer-mamba language model. arXiv preprint arXiv:2403.19887 (2024)
22. Liu, Z., et al.: Enhancing deep knowledge tracing with auxiliary tasks. In: Proceedings of the ACM Web Conference 2023, pp. 4178–4187 (2023)
23. Liu, Z., Liu, Q., Chen, J., Huang, S., Luo, W.: SIMPLEKT: a simple but tough-to-beat baseline for knowledge tracing. arXiv preprint arXiv:2302.06881 (2023)
24. Liu, Z., Liu, Q., Chen, J., Huang, S., Tang, J., Luo, W.: PYKT: a Python library to benchmark deep learning based knowledge tracing models. In: Thirty-sixth Conference on Neural Information Processing Systems Datasets and Benchmarks Track (2022)
25. Lord, F.: A theory of test scores. Psychometric monographs (1952)
26. Luckin, R., Holmes, W.: Intelligence unleashed: an argument for AI in education (2016)
27. Nagatani, K., Zhang, Q., Sato, M., Chen, Y.Y., Chen, F., Ohkuma, T.: Augmenting knowledge tracing by considering forgetting behavior. In: The World Wide Web Conference, pp. 3101–3107 (2019)
28. Nakagawa, H., Iwasawa, Y., Matsuo, Y.: Graph-based knowledge tracing: modeling student proficiency using graph neural network. In: IEEE/WIC/ACM International Conference on Web Intelligence, pp. 156–163 (2019)
29. Nye, B.D., Graesser, A.C., Hu, X.: Autotutor and family: a review of 17 years of natural language tutoring. Int. J. Artif. Intell. Educ. **24**, 427–469 (2014)
30. Pandey, S., Karypis, G.: A self-attentive model for knowledge tracing. arXiv preprint arXiv:1907.06837 (2019)
31. Piech, C., et al.: Deep knowledge tracing. In: Advances in Neural Information Processing Systems, vol. 28 (2015)
32. Rasch, G.: Probabilistic models for some intelligence and attainment tests. ERIC (1993)
33. Sun, J., Yu, F., Wan, Q., Li, Q., Liu, S., Shen, X.: Interpretable knowledge tracing with multiscale state representation. In: Proceedings of the ACM on Web Conference 2024, pp. 3265–3276 (2024)
34. Vaswani, A., et al.: Attention is all you need. In: Advances in Neural Information Processing Systems, vol. 30 (2017)
35. Waleffe, R., et al.: An empirical study of mamba-based language models. arXiv preprint arXiv:2406.07887 (2024)

36. Wu, T., et al.: Embracing imperfection: simulating students with diverse cognitive levels using LLM-based agents (2025). https://arxiv.org/abs/2505.19997
37. Yen, W.M., Fitzpatrick, A.R.: Item response theory. Educ. Meas. **4**, 111–153 (2006)
38. Yeung, C.K.: Deep-IRT: make deep learning based knowledge tracing explainable using item response theory. arXiv preprint arXiv:1904.11738 (2019)
39. Yeung, C.K., Yeung, D.Y.: Addressing two problems in deep knowledge tracing via prediction-consistent regularization. In: Proceedings of the Fifth Annual ACM Conference on Learning at Scale, pp. 1–10 (2018)
40. Yin, Y., et al.: Tracing knowledge instead of patterns: stable knowledge tracing with diagnostic transformer. In: Proceedings of the ACM Web Conference 2023, pp. 855–864 (2023)
41. Zhang, J., Shi, X., King, I., Yeung, D.Y.: Dynamic key-value memory networks for knowledge tracing. In: Proceedings of the 26th International Conference on World Wide Web, pp. 765–774 (2017)
42. Zhou, Y., Lv, Z., Zhang, S., Chen, J.: Cuff-KT: tackling learners' real-time learning pattern adjustment via tuning-free knowledge state guided model updating (2025). https://arxiv.org/abs/2505.19543
43. Zhou, Y., Yao, C., Chen, J.: COLA: collaborative low-rank adaptation. arXiv preprint arXiv:2505.15471 (2025)

Breaking Free: Decoupling Forced Systems with Laplace Neural Networks

Bernd Zimmering[1]($\boxtimes$), Cecília Coelho[1,2], Vaibhav Gupta[1], Maria Maleshkova[1], and Oliver Niggemann[1]

[1] Institute for Artificial Intelligence, Helmut Schmidt University, Hamburg, Germany
{bernd.zimmering,cecilia.coelho,guptav,
maleshkm,oliver.niggemann}@hsu-hh.de
[2] Centre of Mathematics (CMAT), University of Minho, Braga, Portugal

Abstract. Forecasting the behaviour of industrial robots, power grids or pandemics under changing external inputs requires accurate dynamical models that can adapt to varying signals and capture long-term effects such as delays or memory. While recent neural approaches address some of these challenges individually, their reliance on computationally intensive solvers and their black-box nature limit their practical utility. In this work, we propose Laplace-Net, a decoupled, solver-free neural framework for learning forced and delay-aware dynamical systems. It uses the Laplace transform to (i) bypass computationally intensive solvers, (ii) enable the learning of delays and memory effects and (iii) decompose each system into interpretable control-theoretic components. Laplace-Net also enhances transferability, as its modular structure allows for targeted retraining of individual components to new system setups or environments. Experimental results on eight benchmark datasets–including linear, non-linear and delayed systems–demonstrate the method's improved accuracy and robustness compared to state-of-the-art approaches, particularly in handling complex and previously unseen inputs.

Keywords: Neural Networks · Scientific Machine Learning · Neural Differential Equations · Laplace Transform

1 Introduction

In *forced* dynamical systems, an external controller C (e.g., a motor or human) drives a dynamical system S (e.g., a pendulum) using input signal $x(t)$ to achieve desired objectives over time t (Fig. 1). The system responds with outputs $y(t)$, evolving from its initial state y_0 based on the interaction of the forcing inputs with its internal dynamics [23]. These systems span various domains such as control engineering, robotics, finance, ecosystems and epidemiology, where external

---

Supplementary Information The online version contains supplementary material available at https://doi.org/10.1007/978-3-032-06109-6_15.

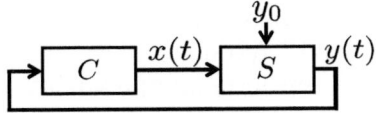

Fig. 1. Control loop with system S that responds with $y(t)$ and is forced by some controller C through excitations $x(t)$. y_0 is the initial state of the system.

inputs (e.g., economic policies, climate, public health measures) strongly influence system behaviour [7,21,27]. Here, modelling S is essential for designing C, enabling effective control of these complex systems.

Traditionally, modelling such systems has relied on hand-crafted ordinary differential equations (ODEs) with predefined forcing terms [23]. These approaches require deep domain expertise and often struggle to generalise beyond their original design [32]. In recent years, data-driven methods like *Neural ODEs* [4] have emerged as powerful tools to learn the dynamics of the system directly from the data. Extensions of Neural ODEs [12,16,18,25] incorporate external excitations $x(t)$ into their models, but rely on iterative ODE solvers. Such solvers can be computationally expensive and prone to numerical drift over long prediction horizons [2]. Although alternative methods [1,14] have been proposed to address these challenges, they often fail to fully decouple the dynamics of the system S from the external controller C, limiting their flexibility in handling arbitrary forcing inputs.

To overcome these limitations, *Neural Operators* (NOs) have been introduced as a solver-free alternative for learning mappings directly from inputs $x(t)$ to outputs $y(t)$ [3,20]. However, NOs frequently struggle to capture critical *memory effects*, such as delays or non-local behaviours (i.e. fractional differential equations (FDEs) as described in [9]), which are essential for accurately modelling many real-world systems. Recent studies [6,22,28] emphasise the importance of addressing these memory effects to improve model fidelity.

Another promising avenue involves leveraging the Laplace Domain (LD) for learning forced dynamical systems. LD-based methods have shown strong performance in capturing both forced dynamics and delays [3,14]. Although the Laplace transform has long been a cornerstone in fields like control theory, fluid dynamics, and systems biology, its integration into modern machine learning frameworks remains relatively under-explored. A recent study [30] highlights the conceptual parallels between classical engineering approaches (e.g., transfer functions, ODE models) and current machine learning methods such as Neural ODEs and Neural Laplace. These similarities are discussed in detail using the Spring-Mass-Damper (SMD) system as a running example, which also serves as a benchmark in this study.

In many real-world scenarios - such as adapting robotic controllers to new hardware configurations or refining economic forecasts under changing regulations - modular and *decoupled* architectures offer significant advantages. By isolating specific components of a model (e.g., internal dynamics vs. external forcing), these architectures enable efficient adaptation to new scenarios without requiring a complete model retraining. This modularity not only reduces computational costs but also enhances interpretability by aligning learned components with classical theoretical insights.

Despite the progress made by existing methods, many remain constrained by specific assumptions about input signals, overlook delays or other memory effects or rely heavily on iterative solvers. These limitations can lead to numerical drift, high computational overheads, or inadequate modelling of long-term dependencies - especially in scenarios involving complex forcing signals or extended prediction horizons.

To address these challenges, we propose a novel modular Laplace-based framework that explicitly handles external forcing and memory effects without relying on iterative solvers (as summarised in Table 1). Our main contributions can be summarized as follows:

- **Decoupled Laplace Representation:** We introduce Laplace-Net, a decoupled NN architecture that employs the Laplace domain with an explicit factorization that separates internal system dynamics from external forcing and initial states, aligning with classical system theory.
- **Arbitrary Forcing and Intervention Handling:** Our approach accepts time-varying or previously unseen inputs without retraining the entire model, facilitating straightforward adaptation to new control signals or external perturbations.
- **Solver-Free, Memory-Aware Inference:** We follow Holt et al. [14] employing numerical inverse Laplace transforms and thus avoiding iterative integration. We mitigate numerical drift and capture memory effects (e.g., delays or fractional dynamics) within the same framework.
- **Enhanced Transferability and Interpretability:** The decoupling into well established subcomponents enables their reuse or pre-training and improves interpretability for experts.
- **Improved Performance:** Laplace-Net consistently outperforms LNO across all datasets and surpasses LSTM on 6 out of 8 datasets, demonstrating its effectiveness in capturing linear, non-linear, chaotic, and memory-dependent dynamics.

The remainder of this paper is structured as follows: Sect. 3 formally defines the problem and introduces key concepts related to Laplace transforms. Section 4 presents the proposed decoupled Laplace-based framework. Section 5 evaluates our approach on linear, non-linear and delayed systems.[1] The conclusions and future directions are discussed in Sect. 6.

2 Related Work

Data-driven modelling of dynamical systems encompasses a wide range of neural approaches, many of which differ in their reliance on time-stepping solvers,

---

[1] Code available at https://github.com/zimmer-ing/Laplace-Net.

ability to model memory effects or inhomogeneous excitations, and degree of modular decomposition. Table 1 summarizes representative methods evaluated across four key aspects:

(i) **Solver-Free** indicates whether the method avoids ODE solvers during training, which are compute intensive.
(ii) **Memory** assesses the capability to explicitly handle delays (as in Delay Differential Equations, DDEs) and non-local behavior (as found in Fractional Differential Equations, FDEs [8]).
(iii) **Arbitrary Forcing** evaluates the ability to generalize to unseen or non-parametric input trajectories $x(t)$.
(iv) **Decoupled** reflects the extent to which the approach separates system dynamics from external inputs and initial conditions, specifically into components that mimic theoretical concepts.

Table 1. Comparison of neural approaches for modelling dynamical systems along four key dimensions: solver-free inference; memory (e.g. delays) ; arbitrary forcing; modularity.

Method	Reference	Solver Free	Memory	Arbitrary Forcing	Decoupled
Neural ODE	[4]	✗	✗	✗	✗
Neural FDE	[6, 29]	✗	✓	✗	✗
Neural DDE	[28]	✗	✓	✗	✗
ODE-RNN	[25]	✗	✗	✓	✗
Fourier NODE	[18]	✓[†]	✗	✓	✗
Neural IM	[12]	✗	✗	✓	✓
Neural CDE	[16]	✗	✗	✓	✗
Neural Flow	[1]	✓	✗	✗	✗
Neural Laplace	[14]	✓	✓	✗	✗
Neural Laplace Control	[13]	✓	✓	✓	✗
DeepONet	[20]	✓	✗	✓	✗[‡]
Laplace NO	[3]	✓	✗	✓	✓
Laplace-Net	This Work	✓	✓	✓	✓

[†] Fourier NODEs eliminate the need for a solver during training but still require one for inference. [‡] DeepONet is partially decoupled: the branch network encodes both initial and external inputs, while the trunk network models system dynamics. However, the separation between initial conditions and external inputs within the branch network is not complete.

Neural ODEs and Solver-Based Extensions. *Neural ODEs* [4] and their immediate variants, such as *ODE-RNN* [25], *ANODE* [11], and *Neural IM* [12], parameterise ODE vector fields in a continuous latent space. These approaches have demonstrated their effectiveness in various scenarios, including homogeneous and some forced systems. However, they still rely on iterative numerical solvers such as Runge-Kutta, which can lead to substantial computational costs during training and error accumulation over extended time horizons. Extensions of this framework include approaches for delayed [22,28] and fractional systems [8]. *Neural Delayed DEs* [28] and *Neural Fractional DEs* [5,29] explicitly embed delay or learn the amount of memory [6] but, like their predecessors, rely on solver-based training loops and do not explicitly separate forcing inputs.

Laplace-Based, Solver-Free Methods. *Neural Laplace* [14] revolutionizes the approach to learning DEs by operating in the Laplace domain, eliminating the need for stepwise integration during both training and prediction. This method employs a numerical inverse Laplace transform algorithm to generate time-domain predictions, enabling the capture of complex memory-like effects such as fractional-order behaviour and delay times. While *Neural Laplace* claims to handle forced differential equations, its implementation is limited to forcing functions that remain constant between training and testing phases, rather than accommodating arbitrary inputs. *Neural Laplace Control* [13] extends the framework for reinforcement learning scenarios. However, it only considers past actions during prediction, not accounting for future actions, restricting its applicability. *Fourier NODE* [18] offers an alternative approach, approximating state derivatives in the frequency domain to avoid using ODE solvers during training. This method explicitly incorporates control inputs for trajectory prediction, enhancing its versatility in handling forced systems. However, *Fourier NODE* still requires a numerical solver during inference. This requirement limits its applicability for resource-constrained scenarios (e.g. edge devices).

Operator Learning for Forced Systems. Modern approaches, such as *DeepONets* [20] and *Laplace Neural Operators* [3], enable *solver-free* evaluations by learning mappings from input (forcing) functions directly to solution functions. While initially developed for Partial Differential Equations (PDE), some works have successfully extended their application to ODEs [3,20]. *DeepONets*, for instance, employ a unique architecture consisting of two key components: a branch network that encodes inputs functions, such as initial conditions and forcing profiles, into a high-dimensional vector; a trunk network that processes evaluation points of the solution. This structure allows *DeepONets* to effectively capture complex solution behaviours across a wide range of input conditions. However, the method's unified approach to encoding both system dynamics and external influences can limit the interpretability and modular reuse of the learned representations. In contrast, *Laplace Neural Operators* introduce a degree of modularization by separating internal system dynamics from external inputs within the Laplace domain. By restricting themselves to a pole–residue representation (Eq. (5) in [3]), these operators enable the inverse Laplace transform to be carried out symbolically, simplifying implementation. However, such a representation struggles to capture delayed or fractional dynamics (Eq. (15) in [15], Theorem 5.4 in [19], and Example 1.25 in [26]), as their Laplace transforms do not generally reduce to simple pole–residue forms. Methods like *Neural Laplace* [14] address this limitation by numerically computing the inverse Laplace transform, thereby allowing for a wider range of dynamical phenomena beyond the pole–residue framework.

Bridging Gaps via Decoupling and Generalized Forcing. As highlighted in Table 1, a recurring shortfall in existing methods is the lack of an *explicit* factorization of the system's internal transfer characteristics, initial conditions, and arbitrary forcing signals – especially in a solver-free framework. Some methods, such as *Neural IM* [12] and *ODE-RNN* [25], partially decouple interventions or control inputs, but they often rely on iterative updates over time or fail to handle continuous forcing seamlessly. Similarly, *Neural Laplace Control* [13] extends Holt et al. [14] by incorporating past actions into a latent state representation, yet it assumes a homogeneous response for predictions and does not account for future forcing inputs, limiting its applicability in scenarios requiring forward-looking control.

3 Preliminaries

We consider a dynamical system $\mathcal{S}$ with input $\mathbf{x}(t) \in \mathbb{R}^{D_x}$ and response $\mathbf{y}(t) \in \mathbb{R}^{D_y}$. Let $\mathbf{t} = (t_1, \ldots, t_{N+M}) \subset [0, T]$ be discrete times ($t_1 < \cdots < t_{N+M}$), where the first N indices partition the *historical* segment $\mathbf{t}_{\text{hist}}$ and the final $(N+1, \ldots, N+M)$ indices partition the *forecast* segment $\mathbf{t}_{\text{fore}}$. We collect samples into $\mathbf{X} \in \mathbb{R}^{(N+M) \times D_x}$ and $\mathbf{Y} \in \mathbb{R}^{(N+M) \times D_y}$ with the partitions $\mathbf{X}_{\text{hist}} \in \mathbb{R}^{N \times D_x}$, $\mathbf{X}_{\text{fore}} \in \mathbb{R}^{M \times p}$, $\mathbf{Y}_{\text{hist}} \in \mathbb{R}^{N \times q}$, and $\mathbf{Y}_{\text{fore}} \in \mathbb{R}^{M \times q}$ defined analogously. Our objective is to predict $\mathbf{Y}_{\text{fore}}$ given $\mathbf{X}_{\text{hist}}, \mathbf{Y}_{\text{hist}}$, and $\mathbf{X}_{\text{fore}}$. Formally, we learn

$$f : (\mathbf{X}_{\text{hist}}, \mathbf{Y}_{\text{hist}}, \mathbf{X}_{\text{fore}}) \mapsto \mathbf{Y}_{\text{fore}}. \tag{1}$$

Although the above forecasting objective is stated in the time domain, a powerful way to analyse and solve differential equations is via the Laplace transform. We therefore briefly recall the key properties of this transform and its inverse as they form the foundation of our solution.

The Laplace transform maps time-domain signals into the complex s-domain, where derivatives become algebraic factors. For a function $\mathbf{y}(t)$, the Laplace transform is:

$$\mathcal{Y}(s) = \mathcal{L}\{\mathbf{y}(t)\} = \int_0^\infty e^{-st}\, \mathbf{y}(t)\, dt, \quad s \in \mathbb{C}. \tag{2}$$

The complex variable s is typically written as $s = \sigma + i\omega$, where $\sigma \in \mathbb{R}$ corresponds to exponential growth/decay and $\omega \in \mathbb{R}$ to oscillatory behaviour. Applied to the n-th derivative, the Laplace transform yields:

$$\mathcal{L}\left\{\frac{d^n \mathbf{y}(t)}{dt^n}\right\} = s^n \mathcal{Y}(s) - \sum_{k=0}^{n-1} s^{n-1-k} \frac{d^k \mathbf{y}(0)}{dt^k}. \tag{3}$$

A pure time delay $\tau \in \mathbb{R}_{>0}$ appears as $e^{-\tau s}$ in the Laplace domain, and fractional derivatives can be treated similarly to Eq. (3) [15,19,26].

Solving an ODE in the Laplace domain calls for the inverse Laplace transform (ILT),

$$\mathbf{y}(t) = \mathcal{L}^{-1}\{\mathcal{Y}(s)\} = \frac{1}{2\pi i} \int_{\sigma-i\infty}^{\sigma+i\infty} \mathcal{Y}(s)\, e^{st}\, ds, \quad (4)$$

which is rarely solvable in closed form.

Since direct evaluation of Eq. (4) is rarely feasible, numerical methods are required. Among them, the Fourier series-based ILT [10] was identified as the most robust for boundary element simulations [17] and proposed for machine learning due to its efficiency and stability [14]. As the name already implies, it employs Fourier transforms at several points in time. It reconstructs smooth, real-valued signals by sampling $\mathcal{Y}(s)$ at a sequence of query points (cf. Eq. (6)) along a vertical line (parallel to the imaginary axis) in the complex plane. The real component of this line is shifted by a time-dependent offset σ. For each time point, this vertical contour is repositioned accordingly. The numerical ILT is given by:

$$\mathbf{y}(t) \approx \frac{1}{\zeta t} e^{\sigma t} \left[\frac{\mathcal{Y}(s_0)}{2} + \sum_{k=1}^{N_{\text{ILT}}} \text{Re}\left\{ \mathcal{Y}(s_k)\, e^{i\frac{k\pi t}{\zeta t}} \right\} \right], \quad t > 0. \quad (5)$$

Here, $\zeta \in \mathbb{R}_{>0}$ controls the frequency resolution, N_{ILT} is the number of frequency terms along the imaginary axis. Together ζ and N_{ILT} determine the bandwidth as well as the maximum frequency to be transformed. Please note, that compared to the original literature [10,17] we follow [14] and directly use ζt as a scaling factor.

The query points s_0, s_k define a discrete *grid* of evaluation points for $\mathcal{Y}(s)$:

$$s_k(t) = \sigma + i\frac{k\pi}{\zeta t}, \quad k \in \mathbb{N}_0, \quad k \leq N_{\text{ILT}}, \quad \text{with} \quad \sigma = \alpha - \frac{\log(\epsilon)}{\zeta t}. \quad (6)$$

Here, $\alpha \in \mathbb{R}_{>0}$ is chosen so that the contour lies to the right of all singularities of $\mathcal{Y}(s)$, ensuring convergence (typically $\alpha = 10e^{-3}$). $\epsilon \in \mathbb{R}_{>0}$ is used for numerical precision in the computation of σ and typically chosen $\epsilon = 10\alpha$. Intuitively, increasing N_{ILT} increases the density of query points along the imaginary axis, allowing finer resolution of frequency components. The time variable t shifts the contour along the real axis, while ζ scales the overall size of the grid in both directions.

4 Solution

To model Eq. (1), we propose Laplace-Net, a Laplace-based neural network (NN) that removes the solver, decouples initial conditions from inputs, and encapsulates system dynamics. We first decompose the system response in line with classical control theory [23] and then integrate NNs into this framework.

4.1 Decomposition of System Responses

To illustrate the decomposition of $\boldsymbol{\mathcal{Y}}(s)$ into decoupled components, we consider a differential equation of the form:

$$\sum_{i=0}^{n} \mathbf{A}_i \frac{d^i \mathbf{y}(t)}{dt^i} = \mathbf{B}\mathbf{x}(t), \tag{7}$$

where $\mathbf{A}_i \in \mathbb{R}^{D_y \times D_y}$ and $\mathbf{B} \in \mathbb{R}^{D_y \times D_x}$ are constant matrices.

Applying the Laplace transform $\mathcal{L}\{\cdot\}$ to both sides and using Eq. (3) yields:

$$\sum_{i=0}^{n} \mathbf{A}_i \left(s^i \boldsymbol{\mathcal{Y}}(s) - \sum_{k=0}^{i-1} s^{i-1-k} \frac{d^k \mathbf{y}(0)}{dt^k} \right) = \mathbf{B}\boldsymbol{\mathcal{X}}(s). \tag{8}$$

Rearranging terms and isolating $\boldsymbol{\mathcal{Y}}(s)$, assuming the invertibility of $\left(\sum_{i=0}^{n} \mathbf{A}_i s^i\right)^{-1}$, results in:

$$\boldsymbol{\mathcal{Y}}(s) = \left(\sum_{i=0}^{n} \mathbf{A}_i s^i\right)^{-1} \left(\mathbf{B}\boldsymbol{\mathcal{X}}(s) + \sum_{i=0}^{n} \mathbf{A}_i \sum_{k=0}^{i-1} s^{i-1-k} \frac{d^k \mathbf{y}(0)}{dt^k} \right). \tag{9}$$

To simplify the structure of the solution, we introduce the notation $\boldsymbol{\mathcal{H}}(s) \in \mathbb{C}^{D_y \times D_y}$ and $\boldsymbol{\mathcal{P}}(s) \in \mathbb{C}^{D_y}$ as follows:

$$\boldsymbol{\mathcal{H}}(s) := \left(\sum_{i=0}^{n} \mathbf{A}_i s^i\right)^{-1}, \quad \boldsymbol{\mathcal{H}}(s) \in \mathbb{C}^{D_y \times D_y}, \tag{10}$$

$$\boldsymbol{\mathcal{P}}(s) := \sum_{i=0}^{n} \mathbf{A}_i \sum_{k=0}^{i-1} s^{i-1-k} \frac{d^k \mathbf{y}(0)}{dt^k}, \quad \boldsymbol{\mathcal{P}}(s) \in \mathbb{C}^{D_y}. \tag{11}$$

Using Eqs. (10) and (11) we can simplify Eq. (9) to:

$$\boldsymbol{\mathcal{Y}}(s) = \boldsymbol{\mathcal{H}}(s)(\mathbf{B}\boldsymbol{\mathcal{X}}(s) + \boldsymbol{\mathcal{P}}(s)), \tag{12}$$

which represents the decomposition of Eq. 7 into separate components: the system dynamics given by $\boldsymbol{\mathcal{H}}(s)$, the influence of initial conditions captured in $\boldsymbol{\mathcal{P}}(s)$, and the external excitations $\mathbf{B}\boldsymbol{\mathcal{X}}(s)$.

4.2 Neural Network-Based Approximation

To generalize the decomposition in Eq. (12), we introduce **Laplace-Net**. Figure 2 provides an overview, and Algorithm 1 details the computational steps. First, historical input-output sequences are encoded into $(\mathbf{P}, \mathbf{z})$, where $\mathbf{P}$ captures initial conditions. Using $\mathbf{P}$ and queries $\mathbf{s}$, $\boldsymbol{\mathcal{P}}(s)$ is formed in the Laplace domain. Second, the external input $\mathbf{X}_{\text{fore}}$ undergoes a numerical Laplace transform and is mapped into the output space via $\mathbf{B}$. Third, a NN approximates the transfer function $\boldsymbol{\mathcal{H}}(s)$, which, together with the other components, is combined using complex-valued operations to compute $\boldsymbol{\mathcal{Y}}(s)$ in the Laplace domain. Finally, an inverse Laplace transform reconstructs the time-domain output $\mathbf{Y}_{\text{fore}}$. To handle long sequences and non-linearities, this process runs recurrently with an adjustable stride δ, resulting in Q steps.

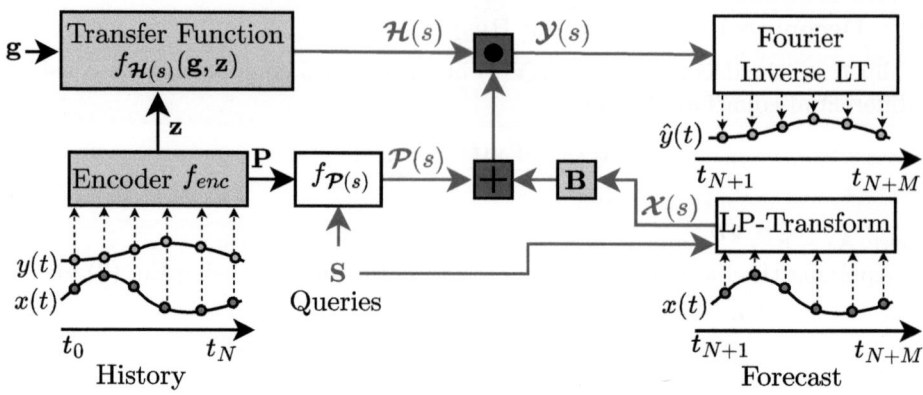

Fig. 2. Overview of the Laplace-Net architecture. Blue elements represent learnable matrices or NNs, including an encoder for historical data and a trainable transfer function. Purple elements denote complex-valued components. (Color figure online)

External Input $X(s)$: The Laplace transform of the external input can be computed numerically using either a discrete summation or a Fourier-based approach. The Discrete Laplace Transform (DLT) follows directly from the definition in Eq. (2):

$$\mathcal{X}(s) = \sum_{k=0}^{N-1} x(t_k) e^{-st_k} \Delta t, \qquad (13)$$

where $\Delta t = t_{k+1} - t_k$ is the time increment.

If $x(t)$ is assumed periodic, it can be represented as a Fourier series [3]:

$$x(t) = \sum_{k=-K}^{K} a_k e^{i\omega_k t}, \quad 0 \leq t < T, \qquad (14)$$

where a_k and ω_k are the Fourier coefficients and frequencies, respectively. Using the Fast Fourier Transform (FFT), these coefficients can be efficiently computed. Applying the Laplace transform yields:

$$\mathcal{X}(s) = \sum_{k=-K}^{K} \frac{a_k}{s - i\omega_k}. \qquad (15)$$

This approach, referred to as the Fast Fourier Laplace Transform (FFLT), exploits the relationship between Fourier and Laplace transforms.

History Encoding and Initial State $\mathcal{P}(s)$. We represent the initial condition term $\mathcal{P}(s)$ via a combination of an encoder network and an analytic structure, rather than explicitly computing its Laplace transform. Specifically, we introduce a history-dependent parameter $\mathbf{P} \in \mathbb{R}^{D_y \times P}$ and a latent variable $\mathbf{z}$, both inferred by a history encoder:

$$f_{\text{enc}} : \mathbb{R}^1 \times \mathbb{R}^{T_{\text{hist}} \times d_x} \times \mathbb{R}^{T_{\text{hist}} \times d_y} \rightarrow \mathbb{R}^{D_z \times P} \times \mathbb{R}^{D_z}, \qquad (16)$$

Algorithm 1. The Laplace-Net algorithm.

Require: $(\mathbf{t}_{\text{hist}}, \mathbf{X}_{\text{hist}}, \mathbf{Y}_{\text{hist}})$, $(\mathbf{t}_{\text{fore}}, \mathbf{X}_{\text{fore}})$, δ, N_{ILT}; **Ensure:** $\mathbf{Y}_{\text{pred}}$
1: **function** LAPLACE-NET($\mathbf{t}_{\text{hist}}, \mathbf{X}_{\text{hist}}, \mathbf{Y}_{\text{hist}}, \mathbf{t}_{\text{fore}}^{(z)}, \mathbf{X}_{\text{fore}}^{(z)}, N_{\text{ILT}}$)
2: $\quad (\mathbf{P}, \mathbf{z}) \leftarrow f_{\text{enc}}(\mathbf{t}_{\text{hist}}, \mathbf{X}_{\text{hist}}, \mathbf{Y}_{\text{hist}})$
3: $\quad$ Compute Queries $\mathbf{s}$ from $\mathbf{t}_{\text{fore}}^{(z)}$ by Eq. (6)
4: $\quad \mathcal{P}(s) \leftarrow f_{\mathcal{P}(s)}(\mathbf{P}, \mathbf{s})$ $\quad\quad\quad\quad\quad\quad\quad\quad\quad\quad\quad\quad\quad\quad$ ▷ Eq. (18)
5: $\quad$ Compute grid $\mathbf{g}$ from $\mathbf{t}_{\text{fore}}, N_{ILT}$ by Eq. (19)
6: $\quad \mathcal{H}(s) \leftarrow f_{\mathcal{H}(s)}(\mathbf{g}, \mathbf{z})$ $\quad\quad\quad\quad\quad\quad\quad\quad\quad\quad\quad\quad\quad\quad$ ▷ Eq.(20)
7: $\quad \mathcal{H}(s) \leftarrow \frac{\mathcal{H}(s)}{f_{\text{scale}}(\mathbf{t}_{\text{fore}}) \cdot \kappa_{\mathcal{H}(s)}}$ $\quad\quad\quad\quad\quad\quad\quad$ ▷ optional step (Eq. (22))
8: $\quad \mathcal{X}(s) \leftarrow \mathcal{L}(\mathbf{t}_{\text{fore}}^{(z)}, \mathbf{X}_{\text{fore}}^{(z)}, \mathbf{s})$ $\quad\quad\quad\quad\quad$ ▷ by either Eq. (13) or Eq. (15)
9: $\quad \mathcal{Y}(s) \leftarrow \mathcal{H}(s)(\mathbf{B}\mathcal{X}(s) + \mathcal{P}(s))$ $\quad\quad\quad\quad\quad\quad\quad\quad\quad$ ▷ Eq. (12)
10: $\quad$ **return** Numerical ILT $f_{\mathcal{L}^{-1}}(\mathcal{Y}(s), \mathbf{t}_{\text{fore}})$ $\quad\quad\quad\quad\quad\quad$ ▷ by Eq. (5)
11: **end function**
12: $\mathbf{Y}_{\text{pred}} \leftarrow \emptyset$, $Q \leftarrow \left\lceil \frac{M}{\delta} \right\rceil$
13: **for** $q = 0$ to $Q - 1$ **do**
14: $\quad (\mathbf{t}_{\text{fore}}^{(z)}, \mathbf{X}_{\text{fore}}^{(z)}) \leftarrow$ Extract window
15: $\quad \mathbf{Y}_{\text{pred}}^{(z)} \leftarrow$ Laplace-Net($\mathbf{t}_{\text{hist}}, \mathbf{X}_{\text{hist}}, \mathbf{Y}_{\text{hist}}, \mathbf{t}_{\text{fore}}^{(z)}, \mathbf{X}_{\text{fore}}^{(z)}, N_{\text{ILT}}$)
16: $\quad (\mathbf{t}_{\text{hist}}, \mathbf{X}_{\text{hist}}, \mathbf{Y}_{\text{hist}}) \leftarrow$ Update history
17: $\quad \mathbf{Y}_{\text{pred}} \leftarrow \mathbf{Y}_{\text{pred}} \cup \mathbf{Y}_{\text{pred}}^{(z)}$
18: **end for**
19: **return** $\mathbf{Y}_{\text{pred}}$

such that:
$$\mathbf{P}, \mathbf{z} = f_{\text{enc}}(\mathbf{t}_{\text{hist}}, \mathbf{X}_{\text{hist}}, \mathbf{Y}_{\text{hist}}). \quad (17)$$

Here, $\mathbf{P}$ collects information needed to construct the polynomial representation of the initial state, and $\mathbf{z}$ is a latent state capturing additional system characteristics from historical data.

Comparing $\mathcal{P}(s)$ to the analytic form in (11), we note that $\mathcal{P}(s)$ is a polynomial in s whose coefficients depend on system matrices $\mathbf{A}_i$ and initial states $\frac{d^k \mathbf{y}(0)}{dt^k}$. Thus, the initial state term can be rewritten as:

$$\mathcal{P}(s) = f_{\mathcal{P}(s)}(s, \mathbf{P}) = \sum_{i=0}^{P-1} \mathbf{p}_i s^i \quad \text{with} \quad \mathbf{P} = (\mathbf{p}_0, \mathbf{p}_1, \ldots, \mathbf{p}_{P-1}). \quad (18)$$

Here, $P \in \mathbb{N}_{>0}$ is a hyper parameter that reflects the order n of Eq. (8), which usually only can be guessed for real-world datasets. This formulation preserves the analytic dependence on initial conditions while offering a flexible, data-driven adaptation. By encoding $\mathbf{P}$ and $\mathbf{z}$ jointly, the model can capture system properties without direct knowledge of $\mathbf{A}_i$ or $\mathbf{y}(0)$ and its derivates.

Transfer Function $\mathcal{H}(s)$. Next, we learn the overall transfer function $\mathcal{H}(s)$ via a NN $f_{\mathcal{H}(s)}$, which takes as input a 2D-grid $\mathbf{g} \in \mathbb{R}^{N_{\text{ILT}} \times T}$. Here, N_{ILT} is the number of ILT terms (see Eq. (5)), and T is the forecast horizon. Although the ILT method naturally produces the (complex) query points $s_k(t)$ (Eq. (6)), these can grow unbounded for small t, leading to extreme input values for the NN. This results in large weight updates, potentially causing gradient instability and slowing down convergence. To address this, we map the ILT queries onto a normalized grid $\mathbf{g} = [g_{m,n}]$, ensuring numerical stability while preserving spectral and temporal structure. The ILT axis remains uniform, while irregularly sampled time points t_n are scaled to $[-1, 1]$ using:

$$g_{m,n} = 2\frac{t_n - t_{\min}}{t_{\max} - t_{\min}} - 1. \tag{19}$$

This ensures that $t_{\min}$ maps to -1 and $t_{\max}$ to 1, preserving relative spacing.

The transfer function is then modelled by:

$$\mathcal{H}(s) = f_{\mathcal{H}(s)}(\mathbf{g}, \mathbf{z}), \tag{20}$$

where $\mathbf{z}$ is precisely the latent state inferred by the history encoder (17). Conditioning on $\mathbf{z}$ allows $\mathcal{H}(s)$ to adapt to varying system behaviours and capture locally linear approximations of potentially non-linear processes.

Inverse Laplace Transform and Time-Independent Scaling In Eq. (5), the contour parameter is often set as $\lambda = \zeta t$, making $\mathcal{Y}(s)$ explicitly time-dependent. To remove this dependency, we define the scaling factor[2]:

$$f_{\text{scale}}(t) = \zeta t\, e^{-\sigma t} = \zeta t\, \epsilon^{\frac{1}{\zeta}} e^{-\alpha t}. \tag{21}$$

When scaling is used, we get $\widetilde{\mathcal{H}}(s)$ by Eq. (20) which is transformed into the time dependent transfer function along the t axis by:

$$\mathcal{H}(s) = \frac{\widetilde{\mathcal{H}}(s)}{f_{\text{scale}}(t) \cdot \kappa_{\mathcal{H}(s)}}. \tag{22}$$

Here, the scaling parameter $\kappa_{\mathcal{H}(s)}$ stabilises training by preventing the amplification of small variations in $\widetilde{\mathcal{H}}(s)$ due to division by $f_{\text{scale}}(t)$, ensuring a well-conditioned and robust representation.

5 Evaluation

We evaluate our method by benchmarking it against a sequence-to-sequence LSTM (seq2seq LSTM) and the LNO of [3] on eight univariate dynamical system datasets that differ in complexity and characteristic behaviour. By restricting ourselves to the univariate case, we concentrate on the core dynamics without the complexity of multiple input channels. In this formulation, the input-to-state $\mathbf{B}$ is simply a scalar, set to 1.

---

[2] A full derivation is provided in Appendix A of the supplementary material.

Experimental Setup. All datasets consist of uniformly sampled time series with 50 historical data points and a forecast horizon of 500 steps. We employ a train-validation-test split: the training set is used to learn model parameters, the validation set for hyperparameter tuning, and the test set for final performance.

For the Spring-Mass-Damper System (SMD) and Mackey-Glass data, we generate our own univariate time series by applying three distinct periodic signals for training (sigmoid), validation (decaying sine), and testing (triangular). In contrast, for the Duffing, Lorenz, and driven pendulum datasets, we adopt the data of [3] directly, which rely on decaying sinusoidal input signals $x(t)$ whose decay coefficient varies across samples. To reduce experimental bias, we determine the learning rate and other model-specific hyperparameters[3] via the Tree-Parzen Estimator (TPE) [24] in optuna, using 100 TPE trials per dataset for each method. We then use the best hyper-parameters and train each method six times with different random seeds to assess robustness. All datasets are processed in a single pass (batch size 512) per epoch. Our experiments run on a high-performance cluster with eight GPUs (Nvidia A40 and A100). In total we run 2544 trainings for our setup.

Table 2. Mean ± (standard deviation over six seeds) for MSE on test set. **Bold** values indicate the best result per data set.

Dataset/Model	LNO	LSTM	Laplace-Net
SMD	1.88e−01 (1.48e−01)	**3.56e−04 (4.53e−05)**	8.75e−04 (2.46e−04)
Duffing $c = 0$	7.42e−02 (3.93e−02)	1.21e−01 (2.21e−02)	**1.98e−02 (6.52e−03)**
Duffing $c = 0.5$	1.06e−03 (1.04e−04)	1.33e−03 (8.73e−04)	**5.31e−05 (1.23e−05)**
Lorenz $\rho = 5$	4.05e−02 (1.18e−02)	**1.21e−04 (2.77e−05)**	5.19e−04 (1.09e−04)
Lorenz $\rho = 10$	5.36e+00 (5.97e−01)	2.10e+00 (3.79e−01)	**1.31e+00 (3.27e−01)**
Pendulum $c = 0$	5.81e−01 (9.83e−02)	6.89e−01 (6.43e−02)	**6.61e−03 (1.67e−03)**
Pendulum $c = 0.5$	1.08e−03 (7.37e−04)	6.92e−04 (1.52e−04)	**5.10e−05 (2.00e−05)**
Mackey-Glass	5.90e−01 (2.08e−01)	3.50e−01 (6.99e−02)	**8.83e−03 (3.27e−03)**

Test Systems and Results. Table 2 presents the mean and standard deviation of the MSE on the test set over six repeated runs. Below, we provide a brief overview of each system and comment on the observed results. We start with a simple linear **Spring-Mass-Damper (SMD)** system, also used in [30] as an application example:

$$m\ddot{y}(t) + c\dot{y}(t) + k y(t) = x(t), \quad m, c, k \in \mathbb{R}^+, \tag{23}$$

where m is the mass, c the damping, and k the spring constant. It has an initial displacement $y(0) = y_0$ as well as initial velocity $\dot{y}(0) = v_0$. As the table shows,

---
[3] Details on the best hyperparameters found by the TPE can be found in Appendix B of the supplementary material.

the seq2seq LSTM achieves the lowest error, yet Laplace-Net still surpasses LNO and provides a stable fit. This indicates that, although SMD is comparatively simpler to model, Laplace-Net remains competitive.

The **Duffing oscillator:**

$$m\ddot{y}(t) + c\dot{y}(t) + k_1\, y(t) + k_3\, y^3(t) = x(t), \quad m, c, k_1, k_3 \in \mathbb{R}^+, \tag{24}$$

introduces a cubic spring (constant k_3). Following [3], we use damped ($c = 0.5$), which provides transient behavior as the oscillations decline and undamped ($c = 0$) where oscillatory behaviour dominated. Notably, Laplace-Net achieves the best results for both scenarios, capturing non-linear oscillatory behaviour accurately in the damped case.

The **Lorenz system:**

$$\dot{s}_x = \sigma(y - s_x), \quad \dot{y} = s_x(\rho - s_z) - y, \quad \dot{s}_z = s_x y - \beta s_z - x(t), \quad \sigma, \rho, \beta \in \mathbb{R}^+, \tag{25}$$

is a three-dimensional chaotic model where s_x, s_z are internal states, $\rho = 5$ or $\rho = 10$ sets the degree of chaos. For $\rho = 5$, the table indicates that the LSTM gives the best result. However, at $\rho = 10$, Laplace-Net emerges on top, evidencing superior adaptability under stronger chaotic dynamics.

Another non-linear system is the **Driven pendulum:**

$$\ddot{x}(t) + c\dot{x}(t) + \frac{g}{l}\sin\bigl(x(t)\bigr) = x_{\text{ext}}(t), \quad c, g, l \in \mathbb{R}^+, \tag{26}$$

where g is the gravity and l is the rod length. Again a damped ($c = 0.5$) and undamped ($c = 0$) similar to the Duffing system, a higher damping leads to more transient, decaying behaviour. Here, Laplace-Net clearly outperforms LSTM and LNO in both scenarios, underscoring its strength in modelling non-linear oscillatory phenomena.

The **Mackey-Glass system:**

$$\dot{y}(t) = \beta \frac{y(t - \tau)}{1 + [y(t - \tau)]^n} - \gamma y(t) + x(t), \quad \beta, \gamma, \tau, n \in \mathbb{R}^+, \tag{27}$$

brings explicit time delays τ, which often pose challenges for standard recurrent architectures. Here, β controls the strength of the delayed feedback, while γ represents the dissipation rate. Laplace-Net attains a particularly low error, whereas for the LSTM and LNO we observe that they are not able to capture the behaviour. Because all models share the same training and tuning procedures, this improvement suggests Laplace-Net retains more effective long-range memory, thus handling delayed feedback more robustly.

Taken together, these findings verify that Laplace-Net is accurate and robust across diverse types of dynamical systems. In most cases, it surpasses both seq2seq LSTM and LNO, particularly for non-linear, chaotic, or delay-based dynamics. This ability to handle forced, damping-induced, and chaotic regimes demonstrates the method's versatility for extended forecasting horizons. Table 2 shows that our method, is able to outperform LNO as well as the LSTM for most of the datasets, except for the Lorenz System with $\rho = 5$.

6 Discussion and Limitations

While Laplace-Net offers a flexible, solver-free approach to modelling forced dynamical systems, it has theoretical and practical limitations. A fundamental constraint arises from the Laplace transform: functions growing super-exponentially, i.e., those for which there exist no constants $C, \sigma > 0$ such that $|f(t)| \leq Ce^{\sigma t}$, are not transformable [26]. This limitation is particularly relevant for transforming input signals $\mathcal{X}(s) = \mathcal{L}\{\mathbf{x}(t)\}$. This restriction is mainly of theoretical interest, as, to the best of our knowledge, the current literature does not report typical cases where this limitation is violated. Furthermore, the Laplace transform is widely used and considered broadly applicable in engineering practice, implicitly assuming that real-world signals do not violate these constraints [23].

Although classical error bounds exist for certain numerical ILT algorithms [10, 17], deriving comparable stability or approximation guarantees for Laplace-Net mapping remains an open challenge. Our empirical results indicate robust performance, but a theoretical analysis of the error and stability properties is an important direction for future work. Another challenge lies in the numerical approximation of $\mathcal{X}(s)$ and $\mathcal{Y}(s)$. For signals containing high frequencies (e.g. abrupt jumps), a large number of ILT terms (N_{ILT}) is required for accurate reconstruction. While the computation of the proposed Laplace transforms, such as the Discrete Laplace Transform (DLT) in Eq. (13) and the Fast Fourier Laplace Transform (FFLT) in Eq. (15), can be computationally intensive, it can be performed once prior training.

Memory consumption also presents a constraint, as the computational cost grows linearly with both the number of ILT terms N_{ILT} and the number of prediction time points. Particularly for signals with sharp discontinuities, achieving sufficient accuracy requires large N_{ILT} values, which significantly increases memory requirements. Despite these challenges, the design of Laplace-Net is highly parallelisable, with the exception of time-stepping. However, this overhead is negligible compared to the numerous iterations required by ODE solvers.

One major advantage of Laplace-Net is that the Laplace representation of the input $\mathcal{X}(s)$ is handled independently, allowing for pre-validation or even manual refinement before joint training. This makes debugging and refining the forcing component significantly easier. Moreover, if certain components of the system transfer function $\mathcal{H}(s)$ are already known, for instance, from physical principles, they can be directly embedded into the model while learning only the remaining unknown terms. This hybrid approach reduces the learning burden and allows for more effective integration of prior knowledge. Recent work has demonstrated that incorporating such explicit prior knowledge into neural ODE models for electrical circuits can substantially improve performance, consistently outperforming black-box LSTM and standard NODE architectures, particularly in data-limited scenarios [31].

The decoupled structure also enables selective training strategies. When working with controlled experiments where the system is initialized at zero, the initial state term $\mathcal{P}(s)$ can be explicitly set to zero, removing unnecessary degrees of freedom and simplifying optimization. In real-world settings where the initial conditions vary, the full model can then be fine-tuned, leveraging pre-trained components for efficient adaptation.

Furthermore the decoupled structure of Laplace-Net improves interpretability: In many fields, the structure of the dynamical system, learned with $\mathcal{H}(s)$ is of interest (e.g. when designing the controller C). Learning it as a dedicated component enables domain experts to interpret what was learned.

7 Conclusion and Future Work

In this work, we introduced a decoupled, solver-free neural network (NN) framework for learning forced and delay-aware dynamical systems: the Laplace-based Network (Laplace-Net). Laplace-Net explicitly separates internal system dynamics from external control inputs and initial conditions, addressing key limitations of existing approaches. Unlike many prior approaches such as Laplace Neural Operator (LNO), Laplace-Net can learn systems with hard delays or non-local memory, in- cluding those appearing in Fractional Differential Equations (FDE). Laplace-Net enhances transferability by enabling fast retraining or fine-tuning for new forcing signals, which is particularly advantageous in data-limited scenarios. Furthermore, it improves interpretability, as its learned components align with classical theoretical concepts familiar to experts (e.g., transfer functions). Finally, Laplace-Net is highly parallelisable and scales linearly with both the number of frequency terms and prediction time steps.

Laplace-Net demonstrates clear advantages across a wide range of dynamical systems. Evaluated on eight datasets covering linear, non-linear, chaotic, and delayed dynamics, it consistently outperforms the LNO in all cases. Compared to an Long Short-Term Memory (LSTM) model, Laplace-Net achieves superior accuracy on nearly all datasets, with the exception of a linear ODE case and one out of seven non-linear scenarios, as shown in Table 2. These results highlight the effectiveness of Laplace-Net in capturing complex system behaviour across various dynamical systems.

While Laplace-Net shows robust performance on synthetic and univariate datasets, this evidence needs to be enhanced for usage in real-world applications. In particular, the evaluation on real-world datasets as well as on multivariate time series is useful. Also, comparisons to more state-of-the-art algorithms such as Fourier NODE or Neural CDEs remain future work. Furthermore, run-time improvements compared to solver-based algorithms as well as resource requirements need to be quantified on a broader basis. Beyond this, investigating the use of more specialised NN architectures for the components of Laplace-Net beyond fully connected networks may enhance performance or increase interpretability. Also, extending to handle two- and three-dimensional use cases, similar to LNO, would increase the applicability of Laplace-Net.

Disclosure of Interests. The authors have no competing interests to declare that are relevant to the content of this article.

Acknowledgments. We acknowledge ChatGPT-4 for support in writing and for assistance with coding. The authors remain responsible for the ideas, content, and conclusions presented in this work. C. Coelho would like to thank the KIBIDZ project funded by dtec.bw—Digitalization and Technology Research Center of the Bundeswehr; dtec.bw is funded by the European Union—NextGenerationEU, and project PL24-00057: "Inteligência Artificial na Otimização da Rega para Olivais Resilientes às Alterações Climáticas" financially supported by Fundação "la Caixa"|BPI and Fundação para a Ciência e Tecnologia (Portuguese Foundation for Science and Technology) and the funding by FCT through the CMAT projects UIDB/00013/2020 and UIDP/00013/2020.

References

1. Biloš, M., Sommer, J., Rangapuram, S.S., Januschowski, T., Günnemann, S.: Neural Flows: Efficient Alternative to Neural ODEs. In: Neural Information Processing Systems (2021)
2. Butcher, J.C.: A history of Runge-Kutta methods. Appl. Numer. Math. **20**(3), 247–260 (1996). https://doi.org/10.1016/0168-9274(95)00108-5
3. Cao, Q., Goswami, S., Karniadakis, G.E.: Laplace neural operator for solving differential equations. Nat. Mach. Intell. **6**(6), 631–640 (2024). https://doi.org/10.1038/s42256-024-00844-4
4. Chen, T.Q., Rubanova, Y., Bettencourt, J., Duvenaud, D.K.: Neural ordinary differential equations. In: Neural Information Processing Systems (2018)
5. Coelho, C., P. Costa, M.F., Ferrás, L.: Neural fractional differential equations (2025). https://doi.org/10.1016/j.apm.2025.116060
6. Coelho, C., Costa, M.F.P., Ferrás, L.L.: Neural fractional differential equations: optimising the order of the fractional derivative. Fractal Fractional **8**(9), 529 (2024). https://doi.org/10.3390/fractalfract8090529
7. Dafilis, M.P., Frascoli, F., McVernon, J., Heffernan, J.M., McCaw, J.M.: The dynamical consequences of seasonal forcing, immune boosting and demographic change in a model of disease transmission. J. Theor. Biol. **361**, 124–132 (2014)
8. Diethelm, K.: The Analysis of Fractional Differential Equations: An Application-Oriented Exposition Using Differential Operators of Caputo Type. In: Lecture Notes in Mathematics, vol. 2004. Springer, Heidelberg (2010). https://doi.org/10.1007/978-3-642-14574-2
9. Diethelm, K., Ford, N.J.: Analysis of fractional differential equations. J. Math. Anal. Appl. **265**(2), 229–248 (2002). https://doi.org/10.1006/jmaa.2000.7194
10. Dubner, H., Abate, J.: Numerical inversion of laplace transforms by relating them to the finite fourier cosine transform. J. ACM **15**(1), 115–123 (1968). https://doi.org/10.1145/321439.321446
11. Dupont, E., Doucet, A., Teh, Y.W.: Augmented Neural ODEs. In: 33rd Conference on Neural Information Processing Systems (NeurIPS 2019), Vancouver, Canada. (2019)
12. Gwak, D., Sim, G., Poli, M., Massaroli, S., Choo, J., Choi, E.: Neural ordinary differential equations for intervention modeling (2020). https://doi.org/10.48550/ARXIV.2010.08304
13. Holt, S., Hüyük, A., Qian, Z., Sun, H., van der Schaar, M.: Neural laplace control for continuous-time delayed systems. In: Proceedings of the 26th International Conference on Artificial Intelligence and Statistics. Proceedings of Machine Learning Research, vol. 206, pp. 1747–1778. PMLR (2023)

14. Holt, S.I., Qian, Z., van der Schaar, M.: Neural laplace: learning diverse classes of differential equations in the Laplace domain. In: Proceedings of the 39th International Conference on Machine Learning, pp. 8811–8832. Proceedings of Machine Learning Research, PMLR (2022)
15. Kexue, L., Jigen, P.: Laplace transform and fractional differential equations. Appl. Math. Lett. **24**(12), 2019–2023 (2011). https://doi.org/10.1016/j.aml.2011.05.035
16. Kidger, P., Morrill, J., Foster, J., Lyons, T.: Neural controlled differential equations for irregular time series. In: Larochelle, H., Ranzato, M., Hadsell, R., Balcan, M., Lin, H. (eds.) Advances in Neural Information Processing Systems, p. 66966707. Curran Associates, Inc. (2020)
17. Kuhlman, K.L.: Review of inverse laplace transform algorithms for laplace-space numerical approaches. Num. Algorithms **63**(2), 339–355 (2013). https://doi.org/10.1007/s11075-012-9625-3
18. Li, X., et al.: From Fourier to neural ODEs: flow matching for modeling complex systems. In: Proceedings of the 41st International Conference on Machine Learning. Proceedings of Machine Learning Research, vol. 235, pp. 29390–29405. PMLR (2024)
19. Liang, S., Wu, R., Chen, L.: Laplace transform of fractional order differential equations. Electron. J. Differ. Equ. **139**, 2015 (2015)
20. Lu, L., Jin, P., Pang, G., Zhang, Z., Karniadakis, G.E.: Learning nonlinear operators via DeepONet based on the universal approximation theorem of operators. Nat. Mach. Intell. **3**(3), 218–229 (2021). https://doi.org/10.1038/s42256-021-00302-5
21. Ma, J., Cui, Y., Liu, L.: Hopf bifurcation and chaos of financial system on condition of specific combination of parameters. J. Syst. Sci. Complexity **21**(2), 250–259 (2008)
22. Monsel, T., Semeraro, O., Mathelin, L., Charpiat, G.: Time and state dependent neural delay differential equations. In: Proceedings of the 1st ECAI Workshop on "Machine Learning Meets Differential Equations: From Theory to Applications". Proceedings of Machine Learning Research, vol. 255, pp. 1–20. PMLR (2024)
23. Ogata, K.: Modern Control Engineering. Prentice Hall, Upper Saddle River, 5th ed. edn. (2010)
24. Ozaki, Y., Tanigaki, Y., Watanabe, S., Onishi, M.: Multiobjective Tree-Structured Parzen Estimator for Computationally Expensive Optimization Problems. In: Proceedings of the 2020 Genetic and Evolutionary Computation Conference, pp. 533–541. GECCO 2020, Association for Computing Machinery, New York, NY, USA (2020). https://doi.org/10.1145/3377930.3389817
25. Rubanova, Y., Chen, R.T.Q., Duvenaud, D.K.: Latent ordinary differential equations for irregularly-sampled time series. In: Wallach, H., Larochelle, H., Beygelzimer, A., dAlché-Buc, F., Fox, E., Garnett, R. (eds.) Advances in Neural Information Processing Systems, vol. 32. Curran Associates, Inc. (2019)
26. Schiff, J.L.: The Laplace Transform: Theory and Applications. Springer eBook Collection Mathematics and Statistics, Springer, New York, NY (1999). https://doi.org/10.1007/978-0-387-22757-3
27. Valencia, J., Olivar, G., Franco, C.J., Dyner, I.: Qualitative analysis of climate seasonality effects in a model of national electricity market. In: Tost, G., Vasilieva, O. (eds.) Analysis, Modelling, Optimization, and Numerical Techniques: ICAMI, San Andres Island, Colombia, November 2013, pp. 349–362. Springer (2015). https://doi.org/10.1007/978-3-319-12583-1_24

28. Zhu, Q., Guo, Y., Lin, W.: Neural delay differential equations. In: Ninth International Conference on Learning Representations. arXiv (2021). https://doi.org/10.48550/arxiv.2102.10801
29. Zimmering, B., Coelho, C., Niggemann, O.: Optimising neural fractional differential equations for performance and efficiency. In: Proceedings of the 1st ECAI Workshop on "Machine Learning Meets Differential Equations: from Theory to Applications". Proceedings of Machine Learning Research, vol. 255, pp. 1–22. PMLR (2024). https://proceedings.mlr.press/v255/zimmering24a.html
30. Zimmering, B., Niggemann, O.: Integrating continuous-time neural networks in engineering: bridging machine learning and dynamical system modeling. In: ML4CPS – Machine Learning for Cyber-Physical Systems (2024). https://doi.org/10.24405/15313
31. Zimmering, B., Roche, J.P., Niggemann, O.: Enhancing nonlinear electrical circuit modeling with prior knowledge-infused neural ODEs. In: 2024 IEEE 29th International Conference on Emerging Technologies and Factory Automation (ETFA), pp. 01–08. IEEE, Padova, Italy (2024). https://doi.org/10.1109/ETFA61755.2024.10711112
32. Zolock, J., Greif, R.: Application of time series analysis and neural networks to the modeling and analysis of forced vibrating mechanical systems. In: ASME International Mechanical Engineering Congress and Exposition, vol. 37122, pp. 1157–1164 (2003)

Open Access This chapter is licensed under the terms of the Creative Commons Attribution 4.0 International License (http://creativecommons.org/licenses/by/4.0/), which permits use, sharing, adaptation, distribution and reproduction in any medium or format, as long as you give appropriate credit to the original author(s) and the source, provide a link to the Creative Commons license and indicate if changes were made.

The images or other third party material in this chapter are included in the chapter's Creative Commons license, unless indicated otherwise in a credit line to the material. If material is not included in the chapter's Creative Commons license and your intended use is not permitted by statutory regulation or exceeds the permitted use, you will need to obtain permission directly from the copyright holder.

Streaming and Spatiotemporal Data

Self-balancing, Memory Efficient, Dynamic Metric Space Data Maintenance, for Rapid Multi-kernel Estimation

Aditya S. Ellendula[✉] and Chandrajit Bajaj[✉]

University of Texas at Austin, Austin, USA
adityase@utexas.edu, cbajaj@cs.utexas.edu

Abstract. We present a dynamic self-balancing octree data structure that fundamentally transforms neighborhood maintenance in evolving metric spaces. Learning systems, from deep networks to reinforcement learning agents, operate as dynamical systems whose trajectories through high-dimensional spaces require efficient importance sampling for optimal convergence. Generative models operate as dynamical systems whose latent representations cannot be learned in one shot, but rather grow and evolve sequentially during training—requiring continuous adaptation of spatial relationships. Our two-parameter (K, α) dynamic octree addresses this challenge by providing a computational fabric that efficiently organizes both the generation flow and querying flow operating on different time scales by enabling logarithmic-time updates and queries without requiring complete rebuilding as distributions evolve. We demonstrate its effectiveness across four key applications: (1) accelerating Stein Variational Gradient Descent by enabling larger particle sets with reduced computation; (2) supporting real-time incremental KNN classification with logarithmic updates; (3) improving retrieval-augmented generation by enabling efficient, incremental semantic indexing; and (4) showing that maintaining both input and latent space structures accelerates convergence and improves sample efficiency. Across all applications, our experimental results confirm exponential performance improvements over standard methods while maintaining accuracy. These improvements are particularly significant for high-dimensional spaces where efficient neighborhood maintenance is crucial to navigate complex latent manifolds. By providing guaranteed logarithmic bounds for both update and query operations, our approach enables more data-efficient solutions to previously computationally prohibitive problems, establishing a new approach to dynamic spatial relationship maintenance in machine learning.

Keywords: Dynamic Octree · Neighborhood Maintenance · Importance Sampling · Logarithmic-Time Updates · Incremental KNN Classification · Retrieval-Augmented Generation

Supplementary Information The online version contains supplementary material available at https://doi.org/10.1007/978-3-032-06109-6_16.

1 Introduction

Generative models represent a cornerstone of modern machine learning, enabling systems to learn complex data distributions and generate new samples. At their core, these models—from variational autoencoders (VAE) to generative adversarial networks (GAN) and diffusion models—rely on transformations between simple distributions and complex data manifolds through latent space navigation. This latent space, often referred to as the generative space or Z space, is not static but evolves continuously throughout training and inference.

Our approach recognizes that generative latent spaces expand and shift during training, demanding efficient kernel-based density estimation. Our dynamic octree structure maintains these evolving distributions with selective indexing and adaptive partitioning. By optimizing the sequence of updates and queries using (K, α) parameters, we achieve consistent performance gains across models and applications.

1.1 The Maintenance Challenge in Generative Spaces

Generative models require efficient navigation of high-dimensional spaces for nearest neighbor searches, importance sampling, and density estimation—operations that scale poorly with traditional spatial indexing. Existing approaches face a fundamental trade-off: rebuild indices when distributions change (expensive) or accept degraded performance. This limitation is critical in:

- **Dynamic Training**: Distribution shifts during training require efficient importance sampling at each epoch.
- **Online Learning**: New data integration demands spatial structure updates without full retraining.
- **Adaptive Inference**: Particle-based methods need maintained spatial relationships as particles transform toward target distributions.

Current spatial structures like KD-trees and R-trees optimize for either query efficiency or update performance, but rarely both. This creates a critical need for structures maintaining logarithmic-time performance for both operations in evolving distributions.

1.2 Our Approach: Self-balancing Dynamic Octree

We introduce a novel self-balancing dynamic octree data structure specifically designed for maintaining neighborhood relationships in evolving metric spaces, featuring:

- **Two-Parameter Adaptivity**: A (K, α) parameterization that enables automatic structure balancing based on local data density.
- **Memory Efficiency**: Reduced footprint through adaptive node capacity and efficient spatial partitioning.

– **Dynamic Rebalancing**: Continuous adaptation to distribution shifts without complete rebuilding, enabling efficient maintenance of spatial relationships in evolving generative spaces.

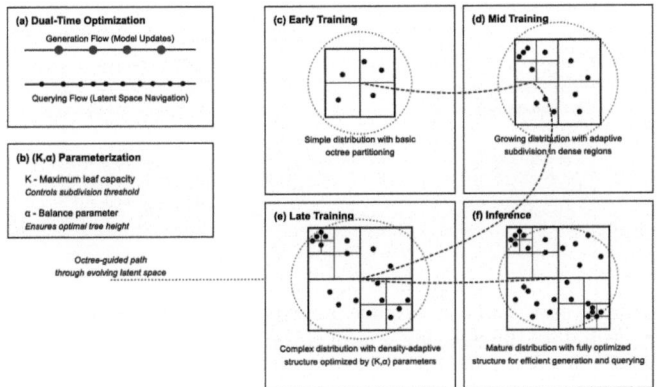

Fig. 1. Dynamic Octree Adaptation in Evolving Latent Spaces. (a) Dual-time optimization highlighting differing update/query frequencies. (b) (K, α) parameters controlling depth and balance. (c–f) Octree evolution across training: (c) early with coarse partitions, (d) mid with initial refinement, (e) late with density-aware subdivision, and (f) inference with optimized structure.

Figure 1 demonstrates that generative spaces expand during training and structured latent spaces emerge iteratively, with our dynamic octree serving as computational fabric for both generation and querying flows. We validate this approach across four applications: **SVGD** (5.6× acceleration, 10× more particles), **Incremental KNN** (5.3× faster updates, logarithmic queries), **RAG systems** (efficient semantic retrieval with domain adaptation), and **dual-space representation** (faster convergence, improved sample efficiency) (Fig. 2 and Table 1).

The remainder of this paper is organized as follows. Section 2 reviews related work, Sect. 3 presents our theoretical framework and algorithmic contributions, Sect. 4 demonstrates our approach through comprehensive case studies spanning diverse machine learning applications, and Sect. 5 concludes with implications and future directions.

2 Related Works

The evolution of efficient data maintenance structures has progressed from classical approaches to specialized spatial structures, yet significant limitations remain when handling evolving distributions.

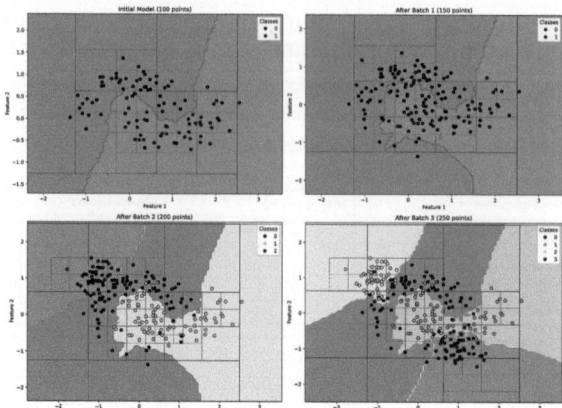

Fig. 2. Adaptive spatial partitioning in incremental KNN classification. Panels show classifier evolution as new data batches are incorporated, with octree structure adapting to data density and class boundaries, maintaining high accuracy and efficiency.

Classical Structures: Self-balancing trees like AVL [6], Red-Black [7], and probabilistic structures like Skip Lists [8] provide O(log n) guarantees for one-dimensional data but lack explicit support for spatial relationships. Structures such as treaps [9] and splay trees [10] adapt well to non-uniform distributions through rotations but are limited to one-dimensional data.

Spatial Data Structures: The fundamental challenge in spatial structures stems from the tension between maintaining spatial relationships and supporting dynamic updates. KD-trees extended binary search principles to spatial organization but struggle with balanced partitioning in higher dimensions. Previous approaches to improve dynamic capabilities include hardware acceleration [11] and structural modifications like iKD-Tree [4], cKD-Tree [13], and BKD-Tree [12], yet they fail to resolve the core trade-off between spatial organization and adaptation to non-uniform distributions.

Recent Advances: The i-Octree [3] improved performance through leaf-based organization and local updates. FLANN [15] offers practical solutions for point cloud processing but still requires complete rebuilding for balance maintenance. Kinetic Data Structures [16] model object motion explicitly but incur substantial overhead with unpredictable updates. Dynamic variants of classical structures like R*-trees [5] and progressive KD-trees [17] improved update handling but still face efficiency trade-offs, particularly in high-dimensional or non-uniform spaces.

Learning-Enhanced Approaches: Recent work has explored integrating machine learning into data structure design [18]. Learned Indexes [19] optimize structure parameters based on data distributions but typically focus on static optimization rather than continuous adaptation to streaming data.

Table 1. Feature Comparison of Spatial Data Structures for Dynamic Datasets

Feature/Capability	DynamicOctree (Ours)	i-Octree	kd-tree	ikd-Tree	R*-tree
Structure Properties					
Dynamic Insertion[a]	✓	✓	×	✓	Ⓟ
Dynamic Deletion[b]	✓	✓	×	✓	Ⓟ
Self-balancing[c]	✓	Ⓟ	×	Ⓟ	Ⓟ
Adaptive Node Capacity[d]	✓	×	×	×	×
Query Capabilities					
Nearest Neighbor Search	✓	✓	✓	✓	✓
Range Queries	✓	✓	✓	✓	✓
Down-sampling Support[e]	✓	✓	×	✓	×
Multi-resolution Queries[f]	✓	×	×	×	Ⓟ
Performance Features					
Constant-time Node Access[g]	✓	✓	×	×	×
Cache-friendly Operations[h]	✓	✓	Ⓟ	Ⓟ	Ⓟ
Memory-efficient Storage	✓	✓	✓	✓	×
Dynamic Memory Management[i]	✓	Ⓟ	×	Ⓟ	Ⓟ
Real-time Performance					
Streaming Updates[j]	✓	Ⓟ	×	✓	×
Low Update Latency[k]	✓	✓	×	Ⓟ	×
Bounded Operation Time[l]	✓	✓	×	Ⓟ	×
Spatial Adaptation					
Density-aware Partitioning[m]	✓	×	×	×	Ⓟ
Local Structure Optimization[n]	✓	Ⓟ	×	Ⓟ	Ⓟ
Advanced Features					
Concurrent Operations[o]	✓	×	×	Ⓟ	×
Box-wise Operations[p]	Ⓟ	✓	×	✓	×

[a] $O(\log n)$ insertion maintaining structure properties
[b] $O(\log n)$ deletion with structure preservation
[c] Maintains balance without complete reconstruction
[d] Dynamically adjustable node capacity based on the parameters
[e] Integrated point cloud down-sampling during updates
[f] Ability to perform queries at different granularity levels without restructuring
[g] Direct access to nodes without traversal overhead
[h] Optimized memory layout for CPU cache efficiency
[i] Efficient memory allocation/deallocation during updates
[j] Efficient handling of continuous real-time updates
[k] Consistently low latency for update operations
[l] Guaranteed upper bounds on operation times
[m] Partition adjustment based on local point density
[n] Local optimization of structure without global rebuilding
[o] Support for parallel operations with thread safety
[p] Efficient operations on groups of points within spatial regions
Legend: ✓: Fully Supported, Ⓟ: Partially Supported, ×: Not Supported
Structure-Specific Notes: - Dynamic Octree: Uses the parameters for adaptive control but fixed after initialization - ikd-Tree: Partial rebuilding required for balance, parallel support limited to rebuilding - i-Octree: Fixed structure parameters but efficient updates - R*-tree: Forced reinsertions affect dynamic performance - kd-tree: Static structure requiring full rebuilding for updates

Despite these advances, current approaches remain limited by fixed parameters and rigid structure rules that constrain adaptability to varying data distributions—a critical requirement for modern machine learning applications with continuously evolving metric spaces.

3 Theoretical Framework and Implementation

Our work extends the (K,α)-octree of Chowdhury et al. [20] to dynamic settings, inheriting proven complexity bounds: $O(n \log n)$ construction, $\Theta(n)$ space, $O(\log n)$ amortized updates, and $O(nd^2(\delta d + K^{1/3}))$ interaction computation.

Definition 1 ((K, α)-admissible octree). *An octree T is (K, α)-admissible if every leaf contains at most αK points and every internal node contains more than K/α points, where $K > 0$ and $\alpha \geq 1$.*

Novel Contributions. Our implementation extends three mechanisms: (i) dynamic root expansion for evolving bounding volumes, (ii) multi-radius queries with distance-based pruning, and (iii) density-aware local rebalancing. The theorems below establish complexity and correctness guarantees for these extensions; complete proofs appear in Appendix A with code correspondence in Appendix B.

3.1 Theoretical Guarantees

Lemma 1 (Tree height preservation). *Let $\Delta_{\max}$ denote the maximum observed domain size and $\ell_{\min}$ the minimum leaf dimension. The tree height satisfies $\text{height}(T) \leq \lceil \log_2(\Delta_{\max}/\ell_{\min}) \rceil + O(1)$ at all times.*

Theorem 1 (Update complexity preservation). *Point insertion, deletion, or position update requires $O(\log n)$ amortized time, including dynamic root expansion and local rebalancing.*

Proof (Sketch). Our potential function $\Phi = \sum_v w(v) \cdot ||\text{atoms}(v)| - K|$ counts deviation from target capacity. Root expansion increases Φ by $O(\log n)$, but subsequent splits amortize this cost. Update operations (`pullUp`/`pushDown`) traverse $O(\log n)$ levels by Lemma 1. □

Lemma 2 (Pruning correctness). *For a node v with center $c(v)$ and half-diagonal $r(v) = \frac{\sqrt{3}}{2} s(v)$, if $\|c(v) - q\| > d + r(v)$ for query point q and radius d, then no point in v lies within distance d of q.*

Proof. For any point $p \in v$, by the triangle inequality: $\|p - q\| \geq \|c(v) - q\| - \|p - c(v)\| \geq \|c(v) - q\| - r(v) > d$. □

Theorem 2 (Query complexity bounds). *Range queries and k-NN search visit $O(d^2(\delta d + K^{1/3}))$ points per query, where δ is the per-point processing cost, preserving the bounds of Chowdhury et al. [20].*

Proof (Sketch). Pruning (Lemma 2) eliminates nodes whose closest point exceeds query radius. The number of visited nodes is bounded by the surface area of the query region and tree structure, yielding the stated complexity. □

3.2 Algorithmic Core

The foundational octree construction, node expansion, and (K, α)-admissibility maintenance algorithms follow directly from Chowdhury et al. [20] and are summarized in Appendix B for completeness. Our algorithmic contributions lie in the extensions for dynamic point management: the `pullUp/pushDown` migration procedures, geometric pruning optimizations for spatial queries, and the neighborhood list construction algorithm `_accum_inter()`.

These extension algorithms achieve direct correspondence between theoretical analysis and implementation through optimizations including 28-bit atom addressing for $O(1)$ lookup, dynamic memory management with exponential resize policies, and squared distance computations. Complete algorithmic specifications for both inherited and novel procedures appear in Appendix B. The full implementation and experiments are available at: https://github.com/SetasAditya/Dynamic-Octree.

4 Experimental Evaluations and Results

Our evaluation demonstrates this unifying principle through four representative case studies, each highlighting different aspects of the dynamic maintenance challenge while validating our (K, α) self-balancing octree across diverse computational scenarios.

4.1 Synthetic Benchmarks: Establishing Fundamental Properties

We validate our theoretical claims through controlled experiments comparing our dynamic octree against kd-trees and i-Octree using time-series data (100K–500K points) with varying density distributions.

Scaling Performance. Figure 3 demonstrates our Dynamic Octree's (DO) scaling advantages from 10K to 200K points: (1) **Logarithmic Scaling:** Maintains $O(\log n)$ complexity for queries and updates, whereas traditional structures exhibit quadratic scaling. (2) **Self-Balancing:** Achieves 22× faster updates than i-Octree at 20K objects through localized rebalancing. (3) **Memory Efficiency:** Uses 10.6% less memory than i-Octree at 100K points.

Neighborhood construction—critical for spatial ML—shows our approach (0.57 s) outperforming i-Octree (8.17 s) by 14.3× at 200K points, with performance gaps growing exponentially.

Adaptive Rebalancing. We evaluated performance across four distribution patterns: varying density, step-wise transitions, exponential growth/decay, and multi-modal clustering using 100K-point clouds over 10 time steps (Table 2).

By adjusting (K, α) parameters, we achieve 36× performance variation in neighborhood construction—from 6.58 s (DO($K=1000$)) to 0.17 s (DO($K=10$))—demonstrating adaptive optimization without structural redesign.

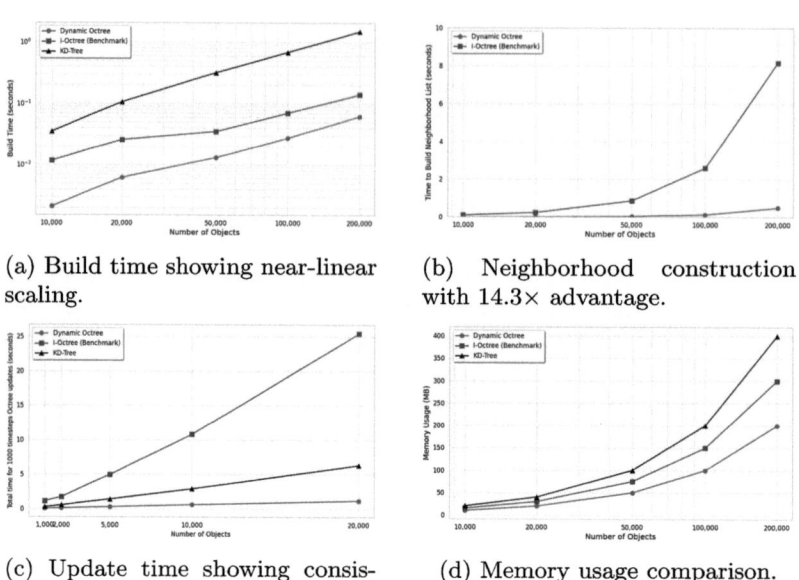

(a) Build time showing near-linear scaling.

(b) Neighborhood construction with 14.3× advantage.

(c) Update time showing consistent efficiency.

(d) Memory usage comparison.

Fig. 3. Synthetic benchmark results: Dynamic Octree (DO) vs. i-Octree (OM) and KD-Tree. Performance gaps widen with scale, confirming theoretical $O(\log n)$ bounds.

Table 2. Performance across distribution patterns. Parameter tuning enables 36× performance variation in neighborhood construction.

Method	Varying Density			Step-wise			Exponential			Multi-modal		
	Build	Update	NB	Build	Update	NB	Build	Update	NB	Build	Update	NB
DO($K=1000$)	**0.00072**	**0.05192**	2.10448	**0.00493**	**0.21182**	6.58040	**0.00006**	**0.04630**	1.65657	**0.00006**	**0.05760**	1.86797
DO($K=10$)	0.00165	0.11467	**0.06234**	0.00575	0.31715	**0.16876**	**0.00006**	0.08393	**0.04575**	0.00008	0.10379	**0.05535**
OM	0.71961	0.71961	6.62204	1.78774	1.78774	21.54342	0.61151	0.61151	4.98176	1.04049	1.04049	7.77186
KD	0.22446	0.22446	0.35293	0.83312	0.83312	1.32703	0.19704	0.19704	0.30873	0.24661	0.24661	0.39029

Continuous Updates. Unlike static structures that degrade under modifications, our approach maintains query efficiency after thousands of updates, providing the continuous performance required by modern generative models during training and inference.

4.2 Case Studies: Transforming Machine Learning Applications

Building on these synthetic foundations, we now demonstrate how the (K, α) dynamic octree transforms real machine learning applications. Modern generative models—from variational autoencoders and normalizing flows to diffusion models and flow matching—share the fundamental computational pattern revealed by our synthetic benchmarks: they require efficient maintenance of neighborhood relationships in continuously evolving metric spaces.

Case Study 1: Particle-Based Bayesian Inference

Computational Challenge. Stein Variational Gradient Descent (SVGD) [30] and related particle-based inference methods face a fundamental bottleneck: computing pairwise kernel interactions between particles scales as $O(n^2)$, limiting practical implementations to hundreds of particles. As particles evolve during inference, their spatial relationships change continuously, requiring repeated neighbor searches within adaptive bandwidth radii.

Access Patterns and Maintenance Requirements. The SVGD update rule, $\phi(x_i) = \frac{1}{n} \sum_{j:\|x_i-x_j\| \leq h}[k(x_j, x_i)\nabla_{x_j} \log p(x_j) + \nabla_{x_j} k(x_j, x_i)]$, relies on an adaptive bandwidth h and induces two core challenges: **dynamic neighborhoods**, as particle proximity changes over iterations, and **adaptive bandwidth**, where h evolves with particle density, requiring continuous structural updates.

Traditional approaches recompute all $O(n^2)$ pairwise distances at each iteration. Our dynamic octree maintains spatial relationships as particles evolve, enabling $O(n \log n)$ complexity through distance-based pruning.

Implementation and Results. We integrated our octree with the reference SVGD implementation from Liu and Wang [30] by maintaining particles in leaf nodes and using range queries to find neighbors within the current bandwidth. When particles move during gradient updates, our update procedure locally rebalances them while preserving the (K, α)-admissible structure. The integration required modifying the kernel computation to use our spatial queries instead of brute-force distance calculations.

Figure 4 demonstrates the transformative impact: our approach achieves 40× speedup at 1,000 particles while actually improving posterior approximation quality (Wasserstein distance reduced from 0.23 to 0.18). This enables practical uncertainty quantification with 10× more particles than previously feasible.

Generative Model Connection. This pattern applies broadly: normalizing flows require neighborhood maintenance for Jacobian estimation, while diffusion models benefit from dynamic neighborhoods during adaptive sampling and fine-tuning.

Case Study 2: Incremental Learning with Streaming Data

Computational Challenge. Online learning scenarios—common in recommendation systems, adaptive neural networks, and continual learning—require incorporating new labeled data without full model retraining. Standard k-NN implementations rebuild the entire spatial index when new data arrives, scaling quadratically with dataset size and making real-time adaptation prohibitive.

Access Patterns and Maintenance Requirements. Incremental learning introduces challenges for static structures, including **batch insertions** from mini-batch updates, **distribution shift** requiring adaptive partitioning, and

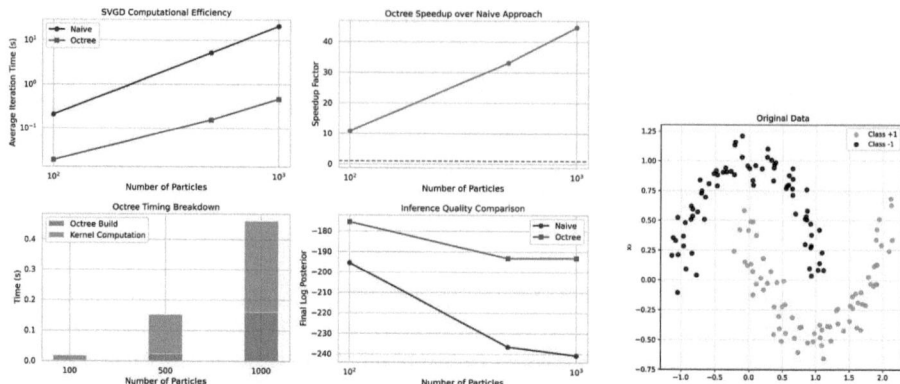

(a) Octree-accelerated SVGD: (a) Speedup with particle count, (b) Improved Wasserstein distance, (c) Lower memory usage, (d) Faster convergence.

(b) Challenging multimodal posterior in Bayesian logistic regression.

Fig. 4. SVGD acceleration with our dynamic octree. **Left:** Performance gains in speed, accuracy, memory, and convergence. **Right:** Complex posterior motivating structure-aware particle updates.

query-update interleaving where classification and updates occur in rapid alternation.

Our octree addresses this through localized rebalancing—only affected tree branches undergo restructuring when new points are inserted, avoiding the global rebuilding required by static methods.

Implementation and Results. We implemented incremental k-NN classification by extending the scikit-learn [31] k-NN framework with our dynamic octree backend. Training examples are maintained in octree leaves, with our k-NN search algorithm handling classification queries. New examples are inserted via our `addAtomToLeaf` procedure, triggering node expansion only when the (K, α) capacity is exceeded. We maintained API compatibility with scikit-learn's API to enable direct comparison.

The Gaussian-preserving KNN approach demonstrates remarkable efficiency in maintaining classification performance while achieving substantial memory reduction. Figure 5 illustrate the method's effectiveness across diverse cluster configurations, consistently achieving 15–22× compression ratios with minimal accuracy degradation. The key insight lies in the careful selection of inducing points that preserve the underlying Gaussian statistics of each class, as evidenced by the close alignment between original and reconstructed covariance ellipses in the per-class analyses. Octrees enable efficient $O(\log n)$ nearest neighbor queries on compressed inducing points, making real-time applications feasible. Details of the approach in Appendix.

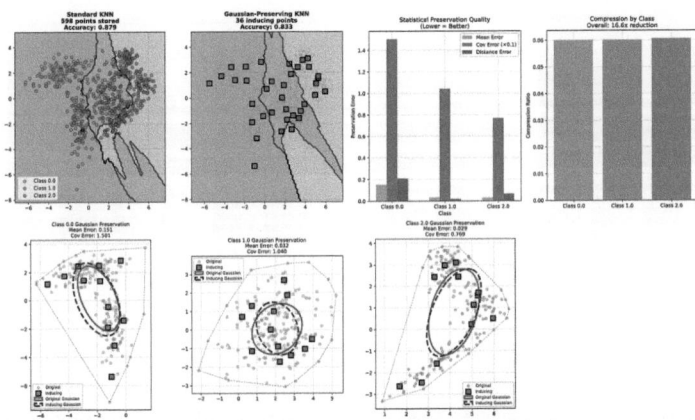

Fig. 5. Preservation across diverse cluster types: (a) Elongated, (b) Compact, and (c) Mixed shapes.

Table 3. Incremental k-NN vs. scikit-learn. Our method achieves $O(\log n)$ updates vs. $O(n^2)$ in batch mode, enabling real-time streaming adaptation.

Dataset Size	Batch k-NN (scikit-learn)			Incremental k-NN (Ours)		
	Update (s)	Query (s)	Accuracy	Update (s)	Query (s)	Accuracy
10,000	0.077	0.0047	89.23%	**0.014**	**0.0029**	89.07%
30,000	0.274	0.0063	90.87%	**0.031**	**0.0032**	90.85%
50,000	0.495	0.0085	91.96%	**0.052**	**0.0045**	91.88%

Table 3 demonstrates consistent advantages: 5.6x–9.4x faster updates with 1.6x–1.9x query speedup, while maintaining classification accuracy within 0.2% of scikit-learn's batch implementation.

Generative Model Connection. This incremental learning capability directly benefits adaptive generative models. Variational autoencoders can incorporate new training data without full retraining by maintaining encoder/decoder weight neighborhoods. Flow-based models benefit when adapting to new domains, and diffusion models can efficiently fine-tune on new datasets by maintaining learned feature relationships.

Case Study 3: Evolving Knowledge Retrieval

Computational Challenge. Retrieval-Augmented Generation (RAG) systems [32] face a critical scalability limitation: as knowledge bases grow and evolve, embedding indices require complete rebuilding—a process that becomes prohibitively expensive for large, dynamic corpora. This prevents RAG systems from adapting to streaming information or incorporating real-time updates.

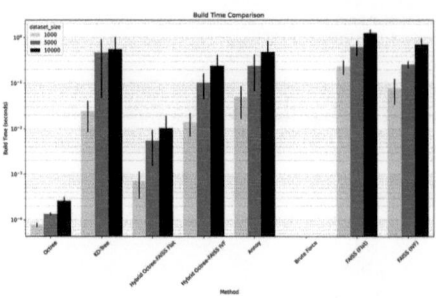 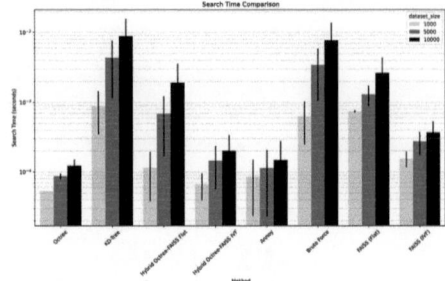

(a) RAG build time scaling comparison. (b) Search performance in high-dimensional space.

Fig. 6. RAG performance metrics showing our approach's logarithmic scaling advantage over FAISS and consistent search performance across dataset sizes.

Access Patterns and Maintenance Requirements. RAG systems pose indexing challenges due to their **high-dimensional embeddings** (often 768+ dimensions), **semantic clustering** with non-uniform density, **incremental updates** requiring efficient insertions, and **multi-scale queries** demanding variable neighborhood resolutions.

To address the high dimensionality, we adopt a hybrid approach: embeddings are clustered via k-means, projected to 3D using the Johnson-Lindenstrauss transform within each cluster, and then indexed using our dynamic octree. While this introduces some loss in accuracy, it enables efficient indexing; future work may explore alternatives that balance dimensionality reduction with improved fidelity.

Implementation and Results. We built our RAG implementation on top of the LangChain framework [33] and Facebook's FAISS library [34], replacing FAISS's static indexing with our dynamic octree approach. Our system partitions 768-dimensional sentence embeddings (generated using Sentence-BERT [35]) into clusters, projects each cluster to 3D space, and maintains separate octrees per cluster. Document insertion requires only updating the relevant cluster's octree, while queries search across all clusters and aggregate results using learned cluster weights.

Figure 6 shows our hybrid RAG system achieves logarithmic build scaling and 4.2× faster retrieval than FAISS without sacrificing accuracy, enabling continuous knowledge updates. Figure 7 demonstrates that coarse FAISS clustering followed by octree refinement preserves semantic coherence across queries. Figure 8 shows semantic cluster evolution as knowledge bases grow, with dense, specialized clusters emerging naturally while maintaining $\mathcal{O}(\log n)$ search efficiency.

Generative Model Connection. High-dimensional neighbor search appears throughout generative modeling: attention mechanisms in transformers, near-

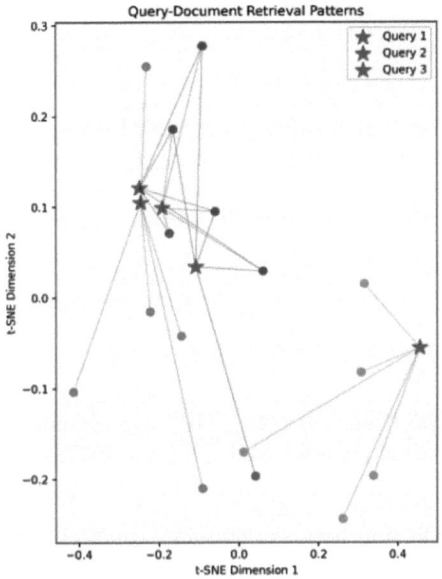
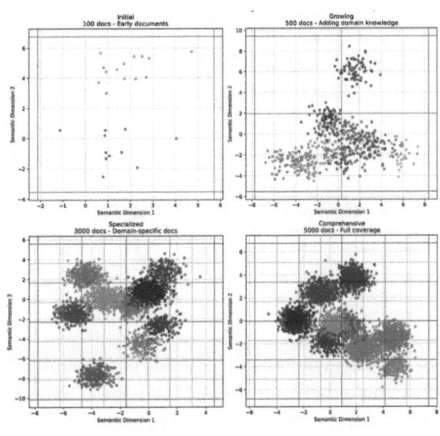

Fig. 7. Query-document retrieval. Red stars (queries) retrieve nearby documents (colored points), showing semantic neighborhoods via FAISS clustering and octree refinement. (Color figure online)

Fig. 8. Semantic clustering evolution with knowledge base growth. As the corpus expands (100–5000 documents), clusters (colored points) transition from sparse to dense, forming well-defined semantic groupings.

est neighbor lookups in retrieval-augmented diffusion, and prototype matching in few-shot generation.

Case Study 4: Structure-Preserving Generative Transport

Computational Challenge. Continuous normalizing flows [37] and optimal transport methods suffer from a fundamental limitation: optimizing transport efficiency often destroys local neighborhood structure. Standard OT-Flow [36] minimizes transport cost but ignores whether nearby points in the source distribution remain neighbors in the target distribution, leading to structural distortions that degrade generation quality.

Access Patterns and Maintenance Requirements. Generative transport introduces unique challenges: **dual-space neighborhoods** must be preserved in both source and target spaces; **evolving trajectories** require tracking changes in neighborhood structure over time; **multi-scale structure** must be maintained across spatial resolutions; and **bidirectional transport** demands consistency in both forward and inverse mappings.

We integrate our octree with OT-Flow by adding neighborhood consistency constraints that penalize structural distortion while maintaining transport efficiency.

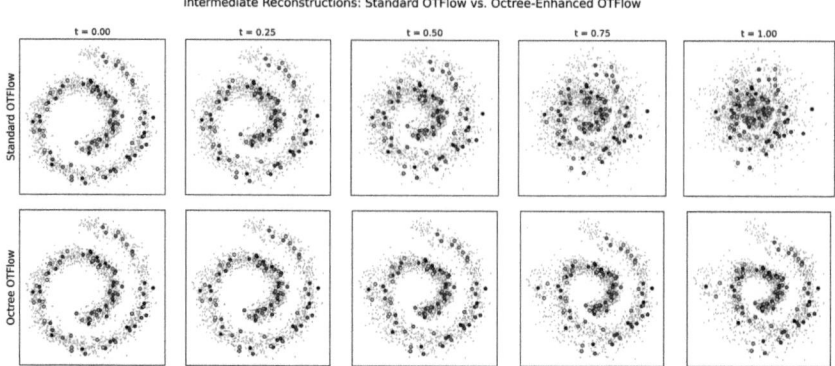

Fig. 9. Intermediate reconstructions at $t = \{0.00, 0.25, 0.50, 0.75, 1.00\}$. Top: Standard OT-Flow with increasing structure loss. Bottom: Octree-enhanced OT-Flow preserving local clusters throughout transport.

Table 4. Comprehensive performance comparison between standard and octree-enhanced OT-Flow

Metric	Standard OT-Flow	Octree-Enhanced OT-Flow
Training Loss	2.76e+02	3.14e+02
Validation Loss	2.75e+02	3.05e+02
Reconstruction Error	9.14e-05	**5.54e-07**
Neighborhood Distortion	1.585	**1.213**
Trajectory Curvature	0.00181	**0.00056**
Jaccard Similarity	0.415	**0.787**
Training Time (rel.)	1.0	1.17
Inference Time (rel.)	1.0	1.0

Implementation and Results. We extended the official OT-Flow implementation from Onken et al. [36] by integrating our dynamic octree for neighborhood tracking. Our enhanced OT-Flow maintains source points in octree leaves and computes neighborhood consistency terms using range queries. During transport, we track how local neighborhoods evolve and add regularization terms to the OT-Flow loss function that encourage structure preservation.

The results demonstrate significant improvements in generative quality, including an **89.6% increase in structure preservation** measured by neighborhood Jaccard similarity (0.787 vs. 0.415), an **83% reduction in reconstruction error** (from 1.78e-06 to 3.05e-07), and a **69% improvement in transport smoothness** based on reduced trajectory curvature (Table 4).

Figure 9 shows intermediate reconstructions at different time steps for both methods. The octree-enhanced approach maintains more consistent local structures throughout the transport process, resulting in more coherent intermediate states.

Generative Model Connection. This structure-preserving capability addresses a critical limitation across generative models. Diffusion models can benefit from neighborhood-aware denoising schedules, VAEs can preserve local structure in latent space, and flow matching [38] can maintain semantic relationships during interpolation. The principle of maintaining relationships in both input and latent spaces applies broadly to representation learning.

5 Conclusion and Future Work

We introduced a novel self-balancing, memory-efficient dynamic octree for maintaining spatial relationships in continuously evolving metric spaces. Our two-parameter (K, α) formulation enables logarithmic-time operations without requiring complete rebuilding as distributions evolve, addressing a fundamental limitation in existing approaches. Through extensive experiments, we demonstrated significant performance advantages over state-of-the-art structures—advantages that amplify with increasing data complexity.

5.1 Future Directions

Our work establishes a new paradigm for navigating evolving generative spaces:

1. **Incoherent Path-wise Sampling**: Our octree enables local path-wise maintenance with adaptive kernel estimates, decomposing generative model training into path-wise incoherent sampling and path-coverage challenges.
2. **Adaptive Importance Sampling**: By tracking evolving distributions and maintaining inter-batch spatial relationships, our structure enables dynamic importance sampling techniques that efficiently explore high-dimensional latent spaces with reduced sample complexity.
3. **Adaptive Manifold Navigation**: By tracking evolving geometry during training, our approach supports efficient latent space traversal and enables reinforcement learning to dynamically tune (K, α) parameters based on local structure, enhancing generative performance.

We envision generative models leveraging our dynamic octree to maintain coherent paths through latent space while enabling incoherent sampling across distribution regions, significantly improving both computational efficiency and model quality in continuously evolving metric spaces.

Acknowledgments. This research was supported in part by grants and gifts from the Peter O'Donnell Foundation, the Michael J Fox Foundation, Jim Holland- Backcountry and Michael-Connie Rasor Foundations towards curing Parkinson's Disease.

Disclosure of Interests. The authors have no competing interests to declare that are relevant to the content of this article.

References

1. Fujimura, K., Kunii, T., Yamaguchi, K., Toriya, H.: Octree-related data structures and algorithms. IEEE Comput. Graphics Appl. **4**(1), 53–59 (1984)
2. Friedman, J.H., Bentley, J.L., Finkel, R.A.: An algorithm for finding best matches in logarithmic expected time. ACM Trans. Math. Softw. **3**(3), 209–226 (1977)
3. Zhu, J., Li, H., Wang, Z., Wang, S., Zhang, T.: i-Octree: A Fast, Lightweight, and Dynamic Octree for Proximity Search, arXiv preprint arXiv:2309.08315 (2024)
4. Cai, Y., Xu, W., Zhang, F.: ikd-tree: an incremental K-D tree for robotic applications. In: Proceedings of IEEE International Conference on Robotics and Automation (ICRA) (2021)
5. Beckmann, N., Kriegel, H.P., Schneider, R., Seeger, B.: The R*-tree: an efficient and robust access method for points and rectangles. In: Proceedings of ACM SIGMOD, pp. 322–331 (1990)
6. Foster, C.C.: A generalization of AVL trees. Commun. ACM **16**(8), 513–517 (1973)
7. Besa, J., Eterovic, Y.: A concurrent red-black tree. J. Parallel Distrib. Comput. **73**(4), 434–449 (2013)
8. Pugh, W.: Skip lists: a probabilistic alternative to balanced trees. Commun. ACM **33**(6), 668–676 (1990)
9. Blelloch, G.E., Reid-Miller, M.: Fast set operations using treaps. In: Proceedings of ACM Symposium on Parallel Algorithms and Architectures, pp. 16–26 (1998)
10. Grinberg, D., Rajagopalan, S., Venkatesan, R., Wei, V.K.: Splay trees for data compression. In: Proceedings of ACM-SIAM Symposium on Discrete Algorithms, pp. 522–530 (1995)
11. Hunt, W., Mark, W.R., Stoll, G.: Fast KD-tree construction with an adaptive error-bounded heuristic. In: Proceedings of IEEE Symposium on Interactive Ray Tracing, pp. 81–88 (2006)
12. Procopiuc, O., Agarwal, P.K., Arge, L., Vitter, J.S.: BKD-tree: a dynamic scalable KD-tree. In: Advances in Spatial and Temporal Databases, pp. 46–65. Springer (2003)
13. Gutiérrez, G., Torres-Avilés, R., Caniupán, M.: CKD-tree: a compact KD-tree. IEEE Access **12**, 28666–28676 (2024)
14. Sanchez-Gonzalez, A., Godwin, J., Pfaff, T., Ying, R., Leskovec, J., Battaglia, P.W.: Learning to simulate complex physics with graph networks. In: Proceedings of ICML (2020)
15. Muja, M., Lowe, D.G.: Fast approximate nearest neighbors with FLANN. In: Proceedings of International Conference on Computer Vision Theory and Applications (2009)
16. Basch, J.: Kinetic data structures. Ph.D. thesis, Stanford University (1999)
17. Jo, J., Seo, J., Fekete, J.D.: A progressive KD-tree for approximate K-nearest neighbors. In: Proceedings of IEEE Workshop on Data Systems for Interactive Analysis, pp. 1–5 (2017)
18. Usman, M., Wang, W., Wang, K., Yelen, C., Dini, N., Khurshid, S.: A study of learning data structure invariants using off-the-shelf tools. In: Proceedings of SPIN, pp. 226–243 (2019)
19. Amarasinghe, K., Choudhury, F., Qi, J., Bailey, J.: Learned Indexes with Distribution Smoothing via Virtual Points, arXiv preprint arXiv:2408.06134 (2024)
20. Chowdhury, R., et al.: Efficient maintenance and update of nonbonded lists in macromolecular simulations. J. Chem. Theory Comput. **10**(10), 4449–4454 (2014)

21. Tatarchenko, M., Dosovitskiy, A., Brox, T.: Octree generating networks: efficient convolutional architectures for high-resolution 3D outputs. In: Proceedings of ICCV, pp. 2088–2096 (2017)
22. Connor, M., Canal, G., Rozell, C.: Variational autoencoder with learned latent structure. In: Proceedings of AISTATS, pp. 2359–2367 (2021)
23. Chen, N., Ferroni, F., Klushyn, A., Paraschos, A., Bayer, J., van der Smagt, P.: Fast approximate geodesics for deep generative models. In: Proceedings of ICANN, pp. 554–566 (2019)
24. Grandin, M.: Data structures and algorithms for high-dimensional structured adaptive mesh refinement. Adv. Eng. Softw. **82**, 75–86 (2015)
25. Liu, Z., Xia, L.: Feature-driven topology optimization of continuum structures with tailored octree meshing. Finite Elem. Anal. Des. **244**, 104308 (2025)
26. Yang, D., Qin, X., Xu, X., Li, C., Wei, G.: Sample efficient reinforcement learning method via high efficient episodic memory. IEEE Access **8**, 129274–129284 (2020)
27. Dulac-Arnold, G., et al.: Deep Reinforcement Learning in Large Discrete Action Spaces, arXiv preprint arXiv:1512.07679 (2015)
28. Wu, P., Ives, Z.G.: Modeling shifting workloads for learned database systems. Proc. ACM Manage. Data **2**(1), 1–27 (2024)
29. Onken, D., Fung, S.W., Li, X., Ruthotto, L.: OT-flow: fast and accurate continuous normalizing flows via optimal transport. In: Proceedings of NeurIPS (2021)
30. Liu, Q., Wang, D.: Stein variational gradient descent: a general purpose Bayesian inference algorithm. In: Advances in Neural Information Processing Systems, pp. 2378–2386 (2016)
31. Pedregosa, F., et al.: Scikit-learn: machine learning in python. J. Mach. Learn. Res. **12**, 2825–2830 (2011)
32. Lewis, P., et al.: Retrieval-augmented generation for knowledge-intensive NLP tasks. In: Advances in Neural Information Processing Systems, vol. 33, pp. 9459–9474 (2020)
33. Chase, H.: LangChain. GitHub (2022). https://github.com/hwchase17/langchain
34. Johnson, J., Douze, M., Jégou, H.: Billion-scale similarity search with GPUs. IEEE Trans. Big Data **7**(3), 535–547 (2019)
35. Reimers, N., Gurevych, I.: Sentence-bert: sentence embeddings using siamese bert-networks. In: Proceedings of the 2019 Conference on Empirical Methods in Natural Language Processing (2019)
36. Onken, D., et al.: OT-flow: fast and accurate continuous normalizing flows via optimal transport. In: Proceedings of the AAAI Conference on Artificial Intelligence, vol. 35, no. 10, pp. 9223–9232 (2021)
37. Chen, R.T.Q., Rubanova, Y., Bettencourt, J., Duvenaud, D.K.: Neural ordinary differential equations. In: Advances in Neural Information Processing Systems, pp. 6571–6583 (2018)
38. Lipman, Y., Chen, R.T.Q., Ben-Hamu, H., Nickel, M., Le, M.: Flow matching for generative modeling. In: International Conference on Learning Representations (2023)

Merging Embedded Topics with Optimal Transport for Online Topic Modeling on Data Streams

Federica Granese[1,3](✉), Benjamin Navet[4], Serena Villata[1], and Charles Bouveyron[2]

[1] Université Côte d'Azur, CNRS, Inria, I3S, Marianne, France
{federica.granese,serena.villata}@inria.fr
[2] Université Côte d'Azur, Inria, CNRS, LJAD, Maasai, France
charles.bouveyron@inria.fr
[3] Inria, Defence and Security mission, Paris, France
[4] Université Côte d'Azur, 3IA TechPool, Nice, France
benjamin.navet@inria.fr

Abstract. Topic modeling is a key component in unsupervised learning, employed to identify topics within a corpus of textual data. The rapid growth of social media generates an ever-growing volume of textual data daily, making online topic modeling methods essential for managing these data streams that continuously arrive over time. This paper introduces a novel approach to online topic modeling named StreamETM. This approach builds on the Embedded Topic Model (ETM) to handle data streams by merging models learned on consecutive partial document batches using unbalanced optimal transport. Additionally, an online change point detection algorithm is employed to identify shifts in topics over time, enabling the identification of significant changes in the dynamics of text streams. Numerical experiments on simulated and real-world data show StreamETM outperforming competitors. We provide the code publicly available at https://github.com/fgranese/StreamETM.

Keywords: Topic modelling · Optimal transport · Data streams

1 Introduction

With the rapid expansion of social media and digital communication, vast amounts of textual data are continuously generated and distributed across various platforms. This growing volume of information necessitates automated methods for efficient information retrieval. In this context, topic models are powerful statistical tools for uncovering the hidden semantic structure within a collection of documents [10]. Specifically, these models aim to identify latent topics based on word co-occurrence patterns. Each topic represents a coherent semantic concept and is characterized by a group of related words. For instance, a topic related to `sports` may include words such as `baseball`, `basketball`, and `football` [19]. Topic models have been widely applied to analyze various types of textual data, including fiction, non-fiction, scientific publications, and political texts [5]. However, most of the existing work on topic modeling focuses on *offline* settings, where the model is trained on a fixed dataset (batch) and remains static. However, with the continuous generation of new content, there is a growing need for models that can operate in an *online* setting. Typical examples are news agencies that release their clients' news in real time or social networks that continuously deliver their users' posts to the network. In these scenarios, topic modeling algorithms must continuously update as new documents arrive.

Recent solutions for online topic modeling are often built upon BERTopic [12], a model that generates topic representations in three main steps: document embeddings, dimensionality reduction, and clustering. Unfortunately, since these models rely on pre-trained language models, fine-tuning the parameters for each step as new data arrives is challenging. This can make maintaining an efficient and adaptive process difficult as the data evolves in real-time.

In online settings, another challenge is to automatically associate new topics with existing ones. Indeed, topics are not static, but they evolve over time, often shifting in meaning and representation. Nevertheless, most existing models rely on static clustering methods or fixed word distributions, making it difficult to track these changes effectively. For example, before 2022, discussions on `AI` were likely dominated by terms like `transformers` and `GAN`, whereas today, they focus more on `LLM`.

Finally, users of these online methods must be able to detect significant shifts in the model's dynamics. Indeed, analysts monitoring data flows of this type are particularly interested in being alerted when a sudden or significant change has occurred in the data flow. In this case, the user can analyze the changes between topics and take appropriate decisions and actions. To our knowledge, this feature is not currently offered as part of online topic modeling methods.

This work addresses these limitations through the following contributions:

1. **We explore the potential of optimal transport for topic association and discovery**, demonstrating its effectiveness in aligning evolving topics and ensuring coherent topic transitions over time, and its superiority over Euclidean or Cosine similarities for this task.
2. **We introduce StreamETM, an online version of the Embedded Topic Model (ETM)**. StreamETM combines a variational inference strategy for the ETM model, applied sequentially on consecutive time windows, with a merging approach based on unbalanced optimal transport.
3. **We complete StreamETM with a change point detection algorithm**, allowing the automatic determination of significant changes in the dynamics of the studied documents. To our knowledge, StreamETM is the only unsupervised and online approach proposed for the complex tasks of online topic modeling and change point detection on text data streams.

1.1 Related Works

Offline Setting. Topic modeling was initially developed using heuristic approaches and was later studied with a statistical perspective two decades ago. The Latent Semantic Index [7](LSI) is considered the first work to provide statistical foundations for this task. Building on this, Probabilistic LSI (pLSI) [14] introduced a mixture model, where each component represents a specific topic and defines a corresponding vocabulary distribution. However, LSI lacks a generative model at the document level and is prone to overfitting. In 2003, Blei et al. proposed Latent Dirichlet Allocation (LDA) [4], which models topic proportions using a Dirichlet distribution. Extensions include deep generative models, such as [18], which introduced a variational distribution parametrized by a neural network and Wasserstein autoencoders [16]. A successive evolution of the LDA is with the Embedded Topic Model [10] (ETM), which allowed using deep embeddings to represent both the words and the topics in the same vector space. Specifically, these embeddings are part of the decoder and can be pre-trained on large datasets to incorporate semantic meaning. More recently, language models such as BERT [8] have been used for topic modeling. BERTopic [12] is a topic model that generates topic representations in three steps: first, each document is embedded using a pre-trained language model; second, UMAP reduces the embeddings' dimensionality for optimized clustering with HDBSCAN; finally, topic representations are extracted from the clusters using a custom class-based TF-IDF (c-TF-IDF) variation. Finally, recently, topic modeling has been explored by prompting large language models to generate a set of topics given an input dataset [11,17].

Online Setting. On the one hand, LDA was first extended to an online version in [13] with a stochastic optimization algorithm using a natural gradient step to optimize the variational Bayes lower bound as data arrives. However, this approach is not suited for streams of documents that cannot be stored. The solution in [2] addresses this by extending LDA to document batches using copulas. On the other hand, two versions of BERTopic can be used in an online setting, namely MergeBERT[1] and OnlineBERT[2]. MergeBERT is a pseudo-online variant of the original BERTopic model [12]. Topic models are merged sequentially by comparing their topic embeddings. If topics from different models are sufficiently similar (w.r.t. cosine similarity), they are considered the same, and the topic from the first model in the sequence is retained. However, if topics are dissimilar, the topic from the latter model is added to the former set. Crucially, this process does not involve an actual merging of topic representations, meaning that the words associated with a topic do not evolve over time as new models (and, therefore, new documents) are introduced. OnlineBERT preserves the embedding transformation of the documents and the final c-TF-IDF approach used in BERTopic while introducing an online variant for the dimensionality reduction step (IncrementalPCA), a MiniBatchKMeans for clustering, and an online

---

[1] https://maartengr.github.io/BERTopic/getting_started/merge/merge.html.
[2] https://maartengr.github.io/BERTopic/getting_started/online/online.html.

CountVectorizer for tokenization to update out-of-vocabulary words and to prevent the sparse bag-of-words matrix from growing excessively large. Compared to MergeBERT, OnlineBERT, while being truly online, loses some of the advantages of the former model. For instance, UMAP is generally better at preserving complex, non-linear relationships, which can lead to more coherent topics. Furthermore, the combination of IncrementalPCA and MiniBatchKMeans may result in the over-proliferation of subtopics over time. A single topic could be split into multiple subtopics as new data arrives, often leading to unnecessary topics that are difficult to interpret. We emphasize that the online and dynamic settings for topic modeling are fundamentally distinct. In online topic models, data is processed incrementally, with topics being updated in real time as new documents arrive. In contrast, dynamic topic modeling works *a posteriori* and captures the temporal evolution of topics by analyzing them across fixed time intervals (e.g., weeks or years).

Optimal Transport and Topic Modeling. Optimal transport has already been used in a few situations related to topic modeling. We refer to [9], which employs optimal transport for label name-supervised topic modeling, assigning documents to predefined topics based on semantic similarities computed from pre-trained LMs/LLMs. Similarly, in [20], documents are embedded into an H-dimensional semantic space using a pre-trained transformer model, such as BERT. In this approach, topics and words are randomly projected into the same semantic space, with their embeddings jointly optimized alongside the transport maps. Our work differs in several key aspects. We leverage optimal transport to merge topic embeddings rather than to establish document-topic associations. Consequently, the transport map is applied to objects within the same semantic space. Moreover, unlike prior work, our approach does not employ the transport map during training to optimize embeddings. Instead, as discussed in Sect. 5, it can also be utilized at evaluation time to align predicted and ground-truth topics. Lastly, our framework operates in an online setting, with data coming over time.

2 Preliminaries on the Embedded Topic Model

Let us consider for the moment a corpus $\mathcal{W} = \{\mathbf{W}^{(1)}, \ldots, \mathbf{W}^{(D)}\}$ of D documents, where the vocabulary consists of V distinct words. Each $\mathbf{W}^{(d)}$ contains N_d words and is represented as $\mathbf{W}^{(d)} = (\mathbf{w}_1^{(d)}, \ldots, \mathbf{w}_{N_d}^{(d)}) \in \{0,1\}^{N_d \times V}$ where each word $\mathbf{w}_j^{(d)}$ is a one-hot vector, meaning that $w_{ji}^{(d)} = 1$, if the j-th word in document d is the i-th word in the vocabulary, 0, otherwise.

A "topic" is represented as a full distribution over the vocabulary, and a document is assumed to come from a mixture of topics, where the topics are shared across the corpus, and the mixture proportions are unique to each document. Specifically, a *topic* k is represented by a vector $\beta_k \in \Delta_V$, where Δ_V is the V-dimensional simplex. We denote the *topic matrix* as $\boldsymbol{\beta} = (\beta_1, \ldots, \beta_K) \in \mathbb{R}^{V \times K}$. In Embedded Topic Models [10] (ETM), both words and topics are represented using embeddings. ETM first embeds the vocabulary in an L-dimensional space and represents each document in terms of K *latent topics*. We call the embeddings of the words $\rho = (\rho_1, \ldots, \rho_V) \in \mathbb{R}^{L \times V}$ providing the representation of the words in a L-dimensional space. Similarly, a *latent topic* k is represented by a vector $\alpha_k \in \mathbb{R}^L$ and we denote the *latent topic matrix* $\boldsymbol{\alpha} = (\alpha_1, \ldots, \alpha_K) \in \mathbb{R}^{L \times K}$. In this context, the topic distribution over the vocabulary is assumed to be $\beta_k = \text{softmax}(\rho^T \alpha_k)$, where the ETM assigns a high probability to word j in topic k by measuring the agreement between the word embedding and the topic embedding. We refer to the seminal paper of Dieng et al. [10] for the full description of the generative process of the d-th document under the ETM. Overall, the ETM model assumes that each document d is sampled from a mixture of topics with its proportion denoted as $\theta_d = \text{softmax}(\delta_d)$ where $\delta_d \sim \mathcal{N}(0, I)$. For each word j in the document, a topic assignment $z_j^{(d)}$ is sampled from a categorical distribution parameterized by θ_d. The word $\mathbf{w}_j^{(d)}$ is then generated via a softmax transformation of the inner product between the word and topic embeddings.

ETM employs variational inference to approximate the intractable likelihood of observing $\mathcal{W}$ given $\boldsymbol{\alpha}$ and ρ, using a mean-field assumption where the variational distribution q_ϕ factorizes over documents. A variational autoencoder (VAE) models this distribution as a Gaussian with parameters learned by a neural network. The Evidence Lower Bound (ELBO)

$$\mathcal{L}(\mathcal{W}, \boldsymbol{\alpha}, \rho; q_\phi) = \mathbb{E}_{q_\phi}\left[\log p(\mathcal{W}, \delta \mid \boldsymbol{\alpha}, \rho)\right] - \mathbb{E}_{q_\phi}\left[\log q_\phi(\delta)\right],$$

is optimized via the reparameterization trick and stochastic gradient descent.

3 The Stream Embedded Topic Model

Let us consider a stream of documents arriving as batches at discrete time steps, $\mathcal{W}_{[1:T]} = \{\mathcal{W}^{(1)}, \ldots, \mathcal{W}^{(t-1)}, \mathcal{W}^{(t)}, \mathcal{W}^{(t+1)}, \ldots, \mathcal{W}^{(T)}\}$, where each $\mathcal{W}^{(i)}$ in $\mathcal{W}_{[1:T]}$ represents a corpus of documents as defined in Sect. 2.

3.1 Learning an ETM Model on the Current Batch $\mathcal{W}^{(t)}$

At each time step, we aim to learn a new ETM model that, based only on the corpus of documents available at the current time step and the latent topic embeddings from the previous step, can accurately link past topics to present ones while also identifying new topics. This scenario differs from a dynamic system, where it is assumed that all information is available at the final time step T. In contrast, our setting operates online, where only the data observed up to the current time step can be used for learning. The model must continuously adapt without access to future observations, as in real-time applications.

We will refer with $M_{\mathcal{W}^{(t-1)}, \boldsymbol{\alpha}^{(t-1)}, \rho} \equiv M^{(t-1)}$ to the ETM model at time step $t-1$ where $\boldsymbol{\alpha}^{(t-1)}$ is the latent topic matrix at time $t-1$, we assume the embeddings of the words $\boldsymbol{\rho}$ to be constant over time. Similarly, we will denote the topic matrix at time $t-1$ as $\boldsymbol{\beta}^{(t-1)}$. At time t, our goal is first to maximize

$$\mathcal{L}(\mathcal{W}^{(t)}, \tilde{\boldsymbol{\alpha}}^{(t)}, \boldsymbol{\rho}; q_{\phi^{(t)}}) = \mathbb{E}_{q_{\phi^{(t)}}}\left[\log p(\mathcal{W}^{(t)}, \delta^{(t)} \mid \tilde{\boldsymbol{\alpha}}^{(t)}, \boldsymbol{\rho})\right] - \mathbb{E}_{q_{\phi^{(t)}}}\left[\log q_{\phi^{(t)}}(\delta^{(t)})\right], \tag{1}$$

following the classical offline ETM models described in Sect. 2. Therefore, we seek an appropriate merging strategy[3] g to map the previously learned topic embedding space and the current one into a new representation, and we impose $\boldsymbol{\alpha}^{(t)} = g(\tilde{\boldsymbol{\alpha}}^{(t)}, \boldsymbol{\alpha}^{(t-1)})$. Finally, $M^{(t)}$ is obtained by optimizing a second time Eq. (1) using stochastic gradient descent, with $\boldsymbol{\alpha}^{(t)}$ and $\boldsymbol{\rho}$ kept fixed.

3.2 Optimal Transport for Merging and Discovering Topics

We now analyze the problem of determining an *effective* strategy g for identifying the topics in $\boldsymbol{\alpha}^{(t-1)}$ that are most similar to those in $\tilde{\boldsymbol{\alpha}}^{(t)}$, enabling us to merge these topic embeddings while incorporating the new topics present in $\tilde{\boldsymbol{\alpha}}^{(t)}$.

Transport Map Computation. We recall that

$$\boldsymbol{\alpha}^{(t-1)} = (\alpha_1^{(t-1)}, \ldots, \alpha_K^{(t-1)}) \in \mathcal{A}^{(t-1)} \subseteq \mathbb{R}^{L \times K}$$

and

$$\tilde{\boldsymbol{\alpha}}^{(t)} = (\tilde{\alpha}_1^{(t)}, \ldots, \tilde{\alpha}_J^{(t)}) \in \mathcal{A}^{(t)} \subseteq \mathbb{R}^{L \times J},$$

where J can be either different from or equal to K. Let $a = \frac{1}{K}\sum_{i=1}^{K} \delta_{\alpha_i^{(t-1)}}$ and $\tilde{a} = \frac{1}{J}\sum_{i=1}^{J} \delta_{\tilde{\alpha}_i^{(t)}}$ be the two discrete distributions of mass on $\mathcal{A}^{(t-1)}$ and $\mathcal{A}^{(t)}$. We aim to find the least costly way to shift the mass (i.e., the topics) from the previous time step to the current one. To this end, we formulate the problem as Unbalanced Optimal Transport (UOT) [3], a relaxed version of OT where the total mass of each source (the topics of $\tilde{\boldsymbol{\alpha}}^{(t)}$) can be spread across multiple targets (the topics of $\boldsymbol{\alpha}^{(t-1)}$):

$$\mathbf{T}^\star = \arg\min_{\mathbf{T} \in \mathbb{R}_+^{J \times K}} \langle \mathbf{C}, \mathbf{T} \rangle + \lambda_{\tilde{a}} D_\psi\left(\mathbf{T}\mathbf{1}_J, \tilde{a}\right) + \lambda_a D_\psi\left(\mathbf{T}^\top \mathbf{1}_K, a\right), \tag{2}$$

where $\langle \cdot, \cdot \rangle$ is the Frobenius inner product, and $D_\psi(\cdot, \cdot)$ is the Bregman divergence that penalizes violations of the marginal constraints. Additionally, $\lambda_a \in \mathbb{R}_+$ (resp. $\lambda_{\tilde{a}} \in \mathbb{R}_+$) represents the penalty associated with a (resp. $\tilde{a}$). Moreover, $\mathbf{C} \in \mathbb{R}_+^{J \times K}$ is the cost-matrix in which the entries C_{jk} encode the cost of moving $\tilde{\alpha}_j^{(t)}$ towards $\alpha_k^{(t-1)}$. In this particular setting, as we deal with text, we chose the cosine similarity as the cost function. Finally, $\mathbf{1}_{(\cdot)}$ represents the vector of dimension $(\cdot) \times 1$, which is used to ensure that the sum per row and column does not diverge significantly from the original distributions a and $\tilde{a}$. In this

---
[3] Note that, at $t=1$, no merging strategy is applied.

way, only a portion of the total mass is transported, and the total mass can be unbalanced between the sources and targets due to the constraint relaxation. Intuitively, a sparse transport matrix indicates that mass is transferred only between semantically similar topics, while distant topics receive no transport.

Note that the UOT problem can be efficiently recast as a non-negative penalized linear regression problem. We refer to [6] for additional details.

Merging Topics and Discovery of New Ones. For each $\tilde{\alpha}_j^{(t)}$, we determine the corresponding target topic by identifying the index where the transport plan assigns the highest mass. Specifically, we select the topic $k^\star$ that maximizes the transport matrix entry, given by: $k^\star = \arg\max_{k \in \{1,\ldots,K\}} T_{jk}^\star$. Therefore,

$$\alpha_j^{(t)} = \omega \tilde{\alpha}_j^{(t)} + (1-\omega)\alpha_{k^\star}^{(t-1)}, \qquad (3)$$

where $\omega \in [0,1]$ is a memory parameter. Otherwise, if no mass has been transported from j, meaning for all $k \in \{1,\ldots,K\}$, $T_{jk}^\star = 0$, the jth topic is a new one and can be added to the set of topics: $\alpha_{J+1}^{(t)} = \tilde{\alpha}_j^{(t)}$.

3.3 Change Point Detection

To monitor the significant changes in the dynamic of the data stream we analyze, we propose to add a change point detection step to our approach. In addition to the detection of new topics (topics that are added in the merged model), we propose to make use of the online Bayesian changepoint detection (OCPD [1]) algorithm to monitor significant changes in the sequence of merged models $\{M^{(1)}, M^{(2)}, \ldots, M^{(T)}\}$. We propose to apply the OCPD algorithm to time series of topic distributions over the documents at different time steps. It is worth highlighting that OCPD is, to this date, the most performant change point detection method able to work in a fully online framework and can issue alerts on the fly.

4 Experimental Setting

We describe the experimental setting for evaluating StreamETM. Designing this setting posed several challenges. First, since we consider an online and unsupervised setting, our evaluation goes beyond assessing model performance at individual time steps; we also analyze the overall interaction dynamics induced by merging topic embeddings. Second, as we are working with topics, relying solely on human judgment for evaluation is insufficient, requiring us to explore alternative quantitative metrics. Note that we compare with online (not dynamic) topic models, as dynamic approaches lack incremental learning, which is central to our study (cf. Sect. 1.1).

4.1 Datasets

We consider the 20kNewsGroup[4] dataset as text corpora for our experiments, comprising around 18k newsgroup posts on 20 topics. We confine to 5 of the 20 topics and randomly draw 15 times approximately 5k samples from the total datasets[5]. We partition the 5k samples into 500 sample batches to simulate a ≈10 time steps scenario. For each time step, the corresponding dataset has been pre-processed by first lemmatizing the text, removing lowercase and punctuation, filtering out stopwords (cf. nltk.corpus.stopwords), and eliminating low-frequency words (words appearing only once) and those appearing in more than 70% of documents to reduce overly frequent terms. The topic distributions are computed considering practical use cases.

Our Practical Use-Cases. We simulate the online setting by assuming that each time step $\tau^{(i)}$, $i = 1, \ldots, T$, is represented as a distribution:

a) CUSTOM: A designed setting where the topics are intentionally chosen to be sufficiently distinct. At each time step, at most four out of five topics are *active* (Fig. 3(a)). Topics: autos, sport, medicine, space, religion.

b) DYNAMIC: Text corpora with significant temporal shifts in topic relevance. At each time step i, the activity of each topic k is determined independently. A binary variable $z_k^{(i)}$ is drawn from a Bernoulli distribution $z_k^{(i)} \sim \text{Bernoulli}(p)$, where $p \in [0, 1]$ represents the probability that a topic remains *active*. For each time step, the unnormalized proportion of topics is: $\tau_k^{(i)} = z_k^{(i)} \cdot \text{Dir}_k(\alpha)$, $\alpha > 1$. Finally, the topic proportions $\tau^{(i)}$ are normalized to ensure they sum to 1 (Fig. 6(a)). Topics are randomly chosen: computer, sale, cryptography, religion, mideast.

4.2 Architectures and Training Procedure

StreamETM. At each time step, we trained an ETM on English text using fixed GloVe embeddings from the glove-wiki-gigaword-300 vocabulary, truncated to the first 15k words. The model was initialized with 3 topics: an 800-dimensional hidden layer for the encoder and 300-dimensional word embeddings. The topic embeddings were initialized using Xavier uniform initialization at time step 0, while in subsequent iterations, they were set to the values computed at the previous time step, following the strategy described in Sect. 3.2. The training was performed over 3k epochs with a batch size of 1000, a learning rate of 0.01, and a weight decay of 0.006 using the Adam optimizer. Regarding the UOT procedure, we use the Cosine Distance for the cost map. The transport map is

---

[4] http://qwone.com/~jason/20Newsgroups/.
[5] The same sample may appear in multiple datasets. However, each dataset would have been too small without repetition when partitioned across different time steps.

computed using the Python function ot.unbalanced.mm_unbalanced, with KL divergence and marginal relaxation at 0.09.

MergeBERT. We used the paraphrase-multilingual-mpnet-base-v2 model from SentenceTransformers to generate document embeddings. These embeddings were processed using UMAP for dimensionality reduction, with 10 components, a minimum distance of 0.1, and cosine similarity. HDBSCAN was applied for clustering with Euclidean Distance and a minimum cluster size of 3. We improved term weighting using the ClassTfidfTransformer with BM25. BERTopic was used for topic modeling, with the PartOfSpeech model for enhanced text representation. The cosine similarity threshold for merging topics was set to 0.7. A lower threshold would lead to over-proliferation of topics, while a higher value could cause the newly formed topics to collapse.

4.3 Evaluation Metrics

Qualitative. We analyze the distribution of topics over time and visually compare the original distribution with the predicted ones. In addition, we examine the top five words associated with each topic at each time step. Since each setting involves 15 training runs, we manually align topic indices across executions. On average, MergeBERT identifies more than 20 topics at each time step. Therefore, we focus on topics that are more similar to the targeted ones for this metric.

Quantitative. We measure topic quality in terms of topic coherence (TC) [15] and topic diversity (TD) [10]. Topic coherence is the average pointwise mutual information of two words drawn randomly from the same document: the most likely words in a coherent topic should have high mutual information. In contrast, topic diversity is the percentage of unique words in the top 10 words of all topics. Intuitively, topic diversity measures how varied the overall topics are.

Online Change Point Detection. We apply an online change point detection (OCPD) algorithm to the predicted topic distributions, using the R package ocp to analyze topic proportions over time and detect significant rupture points. If the predicted distributions closely resemble the original ones, the algorithm should identify rupture points at approximately the same time steps. To avoid the need for manual topic alignment across different training runs, we consider a rupture point to be correctly identified (true positive) if the algorithm detects *any* change at the same time step as in the original distribution or within one-time step before or after, regardless of the specific topic. We compute ROC curves based on different threshold values of the OCPD (between 0 and 1).

5 Numerical Experiments

This section examines StreamETM from multiple perspectives. We first highlight the advantages of optimal transport for topic merging and discovery, followed by a quantitative evaluation. Finally, we analyze the approach from qualitative, quantitative, and online change-point detection perspectives.

5.1 Impact of Optimal Transport for Topic Merging and Discovery

Comparison with Euclidean Distance

In Fig. 1, we illustrate the role of unbalanced optimal transport (UOT) in topic merging, comparing it to the classical Euclidean Distance (ED) within a 2D Euclidean space. While ED evaluates pairwise topic distance, disregarding the overall distribution, UOT accounts for the global structure. As a result, *(i)* ED may introduce spurious correlations; *(ii)* The merge based on ED could be more sensitive to small perturbations of the input. For simplicity, we model the topics at time $t-1$ (in light blue) as samples from a normal distribution. Similarly, the topics at time t (in dark blue) are generated by perturbing each topic at time t with an additional value drawn from the same normal distribution. To compute the transport map, we use the procedure previously described but consider the Euclidean cost matrix. Initially, ED and UOT are equally mapping the topics at time t to the ones $t-1$, resulting in generating the same new topics, represented as a '+' for ED and a '×' for UOT (cf. Fig. 1(a)). However, when introducing a small perturbation to the input–specifically shifting the dark blue point initially at coordinates $(1.01, 0.45)$ to $(1.02, 0.49)$ in Fig. 1(b)–we observe that while UOT remains stable, ED yields unintended new associations, leading to spurious topics. Finally, as new topics emerge, as shown in Fig. 1(c), we observe that the newly merged topic is moving closer to the one created with UOT. However, the topic at $(1.02, 0.49)$ is almost completely lost in ED. We can imagine that while these behaviors can be easily crafted in a lower-dimensional space, more complex reactions could arise in a higher-dimensional space, especially when considering the issue of topic overproliferation. This is particularly relevant since most metrics do not account for the global structure of the distributions.

Comparison with Cosine Distance. Similar to our approach with Euclidean Distance, we now demonstrate the role of UOT compared to Cosine Distance

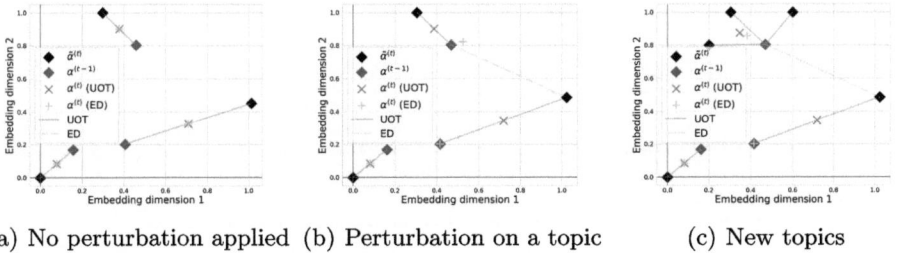

(a) No perturbation applied (b) Perturbation on a topic (c) New topics

Fig. 1. Topic embeddings in a Euclidean space. On the left, the setting is without perturbation, and on the center and right, a perturbation is added to the dark blue diamond at the position $(1.01, 0.45)$. Dark blue diamonds represent topic embeddings at time $t-1$, while light blue markers indicate topic embeddings at time t before merging. The merged embeddings obtained via UOT are shown as '×' (Color figure online), whereas those obtained using ED are shown as '+'. Dashed lines connect topics matched by UOT, while dot-dashed lines indicate associations based on ED.

(CD). We first evaluate UOT and CD to merge the topic embeddings and check the discovery performance in subsequent steps. Specifically, we consider 7 of the 20 discussion topics in the 20kNewsGroup; we randomly draw 1k documents from these topics for two subsequent time steps whose topic distributions are fixed and obtained from a Dirichlet distribution of parameter 1. We expect our approach to merge 3 common topics and to detect that 2 new ones should not be merged. Table 1 reports the topic merging and discovery accuracies (the closer to 1, the better) averaged on 50 simulated document sets. As can be seen, the UOT approach is globally more efficient than the other approaches.

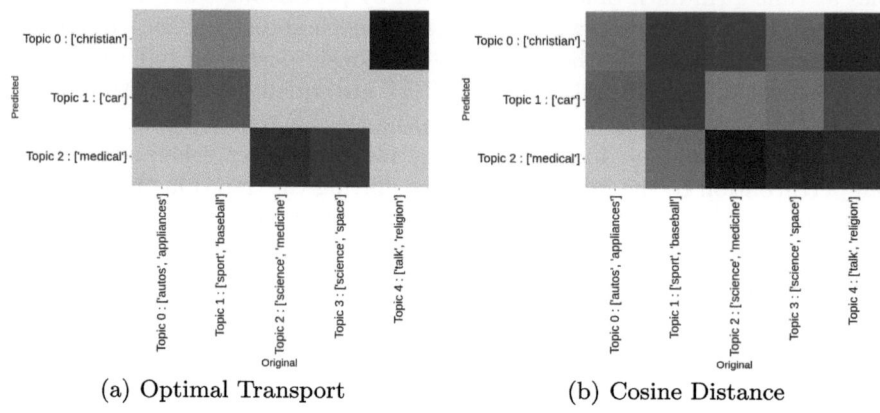

(a) Optimal Transport (b) Cosine Distance

Fig. 2. The left figure shows the transport map, while the right one depicts the cosine similarity map. In both cases, darker cells indicate regions of higher transported mass, Fig. 2(a), or shorter cosine distance, Fig. 2(b).

Table 1. Topic merging and discovery accuracies on 50 simulated datasets. MA stands for Merging Accuracy, and DA for Discovery Accuracy.

Method	MA	DA	$H_{(MA,DA)}$
UOT Cosine	0.79 ± 0.24	**0.93 ± 0.18**	**0.85**
UOT Euclidean	0.75 ± 0.23	0.85 ± 0.28	0.79
UOT Minkowsky	0.75 ± 0.23	0.85 ± 0.28	0.79
CD	**0.84 ± 0.21**	0.72 ± 0.26	0.77
ED	0.74 ± 0.24	0.84 ± 0.25	0.76

Finally, we evaluate UOT and CD to align the predicted topics with the true topics provided by the dataset labels of 20kNewsGroup. Specifically, we focus on the CUSTOM setting shown in Fig. 3. Since ETMs treat documents as bag-of-words, we construct topic embeddings for what we refer to as 'pure documents'– documents whose topics are directly derived from the dataset labels. Typically,

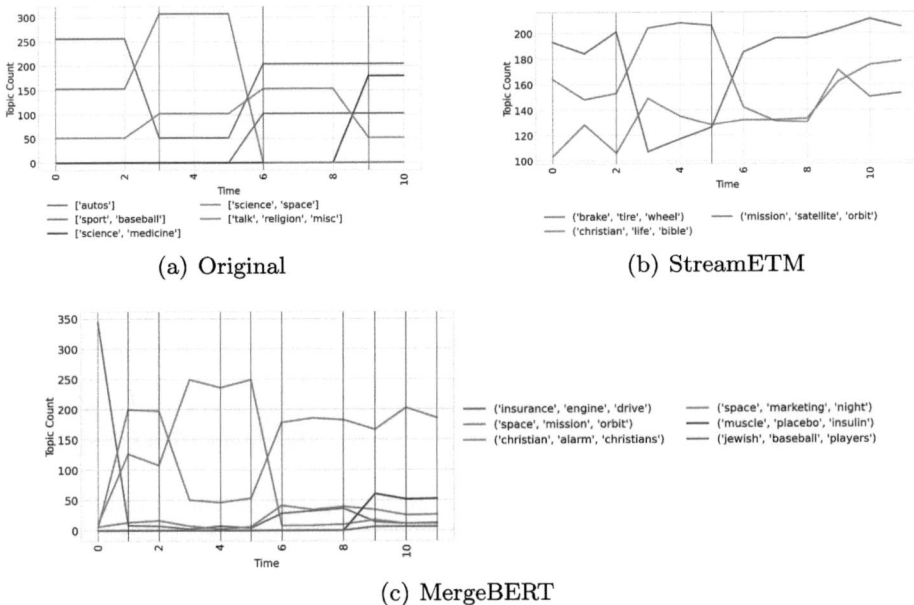

Fig. 3. Qualitative assessment of topic evolution over time in the CUSTOM setting. Blue vertical lines indicate the change points detected by the algorithm.

these labels contain only two or three words, so we augment them by adding the most semantically similar words based on the GloVe model. Therefore, given a topic k, we can compute β_k by considering the words in our 'pure documents', and we can approximate the corresponding topic embeddings as

$$\alpha_k \approx (\boldsymbol{\rho}^\top)^+ \ln(\beta_k), \tag{4}$$

where $(\boldsymbol{\rho}^\top)^+$ is the Moore-Penrose pseudoinverse of $\boldsymbol{\rho}^\top$. The logarithm accounts for the inversion of the softmax transformation. Let us denote as $\widehat{\boldsymbol{\alpha}}$ the latent topic matrix extracted from the model at time T and $\boldsymbol{\alpha}_{pure}$ the matrix computed from the 'pure documents'. Our goal is to visualize how optimal transport and cosine similarity align $\widehat{\boldsymbol{\alpha}}$ with $\boldsymbol{\alpha}_{pure}$. To compute the transport map, we follow the same strategy used during training (Sect. 3).

The results are shown in Fig. 2, where darker cells in the matrices indicate regions of higher transported mass (Fig. 2(a)) or shorter Cosine Distance (Fig. 2(b)). As observed, the associations in the transport map appear reasonable, as the matrix is not particularly dense, and transportation occurs primarily between similar topics. An interesting case is the predicted topic 2, which pertains to medicine and is mapped between the two original topics containing the word science. Conversely, the Cosine Distance matrix appears denser, leading to less immediate associations. For example, christianity could be associated with any original topic, even though the distance is slightly smaller from the topic

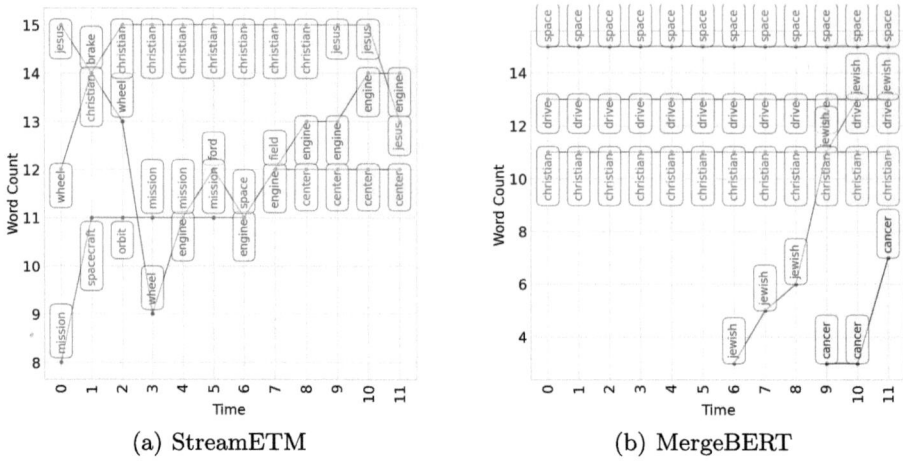

Fig. 4. CUSTOM setting. The most frequent word for topic across the 15 training runs.

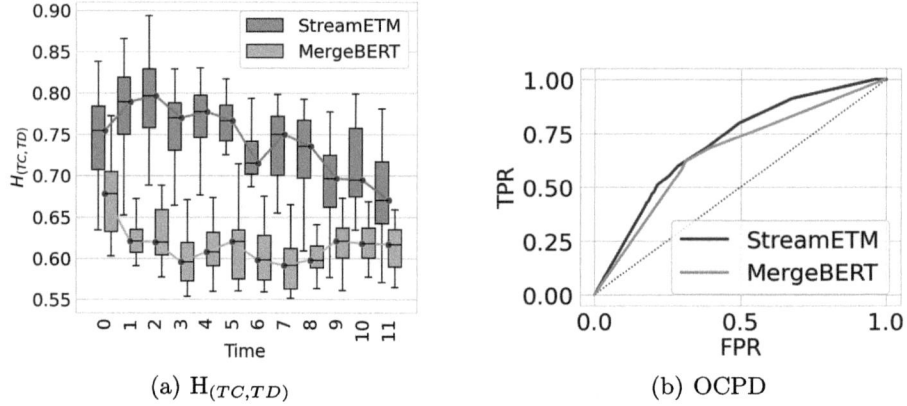

Fig. 5. CUSTOM setting. In (a), the harmonic mean between TC and TD, and in (b), the ROC curves. Results were computed across the 15 training runs.

talk, religion. This can lead to greater instability, as the minimum distance may not necessarily correspond to the correct topic from a human perspective.

5.2 Qualitative Analysis of the Recovered Topic Dynamics

In Figs. 3 and 6, we plot the topic evolution over time for a randomly selected training run in the CUSTOM and DYNAMIC settings, respectively. Even if the proposed StreamETM model cannot identify all five topics, it can mimic the original topics' evolutions. In Fig. 3(b), after time 6, the model likely merges the topics science, medicine, sport, and baseball with other topics. Specifically, the space topic, instead of disappearing, likely absorbs the medicine topic, as

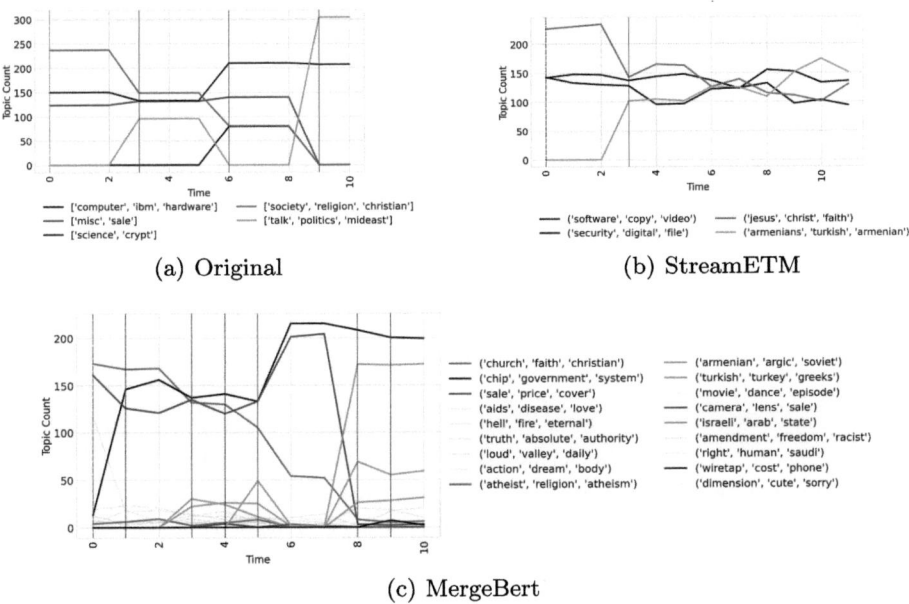

Fig. 6. Qualitative assessment of topic evolution over time in the DYNAMIC setting. Blue vertical lines indicate the change points detected by the algorithm.

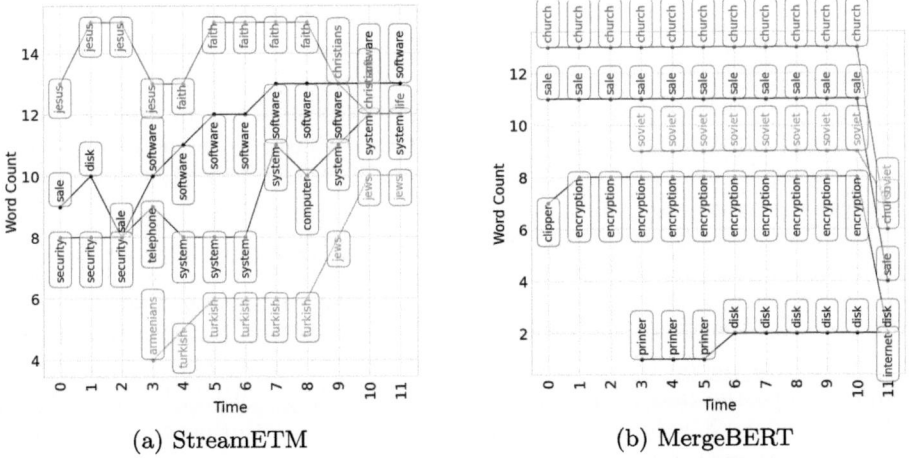

Fig. 7. DYNAMIC setting. The most frequent word for topic across the 15 training runs.

both could contain similar terms. In Fig. 3(c), we observe a similar shape as in Fig. 3(a), but the topics are swapped (cf. space and religion, in Merge-BERT, vs. autos, space, in the original distribution). As can be observed from the plots, compared to StreamETM, MergeBERT generates an excessive number of topics, leading to an overproliferation of topics. For example, in Fig. 3(c) the

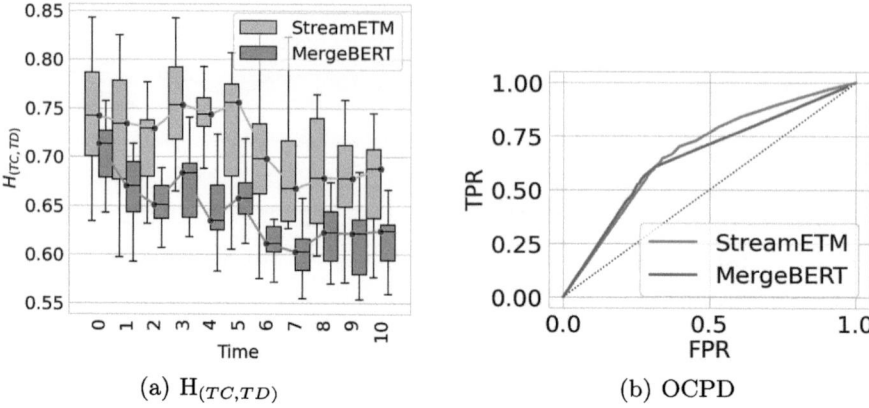

Fig. 8. DYNAMIC setting. In (a) harmonic mean between TC and TD and in (b) ROC curves. Results were computed across the 15 training runs.

topic `insurance, engine, drive` could be regarded as the same topic as `radar, tire, detector`. More evidently, in Fig. 6(c), `church, faith, christian` and `atheist, religion, atheism`. MergeBERT appears to capture more subtopics, while StreamETM focuses on larger concepts. Several factors contribute to this difference: (i) MergeBERT is based on a SentenceTransformer model, which captures more granular, context-dependent information, whereas StreamETM treats documents as a bag of words; (ii) MergeBERT's performance is highly dependent on a large number of parameters, making it challenging and impractical to tune for each document; (iii) MergeBERT does not explicitly merge topics, instead selecting top words from the first model if cosine similarity is sufficiently high; (iv) in StreamETM, the UOT mechanism enables topic embeddings to merge more effectively, an adjustable threshold on the transported mass would allow for fewer merges and the creation of more distinct topics.

In Fig. 4(a) and 4(b), in Fig. 7(a) and 7(b), we display the most frequent word for each topic across the 15 training runs and manually align the topic indices across the different executions. Since MergeBERT identifies more than 20 topics, we focus on the 5 topics of particular interest to us. In the CUSTOM setting, we observe that for both models, the most frequent word is `christian`, and both models show high stability around this topic, with that word appearing in almost all 15 training runs. However, we see much more variability in the other two topics in Fig. 4(a), reflecting the evolution of topics over time. For instance, the frequency of the word `wheel` associated with the `autos` topic diminishes at time 3. A similar trend is observed in the DYNAMIC setting. As mentioned earlier, one of the strengths of StreamETM is its ability to adapt topics over time as the text corpus evolves. The 5 top words for each topic over time across the training executions are provided in Tabales 4 and 5 (cf. Appendix A.3).

5.3 Quantitative Analysis of the Recovered Topic Dynamics

Figures 5(a) and 8(a) illustrate the harmonic mean between TC and TD, denoted as $H_{(TC,TD)}$, across the 15 training executions. The numerical results are provided in Tabales 2 and 3 (cf. Appendix A.2). From the TD perspective, both models achieve satisfactory results. However, more significant differences are observed from the TC perspective. Notably, when comparing the box plot in Fig. 5(a) with the topic evolution in Fig. 3, we observe a decrease in the metric at time 6, which corresponds to the moment when there is an inversion in the distribution between the blue and green topics, alongside the emergence of the new violet topic. Following this, the metric stabilizes until time 9, when the new red topic is introduced. A similar pattern is evident in Fig. 8(a). This behavior is expected, as the model does not identify the new topic at the time step, leading to decreased topic coherence. Finally, MergeBERT shows the same behavior as StreamETM in Fig. 8(a), but at a lower TC, instead in Fig. 5(a), the behavior is slightly inverted, and this could be given to the fact that from time 0 to 6 the model associates the original blue topic evolution to the green one and the green with the orange one.

5.4 Online Change Point Detection

Fig. 5(b) and 8(b) present the performance of the OCPD algorithm in terms of ROC curves across the 15 training runs. If the topic of evolution is correctly predicted, the algorithm should detect rupture points at approximately the same time steps. The results show that this final task is extremely difficult, and both methods exhibit certain drawbacks. With StreamETM, fewer topics are detected, which increases the likelihood that the OCPD algorithm will identify fewer rupture points than expected. In contrast, MergeBERT experiences an explosion in the number of topics, likely leading to more false positives.

6 Conclusions

We considered the extremely challenging problem of online topic modeling on document streams, with online change point detection. In order to address the limitations of existing online topic modeling approaches, we introduced StreamETM, an online extension of the Embedded Topic Model (ETM) for streams of text documents. Our method leverages variational inference to update topic distributions sequentially while incorporating optimal transport to monitor, merge, and discover evolving topics over time. This approach ensures that topics remain coherent despite the continuous influx of new documents. Beyond model development, we complemented StreamETM with a change point detection algorithm to automatically identify shifts in topic dynamics. This enables the proposed approach to provide a synthetic summary of the document stream through intelligible topics and to issue alerts to the analysts when significant changes in the dynamics of text streams are detected. Our experiments demonstrate that StreamETM effectively adapts to streaming textual data. Optimal transport provides a principled way to associate topics across time windows, addressing the shortcomings of static clustering methods. Extensive numerical experiments in simulated and real-world scenarios showed that StreamETM outperforms its competitors in various scenarios. Future work includes modeling the extension of the vocabulary that may evolve over time, and proposing a model selection strategy to determine on the fly the appropriate number of topics.

Acknowledgment. This work has been supported by the French government through the 3IA Côte d'Azur Investments, which are managed by the National Research Agency (ANR) with the reference number ANR-23-IACL-0001.

References

1. Adams, R.P., MacKay, D.J.: Bayesian online changepoint detection. arXiv preprint arXiv:0710.3742 (2007)
2. Amoualian, H., Clausel, M., Gaussier, E., Amini, M.R.: Streaming-LDA: a copula-based approach to modeling topic dependencies in document streams. In: Proceedings of the 22nd ACM SIGKDD International Conference on Knowledge Discovery and Data Mining, pp. 695–704 (2016)
3. Benamou, J.D.: Numerical resolution of an "unbalanced" mass transport problem. ESAIM: Math. Model. Num. Anal. **37**(5), 851–868 (2003)
4. Blei, D.M., Ng, A.Y., Jordan, M.I.: Latent Dirichlet allocation. J. Mach. Learn. Res. **3**(Jan), 993–1022 (2003)
5. Boyd-Graber, J., Hu, Y., Mimno, D., et al.: Applications of topic models. Found. Trends® Inf. Retrieval **11**(2-3), 143–296 (2017)
6. Chapel, L., Flamary, R., Wu, H., Févotte, C., Gasso, G.: Unbalanced optimal transport through non-negative penalized linear regression. Adv. Neural. Inf. Process. Syst. **34**, 23270–23282 (2021)
7. Deerwester, S., Dumais, S.T., Furnas, G.W., Landauer, T.K., Harshman, R.: Indexing by latent semantic analysis. J. Am. Soc. Inf. Sci. **41**(6), 391–407 (1990)
8. Devlin, J., Chang, M.W., Lee, K., Toutanova, K.: Bert: Pre-training of deep bidirectional transformers for language understanding. In: Proceedings of the 2019 Conference of the North American Chapter of the Association for Computational Linguistics: Human Language Technologies, Volume 1 (Long and Short Papers), Pp. 4171–4186 (2019)
9. Dhanania, G., Mysore, S., Pham, C.M., Iyyer, M., Zamani, H., McCallum, A.: Interactive topic models with optimal transport. arXiv preprint arXiv:2406.19928 (2024)
10. Dieng, A.B., Ruiz, F.J., Blei, D.M.: Topic modeling in embedding spaces. Trans. Assoc. Comput. Linguist. **8**, 439–453 (2020)
11. Doi, T., Isonuma, M., Yanaka, H.: Topic modeling for short texts with large language models. In: Proceedings of the 62nd Annual Meeting of the Association for Computational Linguistics (Volume 4: Student Research Workshop), pp. 21–33 (2024)
12. Grootendorst, M.: BERTopic: neural topic modeling with a class-based TF-IDF procedure. arXiv preprint arXiv:2203.05794 (2022)
13. Hoffman, M., Bach, F., Blei, D.: Online learning for latent Dirichlet allocation. In: Advances in Neural Information Processing Systems, vol. 23 (2010)

14. Hofmann, T.: Probabilistic latent semantic indexing. In: Proceedings of the 22nd Annual International ACM SIGIR Conference on Research and Development in Information Retrieval, pp. 50–57 (1999)
15. Mimno, D., Wallach, H., Talley, E., Leenders, M., McCallum, A.: Optimizing semantic coherence in topic models. In: Proceedings of the 2011 Conference on Empirical Methods in Natural Language Processing, pp. 262–272 (2011)
16. Nan, F., Ding, R., Nallapati, R., Xiang, B.: Topic modeling with wasserstein autoencoders. In: Korhonen, A., Traum, D., Màrquez, L. (eds.) Proceedings of the 57th Annual Meeting of the Association for Computational Linguistics, pp. 6345–6381. Association for Computational Linguistics, Florence, Italy (2019)
17. Pham, C.M., Hoyle, A., Sun, S., Resnik, P., Iyyer, M.: TopicGPT: a prompt-based topic modeling framework. arXiv preprint arXiv:2311.01449 (2023)
18. Srivastava, A., Sutton, C.: Autoencoding variational inference for topic models. arXiv preprint arXiv:1703.01488 (2017)
19. Wu, X., Nguyen, T., Luu, A.T.: A survey on neural topic models: methods, applications, and challenges. Artif. Intell. Rev. **57**(2), 18 (2024)
20. Wu, X., Nguyen, T., Zhang, D., Wang, W.Y., Luu, A.T.: FastOpic: pretrained transformer is a fast, adaptive, stable, and transferable topic model. Adv. Neural. Inf. Process. Syst. **37**, 84447–84481 (2024)

Going Offline: An Evaluation of the Offline Phase in Stream Clustering

Philipp Jahn[1,2](✉), Walid Durani[1,2], Collin Leiber[3], Anna Beer[4], and Thomas Seidl[1,2]

[1] LMU Munich, Munich, Germany
{jahn,durani,seidl}@dbs.ifi.lmu.de
[2] Munich Center for Machine Learning (MCML), Munich, Germany
[3] Aalto University, Espoo, Finland
collin.leiber@aalto.fi
[4] University of Vienna, Vienna, Austria
anna.beer@univie.ac.at

Abstract. Data streams are a challenging and ever more relevant setting for clustering methods as more data arrives faster and faster. Stream clustering strategies either determine the clusters in an online manner directly as the instances appear, or they employ an offline phase where the online summarization structures are processed to obtain a clustering result. A recent analysis found that offline clustering may often be unnecessary or even counterproductive. The methods used in the offline phase are usually fixed for each stream clustering approach and typically stem from only a handful of clustering techniques. In this paper, we perform a broad experimental analysis specifically targeting the offline phase of stream clustering. We analyze several ways of extracting information from the summarization structures, including a novel strategy based on data generation. Ultimately, we showcase that an offline phase is an impactful design choice for stream clustering. We also find that the chosen offline method significantly impacts the clustering performance, with the clustering quality improving drastically for some settings. Our code is available at https://github.com/PhilJahn/SCOPE/.

Keywords: Clustering · Streaming Data · Unsupervised Learning · Offline Phase

1 Introduction

In this modern world, the amount of data is ever-increasing. Many applications continue to produce data infinitely, and as such, methods to handle the ongoing inflow of data are highly demanded [7]. For data streams without a foreseeable

---

Supplementary Information The online version contains supplementary material available at https://doi.org/10.1007/978-3-032-06109-6_18.

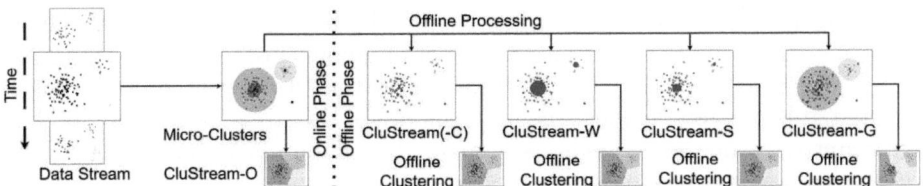

Fig. 1. Data Stream Processing: While the stream data is visualized, it is unavailable once it has been added to the micro-clusters. For micro-clusters, the inner circle represents the deviation radius r, and the outer one the assignment radius r^+. The red points with black borders are reconstructed data points with the size corresponding to the number of data points. The CluStream variants are different processing strategies and will be explained in Sect. 3.

end, the amount of data becomes too large to store, which led to the development of stream learning methods such as stream clustering [4,40]. As with clustering of static data, the goal is to find groupings of data where similar data points are assigned to the same groups and dissimilar data points are kept separate.

A popular strategy for dealing with the constraints of the stream setting is to split the clustering process into an online and an offline phase, where the online phase deals with the ongoing stream, and the offline phase determines the actual clustering [2]. Most stream clustering approaches are limited to a single specific offline clustering approach [14]. A recent study [61] has called offline processing into question and has shown that it may be unneeded or even disadvantageous. This study included leaving out the offline processing for two preexisting stream clustering approaches, the partitioning StreamKM++ [1] and the density-based DenStream [13]. Aside from this, they applied k-Means++ [6] and DBSCAN [20], the offline algorithms used in StreamKM++ and DenStream, respectively, to their own approach using micro-clusters, resulting in the pure online summarization outperforming the offline-processed method.

However, evaluating the usefulness of clustering in the offline phase based on the performance of only a few classical clustering methods can be misleading, raising the question of whether the limitations generally lie in the offline processing or merely in the specific selected offline clustering method. Due to the typical lack of strict time constraints [14], the offline phase is also more suitable for optimization than the online phase, which can not be replayed and is more resource-constrained. Thus, in this paper, we investigate the clustering step in the offline phase by incorporating a wide variety of offline clustering methods into a preexisting stream clustering approach. We compare them among each other and against the approach without any offline clustering. As the previous work only examined partitioning and density-based techniques in this context [61], our examination also focuses on these categories. In this study, CluStream [2] serves as a representative, as it is one of the most well-known stream clustering algorithms and the basis [14] built upon by other widely used stream clustering methods like StreamKM++ [1] and DenStream [13]. Figure 1 visualizes our study design. To the best of our knowledge, we are the first to investigate the offline phase of stream clustering with a diverse set of offline clustering algorithms. For the examined datasets, our results have shown that if the offline processing is adjusted, it is possible to boost the performance of the stream clustering method significantly. In one experiment, swapping the offline clustering algorithm for CluStream resulted in almost a doubling of performance compared to the typical configuration of CluStream. Interestingly, using CluStream with the same underlying clustering as some competitor techniques outperforms them in multiple cases. As such, future evaluations of online summarization techniques should be done with awareness of this factor, as a correctly chosen offline algorithm may dominate the performance of the overall evaluation. Based on CluStream as a leading example, our main contributions are:

- We investigate 12 different offline clustering approaches as processing techniques for the offline phase.
- We introduce a novel way of replicating data from online summaries.
- We investigate and compare multiple ways of processing the summaries.
- We perform an extensive evaluation in the context of other stream clustering approaches and pure online summarization as clustering.

2 Related Work

2.1 Clustering

Clustering methods group similar data objects together while separating dissimilar objects. There are many types of offline clustering algorithms [47] that handle different concepts of data similarity. Here, we put our focus on partitioning and density-based clustering approaches. While there are many more techniques, like hierarchical and grid-based methods, we do not cover them in this work.

Partitioning Clustering. Partitioning approaches split the data into distinct partitions. Their most prominent representative is k-Means [37], which finds k clusters by iteratively assigning each point to its closest center and updating the k centroids. It has led to many derived techniques. SubKMeans [41] performs a dimensionality-reduction simultaneously with the clustering. A major focus is the automatic determination of the cluster number k. X-Means [49] does this k-estimation by optimizing information criteria. Projected Dip-Means (P-DipM) [15] applies a test for unimodality on multiple different one-dimensional projections. Aside from these k-Means-based approaches, Spectral Clustering (SC) [38] is a popular approach that transfers the task to a k-dimensional representation based on the similarity graph. Other clustering algorithms, though usually k-Means, can be applied to obtain the final clustering. SpectACl [28] incorporates the average density into the process of SC.

Density-based Clustering. In density-based clustering, clusters are dense regions with many data points that are separated by areas of lower point density. A common variant is searching for density-*connected* clusters, such as in

DBSCAN [20], where clusters are comprised of density-connected points within dense areas. However, DBSCAN cannot find clusters with varying levels of density. Later innovations have attempted to address this issue. HDBSCAN [12] uses hierarchical clustering concepts to do so. RNN-DBSCAN (RNN-DBS) [11] uses reverse nearest neighborhood sizes to define dense points and uses neighborhood relations rather than distances to handle connectivity. In contrast to these density-connectivity-based approaches, there are also methods based on detecting density-peaks, e.g., DPC [52]. Density peaks are characterized by high local density and large distances to other candidates for density peaks. These peaks serve as centroids for the clusters. SNN-DPC [36] introduces an allocation strategy based on the incorporation of shared nearest neighbors. DBHD [18] uses local density to determine clusters with the help of the k-nearest neighborhood while allowing for some density variation within clusters.

2.2 Stream Clustering

The stream setting adds many additional constraints to tasks like clustering [4]. Stream data may be infinite and arrive continuously in an uncontrollable order. As such, storage is only possible in a limited manner. Additionally, the underlying distribution of the data can change over time [23]. Thus, stream clustering requires both a summarization structure and a window or forgetting mechanism [61]. Summarization structures maintain temporary information about data points but may differ in what information is saved. As with regular clustering, stream clustering offers a diverse set of different strategies and underlying concepts [4,14,40,65]. In this paper, we focus solely on partitioning and density-based methods. A wide array of methods outside these constraints exist, such as hierarchical [51] and grid-based [57] stream clustering techniques.

Most stream clustering methods can be grouped into either online or online-offline methods [40]. Online methods directly return the clusters upon processing the data. In contrast, online-offline methods perform postprocessing, typically with an offline clustering method, either at fixed timesteps or based on user input. Unlike online processing, offline processing is usually not time-critical [14]. The chosen offline clustering method impacts the resulting cluster shapes [4] and is often not specific to a method. Instead, it could also be combined with different online methods [14], though generally, this is not addressed by stream clustering approaches. Instead, most approaches describe one specific offline processing behavior that usually corresponds to one of a few clustering approaches (e.g., k-Means [37], DBSCAN [20]) or a modification thereof. Kranen et al. [31] note that the summaries of their method ClusTree could be used with any offline clustering algorithm, including both partitioning and density-based approaches. However, they did not evaluate this aspect in their experiments. In their follow-up approach LiarTree [32] they do not elaborate further on this aspect or specify the offline clustering approach.

CluStream. CluStream [2] is a fundamental stream clustering method which had a major influence on subsequent stream clustering approaches [14]. CluStream maintains a set of micro-clusters to summarize regions of interest. The radius r of a micro-cluster is based on the deviation of the assigned points. Here, there are differences depending on the implementation. For MOA [10], the maximum deviation value for any dimension is used, whereas River [43] uses the average across all dimensions. Data point assignment occurs if a data point falls within a maximum boundary factor $mbf \cdot r$ of the centroid. We call this assignment radius r^+. A new micro-cluster is created if a new point falls outside of this range for their closest micro-cluster. To maintain a limited number of micro-clusters, they are merged based on the closest pairs. Alternatively, micro-clusters that have not received a new data point for too long are aged out. The micro-clusters are then employed in the offline phase to determine the actual clusters using weighted k-Means (Wk-Means) [37]. CluStream has led to the development of multiple related techniques. Spark-CluStream [8] employs a weighted sampling of the micro-cluster centroids. While some variants change the micro-cluster processing procedure, most perform a k-Means-based offline clustering, with some introducing k-estimation techniques [5]. Still, the recent DynamicCluStream [3] instead merges overlapping micro-clusters to form clusters.

Competitors. As competitors for this work, we included a collection of both traditional and recent stream clustering approaches. STREAMKmeans [46] is a variant of STREAMLSEARCH [46], where the k-median clustering is replaced with k-Means. It works on the basis of performing clustering chunk-wise and then storing the resulting centers. The final clustering is produced using a weighted clustering on a fixed number of these centers. DenStream [13] incorporates the density-connectivity principles of DBSCAN [20] into an online-offline stream clustering framework. Micro-clusters mimic the typical hierarchical structure of DBSCAN based on the weight and radius of the micro-cluster. The weights of micro-clusters decay over time. Points are assigned based on a distance-parameter ε that is also used for the DBSCAN clustering in the offline phase. DBSTREAM [26] tracks the number of data points that would be assigned to each pair of micro-clusters. These values are then used to merge micro-clusters into full clusters in the offline phase, rather than a traditional offline clustering algorithm. EMCStream [66] is a recent method that works by clustering UMAP [42] embeddings with k-Means [37]. EMCStream includes a rewind function when concept drift is detected, though the rewind is limited to a set amount of input data. MCMSTStream [19] is another recent approach that represents the stream by micro-clusters with a fixed radius. Clusters are determined through minimum spanning trees [24], where micro-clusters within a certain range of another are included in the same cluster. The recent GB-FuzzyStream [62] introduces a two-level architecture of fuzzy summarization structures, called Fuzzy Granular-Balls (FGBs) and Fuzzy Micro-Balls (FMBs). FGBs summarize incoming data, whereas FMBs are formed through the combination of FGBs. In the offline phase, DPC [52] is applied on the centers of the FMBs to determine the clusters.

2.3 Data Generation

Many different types of data generation methods are available that generate new synthetic instances based on given instructions, often in the form of sampling distributions. These distributions either receive their own label or are combined to form more complex clusters [30]. While commonly applied in benchmarking and evaluation, in the case of SMOTE [16], data generation is used to deal with imbalanced data by artificially increasing the number of minority class samples. Especially relevant for this work is SMOClust [17], a stream-based variant of the SMOTE approach. SMOClust makes use of the online summaries of stream clustering approaches to generate new samples for the minority class.

3 Offline Handling for CluStream

Offline Processing. The offline phase of CluStream works by taking the centroids of the micro-clusters and using them as input for a traditional clustering algorithm. The reported cluster label for a specific centroid then serves as the label for the whole micro-cluster. Regular CluStream uses Wk-Means with the micro-cluster weights as weights. Since we want to evaluate the impact of various offline clustering algorithms, we substitute Wk-Means with 12 different clustering algorithms selected from both traditional methods and more recent techniques. These are put into contrast with **CluStream-O**, a CluStream variant that directly uses the micro-clusters determined in the online phase for the cluster assignment rather than performing an offline phase. When incorporating other offline clustering algorithms into the base CluStream, the process is similar to Wk-Means. The centroids of the micro-clusters are used as prototypes to reconstruct the real data points when training the offline clustering algorithms. We refer to the form of CluStream, which directly replaces Wk-Means and uses only the centroids as inputs, as **CluStream-C** (Centroid CluStream). Unlike k-Means, most offline clustering approaches do not offer a weighted variant and thus need other ways to introduce weights to fully exploit the online summaries.

Weighted Data Reconstruction. As with Spark-CluStream [8], a fake weighting scheme can be introduced independently of the choice of offline clustering method on the side of the data reconstruction technique. A naive approach is to multiply the centroids by the weight of the micro-cluster. This would correspond to a true weighted clustering. We refer to this approach as **CluStream-W** (Weighted CluStream). Furthermore, we include **CluStream-S** (Sampled CluStream), which is similar to Spark-CluStream, where we sample a limited number of points from the centroids based on their relative weight ratios rather than the absolute values. All centroids are present in the reconstructed data at least once, so no micro-cluster is lost due to the sampling. The label assignment uses the clustering label determined for the closest centroid.

Generative Processing. Additionally, we introduce a generative approach to produce suitable input data for offline clustering algorithms. As the micro-clusters offer both a centroid and a radius, we can use them as definitions for distributions for synthetic data generation. Since the real distribution of the data points within a micro-cluster is no longer available, we instead use a uniform distribution over the hypersphere defined by the micro-cluster (see, e.g.,

Table 1. Properties of used datasets

Name	Key	Type	Shuffled?	# Dim.	# Obj.	k	One-off?
Complex-9 [9]	Comp-9	Synthetic	Yes	2	3031	9	No
DENSIRED-2 [30]	DEN-2	Synthetic	Yes	2	5000	11	Yes
DENSIRED-10 [30]	DEN-10	Synthetic	Yes	10	5000	11	No
DENSIRED-100 [30]	DEN-100	Synthetic	Yes	100	5000	11	Yes
RBF-3 40000[a]	RBF-3	Synthetic	No	2	40000	8	No
Fertility-vs-Income[b] [59]	FvI	Real-World	No	2	4014	2	Yes
Electricty [54]	Elec	Real-World	No	8	45312	2	Yes
KDDCUP99 [54]	KDD99	Real-World	No	41	494021	23	No
Gas Sensor Array [54]	Gas	Real-World	No	128	13910	6	No
Star Light Curves [54]	SLC	Real-World	No	1024	9236	3	Yes

[a] https://github.com/CIG-UFSCar/DS_Datasets/tree/master, last accessed 25.02.2025, based on data generation from MOA [10]. [b] Dataset created from data from the Gapminder data repository https://www.gapminder.org/data/, last accessed: 05.06.2025.

[30]). As with River [43], we define r as the average standard deviation across all dimensions. Since points assigned to a micro-cluster may lie outside of this micro-cluster radius r, the assignment radius $mbf \cdot r = r^+$ is instead used as the radius of the generating hypersphere. This approach is denoted **CluStream-G** (Generative CluStream) and generates a limited number of data points. The centroid of every micro-cluster is also included, meaning that, as with CluStream-S, all micro-clusters are represented. The mapping of data points to clusters in CluStream happens on a micro-cluster basis. Every evaluated point is simply assigned to the closest micro-cluster. The label of that micro-cluster is then used as the label for the data point. However, the micro-clusters may not be homogenous, adding some level of granularity to this. When using generative approaches, the points are not just focused on the centroid of each micro-cluster, but are instead more spread out. As a result, the clustering approaches can produce different labels for different reconstruction points even if they are created from the same micro-cluster. These points are then used to label the data rather than just the centroid. The assigned labels for CluStream-G are based on the labels of the nearest neighbor within the generated dataset rather than just considering the centroids as done in regular CluStream. Thus, the final step is comparable to the nearest neighbor classifier [21]. A more formalized description of the CluStream variants can be found in the supplementary file.

4 Experiments

4.1 Experiment Setup

We present the properties of all used datasets in Table 1, though some were only one-off datasets used for either Sect. 4.5 or Sect. 4.6. Some datasets (Complex-9 and DENSIRED variants) were shuffled for the experiments as they were presorted based on the ground truth labels. All other datasets were not shuffled and retain any present concept drift [23]. We examine the effects of this drift using the FvI dataset in Sect. 4.5. We used the River stream learning library[1] [43] as a base for our evaluation. We used their implementations of DenStream, DBStream, and STREAMKmeans, as well as a modified version of their CluStream code. EMCStream[2], MCMSTStream[3] and GB-FuzzyStream[4] were adapted from the linked repositories. k-Means(++), SC, DBSCAN and HDBSCAN were from scikit-learn[5] [48]. SubKMeans, X-Means and Projected Dip-Means were from ClustPy[6] [34]. SpectACl[7], SNN-DPC[8] and DPC[9] were taken from the linked repositories. Our implementations of RNN-DBS and DBHD are available in our repository. There was a 7-day time limit for experiments, which was exceeded by some approaches.

4.2 Parameter Selection

We used the AutoML approach SMAC3[10] [35] to look for the best parameters for both the CluStream variants and the competitors. We apply the same parameters across the full stream and optimize based on batches, circumventing the problems arising from using traditional AutoML for stream clustering methods [14]. We downsample large datasets for AutoML, as recommended (e.g., in [64]). As in prior research on AutoML for clustering [53], we give a fixed time limit for all approaches. All experiments were executed on the same hardware (Intel(R) Xeon(R) CPU E5-4640 v4 @ 2.10GHz). For CluStream variants, we split the time budget so that 20% of the time was spent on the online phase and 80% on the offline phase. Most CluStream variants use the parameters obtained from the same online phase optimizations for comparability and use 100 micro-clusters. CluStream-O variants with different micro-cluster numbers are optimized separately. CluStream-S and CluStream-G generate around 1000 points for each evaluation batch. We use the ground-truth cluster number for methods requiring an input cluster number. For more details, see the supplementary file.

4.3 Metrics

For evaluating the clustering results, we used adjusted rand index (ARI) [29] and adjusted mutual information (AMI) [45]. Both metrics have a maximum value of

---

[1] https://github.com/online-ml/river, last accessed: Feb 20th, 2025.
[2] https://gitlab.com/alaettinzubaroglu/emcstream, last accessed: Feb 20th, 2025.
[3] https://github.com/senolali/MCMSTStream, last accessed: Feb 20th, 2025.
[4] https://github.com/xjnine/GBFuzzyStream, last accessed: Feb 20th, 2025.
[5] https://scikit-learn.org, last accessed: Feb 20th, 2025.
[6] https://github.com/collinleiber/ClustPy, last accessed: Feb 20th, 2025.
[7] https://bitbucket.org/Sibylse/spectacl, last accessed: Feb 20th, 2025.
[8] https://github.com/liurui39660/SNNDPC, last accessed: Feb 20th, 2025.
[9] https://github.com/colinwke/dpca, last accessed: Feb 20th, 2025.
[10] https://github.com/automl/SMAC3, last accessed 30.01.2025.

1, where higher is better. We use the sum of both to optimize the results of the parameter selection. For fairness, the metrics are calculated in batches of 1000, and the mean value over 5 seeds is reported for the best-performing parameters.

Many definitions for the similarity between datasets have been proposed [56]. For the paper, we focus on strategies that do not require ground-truth labels. Bag of prototypes (BoP)[11] [58] is a method of representing datasets by determining patches within the dataset. The Jensen-Shannon divergence [22] between the histogram for the patches in the original dataset and the histogram produced by the assignment of the points of the projected compared dataset is then used as a similarity score. Furthermore, the Maximum Mean Discrepancy (MMD) is also a common method for comparing distributions [25,50]. We used the PyTorch-based implementation from [60][12] to compute the MMD, which, by default, examines the distributions using five different kernel functions. Aside from distributions, Classifier Two-Sample Tests [50,63] are also used to assess the similarity between datasets. Here, a binary nearest-neighbor classifier [21] is trained to discriminate between the data of both datasets. We distinguish between the leave-one-out accuracy using the real data points (CA_r) and the offline points (CA_o) based on which points the accuracy is calculated for. We also report the average distance of the real data points to the closest offline data point (NNd) and the average distance of an offline data point to its closest real data point. The scores are calculated in batches of 1000, and the weighted average score is reported. Smaller values denote a closer resemblance of data. The purity of a clustering [39] is the accuracy if each cluster is assigned its majority ground-truth label. We treat all unique offline data points as potential cluster labels and report the purity for assigning the real data points to their closest offline data point. This value represents a hard boundary for the performance of the stream clustering algorithm, as the CluStream-based approaches can not distinguish clusters beyond this. To maintain the logic of smaller values denoting a better score, we instead track the Impurity (Imp.), defined as $1-$Purity. Purity has also been used as the primary metric for evaluating the offline phase in a prior work [61]. However, we opted for ARI and AMI, as the usage of Purity requires a restriction to a similar number of clusters to allow for a meaningful comparison, and we aimed for multiple methods without a specified number of clusters. Still, we report the Purity performance in our supplementary file.

For evaluating the cluster evolution, we use the Temporal Silhouette index (TS)[13] [59] and the Cluster Mapping Measure (CMM) [33]. TS is an unsupervised cluster validation index designed to handle concept drift, whereas CMM is a supervised evaluation metric designed for stream data. We use the objects within the smallest hypersphere that covers all objects with the same label as the ground truth clusters. We include our implementation of the CMM in our repository. While TS is calculated for the full clustering with the most suitable clusters per

---

[11] https://github.com/Klaus-Tu/Bag-of-Prototypes, last accessed: 02.12.2024.
[12] https://github.com/jindongwang/transferlearning, last accessed: 08.03.2025.
[13] https://github.com/CN-TU/py-temporal-silhouette, last accessed: 05.06.2025.

Table 2. Mean metric scores over 5 seeds for evaluated datasets for best-performing parameters according to the sum of ARI and AMI (×100). The best scores are marked as **bold**, and the second-best scores are underlined.

Name	Comp-9 ARI	Comp-9 AMI	DEN-10 ARI	DEN-10 AMI	RBF-3 ARI	RBF-3 AMI	KDD99 ARI	KDD99 AMI	Gas ARI	Gas AMI
STREAMKmeans	41.6	61.6	28.8	52.6	68.4	74.6	**94.0**	**87.0**	11.6	17.0
DenStream	50.0	70.5	60.0	73.2	63.3	69.9	79.2	75.9	<u>35.3</u>	<u>53.0</u>
DBSTREAM	56.9	69.3	<u>67.8</u>	<u>74.9</u>	69.6	76.1	<u>92.5</u>	<u>85.2</u>	26.3	50.1
EMCStream	57.3	80.4	60.3	73.9	53.6	66.3	81.6	76.8	35.1	41.7
MCMSTStream	65.3	74.5	**73.7**	**84.7**	74.8	78.1	90.3	82.7	16.4	38.4
GB-FuzzyStream	20.0	57.5	19.8	43.4	31.0	51.4	-	-	5.8	20.4
CluStream-O - var. k	48.7	66.9	53.2	70.7	65.2	73.2	89.5	83.5	27.4	50.1
CluStream-O - fixed k	41.6	64.7	16.0	34.3	60.2	71.2	87.1	80.6	25.5	37.8
CluStream-O - k=100	9.5	53.0	49.7	69.8	41.9	60.3	80.3	67.5	24.2	50.5
CluStream - Wk-Means	36.8	62.8	54.5	67.9	<u>75.3</u>	78.4	89.7	77.5	32.0	45.2
CluStream-C - k-Means	37.6	63.4	14.4	37.2	73.5	77.8	90.4	79.6	24.7	39.4
CluStream-C - SubKMeans	35.7	61.3	35.9	53.9	73.5	77.5	90.4	79.6	24.2	38.7
CluStream-C - X-Means	49.9	66.7	26.6	47.3	<u>76.3</u>	<u>79.3</u>	90.2	79.6	29.8	52.4
CluStream-C - P-Dip-M	0.0	0.0	0.0	0.0	18.3	24.4	89.6	79.0	12.7	20.3
CluStream-C - SC	47.7	72.8	49.6	64.7	**76.8**	79.0	91.2	81.4	31.6	45.3
CluStream-C - SpectACl	60.8	79.0	55.9	74.5	66.5	76.4	89.6	80.0	26.4	39.0
CluStream-C - DBSCAN	**73.4**	**86.5**	52.8	70.3	63.7	77.1	90.6	78.0	26.5	50.9
CluStream-C - HDBSCAN	<u>71.9</u>	<u>85.7</u>	58.3	73.2	72.0	**79.6**	90.7	80.5	34.7	51.4
CluStream-C - RNN-DBS	37.0	69.2	9.5	22.1	65.1	71.9	87.6	79.8	32.4	49.0
CluStream-C - DPC	45.0	75.7	56.5	70.2	69.3	76.7	92.1	83.7	31.5	52.2
CluStream-C - SNN-DPC	46.3	68.0	25.6	49.4	59.0	69.2	86.1	77.6	29.6	47.0
CluStream-C - DBHD	52.3	75.9	57.7	69.9	73.4	78.5	88.4	79.4	**35.6**	**54.0**

batch based on the overlap mapped to the ground truth, CMM is calculated in batches of 1000, and the weighted average is reported.

4.4 Performance Impact of the Offline Phase

The metrics for best-performing parameters when directly replacing Wk-Means in CluStream (CluStream-C) and all competitors are given in Table 2. Colored cells denote the relationship in performance between CluStream-O and other approaches, where red/blue means it is worse/better than the best variant of CluStream-O, with saturation indicating the relative performance. The results show that the chosen offline strategy has a strong impact on CluStream's performance. This can be seen best for Comp-9, where the best-performing offline clustering technique has almost double the ARI score of the default case. CluStream-C, with a properly chosen offline phase method, often beats the competing strategies. Still, it is noticeable that the best offline strategy depends on the dataset. This lines up with the statement that the offline phase method determines the final cluster shapes [4]. Specifically, density-based approaches work best for datasets with arbitrarily shaped clusters (like Comp-9). DEN-10 has multiple density levels, leading to more difficulty for DBSCAN. In contrast, centroid-based techniques perform well for RBF-3, where the dataset consists of multiple moving distributions. Despite CluStream originally working with Wk-Means, a density-based offline clustering often results in a better performance.

We also compared the results against CluStream-O with different settings for cluster count k. Clustream-O var. k allows for a flexible choice of clusters beyond the ground-truth cluster number, which was used for CluStream-O fixed k and all other approaches requiring the cluster number. CluStream-O with k=100 uses the same micro-clusters as CluStream-C. In the results we see that CluStream-O is a viable strategy that can outperform CluStream when using an offline phase, especially for the default setup of CluStream. This reinforces the observations made by Wang et al. [61]. For CluStream, the micro-clusters already roughly adhere to the same ideas as k-Means, where points are assigned to centroids that adjust based on the data. The online phase also has the advantage of accessing real data points, whereas the offline phase can only use summaries. Despite this, an appropriate choice of the offline clustering algorithm still often leads to CluStream outperforming CluStream-O. For all examined datasets, there is at least one configuration that manages to perform better than the best CluStream-O variant, though these are not necessarily the same variants on all datasets.

When using the same underlying clustering methods as CluStream-C, some competitors can have a worse performance. Specifically, DenStream is similar to CluStream, but introduces concepts of DBSCAN in its summaries. Despite its less specialized micro-clusters, CluStream-C outperforms DenStream when using DBSCAN in the offline phase for three of the five datasets in Table 2. Still, on one of these three, DenStream outperforms the default CluStream variant. Thus, stream clustering methods should also be compared using the same offline methods, as the final performance is impacted by the chosen offline method.

4.5 Cluster Evolution

Concept drift [23] and subsequent cluster evolution [33,55] are important factors for the real-world application of stream clustering [44]. To examine the cluster evolution, we drew on prior research [59]. Like them, we use the FvI dataset to showcase this and aimed to use the same parameters they did. They provide the code they used for evaluating the real datasets in their repository[14]. We set the parameters for TS [59] to the default parameters described in their paper, which also correspond to the ones they used in their code. These are a window-size w of 100, the number of neighbors k to 1000, and ς to 1. CMM [33] requires

---

[14] https://github.com/CN-TU/py-temporal-silhouette, last accessed: 05.06.2025.

a neighborhood size k, which was set to 5. In the description of CMM, this parameter is noted to only have a minor impact when varied between 1 and 10.

The clustering results for several stream clustering algorithms are presented in Fig. 2. Here, we selected the best run among five runs with default parameters and five with optimized parameters, based on the sum of ARI and AMI. The mapping to the ground truth clusters was done based on the largest overlap within each batch of size 1000. The chosen offline algorithm has a significant impact on the ability to handle cluster evolution. A major factor appears to be the ability of methods to determine the cluster number on their own. Here, these estimations often lead to overestimation, which negatively impacts the TS index. Still, oversegmenting appears to have the advantage with CMM. This behavior can be attributed to CMM performing its own matching and, as such, handling the additional cluster labels without an additional malus. As the oversegmented clusters may be comparatively pure, this leads to high performance with CMM. This again highlights the importance of aligning metrics and goals during evaluation and of selecting offline clustering methods that suit the problem setting.

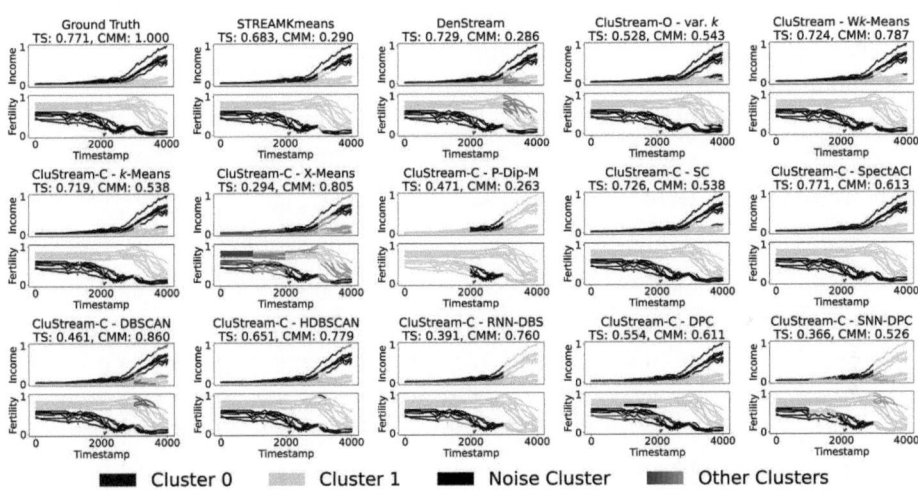

Fig. 2. Clustering behavior of the best-performing run according to ARI and AMI for selected stream clustering algorithms on the FvI dataset

4.6 Offline Replication Quality

In Table 3, some values for centroid-based offline approaches (CluStream-C (CS-C), CluStream-W (CS-W), and CluStream-S (CS-S)) are the same, and thus reported only once. These are the metrics that cover the assignment of real data points to offline data points. Here, CluStream-G always outperforms the other approaches. This is inherently the case as CluStream-G includes all centroids. Nonetheless, the Impurity score showcases a significantly higher ceiling for

Table 3. Dataset replication scores for CluStream offline clustering inputs for default parameters (×100). The best scores are marked in **bold**.

Key	CS-C	CS-W	CS-S	Centroid				CluStream-G			
	iNNd	iNNd	iNNd	NNd		CA_r	Imp.	iNNd	NNd	CA_r	Imp.
Comp-9	**0.88**	0.97	0.96	2.62		86.0	0.10	1.07	**1.19**	46.5	0.00
DEN-2	0.82	**0.58**	0.59	1.85		86.4	4.98	0.80	**0.84**	57.3	0.60
DEN-10	7.52	**4.03**	4.12	7.90		86.2	9.28	5.89	**6.54**	84.8	0.80
DEN-100	**0.27**	11.25	10.72	27.14		89.1	37.56	13.05	**26.37**	88.9	13.54
RBF-3	0.79	**0.49**	0.51	1.86		86.5	4.60	0.58	**0.75**	47.2	2.30
Elec	**2.82**	3.06	3.05	6.91		85.3	18.39	3.86	**5.94**	79.3	9.19
KDD99	4.22	**1.93**	2.03	3.21		69.2	0.37	2.12	**3.14**	68.9	0.12
Gas	4.11	**3.82**	3.84	7.99		78.5	6.11	3.96	**7.90**	78.0	1.63
SLC	**26.50**	45.42	45.09	100.09		80.1	13.71	45.50	**99.89**	80.0	6.93

the clustering performance. However, with increasing dimensionalities, the gap between CluStream-G and the other approaches in terms of the nearest neighborhood diminishes. This behavior is expected due to the Curse of Dimensionality as the generated points are typically close to the hypersphere boundaries [27].

Table 4. Additional dataset replication scores for CluStream offline clustering inputs for default parameters (×100). The best scores are marked as **bold**.

Name	CluStream-C			CluStream-W			CluStream-S			CluStream-G		
	CA_o	BoP	MMD	CA_o	BoP	MMD	CA_o	BoP	MMD	CA_o	BoP	MMD
Comp-9	**0.6**	7.2	**0.6**	98.8	9.5	0.7	99.6	9.0	**0.6**	53.4	**2.7**	**0.6**
DEN-2	0.0	18.3	37.0	97.0	14.5	**3.4**	98.5	14.1	3.5	60.1	**5.1**	3.6
DEN-10	0.2	29.3	109.1	92.6	11.7	**5.6**	97.7	11.5	5.7	82.8	**8.4**	5.8
DEN-100	0.0	39.0	214.4	87.5	29.7	9.2	98.0	**29.0**	6.4	98.0	**29.0**	**6.0**
RBF-3	0.0	20.2	15.1	97.1	13.9	1.0	98.3	13.6	**0.9**	53.4	**3.1**	**0.9**
Elec	0.1	8.4	**2.6**	99.6	9.4	1.3	99.8	9.0	1.2	89.2	**6.4**	1.2
KDD99	1.1	34.3	124.8	92.9	11.4	23.0	98.9	11.3	23.6	97.0	**10.8**	23.6
Gas	0.3	20.2	42.6	97.2	13.7	**1.4**	98.8	13.5	1.5	98.8	**13.0**	1.5
SLC	0.6	22.9	36.1	91.4	31.4	7.4	97.1	30.6	**7.1**	97.1	**30.4**	**7.1**

For the iNNd score in Table 3, CluStream-G consistently performs worse than other approaches as it spreads its offline points further. Especially for higher dimensionalities, this can lead to some points being far apart from real data points. For CA_o in Table 4, using CluStream centroids without weighting returns the best results. Since there is only one replicated point per micro-cluster, it only requires a real data point to be closer to a centroid than another microcluster. When evaluating the distributions, which are covered by BoP and MMD in Table 4, CluStream-G again performs well, though it does not outperform other techniques for all examined datasets. However, even when performing worse than other approaches, the scores are still fairly close to the best-performing ones. Depending on the dataset, the weighting can be both advantageous and disadvantageous. Although weighting allows for better mimicking of the real data regarding point presence, the lack of weight reduction over time can lead to deviations from the current real distributions during later timesteps.

4.7 Performance Impact of the Offline Replication

Another aspect to evaluate is the impact of the offline replication technique on the clustering performance. An overview of the results for the best-performing parameters can be seen in Fig. 3. As CluStream does not include decay of the micro-cluster weights, they accumulate for streams where micro-clusters survive for a long time and summarize many data points. This could lead to large sizes of the generated data for CluStream-W, which can result in scalability issues and does not align with the constraints of stream clustering, as the weights could grow infinitely. Despite most clearly approximating a weighted clustering, it is often outperformed by the other weighted approaches or CluStream-C.

Although CluStream-G generally results in a better representation of the real data according to the dataset similarity metric, this does not necessarily result in a better clustering performance. The introduction of weights appears to be advantageous for many methods, though it can lead to mixed results for some approaches, which is particularly noticeable in RNN-DBS and X-Means. For the case of density-connectivity approaches, the introduction of weights translates to a shift from connecting singleton micro-clusters to connecting primarily within the micro-clusters themselves for higher-weight micro-clusters for CluStream-S. This can be interpreted as a shift between a global representation for singleton micro-clusters, where the broader structure is made clearer, and a more local representation when weights are introduced, leading to some trade-offs. For CluStream-G, the higher spread can lead to individual generated points becoming their own clusters while the overall distances between micro-clusters are reduced, making them harder to separate for density-connectivity approaches. Still, it can also lead to connections between micro-clusters with a large radius that belong to the same ground-truth cluster. For density-peak and partitioning methods, the introduction of weights helps differentiate between micro-clusters in terms of relevance. Generating the data points also allows for a better mimicking of the distributions. This is most noticeable for P-DipM, which improves significantly due to a better representation of the distributions used in the unimodality test. In contrast, P-DipM consistently failed during the parameter optimization for approaches that only multiply the centroids for higher-dimensional data.

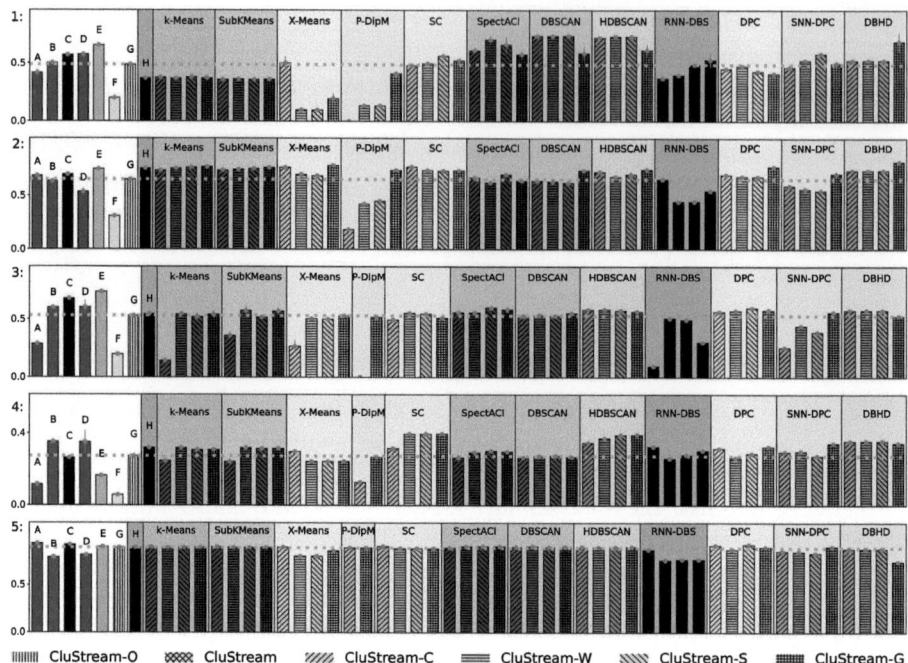

Fig. 3. Mean ARI results over 5 seeds for the datasets Complex-9 (1), RBF-3 40000 (2), DENSIRED-10 (3), Gas Sensor Array (4), and KDDCUP99 (5) for the best-performing runs of STREAMKmeans (A), DenStream (B), DBSTREAM (C), EMCStream (D), MCMSTStream (E), GB-FuzzyStream (F), CluStream-O (G) (also marked by the horizontal line), as well as the CluStream variants (denoted by hatch) for the respective offline clustering algorithms, including the default case of Wk-Means (H). The color indicates the offline clustering. The standard deviation over the different seeds is denoted by gray bars at the top. (Color figure online)

5 Discussion and Conclusion

We performed a broad evaluation of the offline phase on the example of CluStream, investigating different offline clustering strategies from different categories. We also investigated different approaches to reconstruct the data from summaries, which support this offline clustering. We tackled the observation made by Wang et al. [61] that the offline phase may be superfluous in many cases. With suitable parameters and offline clustering approaches, it is possible to outperform the purely online CluStream as well as many competitors. However, it is also important to note that there is no universal solution that always performs best. Although a generative reconstruction offers the best representation based on our evaluation, it does not necessarily lead to the best clustering performance in all cases. It is sensible to treat both the offline reconstruction and the actual offline clustering algorithm as additional constraints for evaluation. Rather than using a single fixed offline approach specific to each stream clustering algorithm, it instead is better to treat the offline phase as something flexible where the same offline approach is either used for all strategies or the performance is measured across a broader spectrum of offline strategies. In the future, we want to expand the evaluation to more online summarization principles, especially those that include weight decay, an aspect that CluStream lacks.

Disclosure of Interests. The authors have no competing interests to declare that are relevant to the content of this article.

References

1. Ackermann, M.R., Märtens, M., Raupach, C., Swierkot, K., Lammersen, C., Sohler, C.: StreamKM++: A clustering algorithm for data streams. ACM J. Exp. Algorithmics **17**(1) (2012)
2. Aggarwal, C.C., Han, J., Wang, J., Yu, P.S.: A framework for clustering evolving data streams. In: VLDB, pp. 81–92. Morgan Kaufmann (2003)
3. Ahsani, S., Yousef Sanati, M., Mansoorizadeh, M.: DynamicClustream: an algorithm based on clustream to improve clustering quality. Int. J. Web Res. **6**(2), 77–87 (2023)
4. de Andrade Silva, J., Faria, E.R., Barros, R.C., Hruschka, E.R., de Leon Ferreira de Carvalho, A.C.P., Gama, J.: Data stream clustering: a survey. ACM Comput. Surv. **46**(1), 13:1–13:31 (2013)
5. de Andrade Silva, J., Hruschka, E.R.: A support system for clustering data streams with a variable number of clusters. ACM Trans. Auton. Adapt. Syst. **11**(2), 11:1–11:26 (2016)
6. Arthur, D., Vassilvitskii, S.: k-means++: the advantages of careful seeding. In: SODA, pp. 1027–1035. SIAM (2007)
7. Babcock, B., Babu, S., Datar, M., Motwani, R., Widom, J.: Models and issues in data stream systems. In: PODS, pp. 1–16. ACM (2002)
8. Backhoff, O., Ntoutsi, E.: Scalable online-offline stream clustering in apache spark. In: ICDM Workshops, pp. 37–44. IEEE Computer Society (2016)
9. Barton, T.: Clustering-benchmark repository. https://github.com/deric/clustering-benchmark (2015)
10. Bifet, A., Holmes, G., Kirkby, R., Pfahringer, B.: MOA: massive online analysis. J. Mach. Learn. Res. **11**, 1601–1604 (2010)
11. Bryant, A., Cios, K.J.: RNN-DBSCAN: a density-based clustering algorithm using reverse nearest neighbor density estimates. IEEE Trans. Knowl. Data Eng. **30**(6), 1109–1121 (2018)
12. Campello, R.J.G.B., Moulavi, D., Sander, J.: Density-based clustering based on hierarchical density estimates. In: Pei, J., Tseng, V.S., Cao, L., Motoda, H., Xu, G. (eds.) PAKDD 2013. LNCS (LNAI), vol. 7819, pp. 160–172. Springer, Heidelberg (2013). https://doi.org/10.1007/978-3-642-37456-2_14
13. Cao, F., Ester, M., Qian, W., Zhou, A.: Density-based clustering over an evolving data stream with noise. In: SDM, pp. 328–339. SIAM (2006)
14. Carnein, M., Trautmann, H.: Optimizing data stream representation: an extensive survey on stream clustering algorithms. Bus. Inf. Syst. Eng. **61**(3), 277–297 (2019)
15. Chamalis, T., Likas, A.: The projected dip-means clustering algorithm. In: SETN, pp. 14:1–14:7. ACM (2018)

16. Chawla, N.V., Bowyer, K.W., Hall, L.O., Kegelmeyer, W.P.: Smote: synthetic minority over-sampling technique. J. Artif. Intell. Res. **16**, 321–357 (2002)
17. Chiu, C.W., Minku, L.L.: Smoclust: synthetic minority oversampling based on stream clustering for evolving data streams. Mach. Learn. **113**(7), 4671–4721 (2024). https://doi.org/10.1007/s10994-023-06420-y
18. Durani, W., Mautz, D., Plant, C., Böhm, C.: DBHD: density-based clustering for highly varying density. In: ICDM, pp. 921–926. IEEE (2022)
19. Erdinç, B., Kaya, M., Senol, A.: MCMSTStream: applying minimum spanning tree to KD-tree-based micro-clusters to define arbitrary-shaped clusters in streaming data. Neural Comput. Appl. **36**(13), 7025–7042 (2024)
20. Ester, M., Kriegel, H., Sander, J., Xu, X.: A density-based algorithm for discovering clusters in large spatial databases with noise. In: KDD, pp. 226–231. AAAI Press (1996)
21. Fix, E.: Discriminatory analysis: nonparametric discrimination, consistency properties, vol. 1. USAF school of Aviation Medicine (1985)
22. Fuglede, B., Topsoe, F.: Jensen-Shannon divergence and Hilbert space embedding. In: ISIT 2004. Proceedings, p. 31. IEEE (2004)
23. Gama, J., Zliobaite, I., Bifet, A., Pechenizkiy, M., Bouchachia, A.: A survey on concept drift adaptation. ACM Comput. Surv. **46**(4), 44:1–44:37 (2014)
24. Graham, R.L., Hell, P.: On the history of the minimum spanning tree problem. IEEE Ann. Hist. Comput. **7**(1), 43–57 (1985)
25. Gretton, A., Borgwardt, K.M., Rasch, M.J., Schölkopf, B., Smola, A.J.: A kernel two-sample test. J. Mach. Learn. Res. **13**, 723–773 (2012)
26. Hahsler, M., Bolaños, M.: Clustering data streams based on shared density between micro-clusters. IEEE Trans. Knowl. Data Eng. **28**(6), 1449–1461 (2016)
27. Hastie, T., Tibshirani, R., Friedman, J.: The Elements of Statistical Learning. SSS, Springer, New York (2009). https://doi.org/10.1007/978-0-387-84858-7
28. Hess, S., Duivesteijn, W., Honysz, P., Morik, K.: The SpectACl of nonconvex clustering: a spectral approach to density-based clustering. In: AAAI, pp. 3788–3795. AAAI Press (2019)
29. Hubert, L., Arabie, P.: Comparing partitions. J. Classif. **2**, 193–218 (1985)
30. Jahn, P., Frey, C.M.M., Beer, A., Leiber, C., Seidl, T.: Data with density-based clusters: a generator for systematic evaluation of clustering algorithms. In: ECML/PKDD (7). LNCS, vol. 14947, pp. 3–21. Springer (2024). https://doi.org/10.1007/978-3-031-70368-3_1
31. Kranen, P., Assent, I., Baldauf, C., Seidl, T.: The clustree: indexing micro-clusters for anytime stream mining. Knowl. Inf. Syst. **29**(2), 249–272 (2011)
32. Kranen, P., Reidl, F., Sanchez Villaamil, F., Seidl, T.: Hierarchical clustering for real-time stream data with noise. In: Bayard Cushing, J., French, J., Bowers, S. (eds.) SSDBM 2011. LNCS, vol. 6809, pp. 405–413. Springer, Heidelberg (2011). https://doi.org/10.1007/978-3-642-22351-8_25
33. Kremer, H., et al.: An effective evaluation measure for clustering on evolving data streams. In: KDD, pp. 868–876. ACM (2011)
34. Leiber, C., Miklautz, L., Plant, C., Böhm, C.: Benchmarking deep clustering algorithms with Clustpy. In: ICDM (Workshops), pp. 625–632. IEEE (2023)
35. Lindauer, M., et al.: SMAC3: A versatile Bayesian optimization package for hyperparameter optimization. J. Mach. Learn. Res. **23**, 54:1–54:9 (2022)
36. Liu, R., Wang, H., Yu, X.: Shared-nearest-neighbor-based clustering by fast search and find of density peaks. Inf. Sci. **450**, 200–226 (2018)
37. Lloyd, S.P.: Least squares quantization in pcm. IEEE Trans. Inf. Theory **28**(2), 129–136 (1982)

38. von Luxburg, U.: A tutorial on spectral clustering. Stat. Comput. **17**(4), 395–416 (2007)
39. Manning, C.D., Raghavan, P., Schütze, H.: Introduction to Information Retrieval. Cambridge University Press (2008)
40. Mansalis, S., Ntoutsi, E., Pelekis, N., Theodoridis, Y.: An evaluation of data stream clustering algorithms. Stat. Anal. Data Min. **11**(4), 167–187 (2018)
41. Mautz, D., Ye, W., Plant, C., Böhm, C.: Towards an optimal subspace for k-means. In: KDD, pp. 365–373. ACM (2017)
42. McInnes, L., Healy, J.: UMAP: uniform manifold approximation and projection for dimension reduction. CoRR abs/1802.03426 (2018)
43. Montiel, J., et al.: River: machine learning for streaming data in python. J. Mach. Learn. Res. **22**, 110:1–110:8 (2021)
44. Namitha, K., Kumar, G.S.: Concept drift detection in data stream clustering and its application on weather data. Int. J. Agric. Environ. Inf. Syst. **11**(1), 67–85 (2020)
45. Nguyen, X.V., Epps, J., Bailey, J.: Information theoretic measures for clusterings comparison: variants, properties, normalization and correction for chance. J. Mach. Learn. Res. **11**, 2837–2854 (2010)
46. O'Callaghan, L., Meyerson, A., Motwani, R., Mishra, N., Guha, S.: Streaming-data algorithms for high-quality clustering. In: ICDE, pp. 685–694. IEEE Computer Society (2002)
47. Oyewole, G.J., Thopil, G.A.: Data clustering: application and trends. Artif. Intell. Rev. **56**(7), 6439–6475 (2023)
48. Pedregosa, F., et al.: Scikit-learn: machine learning in Python. J. Mach. Learn. Res. **12**, 2825–2830 (2011)
49. Pelleg, D., Moore, A.W.: X-means: extending k-means with efficient estimation of the number of clusters. In: ICML, pp. 727–734. Morgan Kaufmann (2000)
50. Plesovskaya, E., Ivanov, S.: An empirical analysis of kde-based generative models on small datasets. Procedia Comput. Sci. **193**, 442–452 (2021)
51. Rajagopalan, A., Vitale, F., Vainstein, D., Citovsky, G., Procopiuc, C.M., Gentile, C.: Hierarchical clustering of data streams: Scalable algorithms and approximation guarantees. In: ICML. Proceedings of Machine Learning Research, vol. 139, pp. 8799–8809. PMLR (2021)
52. Rodriguez, A., Laio, A.: Clustering by fast search and find of density peaks. Science **344**(6191), 1492–1496 (2014)
53. da Silva, M.C., Licari, B., Tavares, G.M., Junior, S.B.: Benchmarking AutoML clustering frameworks. In: AutoML Conference 2024 (ABCD Track) (2024)
54. de Souza, V.M.A., dos Reis, D.M., Maletzke, A.G., Batista, G.E.A.P.A.: Challenges in benchmarking stream learning algorithms with real-world data. Data Min. Knowl. Discov. **34**(6), 1805–1858 (2020)
55. Spiliopoulou, M., Ntoutsi, I., Theodoridis, Y., Schult, R.: MONIC: modeling and monitoring cluster transitions. In: KDD, pp. 706–711. ACM (2006)
56. Stolte, M., Kappenberg, F., Rahnenführer, J., Bommert, A.: Methods for quantifying dataset similarity: a review, taxonomy and comparison. Stat. Surv. **18** (2024). https://doi.org/10.1214/24-ss149
57. Tareq, M., Sundararajan, E.A., Harwood, A., Bakar, A.A.: A systematic review of density grid-based clustering for data streams. IEEE Access **10**, 579–596 (2021)
58. Tu, W., Deng, W., Gedeon, T., Zheng, L.: A bag-of-prototypes representation for dataset-level applications. In: CVPR, pp. 2881–2892. IEEE (2023)
59. Vázquez, F.I., Zseby, T.: Temporal silhouette: validation of stream clustering robust to concept drift. Mach. Learn. **113**(4), 2067–2091 (2024)

60. Wang, J., et al.: Everything about transfer learning and domain adapation. http://transferlearning.xyz
61. Wang, X., Wang, Z., Wu, Z., Zhang, S., Shi, X., Lu, L.: Data stream clustering: an in-depth empirical study. Proc. ACM Manag. Data **1**(2), 162:1–162:26 (2023)
62. Xie, J., Dai, M., Xia, S., Zhang, J., Wang, G., Gao, X.: An efficient fuzzy stream clustering method based on granular-ball structure. In: ICDE, pp. 901–913. IEEE (2024)
63. Xu, Q., et al.: An empirical study on evaluation metrics of generative adversarial networks. CoRR abs/1806.07755 (2018)
64. Zogaj, F., Cambronero, J.P., Rinard, M.C., Cito, J.: Doing more with less: characterizing dataset downsampling for automl. Proc. VLDB Endow. **14**(11), 2059–2072 (2021)
65. Zubaroglu, A., Atalay, V.: Data stream clustering: a review. Artif. Intell. Rev. **54**(2), 1201–1236 (2021)
66. Zubaroglu, A., Atalay, V.: Online embedding and clustering of evolving data streams. Stat. Anal. Data Min. **16**(1), 29–44 (2023)

Adaptive Options for Decision Trees in Evolving Data Stream Classification

Daniel Nowak Assis[(✉)], Jean Paul Barddal, and Fabrício Enembreck

Programa de Pós-Graduação em Informática (PPGIa), Pontifícia Universidade
Católica do Paraná, Curitiba, Paraná, Brazil
{daniel.nassis,jean.barddal,fabricio}@ppgia.pucpr.br

Abstract. Decision trees are fundamental components of data stream mining frameworks and pipelines. However, their inherent instability - where small variations in training data can lead to significant structural changes- has motivated research into methods that either (i) mitigate this instability or (ii) exploit it for improved performance. Option trees provide an alternative approach to instability reduction by allowing non-leaf nodes to have multiple subtrees as child nodes. This enables instances to traverse multiple paths within a single decision tree structure, offering greater processing time and memory efficiency compared to ensemble methods–key advantages for streaming data mining, where data arrives continuously and potentially without bounds. This paper introduces LASTO, an algorithm with adaptive mechanisms for splitting and dynamically adding option nodes. Our primary contribution lies in the option node addition mechanism, where change detectors monitor branch performance and introduce option nodes when a decline in predictive quality is observed. An option node is only added if the split gain surpasses that of the previous split, ensuring its necessity and effectiveness. Experimental results demonstrate that LASTO achieves statistically significant differences in predictive performance while maintaining computational efficiency comparable to state-of-the-art decision trees for data stream classification.

Keywords: Decision Tree · Data Stream · Option Nodes

1 Introduction

Streaming data is integral to today's evolving digital landscape, and mining its concepts can reveal valuable insights. Researchers and practitioners in data stream mining focus on developing machine learning algorithms capable of efficiently processing high-speed, continuous, and potentially infinite data. These algorithms must provide high predictive quality and ensure anytime response, fast processing, and low memory consumption to prevent excessive instance storage. Otherwise, memory limitations or the need to discard instances could overwhelm the system and lead to failure [1].

Another fundamental challenge in streaming data mining is its evolving nature. Unlike traditional machine learning settings, the assumption that data distributions remain stable over time does not hold. This phenomenon, known as concept drift [2], refers to changes in the probability distribution of data over time. Concept drift can severely impact predictive performance, making it essential for machine learning models to detect and adapt to these changes promptly to maintain reliable learning outcomes. Hoeffding Trees [3] offer an efficient approach to stream classification, resembling batch decision tree algorithms such as C4.5 [4] and CART [5]. These trees continuously learn and predict from incoming instances, performing periodic split evaluations based on the Hoeffding Theorem [6]. This theorem enables incremental learning by distributing the computational cost of evaluating splits at leaf nodes across the data stream. As a result, Hoeffding Trees are among the most widely used and efficient methods for mining streaming data. Several studies, such as [7] and [8], have extended Hoeffding Trees, demonstrating improved predictive performance over the standard approach. Among these, we highlight the Local Adaptive Streaming Tree (LAST) [9], which addresses a key limitation of Hoeffding-based trees: their static split evaluation, which does not account for the evolving state of the tree over time. LAST introduces change detectors [2] at leaf nodes to monitor their statistics dynamically and determine optimal split moments. Experimental results have shown that LAST not only achieves competitive predictive performance against state-of-the-art decision trees but also improves processing efficiency.

Decision trees, however, suffer from limited lookahead ability, making them inherently unstable. Since they make splitting decisions based only on local statistics, they may not always select the best long-term splits [10]. Ensemble methods mitigate this instability by combining multiple decision trees into a single, stronger learner [11]. While ensembles are state-of-the-art in many applications, they introduce significant computational costs due to the need to train and maintain multiple base models–making them less suitable for data stream mining systems with strict memory and time constraints. An alternative to ensembles is Option Trees [12,13], which reduce decision tree instability while maintaining a single tree structure. Option Trees introduce option nodes, which allow instances to follow multiple decision paths simultaneously. This design enhances predictive robustness without the overhead of training multiple trees. In [10], the authors extended Hoeffding Trees to incorporate option nodes. In this paper, we propose Local Adaptive Streaming Tree with Options (LASTO), a novel approach that integrates adaptivity in both the splitting mechanism and the addition of option nodes. Using change detection algorithms, LASTO continuously monitors node statistics to dynamically determine when to introduce new option nodes, further enhancing model stability and predictive performance.

This paper is structured as follows: Sect. 2 discusses Hoeffding-based Trees and LAST. Section 3 introduces our proposed method. Section 4 presents experimental results. Finally, Sect. 5 concludes the paper and outlines future research directions.

2 Related Works on Decision Trees for Data Streams

In this section, we bring forward existing works on decision trees focusing on Hoeffding Trees and the Local Adaptive Streaming Tree (LAST).

2.1 Hoeffding Trees

Hoeffding Trees [3] are incremental and online decision trees designed for classification problems. The tree structure is periodically updated with split attempts when the number of samples observed in a leaf node achieves a user-given parameter called *grace period* (GP). For instance, if GP = 50, a split attempt will occur when a leaf node observes $50, 100, 150, 200, \ldots$ samples until a split ensues.

A split occurs if it passes the Hoeffding-bound constraint. Given a level of confidence δ (user-given), a split occurs if:

$$\Delta G(X_a) - \Delta G(X_b) \geq \sqrt{\frac{R^2 \log(\frac{1}{\delta})}{2n}} \qquad (1)$$

where $\Delta G(\cdot)$ is the impurity measure applied, (such as gini index [5] or information gain [4]), X_a is the feature that maximizes $\Delta G(\cdot)$, X_b is the feature that presents second best $\Delta G(\cdot)$ value, R is the range of $\Delta G(\cdot)$ function and n is the number of samples in the leaf nodes before splitting.

Figure 1 illustrates the training process of Hoeffding Trees, where ϵ is the Hoeffding bound.

Since $\lim_{n \to +\infty} \epsilon = 0$, and if in a node $\Delta G(X_a)$ and $\Delta G(X_b)$ have similar values, a split will potentially take many observations to split. To relax the Hoeffding constraint in these situations, Hoeffding trees also present a tie threshold. Given τ (user-given threshold), a split will ensue when $\tau > \epsilon$.

In [14], the authors observed that Naive Bayes could enhance predictive quality at leaf nodes. Authors in [15] noticed that selecting Naive Bayes or majority class strategy prediction according to the method with the highest accuracy at the leaf could further enhance Hoeffding Trees, which is commonly used.

2.2 Hoeffding Adaptive Tree

Hoeffding Adaptive Tree (HAT) [7] extend the Hoeffding Tree algorithm by adding the ADaptive WINdowing (ADWIN) [16] change detection algorithm to each non-terminal node. ADWIN [16] is a widely used change detector that maintains a window W of recent observations and attests that no change is present in the window if the mean value of subwindows of W has a similar value according to Hoeffding's theorem. If ADWIN flags a change in the accuracy of the instances that traverse the tree, a new subtree is created and replaces the node and its branch if the subtree is more accurate.

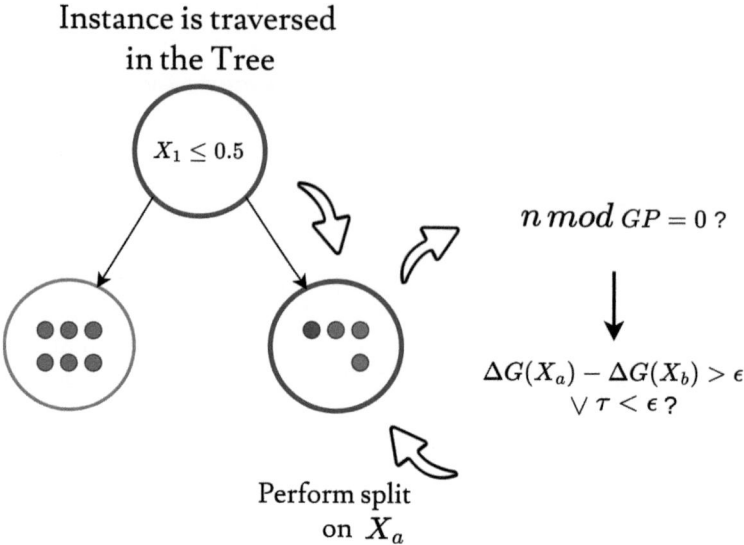

Fig. 1. Hoeffding Tree training process for an instance

2.3 Extremely Fast Decision Tree

In [8], the authors propose the Extremely Fast Decision Tree (EFDT). The first difference between EFDT and Hoeffding Trees is that EFDT applies a softer split constraint. Instead of comparing $\Delta G(X_a) - \Delta G(X_b) \geq \epsilon$, the authors propose comparing $\Delta G(X_a)$ with the occasion of any split occurrence, or $\Delta G(X_a) - \Delta G(X_\emptyset) \geq \epsilon \equiv \Delta G(X_a) \geq \epsilon$, thus resulting in deeper trees.

Similar to HAT, EFDT has a split reevaluation mechanism. This process is similar to the split attempt. A split reevaluation is performed at each GP_2 (user-given) sample traversed in non-terminal nodes. Given X_c, the feature used for splitting at the non-terminal node before the reevaluation and $\Delta G(X_c)$ the impurity at the non-terminal node, the sub-tree and its child nodes are substituted for a newly evaluated split on X_a if:

$$\Delta G(X_a) - \Delta G(X_c) \geq \epsilon \qquad (2)$$

In other words, if a new split is more beneficial than the previous one done at the terminal node, the new split replaces the sub-tree and its child nodes.

2.4 Local Adaptive Streaming Trees

The trees described earlier perform a static and periodic evaluation of splits. A split attempt will only occur at every GP samples observed at a leaf node, but a change in the purity or accuracy of the leaf node may occur earlier, and the tree would be unable to anticipate it. Even when small changes occur in a leaf node, the greedy evaluation of attributes and their values that compose the best split will still be performed and might not result in significant changes in the tree and consume more processing time.

Depicting these points, the authors in [9] propose the Local Adaptive Streaming Tree (LAST) algorithm. At each leaf node, LAST maintains a change detector [2] that constantly monitors leaf node statistics to determine ideal moments for splitting. Change detectors are often tailored to handle binomial distributions, i.e., error rates. If a change detector triggers a change, a split will ensue if $\Delta G(X_a) > 0.0$, the softest split constraint possible, which means change detectors control how the tree grows. Since change detectors constantly monitor new upcoming instances, they track how the stream evolves on an instance basis rather than in chunks.

Figure 2 illustrates the training process of LAST.

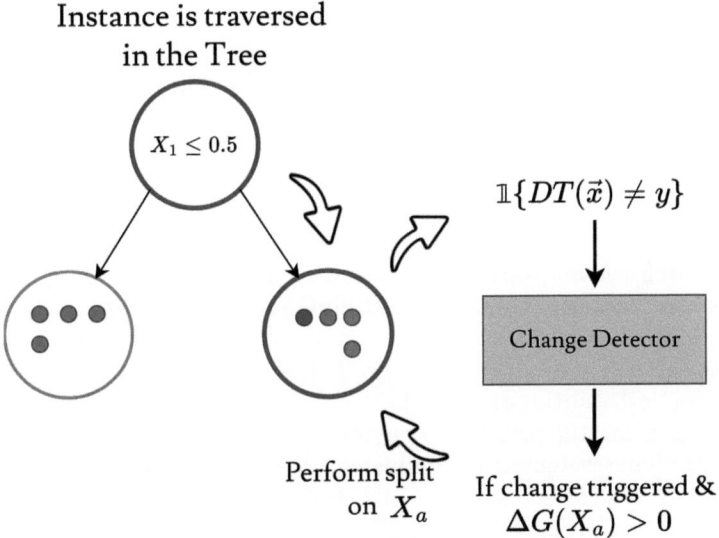

Fig. 2. LAST training process for an instance

2.5 Hoeffding Option Trees

Option nodes let an instance traverse more than one decision path. If an instance reaches an option node, it traverses all the child node paths. For example, if the instance reaches the option node in the tree in Fig. 4, it will follow all paths to the child nodes $\{X_3 \leq 3.7, X_2 \leq 9\}$ (Fig. 3).

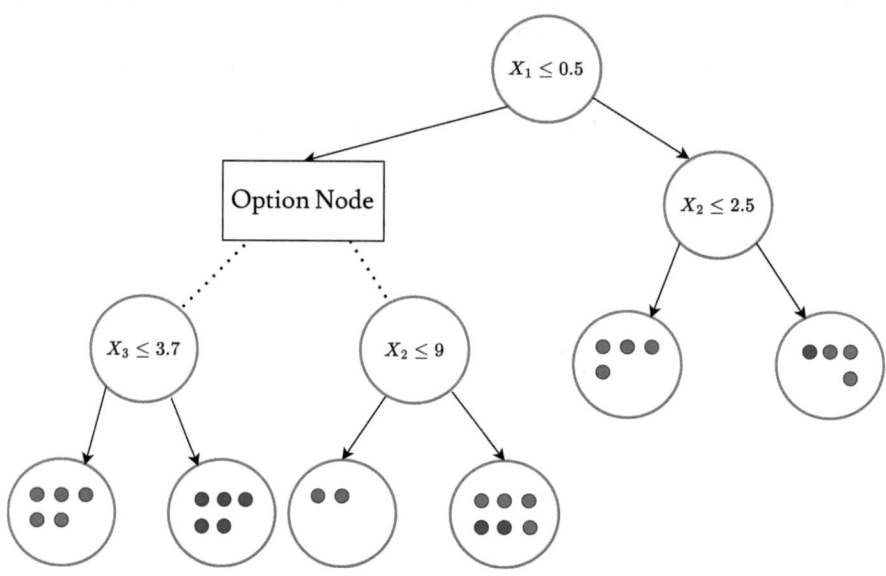

Fig. 3. An Option Tree

In the batch setting, option nodes are created in the training phase with restrictions, for instance, the maximum number of child nodes in option nodes [13]. For voting, since an instance can arrive in more than one leaf node, it is possible to perform majority voting, as in [13], or weighted voting, as in [12], such that the probabilities of each class at each leaf node are summed.

The authors in [10] proposed constraining the maximum number of child nodes and applying weighted voting instead of a simple majority voting scheme. The authors also propose adding child nodes for option nodes that split on features not previously used in the option node children.

Since the tree induction is incremental, adding child nodes to option nodes is also incremental. The authors use a similar approach to the splitting phase. Given a feature X_{max}, the feature with a maximum value of $\Delta G(\cdot)$ in the option node and X_{cand} the candidate feature for splitting in a new child node, a new child node split in X_{cand} is added if pass the constraint in Eq. 3.

$$\Delta G(X_{cand}) - \Delta G(X_{max}) \geq \sqrt{\frac{R^2 \log(\frac{1}{\delta'})}{2n}} \quad (3)$$

In this case, the authors apply a softer confidence $1-\delta' = 0.955$ since the one used in the splitting [3] is $\delta = 10^{-8}$ with confidence $(1-\delta) = 0.99\ldots$, avoiding the creation of few option nodes.

3 Local Adaptive Streaming Tree with Options (LASTO)

In this section, we introduce our proposal called *Local Adaptive Streaming Tree with Options* (LASTO). Compared to traditional Hoeffding Option Trees [10], our approach presents two distinctive characteristics: (i) the adaptive addition of option nodes and (ii) the determination of split attempt moments via adaptive leaf statistics monitoring following the work of [9].

As depicted in [9], the periodic split attempt cannot anticipate changes in the accuracy of the leaf node between two split attempts, and even when little change occurred in the leaf node, the greedy evaluation of attributes and their values that compose the best split will still be performed and might not result in a significant tree change and consume more processing time. The same follows for adding option nodes in non-leaf nodes in [10]. Hoeffding Option Tree cannot anticipate decays in performance between two periodic evaluations for adding new option nodes, and the periodic review of split nodes is costly since multiple nodes will perform split evaluations constantly. In contrast, our algorithm performs split evaluations only in moments where a decay in performance is observable according to the change detector.

Algorithm 1 presents LASTO pseudocode. Lines 1–19 present the LAST algorithm's adaptive splitting mechanism performed at leaf nodes. Lines 19–33 show the adaptive addition of new option nodes for non-terminal nodes of the tree. For the addition of option nodes, since the change detector determines the moment of node addition to the option node and applies a hard constraint for detecting a change in accuracy, we use a softer constraint for the addition of the option node (Algorithm 1, line 23). In this case, the gain of a new split must result in a value superior to the maximum gain of the nodes in the option node, justifying the addition of a new node to the option node.

Algorithm 1 LASTO

Input: S: a data stream, X: a set of attributes, $\Delta G(\cdot)$: a split evaluation function, $maxOptions$: the maximum number of options reachable by a single example, ψ: Change detector used in nodes.

1: **for** each sample $(x, y) \in S$ **do**
2:     Sort x into option nodes L using LASTO
3:     **for** all option nodes l of the set L **do**
4:         Update l statistics using (x, y)
5:         $n_l \leftarrow n_l + 1$
6:         Update l_ψ with $\mathbb{1}\{DT(x) \neq y\}$
7:         **if** l_ψ detected change $\wedge \neg(l$ contains samples from only one class) **then**
8:             **if** l has no children **then**
9:                 Compute $\Delta G(X_i)$ for each $X_i \in X_l$ stored in l
10:                 Let X_a be the attribute with highest ΔG
11:                 **if** $(\Delta G(X_a) > 0.0)$ **then**
12:                     Add nodes below l that split on X_a
13:                     **for** each leaf node l_i from splitting on X_a **do**
14:                         Let $n_{l_i} \leftarrow 0$
15:                         $l_{i\psi} \leftarrow \psi$
16:                     **end for**
17:                 **end if**
18:             **else**
19:                 **if** $l.optionCount < maxOptions$ **then**
20:                     Compute $\Delta G(X_i)$ for existing splits and (non-used) attributes
21:                     Let X_{max} be existing child split with highest ΔG
22:                     Let X_{cand} be (non-used) attribute with highest ΔG
23:                     **if** $\Delta G(X_{cand}) > \Delta G(X_{max})$ **then**
24:                         Add an additional child option to l that splits on X_{cand}
25:                         **for** each leaf node l_i from splitting on X_{cand} **do**
26:                             Let $n_{l_i} \leftarrow 0$
27:                             $l_{i\psi} \leftarrow \psi$
28:                         **end for**
29:                     **end if**
30:                 **else**
31:                     Remove attribute statistics stored at l
32:                 **end if**
33:             **end if**
34:         **end if**
35:     **end for**
36: **end for**

Figure 4 illustrates the LASTO training process, highlighting the paper's main contribution. Specifically, the figure demonstrates the addition of option nodes when a change in accuracy is detected in the subsequent nodes under a decision node. Additionally, it incorporates the information gain constraint, ensuring that an option node is added only if its information gain exceeds the maximum gain among existing option nodes. In the case of Fig. 4, this condition is represented as $\Delta G(X_a) > \Delta G(X_5)$, since there is only one option node in the decision node $\{X_5 \leq 3.2\}$.

Unlike in [10], as the change detectors take into account the performance of the tree, parts of the tree where the performance is decaying, and the split decision at these parts turn out to be not the best option in the long term (instability), the addition of option nodes can mitigate the instability of the tree by aggregating the predictions with more options nodes and decision paths.

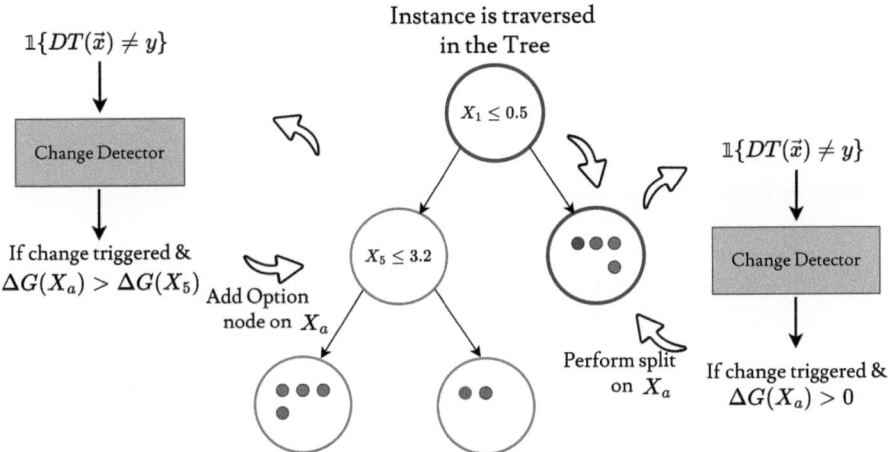

Fig. 4. LASTO training process for an instance

One of the method's main advantages is that the user does not have to specify the *Grace Period*, τ, δ, and δ' hyperparameters. These are crucial hyperparameters for the algorithm's performance, and the optimal value of these parameters can differ in multiple scenarios. Change detectors can also have hyperparameters, but some are well-established regarding change detection, and some have no hyperparameters.

As in [10], we maintain the weighted voting scheme if an instance traverses more than one path and set the maximum number of option nodes to five.

4 Experiments and Results

This section introduces the experimental protocol adopted, followed by the results obtained and discussion.

4.1 Experimental Protocol

All algorithms were implemented in the Massive Online Analysis (MOA) framework [17]. All experiments were done in an Intel(R) Xeon(R) CPU E5649 @ 2.53 GHz with 32 GB of RAM.

The code of the proposal is available in[1] for the MOA framework.

---

[1] https://sites.google.com/view/lasto-paper.

All the Hoeffding Tree-based algorithms evaluated had default hyperparameters from MOA (*Grace Period* = 200, level of confidence = 10^{-7}, impurity measure is information gain). LAST and LASTO had ADWIN [16] as change detectors with default hyperparameters.

We assess the predictive performance using accuracy computed in a prequential validation strategy, where every instance is used first for testing and then for training. Additionally, we measured computational resource usage in terms of CPU-Time (in seconds), RAM-Hours (GB/h), and tree size (number of nodes). CPU-Time reports the full experiment duration, while RAM-Hours and tree size reflect the peak values observed throughout the stream.

Experiments were held with 21 datasets reported in Table 1, with twelve real-world and nine synthetic datasets. The synthetic datasets and parameters used are discussed as follows.

LED [5]. This generator produces 24 boolean features, while 17 are irrelevant. Each feature has a 10% of being inverted, simulating noise. We simulated three abrupt (LED_a) and gradual (LED_g) drifts.

SEA [19]. This generator produces 3 numerical features (f_1, f_2, f_3). If $f_1+f_2 \leq \theta$, the class has value 1, otherwise 0. In this dataset, we simulated three abrupt (SEA_a) and gradual (SEA_g) drifts by changing θ values.

AGRAWAL [18] This generator has six nominal and three numerical features. Ten distinct functions map two classes. In this dataset, we simulate three abrupt (AGR_a) and gradual(AGR_g) datasets.

RBF [17]. This generator produces ten features and 5 class values. Data is generated based on the radial basis function (RBF). Centroids are generated randomly and mapped with a standard deviation value, a weight, and a class label. In this dataset, incremental drifts are simulated by continuously changing the centroids' position. The parameters used were 50 centroids at a speed change of 10^{-4} (moderate, RBF_m) and 10^{-3} (fast, RBF_f).

HYPER [20]. A hyperplane is a flat, $(n-1)$ dimensional subset of that space that divides it into two disconnected parts. Drifts can be simulated incrementally by changing the decision boundary implied. HYPER was set up with 10 features and a magnitude of change of 10^{-3}.

The real-world datasets used were Outdoor, Rialto, Airlines, CovType, Nomao, Poker, NOAA, and three versions of the INSECTS dataset with abrupt, gradual, and incremental drifts, respectively. All real-world datasets were collected from [21].

4.2 Discussion

Table 2 presents the prequential accuracy of the decision trees evaluated, where bold values indicate the best result per dataset, and Fig. 5 provides a critical

Table 1. Description of the evaluated datasets.

Dataset	# examples	# features	# classes	Majority class (%)
LED_a	1,000,000	24	10	10.28
LED_g	1,000,000	24	10	10.28
SEA_a	1,000,000	3	2	59.91
SEA_g	1,000,000	3	2	59.91
AGR_a	1,000,000	9	2	52.83
AGR_g	1,000,000	9	2	52.83
RBF_m	1,000,000	10	5	30.01
RBF_f	1,000,000	10	5	30.01
HYPER	1,000,000	10	2	50
Outdoor	4,000	21	40	4.11
Rialto	82,250	27	10	10
Airlines	539,383	7	2	55.47
CoverType	581,012	54	7	48.75
Nomao	34,465	119	2	71.44
Poker	829,201	10	10	47.78
NOAA	18,158	8	2	69.74
$INSECTS_a$	52,848	33	6	16.07
$INSECTS_i$	57,018	33	6	11.56
$INSECTS_g$	24,150	33	6	15.76
LADPU	22,950	96	10	10
Asfault	8,066	62	5	55.59

distance plot of a pairwise one-sided Wilcoxon signed-rank tests with $\alpha = 0.1$ and form cliques using the Holm correction for multiple testing as performed in [22,23]. LASTO has been shown to improve the results of LAST, as it presented the best ranking overall and statistical difference to all methods. LASTO presented the best ranking in real-world datasets and the second-best ranking in synthetic datasets. Hoeffding Adaptive Trees (HAT) could present the best results in synthetic datasets but could not outperform EFDT in real-world datasets and show no statistical difference to EFDT.

Figure 6 shows a comparison between LASTO and HAT across the evaluated datasets in this work in a scatter plot, while Fig. 7 presents a comparison between LASTO and LAST. LASTO had 14 wins against HAT, and the difference in accuracy is more noticeable than LASTO against LAST. LASTO had 17 wins against LAST.

Figures 8, 9, 10 and 11 present the accuracy throughout time for the datasets LED_a, LED_g, $INSECTS_a$ and $INSECTS_g$, respectively. In the $INSECTS_a$ dataset, HAT showed a significant decrease in accuracy, while LAST and LASTO achieved stabler and higher accuracy. In the third drift of the dataset, LAST had

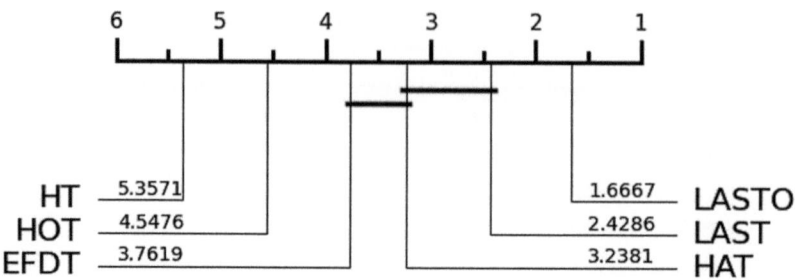

Fig. 5. Critical distance on accuracy with Wilcoxon signed-rank test and $\alpha = 0.01$.

an accuracy decrease bigger than LASTO, and LASTO ended as the most accurate classifier. In the INSECTS$_g$ dataset, HAT presented an accuracy lower than LAST and LASTO, but after the drift, HAT had an accuracy decrease greater than LAST and LASTO. In the LED$_a$ dataset, all methods reacted similarly to drifts, but HAT presented lower accuracy compared to LAST and LASTO. In the LED$_g$ dataset, the methods presented similar behavior, and HAT presented lower accuracy compared to LAST and LASTO until the third drift occurred, and LAST had a big drop in accuracy, while HAT and LASTO remained stable.

Table 3 shows the tree size of decision trees. LASTO presented the worst tree size ranking but presented a lower tree size ranking compared to HT and EFDT in synthetic datasets. In some real-world datasets, LASTO presents smaller tree sizes and higher accuracy than EFDT, such as in Asphalt and INSECTS$_i$. In synthetic data, with the exception of the RBF *dataset*, LASTO had a smaller tree size while achieving higher accuracy. RBF is a dataset that incremental changes occur, such that the detector flags changes recurrently because a change includes multiple intermediary concepts, affecting both LAST and LASTO high complexity in this dataset. Regularization pre-pruning techniques to avoid high complexity [24] or simply a stricter splitting condition that guarantees the split with maximized gain is indeed better than the other possible splits in LAST and LASTO could come to good use.

Figures 12 and 13 present box plots for CPU-Time (in seconds and log scale), and the methods were ordered by the median value. LASTO presented a higher median and upper quartile compared to other methods. In real-world data, LASTO also presented a higher lower quartile greater than other methods, while in synthetic data, HAT was the only method that presented a greater lower quartile compared to LASTO. No more than one clique was identified in a pairwise Wilcoxon signed-rank test with a Holm correction. One must be careful in analyzing log-scaled box plots, as values are small, and slight changes are still feasible as efficient learners for mining data streams.

Table 2. Prequential Accuracy of decision trees

Data Stream	HT	EFDT	HAT	LAST	HOT	LASTO
LED_a	69.03	69.87	73.73	73.93	70.50	**73.94**
LED_g	68.65	69.72	**72.60**	71.49	69.59	72.55
SEA_a	86.42	86.41	**88.81**	86.61	86.42	86.58
SEA_g	86.42	86.37	**88.51**	86.38	86.43	86.67
AGR_a	81.05	82.87	**91.05**	83.94	81.09	84.88
AGR_g	77.37	80.09	**86.53**	80.58	77.50	80.97
RBF_m	45.49	51.27	61.75	64.11	56.55	**72.60**
RBF_f	32.29	31.87	39.16	36.70	33.94	**42.15**
HYPER	78.77	81.59	**86.69**	79.41	79.72	80.10
Outdoor	57.33	59.58	57.27	**60.40**	57.33	60.35
Rialto	31.35	**57.74**	30.62	56.33	27.14	56.71
Airlines	65.08	65.27	63.81	65.52	64.77	**69.83**
CovType	80.31	84.67	81.89	87.52	84.92	**89.27**
Nomao	92.13	93.93	93.97	**94.68**	93.04	93.34
Poker	76.07	76.60	66.87	76.40	76.23	**78.73**
NOAA	73.43	73.23	73.53	73.92	73.64	**74.09**
$INSECTS_a$	53.83	62.24	61.50	63.79	55.95	**64.74**
$INSECTS_i$	52.16	57.06	54.01	58.19	52.16	**59.02**
$INSECTS_g$	60.61	66.42	61.70	**67.61**	60.61	66.68
LADPU	51.20	59.78	51.25	60.63	51.20	**65.42**
Asfault	71.85	83.61	71.86	85.88	71.85	**87.30**
Avg. $Rank_{Synth}$	5.56	4.67	**1.56**	3.11	4.22	1.89
Avg. $Rank_{Real}$	5.21	3.08	4.50	1.92	4.79	**1.50**
Avg. Rank	5.36	3.76	3.24	2.43	4.55	**1.67**

Figures 14 and 15 present box plots for RAM-Hours (in GB/h and log scale), and the methods were ordered by the median value. In real-world data, LASTO presented the highest lower quartile, median, and upper quartile. In synthetic data, LASTO presented lower quartile, median, and upper quartiles that were greater than HOT and HT. No more than one clique was identified in a pairwise Wilcoxon signed-rank test with a Holm correction.

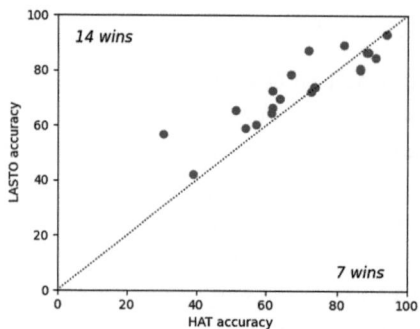

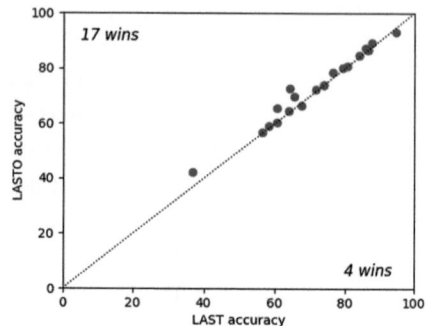

Fig. 6. Comparison of LASTO and HAT accuracy.

Fig. 7. Comparison of LASTO and LAST accuracy.

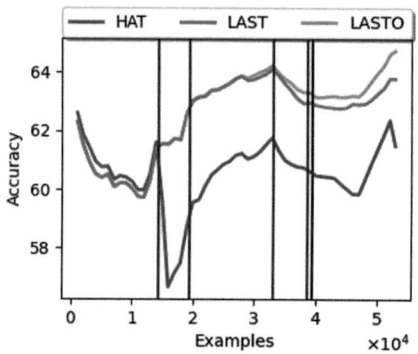

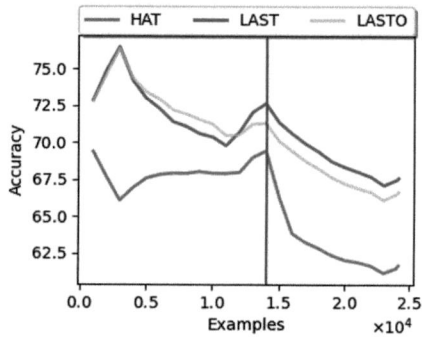

Fig. 8. Accuracy over time in the INSECTS$_a$ dataset.

Fig. 9. Accuracy over time in the INSECTS$_g$ dataset.

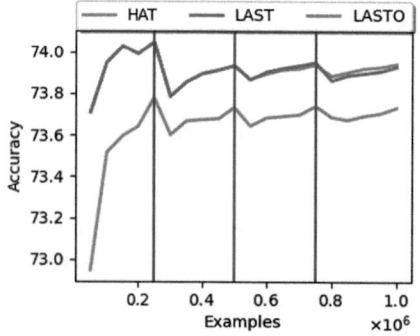

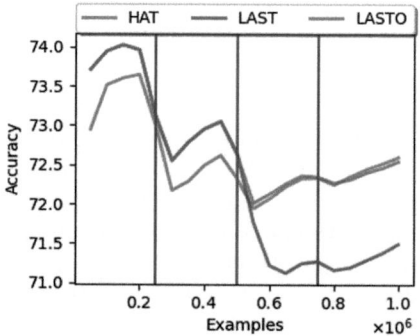

Fig. 10. Accuracy over time in the LED$_a$ dataset.

Fig. 11. Accuracy over time in the LED$_g$ dataset.

Table 3. Tree size (# nodes) of decision trees

Data Stream	HT	EFDT	HAT	LAST	HOT	LASTO
LED_a	229	278	37	**15**	598	37
LED_g	221	299	78	**29**	634	56
SEA_a	753	357	541	**7**	828	19
SEA_g	743	350	1049	**11**	822	46
AGR_a	1056	966	157	**53**	1429	246
AGR_g	1190	623	1220	**187**	1563	843
RBF_m	219	1112	**46**	3277	726	16066
RBF_f	139	170	**82**	1455	290	6022
HYPER	1087	795	618	**225**	3566	1084
Outdoor	**1**	17	**1**	11	**1**	19
Rialto	**9**	164	**9**	185	26	914
Airlines	8582	15146	91376	8873	**1208**	1840
CovType	339	893	**168**	941	1392	2738
Nomao	34	31	**8**	36	98	110
Poker	297	543	**3**	683	1484	3392
NOAA	13	15	**1**	7	28	22
$INSECTS_a$	9	69	**1**	35	22	118
$INSECTS_i$	**7**	65	11	11	10	56
$INSECTS_g$	3	32	**1**	25	4	72
LADPU	**1**	42	**1**	35	**1**	132
Asfault	**1**	23	**1**	5	**1**	20
Avg. $Rank_{Synth}$	3.89	3.56	3.06	**1.89**	5.33	3.28
Avg. $Rank_{Real}$	**1.88**	4.62	2.29	3.62	3.17	5.42
Avg. Rank	2.74	4.17	**2.62**	2.88	4.10	4.50

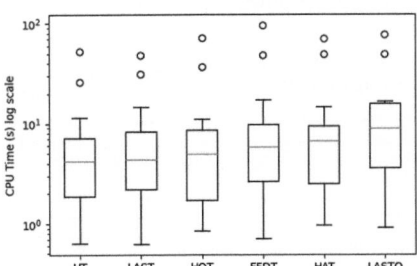

Fig. 12. CPU-Time (seconds, log scale) in real-world datasets.

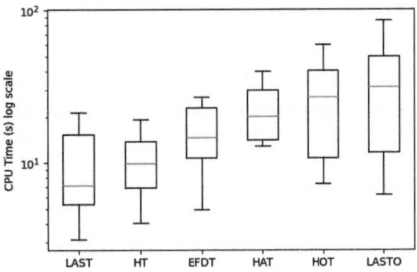

Fig. 13. CPU-Time (seconds, log scale) in synthetic datasets.

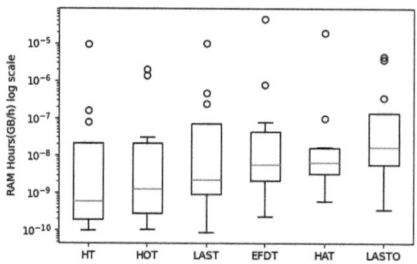
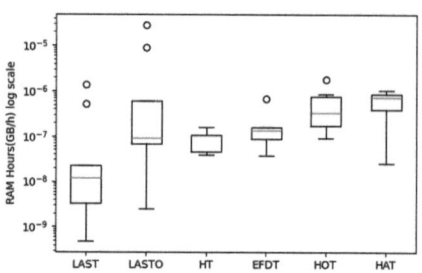

Fig. 14. RAM-Hours (GB/h, log scale) in real-world datasets.

Fig. 15. RAM-Hours (GB/h, log scale) in synthetic datasets.

5 Conclusions

In this work, we propose the *Local Adaptive Streaming Tree with Options (LASTO)* algorithm. LASTO extends the LAST algorithm to allow the creation of option nodes throughout the stream, and the main contribution of this paper is the adaptive creation of option nodes through change detection algorithms. LASTO further leverages the results of LAST and outperforms state-of-the-art decision tree algorithms. LASTO presented higher computational costs in tree size ranks in real-world datasets and lower quartiles, medians, and upper quartiles in CPU-Time and RAM-Hours than most methods, yet no statistical difference in computational cost is observed.

In future works, we plan to propose a tree with an adaptive split reevaluation, as in HAT, that can replace branches with decreasing accuracy in the tree with newer ones, and an adaptive splitting strategy, as in LAST, that can react to changes in the leaf nodes accuracy by splitting the tree. We also plan to adapt LAST and LASTO to regression problems.

Acknowledgments. This work was financed by the Pontifícia Universidade Católica do Paraná (PUCPR) through the PIBIC Master âĂŞ Combined Degree program.

Disclosure of Interests. The authors have no competing interests to declare that are relevant to the content of this article.

References

1. Gomes, H.M., et al.: Adaptive random forests for evolving data stream classification. Mach. Learn. **106**(9–10), 1469–1495 (2017)
2. Lu, J., Liu, A., Dong, F., Gu, F., Gama, J., Zhang, G.: Learning under concept drift: a review. IEEE Trans. Knowl. Data Eng. **31**(12), 2346-2363 (2019). https://doi.org/10.1109/TKDE.2018.2876857
3. Domingos, P., Hulten, G.: Mining high-speed data streams. In: Proceedings of the sixth ACM SIGKDD International Conference on Knowledge Discovery and Data Mining (KDD '00). Association for Computing Machinery, New York, NY, USA, pp. 71–80, 2000. https://doi.org/10.1145/347090.347107

4. Quinlan, J.R.: C4.5: Programs for Machine. Morgan Kaufmann Publishers, 340 Pine Street, 6th Floor San Francisco, CA 94104 USA, 1992
5. Breiman, L.: Classification and Regression Trees. Wadsworth Statistics, Wadsworth, Belmont, CA (1984)
6. Hoeffding, W.: Probability inequalities for sums of bounded random variables, pp. 409–426. The collected works of Wassily Hoeffding, Springer (1963)
7. Bifet, A., Gavaldà, R.: Adaptive learning from evolving data streams. In: Adams, N.M., Robardet, C., Siebes, A., Boulicaut, JF. (eds.) Advances in Intelligent Data Analysis VIII. IDA 2009. LNCS, vol. 5772, pp. 249–260. Springer, Berlin, Heidelberg (2009). https://doi.org/10.1007/978-3-642-03915-7_22
8. Manapragada, C., Webb, G., Salehi, M.: Extremely fast decision tree. In: Proceedings of the 24th ACM SIGKDD International Conference on Knowledge Discovery and Data Mining (KDD '18). ACM, New York, NY, USA, pp. 1953–1962. https://doi.org/10.1145/3219819.3220005
9. Assis, D.N., Barddal, J.P., Enembreck, F.: Just change on change: adaptive splitting time for decision trees in data stream classification. In: Proceedings of ACM SAC Conference (SAC'24). ACM, New York, NY, USA, Article 4, p. 7, 2024. https://doi.org/10.1145/3605098.3635899
10. Pfahringer, B., Holmes, G., Kirkby,R.: New options for hoeffding trees. In: Orgun, M.A., Thornton, J. (eds.) AI 2007: Advances in Artificial Intelligence. AI 2007. LNCS, vol. 4830, pp. 90–99. Springer, Berlin, Heidelberg (2007). https://doi.org/10.1007/978-3-540-76928-6_11
11. Gomes, H.M, Barddal, J.P., Enembreck, F., Bifet, A.: A survey on ensemble learning for data stream classification. ACM Comput. Surv. **50**(2), Article 23, 36 (2018). https://doi.org/10.1145/3054925
12. Buntine, W.: Learning classification trees. Stat. Comput. **2**, 63–73 (1992). https://doi.org/10.1007/BF01889584
13. Kohavi, R., Kunz, C.: Option decision trees with majority votes. In: Proceedings of the Fourteenth International Conference on Machine Learning (ICML '97). Morgan Kaufmann Publishers Inc., San Francisco, CA, USA, pp. 161–169, 1997
14. Gama, J., Rocha, R., Medas, P.: Accurate decision trees for mining high-speed data streams. In: Proceedings of the ninth ACM SIGKDD International Conference on Knowledge Discovery and Data Mining (KDD '03). Association for Computing Machinery, New York, NY, USA, pp. 523–528, 2003. https://doi.org/10.1145/956750.956813
15. Jorge, A.M., Torgo, L., Brazdil, P., Camacho, R., Gama, J. (eds.): PKDD 2005. LNCS (LNAI), vol. 3721. Springer, Heidelberg (2005). https://doi.org/10.1007/11564126
16. Bifet, A., Gavaldà, R.: Learning from time-changing data with adaptive windowing. In: Proceedings of the 7th SIAM International Conference on Data Mining, vol. 7 (2007). https://doi.org/10.1137/1.9781611972771.42
17. Bifet, A., et al.: Moa: massive online analysis, a framework for stream classification and clustering. volume 11 of Proceedings of Machine Learning Research, pp. 44–50, Cumberland Lodge, Windsor, UK, 01–03 September 2010. PMLR
18. Agrawal, R., Imielinski, T., Swami, A.: Database mining: a performance perspective. IEEE Trans. Knowl. Data Eng. **5**(6), 914–925 (1993). https://doi.org/10.1109/69.250074
19. Street, W.N., Kim, Y.: A streaming ensemble algorithm (SEA) for large-scale classification. In: Proceedings of the seventh ACM SIGKDD International Conference on Knowledge Discovery and Data Mining (KDD '01). Association for Computing Machinery, New York, NY, USA, pp. 377–382, 2001

20. Hulten, G., Spencer, L., Domingos, P.: Mining time-changing data streams. In: Proceedings of the Seventh ACM SIGKDD International Conference on Knowledge Discovery and Data Mining (San Francisco, California) (KDD '01). Association for Computing Machinery, New York, NY, USA, pp. 97–106 (2001)
21. Souza, V.M., dos Reis, D.M., Maletzke, A.G., Batista, G.E.: Challenges in benchmarking streaming learning algorithms with real-world data. Data Min. Knowl. Discov. **34**, 1805–1858 (2020)
22. García, S., Herrera, F.: An extension on "statistical comparisons of classifiers over multiple data sets" for all pairwise comparisons. J. Mach. Learn. Res. **9**, 2677–2694 (2008)
23. Benavoli, A., Corani, G., Mangili, F.: Should we really use post-hoc tests based on mean-ranks? J. Mach. Learn. Res. **17**, 1–10 (2016)
24. Barddal, J.P., Enembreck, F.: Learning regularized hoeffding trees from data streams. In: Proceedings of the Annual ACM Symposium on Applied Computing, SAC 2019, Limassol, Cyprus, 08–12 April 2019

ST-LoRA: Low-Rank Adaptation for Spatio-Temporal Forecasting

Weilin Ruan[1], Wei Chen[1], Xilin Dang[2], Jianxiang Zhou[1], Weichuang Li[1], Xu Liu[3], and Yuxuan Liang[1,4](✉)

[1] The Hong Kong University of Science and Technology (Guangzhou), Guangzhou, China
{jzhou814,wli043}@connect.hkust-gz.edu.cn
[2] The Chinese University of Hong Kong, Sha Tin, Hong Kong, China
xldang23@cse.cuhk.edu.hk
[3] National University of Singapore, Singapore, Singapore
liuxu@comp.nus.edu.sg
[4] State Key Lab of Resources and Environmental Information System, Chinese Academy of Sciences, Beijing, China
yuxliang@outlook.com

Abstract. Spatio-temporal forecasting is essential for understanding future dynamics within real-world systems by leveraging historical data from multiple locations. Existing methods often prioritize the development of intricate neural networks to capture the complex dependencies of the data. These methods neglect node-level heterogeneity and face over-parameterization when attempting to model node-specific characteristics. In this paper, we present a novel <u>lo</u>w-<u>r</u>ank <u>a</u>daptation framework for existing <u>s</u>patio-<u>t</u>emporal prediction models, termed ST-LoRA, which alleviates the aforementioned problems through node-level adjustments. Specifically, we introduce the node-adaptive low-rank layer and node-specific predictor, capturing the complex functional characteristics of nodes while maintaining computational efficiency. Extensive experiments on multiple real-world datasets demonstrate that our method consistently achieves superior performance across various forecasting models with minimal computational overhead, improving performance by 7% with only 1% additional parameter cost. The source code is available at https://github.com/RWLinno/ST-LoRA.

1 Introduction

With the rapid advancement of data acquisition technologies and mobile computing, vast spatio-temporal data are being generated for urban analysis and related applications [6,51]. Spatio-temporal forecasting aims to predict future changes based on dynamic temporal observations recorded at static locations with spatial associations [52]. Modeling and analyzing these spatio-temporal dynamic systems can be applied to various prediction scenarios, such as traffic speed forecasting [45,48], taxi demand prediction [47], and air quality prediction [23,25]. Early research primarily focused on traditional time-series models,

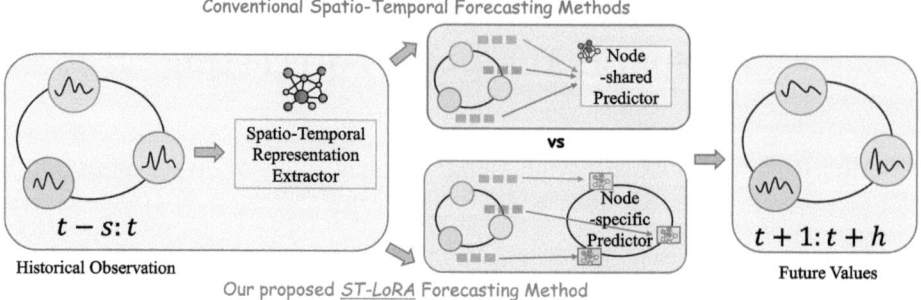

Fig. 1. Comparison between conventional STF methods and our proposed ST-LoRA framework featuring node-specific predictors for node-level fine-tuning.

such as the Historical Average (HA) [36] method and the Auto-Regressive Integrated Moving Average (ARIMA) [26] model, as well as machine learning-based models [38], including Vector Auto-Regression (VAR) [55] and Artificial Neural Networks (ANN) [13]. These methods were applied directly to spatio-temporal forecasting (STF) without considering spatial dependencies, leading to suboptimal performance. With the accumulation of spatio-temporal big data, recent approaches have shifted towards data-driven deep learning models, which are capable of capturing the inherent spatio-temporal dependencies within dynamic systems. Simple yet effective strategies involve using convolutional neural networks (CNNs) [9] to capture spatial dependencies and recurrent neural networks (RNNs) [4,11,49,50] for temporal dependencies, thereby improving performance.

Given the non-Euclidean nature of spatial dependencies, deep learning methods have evolved to combine sophisticated temporal models with Graph Neural Networks (GNNs) [19,44] for capturing both global temporal dependencies and regional patterns. Spatio-temporal graph neural networks (STGNNs) [20,48] have emerged as powerful tools for learning robust high-level spatio-temporal representations through local information aggregation [16]. Recent years have witnessed significant advances in this field, including innovations in graph convolution architectures [7,42], dynamic graph structure learning [15,45], and efficient attention mechanisms [43,53]. Furthermore, researchers have explored integrating advanced techniques such as self-supervised learning [34] and large language models [54] into spatio-temporal prediction tasks. While these sophisticated approaches have achieved remarkable performance improvements, they often come at the cost of increased computational complexity and memory requirements, making it challenging to balance model effectiveness with operational efficiency.

To better understand the landscape of spatio-temporal forecasting, we present a systematic analysis of existing architectures, revealing their common structural patterns as illustrated in Fig. 1. Existing spatio-temporal forecasting methods typically consist of two main components. The first component is the *Spatio-Temporal Representation Extractor*, which serves as the core framework

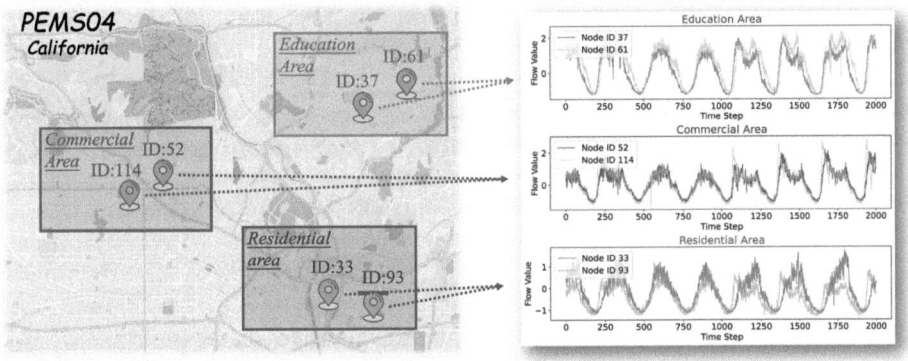

Fig. 2. Traffic flow visualization of each node in different areas on the PEMS04.

and is responsible for capturing high-order complex spatio-temporal relationships. This component can be implemented using various architectures, such as CNNs, RNNs, and STGNNs. The second component is the *Node-Shared Predictor*, which takes the advanced spatio-temporal representations extracted by the first component and predicts future changes for each location. This predictor typically consists of parameter-sharing fully connected layers.

While this two-component architecture has been widely adopted in existing methods, it suffers from a significant limitation: the parameter-sharing node predictor fundamentally struggles to address **node-level heterogeneity**. This shared parameterization approach assumes all nodes exhibit similar behavior patterns that can be modeled using identical parameters. However, in real-world scenarios, nodes frequently display distinct temporal dynamics and behavioral characteristics that shared predictors cannot adequately capture. This heterogeneity is particularly pronounced in urban traffic networks, where sensors distributed across diverse functional areas exhibit unique patterns influenced by their specific contexts and surrounding environments. To illustrate this problem intuitively, we analyze the PEMS04 traffic flow dataset [3] from California, examining nodes across different urban zones (Fig. 2). Our analysis reveals that even nodes 33 and 93, situated within the same residential area, exhibit substantially different temporal evolution patterns between time steps 1250 and 2000. This finding underscores the limitations of current parameter-sharing approaches in modeling node-specific behavioral characteristics. Consequently, existing spatio-temporal forecasting models attempting to address heterogeneity through extensive shared parameterization inevitably confront the **over-parameterization dilemma**. Maintaining separate parameters for each node not only incurs prohibitive computational and memory costs, especially for large-scale networks with hundreds or thousands of nodes, but also significantly increases the risk of model overfitting and compromised generalization performance.

To address these challenges, we draw inspiration from low-rank matrix factorization techniques [33]. Specifically, we first customize a node-adaptive low-rank layer containing multiple trainable matrices, utilizing low-rank decomposition techniques to effectively reduce computational complexity and enhance model training efficiency. Subsequently, we propose a novel lightweight and efficient low-rank adaptation framework named ST-LoRA. This framework seamlessly integrates the low-rank layer into existing spatio-temporal forecasting models through a multi-layer fusion residual stacking approach, thereby achieving node-specific predictors and mitigating the effects of overparameterization. Experimental results on real-world traffic datasets show that our framework significantly improves performance over various baseline methods in spatio-temporal forecasting tasks. Our major contributions can be summarized as follows:

1) A node-level heterogeneity perspective for STF. We are the first to introduce low-rank adaptation techniques to the spatio-temporal domain to explicitly account for the node-level heterogeneity. Our proposed Node Adaptive Low-rank Layers capture diverse node-level patterns and distributions by leveraging low-rank matrix factorization while maintaining computational efficiency.

2) A general low-rank adaptation method for existing ST models. We developed node-specific predictors along with a framework called ST-LoRA, which, in a lightweight and efficient manner, allows existing spatio-temporal prediction models to serve as backbone networks to enhance overall performance.

3) Extensive empirical studies. We rigorously evaluate our proposed method on various models and six public traffic datasets. The experimental results demonstrate that our method significantly enhances prediction accuracy across all baseline models while requiring less than **1%** additional learnable parameters, achieving remarkable more than **7%** performance improvements in terms of average RMSE across prediction horizons.

2 Preliminaries

2.1 Formulation

The objective of STF is to predict future values based on previously observed time series data from N correlated sensors. This sensor network can be represented as a weighted directed graph $\mathcal{G} = (\mathcal{V}, \mathcal{E}, \mathcal{W})$, where $\mathcal{V}$ is the node set with $|\mathcal{V}| = N$, $\mathcal{E}$ is the edge set, and $\mathcal{W} \in \mathbb{R}^{N \times N}$ is a weighted adjacency matrix that encodes the relationships between nodes. The spatio-temporal data observed on $\mathcal{G}$ can be represented as a graph signal $X \in \mathbb{R}^{N \times F}$, where F is the number of features associated with each node. Let $X^{(t)}$ denote the graph signal observed at time t. The spatio-temporal forecasting problem aims to learn a function $\mathcal{F}(\cdot)$ that maps s historical graph signals to h future graph signals, given a graph $\mathcal{G}$:

$$[X^{(t-s+1)}, \ldots, X^{(t)}; \mathcal{G}] \xrightarrow{\mathcal{F}(\cdot)} [X^{(t+1)}, \ldots, X^{(t+h)}]. \tag{1}$$

2.2 Related Work

Spatio-Temporal Forecasting has evolved into a foundational paradigm for predicting future states by leveraging historical observations across spatial and temporal dimensions. Traditional methods grounded in statistical and time series analysis achieved modest success but exhibited significant limitations in modeling complex spatial structures and intricate ST relationships [16,42]. To address these shortcomings, deep learning frameworks have increasingly been embraced, which demonstrate superior capability in extracting latent feature representations, including non-linear spatial and temporal correlations from historical data [29,40,41]. Among these advanced frameworks, Spatio-Temporal Graph Neural Networks (STGNNs) have emerged as powerful tools for prediction tasks. By integrating Graph Neural Networks (GNNs) [19] with sophisticated temporal modeling techniques [49], these architectures effectively capture complex spatio-temporal dynamics through local information aggregation. Over the past decade, several influential STGNN architectures have been proposed, including GWNet [45], STGCN [48], DCRNN [20], and AGCRN [2], each demonstrating remarkable performance across diverse spatio-temporal prediction tasks. Complementing these developments, attention mechanisms [30,39] have gained substantial traction due to their effectiveness in modeling dynamic dependencies inherent in spatio-temporal data. Despite the proliferation and diversification of STGNN architectures, performance improvements have begun to plateau, prompting researchers to explore integrating Self-Supervised Learning (SSL) [22,34] and Large Language Models (LLMs) [17,46,54]. Recent studies have further investigated methods to capture spatio-temporal heterogeneity through techniques such as spatial-temporal decoupled masked pre-training [8] and heterogeneity-informed learning approaches [5].

However, these methods often introduce substantial computational overhead and model complexity. Against this backdrop, we introduce a parameter-efficient node-specific adaptation method that significantly enhances existing forecasting frameworks while maintaining minimal parameter and computational costs.

Low-rank Adaptation is the technique that decomposes high-dimensional parameter spaces into products of low-rank matrices, reducing computational complexity while preserving essential information. The foundational work on LoRA [10,12] demonstrated that injecting trainable low-rank matrices into pre-trained models enables efficient adaptation with minimal parameter overhead. This approach has been refined through variants like DyLoRA [37] with dynamic adaptation mechanisms and Compacter [18] leveraging parameterized complex multiplication layers for task-specific optimization. The extension of low-rank adaptation to multi-modal and spatio-temporal domains represents a significant advancement for complex applications. MTLoRA [1] adapted this approach for multi-task learning scenarios, while robust low-rank reconstruction techniques [14] have shown effectiveness for preserving invariant features across domains. In spatio-temporal forecasting, MFSTN [32] and DeepLGN [24] use matrix or tensor factorization for region-specific parameter decomposition, but

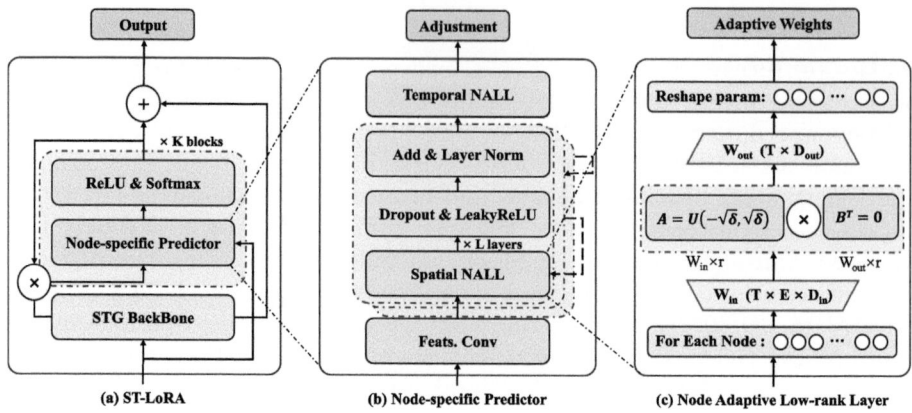

Fig. 3. Overview of the proposed ST-LoRA framework.

their grid-based modeling limits node-level granularity. ST-Adapter [31] introduced low-rank adaptation for cross-modality transfer in spatio-temporal tasks but focused on modality transfer rather than node-specific adaptation.

However, these approaches rely predominantly on region-level predictions, limiting their ability to capture fine-grained node-level heterogeneity and compromising generalizability across diverse spatial configurations. Our proposed framework addresses these limitations by adapting low-rank optimization for node-level heterogeneity in spatio-temporal forecasting.

3 Methodology

In this section, we present ST-LoRA, a lightweight yet effective framework that enhances spatio-temporal models by addressing the node heterogeneity and over-parameterization challenges. As illustrated in Fig. 3, our framework consists of three key components: (a) the gated integration mechanism that enhances existing backbone STGNNs, (b) Node-specific Predictors (NSPs) that capture patterns with node-level fine-tuning, and (c) Node-Adaptive Low-rank Layers (NALLs) that leverage low-rank adaptation for parameter customization.

3.1 Node-Adaptive Low-Rank Layers

The core innovation of ST-LoRA lies in the Node-Adaptive Low-rank Layers (NALL), which introduce learnable low-rank matrices to efficiently customize the base model parameters for different nodes. Let $\mathbf{W} \in \mathbb{R}^{d_{out} \times d_{in}}$ represent the base weight matrix, where d_{in} and d_{out} are the input and output dimensions, respectively. Traditional approaches would require a complete set of parameters for each node, leading to $\mathcal{O}(N \cdot d_{in} \cdot d_{out})$ parameters for N nodes, which is computationally prohibitive for large-scale spatio-temporal networks. Drawing inspiration from low-rank matrix factorization theory [21], NALL decomposes the parameter matrix $\Delta \mathbf{W}$ into the product of two low-rank matrices. For node v_i with input $\mathbf{x}$, the adaptation process can be formally expressed as:

$$\Delta \mathbf{W}_{v_i} = \mathbf{BA}_{v_i} \cdot \frac{\alpha}{r}, \quad \hat{\mathbf{y}}_\mathbf{i} = \sigma \left(\mathbf{Wx} + \Delta \mathbf{W}_{v_i} \mathbf{x} + \mathbf{b} \right), \tag{2}$$

where $\mathbf{B} \in \mathbb{R}^{d_{out} \times r}$ and $\mathbf{A}_i \in \mathbb{R}^{r \times d_{in}}$ are learnable low-rank matrices with rank r, α is a scaling factor controlling the adaptation magnitude, and σ is a non-linear activation function (e.g., LeakyReLU). This formulation reduces the parameter complexity from $\mathcal{O}(N \cdot d_{in} \cdot d_{out})$ to $\mathcal{O}(r \cdot (d_{in} + d_{out}) + N \cdot r^2)$, representing a significant reduction when $r \ll \min(d_{in}, d_{out})$. By constraining adaptations to lower-dimensional node-specific patterns, NALL efficiently captures meaningful behavioral differences while preventing overfitting to node-specific noise patterns. During inference, while $\mathbf{W}$ remains frozen to preserve the pre-trained knowledge, $\mathbf{A}_i$ and $\mathbf{B}$ continue to adapt and capture node-specific patterns. Our implementation further enhances NALL with dropout with $p = 0.3$ and Kaiming initialization to stabilize training dynamics and improve convergence stability.

3.2 Node-Specific Predictors

While a single NALL layer provides efficient parameter adaptation, capturing complex spatio-temporal dependencies requires a more sophisticated architectural design. We propose Node-Specific Predictors (NSP) that hierarchically stack multiple NALL layers with residual connections to model heterogeneous patterns across different nodes. Given an input sequence $\mathbf{X}_{t-T:t} \in \mathbb{R}^{T \times N \times D}$, where T is the sequence length, N is the number of nodes, and D is the feature dimension, NSP processes the input through following integrated components:

$$\begin{aligned} \mathbf{H}^{(0)} &= \mathrm{Conv2D}(\mathbf{X}_{t-T:t}), \\ \mathbf{H}^{(l)} &= \mathbf{H}^{(l-1)} + \mathrm{NALL}^{(l)}(\sigma(\mathbf{H}^{(l-1)})), \quad l = 1, 2, ..., L \\ \hat{\mathbf{Y}}_t &= \mathcal{G}_t(\mathbf{H}^{(L)}), \end{aligned} \tag{3}$$

where $\mathbf{H}^{(l)} \in \mathbb{R}^{T \times N \times D}$ represents the hidden feature representations at layer l, $\mathrm{Conv2D}(\cdot)$ first extracts temporal features using convolution operations with optimized kernel configurations, multiple NALL layers then process spatial information through residual connections, and finally $\mathcal{G}_t$ projects the features for temporal prediction. The activation function σ incorporates RMSNorm and dropout to control model complexity and enhance training stability.

The key innovation of NSP lies in its unified approach to spatio-temporal modeling. Unlike traditional GNNs that rely on fixed graph convolutions, NSP leverages the low-rank structure of NALLs to achieve both spatial and temporal adaptability. Specifically, the spatial patterns are captured through the rank-constrained weight matrices in NALLs, which naturally aggregate node-specific information, while the temporal dependencies are modeled through the sequential application of adapted transformations. This design enables NSP to efficiently capture complex node-specific patterns while maintaining computational efficiency through the low-rank structure of NALL layers. The effectiveness of this architecture is particularly evident in scenarios with heterogeneous node behaviors, where traditional fixed-parameter approaches often struggle to capture diverse patterns simultaneously. Importantly, while NSP provides node-specific adaptations, it preserves spatial dependencies captured by the backbone model by operating on representations that already encode inter-node relationships, thus complementing rather than replacing existing spatial modeling mechanisms.

3.3 ST-LoRA Integration

To enhance model generalization and adaptability to diverse spatio-temporal patterns, we propose ST-LoRA, a novel low-rank adaptation framework for spatio-temporal data that seamlessly integrates existing backbone models with our NSP module. Let f_θ denote a pre-trained spatio-temporal backbone model and $\mathcal{H}(\cdot)$ represent our NSP-based enhancement operator. The ST-LoRA framework employs a hierarchical architecture with multiple NSP blocks to capture complex spatio-temporal dependencies at different scales. Given input sequence $\mathbf{X}_{t-T:t}$, the integration process can be formulated as:

$$\begin{aligned}
\mathbf{Y}_{\text{base}} &= f_\theta(\mathbf{X}_{t-T:t}), \\
\mathbf{Z}^{(1)} &= \mathcal{H}^{(1)}(\sigma(\mathbf{Y}_{\text{base}})), \\
\mathbf{Z}^{(k)} &= \mathcal{H}^{(k)}(\sigma([\mathbf{X}_{t-T:t}, \mathbf{Z}^{(k-1)}])), \quad k=2,\ldots,K \\
\mathbf{R} &= \sigma(\mathcal{F}([\mathbf{X}_{t-T:t}, \frac{1}{K}\sum_{k=1}^{K}\mathbf{Z}^{(k)}])), \\
\mathbf{Y}_{\text{final}} &= \mathbf{R} \odot \mathbf{Y}_{\text{base}} + (1-\mathbf{R}) \odot \frac{1}{K}\sum_{k=1}^{K}\mathbf{Z}^{(k)},
\end{aligned} \quad (4)$$

where K is the number of NSP blocks, σ is a non-linear activation function (e.g., ReLU), $[\cdot,\cdot]$ denotes feature concatenation, $\mathcal{F}$ is a learnable fusion layer that generates adaptive blending weights, and $\mathbf{R} \in [0,1]$ is a node-specific gating tensor that controls the contribution of the adaptation mechanism. This allows NSP blocks to access both original historical context and refined node-specific representations, enabling the framework to capture diverse spatio-temporal patterns at different scales while maintaining stability through averaging.

The framework is optimized end-to-end using a temporal Mean Absolute Error (MAE) loss with L2 regularization over the prediction horizon T':

$$\mathcal{L} = \frac{1}{T'}\sum_{i=1}^{T'} \|\mathbf{X}_{t+i} - \mathbf{Y}_{\text{final}}^{(t+i)}\|_1 + \lambda\|\alpha\|_2, \quad (5)$$

where λ controls the strength of the regularization term on the gating parameter. This formulation ensures accurate predictions through the MAE term while preventing over-reliance on either the backbone model or the adaptation.

The effectiveness of ST-LoRA stems from its ability to preserve the backbone model's general prediction capability while introducing node-specific adaptations through the NSP blocks, making it suitable for complex real-world scenarios with heterogeneous spatio-temporal patterns. By integrating NALLs and NSPs, ST-LoRA provides an efficient solution to the fundamental trade-off between modeling node-level heterogeneity and managing computational complexity.

4 Experiments

In this section, we conduct extensive experiments to investigate the following Research Questions (RQ):

- **RQ1:** Can ST-LoRA be seamlessly integrated with various spatio-temporal prediction models?
- **RQ2:** How effectively does our framework improve prediction performance across different scenarios?
- **RQ3:** What are the computational overhead and parameter costs of our framework?
- **RQ4:** How do different architectural choices affect the model's performance?

4.1 Experimental Setup

Datasets. We evaluate our approach on six public traffic datasets that are widely used in spatio-temporal forecasting research. As summarized in Table 1, these datasets encompass both traffic speed measurements (METR-LA, PEMS-BAY) and traffic flow records (PEMS03/04/07/08), featuring diverse spatial scales ranging from 170 to 883 sensor nodes and temporal ranges spanning 16,992 to 52,116 timestamps. Following standard practice, we split each dataset chronologically into training, validation, and testing sets with ratios of 7:1:2 for speed datasets and 6:2:2 for flow datasets. All above datasets are divided along the time axis into three non-overlapping parts, including training, validation, and test sets. METR-LA and PEMS-BAY are divided in a fraction of 7:1:2 while PEMS03, PEMS04, PEMS07, and PEMS08 are divided in a fraction of 6:2:2.

Table 1. Statistics and description of datasets we used.

Dataset	#Nodes	#Edges	#Frames	Time Range	Type
METR-LA	207	1515	34,272	03/01/2012 - 06/27/2012	Traffic speed
PEMS-BAY	325	2369	52,116	01/01/2017 - 06/30/2017	Traffic speed
PEMS03	358	547	26208	09/01/2018 - 11/30/2018	Traffic flow
PEMS04	307	340	16992	01/01/2018 - 02/28/2018	Traffic flow
PEMS07	883	866	28224	05/01/2017 - 08/06/2017	Traffic flow
PEMS08	170	295	17856	07/01/2016 - 08/31/2016	Traffic flow

Evaluation Protocol. We adopt three standard metrics for evaluation: Mean Absolute Error (MAE), Root Mean Square Error (RMSE), and Mean Absolute Percentage Error (MAPE). For comprehensive assessment, we examine model performance across different prediction horizons (15-min, 30-min, and 60-min) and report both the horizon-specific and average results. Each experiment is repeated five times with different random seeds to ensure statistical reliability.

Baselines. We evaluate six representative spatio-temporal prediction models as backbone networks to validate the effectiveness of the ST-LoRA framework. Long Short-Term Memory (LSTM) [11] controls the flow of information by introducing a gating mechanism to selectively keep and forget temporal data. Spatio-temporal Graph Convolution Network (STGCN) [48] combines graph convolution and 1D convolution to process spatio-temporal data. Graph WaveNet (GWN) [45] utilizes adaptive adjacency matrices and dilation convolution to capture spatial and temporal correlations in traffic data. Adaptive Graph Convolutional Recurrent Network (AGCRN) [2] infers dependencies between streaming time series through node adaptive parameter learning and data-adaptive graph generation modules. Decoupled Dynamic Spatio-Temporal Graph Neural Network (D2STGNN) [35] is able to separate diffuse and intrinsic traffic information, thus enhancing dynamic graph learning. Finally, Spatio-Temporal Adaptive Embedding transformer (STAE) [27] encodes nodal, spatial, and temporal features through linear layers and multiple embedding layers respectively.

4.2 Model Settings of ST-LoRA (RQ1)

All experiments are conducted using the PyTorch framework on a Linux server equipped with NVIDIA RTX A6000 GPUs. For model training, we employ Adam optimizer with an initial learning rate of 0.001 and weight decay of 0.0005. The evaluation metrics include MAE, RMSE, and MAPE, which are standard in traffic forecasting tasks. For comprehensive assessment, we reported the average performance across all 12 prediction horizons on four traffic flow datasets (PEMS03, PEMS04, PEMS07, and PEMS08).

We directly converted the original baselines to ST-LoRA framework as backbones. The learning rate is set to be adjusted in step 10, and the ratio is 0.1. Various models are implemented concerning the benchmark LargeST [28] and their official source code. For hyper-parameters in the framework, such as the number of NSPs is usually taken as 1, the number of node adaptive low-rank layers is usually taken as 4, and the maximum rank of the low-rank space is usually taken as 16, which is generally adjusted according to the original model. This setup ensures that we seamlessly integrate existing methods into our framework. Experiments show that our proposed framework supports multiple spatio-temporal prediction models, including the aforementioned baselines.

4.3 Performance Comparisons (RQ2)

To validate the effectiveness of our framework, we conducted comprehensive experiments across multiple models and datasets. Specifically, we analyze the performance improvements of different baseline models on the PEMS04 dataset (Table 2), and the generalization capability of our framework across multiple traffic datasets (Table 3). For statistical reliability, each experiment was repeated five times, with models enhanced by our framework denoted with a "+" suffix.

Table 2. The improvement of different models in the PEMS04 dataset. Here, lower values indicate better performance. All six baselines have achieved significant improvements, denoted by Δ. The subscripts indicate standard deviations.

Model	15min MAE ↓	15min RMSE ↓	15min MAPE% ↓	30min MAE ↓	30min RMSE ↓	30min MAPE% ↓	60min MAE ↓	60min RMSE ↓	60min MAPE% ↓	Avg MAE ↓	Avg RMSE ↓	Avg MAPE% ↓
HA	$28.92_{\pm1.28}$	$42.69_{\pm1.82}$	$20.31_{\pm0.89}$	$33.73_{\pm1.28}$	$49.37_{\pm1.85}$	$24.01_{\pm0.91}$	$46.97_{\pm1.31}$	$67.43_{\pm1.89}$	$35.11_{\pm0.92}$	$38.03_{\pm1.28}$	$59.24_{\pm1.85}$	$27.88_{\pm0.91}$
VAR	$21.94_{\pm0.62}$	$34.30_{\pm1.02}$	$16.42_{\pm0.48}$	$23.72_{\pm0.71}$	$36.58_{\pm1.08}$	$18.02_{\pm0.52}$	$26.76_{\pm0.82}$	$40.28_{\pm1.23}$	$20.94_{\pm0.64}$	$23.51_{\pm0.72}$	$36.39_{\pm1.11}$	$17.85_{\pm0.55}$
SVR	$22.52_{\pm0.68}$	$35.30_{\pm1.12}$	$14.71_{\pm0.45}$	$27.63_{\pm0.78}$	$42.23_{\pm1.25}$	$18.29_{\pm0.49}$	$37.86_{\pm1.15}$	$56.01_{\pm1.70}$	$26.72_{\pm0.82}$	$28.66_{\pm0.87}$	$44.59_{\pm1.36}$	$19.15_{\pm0.59}$
LSTM	$21.94_{\pm0.59}$	$33.37_{\pm0.93}$	$15.32_{\pm0.40}$	$25.83_{\pm0.66}$	$39.10_{\pm1.04}$	$20.35_{\pm0.43}$	$36.41_{\pm0.82}$	$50.73_{\pm1.28}$	$29.92_{\pm0.56}$	$27.14_{\pm0.69}$	$41.59_{\pm1.08}$	$18.20_{\pm0.46}$
LSTM+	$18.89_{\pm0.58}$	$29.96_{\pm0.91}$	$13.02_{\pm0.40}$	$21.31_{\pm0.65}$	$34.22_{\pm1.04}$	$13.96_{\pm0.43}$	$26.34_{\pm0.80}$	$41.30_{\pm1.26}$	$18.26_{\pm0.56}$	$22.18_{\pm0.68}$	$35.16_{\pm1.07}$	$15.08_{\pm0.46}$
Δ	$-3.05_{\pm0.18}$	$-3.41_{\pm0.20}$	$-2.30_{\pm0.14}$	$-4.52_{\pm0.27}$	$-4.88_{\pm0.29}$	$-6.39_{\pm0.38}$	$-10.07_{\pm0.60}$	$-9.43_{\pm0.57}$	$-11.66_{\pm0.70}$	$-4.96_{\pm0.30}$	$-6.43_{\pm0.39}$	$-3.12_{\pm0.19}$
STGCN	$19.45_{\pm0.59}$	$30.12_{\pm0.92}$	$14.21_{\pm0.43}$	$21.85_{\pm0.62}$	$34.43_{\pm0.97}$	$14.13_{\pm0.44}$	$26.97_{\pm0.68}$	$41.11_{\pm1.06}$	$16.84_{\pm0.48}$	$22.70_{\pm0.63}$	$35.55_{\pm0.98}$	$14.59_{\pm0.45}$
STGCN+	$19.12_{\pm0.58}$	$29.72_{\pm0.91}$	$13.89_{\pm0.42}$	$19.92_{\pm0.61}$	$31.63_{\pm0.96}$	$13.77_{\pm0.42}$	$22.07_{\pm0.67}$	$34.47_{\pm1.05}$	$15.42_{\pm0.47}$	$20.37_{\pm0.62}$	$31.94_{\pm0.97}$	$14.36_{\pm0.44}$
Δ	$-0.33_{\pm0.02}$	$-0.40_{\pm0.02}$	$-0.32_{\pm0.02}$	$-1.93_{\pm0.12}$	$-2.80_{\pm0.17}$	$-0.36_{\pm0.02}$	$-4.90_{\pm0.29}$	$-6.64_{\pm0.40}$	$-1.42_{\pm0.09}$	$-2.33_{\pm0.14}$	$-3.61_{\pm0.22}$	$-0.23_{\pm0.01}$
GWNet	$18.65_{\pm0.57}$	$29.24_{\pm0.89}$	$13.82_{\pm0.42}$	$19.57_{\pm0.60}$	$30.62_{\pm0.92}$	$13.28_{\pm0.39}$	$23.07_{\pm0.70}$	$35.35_{\pm1.08}$	$17.34_{\pm0.53}$	$25.45_{\pm0.62}$	$39.70_{\pm0.97}$	$17.29_{\pm0.45}$
GWNet+	$17.89_{\pm0.55}$	$28.52_{\pm0.87}$	$12.64_{\pm0.39}$	$18.88_{\pm0.58}$	$29.38_{\pm0.89}$	$13.06_{\pm0.40}$	$20.89_{\pm0.64}$	$32.96_{\pm1.00}$	$14.92_{\pm0.46}$	$19.22_{\pm0.59}$	$30.62_{\pm0.93}$	$13.54_{\pm0.41}$
Δ	$-0.76_{\pm0.05}$	$-0.72_{\pm0.04}$	$-1.18_{\pm0.07}$	$-0.69_{\pm0.04}$	$-1.24_{\pm0.07}$	$-0.22_{\pm0.01}$	$-2.18_{\pm0.13}$	$-2.39_{\pm0.14}$	$-2.42_{\pm0.15}$	$-6.23_{\pm0.37}$	$-9.08_{\pm0.54}$	$-3.75_{\pm0.23}$
AGCRN	$18.12_{\pm0.55}$	$29.45_{\pm0.90}$	$12.85_{\pm0.39}$	$18.77_{\pm0.57}$	$30.08_{\pm0.92}$	$12.97_{\pm0.40}$	$20.41_{\pm0.62}$	$32.87_{\pm1.00}$	$14.38_{\pm0.44}$	$19.83_{\pm0.58}$	$32.26_{\pm0.94}$	$13.40_{\pm0.41}$
AGCRN+	$17.83_{\pm0.54}$	$29.16_{\pm0.89}$	$12.55_{\pm0.38}$	$18.63_{\pm0.57}$	$29.99_{\pm0.91}$	$12.82_{\pm0.39}$	$19.97_{\pm0.61}$	$32.37_{\pm0.99}$	$13.78_{\pm0.42}$	$18.81_{\pm0.57}$	$30.51_{\pm0.93}$	$13.05_{\pm0.40}$
Δ	$-0.29_{\pm0.02}$	$-0.29_{\pm0.02}$	$-0.30_{\pm0.02}$	$-0.14_{\pm0.01}$	$-0.09_{\pm0.01}$	$-0.15_{\pm0.01}$	$-0.44_{\pm0.03}$	$-0.50_{\pm0.03}$	$-0.60_{\pm0.04}$	$-1.02_{\pm0.06}$	$-1.75_{\pm0.11}$	$-0.35_{\pm0.02}$
STAE	$17.95_{\pm0.55}$	$29.12_{\pm0.89}$	$12.65_{\pm0.39}$	$18.92_{\pm0.58}$	$30.09_{\pm0.92}$	$13.35_{\pm0.41}$	$21.06_{\pm0.64}$	$33.37_{\pm1.02}$	$15.55_{\pm0.47}$	$19.31_{\pm0.59}$	$30.86_{\pm0.94}$	$13.85_{\pm0.42}$
STAE+	$17.65_{\pm0.54}$	$28.73_{\pm0.88}$	$12.45_{\pm0.38}$	$18.62_{\pm0.57}$	$29.55_{\pm0.90}$	$13.29_{\pm0.41}$	$20.40_{\pm0.62}$	$32.38_{\pm0.99}$	$15.00_{\pm0.46}$	$18.89_{\pm0.58}$	$30.22_{\pm0.92}$	$13.58_{\pm0.41}$
Δ	$-0.30_{\pm0.02}$	$-0.39_{\pm0.02}$	$-0.20_{\pm0.01}$	$-0.30_{\pm0.02}$	$-0.54_{\pm0.03}$	$-0.06_{\pm0.01}$	$-0.66_{\pm0.04}$	$-0.99_{\pm0.06}$	$-0.55_{\pm0.03}$	$-0.42_{\pm0.03}$	$-0.64_{\pm0.04}$	$-0.27_{\pm0.02}$
D2STGNN	$18.95_{\pm0.58}$	$29.85_{\pm0.91}$	$14.82_{\pm0.45}$	$19.96_{\pm0.61}$	$31.34_{\pm0.95}$	$15.52_{\pm0.47}$	$23.34_{\pm0.71}$	$35.89_{\pm1.09}$	$17.39_{\pm0.53}$	$20.75_{\pm0.63}$	$32.36_{\pm0.99}$	$15.91_{\pm0.49}$
D2STGNN+	$18.25_{\pm0.56}$	$28.92_{\pm0.88}$	$14.12_{\pm0.43}$	$19.21_{\pm0.59}$	$30.50_{\pm0.93}$	$13.46_{\pm0.41}$	$21.73_{\pm0.66}$	$33.73_{\pm1.03}$	$17.00_{\pm0.52}$	$19.73_{\pm0.60}$	$31.05_{\pm0.95}$	$14.86_{\pm0.45}$
Δ	$-0.70_{\pm0.04}$	$-0.93_{\pm0.06}$	$-0.70_{\pm0.04}$	$-0.75_{\pm0.05}$	$-0.84_{\pm0.05}$	$-2.06_{\pm0.12}$	$-1.61_{\pm0.10}$	$-2.16_{\pm0.13}$	$-0.39_{\pm0.02}$	$-1.02_{\pm0.06}$	$-1.31_{\pm0.08}$	$-1.05_{\pm0.06}$

Table 3. Performance Improvements of one of the backbone STGNNs on Multiple Traffic Datasets. We use STGCN in the table as an example to illustrate the significant enhancement of our method from the perspective of the dataset.

Dataset	15min MAE	15min RMSE	15min MAPE%	30min MAE	30min RMSE	30min MAPE%	60min MAE	60min RMSE	60min MAPE%	Avg MAE	Avg RMSE	Avg MAPE%
PEMS04	$-0.33_{\pm0.02}$	$-0.40_{\pm0.03}$	$-0.07_{\pm0.01}$	$-1.45_{\pm0.09}$	$-2.50_{\pm0.15}$	$-0.10_{\pm0.01}$	$-4.94_{\pm0.30}$	$-6.61_{\pm0.40}$	$-1.28_{\pm0.08}$	$-2.24_{\pm0.14}$	$-3.17_{\pm0.19}$	$-0.48_{\pm0.03}$
PEMS08	$-0.20_{\pm0.01}$	$-1.09_{\pm0.07}$	$-0.57_{\pm0.03}$	$-1.37_{\pm0.08}$	$-1.79_{\pm0.11}$	$-0.30_{\pm0.02}$	$-7.63_{\pm0.46}$	$-5.86_{\pm0.35}$	$-1.28_{\pm0.08}$	$-3.07_{\pm0.18}$	$-2.91_{\pm0.17}$	$-0.72_{\pm0.04}$
PEMS03	$-0.31_{\pm0.02}$	$-0.51_{\pm0.03}$	$-0.72_{\pm0.04}$	$-0.22_{\pm0.01}$	$-0.23_{\pm0.01}$	$-0.60_{\pm0.04}$	$-0.45_{\pm0.03}$	$-0.35_{\pm0.02}$	$-1.25_{\pm0.08}$	$-0.33_{\pm0.02}$	$-0.36_{\pm0.02}$	$-0.86_{\pm0.05}$
PEMS07	$-0.26_{\pm0.02}$	$-0.29_{\pm0.02}$	$-0.16_{\pm0.01}$	$-0.38_{\pm0.02}$	$-0.35_{\pm0.02}$	$-0.31_{\pm0.02}$	$-0.59_{\pm0.04}$	$-0.59_{\pm0.04}$	$-0.32_{\pm0.02}$	$-0.41_{\pm0.03}$	$-0.41_{\pm0.03}$	$-0.26_{\pm0.02}$
METR-LA	$-0.10_{\pm0.01}$	$-0.36_{\pm0.02}$	$-0.03_{\pm0.00}$	$-0.33_{\pm0.02}$	$-0.83_{\pm0.05}$	$-0.80_{\pm0.05}$	$-1.05_{\pm0.06}$	$-1.97_{\pm0.12}$	$-2.30_{\pm0.14}$	$-0.49_{\pm0.03}$	$-1.05_{\pm0.06}$	$-1.04_{\pm0.06}$
PEMSBAY	$-0.04_{\pm0.00}$	$-0.06_{\pm0.00}$	$-0.11_{\pm0.01}$	$-0.10_{\pm0.01}$	$-0.45_{\pm0.03}$	$-0.23_{\pm0.01}$	$-0.50_{\pm0.03}$	$-1.14_{\pm0.07}$	$-1.02_{\pm0.06}$	$-0.21_{\pm0.01}$	$-0.55_{\pm0.03}$	$-0.45_{\pm0.03}$

As shown in Table 2, ST-LoRA demonstrates consistent performance improvements across various baseline models, ranging from traditional models to state-of-the-art approaches. For traditional methods, LSTM achieves remarkable improvements with MAE reductions of 3.05, 4.52, and 10.07 at 15-min, 30-min, and 60-min horizons, respectively. The enhancement is particularly evident in long-term predictions, where STGCN shows MAE reductions of 0.33, 1.93, and 4.90 across different horizons. Even sophisticated models like D2STGNN and AGCRN benefit from our framework, with D2STGNN achieving consistent MAE reductions of 0.70, 0.75, and 1.61, while AGCRN shows stable improvements with an average MAE reduction of 1.02. These results validate the effectiveness of our framework in enhancing STGNNs through node-level low-rank adaptations.

The results in Table 3 demonstrate our framework's generalization capability across diverse datasets. Using STGCN as an example, we observe substantial improvements on all datasets. On PEMS04, MAE reductions of 0.33, 1.45, and 4.94 are achieved for 15-min, 30-min, and 60-min horizons respectively, with an average reduction of 2.24. PEMS08 shows even stronger improvements with MAE reductions up to 7.63 for 60-min predictions. The effectiveness varies systematically across different prediction horizons, with longer-term predictions (60-min) consistently exhibiting more significant improvements. On datasets with distinct spatial structures (PEMS03, PEMS07, METR-LA, and PEMS-BAY), the framework maintains robust performance gains. These improvements across datasets with varying node counts confirm the framework's versatile adaptability to different types of spatio-temporal data.

The superior performance can be attributed to two key aspects. First, our node-adaptive approach provides a precisely calibrated parameter space for fine-tuning predictions while maintaining computational efficiency through low-rank matrix factorization. Second, the additional parameters from low-rank matrices effectively capture complex spatio-temporal dependencies, including regional characteristics, temporal dynamics, and node interactions, all achieved within a compressed parameter space. This synergistic combination of adaptive capacity and computational efficiency enables our framework to enhance various baseline models consistently across diverse prediction scenarios.

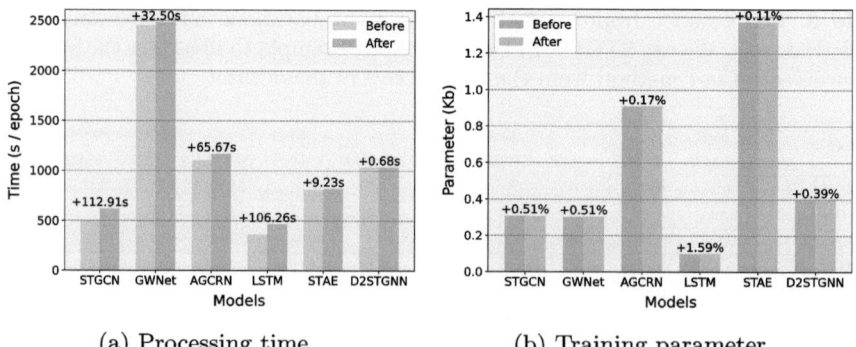

Fig. 4. Efficiency study comparing time and parameter cost of ST-LoRA.

4.4 Efficiency and Scalability Studies (RQ3)

Time Efficiency. In Fig. 4(a), we analyze the computational overhead when integrating our framework with existing models. The results demonstrate that ST-LoRA introduces minimal additional training time while delivering substantial performance gains. With 16 NALLs and 4 MLRFs to enhance, the time increase remains remarkably efficient, adding a mere 0.68 s for D2STGNN. This efficiency stems from our low-rank adaptation strategy, which maintains stable training times even with multiple node-specific predictors.

Framework Scalability. We evaluate parameter efficiency across six baseline models using consistent node adaptive low-rank layer configurations. As shown in Fig. 4(b), our approach achieves remarkable parameter efficiency, requiring less than 1% additional trainable parameters for most models while delivering 4.2% to 7.3% improvements in average RMSE. Notably, the smallest LSTM model maintains overhead below 2% while achieving an impressive 15% reduction in Average RMSE. This demonstrates ST-LoRA's ability to effectively capture and adapt to node heterogeneity with minimal computational overhead.

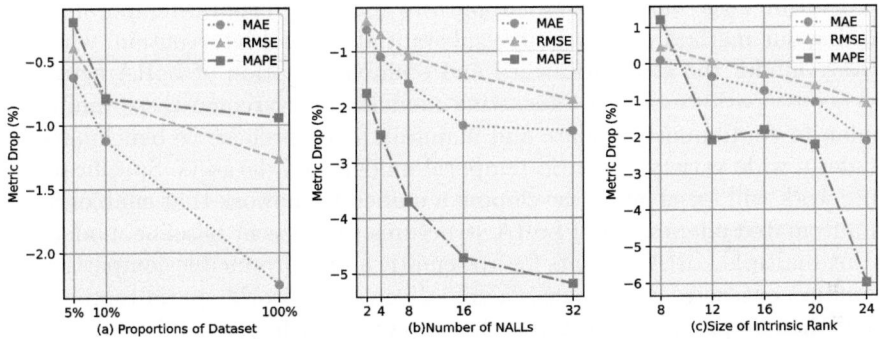

Fig. 5. Parameter sensitivity analysis examining the impact of varying dimensions, placements, and quantities of adaptive components on model performance.

4.5 Parameter Sensitivity Analysis (RQ4)

In our experiments, we fixed the number of layers at 4 and the node embedding dimension at 12, which are the two most critical parameters. The node embedding dimension represents the rank of the low-rank matrix required for the additional parameters of the nodes, which tends to increase as more feature information is included in the data. After stacking multiple layers of NALL, the fine-tuning effect of these additional parameter spaces is amplified. It is important to design these two hyper-parameters in a balanced way because a larger parameter space does not necessarily mean it is easier to learn. We again use the

STGCN model and the PEMS04 dataset as an example to explore the relationship between the size of this dataset as well as the two hyper-parameters and the lifting effect, and the results are shown in Fig. 5.

5 Conclusion

In this paper, we focus on the challenges of node-level heterogeneity and over-parameterization in spatio-temporal modeling. We introduce ST-LoRA, a novel framework featuring Node-Adaptive Low-rank Layers and Node-Specific Predictors that efficiently customize parameters while maintaining computational efficiency. Our proposed approach enhances existing models by effectively capturing heterogeneous features and distributional changes within independent nodes. The improvements demonstrate that efficient low-rank adaptation can significantly enhance forecasting in domains with heterogeneous node behaviors.

6 Limitation and Future Work

Despite the promising improvements brought by ST-LoRA, the development and application of Low-rank adaptation techniques have so far been mostly concentrated within large models. When applied to specialized spatio-temporal models, adapting our method often requires substantial manual intervention, which collectively hinder the straightforward and scalable adoption of LoRA across heterogeneous spatio-temporal forecasting models. To overcome these limitations, we plan to continuously update and maintain a comprehensive benchmark that includes a wide variety of spatio-temporal models and datasets. Specifically, our future work will focus on: 1) developing a unified framework that enables flexible and automated adaptation of LoRA structures to different baseline models, supporting multiple LoRA variants for systematic and reproducible comparison; and 2) conduct extensive experiments across diverse real-world spatio-temporal scenarios, thereby providing the research community with a fair and comprehensive baseline for future studies.

Acknowledgment. This work is supported by the National Natural Science Foundation of China (No. 62402414), the Guangdong Basic and Applied Basic Research Foundation (No. 2025A1515011994), and a grant from State Key Laboratory of Resources and Environmental Information System. This study is also supported by the Guangzhou Municipal Science and Technology Project (No. 2023A03J0011), the Guangzhou Industrial Information and Intelligent Key Laboratory Project (No. 2024A03J0628), and Guangdong Provincial Key Lab of Integrated Communication, Sensing and Computation for Ubiquitous Internet of Things (No. 2023B1212010007).

References

1. Agiza, A., Neseem, M., Reda, S.: Mtlora: low-rank adaptation approach for efficient multi-task learning. In: Proceedings of the IEEE/CVF Conference on Computer Vision and Pattern Recognition, pp. 16196–16205, 2024

2. Bai, L., Yao, L., Li, C., Wang, X., Wang, C.: Adaptive graph convolutional recurrent network for traffic forecasting. Adv. Neural Inf. Process. Syst. **33**, 17804–17815 (2020)
3. Chen, C., Petty, K., Skabardonis, A., Varaiya, P., Jia, Z.: Freeway performance measurement system: mining loop detector data. Transp. Res. Rec. **1748**(1), 96–102 (2001)
4. Chung, J., Gulcehre, C., Cho, K., Bengio, Y.: Empirical evaluation of gated recurrent neural networks on sequence modeling, 2014
5. Dong, Z., et al.: Heterogeneity-informed meta-parameter learning for spatiotemporal time series forecasting. In: Proceedings of the 30th ACM SIGKDD Conference on Knowledge Discovery and Data Mining, 2024
6. Du, R., Santi, P., Xiao, M., Vasilakos, A.V., Fischione, C.: The sensable city: a survey on the deployment and management for smart city monitoring. IEEE Commun. Surv. Tutor. **21**(2), 1533–1560 (2018)
7. Fang, Z., Long, Q., Song, G., Xie, K.: Spatial-temporal graph ode networks for traffic flow forecasting. In: Proceedings of the 27th ACM SIGKDD Conference on Knowledge Discovery & Data Mining, pp. 364–373, 2021
8. Gao, H., Jiang, R., Dong, Z., Deng, J., Ma, Y., Song, X.: Spatial-temporal-decoupled masked pre-training for spatiotemporal forecasting. arXiv preprint arXiv:2312.00516, 2023
9. Jiuxiang, G., et al.: Recent advances in convolutional neural networks. Pattern Recogn. **77**, 354–377 (2018)
10. Hayou, S., Ghosh, N., Yu, B.: Lora+: efficient low rank adaptation of large models. arXiv preprint arXiv:2402.12354, 2024
11. Hochreiter, S., Schmidhuber, J.: Long short-term memory. Neural Comput. **9**(8), 1735–1780 (1997)
12. Hu, E.J., et al.: Lora: low-rank adaptation of large language models, 2021
13. Huang, W., Song, G., Hong, H., Xie, K.: Deep architecture for traffic flow prediction: deep belief networks with multitask learning. IEEE Trans. Intell. Transp. Syst. **15**(5), 2191–2201 (2014)
14. Jhuo, I.H., Liu, D., Lee, D.T., Chang, S.F.: Robust visual domain adaptation with low-rank reconstruction. In: 2012 IEEE Conference on Computer Vision and Pattern Recognition, pp. 2168–2175. IEEE, 2012
15. Jiang, R., et al.: Spatio-temporal meta-graph learning for traffic forecasting. In: Proceedings of the AAAI Conference on Artificial Intelligence, vol. 37, pp. 8078–8086 (2023)
16. Jin, G., et al.: Spatio-temporal graph neural networks for predictive learning in urban computing: a survey. IEEE Trans. Knowl. Data Eng. (2023)
17. Jin, M., et al.: Position: what can large language models tell us about time series analysis. In: Forty-first International Conference on Machine Learning, 2024
18. Karimi Mahabadi, R., Henderson, J., Ruder, S.: Compacter: efficient low-rank hypercomplex adapter layers. Adv. Neural Inf. Process. Syst. **34**, 1022–1035 (2021)
19. Kipf, T.N., Welling, M.: Semi-supervised classification with graph convolutional networks, 2016
20. Li, Y., Yu, R., Shahabi, C., Liu, Y.: Diffusion convolutional recurrent neural network: data-driven traffic forecasting (2017)
21. Li, Y., Ma, T., Zhang, H.: Algorithmic regularization in over-parameterized matrix sensing and neural networks with quadratic activations. In: Conference On Learning Theory, pp. 2–47. PMLR, 2018

22. Li, Z., Huang, C., Xia, L., Xu, Y., Pei, J. : Spatial-temporal hypergraph self-supervised learning for crime prediction. In: 2022 IEEE 38th International Conference on Data Engineering (ICDE), pp. 2984–2996. IEEE, 2022
23. Liang, Y., Ke, S., Zhang, J., Yi, X., Zheng, Y.: Geoman: multi-level attention networks for geo-sensory time series prediction. In: IJCAI 2018, pp. 3428–3434 (2018)
24. Liang, Y., et al.: Revisiting convolutional neural networks for citywide crowd flow analytics. In: Hutter, F., Kersting, K., Lijffijt, J., Valera, I. (eds.) Machine Learning and Knowledge Discovery in Databases. ECML PKDD 2020. LNCS, vol. 12457, pp. 578–594. Springer, Cham (2021). https://doi.org/10.1007/978-3-030-67658-2_33
25. Liang, Y., et al.: Airformer: predicting nationwide air quality in China with transformers. In: Proceedings of the AAAI Conference on Artificial Intelligence, pp. 14329–14337, 2023
26. Lippi, M., Bertini, M., Frasconi, P.: Short-term traffic flow forecasting: an experimental comparison of time-series analysis and supervised learning. IEEE Trans. Intell. Transp. Syst. **14**(2), 871–882 (2013)
27. Liu, H., et al.: Spatio-temporal adaptive embedding makes vanilla transformer sota for traffic forecasting. In: Proceedings of the 32nd ACM International Conference on Information and Knowledge Management, pp. 4125–4129, 2023
28. Liu, X., et al.: Largest: a benchmark dataset for large-scale traffic forecasting. Adv. Neural Inf. Process. Syst. **36** (2024)
29. Lv, Y., Duan, Y., Kang, W., Li, Z., Wang, F.-Y.: Traffic flow prediction with big data: a deep learning approach. IEEE Trans. Intell. Transp. Syst. **16**(2), 865–873 (2014)
30. Ma, Y., Lou, H., Yan, M., Sun, F., Li, G.: Spatio-temporal fusion graph convolutional network for traffic flow forecasting. Information Fusion **104**, 102196 (2024)
31. Pan, J., Lin, Z., Zhu, X., Shao, J., Li, H.: St-adapter: parameter-efficient image-to-video transfer learning. Adv. Neural Inf. Process. Syst. **35**, 26462–26477 (2022)
32. Pan, Z., Wang, Z., Wang, W., Yu, Y., Zhang, J., Zheng, Y.: Matrix factorization for spatio-temporal neural networks with applications to urban flow prediction. In: Proceedings of the 28th ACM International Conference on Information and Knowledge Management, pp. 2683–2691, 2019
33. Sainath, T.N., Kingsbury, B., Sindhwani, V., Arisoy, E., Ramabhadran, B.: Low-rank matrix factorization for deep neural network training with high-dimensional output targets. In: 2013 IEEE International Conference on Acoustics, Speech and Signal Processing, pp. 6655–6659. IEEE, 2013
34. Shao, Z., Zhang, Z., Wang, F., Xu, Y.: Pre-training enhanced spatial-temporal graph neural network for multivariate time series forecasting. In: Proceedings of the 28th ACM SIGKDD Conference on Knowledge Discovery and Data Mining, pp. 1567–1577, 2022
35. Shao, Z., et al.: Decoupled dynamic spatial-temporal graph neural network for traffic forecasting. Proc. VLDB Endow. **15**(11), 2733–2746 (2022)
36. Smith, B.L., Demetsky, M.J.: Traffic flow forecasting: comparison of modeling approaches. J. Transp. Eng. **123**(4), 261–266 (1997)
37. Valipour, M., Rezagholizadeh, M., Kobyzev, I., Ghodsi, A.: Dylora: parameter efficient tuning of pre-trained models using dynamic search-free low-rank adaptation. arXiv preprint arXiv:2210.07558, 2022
38. Lint, J.W.C., Hinsbergen, C.P.I.J.: Short-term traffic and travel time prediction models. Artif. Intell. Appl. Crit. Transp. Issues **22**(1), 22–41 (2012)
39. Vaswani, A., et al.: Attention is all you need. Adv. Neural Inf. Process. Syst. **30** (2017)

40. Wang, H., Zhang, R., Cheng, X., Yang, L.: Hierarchical traffic flow prediction based on spatial-temporal graph convolutional network. IEEE Trans. Intell. Transp. Syst. **23**(9), 16137–16147 (2022)
41. Wang, S., Cao, J., Philip, S.Y.: Deep learning for spatio-temporal data mining: a survey. IEEE Trans. Knowl. Data Eng. **34**(8), 3681–3700 (2020)
42. Wang, X., et al.: Traffic flow prediction via spatial temporal graph neural network. In: Proceedings of the Web Conference 2020, pp. 1082–1092 (2020)
43. Haixu, W., Jiehui, X., Wang, J., Long, M.: Autoformer: decomposition transformers with auto-correlation for long-term series forecasting. Adv. Neural Inf. Process. Syst. **34**, 22419–22430 (2021)
44. Wu, Z., Pan, S., Chen, F., Long, G., Zhang, C., Yu, P.S.: A comprehensive survey on graph neural networks. IEEE Trans. Neural Netw. Learn. Syst. **32**(1), 4–24 (2020)
45. Wu, Z., Pan, S., Long, G., Jiang, J., Zhang, C.: Graph wavenet for deep spatial-temporal graph modeling. In: Proceedings of the 28th International Joint Conference on Artificial Intelligence, pp. 1907–1913, 2019
46. Yan, Y., et al.: Urbanclip: learning text-enhanced urban region profiling with contrastive language-image pretraining from the web. In: Proceedings of the ACM on Web Conference 2024, pp. 4006–4017 (2024)
47. Yao, H., et al.: Deep multi-view spatial-temporal network for taxi demand prediction. In: Proceedings of the AAAI Conference on Artificial Intelligence, 2018
48. Yu, B., Yin, H., Zhu, Z.: Spatio-temporal graph convolutional networks: a deep learning framework for traffic forecasting. In: Proceedings of the 27th International Joint Conference on Artificial Intelligence, pp. 3634–3640, 2018
49. Yong, Yu., Si, X., Changhua, H., Zhang, J.: A review of recurrent neural networks: lstm cells and network architectures. Neural Comput. **31**(7), 1235–1270 (2019)
50. Zhang, D., Kabuka, M.R.: Combining weather condition data to predict traffic flow: a gru-based deep learning approach. IET Intell. Transp. Syst. **12**(7), 578–585 (2018)
51. Zhang, J., Wang, F.-Y., Wang, K., Lin, W.-H., Xin, X., Chen, C.: Data-driven intelligent transportation systems: a survey. IEEE Trans. Intell. Transp. Syst. **12**(4), 1624–1639 (2011)
52. Zhang, Q., Chang, J., Meng, G., Xiang, S., Pan, C.: Spatio-temporal graph structure learning for traffic forecasting. In: Proceedings of the AAAI Conference on Artificial Intelligence, vol. 34, pp. 1177–1185 (2020)
53. Zhou, T., Ma, Z., Wen, Q., Wang, X., Sun, L., Jin, R.: Fedformer: frequency enhanced decomposed transformer for long-term series forecasting. In: International Conference on Machine Learning, pp. 27268–27286. PMLR, 2022
54. Zhou, T., Niu, P., Sun, L., Jin, R., et al.: One fits all: power general time series analysis by pretrained lm. Adv. Neural Inf. Process. Syst. **36** (2024)
55. Zivot, E., Wang, J.: Vector autoregressive models for multivariate time series. In: Modeling Financial Time Series with S-PLUS®, pp. 385–429. Springer, New York (2006). https://doi.org/10.1007/978-0-387-21763-5_11

Identifiable Autoregressive Variational Autoencoders for Nonlinear and Nonstationary Spatio-Temporal Blind Source Separation

Mika Sipilä[1](✉), Klaus Nordhausen[2], and Sara Taskinen[1]

[1] Department of Mathematics and Statistics, University of Jyvaskyla, Jyvaskyla, Finland
mika.e.sipila@jyu.fi
[2] Department of Mathematics and Statistics, University of Helsinki, Helsinki, Finland

Abstract. The modeling and prediction of multivariate spatio-temporal data involve numerous challenges. Dimension reduction methods can significantly simplify this process, provided that they account for the complex dependencies between variables and across time and space. Nonlinear blind source separation has emerged as a promising approach, particularly following recent advances in identifiability results. Building on these developments, we introduce the identifiable autoregressive variational autoencoder, which ensures the identifiability of latent components consisting of nonstationary autoregressive processes. The blind source separation efficacy of the proposed method is showcased through a simulation study, where it is compared against state-of-the-art methods, and the spatio-temporal prediction performance is evaluated against several competitors on air pollution and weather datasets.

Keywords: variational autoencoder · identifiability · multivariate spatio-temporal data · nonlinear ICA

1 Introduction

In multivariate spatio-temporal data, the multivariate observations $x(s,t) := x^t := x \in \mathcal{X} \subset \mathbb{R}^S$ are collected in various spatial locations $s \in \mathcal{S} \subset \mathbb{R}^D$ at times $t \in \mathcal{T} \subset \mathbb{R}$, where $\mathcal{X}$ is the domain of x, $\mathcal{S}$ and $\mathcal{T}$ are spatial and temporal domains, respectively, and D is a spatial dimension. Modeling and predicting such data are highly challenging and computationally demanding due to the

---

This research was supported by the Research Council of Finland (363261, 453691) and the Vilho, Yrjö and Kalle Väisälä foundation.

Supplementary Information The online version contains supplementary material available at https://doi.org/10.1007/978-3-032-06109-6_21.

© The Author(s), under exclusive license to Springer Nature Switzerland AG 2026
R. P. Ribeiro et al. (Eds.): ECML PKDD 2025, LNAI 16019, pp. 362–380, 2026.
https://doi.org/10.1007/978-3-032-06109-6_21

fact that the spatio-temporal dependency structures, as well as the dependencies between the variables, have to be accounted for. These dependencies are often modeled through $S \times S$ dimensional covariance function $\boldsymbol{C}(\boldsymbol{x}(\boldsymbol{s},t), \boldsymbol{x}(\boldsymbol{s}',t'))$. Modeling the covariance function is especially complicated in case of nonstationary data [20,21], which means that the covariance function $\boldsymbol{C}$ cannot be simplified to stationary form $\boldsymbol{C}(\boldsymbol{x}(\boldsymbol{s},t), \boldsymbol{x}(\boldsymbol{s}',t')) = \boldsymbol{C}(\|\boldsymbol{s}-\boldsymbol{s}'\|, |t-t'|)$. Instead, for nonstationary data, the covariance function $\boldsymbol{C}$ changes when spatial or temporal locations are shifted.

Spatio-temporal data modeling can be simplified without restrictive assumptions like stationarity, by using blind source separation. In blind source separation, it is assumed that the observation $\boldsymbol{x}$ is generated from the independent latent component $\boldsymbol{z}(\boldsymbol{s},t) := \boldsymbol{z}^t := \boldsymbol{z} \in \mathbb{R}^P$ through a mixing function $\boldsymbol{f}$ as

$$\boldsymbol{x} = \boldsymbol{f}(\boldsymbol{z}). \tag{1}$$

Once the latent components are successfully recovered, they can be modeled independently due to their assumed statistical independence. The dependencies among the components of the observed variable vector $\boldsymbol{x}$ are therefore presumed to arise exclusively from the mixing function $\boldsymbol{f}$. Blind source separation (BSS) aims to recover the latent components by estimating the mixing and unmixing functions from the observed data.

While most traditional BSS methods, such as spatio-temporal BSS (STBSS) [19], are limited only to linear mixing function $\boldsymbol{f}(\boldsymbol{z}) = \boldsymbol{A}\boldsymbol{z}$, where $\boldsymbol{A}$ is a $S \times P$ matrix, nonlinear BSS variants have also been recently developed. In the nonlinear case however stronger assumptions are needed for identifiability. One such approach for nonlinear BSS assumes, for example, structural sparsity [16]. Other recent developments are mostly for time series, and they solve nonlinear BSS by exploiting either stationary autocorrelation structure or nonstationary variances. For these methods, see [9] and the references therein.

In particular, [13] introduced identifiable variational autoencoder (iVAE) for nonlinear and nonstationary temporal BSS. Later, iVAE have been extended to nonstationary spatial data in [23] and to nonstationary spatio-temporal data in [22]. However, all previous iVAE methods are identifiable only if the latent components possess nonstationary variance, and they do not incorporate previous observations in time in the model. Instead, the previous methods model the nonstationary variance only based on the spatial and temporal location of the observations.

In this paper, we assume that each latent component z_i, for $i = 1, \ldots, P$, is generated by a nonstationary autoregressive process defined as follows:

$$z_i(\boldsymbol{s},t) = \mu_i(\boldsymbol{s},t) + \sum_{r=1}^{R} \gamma_{i,r}(\boldsymbol{s},t)\Big(z_i(\boldsymbol{s},t-r) - \mu_i(\boldsymbol{s},t-r)\Big) + \omega_i(\boldsymbol{s},t), \tag{2}$$

where μ_i is a nonstationary trend function, R is the autoregressive order, $\gamma_{i,r}$ is a time- and location-dependent autoregressive coefficient function, and ω_i is the innovation term, also varying over location $\boldsymbol{s}$ and time t. A similar model to (2) is considered in [5] in the context of stationary subspace analysis for time series.

We propose an identifiable autoregressive variational autoencoder (iVAEar) which extends the identifiability also to nonstationary autoregressive coefficients. In Sect. 2, we discuss iVAEar's model assumptions and identifiability conditions, and in Sect. 3 we introduce the iVAEar method to estimate the model. We demonstrate iVAEar's latent component estimation performance through comprehensive simulation studies in Sect. 4, and illustrate its multivariate spatio-temporal forecasting potential in Sect. 5. Finally, the paper is concluded in Sect. 6. All proofs are given in the supplement[1] together with some additional material.

2 Autoregressive Latent Component Model and Identifiability

In this section, we introduce an autoregressive latent component model and its identifiability results under nonstationary data. We begin by establishing general identifiability conditions for autoregressive latent component models in Definition 1 and Theorems 1 and 2. We then examine specific cases that yield stronger identifiability results: first, we provide general results for the case where $R = 0$ (Proposition 1), followed by results for Gaussian latent components and Gaussian autoregressive latent components (Propositions 2 and 3, respectively). Note, that although we focus on spatio-temporal data in the paper, all the results and estimation methods apply also for time series data by dropping the spatial location out of the equations.

In original iVAE [13], the main assumption leading to identifiability of the latent component model is that an additional variable $u \in \mathcal{U}$, where $\mathcal{U}$ is the domain of u, is observed so that the latent components z have a conditional distribution $p(z|u) = \prod_{i=1}^{P} p(z_i|u)$. In all previous iVAE methods, u has included information on temporal, spatial, or spatio-temporal location of the observation. In iVAEar, we assume that in addition to spatio-temporal location, we also have the previous R observations in time, $\{x(s, t-1), \ldots, x(s, t-R)\} := x^-$, as the additional data. The autoregressive assumption leads to the following generative deep latent variable model:

$$p(x, z | x^-; u) = p(x|z) p(z|z^-; u), \quad (3)$$

where $z^- = \{z(s, t-1), \ldots, z(s, t-R)\}$ is the set of previous latent components in time. Following [13], the distribution $p(x|z)$ is defined as

$$p(x|z) = p_\epsilon(x - f(z)), \quad (4)$$

meaning that x decomposes into $x = f(z) + \epsilon$, where ϵ is an independent noise vector. In non-noisy nonlinear BSS (1), p_ϵ can be modeled with a zero mean Gaussian distribution with infinitesimal variance. Further, it is assumed that

---

[1] https://github.com/mikasip/iVAEar.

the conditional latent distribution is part of the exponential family:

$$p_{T,\lambda}(z|z^-, u) = \prod_{i=1}^{P} \frac{Q_i(z_i, z_i^-)}{Z_i(u)} \exp\left[\sum_{j=1}^{k} T_{i,j}(z_i, z_i^-) \lambda_{i,j}(u)\right], \quad (5)$$

where $Q_i(z_i, z_i^-)$ is a base measure, $Z_i(u)$ is a normalizing constant, $\boldsymbol{T}_i(z_i, z_i^-) = (T_{i,1}(z_i, z_i^-), \ldots, T_{i,k}(z_i, z_i^-))^\top$ contains sufficient statistics, and $\boldsymbol{\lambda}_i(u) = (\lambda_{i,1}(u), \ldots, \lambda_{i,k}(u))^\top$ contains the parameters depending on u. The dimension k of each sufficient statistic $\boldsymbol{T}_i(z_i, z_i^-)$ and $\boldsymbol{\lambda}_i(u)$ is assumed to be fixed. The formulation (5) reduces to general exponential family formula if the autoregressive order $R = 0$. The exponential family form in (5) includes variables z_i generated through AR processes with any exponential family innovations if the location μ_i and AR coefficients γ_i^r are constant. Some AR processes, such as processes with Gaussian or exponential distributed innovations, fall in this form even with non-stationary location and AR coefficients. The properties of Gaussian AR processes are discussed in more detail later in this section.

Assuming the generative model defined by the Eqs. (3)–(5), and nonlinear BSS (1) problem, it is of interest to identify the latent components z as well as possible to obtain information about the true generative process behind the observed data. Hence, we next define two identifiability classes that can be obtained with sufficient assumptions. In following, we use the notation $\{\boldsymbol{f}^{-1}(\boldsymbol{x}(s, t-1)), \ldots, \boldsymbol{f}^{-1}(\boldsymbol{x}(s, t-R))\} := \boldsymbol{f}^{-1}(\boldsymbol{x}^-)$ to denote the unmixing function applied to previous R observations in time individually.

Definition 1. *Consider the real parameter set $(\boldsymbol{f}, \boldsymbol{T}, \boldsymbol{\lambda})$ and the estimated one $(\tilde{\boldsymbol{f}}, \tilde{\boldsymbol{T}}, \tilde{\boldsymbol{\lambda}})$ of mixing functions, sufficient statistics and natural parameters such that $p_{f,T,\lambda}(\boldsymbol{x}|\boldsymbol{x}^-, \boldsymbol{u}) = p_{\tilde{f},\tilde{T},\tilde{\lambda}}(\boldsymbol{x}|\boldsymbol{x}^-, \boldsymbol{u})$ for all $\boldsymbol{x}, \boldsymbol{x}^- \in \mathcal{X}$ and $\boldsymbol{u} \in \mathcal{U}$. If there exists an invertible $Pk \times Pk$ matrix $\boldsymbol{A}$ and a vector $\boldsymbol{c}$ so that*

$$\tilde{\boldsymbol{T}}(\tilde{\boldsymbol{f}}^{-1}(\boldsymbol{x}), \tilde{\boldsymbol{f}}^{-1}(\boldsymbol{x}^-)) = \boldsymbol{A}\boldsymbol{T}(\boldsymbol{f}^{-1}(\boldsymbol{x}), \boldsymbol{f}^{-1}(\boldsymbol{x}^-)) + \boldsymbol{c} \quad (6)$$

for all $\boldsymbol{x}, \boldsymbol{x}^- \in \mathcal{X}$, the set $(\boldsymbol{f}, \boldsymbol{T}, \boldsymbol{\lambda})$ is identifiable up to an affine transformation. If $\boldsymbol{A}$ is a block permutation matrix, then the set $(\boldsymbol{f}, \boldsymbol{T}, \boldsymbol{\lambda})$ is identifiable up to block-affine transformation.

The block-affine identifiability is a stronger result, and often desirable. Block-affine identifiability is closely related to permutation and signed scale indeterminacy of z of linear BSS. To build intuition about how block-affine identifiability relates to the identifiability of the latent components z, we next provide sufficient conditions on the sufficient statistics $\boldsymbol{T}$ in the case $R = 0$ that ensure identifiability of z up to permutation and component-wise nonlinearity.

Proposition 1. *Assume that the set $(\boldsymbol{f}, \boldsymbol{T}, \boldsymbol{\lambda})$ is identifiable up to block-affine transformation and that the autoregressive order $R = 0$. Further assume:*

(i) A non-noisy BSS model (1), i.e. that $\boldsymbol{z} = \boldsymbol{f}^{-1}(\boldsymbol{x})$.

(ii) There is a function $\tilde{g}_i : \mathbb{R}^k \to \mathbb{R}$ for all $i = 1, \ldots P$ such that $\tilde{g}_i(\tilde{\boldsymbol{T}}_i(\tilde{z}_i)) = a_i \tilde{z}_i$, where $a_i \neq 0$.

Then we have that $\tilde{\boldsymbol{f}}^{-1}(\boldsymbol{x}) = \tilde{\boldsymbol{z}} = \boldsymbol{P}(g_1(z_1), \ldots, g_P(z_P))^\top$, where $\boldsymbol{P}$ is a $P \times P$ permutation matrix and $g_1, \ldots g_P$ are component-wise nonlinearities.

Assumption (ii) of Proposition 1 holds for most of common exponential family distributions such as Gaussian, beta, gamma, Pareto, Poisson and exponential distributions, which have sufficient statistic of the form $T(x) = x$ or $T(x) = \log(x)$. If we have a noisy nonlinear BSS instead of non-noisy, there is an additional noise indeterminacy for each component. For the case $R > 0$ with autoregressive dependencies, similar results can be derived so that the component-wise nonlinearities would depend also on their previous values, i.e., that $\tilde{\boldsymbol{f}}^{-1}(\boldsymbol{x}) = \tilde{\boldsymbol{z}} = \boldsymbol{P}(g_1(z_1, z_1^-), \ldots, g_P(z_P, z_P^-))^\top$. However, for specific autoregressive models, stronger identifiability results can be obtained. In particular, later in this section we demonstrate that for Gaussian autoregressive latent processes, the latent components can be identified up to permutation, location and scale transformations.

Next, we introduce two theorems that give sufficient conditions to achieve affine or block-affine identifiability. The main identifiability theorem is as follows:

Theorem 1. *When the data are generated according the generative model in (3)–(5), and the following holds:*

(i) *The set $\{\boldsymbol{x} \in \mathcal{X} | \rho_\epsilon(\boldsymbol{x}) = 0\}$ has measure zero, where $\mathcal{X}$ is a domain of $\boldsymbol{x}$ and ρ_ϵ is a characteristic function of the density p_ϵ in (4).*
(ii) *The mixing function $\boldsymbol{f}$ in (4) is injective.*
(iii) *The sufficient statistics $T_{i,j}$ in (5) are differentiable with respect to z_i almost everywhere, and the functions $T_{i,1}, \ldots, T_{i,k}$ are linearly independent on any subset of $\mathcal{X}$ with positive measure.*
(iv) *There exist $Pk+1$ distinct points $\boldsymbol{u}_0, \ldots, \boldsymbol{u}_{Pk}$ so that the $Pk \times Pk$ matrix $\boldsymbol{L} = (\boldsymbol{\lambda}(\boldsymbol{u}_1) - \boldsymbol{\lambda}(\boldsymbol{u}_0), \ldots, \boldsymbol{\lambda}(\boldsymbol{u}_{Pk}) - \boldsymbol{\lambda}(\boldsymbol{u}_0))$ is invertible.*

Then, the set $(\boldsymbol{f}, \boldsymbol{T}, \boldsymbol{\lambda})$ is identifiable up to affine transformation.

While the assumptions (i)–(iii) are not very restrictive, the assumption (iv) is crucial to understand as it restricts the identifiability only to cases where the parameters $\boldsymbol{\lambda}(\boldsymbol{u})$ vary enough when $\boldsymbol{u}$ changes. Because of this assumption, the latent components are identifiable only when the exponential family parameters are nonstationary.

Although identifiability up to a affine transformation might already be useful, in most cases it is desirable to achieve block-affine identifiability. The next theorem gives sufficient conditions for such identifiability.

Theorem 2. *Assume that the assumptions of Theorem 1 hold. Further assume:*

(i) *The dimension of sufficient statistics is $k \geq 2$.*
(ii) *The sufficient statistics $T_{i,j}$ are twice differentiable with respect to z_i.*

(iii) The mixing function $\boldsymbol{f}$ has all second-order cross derivatives.

Then, the set $(\boldsymbol{f}, \boldsymbol{T}, \boldsymbol{\lambda})$ is identifiable up to block-affine transformation.

Theorem 2, combined with the additional conditions of Proposition 1, essentially guarantees that latent components can be recovered up to permutation and component-wise nonlinearity. For example, Gaussian distributed latent components with unknown nonstationary mean and variance, with sufficient statistics $\boldsymbol{T}_i(z_i) = (z_i, z_i^2)^\top$, fall within Theorem 2. In fact, we can show that for such Gaussian data the identifiability can be further reduced to permutation, scale and location shift, which is in par with identifiability results of linear BSS:

Proposition 2. *Assume that the assumptions of Theorem 2 hold and that the data are generated through BSS model (1). Further, assume that the latent components z_i and the respective estimates $\tilde{z}_i$ are Gaussian, meaning that $\boldsymbol{T}_i(z_i) = (z_i, z_i^2)^\top$ and $\tilde{\boldsymbol{T}}_i(\tilde{z}_i) = (\tilde{z}_i, \tilde{z}_i^2)^\top$. Then we have that $\tilde{\boldsymbol{z}} = \boldsymbol{P\Lambda z} + \boldsymbol{d}$, where $\boldsymbol{P}$ is a permutation matrix and $\boldsymbol{\Lambda}$ is a diagonal matrix with non-zero diagonal elements.*

Since our main focus in this paper is on Gaussian autoregressive latent components which always has $k \geq 2$, we refer the reader to [13] for $k = 1$ case, where sufficient conditions are provided for exponential family with $R = 0$. When the autoregressive process (3) is assumed for the latent components with Gaussian innovations, we have the following distribution:

$$p(\boldsymbol{z}|\boldsymbol{z}^-, \boldsymbol{u}^t, \ldots, \boldsymbol{u}^{t-R}) =$$

$$\prod_{i=1}^{P} \frac{1}{2\pi\sigma_i(\boldsymbol{u}^t)} \exp\left[\frac{\left(z_i - \mu_i(\boldsymbol{u}^t) - \sum_{r=1}^{R}(\gamma_{i,r}(\boldsymbol{u}^t)z_i^{t-r} - \mu_i(\boldsymbol{u}^{t-r}))\right)^2}{2\sigma^2(\boldsymbol{u}^t)}\right], \quad (7)$$

where $\boldsymbol{u}^t$ denotes the auxiliary variable for the observation $\boldsymbol{x}^t$.

Proposition 3. *Assume that the assumptions of Theorem 2 hold and that the data are generated through BSS model (1). Further assume that the latent components z_i and the respective estimates $\tilde{z}_i$ are generated through the Gaussian AR process (2) with $R \geq 1$. Then we have that $\tilde{\boldsymbol{z}} = \boldsymbol{P\Lambda z} + \boldsymbol{d}$, where $\boldsymbol{P}$ is a permutation matrix, $\boldsymbol{\Lambda}$ is a diagonal matrix with non-zero diagonal elements and $\boldsymbol{d}$ is a constant vector.*

Proposition 3 gives the main identifiability conditions for the Gaussian autoregressive latent components. In practice, the conditions on the mixing function are not very restrictive. However, condition (iv) of Theorem 1 requires sufficient nonstationarity either in the AR coefficients $\gamma_{i,r}$ or in the variance σ_i. In Sect. 3, we introduce an estimation method for estimating the generative model defined by Eqs. (3)–(5).

3 Autoregressive Identifiable Variational Autoencoder

The iVAEar method is an autoregressive extension of spatio-temporal iVAE, introduced in [22]. It consists of an encoder $g(x, u)$, a decoder $h(x)$ and an auxiliary function $w(u)$. As the true AR order R is in general unknown, we use W to refer to the AR order used in the iVAEar method. The method takes as an input the current observations x and their auxiliary data u, and the W previous observations in time and their auxiliary data (x^{t-r}, u^{t-r}), $r = 1, \ldots, W$.

The encoder aims to estimate the unmixing function q. It maps the observation and auxiliary data pair (x, u) into the mean vector $\mu_{z|x} \in \mathbb{R}^P$ and the variance vector $\sigma_{z|x} \in \mathbb{R}^P$. For the current observation x, the encoder's output is used for reparametrization trick [14] to obtain a new latent representation z'. The decoder aims then to estimate the mixing function f by trying to construct the original input x from z'. For the previous observations x^{t-r}, the encoder is used to obtain the corresponding latent component estimates $u_{z|x,u}^{t-r}$, which are provided by the mean function $\mu_{z|x,u}(x^{t-r}, u^{t-r})$. These are used to calculate the mean of the Gaussian latent distribution (7).

The auxiliary function w aims to estimate the function λ by mapping the auxiliary data u into parameters $\mu_{z|u}, \sigma_{z|u}, \gamma_{z|u}^1, \ldots, \gamma_{z|u}^W$, that estimate the true parameters of the autoregressive Gaussian distribution (7). In addition, the auxiliary function is used to obtain the mean estimates $\mu_{z|u}^{t-r}$ based on the auxiliary data u^{t-r} of the previous observations.

The encoder, the decoder and the auxiliary function are modeled using deep neural networks with parameters $\theta_g, \theta_h, \theta_w$, that refer to the weights and biases of encoder, decoder and auxiliary function, respectively. The parameters $\theta = (\theta_g, \theta_h, \theta_u)^\top$ of the neural networks are optimized by minimizing the lower bound of the data log-likelihood, or evidence lower bound (ELBO):

$$\text{ELBO} = E_{q_\theta(z|x,u)}\big(\log p_{\theta_h}(x|z) + \log p_{\theta_w}(z|z^-, u) - \log q_{\theta_g}(z|x, u)\big), \quad (8)$$

where the first part, $p_{\theta_h}(x|z)$, controls the reconstruction accuracy and the second part, $\log p_{\theta_w}(z|z^-, u) - \log q_{\theta_g}(z|x, u)$, is the Kullback-Leibler divergence, which tries to keep the variational distribution $\log q_{\theta_g}(z|x, u)$ close to the prior distribution $\log p_{\theta_w}(z|z^-, u)$. Because Gaussian autoregressive latent data is assumed (7), the distributions $p_{\theta_w}, q_{\theta_g}$ and p_{θ_h} are assumed Gaussian, ensuring that the estimated components follow the same distribution (7). Specifically, we set $p_{\theta_w} = N(z|\mu^*, \text{diag}(\sigma_{z|u}))$, where $\mu^* = \mu_{z|u} + \sum_{i=1}^R \gamma_{z|u}^{t-r}(\mu_{z|x,u}^{t-R} - \mu_{z|u}^{t-R})$, $q_{\theta_g} = N(z|\mu_{z|x,u}, \text{diag}(\sigma_{z|x,u}))$ and $p_{\theta_h} = N(x|x', \beta I)$, where $\beta > 0$ is a small constant that represents the variance of (4). By decreasing β, the weight of the reconstruction loss is increased in the loss function similarly as in β-VAE [8]. The whole iVAEar framework is illustrated in $R = 1$ case in Fig. 1. For more details of iVAE framework, see [13,22,23].

For iVAEar, we construct the auxiliary data following [22] based on either spatial and temporal segmentation or spatial and temporal radial basis functions. In segmentation based algorithm, the spatial domain in divided into equally sized two dimensional square segments, and the temporal domain into equally sized

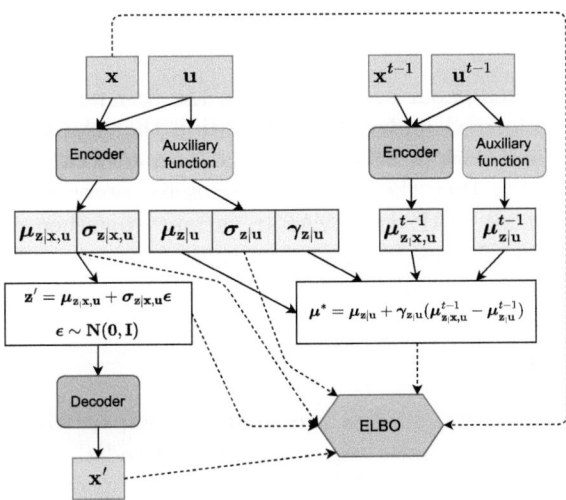

Fig. 1. Schematic presentation of iVAEar method in $R = 1$ case.

one dimensional segments. The auxiliary variable then gives the spatial and temporal segments corresponding to the observation. In radial basis function based algorithm, multiple spatial and temporal node points are selected from spatial and temporal domains. The auxiliary variable, i.e. radial basis functions, are then constructed based on distance between the location of the observation and each of the node points. Segmentation based iVAEar is denoted iVAEar_s and radial basis function based iVAEar is denoted iVAEar_r in the rest of the paper. For further details of constructing the auxiliary data, see [22].

If the underlying latent components satisfy the assumptions of Theorem 1 or Theorem 2, then we have the following consistency result.

Theorem 3. *Assume that the Theorem 1 or Theorem 2 hold. Further assume that the family of the variational distributions $q_{\theta_g}(z|x, x^-, u)$ contains the distribution $p_{\tilde{f}, \tilde{T}, \tilde{\lambda}}(z|x, x^-, u)$. Then iVAEar learns the true set (f, T, λ) up to the identifiability classes given by Theorems 1 and 2 in the limit of infinite data.*

In AR Gaussian latent data case, when also q_{θ_g} is Gaussian, then by Proposition 3, iVAEar estimates the true latents z up to permutation, signed scale and location shift in the limit of infinite data.

The auxiliary function of iVAEar enables the method to be used for spatio-temporal interpolation or forecasting purposes. Particularly, iVAEar_r method provides smooth estimates of the spatio-temporal functions $\mu_i(u^t)$, $\gamma_{i,r}(u^t)$ and $\sigma_i(u^t)$, $i = 1, \ldots, P$, $r = 1, \ldots, R$. These can be used to predict the latent components to new spatio-temporal locations, after which the predictions can be transformed into observation space by using the decoder of the trained iVAEar. The prediction capabilities of iVAEar are illustrated later in Sect. 5.

4 Simulations

The simulations of this paper are two-fold; in the first part in Sect. 4.1, various simulations are performed under the assumption that the true AR order R is known. In the second part in Sect. 4.2, the performance of iVAEar_r is studied under the assumption that the true autoregressive order R is unknown. The implementations of all iVAE and iVAEar variants together with the code to simulate the data in all considered settings and to reproduce the case study of Sect. 5, are available in GitHub[2,3].

4.1 Main Simulations

In this section, simulation studies are used to compare the performances of iVAEar_r and iVAEar_s against segmentation and radial basis function based spatio-temporal iVAE methods, iVAEs and iVAEr, respectively, as proposed in [22], STBSS, and symmetric FastICA (FICA) with hyperbolic tangent nonlinearity [10]. In simulations, we generate the latent spatio-temporal fields z and a mixing function f. We are particularly interested in performance in settings, where the variance and/or the AR coefficients of the latent fields z are varying in space and in time. Hence, we select one setting with nonstationary AR1 coefficient, one with nonstationary variance and one with both AR1 coefficient and variance nonstationary. In addition, each of the settings is considered with and without nonstationary spatio-temporal trend function. Next, we give all the simulation details and explain how z and f are generated.

In all simulations, we set the observed dimension $S = 6$ and the latent dimension $P = 6$. The number of spatial locations is $n_s = 100$ and the number of time points is $n_t = 500$. The spatial locations $s_1, \ldots s_{n_s}$ are generated uniformly in the domain $[0,1] \times [0,1]$, and the observations over time are set at times $t = 1, \ldots, n_t$. The latent spatio-temporal fields are generated using the following vector AR process. Assume the spatial field at time t to be $\boldsymbol{\delta}(t) = (\delta(s_1, t), \ldots, \delta(s_{n_s}, t))$. By using the vector AR process we have then

$$\boldsymbol{\delta}(t) = \sum_{r=1}^{R} \rho_r \boldsymbol{K}_r(t) \boldsymbol{\delta}(t-r) + \boldsymbol{\epsilon}_\delta(t), \tag{9}$$

where $r = 1, \ldots, R$ is the order of AR process, ρ_r is the baseline AR coefficient for the rth order, $\boldsymbol{K}_r(t)$ is a spatial kernel matrix for time t, which determines the temporal correlation with spatial locations, and $\boldsymbol{\epsilon}_\delta(t)$ is a n_s-dimensional Gaussian noise vector with spatial covariance function $C(\epsilon_\delta(s,t), \epsilon_\delta(s',t)), s, s' \in \{s_1, \ldots, s_{n_s}\}$. If the kernel matrices $\boldsymbol{K}_r(t)$ are diagonal, the generated data have separable spatio-temporal covariance function, i.e., data do not have any spatio-temporal interaction. For the simulations, we set $R = 1$. As spatial covariance

---

[2] https://github.com/mikasip/NonlinearBSS.
[3] https://github.com/mikasip/iVAEar.

function for time t we use variance modulated Matern covariance function

$$C(\epsilon_\delta(\boldsymbol{s},\boldsymbol{s}',t)) = \sigma(\boldsymbol{s},t)\sigma(\boldsymbol{s}',t)\frac{1}{2^{\nu-1}\Gamma(\nu)}\left(\frac{\|\boldsymbol{s}-\boldsymbol{s}'\|}{\phi}\right)^\nu K_\nu\left(\frac{\|\boldsymbol{s}-\boldsymbol{s}'\|}{\phi}\right), \quad (10)$$

where σ modulates the variance based on the time and spatial location, K_ν is a modified Bessel function of second kind, and ϕ and ν are range and shape parameters, respectively. The common Matern parameters for all settings are provided in the supplementary material. In the simulations, we consider data with and without trend. The spatio-temporal trend is generated as composition of cyclical and liner trends as follows:

$$\mu(s_1, s_2, t) = \theta_{s_1} s_1 + \theta_{s_2} s_2 + \theta_t t + \alpha \sin(\omega_{s_1} s_1 + \omega_{s_2} s_2 + \omega_t t + \omega_c). \quad (11)$$

The parameters are generated so that $\theta_{s_1}, \theta_{s_2} \sim \mathrm{Unif}(-3,3)$, $\theta_t \sim \mathrm{Unif}(-0.01, 0.01)$, $\omega_{s_1}, \omega_{s_2} \sim \mathrm{Unif}(0.2, 4)$, $\omega_t \sim \mathrm{Unif}(0.01, 0.1)$, $\omega_c \sim \mathrm{Unif}(0, 2\pi)$ and $\alpha \sim \mathrm{Unif}(-2, 2)$.

Setting 1. The latent fields have constant variance $\sigma(\boldsymbol{s}, t) = 1$ and varying AR1 coefficients over space and time. The kernel matrix $\boldsymbol{K}_1(t)$ is a diagonal matrix with AR1 coefficients $\gamma(\boldsymbol{s}_1, t), \ldots, \gamma(\boldsymbol{s}_{n_s}, t)$ in the diagonal for each spatial location $\boldsymbol{s}_1, \ldots, \boldsymbol{s}_{n_s}$. The parameters $\gamma(\boldsymbol{s}, t)$ are generated as

$$\gamma(\boldsymbol{s}, t) = \cos\left(\frac{2\pi t b}{n_t} - c(\boldsymbol{s})\right), \quad (12)$$

where b is a scale parameter and $c(\boldsymbol{s})$ is a shift parameter. To obtain variability in space, we generate the shift parameters $c(\boldsymbol{s})$ from the Gaussian distribution $N(0, 0.3)$ with Matern spatial covariance function with parameters ϕ_c, ν_c. The Matern parameters for shift are $\phi_{c_1}, \nu_{c_1} = (0.25, 5)$, $\phi_{c_2}, \nu_{c_2} = (0.15, 2)$, $\phi_{c_3}, \nu_{c_3} = (0.1, 3)$, $\phi_{c_4}, \nu_{c_4} = (0.3, 4)$, $\phi_{c_5}, \nu_{c_5} = (0.2, 1)$ for the latent components $z_1, \ldots, z_5$. The scale parameters b are generated from $\mathrm{Unif}(1, 10)$ and the baseline AR1 parameters ρ_r are generated from $\mathrm{Unif}(0.6, 0.99)$ for each latent component.

Setting 2. The zero-mean latent fields z_i^* are generated as in Setting 1. Then, the final latent fields are obtained as $z_i(\boldsymbol{s}, t) = z_i^*(\boldsymbol{s}, t) + \mu_i(\boldsymbol{s}, t)$, where $\mu_i(\boldsymbol{s}, t)$ is generated as in (11).

Setting 3. The latent fields have constant AR1 coefficients and varying variance over space and time. The kernel matrix is $\boldsymbol{K}_1(t)$ is identity matrix for all t. The spatial domain is divided randomly into 5 clusters and the time domain into 10 segments providing 50 spatio-temporal segments $S_1, \ldots, S_{50}$, each having their own standard deviation $\sigma_1, \ldots, \sigma_{50}$. The function σ is then $\sigma(\boldsymbol{s}, t) = \sum_{k=1}^{50} \mathbb{1}((\boldsymbol{s}, t) \in S_k)\sigma_k$, where $\mathbb{1}$ is an indicator function giving 1, if the location $(\boldsymbol{s}, t)$ belongs in segment S_k, otherwise it gives 0. The baseline AR1 parameters ρ_r are generated from $\mathrm{Unif}(0.1, 0.9)$ for each latent component.

Setting 4. The zero-mean latent fields z_i^* are generated as in Setting 3. Then, the final latent fields are obtained as $z_i(\boldsymbol{s}, t) = z_i^*(\boldsymbol{s}, t) + \mu_i(\boldsymbol{s}, t)$, where $\mu_i(\boldsymbol{s}, t)$ is generated as in (11).

Setting 5. The latent fields have varying variances and varying AR1 coefficients over space and time. The fields are generated by combining settings 1 and 2. That is, we have an identical situation to Setting 2, but the function σ is defined as in Setting 4.

Setting 6. The zero-mean latent fields z_i^* are generated as in Setting 5. Then, the final latent fields are obtained as $z_i(\boldsymbol{s},t) = z_i^*(\boldsymbol{s},t) + \mu_i(\boldsymbol{s},t)$, where $\mu_i(\boldsymbol{s},t)$ is generated as in (11).

These simulation settings are considered to investigate how different types of nonstationarities affect the performance of the algorithms. The Settings 1 and 2 do not have any nonstationarity in variance, but do have nonstationary AR1 coefficient, meaning that the identifiability results hold for iVAEar methods, but not for iVAEs and iVAEr. In Settings 3–6 the variance is nonstationary, and hence the identifiability holds for all iVAE methods. Nonetheless, these settings are of interest when comparing performances when there are additional stationary or nonstationary autocorrelation present. Nonstationary trend is considered in Settings 2, 4 and 6 to see if that affects the performance.

Mixing Function. The observations $\boldsymbol{x}$ are obtained by applying a linear or nonlinear mixing function $\boldsymbol{f}_L$ to the generated latent components $\boldsymbol{z}$. The function $\boldsymbol{f}_L$ is generated using multilayer perceptron (MLP) following, e.g. [11–13]. The parameter L denotes the number of mixing layers used in MLP. Each layer i consists of a $P \times P$ mixing matrix $\boldsymbol{B}_i$ and an activation function ψ_i. The matrices $\boldsymbol{B}_i$ are normalized to have unit length rows and colums in order to avoid vanishing of any of the latent components in the mixing process. The mixing function $\boldsymbol{f}_L$ can be then defined recursively as

$$\boldsymbol{f}_L(\boldsymbol{z}) = \begin{cases} \psi_L(\boldsymbol{B}_L \boldsymbol{z}), & L = 1, \\ \psi_L(\boldsymbol{B}_L \boldsymbol{f}_{L-1}(\boldsymbol{z})), & L \in \{2, 3, \dots\}, \end{cases}$$

where the activation function ψ_L is linear for the first layer and exponential linear unit (ELU), given as

$$\psi_i(x) = \begin{cases} x, & x \geq 0, \\ \exp(x) - 1, & x < 0, \end{cases}$$

for the other layers. This results $\boldsymbol{f}_1$ with one layer being linear mixing, and when L increases, the mixing function becomes increasingly nonlinear.

Performance Index. The performance of the algorithms is measured using the mean correlation coefficient (MCC), which is also used for example in [7,12,22,23]. MCC is a function of correlation matrix $\boldsymbol{\Omega} = \mathrm{Cor}(\boldsymbol{z}, \hat{\boldsymbol{z}})$ of the true and estimated latent components. MCC measures how similar the optimal permutation of $\boldsymbol{\Omega}$ is to $P \times P$ identity matrix, and is calculated as

$$\mathrm{MCC}(\boldsymbol{\Omega}) = \frac{1}{P} \sup_{\boldsymbol{P} \in \mathcal{P}} \mathrm{tr}(\boldsymbol{P} \, \mathrm{abs}(\boldsymbol{\Omega})), \tag{13}$$

where $\mathcal{P}$ is a set of all possible $P \times P$ permutation matrices, $\mathrm{tr}(\cdot)$ is the trace of a matrix and $\mathrm{abs}(\cdot)$ denotes taking elementwise absolute values of a matrix. The values of MCC vary in range $[0,1]$, where 1 is the optimal value, meaning that estimated components $\hat{\boldsymbol{z}}$ correlate perfectly with the true components $\boldsymbol{z}$.

Model Specifications. All iVAE models have 3 hidden layers with 128 units in encoder, decoder and auxiliary functions. All hidden layers use leaky rectified unit (ReLU) activation function [18]. iVAEar_r and iVAEr are set up with spatial resolution levels $H = (2,9)$ and temporal resolution levels $G = (9, 17, 37)$. In iVAEar1_s and iVAEs, 10×10 spatial segmentation is used by producing 100 equally sized segments, and temporal domain is divided into 100 segments, each of which contains 5 consecutive time points. For details of constructing the radial basis function based and segmentation based auxiliary variables, see [22]. All models are trained for 60 epochs with batch size of 64, and use the learning rate of 0.001 with polynomial decay of second-order over 10000 training steps, where the learning rate after the first 10000 training steps is 0.0001. STBSS uses two spatial ring kernels $(0, 0.15)$ and $(0.15, 0.3)$, and time lag of 1. These parameters were selected by training STBSS with multiple different parameters in each setting, and selecting the parameters that provided the best results on average. For more about STBSS and its parameters, see [19].

Simulation Results. The results of the simulations are provided in Fig. 2. Overall, the best results, especially in nonlinear scenarios, are obtained by iVAEar_r, followed by iVAEar_s in all settings. Nonstationary trend (Settings 2, 4 and 6) results in worse performance for all of the methods compared to settings where the trend is not present (Settings 1, 3 and 6).

In Setting 1, where only AR1 coefficient is nonstationary, the latent components are successfully recovered only by iVAEar_r and iVAEar_s under nonlinear mixing. Under linear mixing, FICA performs nearly as well as iVAEar_r and iVAEar_s. STBSS is the fourth best performing method, followed by iVAEs and iVAEr.

In Setting 2, where also nonstationary trend is added, iVAEar_r and iVAEar_s are the only methods with decent performance, although their performance also drops considerably in nonlinear settings.

In Setting 3 with nonstationary variance, all of the methods perform relatively well. FICA and all iVAE based methods perform almost equally well under the linear mixing, but under the nonlinear mixing, FICA's performance suffers more. iVAEar based methods perform better than their iVAE counterparts, which is probably due to the fact that there are still stationary autocorrelation present in the latent components.

In Setting 4, where the nonstationary trend is included into scenario of Setting 3, all of the methods lose performance. However, iVAEar_r still maintains its performance nearly as well as in Setting 3, being clearly the best method.

In Settings 5 and 6, where the variance and the AR1 coefficient are nonstationary, the results are very similar to the results of Settings 3 and 4, but the performances of FICA and iVAE methods are consistently slightly better due to the stronger nonstationarity. iVAE based methods maintain their performances better in nonlinear cases, and all of the methods perform slightly worse when the nonstationary trend is included.

Overall, autoregressive iVAE methods bring considerable improvement in performance as compared to the existing nonlinear STBSS methods. Based on the results, the methods can successfully estimate the latent components if there is either nonstationarity in autocorrelation or in variance. Nonstationary trend seems to be more challenging to tackle for the methods. Radial basis function based iVAEar, iVAEar_r, is the best performing method in all of the settings, and is the recommended choice for nonlinear nonstationary STBSS problems.

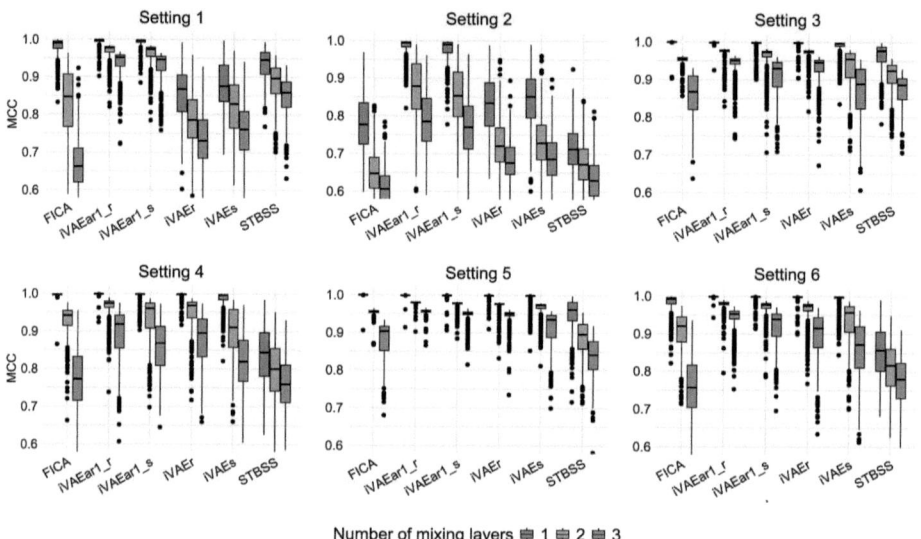

Fig. 2. Mean correlation coefficients from 500 trials for Settings 1–6. The y-axis shows MCC (optimal value = 1), while the x-axis represents different methods. Box colors indicate the number of mixing layers in the mixing function.

4.2 Sensitivity for AR Order Mismatch

In this section, we study how sensitive the best performing method, iVAEar_r, is for AR order mismatch. The data are generated from Settings 1 and 5 with the true AR orders $R = 1$ and $R = 3$, and the latent components z are estimated using the iVAEar_r with AR orders $W = 1, 3, 5$, denoted iVAEar1_r, iVAEar3_r and iVAEar5_r.

In $R = 1$ scenario, the settings are identical to Settings 1 and 5 of the Sect. 4.1. In $R = 3$ scenario, the data are generated as in Settings 1 and 5, but the AR coefficients $\gamma_r(s_i, t)$, $r = 1, \ldots, R$, $i = 1, \ldots, n_s$, are generated as in (12). The coefficients are then multiplied by constants d_r, where $d_r \sim \text{Unif}(0, 1)$, to create varying magnitudes to the components. The baseline AR coefficients are set to $\rho_r = 1, r = 1, \ldots, R$. To guarantee the weak-sense stationarity of the AR process, defined in Definition 2 (supplementary material), the AR coefficients are scaled as follows:

$$\gamma_r(s_i, t) = \frac{\gamma_r(s_i, t)}{\max_{i,t}(|\gamma_r(s_i, t)| + |\gamma_r(s_i, t)| + |\gamma_r(s_i, t)|) + 0.01}, \quad (14)$$

for each latent component $j = 1, \ldots, P$. This procedure guarantees $|\gamma_r(s_i, t)| + |\gamma_r(s_i, t)| + |\gamma_r(s_i, t)| < 1$ for all $r = 1, \ldots, R$, $i = 1, \ldots, n_s$, which is a sufficient condition for fulfilling the weak-sense stationarity.

The results are presented in Fig. 3. In the case where only AR coefficients are nonstationary, the best performance is achieved when the true AR order $W = R$ is used in the model. Based on the results, it is safer to use larger W as the performance drops only by little when $W > R$. The performance drops more significantly when too small W is used in the model. In the case where also variance is nonstationary, the effect of incorrect AR order is negligible, although the correct AR order still produces the best performance. In general, based on the results, it is safer to use $W = 3$ or $W = 5$ in the model rather than $W = 1$.

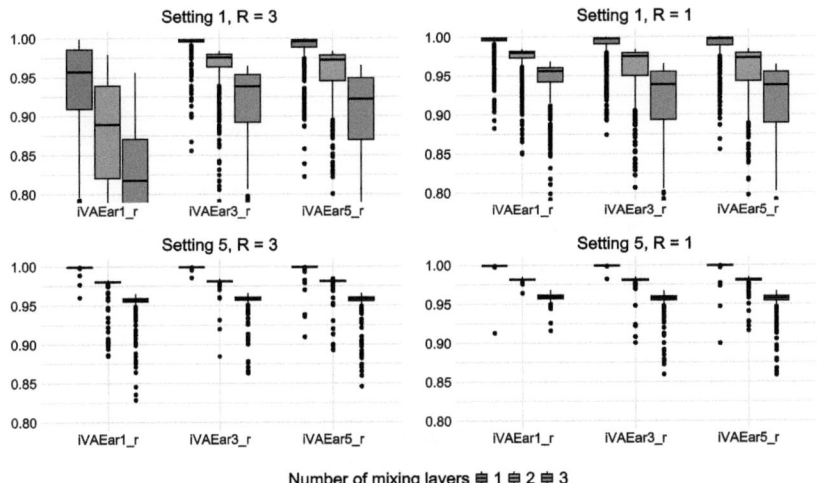

Fig. 3. Mean correlation coefficients of 500 trials for Setting 1 (top) and Setting 5 (bottom) with $R = 1$ and $R = 3$. The y-axis shows MCC (optimal value $= 1$), while the x-axis represents different methods. Box colors indicate the number of mixing layers in the mixing function.

5 Case Study

We apply the iVAEar_r and iVAEar_s methods to an air pollution dataset [1] to predict future values and compare their accuracy against iVAEr, spatio-temporal kriging [3], ARIMA [2] and vector ARIMA (VARIMA) [17]. Spatio-temporal kriging considers both spatial and temporal dependencies, while ARIMA models only temporal structures, making predictions separately for each station. Both kriging and ARIMA fit models univariately and do not account for cross-variable dependencies. In contrast, VARIMA models cross-dependencies between the variables through multivariate autoregressive process, but does modeling individually for each station. iVAEar_r and iVAEr incorporate cross-variable dependencies through latent component decomposition and spatio-temporal trends. Additionally, iVAEar_r estimates autoregressive structures of latent components for improved prediction.

The data consist of hourly air pollution and weather measurements from 64 stations in Athens, Greece, spanning 2020–2023. We use daily observations at 12 PM, resulting in $n_t = 1124$. The data include seven weather variables (wind speed U, wind speed V, dew point temperature, soil temperature, air temperature, relative humidity, precipitation) and four air pollution variables (PM10, PM2.5, NO2, O3). Precipitation is removed due to its predominantly zero values, yielding $S = 10$. Six stations lacking complete data are excluded, leaving $n_s = 58$. The remaining 162 missing observations are imputed using CUTOFF [4]. The last 24 time points serve as test data, while the first 1100 are used for training.

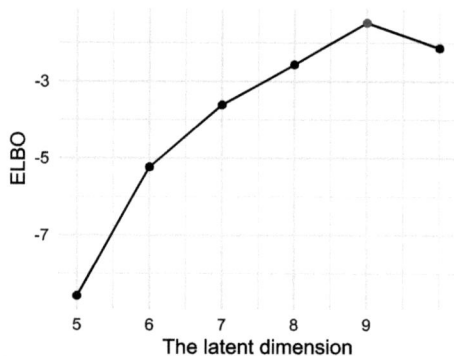

Fig. 4. ELBO for different latent dimensions.

We estimate the latent dimension P by fitting iVAEar_r models with $P = 5, \ldots, 10$, selecting the best model using knee-point detection and profile AIC (pAIC) [22]. ELBOs for different latent dimensions are shown in Fig. 4. Both methods indicate $P = 9$ as optimal, which is used in final models.

For forecasting with iVAEar_r, iVAEar_s and iVAEr, auxiliary data must remain within the training data bounds. Hence, we use seasonal periods $t_s = 1, \ldots, 365$ instead of absolute time $t = 1, \ldots, 1124$ and introduce a one-hot encoded year factor to allow inter-year variability. Spatial resolution levels are set to $H = (2, 9)$, learning rate to 0.0001, variance parameter $\beta = 0.02$, batch size to 64, and training spans 40 epochs. A hyperparameter search optimizes temporal resolution for iVAEar_r and iVAE_r, segmentation sizes for iVAEar_s, hidden units in the auxiliary function, and autoregressive order for iVAEar_r and iVAEar_s. The best parameters are selected by leaving 10 last time points of the training data for validation. Selected parameters are $G = (9, 17)$, $n_{\theta_w} = 16$, and $R = 2$ for iVAEar_r, $G = (9, 17)$, $n_{\theta_w} = 16$ for iVAE_r and spatial segment size of 5000, temporal segment size of 5 and $R = 3$ for iVAEar_s.

For ARIMA, VARIMA and kriging, seasonal trends are removed as these methods assume seasonal stationarity. Seasonality is modeled as

$$x_i(s, t) = \beta_{0,i} + \beta_{1,i}\cos(2\pi t/365) + \beta_{2,i}\sin(2\pi t/365) + x_{res,i}(s, t),$$

where residuals $x_{res,i}$ are predicted using ARIMA and kriging. Kriging uses product-sum covariance models, while ARIMA selects the best model for each station via corrected AIC with AR orders $0, \ldots, 5$, MA orders $0, \ldots, 5$, and integration determined by the KPSS test [15]. In VARIMA, we select the best model for each station based on AIC. The options are models with AR $= 1, \ldots, 8$ and MA $= 0$, or a model with AR $= 1$ and MA $= 1$. Integration order was selected to be 1 for whole data, from options 1 or 0, based on better validation accuracy. VARIMA models with larger number of parameters caused numerical instability, and were hence not considered.

Prediction accuracy is measured using mean squared error (MSE):

$$MSE(\boldsymbol{x}_i, \hat{\boldsymbol{x}}_i) = \frac{1}{n}\sum_{j=1}^{n}(x_{i,j} - \hat{x}_{i,j})^2,$$

where $\boldsymbol{x}_i$ contains true values and $\hat{\boldsymbol{x}}_i$ predicted ones. Combined accuracy is assessed via weighted MSE (wMSE):

$$wMSE(\boldsymbol{X}, \hat{\boldsymbol{X}}) = \frac{1}{S}\sum_{i=1}^{S}\frac{MSE(\boldsymbol{x}_i, \hat{\boldsymbol{x}}_i)}{\sigma^2(\boldsymbol{x}_i)},$$

where $\sigma^2(\boldsymbol{x}_i)$ is the variance of the deseasonalized variable.

Table 1 presents forecasting results. iVAEar_r outperforms competitors based on wMSE. VARIMA has the second best combined performance, and the best performance for predicting wind speeds. ARIMA has the second worst combined performance but excels for PM10, PM2.5, and NO2. Kriging and iVAEr perform similarly, with kriging being slightly better overall and excelling in soil temperature predictions. iVAEar_r achieves the lowest errors for dew point temperature, air temperature and O3. iVAEar_s has the best prediction performance for relative humidity, and has high accuracy for O3 as well, but its high errors on soil temperature, air temperature and NO2 makes it the worst method when considering the overall performance. Notably, O3 and relative humidity predictions benefit significantly from incorporating cross-variable dependencies, underscoring the advantage of iVAEar_r, iVAEar_s and VARIMA over univariate models. However, iVAEar_s shows inconsistent performance in prediction and is suboptimal for this task. Its segmentation-based auxiliary variables lead to a highly non-continuous estimate of the trend function, which hinders the model's ability to generalize to future data. Therefore, iVAEar_r is the preferred method for forecasting purposes.

Table 1. Mean squared errors for predictions in time.

	Wind Speed U	Wind Speed V	Dewpoint Temp	Soil Temp	Temp	Rel. Humidity	PM10	PM2.5	NO2	O3	wMSE
iVAEar_r	1.57	6.16	**3.42**	1.08	**3.44**	64.15	81.31	30.42	106.87	**93.09**	**0.49**
iVAEar_s	1.70	7.25	4.70	8.75	7.22	**47.29**	81.56	30.71	200.20	94.91	0.84
iVAEr	2.05	11.36	4.24	0.60	4.60	96.40	84.60	31.89	114.69	174.50	0.63
Kriging	1.71	8.41	4.73	**0.44**	5.49	131.21	82.92	43.65	104.03	141.89	0.62
ARIMA	1.79	6.22	4.85	3.08	9.22	119.62	**75.15**	**27.26**	**97.98**	190.36	0.67
VARIMA	**1.54**	**5.75**	4.11	1.64	8.29	65.68	75.70	35.80	99.06	121.81	0.56

6 Conclusions and Discussion

We have proposed a novel autoregressive iVAE method for nonlinear spatio-temporal BSS, extending identifiability results to cases with nonstationary autoregressive coefficients. Our simulation studies demonstrate superior latent component estimation compared to state-of-the-art methods, and real-world applications to air pollution and weather datasets show that iVAEar achieves significantly improved multivariate spatio-temporal prediction accuracy. Furthermore, we establish strong identifiability results, particularly for autoregressive Gaussian latent components.

A limitation of iVAEar is its reliance on a strict autoregressive assumption in time, making it optimal for separable spatio-temporal processes. Future work should explore extensions to nonseparable models and to more general graph structured data. As the identifiability under nonstationary AR coefficients was studied in this paper mainly for Gaussian innovations, the robustness of the method against innovations from other distributions should be studied in future.

In prediction tasks, careful hyperparameter selection and validation are necessary to prevent overfitting, and auxiliary variables must be chosen to ensure compatibility between training and test data. Additionally, iVAEar can be combined with univariate spatio-temporal prediction methods such as graphLSTM [6], allowing latent components to be predicted separately before reconstructing the observed data.

As iVAEar can be used for both time series and spatio-temporal data, it is a valuable method for latent component estimation and multivariate prediction across various fields, including environmental sciences, meteorology, and neuroscience, where applications often involve multiple temporal or spatio-temporal variables representing the same underlying phenomenon.

Acknowledgments. We gratefully acknowledge support from the Vilho, Yrjö, and Kalle Väisälä Foundation (MS), the Research Council of Finland (grants 453691 to ST and 363261 to KN), and the HiTEc COST Action (CA21163) (KN, ST). We also thank CSC IT Center for Science, Finland, for providing computational resources. Finally, we thank the three anonymous referees for their insightful feedback.

Disclosure of Interests. The authors have no competing interests to declare that are relevant to the content of this article.

References

1. Angelis, G.F., Emvoliadis, A., Theodorou, T.I., Zamichos, A., Drosou, A., Tzovaras, D.: Regional datasets for air quality monitoring in European cities. In: IGARSS 2024 - 2024 IEEE International Geoscience and Remote Sensing Symposium, pp. 6875–6880 (2024)
2. Box, G.E.P., Jenkins, G.M., Reinsel, G.C., Ljung, G.M.: Time Series Analysis: Forecasting and Contro, 5th edn.. Wiley, Hoboken (2015)
3. Cressie, N., Wikle, C.K.: Statistics for Spatio-Temporal Data. Wiley, Hoboken (2011)
4. Feng, L., Nowak, G., O'Neill, T., Welsh, A.: Cutoff: a spatio-temporal imputation method. J. Hydrol. **519**, 3591–3605 (2014)
5. Flumian, L., Matilainen, M., Nordhausen, K., Taskinen, S.: Stationary subspace analysis based on second-order statistics. J. Comput. Appl. Math. **436**, 115379 (2024)
6. Gao, X., Li, W.: A graph-based LSTM model for PM2.5 forecasting. Atmos. Pollut. Res. **12**(9), 101150 (2021)
7. Hälvä, H., Hyvärinen, A.: Hidden Markov nonlinear ICA: unsupervised learning from nonstationary time series. In: Conference on Uncertainty in Artificial Intelligence, pp. 939–948. PMLR (2020)
8. Higgins, I., et al.: β-VAE: learning basic visual concepts with a constrained variational framework. In: International Conference on Learning Representations (2017)
9. Hyvärinen, A., Khemakhem, I., Morioka, H.: Nonlinear independent component analysis for principled disentanglement in unsupervised deep learning. Patterns **4**(10) (2023)
10. Hyvärinen, A.: Fast and robust fixed-point algorithms for independent component analysis. IEEE Trans. Neural Netw. **10**(3), 626–634 (1999)
11. Hyvärinen, A., Morioka, H.: Unsupervised feature extraction by time-contrastive learning and nonlinear ICA. Adv. Neural Inf. Process. Syst. **29** (2016)
12. Hyvärinen, A., Sasaki, H., Turner, R.: Nonlinear ICA using auxiliary variables and generalized contrastive learning. In: The 22nd International Conference on Artificial Intelligence and Statistics, pp. 859–868. PMLR (2019)
13. Khemakhem, I., Kingma, D., Monti, R., Hyvärinen, A.: Variational autoencoders and nonlinear ICA: a unifying framework. In: International Conference on Artificial Intelligence and Statistics, pp. 2207–2217. PMLR (2020)
14. Kingma, D.P., Welling, M.: Auto-encoding Variational Bayes. arXiv preprint arXiv:1312.6114 (2013)
15. Kwiatkowski, D., Phillips, P.C., Schmidt, P., Shin, Y.: Testing the null hypothesis of stationarity against the alternative of a unit root: how sure are we that economic time series have a unit root? J. Econom. **54**(1–3), 159–178 (1992)
16. Lachapelle, S., et al.: Disentanglement via mechanism sparsity regularization: a new principle for nonlinear ICA. In: Conference on Causal Learning and Reasoning, pp. 428–484. PMLR (2022)

17. Lütkepohl, H.: New Introduction to Multiple Time Series Analysis. Springer, Berlin, Heidelberg (2005). https://doi.org/10.1007/978-3-540-27752-1
18. Maas, A.L., Hannun, A.Y., Ng, A.Y.: Rectifier nonlinearities improve neural network acoustic models. In: Proceedings of the ICML Workshop on Deep Learning for Audio, Speech, and Language Processing (2013)
19. Muehlmann, C., De Iaco, S., Nordhausen, K.: Blind recovery of sources for multivariate space-time random fields. Stoch. Env. Res. Risk Assess. **37**, 1593–1613 (2023)
20. Porcu, E., Furrer, R., Nychka, D.: 30 years of space-time covariance functions. WIREs Comput. Stat. **13**(2), e1512 (2021)
21. Salvana, M.L.O., Genton, M.G.: Nonstationary cross-covariance functions for multivariate spatio-temporal random fields. Spat. Stat. **37**, 100411 (2020)
22. Sipilä, M., Cappello, C., De Iaco, S., Nordhausen, K., Taskinen, S.: Modelling multivariate spatio-temporal data with identifiable variational autoencoders. Neural Netw. **181**, 106774 (2025)
23. Sipilä, M., Nordhausen, K., Taskinen, S.: Nonlinear blind source separation exploiting spatial nonstationarity. Inf. Sci. **665**, 120365 (2024)

Text and Natural Language Processing

PromptDSI: Prompt-Based Rehearsal-Free Continual Learning for Document Retrieval

Tuan-Luc Huynh[1](✉), Thuy-Trang Vu[1], Weiqing Wang[1], Yinwei Wei[2], Trung Le[1], Dragan Gasevic[2], Yuan-Fang Li[1], and Thanh-Toan Do[1]

[1] Department of Data Science and AI, Monash University, Melbourne, Australia
tuan.huynh1@monash.edu
[2] Department of Human-Centred Computing, Monash University, Melbourne, Australia

Abstract. Differentiable Search Index (DSI) utilizes pre-trained language models to perform indexing and document retrieval via end-to-end learning without relying on external indexes. However, DSI requires full re-training to index new documents, causing significant computational inefficiencies. Continual learning (CL) offers a solution by enabling the model to incrementally update without full re-training. Existing CL solutions in document retrieval rely on memory buffers or generative models *for rehearsal*, which is infeasible when accessing previous training data is restricted due to privacy concerns. To this end, we introduce PromptDSI, a prompt-based, *rehearsal-free* continual learning approach for document retrieval. PromptDSI follows the Prompt-based Continual Learning (PCL) framework, using learnable prompts to efficiently index new documents without accessing previous documents or queries. To improve retrieval latency, we remove the initial forward pass of PCL, which otherwise greatly increases training and inference time, with a negligible trade-off in performance. Additionally, we introduce a novel topic-aware prompt pool that employs neural topic embeddings as fixed keys, eliminating the instability of prompt key optimization while maintaining competitive performance with existing PCL prompt pools. In a challenging rehearsal-free continual learning setup, we demonstrate that PromptDSI variants outperform rehearsal-based baselines, match the strong cache-based baseline in mitigating forgetting, and significantly improving retrieval performance on new corpora (Code is available at: https://github.com/LouisDo2108/PromptDSI).

Keywords: Continual Learning · Document Retrieval

1 Introduction

Differentiable Search Index (DSI) [33] leverages a Transformer model [34] to encode corpus information directly into the model parameters through end-to-end optimization. This end-to-end retrieval paradigm eliminates the need to construct traditional inverted indices or vector databases used in sparse [29] or dense retrieval [12]. However, in real-world scenarios where new documents are continually added, re-training DSI from scratch for each update is computationally prohibitive, necessitating continual learning (CL) methods [8,22]. This challenging setting is known as dynamic corpora [23], or lifelong information retrieval [9]. DSI++ [23] employs generative replay, while IncDSI [15] uses constrained optimization in an instance-wise continual learning setup. However, DSI++ requires an additional query generation model, leading to substantial computational overhead during training and introducing the challenge of maintaining this model for continual indexing. Meanwhile, IncDSI relies on caching queries for all previously indexed documents, resulting in high memory demands and potential data privacy concerns [6].

Rehearsal-free prompt-based continual learning (PCL) methods [30,35,37,39,40] offer a promising approach to alleviate the need to access previous documents or queries. These methods have shown competitive performance compared to rehearsal-based techniques in class-continual learning settings within the vision domain [35]. However, adapting PCL methods to document retrieval remains unexplored due to the extreme classification problem caused by the instance-wise nature, in which each document is a unique class and there are usually at least 100k documents. Moreover, existing PCL methods require two forward passes through the Transformer model, which is not suitable for retrieval systems with low latency requirements.

In this work, we propose PromptDSI, a prompt-based *rehearsal-free* continual learning DSI for document retrieval. PromptDSI uses learnable prompts to index new documents while keeping the DSI backbone frozen, while not accessing previous documents or queries. To overcome the inefficiencies of PCL methods and tailor them for retrieval, we introduce several model-agnostic modifications. We eliminate the inefficient initial forward pass in PCL methods by using intermediate layer representations instead of the pre-trained language model's final layer [CLS] token for query-key matching. This reduces computational overhead with a minimal performance trade-off. Furthermore, due to the lack of distinct semantics across new corpora, PromptDSI often collapses to using a limited set of prompts, leading to underutilized parameters. Inspired by neural topic modeling [9,11], we propose using neural topic embeddings mined from the initial corpus as fixed keys in the prompt pool of PCL methods. This strategy eliminates the training instability of prompt keys and improves the interpretability of prompt selection. Finally, while existing PCL methods follow multi-layer prompting [30,35,39], it is unclear if this is optimal for document retrieval. To explore the stability-plasticity trade-off, we conduct a comprehensive layer-wise prompting study to identify the most effective prompting layers. Overall, our work makes the following contributions:

- We introduce PromptDSI, the first PCL method for classification-based, end-to-end document retrieval.
- We propose two novel approaches to adapt existing PCL methods to document retrieval: (i) an efficient single-pass PCL approach for low-latency

retrieval and (ii) using neural topic embeddings as fixed prompt keys to stabilize query-key matching in PCL's prompt pool, addressing prompt underutilization and enhancing interpretability.
- We conduct a thorough analysis which verifies that single-layer prompting is sufficient for optimal performance when adapting existing PCL methods to continual learning for document retrieval.
- Experimental results on the NQ320k and MSMARCO 300k datasets under the challenging rehearsal-free setup show that PromptDSI performs on par with IncDSI, a strong baseline that requires caching previous training data.

2 Related Work

2.1 End-to-End Retrieval

End-to-end retrieval is an emerging paradigm that aims to replace the conventional "retrieve-then-rank" pipeline [12,29] with a single Transformer model [34], pioneered by Differentiable Search Index (DSI) [33]. By integrating corpus information into the model parameters, DSI eliminates specialized search procedures, and enables end-to-end optimization. DSI can be divided into two subcategories: classification-based [15] and generative retrieval [4,23], with the former being more resilient to catastrophic forgetting during continual indexing [23]. Therefore, we focus on the classification-based DSI approach in this work. Improving document identifier representation remains the main research focus of the community [45,46], while the challenging continual learning (CL) setting is receiving increasing attention [4,15,23]. However, existing solutions either rely on caching previous queries or a generative model for rehearsal. PromptDSI builds upon IncDSI [15], which handles CL by caching all previous queries, and pushes DSI towards rehearsal-free CL.

2.2 Continual Learning (CL)

Addressing catastrophic forgetting in continual learning (CL) has been an active research area [36]. Two popular approaches are regularization-based methods, which constrain model updates via regularization terms or knowledge distillation [14,20], and replay-based methods, which use memory buffers or generative models for rehearsal [2,3]. These approaches dominate lifelong information retrieval studies [4,23]. Recently, Prompt-based Continual Learning (PCL) has emerged as a solution for scenarios where historical data access is restricted due to privacy regulations [6]. Various studies [30,37,39,40] have explored the use of prompts to guide frozen pre-trained models in learning new tasks without memory buffers. Concurrent to our work, [13] introduces one-stage prompt-based continual learning; however, their method is applied only to CODA-Prompt [30] and evaluated exclusively in the vision domain. In contrast, PromptDSI adapts vision-domain PCL methods to a more challenging instance-wise continual learning setting, where each document is a unique class, with at least 100k documents.

We propose a model-agnostic modification: efficient single-pass PCL, and validate its performance across three popular PCL methods. Additionally, we introduce fixed neural topic embeddings as prompt keys to mitigate prompt pool underutilization observed in certain PCL methods and to enhance explainability.

3 Background

3.1 Differentiable Search Index (DSI)

Indexing Stage. A Transformer model [34] f_Θ parameterized by Θ is trained to learn a mapping function from a document $d \in \mathcal{D}$ to its document identifier (docid) $id \in \mathcal{I}$ during the indexing stage: $f_\Theta : \mathcal{D} \to \mathcal{I}$. **Document representation** and **docid representation** are two crucial aspects of DSI that need to be predefined.

Document Representation. The original DSI is trained to map a document's texts to its corresponding docid. However, the model may need to process queries that are distributionally different from training documents at retrieval time, leading to a mismatch between indexing and retrieval. To bridge this gap, the current standard approach is to generate pseudo-queries that serve as document representations during indexing [26,47]. Following this, we leverage docT5query [25] to generate pseudo-queries that supplement annotated queries, which are collectively used as inputs during the indexing stage: $f_\Theta : \mathcal{Q} \to \mathcal{I}$.

Docid Representation. We adopt atomic docids, where each document is assigned a unique integer identifier. Denote the classification-based DSI model as f_Θ, parameterized by $\Theta = \{\theta_e, \theta_l\}$, where θ_e represents the encoder weights, and $\theta_l \in \mathbb{R}^{\dim \times |\mathcal{D}|}$ denotes the linear classifier weights, with $|\mathcal{D}|$ being the total number of documents. Each docid corresponds to a unique column vector $V \in \mathbb{R}^{\dim}$ in θ_l, where the docid (i.e., the unique integer) specifies the position of the column vector in θ_l. Unlike dense retrieval, which uses dual encoders and an external index with contrastive learning [12,43], classification-based DSI uses a single encoder and stores document embeddings as classifier weights, training with a seq2seq objective [32] to map queries to docids.

Retrieval Stage. Given a query $q \in \mathcal{Q}$, DSI returns a ranked list of documents by sorting the inner products of the query embedding $h_q = f_{\theta_e}(q)[0] \in \mathbb{R}^{\dim}$ (i.e., the [CLS] token) and the linear classifier weight in descending order:

$$f_\Theta(q) = \left[\underset{id \in \mathcal{I}}{\operatorname{argmax}}^{(1)}(\theta_l^\top \cdot h_q), \underset{id \in \mathcal{I}}{\operatorname{argmax}}^{(2)}(\theta_l^\top \cdot h_q), \ldots \right],$$

where $\underset{id \in \mathcal{I}}{\operatorname{argmax}}^{(i)}(\theta_l^\top \cdot h_q)$ denotes the ith ranked docid.

3.2 Continual Learning in DSI

The continual learning setup in DSI assumes that there are $T+1$ corpora: $\{D_0, \ldots, D_T\}$ with corresponding query sets $\{Q_0, \ldots, Q_T\}$ and corresponding docid sets $\{I_0, \ldots, I_T\}$, where $D_t = \{d_1^t, \ldots, d_{|D_t|}^t\}$. D_0 is often a large-scale corpus with annotated query-document pairs. $D_{>0} = \{D_1, \ldots, D_T\}$ are new corpora with completely new documents and no annotated query-document pairs arriving sequentially. Denote the parameters of the DSI model at timestep t (i.e., after indexing $D_{\leq t} = \{D_0, \ldots, D_t\}$) as Θ_t. At every timestep $t>0$, the previous DSI model $f_{\Theta_{t-1}}$ trained upto $D_{\leq t-1}$ has to train on corpus D_t and updates its parameters to Θ_t. The evaluation at timestep t will use f_{Θ_t} on $\{Q_0, \ldots, Q_t\}$ to predict $\{I_0, \ldots, I_t\}$. To index new documents, at timestep t, DSI's linear classifier θ_l is expanded to $\theta_l = \{\theta_l; \theta_{l,t}\}$ where $\theta_{l,t} \in \mathbb{R}^{\dim \times |D_t|}$ denotes the expanded portion and $\{\cdot; \cdot\}$ is concatenation.

3.3 Prompt Tuning

Prompt tuning [18,19] introduces a small set of learnable soft prompts to instruct frozen pre-trained language models on downstream tasks. In this work, we adopt the prefix tuning [19] variant. Given an input sequence $x \in \mathbb{R}^{\dim \times n}$ with length n and embedding dimension of dim, prompt token $p \in \mathbb{R}^{\dim \times m}$ with length m is prepended to the input of self-attention [34] as follows:

$$\text{Attention}(xW_q, [p_k, x]W_k, [p_v, x]W_v),$$

where W_q, W_k, W_v are projection matrices and $p_k, p_v \in \mathbb{R}^{\dim \times \frac{m}{2}}$ are equally split from p.

4 PromptDSI: Single-Pass Rehearsal-Free Prompt-Based Continual Learning for Document Retrieval

PCL methods [30,35,37,40] can be seamlessly integrated into classification-based DSI. However, such an approach is not efficient for a document retrieval system. Moreover, simple adaptation also faces the issue of prompt underutilization. In this section, we will further elaborate on these issues and propose corresponding solutions.

4.1 Prompt-Based Continual Learning (PCL)

PCL methods introduce a prompt pool $\mathbf{P} = \{p_1, \ldots, p_M\}$ with M prompts and a set of corresponding prompt keys $\mathbf{K} = \{k_1, \ldots, k_M\}$, where each prompt $p_i \in \mathbb{R}^{\dim \times m}$ with length m is paired with a key $k_i \in \mathbb{R}^{\dim}$ in a key-value manner. $\mathbf{P}$ acts as an external memory for the pre-trained language model (PLM), enabling storage of new information without disrupting its inherent knowledge or explicitly retaining previous training data.

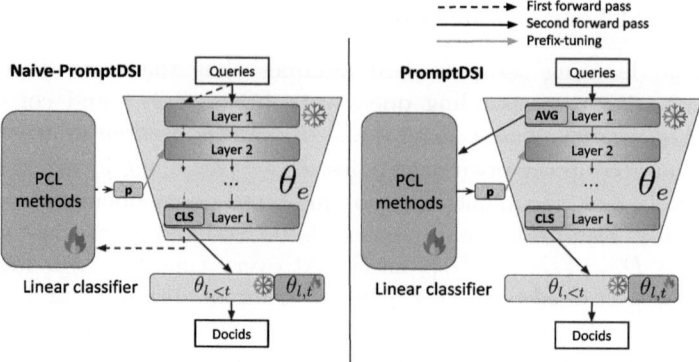

Fig. 1. Naive-PromptDSI (left) integrates PCL methods into DSI using two forward passes, causing increased training/inference time. PromptDSI (right) enhances efficiency by using intermediate layer representations (i.e. average of token embeddings [AVG]) for prompt selection, effectively removing an additional forward pass. In this example, prompts p are prefix tuning to layer 2 of the DSI's encoder θ_e. At timestep $t > 0$, $\theta_{l,<t}$ refers to the frozen portion of the linear classifier, while $\theta_{l,t}$ represents the expanded portion used for training on corpus D_t.

As depicted in Fig. 1 (left), given a query q, the **first pass** extracts the [CLS] token h_q of the input query q from a frozen PLM θ_e. A set of top-N prompt keys from the prompt pool are optimized with cosine distance to align them with the [CLS] token h_q using the following query-key matching mechanism:

$$\mathcal{L}_{\text{match}} = \sum_{i \in S_q} \gamma(h_q, k_i), \quad \text{s.t.} \quad S_q = \operatorname*{argmin}_{\{s_i\}_{i=1}^N \subseteq [1,M]} \sum_{i=1}^N \gamma(h_q, k_{s_i}), \quad (1)$$

where S_q denotes a set of top-N prompt key ids and $\gamma(\cdot,\cdot) = 1 - \cos(\cdot,\cdot)$ is the cosine distance. In the **second pass**, the same query q is reprocessed by θ_e; however, this time the previously selected top-N corresponding prompts $p \subset \mathbf{P}$ are prefix-tuned to the PLM, resulting in an enhanced [CLS] token: $\hat{h}_q = f_{p,\theta_e}(q)[0] \in \mathbb{R}^{\text{dim}}$, which has been instructed by the knowledge from prompts p.

4.2 Single-Pass PCL

As previously discussed, existing PCL methods involve two forward passes during training and inference. Given that a forward pass in Transformer models is already computationally expensive, this two-pass design is unsuitable for retrieval systems, as it exacerbates latency during both training and inference. We refer to this naive adaptation of two-pass PCL methods to DSI as Naive-PromptDSI.

To mitigate the inefficiency of Naive-PromptDSI, we introduce PromptDSI, a streamlined variant that eliminates the first pass typically required by PCL methods. As illustrated on the right side of Fig. 1, instead of using the [CLS] token from the first pass for prompt selection, PromptDSI leverages the average token embeddings [AVG] from the intermediate layer immediately preceding the prompting layer: [AVG] = $\frac{1}{|q|} \sum_{i=1}^{|q|} f_{\theta_e^{l-1}}(q)_i \in \mathbb{R}^{\dim}$, where $|q|$ denotes the sequence length of query q, and $f_{\theta_e^{l-1}}(q)_i$ represents the output of the $(l-1)th$ layer of the encoder θ_e at position i. If $l = 1$, we use the average of the embeddings from the pre-trained language model's embedding layer. This adjustment approximates the semantic richness typically provided by the [CLS] token. In Sect. 5.4, we show that this design incurs only minor task performance degradation while speeding up both training and inference. We hypothesize that this is thanks to queries in document retrieval are semantically simple compared to the images in vision domain, leading to shallow query embeddings are sufficient for prompt selection.

4.3 Topic-Aware Prompt Keys

Given a prompt pool **P**, L2P [40] shares **P** for all incoming tasks, while S-Prompt++ [35,37] allocates a single key-prompt pair for each incoming tasks and freezes previous pairs. Since the learnable prompt keys in the prompt pool are optimized to represent new corpora, the lack of distinct semantic boundaries among corpora in document retrieval (i.e., corpora both consist of documents of similar topics) causes these keys to become highly similar across corpora. This leads to a collapse in prompt selection (i.e., the query-key matching mechanism in Eq. (1)) to a small subset of prompts, resulting in underutilization of parameters, which is visualized and elaborated in Sect. 5.5.

Instabilities in training prompt pools for PCL methods have been reported in the literature [24,44]. We observe that in PCL methods, the query embeddings used for prompt selection are deterministic [40], suggesting that optimizing prompt keys **K** might be unnecessary. Inspired by neural topic modeling techniques [9,11], we propose using neural topic embeddings derived from D_0 as fixed prompt keys. We employ BERTopic [10] to cluster document embeddings and generate neural topic embeddings via a class-based TF-IDF procedure (we refer readers to [10] for details of BERTopic). By assuming each document semantically belongs to a neural topic, we employ these topic-aware fixed prompt keys to stabilize the query-key matching mechanism, addressing underutilization of prompts. Furthermore, this approach facilitates knowledge transfer between documents within the same topic and allows better interpretability compared to general-purpose or corpus-specific prompts in existing PCL methods. We refer to this PromptDSI variant as **PromptDSI$_{\text{Topic}}$**.

4.4 Optimization Objective

Denote PromptDSI's encoder and linear classifier as θ_e and θ_l, respectively. At timestep $t = 0$, PromptDSI is optimized using cross-entropy loss $\mathcal{L}_{CE}$ on D_0:

$$\mathcal{L}_0 = \sum_{q \in Q_0} \mathcal{L}_{CE}(f_{\theta_l}(f_{\theta_e}(q)), \text{id}_q), \tag{2}$$

where $\text{id}_q \in I_0$ is the one-hot encoded ground truth docid of query q.

We study three popular PCL methods: L2P [40], S-Prompt++ (S++) [35,37], and CODA-Prompt (CODA) [30]. During continual indexing, the encoder θ_e is frozen while prompt pool $\mathbf{P}$, prompt keys $\mathbf{K}$, and a portion of the linear classifier θ_l are optimized. We refer to $f_{\text{extra},\theta_e}$ as PromptDSI's encoder parameterized by θ_e and a set of learnable components **extra**. Denote $\mathbf{P}_t$ and $\mathbf{K}_t$ as prompts and prompt keys allocated for indexing D_t, at timestep $t > 0$, the general optimization objective for PromptDSI with L2P or S++ is:

$$\mathcal{L}_t^{\text{L2P}} = \sum_{q \in Q_t} \min_{\mathbf{P}_t, \mathbf{K}_t, \theta_{l,t}} \mathcal{L}_{CE}(f_{\theta_l}(f_{\mathbf{P}_t, \mathbf{K}_t, \theta_e}(q)), \text{id}_q) + \mathcal{L}_{\text{match}}, \tag{3}$$

where $\mathcal{L}_{\text{match}}$ is defined in Eq. (1) and $\text{id}_q \in I_t$. Unlike **PromptDSI$_{\text{L2P}}$**, which optimizes all key-prompt pairs, **PromptDSI$_{\text{S++}}$** optimizes only one key-prompt pair per timestep. **PromptDSI$_{\text{CODA}}$** introduces learnable attention vectors $A \in \mathbb{R}^{\dim}$ for each prompt. Instead of using $\mathcal{L}_{\text{match}}$, it computes a weighted sum of prompts: $P = \sum_{i=1}^{M} \alpha_i p_i$, where $\alpha_i = \cos(h_q \odot A_i, k_i)$ and $\odot$ denotes the Hadamard product. It is trained end-to-end with the following objective:

$$\mathcal{L}_t^{\text{CODA}} = \sum_{q \in Q_t} \min_{\mathbf{P}_t, \mathbf{K}_t, A_t, \theta_{l,t}} \mathcal{L}_{CE}(f_{\theta_l}(f_{\mathbf{P}_t, \mathbf{K}_t, A_t, \theta_e}(q)), \text{id}_q). \tag{4}$$

Using precomputed neural topic embeddings as fixed prompt keys, **PromptDSI$_{\text{Topic}}$** omits optimizing prompt keys $\mathbf{K}_t$ in Eq. 3 and also removes $\mathcal{L}_{\text{match}}$:

$$\mathcal{L}_t^{\text{Topic}} = \sum_{q \in Q_t} \min_{\mathbf{P}_t, \theta_{l,t}} \mathcal{L}_{CE}(f_{\theta_l}(f_{\mathbf{P}_t, \theta_e}(q)), \text{id}_q). \tag{5}$$

5 Experiments

5.1 Experimental Setting

Datasets. We evaluate PromptDSI on two well-known binary relevance document retrieval datasets: Natural Questions (NQ320k) [16] and a modified version of MSMARCO (MSMARCO 300k) [1,5] (Table 1). NQ320k refers to the title-de-duplicated version of the Natural Questions dataset, containing 320k query-document pairs from approximately 108k documents [15,31,38]. MSMARCO 300k is a modified subset of the MS MARCO Document Ranking dataset [1,5] with 300k documents, which is established in previous works [15,23,31]. For each corpus, queries from the official training set are split 80%/20% for training and validation, while the official development set is used for testing. To mimic the continual learning (CL) setup, each dataset is split into an initial corpus (D_0) containing 90% of the total documents, and five new corpora (D_1-D_5), each with 2% of the total documents. Each document in the train set is supplied with up to 15 additional pseudo-queries generated using docT5query [25] along with annotated natural queries. Each query corresponds to one relevant document.

Table 1. The NQ320k and MSMARCO 300k dataset statistics used in our study.

Corpus	Document	Train Queries	Validation Queries	Test Queries	Generated Queries
NQ320k					
D_0	98743	221194	55295	6998	1480538
D_1	2000	4484	1091	152	29997
D_2	2000	4417	1085	153	29992
D_3	2000	4800	1298	177	29991
D_4	2000	4346	1107	116	29992
D_5	1874	4131	964	140	28105
MSMARCO 300k					
D_0	289424	262008	65502	4678	4312150
D_1	2000	1768	480	40	29787
D_2	2000	1799	457	35	29805
D_3	2000	1800	450	30	29774
D_4	2000	1772	475	29	29821
D_5	2000	1851	430	30	29779

Evaluation metrics. We adopt Hits@{1, 10} and Mean Reciprocal Rank (MRR)@10 as document retrieval metrics. To evaluate CL performance, after training on corpus D_t, we report average performance (A_t), forgetting (F_t), and learning performance (LA_t), following previous works [23]. In the main result tables, We report the results of initial corpus D_0 and new corpora D_1-D_5 separately. We emphasize on A_t as it reflects both stability and plasticity [30]. Let $P_{t,i}$ be the performance of the model on corpus D_i in some metrics, after training on corpus D_t, where $i \leq t$. Forgetting of D_0 is calculated as: $\max(P_{5,0} - P_{0,0}, 0)$. With $t > 0$, the CL metrics are defined as follows:

$$A_t = \frac{1}{t}\sum_{i=1}^{t} P_{t,i} \quad LA_t = \frac{1}{t}\sum_{i=1}^{t} P_{i,i} \quad F_t = \frac{1}{t}\sum_{i=0}^{t-1} \max_{i' \in \{0,...,t-1\}} (P_{i',i} - P_{t,i})$$

Baselines. We adopt the well-established BERT [7] and SBERT [28][1] as backbones and compare PromptDSI with both CL and non-CL baselines.[2] While recent dense encoders such as BGE [42], and NV-Embed [17] can also serve as backbones and may yield improved retrieval performance, our goal is not to benchmark classification-based DSI frameworks with state-of-the-art backbones, but to analyze their continual learning behavior. Due to resource and space constraints, we leave such comparisons to future work.

- **Sequential Fine-tuning** sequentially optimizes on new corpora without accessing previous ones, serving as the performance lower bound in CL.
- **DSI++** [23] involves sequential fine-tuning on new corpora, using a query generation model to generate pseudo queries for sparse experience replay.
- **IncDSI** [15] indexes new documents by sequentially caching previous query embeddings and expanding θ_l. The new θ_l's embeddings are determined by solving constrained optimization problems. Since IncDSI is designed for online learning, we include "IncDSI*", a variant that solves the optimization for several epochs. We regard IncDSI as a strong baseline on D_0.
- **Multi-corpora Fine-tuning (Multi)** only fine-tunes on new corpora D_1-D_5, which are merged as one corpus. It is equivalent to the multi-task learning baseline in CL, serving as the performance upper bound on new corpora.
- **Joint Supervised (Joint)** trains on both initial and all new corpora, similar to the conventional supervised learning setup.
- **Dense Passage Retrieval (DPR)** [12] is a popular BERT-based dual-encoder trained with BM25 [29] hard negatives and in-batch negatives. DPR serves as a strong dense retrieval baseline and performs zero-shot retrieval on new corpora.

Implementation Details. We employ AdamW [21] and use a single NVIDIA A100 80GB GPU for all experiments. Following [15], we train BERT/SBERT on D_0 for 20 epochs, using batch size 128 and 1024, learning rate $1e^{-4}$ and $5e^{-5}$ for NQ320k and MSMARCO 300k, respectively. All subsequent methods are trained with batch size 128 and initialized from the same BERT/SBERT checkpoint trained on D_0. We randomly sample pseudo-queries from previous corpora to substitute for the query generation model in DSI++[3]. We reproduce IncDSI [15] using its official implementation. For PCL methods in PromptDSI, we leverage open-source implementations. PromptDSI$_{\text{L2P/S++}}$ use a prompt pool of size 5, prompt length 20 and top-1 prompt selection. PromptDSI$_{\text{CODA}}$ uses a prompt length 10 and 2 prompts per task. For BERT-based PromptDSI, we use learning rate $1e^{-4}$ and $5e^{-4}$; for SBERT-based PromptDSI, we use $1.5e^{-4}$ and

---

[1] HuggingFace model identifiers: `google-bert/bert-base-uncased` and `sentence-transformers/all-mpnet-v2`.
[2] We omit comparisons with regularization-based methods, as they underperform compared to replay-based approaches [41].
[3] Since the code for DSI++ has not been released.

$1e^{-3}$ for NQ320k and MSMARCO 300k, respectively. For PromptDSI$_{\text{Topic}}$, we use BERTopic [10] to mine neural topics from D_0, adhering closely to the author's best practices guide[4]. PromptDSI variants are trained for 10 epochs since prefix-tuning [19] requires longer training to converge. Other full-model fine-tuning baselines are trained for 5 epochs. Results for CL methods are averaged over three runs, with standard deviations reported accordingly. The layer-wise prompting study in Sect. 5.6 is conducted using a fixed random seed.

Table 2. BERT-based methods performance after indexing D_5. H@10 and M@10 denote Hits@10 and MRR@10. **D$_0$** denotes $P_{5,0}$ on D_0's test queries. † denotes results from [15]. Params. denotes number of trainable parameters. **Bold** and underline highlight the top and second best CL methods. The underscript numbers denote the standard deviations.

BERT-based	NQ320k					MSMARCO 300k					Rehearsal free
	$D_0 \uparrow$		$A_5 \uparrow$		Params.↓	$D_0 \uparrow$		$A_5 \uparrow$		Params.↓	
	H@10	M@10	H@10	M@10		H@10	M@10	H@10	M@10		
Non CL Methods (For Reference)											
Multi	0.0	0.0	91.4	83.9	193 M	0.0	0.0	92.2	83.9	340 M	–
Joint	85.9	70.1	84.7	68.4	193 M	76.8	55.2	78.3	53.8	340 M	–
DPR	70.3	51.9	70.1	49.8	220 M	68.8†	–	62.8†	–	220 M	–
CL Methods											
Sequential	0.0$_{0.0}$	0.0$_{0.0}$	27.4$_{2.8}$	22.2$_{1.2}$	193 M	0.0$_{0.0}$	0.0$_{0.0}$	31.9$_{0.8}$	27.2$_{0.6}$	340 M	✓
DSI++	2.6$_{0.0}$	2.6$_{2.6}$	28.6$_{1.9}$	22.1$_{28.6}$	193 M	2.6$_{0.1}$	2.4$_{0.0}$	28.6$_{7.3}$	24.2$_{5.1}$	340 M	✗
IncDSI	86.4$_{0.1}$	**72.2**$_{0.3}$	85.8$_{0.6}$	69.5$_{0.3}$	7.6 M	79.5$_{0.9}$	57.5$_{1.3}$	81.8$_{2.2}$	61.4$_{3.2}$	7.7 M	✗
IncDSI*	**86.5**$_{0.2}$	<u>72.0</u>$_{0.1}$	85.2$_{1.0}$	68.6$_{0.9}$	7.6 M	**80.6**$_{0.0}$	**59.0**$_{0.0}$	84.8$_{0.1}$	65.1$_{0.0}$	7.7 M	✗
PromptDSI (Ours) with											
L2P	86.1$_{0.1}$	71.2$_{0.2}$	**90.8**$_{0.4}$	73.2$_{1.8}$	7.6 M	<u>80.5</u>$_{0.0}$	58.7$_{0.0}$	86.7$_{1.4}$	<u>67.4</u>$_{1.1}$	7.8 M	✓
S++	86.1$_{0.2}$	71.4$_{0.2}$	<u>90.5</u>$_{0.4}$	<u>73.8</u>$_{0.7}$	7.6 M	80.4$_{0.1}$	58.6$_{0.1}$	**86.8**$_{1.5}$	<u>67.4</u>$_{0.8}$	7.8 M	✓
CODA	86.0$_{0.0}$	71.2$_{0.1}$	90.3$_{0.3}$	**74.2**$_{0.8}$	7.7 M	**80.6**$_{0.1}$	<u>58.9</u>$_{0.2}$	**87.9**$_{0.6}$	66.8$_{0.3}$	7.8 M	✓
Topic	86.0$_{0.1}$	71.3$_{0.0}$	<u>90.5</u>$_{0.5}$	**74.2**$_{1.4}$	8.8 M	80.4$_{0.0}$	58.6$_{0.1}$	86.7$_{0.5}$	**67.5**$_{0.5}$	10.4 M	✓

5.2 Main Results

We present our results of BERT/SBERT-based methods in Tables 2 and 3. Performance of the latter is often better thanks to the better representation.

Among non-CL methods, across backbones and datasets, **Multi-corpora Fine-tuning** completely forgets D_0 and heavily overfits D_1-D_5. Both **Joint** and **DPR** achieve a balance between initial and new corpora; however, they generally underperform IncDSI and PromptDSI. Among CL methods, **Sequential Fine-tuning** suffer sfrom severe catastrophic forgetting and significantly

---

[4] https://maartengr.github.io/BERTopic/getting_started/best_practices/best_practices.html.

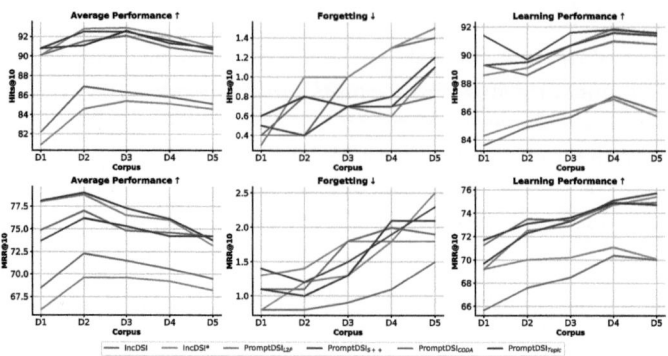

Fig. 2. Continual indexing performance of BERT-based methods on NQ320k

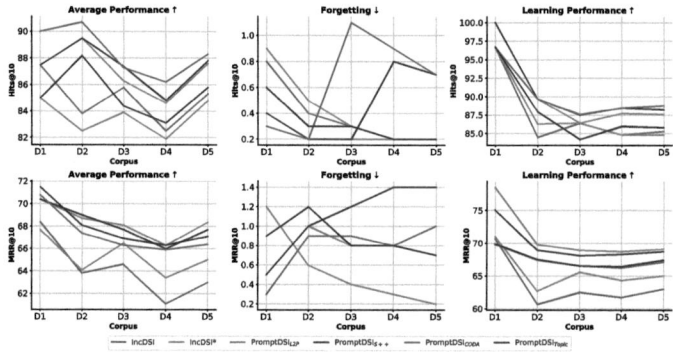

Fig. 3. Continual indexing performance of BERT-based methods on MSMARCO 300k

overfitting the most recent corpora. **DSI++**, even with sparse experience replay, provides only slight improvements over Sequential Fine-tuning, highlighting that maintaining a memory buffer or a generative model for rehearsal is non-trivial. Overall, Sequential Fine-tuning and DSI++ employ full-model fine-tuning CL methods (i.e., huge trainable parameters), but suffers from catastrophic forgetting. In contrast, IncDSI and PromptDSI are significantly more parameter-efficient, as a result of freezing the backbone.

IncDSI maintains strong performance across all corpora, with IncDSI* (10 epochs) further improving overall metrics. However, it still falls short of optimal performance on new corpora. All **PromptDSI** variants outperform IncDSI and IncDSI* in terms of A_5 by large margins across metrics, datasets, and backbones while maintaining D_0 performance close to that of IncDSI. **PromptDSI**$_{\text{Topic}}$ removes prompt-key optimization to stabilize query-key matching, achieving comparable or superior performance among PromptDSI variants.

We further analyze the continual indexing of BERT-based PromptDSI and IncDSI in Figs. 2 and 3. PromptDSI consistently outperforms IncDSI in Aver-

Table 3. SBERT-based methods performance after indexing D_5. $\mathbf{D_0}$ denote $P_{5,0}$ on D_0's test queries. H@10 and M@10 denotes Hits@10 and MRR@10. Params. denotes number of trainable parameters. **Bold** and underline highlight the top and second best CL methods. The underscript numbers denote the standard deviations.

SBERT-based	NQ320k					MSMARCO 300k					Rehearsal free
	$\mathbf{D_0}$ ↑		A_5 ↑		Params.↓	$\mathbf{D_0}$ ↑		A_5 ↑		Params.↓	
	H@10	M@10	H@10	M@10		H@10	M@10	H@10	M@10		
Non CL methods (For reference)											
Multi	0.0	0.0	92.0	83.6	193 M	0.0	0.0	94.7	87.2	340 M	–
Joint	86.8	71.5	86.4	69.7	193 M	76.3	55.5	84.1	61.2	340 M	–
CL methods											
Sequential	$0.0_{0.0}$	$0.0_{0.0}$	$25.2_{2.0}$	$20.3_{0.8}$	193 M	$0.0_{0.0}$	$0.0_{0.0}$	$27.1_{2.1}$	$23.3_{1.2}$	340 M	✓
DSI++	$2.7_{0.0}$	$2.4_{0.1}$	$28.5_{4.8}$	$22.3_{2.7}$	193 M	$2.8_{0.1}$	$2.5_{0.1}$	$29.0_{4.7}$	$23.3_{0.5}$	340 M	✗
IncDSI	$87.1_{0.0}$	$72.3_{1.1}$	$86.6_{0.8}$	$70.5_{2.4}$	7.6 M	$80.9_{1.0}$	$58.6_{1.2}$	$82.8_{1.6}$	$64.0_{3.3}$	7.7 M	✗
IncDSI*	$87.0_{0.0}$	$\mathbf{72.6_{0.0}}$	$87.3_{0.1}$	$73.2_{0.0}$	7.6 M	$\mathbf{82.0_{0.0}}$	$\mathbf{60.0_{0.0}}$	$84.1_{0.1}$	$68.0_{0.2}$	7.7 M	✗
PromptDSI (Ours) with											
L2P	$86.9_{0.1}$	$\mathbf{72.6_{0.1}}$	$\mathbf{91.1_{0.1}}$	$74.0_{3.8}$	7.6 M	$\mathbf{81.6_{0.1}}$	$\underline{59.1_{0.0}}$	$87.4_{0.4}$	$70.1_{0.4}$	$\underline{7.8\text{ M}}$	✓
S++	$86.8_{0.0}$	$\underline{72.5_{0.1}}$	$91.0_{0.5}$	$\mathbf{74.8_{2.7}}$	7.6 M	$81.4_{0.1}$	$58.9_{0.1}$	$\underline{87.5_{0.9}}$	$\mathbf{71.4_{0.3}}$	$\underline{7.8\text{ M}}$	✓
CODA	$\mathbf{87.0_{0.1}}$	$72.1_{0.9}$	$\mathbf{91.1_{0.5}}$	$74.2_{4.1}$	$\underline{7.7\text{ M}}$	$81.5_{0.0}$	$59.0_{0.2}$	$\underline{87.5_{0.7}}$	$70.0_{1.0}$	$\underline{7.8\text{ M}}$	✓
Topic	$86.8_{0.0}$	$72.1_{0.2}$	$\mathbf{91.1_{0.3}}$	$\mathbf{75.1_{1.9}}$	9.0 M	$81.3_{0.1}$	$\underline{59.1_{0.2}}$	$\mathbf{88.1_{1.9}}$	$\underline{70.5_{1.8}}$	10.6 M	✓

age and Learning Performance across datasets, with minimal forgetting, often matching IncDSI or surpassing IncDSI*. These results highlight the superior stability-plasticity trade-off of PromptDSI, despite being rehearsal-free.

5.3 Memory Complexity Analysis

DSI++ requires storing an additional T5 [27] model for query generation and IncDSI requires caching a matrix $\mathbf{Z} \in \mathbb{R}^{\dim \times \sum_{t=0}^{T} |D_t|}$, where each column of $\mathbf{Z}$ represents an average query embedding. Consequently, the memory usage and indexing time of IncDSI increase linearly with the number of documents. For our experiments, caching requires approximately 318 MiB for NQ320k and 977 MiB for MSMARCO 300k. Extending to the full MS MARCO dataset (8.8M passages) requires about 25 GiB of memory. In many cases, loading such a large memory footprint onto conventional GPUs may not be possible. In contrast, PromptDSI is rehearsal-free, eliminating the need to store $\mathbf{Z}$. It employs a prompt pool and a set of prompt keys, i.e., $\mathbf{P} \cup \mathbf{K} \in \mathbb{R}^{\dim \times (M(m+1))}$, which consists of M prompts $p \in \mathbb{R}^{\dim \times m}$ and M prompt keys $k \in \mathbb{R}^{\dim}$. The L2P/S++ variants require approximately 315 KiB, which is about three orders of magnitude smaller than IncDSI's overhead on NQ320k, while the largest "Topic" variant requires approximately 11.9 MiB–roughly one to two orders of magnitude smaller than IncDSI or the additional T5 model used in DSI++.

Table 4. Performance comparison between Naive-PromptDSI and PromptDSI on NQ320k.

Methods	Metric	Naive-PromptDSI		PromptDSI		Single-pass speedup
		Hits@10	MRR@10	Hits@10	MRR@10	
PromptDSI$_{L2P}$	$D_0 \uparrow$	$86.1_{0.1}$	$71.3_{0.1}$	$86.1_{0.1}$	$71.2_{0.2}$	4.3x
	$A_5 \uparrow$	$90.3_{0.5}$	$74.1_{0.3}$	$90.8_{0.4}$	$73.2_{1.8}$	
PromptDSI$_{S++}$	$D_0 \uparrow$	$86.1_{0.1}$	$71.3_{0.2}$	$86.1_{0.2}$	$71.4_{0.1}$	4.2x
	$A_5 \uparrow$	$90.5_{0.2}$	$74.0_{0.9}$	$90.5_{0.4}$	$73.8_{0.7}$	
PromptDSI$_{CODA}$	$D_0 \uparrow$	$86.0_{0.1}$	$71.2_{0.1}$	$86.0_{0.0}$	$71.2_{0.1}$	1.7x
	$A_5 \uparrow$	$90.6_{0.2}$	$74.2_{0.6}$	$90.3_{0.3}$	$74.2_{0.8}$	

5.4 Single-Pass PromptDSI Analysis

Table 4 presents the comparison between Naive-PromptDSI and PromptDSI. Using intermediate layer representations as query embeddings for prompt selection (i.e., bypassing the first forward pass), we observe only a minimal trade-off in performance across all PromptDSI variants. This is primarily reflected in MRR@10, with a maximum drop of just 0.9%. Notably, with our implementations, the single-pass L2P and S++ variants can be up to 4 times faster by omitting the first forward pass. Although the speedup is less significant for the CODA variant, which employs a weighted sum of prompts strategy, it still achieves a notable 1.7x speedup. Overall, these results confirm that the proposed single-pass PCL methods in PromptDSI meet the low-latency requirements of typical information retrieval systems, with only a negligible impact on performance.

5.5 Prompt Pool Utilization Analysis

Figure 4 (left) illustrates the prompt pool utilization of PromptDSI variants.[5] We observe that L2P frequently selects a small subset of prompts across all corpora. While S++ benefits from SBERT's better similarity-based embeddings to achieve more diverse task-specific prompt selection, this effect does not extend to L2P. These findings suggest that optimizing the prompt pool and ensuring diverse selection remain challenging due to instability. With a topic-aware prompt pool, PromptDSI$_{Topic}$ achieves better prompt utilization, leading to improved performance in some cases (Table 3) while mitigating training instability. Notably, in Fig. 4 (bottom-right), prompt pool utilization exceeds 60%, with over 30% of the prompts frequently selected (i.e., above the uniform threshold). Beyond performance improvements, topic-aware prompts enhance interpretability, unlike general-purpose (L2P) or corpus-specific (S++) prompts.

Since we uses two backbones BERT and SBERT, we adopt separate BERTopic models for each, resulting in slightly different topics for the same dataset (Figs. 5 and 6). While effective, topic modeling may benefit further from

---
[5] PromptDSI$_{CODA}$ applies a weighted sum of prompts instead of prompt selection.

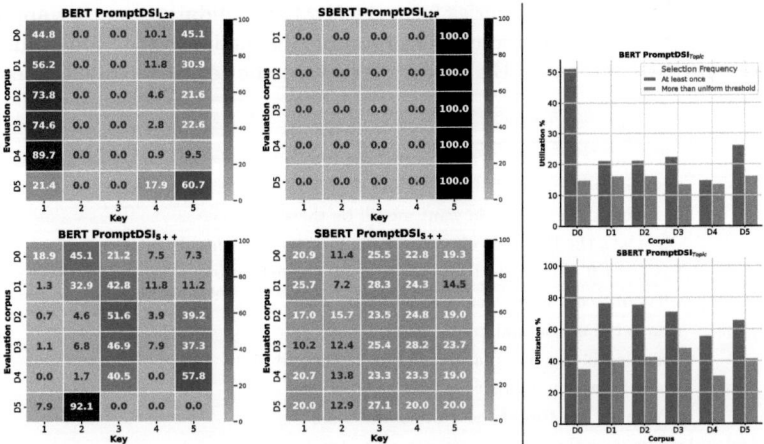

Fig. 4. Prompt pool utilization:PromptDSI$_{L2P/S++}$ (left); PromptDSI$_{Topic}$ (right).

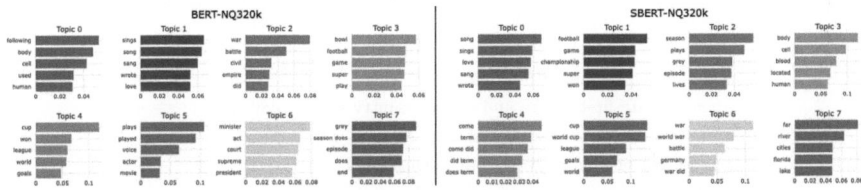

Fig. 5. Top 8 NQ320k topics mined using BERTopic with BERT/SBERT and their corresponding most frequent terms. A total of 80 topics were identified with BERT and 91 with SBERT from D_0.

LLMs due to their superior representational and contextual capabilities. Table 5 presents queries associated with the top 8 topics identified by SBERT-based BERTopic on the NQ320k validation set, which PromptDSI$_{Topic}$ selects during inference. These neural topics reflect frequently queried subjects, with queries often containing recurring or semantically similar terms.

5.6 Layer-Wise Prompting Study

To determine the optimal layers for prompting (i.e., prefix-tuning), we follow the protocol of [39]. We assume prompting layers are contiguous and limit the search space to three layers. Using SBERT-based PromptDSI, we attach prompts to each layer of θ_e to identify effective layers for multi-layer prompting. Given that PromptDSI variants improve A_5 at the cost of a slight degradation in D_0, we define our main criteria as follows: (1) *Lower forgetting on D_0*, (2) *Moderate performance on A_5*, and (3) *Fewer prompting layers are preferable*. For single-layer prompting, Fig. 7 (left) shows that CODA retains more knowledge but performs worse than L2P and S++. Overall, PromptDSI outperforms IncDSI across

Table 5. Examples annotated queries from the NQ320k validation set that are matched correctly to the corresponding topic-aware prompts during inference. Topic embeddings are mined using SBERT-based BERTopic. Topic-specific terms are highlighted.

Topic	Queries
0 (Music)	who **sang** the **song** no other love have i
	who **sings** the **song** it feels like rain
	who **sings** whenever you want me i'll be there
1 (Football)	when was the last time **cleveland browns** were in the playoffs
	has any **nfl** team gone 16–0 and won the **superbowl**
	what **nfl** team never went to the **super bowl**
2 (Movies)	who is the **actor** that **plays** spencer reid
	who died in vampire diaries **season** 1 **episode** 17
	who **played** the mother on father knows best
	how many **season** of the waltons are there
3 (Human biology)	where does the **amino acid** attach to **trna**
	when a person is at rest approximately how much **blood** is being held within the **veins**
	where are **lipids** synthesized outside of the endomembrane system
4 (Origin)	where does the last name broome **come from**
	where does spring water found in mountains **come from**
	where does the last name de leon **come from**
5 (Soccer)	who is going to the 2018 **world cup**
	when did **fifa** first begun and which country was it played
	who came second in the **world cup** 2018
6 (War)	who fought on the western front during **ww1**
	when did the allies start to win **ww2**
	when did the united states declare **war** on **germany**
	what were the most effective weapons in **ww1**
7 (Geograpy)	how wide is the **mississippi** river at davenport **iowa**
	bob dylan musical girl from the north **country**
	what are the four **deserts** in **north america**

prompting layers. However, L2P and S++ exhibit severe forgetting in the top layers (10–12), leading us to exclude them from further analysis. Notably, layer 2 achieves comparable or lower forgetting than IncDSI on D_0 while maintaining strong A_5, making it a promising choice. We select S++ for multi-layer prompting analysis due to its high forgetting on D_0. As shown in Fig. 7 (right), two-layer prompting (first column) slightly reduces forgetting, but the gains in A_5 are marginal ($< 1\%$ for MRR@10, $< 0.5\%$ for Hits@10). Three-layer prompting significantly degrades MRR@10 (up to 2.5%) despite increased computation, offering minimal reduction in forgetting. Since multi-layer prompting incurs higher computational costs, these findings suggest that single-layer prompting, particularly in the lower layers (1-5), achieves the best trade-off between efficiency and performance. Consequently, we primarily perform single-layer prefix-tuning on layer 2 of DSI's encoder in our experiments, which satisfies all desirable criteria.

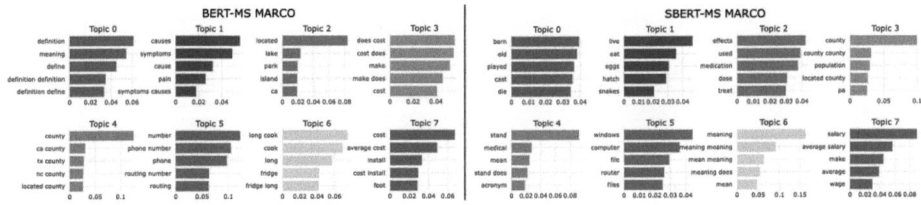

Fig. 6. Top 8 MSMARCO 300k topics mined using BERTopic with BERT/SBERT and their corresponding most frequent terms. A total of 182 topics were identified with BERT and 193 with SBERT from D_0.

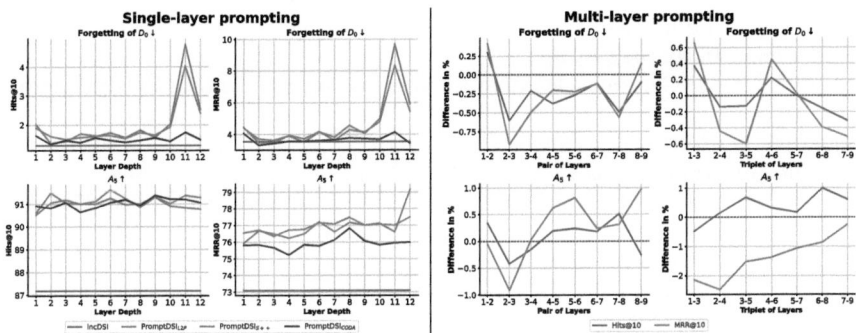

Fig. 7. Layer-wise prompting analysis of SBERT-based PromptDSI on NQ320k. **Left half:** Single-layer prompting analysis of different PromptDSI variants. **Right half:** Multi-layer prompting analysis of SBERT-based PromptDSI$_{S++}$, illustrating the performance changes (i.e., percentage gains and drops) when using 2-layer prompting (first column) and 3-layer prompting (second column) compared to single-layer prompting at layer 1, indicated by the red dashed line.

6 Conclusion

We present PromptDSI, a novel prompt-based approach for rehearsal-free continual learning in document retrieval. We adapt prompt-based continual learning (PCL) methods and introduce single-pass PCL. We validate our approach on three standard PCL methods. Our topic-aware prompt pool addresses parameter underutilization, ensuring diverse and efficient prompt usage, while also enhancing interpretability. Results show that PromptDSI outperforms rehearsal-based DSI++ and matches IncDSI in mitigating forgetting, while achieving superior performance on new corpora.

Acknowledgments. This material is based on research sponsored by Defense Advanced Research Projects Agency (DARPA) under agreement number HR0011-22-2-0047. The U.S. Government is authorised to reproduce and distribute reprints for Governmental purposes notwithstanding any copyright notation thereon. The views and conclusions contained herein are those of the authors and should not be interpreted as necessarily representing the official policies or endorsements, either expressed or implied, of DARPA or the U.S. Government. This work is supported by the Australian Research Council Discovery Early Career Researcher Award DE250100032 and Monash eResearch capabilities, including M3.

References

1. Bajaj, P., Campos, D., Craswell, N., et al.: MS MARCO: a human generated machine reading comprehension dataset. arXiv preprint arXiv:1611.09268 (2016)
2. Buzzega, P., Boschini, M., Porrello, A., Abati, D., Calderara, S.: Dark experience for general continual learning: a strong, simple baseline. In: NeurIPS (2020)
3. Chaudhry, A., Ranzato, M., Rohrbach, M., Elhoseiny, M.: Efficient lifelong learning with a-gem. In: ICLR (2019)
4. Chen, J., et al.: Continual learning for generative retrieval over dynamic corpora. In: CIKM (2023)
5. Craswell, N., Mitra, B., Yilmaz, E., Campos, D., Lin, J.: Overview of the TREC 2021 deep learning track. In: TREC (2021)
6. Custers, B., Sears, A.M., Dechesne, F., Georgieva, I., Tani, T., Van der Hof, S.: EU Personal Data Protection in Policy and Practice. Springer, Cham (2019). https://doi.org/10.1007/978-94-6265-282-8
7. Devlin, J., Chang, M.W., Lee, K., Toutanova, K.: BERT: pre-training of deep bidirectional transformers for language understanding. In: NAACL (2019)
8. French, R.M.: Catastrophic forgetting in connectionist networks. Trends Cognit. Sci. (1999)
9. Gerald, T., Soulier, L.: Continual learning of long topic sequences in neural information retrieval. In: ECIR (2022)
10. Grootendorst, M.: Bertopic: neural topic modeling with a class-based TF-IDF procedure. arXiv preprint arXiv:2203.05794 (2022)
11. Gupta, P., Chaudhary, Y., Runkler, T., Schuetze, H.: Neural topic modeling with continual lifelong learning. In: ICML (2020)
12. Karpukhin, V., Oguz, B., Min, S., et al.: Dense passage retrieval for open-domain question answering. In: EMNLP (2020)
13. Kim, Y., Li, Y., Panda, P.: One-stage prompt-based continual learning. In: Leonardis, A., Ricci, E., Roth, S., Russakovsky, O., Sattler, T., Varol, G. (eds.) ECCV 2024. LNCS, vol. 15071, pp. 163–179. Springer, Cham (2024). https://doi.org/10.1007/978-3-031-72624-8_10
14. Kirkpatrick, J., Pascanu, R., Rabinowitz, N., et al.: Overcoming catastrophic forgetting in neural networks. PNAS (2017)
15. Kishore, V., Wan, C., Lovelace, J., Artzi, Y., Weinberger, K.Q.: INCDSI: incrementally updatable document retrieval. In: ICML (2023)
16. Kwiatkowski, T., Palomaki, J., Redfield, O., et al.: Natural questions: a benchmark for question answering research. TACL (2019)
17. Lee, C., Roy, R., Xu, M., et al.: NV-embed: Improved techniques for training LLMs as generalist embedding models. In: ICLR (2025)
18. Lester, B., Al-Rfou, R., Constant, N.: The power of scale for parameter-efficient prompt tuning. arXiv preprint arXiv:2104.08691 (2021)
19. Li, X.L., Liang, P.: Prefix-tuning: Optimizing continuous prompts for generation. arXiv preprint arXiv:2101.00190 (2021)
20. Li, Z., Hoiem, D.: Learning without forgetting. TPAMI (2017)

21. Loshchilov, I., Hutter, F.: Decoupled weight decay regularization. arXiv preprint arXiv:1711.05101 (2017)
22. McCloskey, M., Cohen, N.J.: Catastrophic interference in connectionist networks: the sequential learning problem. Psych. Learn. Motiv. (1989)
23. Mehta, S., Gupta, J., Tay, Y., et al.: DSI++: updating transformer memory with new documents. In: EMNLP (2023)
24. Moon, J.Y., Park, K.H., et al.: Online class incremental learning on stochastic blurry task boundary via mask and visual prompt tuning. In: ICCV (2023)
25. Nogueira, R., Lin, J., Epistemic, A.: From doc2query to docttttquery. Online preprint (2019)
26. Pradeep, R., et al.: How does generative retrieval scale to millions of passages? In: EMNLP (2023)
27. Raffel, C., Shazeer, N., Roberts, A., et al.: Exploring the limits of transfer learning with a unified text-to-text transformer. JMLR (2020)
28. Reimers, N., Gurevych, I.: Sentence-BERT: Sentence embeddings using Siamese BERT-networks. In: EMNLP-IJCNLP (2019)
29. Robertson, S., Zaragoza, H., et al.: The probabilistic relevance framework: Bm25 and beyond. Found. Trends® Inf. Retrieval (2009)
30. Smith, J.S., Karlinsky, L., Gutta, V., et al.: Coda-prompt: continual decomposed attention-based prompting for rehearsal-free continual learning. In: CVPR (2023)
31. Sun, W., et al.: Learning to tokenize for generative retrieval. In: NeurIPS (2023)
32. Sutskever, I., Vinyals, O., Le, Q.V.: Sequence to sequence learning with neural networks. In: NeurIPS (2014)
33. Tay, Y., Tran, V., Dehghani, M., et al.: Transformer memory as a differentiable search index. In: NeurIPS (2022)
34. Vaswani, A., et al.: Attention is all you need. In: NeurIPS (2017)
35. Wang, L., Xie, J., Zhang, X., et al.: Hierarchical decomposition of prompt-based continual learning: Rethinking obscured sub-optimality. In: NeurIPS (2023)
36. Wang, L., Zhang, X., Su, H., Zhu, J.: A comprehensive survey of continual learning: theory, method and application. TPAMI (2024)
37. Wang, Y., Huang, Z., Hong, X.: S-prompts learning with pre-trained transformers: an Occam's razor for domain incremental learning. In: NeurIPS (2022)
38. Wang, Y., et al.: A neural corpus indexer for document retrieval. In: NeurIPS (2022)
39. Wang, Z., Zhang, Z., Ebrahimi, S., et al.: Dualprompt: complementary prompting for rehearsal-free continual learning. In: ECCV (2022)
40. Wang, Z., et al.: Learning to prompt for continual learning. In: CVPR (2022)
41. Wu, T., Caccia, M., Li, Z., Li, Y.F., Qi, G., Haffari, G.: Pretrained language model in continual learning: a comparative study. In: ICLR (2021)
42. Xiao, S., Liu, Z., Zhang, P., et al.: C-pack: packed resources for general Chinese embeddings. In: SIGIR (2024)
43. Xiong, L., Xiong, C., Li, Y., et al.: Approximate nearest neighbor negative contrastive learning for dense text retrieval. arXiv preprint arXiv:2007.00808 (2020)
44. Yadav, P., Sun, Q., Ding, H., et al.: Exploring continual learning for code generation models. In: ACL (2023)
45. Zeng, H., Luo, C., Jin, B., Sarwar, S.M., Wei, T., Zamani, H.: Scalable and effective generative information retrieval. In: TheWebConf (2024)
46. Zhang, P., Liu, Z., Zhou, Y., Dou, Z., Liu, F., Cao, Z.: Generative retrieval via term set generation. In: SIGIR (2024)
47. Zhuang, S., Ren, H., Shou, L., et al.: Bridging the gap between indexing and retrieval for DSI with query generation. arXiv preprint arXiv:2206.10128 (2022)

A Scalable Model for Frequency Distribution of Low Occurrence Multi-words Towards Handling Very Large Spectrum of Text *Corpora* Sizes

Joaquim F. Silva[✉] and Jose C. Cunha

NOVA LINCS, NOVA School of Science and Technology, Caparica, Portugal
{jfs,jcc}@fct.unl.pt

Abstract. Predicting the diversity of words and multi-words (n-grams) in a text *corpus* and their frequency distributions is important in NLP and language modeling, and is becoming critical to enable the design of modern applications, namely Large Language Models, e.g. for guiding tokenization and *corpus* analysis for pre-training. This requires the ability to model the very large scale *corpora* behaviour, the handling of multi-words as subwords or phrases, and the distribution of n-grams across different frequency ranges, namely the low occurrence n-grams. We present a scalable model to predict the number of distinct n-grams and their frequency distributions targeting an extended range of *corpora* sizes, from hundreds of million words to hundreds of billion words (a 1000 times factor). This led us to a novel approach for explicitly incorporating into the model the parameter dependency behaviour regarding the extended *corpora* size range.

In the presence of such extended range of *corpora* sizes, the model estimates the cumulative numbers of distinct n-grams ($1 \leq n \leq 6$) greater or equal to a given frequency $k \geq 1$, in a *corpus*, and the numbers of n-grams with equal-frequencies, in a given language *corpus*. Unlike most approaches that assume an open, potentially infinite, language word vocabulary, this model relies on the vocabulary finiteness. The model ensures very low and stable average relative errors (*circa* 2%), for the low frequencies starting with singletons, from 1-grams to 6-grams, across the above very large range of *corpora* sizes, in English and German.

Keywords: Scalable Prediction Model · Large Text Corpora · n-gram Frequency Distribution

1 Introduction

A word n-gram is a sequence of n consecutive words. Knowledge on the statistical n-gram frequency distributions in text *corpora* is useful in applications, e.g. indexing, extracting relevant terms, compression, cache design, and translation. In large language modelling, understanding n-gram distributions as a function of *corpus* size is useful for: *a*) Guiding Tokenization Strategies, as tokenizers can be tuned to produce subwords or phrases that approximate frequent n-gram patterns; besides, the balance of distinct 1-grams (words) *versus* higher order n-grams (multi-words) in different frequency ranges can help determine the appropriate tokenization granularity; *b*) *Corpus* Analysis for pre-training, where knowing the number of distinct n-grams across frequency ranges serves as a proxy for a *corpus* linguistic diversity; a *corpus* with n-grams spanning a broad range of frequencies likely captures richer patterns, important for pre-training deep language models; however, if the numbers of distinct n-grams stabilise beyond a certain *corpus* size, it suggests diminishing returns when adding more data, guiding the selection of an optimal *corpus* size for pre-training or fine-tuning.

Most traditional frequency distribution models consider moderate size *corpora* (from thousands to several million words (Mw)) and only apply to single words (1-grams). However, larger *corpora* have impact upon n-gram frequency distributions, as shown by the emergence of Big Data. Also, multi-word n-grams ($n \geq 2$) reveal the language phrase/subphrase structure and express semantic specificity, and are becoming more relevant in an increasingly number of applications. Furthermore, most of the semantic content words and multi-words, e.g. important for topic mining, appear in the low frequency range, occurring 1,2,3... times, and they represent the majority of the distinct n-grams in each given *corpus*. In [11] a language-independent model is proposed for words and multi-words (from 1-grams to 6-grams) of low occurrence frequencies. It predicts the cumulative number of distinct n-grams, $D(k; C)$, with frequencies greater than or equal to k, for $k \geq 1$, in a *corpus* of size C, ($D(C) = D(1, C)$ is the total number of distinct n-grams), as well as the sizes, $W(k, C)$, of groups of n-grams with equal frequencies, as a function of *corpus* size. The principles underlying the model have a great potential for applications mainly when considering extremely large *corpora* sizes, handling words and multi-words, and low-frequency n-grams. All the above motivates the overall goal of this paper, that is to further explore the rationale behind the above model – that we denote as the baseline model – and evaluate its adequacy to predict $D(C)$, $D(k, C)$ and $W(k, C)$ variables, in a wider range (spanning a 1×1000 factor) of very large *corpora*, namely going into the hundred billion words (Gw) scale. The main contributions of this paper are the achievement of very low and stable average relative errors (around 2%) in the prediction of the above variables, encompassing 1-grams to 6-grams, and for the low frequencies starting with singletons, across the above very large range of *corpora* sizes, in English and German. This was achieved by considering the dependence of the model parameters on *corpus* size and their fine tuning, enforcing a sound estimation methodology relying on the separations of the training/validation and testing *corpora*, and by proposing a well-founded method for identifying the frequency limits of the model validity. This is in contrast to the baseline approach, which exhibits a critical issue when assuming the constancy of the model parameters versus C, and whose usage for *corpora* well beyond the 8.6 Gw largest *corpus* size in [11], revealed its inadequacy for large scale *corpora*, having led to significant deviations from real data. Besides, the usage of the same *corpora* sets in the baseline, both for training and testing purposes, is inadequate. We present the background of this work, the new proposed approach, experimental results and conclusions. A guide for the model reproducibility is found at https://github.com/OurName1234/ngrams.

2 Background and Related Work

Several influential word frequency distribution models were proposed [9], including the empirical Zipf's Law [13], showing the word frequency distribution as an approximated power law, but deviating from real data for high and low frequencies, and also theoretical models, e.g. based on preferential attachment [12]. However, firstly, most models only consider word frequencies, ignoring multi-words, although language modeling benefits from the knowledge on n-gram frequency patterns [4–6,10,11]. Secondly, the model predictions often show deviations from the real *corpora* data, in the high and low occurrence frequencies. Often, they ignore the low-frequency words, or are unable to accurately model the large set of less frequent, content words in a *corpus*, being important in many applications. Thirdly, most models have been tested only with small and moderate size *corpora* (up to several million words). However, the emergence of BigData and Web-based very large *corpora* and/or n-gram frequency data [2,3] triggered the development of large-scale applications [2], posing new challenges.

We address a challenge posed by large text *corpora* concerning the growth of the available *corpora* sizes and their effect upon the numbers of distinct n-grams and their frequency distributions, for evaluating the models/applications. The evolution of the number of distinct words (D) wrt to the *corpus* size (C), is modeled by Herdan' s and Heaps' empirical law [1], assuming an infinite word language vocabulary and stating that D would always keeps growing with increasing *corpus* sizes, as a power law with a constant exponent, but empirical evidence from large *corpora* shows that such exponent depends on the *corpus* size [1], suggesting that D will eventually saturate as C tends to infinity. This saturation of D occurs in word frequency distributions in languages with limited word vocabularies, e.g. Chinese, Japanese, Korean [8]. There is a lack of models predicting how the *corpus* size, for a wide range of large *corpora* sizes, explicitly influences the $D(C)$, $W(k,C)$ and $D(k,C)$ distributions for multi-words, namely considering the low occurrence n-grams and the model validation with real large *corpora* from different languages. This is useful to predict the impact of *corpus* growth upon application time and space complexities, thus supporting application design. Only a few models [5,10,11] address the above issues by unified approaches. However, only [11] relies on a principled model – the baseline model –, reflecting to the best of our knowledge, the state of the art of unified approaches for predicting the effect of *corpus* size upon the n-gram frequency distributions, for low frequencies and a wide range of large *corpora* sizes.

3 The Proposed Approach

Brief Review of the Baseline Model. The baseline [11] model assumes that for a fixed temporal epoch, there is an n-gram language L vocabulary with size $V(L,n)$. $D(k,C;L,n)$ is the number of distinct n-grams of size n, occurring at least k times in a *corpus* of size C of language L, also denoted $D(k,C)$ when L and n are implicit. For $k=1$, $D(k,C;L,n)$ is denoted as $D(C;L,n)$ or $D(C)$ if L and n are implicit. Under a continuum approximation, the growth rate of $D(k,C;L,n)$ wrt C, with $k \geq 1$, is modeled by the derivative $dD(k,C;L,n)/dC$, influenced by two factors: one is inspired by a cumulative form of preferential attachment, such that, when the *corpus* size C grows by a given amount, each $D(k,C;L,n)$ tends to increase at a rate proportional to $D(k,C;L,n)/C$, its current relative size in the *corpus*; another is due to the finiteness of the n-gram language vocabulary $V(L,n)$, reflecting a slowdown effect defined by the proportion of remaining n-grams still having a frequency below k, regardless of whether they appear in the current *corpus* or are unseen n-grams: $(V(L,n) - D(k,C;L,n))/V(L,n)$. For $k=1$, this is the proportion of the finite vocabulary n-grams still unseen in the current *corpus* of size C. Thus, $\frac{dD(k,C;L,n)}{dC}$ is given by:

$$\frac{dD(k,C)}{dC} = g_k \frac{D(k,C)}{C} \frac{V - D(k,C)}{V} \tag{1}$$

where V and g_k simplify $V(L,n)$ and the proportionality factor $g_k(L,n)$ respectively. Indeed, $V = \sum_{k=1}^{k=kmax} W(k,C)$ where $W(k,C)$ is the number of distinct n-grams with frequency k and $kmax$ is the highest frequency in the *corpus*, for each n. The solution of Eq. (1) is (h_k standing for an integration constant):

$$D(k,C;L,n) = \frac{V(L,n)}{1 + (h_k(L,n)\,C)^{-g_k(L,n)}} \ . \tag{2}$$

From (2), $W(k,C;L,n)$, the number of equal-frequency (k) distinct n-grams of size n, is predicted by the subtraction of the cumulative numbers $D(k,C;L,n)$ and $D(k+1,C;L,n)$ for two frequency consecutive values, k and $k+1$.

3.1 An Approach to Large-Scale Corpora

The baseline model [11] was trained for English with corpora up to 8.6 Gw and would be able to predict $D(k,C;L,n)$ and $W(k,C;L,n)$ values for any *corpus* size with average relative errors around 3%. However, for the purpose of evaluating that model (as available at "http://bit.ly/3gqM6rS") for extended large *corpora* ranges, we experimented with large scale English *corpora* reaching hundreds of billion words, and the obtained predictions show significant deviations from the empirical values, reflecting relative errors with modules much larger than 3% (generally over 20%). This led us to a new approach considering the dependency of the model parameters $g_k(L,n)$ and $h_k(L,n)$ on the *corpus* size C. Indeed, by considering the above dependencies, we achieved significantly lower errors in the model predictions compared to the baseline. Timewise, this involves typical n-gram counting in large *corpora* – which is computationally heavy, requiring the use of a parallel computing infrastructure – but is done only once, for model parameter estimation, while model utilisation for prediction purposes only needs a fast formula calculation (2). The errors obtained by the new approach kept stable across a much wider range of large *corpora* sizes, spanning a 1×1000 factor, for English, and reaching 373 billion words – a comparison of the relative errors when assuming the $g_k(L,n)$ and $h_k(L,n)$ constancy [11], *versus* when considering their dependency on C is presented on Sect. 5.

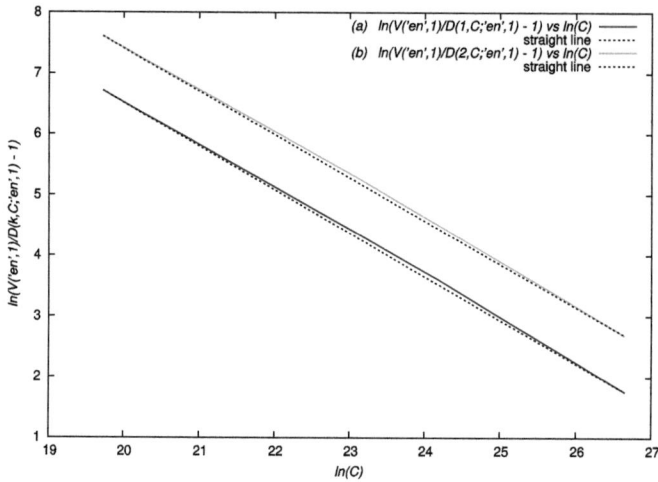

Fig. 1. Dependency of $\ln(\frac{V(L,n)}{D(k,C;L,n)} - 1)$ *versus* $\ln(C)$ for empirical 1-gram counts in English *corpora* (solid lines). Dashed lines refer to constancy assumption.

The Parameters Constancy Assumption in the Baseline Model. From the baseline model (2), the curve for $\ln(\frac{V(L,n)}{D(k,C;L,n)} - 1) = \ln((h_k(L,n)C)^{-g_k(L,n)}) = -g_k(L,n)\ln(h_k(L,n)) - g_k(L,n)\ln(C)$ is a straight line with slope $-g_k(L,n)$ when drawn as function of $\ln(C)$, because the constancy of $g_k(L,n)$ and $h_k(L,n)$ versus C is assumed. However, the experimental curves of $\ln(\frac{V(L,n)}{D(k,C;L,n)} - 1)$ *versus* $\ln(C)$, for the empirical $D(k,C;L,n)$ values (for English 1-grams and $k \in \{1,2\}$), show noticeable deviations from straight lines (in Fig. 1 the experimental curves are solid and straight lines are dashed): this visual perception is consistent with the large numeric values of the relative errors obtained when using the baseline model, as reported in Sect. 5, Tables 1, 2, 3, 4, 5. Note that this figure covers an extended *corpora* range of test *corpora* (beyond the range considered in the baseline): 366 Mw, 11.3 Gw, 31.5 Gw, 82.7 Gw, 172 Gw and 373 Gw. In this experiment, we considered an estimated English 1-gram vocabulary of $V('en',1) = 2.95e9$ – as discussed in Sect. 3.2. Thus, we model $D(k,C;L,n)$ and $W(k,C;L,n)$ with the explicit dependency

$g_k(C; L, n)$ and $h_k(C; L, n)$:

$$D(k, C; L, n) = \frac{V(L, n)}{1 + (h_k(C; L, n) \cdot C)^{-g_k(C;L,n)}} \quad (3)$$

$$W(k, C; L, n) = D(k, C; L, n) - D(k+1, C; L, n) \quad (4)$$

3.2 Estimating the Model Parameters

We present the method for estimating the model parameters – for each (L, n) –, considering the dependence on C: $V(L, n)$, $g_k(C; L, n)$ and $h_k(C; L, n)$. We use a set of training *corpora* to estimate the parameters, and a separate set of testing *corpora* to evaluate the results, with *corpora* up to hundreds of billion words. Overall, this method involves estimating: *i*) the vocabulary size $V(L, n)$; *ii*) the parameters $g_k(C; L, n)$ and $h_k(C; L, n)$ with the training *corpora*; *iii*) the dependency behavior of $g_k(C; L, n)$ and $h_k(C; L, n)$ for general test *corpora*. Concerning *i*), we estimate the vocabulary size to ensure the lowest average relative errors of model $D(k, C; L, n)$ (3) for each k. To avoid the computational complexity of an exhaustive search – which would be $O(S^{2N+1})$, S being the number of considered candidate values for each parameter $(V(L, n), g_k(C; L, n), h_k(C; L, n))$ and N the number of training *corpora* –, in choosing the best parameter combination, we first estimate $V(L, n)$. Concerning *ii*), given the estimated $V(L, n)$, we estimate the pairs $(g_k(C; L, n), h_k(C; L, n))$ for each training *corpus* C. Concerning *iii*), given the collection of the above estimated pairs $(g_k(C; L, n), h_k(C; L, n))$, we rely on regression using *splines* [7] (outperforming piecewise linear methods), thus enabling the estimation of values of $g_k(C; L, n)$ and $h_k(C; L, n)$ for any general *corpora*.

i) Estimating the Vocabulary Size. If we draw a secant line connecting two points (i and j) on one of the curves (a) or (b) of Fig. 1, whose corresponding *corpora* size values are $\ln(C_i)$ and $\ln(C_j)$, then the slope defined by this secant corresponds to a value of $g_k(C; L, n)$ that is valid for both *corpora*. So, there is a $g_k(C; L, n) = g_{k_{i,j}}$ that can fit both *corpora* C_i and C_j. Let h_{k_i} and h_{k_j} be the h_k parameter values corresponding, in (3), respectively, to the *corpora* C_i and C_j. Let V, D_{k_i} and D_{k_j} abbreviate $V(L, n)$, $D(k, C_i; L, n)$ and $D(k, C_j; L, n)$. Under the assumption $g_k(C; L, n) = g_{k_{i,j}}$, we obtain $g_{k_{i,j}}$ from (3), the left-side equation in (5). Also, under the approximation of assuming a common value, $h_{k_{i,j}}$, for $h_{k_i} \approx h_{k_j}$ (discussed below), we obtain the right-side equation in (5).

$$g_{k_{i,j}} = \ln(\frac{(V - D_{k_i}) D_{k_j}}{(V - D_{k_j}) D_{k_i}}) / \ln(\frac{h_{k_j} C_j}{h_{k_i} C_i}) \quad h_{k_{i,j}} = \frac{1}{C_j((V/D_{k_j}) - 1)^{(1/g_{k_{i,j}})}} \quad (5)$$

When using $D(k, C; L, n)$ (3) for several values of k, there must be a $V(L, n)$ value that leads to the model predictions minimizing the average relative errors for the training *corpora* set. We consider a range of k values from 1 to $kmax$

($kmax$ set to 2^{12}, explained in Sect. 5.2), and pairs of values ($g_k(C;L,n)$, $h_k(C;L,n)$), drawn from two distinct candidates ranges: one for $g_k(C;L,n)$ varying around an initial g_{init} value, and another range for $h_k(C;L,n)$, varying around an initial h_{init}. So, to find the initial values g_{init} and h_{init}, to be used as starting points for the above search, we apply (5) to obtain $g_{init} = g_{k_{i,j}}$ and $h_{init} = h_{k_{i,j}}$. Thus, let C_{min} and C_{max} be the smallest and the largest *corpora* from the training set. In Eq. (5) we instantiate $C_i = C_{min}$, $C_j = C_{max}$ and the corresponding empirical (D_{emp}) values of $D_{k_i} = D_{emp}(k, C_{min}; L, n)$, $D_{k_j} = D_{emp}(k, C_{max}; L, n)$. Assuming that, since h_{k_i} and h_{k_j} are relatively close (though not equal) we approximate $h_{k_i} \approx h_{k_j}$ (5). This simplification allows to compute g_{init} and h_{init} using only the empirical values and the estimated $V(L,n)$.

Then, we find the $V(L,n)$ value yielding the lowest average relative error by considering all pairs constructed from the mentioned candidate ranges: for each ($g_k(C;L,n)$, $h_k(C;L,n)$), the error in $D(k, C_i; L, n)$ is calculated for each C_i from the training set; this is performed for each value of k.

ii) **Estimating Parameters** $g_k(C;L,n)$ **and** $h_k(C;L,n)$. Following Sect. 3.1, for each value of k, although the values of $g_k(C;L,n)$ are relatively close for several *corpora*, they are not equal. Thus, $g_k(C;L,n)$ must be fine-tuned for each *corpus* size C in order to achieve accurate $D(k, C_i; L, n)$ predictions on a wide range of large *corpora* sizes. The same applies to $h_k(C;L,n)$. Given the estimated $V(L,n)$, the values of $g_k(C;L,n)$ and $h_k(C;L,n)$ for each training *corpus* C_{tr} are obtained in two phases: *Phase i)* Finding initial points ($g_{init}(C_{tr})$, $h_{init}(C_{tr})$) for this search: we apply (5) to obtain $g_{init}(C_{tr}) = g_{k_{i,j}}$ and $h_{init}(C_{tr}) = h_{k_{i,j}}$, with C_i and D_{k_i} instantiated to C_{tr} and $D_{emp}(k, C_{tr}; L, n)$ respectively, and C_j and D_{k_j} instantiated to the largest training *corpus* C_{max} and $D_{emp}(k, C_{max}; L, n)$. Assuming that, since h_{k_j} and h_{k_j} are relatively close (though not equal) we approximate $h_{k_i} \approx h_{k_j}$, thus quickly finding $g_{init}(C_{tr})$ and $h_{init}(C_{tr})$; *Phase ii)* Searching around $g_{init}(C_{tr})$ and $h_{init}(C_{tr})$ to find ($g_k(C_{tr}; L, n)$, $h_k(C_{tr}; L, n)$) minimizing the $D(k, C_{tr}; L, n)$ relative error.

iii) **Estimating the Dependency Behavior of** $g_k(C;L,n)$ **and** $h_k(C;L,n)$ **for General Test Corpora.** To model the dependencies of $g_k(C;L,n)$ and $h_k(C;L,n)$ on C, for each k, allowing to calculate $D(k, C; L, n)$ (3) for each test *corpus*, we use *splines*, based on the training learned values. The *spline* implementation uses two hyperparameters, degree (dg) and smoothing level (s), denoted (dg_g, s_g) and (dg_h, s_h), respectively, for $g_k(C;L,n)$ and $h_k(C;L,n)$, tuned by cross-validation. Thus, to choose the quadruple that leads to the most accurate $D(k, C; L, n)$ predictions, a set of quadruple values (dg_g, s_g, dg_h, s_h) is generated such that $dg_g, dg_h \in \{3, 4, 5\}$ and $s_g, s_h \in \{0, 0.5, 1, 1.5 \ldots 7\}$. For each quadruple, leave-one-out cross-validation is employed: for each of N iterations (where N is the size of the training set, now used as cross-validation set), one *corpus* is used for validation, and the remaining $N-1$ *corpora* are used for training. Each iteration uses a different validation *corpus*.

In further detail, the training part of the cross-validation uses the specific values of $g_k(C;L,n)$ and $h_k(C;L,n)$ obtained for each *corpus*, and builds the *splines* for modeling $g_k(C; L, n)$ and for $h_k(C; L, n)$ vs C. These *splines* are then used to interpolate values of $g_k(C_{val}; L, n)$ and $h_k(C_{val}; L, n)$, where C_{val} is the out-of-one *corpus* for validation in each iteration of the cross-validation. Firstly, $g_k(C_{val}; L, n)$ and $h_k(C_{val}; L, n)$ are used to obtain $D(k, C_{val}; L, n)$ prediction (using (3)) and the corresponding relative error. Secondly, we calculate the root mean square of the relative errors (in absolute values), considering all iterations of the cross-validation for the quadruple. Finally, the quadruple that shows the lowest error is chosen to model the dependencies of $g_k(C; L, n)$ and $h_k(C; L, n)$ on C using the full cross-validation set as training *corpora*. Then, $g_k(C; L, n)$ and $h_k(C; L, n)$ can be obtained from the *splines* for test *corpora*.

4 Maxima k Values for Reliable $W(k, C; L, n)$ Predictions

To assess the predictions accuracy of $W(k, C; L, n)$ using the *corpora* test set, the range of k must allow reliable predictions. Due to the stochastic variability of empirical $D(k, C; L, n)$ and $D(k+1, C; L, n)$, they can deviate from their means. Since $W(k, C; L, n) = D(k, C; L, n) - D(k+1, C; L, n)$, such variations may significantly affect the empirical $W(k, C; L, n)$ values, specially when the means of $D(k, C; L, n)$ and $D(k+1, C; L, n)$ are too close. For the empirical $W(k, C; L, n)$ to be reliable, the means of $D(k, C; L, n)$ and $D(k+1, C; L, n)$ must be sufficiently distant to reduce the probability of the corresponding empirical values being close. While the exact means are unknown, we use the empirical values from *corpora* as approximations. This introduces some risk, but obtaining large *corpora* to estimate these means is impractical. The results support this assumption (Sect. 5). Thus, let D_k and D_{k+1} follow Poisson distributions with $\lambda_k = D(k, C; L, n)$ and $\lambda_{k+1} = D(k+1, C; L, n)$ as their means, reflecting the values for *corpora* with equal C, given L and n. Then, $W_k = D_k - D_{k+1}$, with variances $Var(D_k) = k$ and $Var(D_{k+1}) = k+1$. Since λ_k and λ_{k+1} are large enough, Normal distribution can be used. Hence, $W_k \sim \mathcal{N}(\mu, \sigma^2)$ where $\mu = \lambda_k - \lambda_{k+1}$ and $\sigma^2 = \lambda_k + \lambda_{k+1}$. Thus, for W_k to be reliable we state that the relative deviation of W_k from μ should be smaller than a threshold ϵ (a small positive number) with a confidence probability P. Using the Cumulative Distribution Function ($\Phi()$) of the Normal distribution, we express the probability as: $P = 2\Phi\left(\frac{\epsilon\mu}{\sigma}\right) - 1$ leading to $\epsilon = \frac{\sigma}{\mu}\Phi^{-1}\left(\frac{P+1}{2}\right)$. Thus, for reliability, the relative deviation ϵ should satisfy:

$$\epsilon > \frac{\sqrt{\lambda_k + \lambda_{k+1}}}{\lambda_k - \lambda_{k+1}} \Phi^{-1}\left(\frac{P+1}{2}\right) . \qquad (6)$$

As k increases, D_k and D_{k+1} tend to become closer, leading to a maximum k value: the k-threshold for W_k reliability. As the difference between D_k and D_{k+1} increases with *corpus* size, larger *corpora* tend to have larger k-thresholds.

In summary, for a given $P = 0.95$ and $\sigma = 0.03$, the k-threshold of a *corpus* of size C, is the maximum k such that $0.03 > \frac{\sqrt{\lambda_k + \lambda_{k+1}}}{\lambda_k - \lambda_{k+1}} \Phi^{-1}\left(\frac{0.95+1}{2}\right)$ where λ_k and λ_{k+1} are the empirical $D(k, C; L, n)$ and $D(k+1, C; L, n)$ values, respectively. This represents the maximum k for which the relative error of the prediction

$W(k,C;L,n)$ using Eq. (4) is reliable, as it requires the empirical $W(k,C;L,n)$ value to be measured. The k-threshold values are in Sect. 5.

5 Results

5.1 The Corpora Sets

We extracted files from *oscar-project* (https://oscar-project.org/) in order to build separate sample *corpora* collections: one in English and one in German. Files were randomly selected obtaining a collection of English *corpora* with the following sizes: 299 Mw, 365 Mw, 366 Mw, 5.48 Gw, 7.31 Gw, 11.3 Gw, 15.0 Gw, 20.5 Gw, 31.5 Gw, 40.6 Gw, 66.3 Gw, 82.7 Gw, 84.5 Gw, 101 Gw, 172 Gw and 373 Gw. For German, the following *corpora* collection was formed: 170 Mw, 281 Mw, 307 Mw, 1.23 Gw, 2.46 Gw, 4,93 Gw, 9.85 Gw, 19.4 Gw, 24.3 Gw, 27.1 Gw, 39.1 Gw, 48.9 Gw and 52.2 Gw. To ensure that the test *corpora* sets covered sizes ranging from the magnitude of the smallest *corpus* to the magnitude of the largest one for each language, without sacrificing the size of the training sets, we selected *corpora* of the following sizes from the English collection: 366 Mw, 11.3 Gw, 31,5 Gw and 82.7 Gw, 172 Gw and 373 Gw, and from the German collection: 307 Mw, 4.93 Gw, 24.3 Gw and 48.9 Gw. The remaining *corpora* were assigned to training or to cross-validation sets, depending on the needs.

To ensure fair counts while preserving text semantics, a space was added next to each of the following characters: {':',';',',', '(',')',']',',',',']',',','<','>','"', '!', '?'}. Inflected forms are counted as distinct words in *corpora*, affecting the estimated vocabulary sizes for each n-gram size. For all the *corpora* in those collections, n-gram counts ($1 \leq n \leq 6$) were performed for each *corpus*, except for the 172 Gw and 373 Gw English *corpora*, for which, due to the long computation times required, only the 1-gram counts are reported in this paper.

5.2 Experimental Results

The estimated vocabulary sizes for each n-gram size are: 2.95×10^9, 1.995×10^{10}, 3.335×10^{10}, 1.51×10^{11}, 2.48×10^{11} and $7,2 \times 10^{11}$, for English 1-grams, 2-grams,...,6-grams, respectively, and 1.80×10^9, 6.76×10^9, 2.48×10^{10}, 7.30×10^{10}, 2.20×10^{11} and 7.25×10^{11}, for German 1-grams, 2-grams,..., 6-grams, respectively. Note that these estimated vocabulary values are affected by the inclusion of all word inflections in the n-gram counting. The following values give an insight of the magnitude of the numbers of distinct n-grams: 3 579 008, 1 461 558 and 266 894 for the 1-gram of the 366 Mw English *corpus*, for $k=1$, $k=2$ and $k=15$, respectively, and 7 560 504 911, 2 624 427 472, 317 955 329 for the 3-gram of the 82.7 Gw English *corpus*, for $k=1$, $k=2$ and $k=15$, respectively.

Metrics for Evaluation. For a language L and an n-gram size, let $D_{pred}(k,C)$ to be a prediction value obtained from $D(k,C;L,n)$, and $D_{emp}(k,C)$ to be the corresponding empirical value. Let $RED(k,C) = \left|\frac{D_{pred}(k,C) - D_{emp}(k,C)}{D_{emp}(k,C)}\right|$ represent the module of the Relative Error of that prediction. Similarly, $REW(k,C) = \left|\frac{W_{pred}(k,C) - W_{emp}(k,C)}{W_{emp}(k,C)}\right|$ gives the module of the Relative Error of a $W(k,C;L,n)$ prediction. The mean of $RED(k,C)$ for a given frequency k across a set of C values is denoted as $MRED(k)$. The mean of $RED(k,C)$ for a given $corpus$ size C over a set of k values is denoted as $MRED(C)$. Similarly, $MREW(k)$ and $MREW(C)$ are used for $REW(k,C)$. Also, $SRED(k) = \sqrt{\frac{1}{|\mathcal{C}|}\sum_{C\in\mathcal{C}} RED(k,C)^2}$ represents the Root Mean Square of the Relative Error of the $D(k,C)$ predictions given k, across a set of C values. This measures the stability of $RED(k,C)$ wrt a given k along the set $\mathcal{C}$; the closer $SRED(k)$ is to $MRED(k)$, the more stable $RED(k,C)$ is for that specific k value. Also, $SRED(C) = \sqrt{\frac{1}{|\mathcal{K}|}\sum_{k\in\mathcal{K}} RED(k,C)^2}$ measures the stability of $RED(k,C)$ wrt C across a set of k values, where $\mathcal{K}$ is the set of k values used. Likewise, to measure the stability of $REW(k,C)$ for a specific value of k or C, we define $SREW(k) = \sqrt{\frac{1}{|\mathcal{C}|}\sum_{C\in\mathcal{C}} REW(k,C)^2}$ and $SREW(C) = \sqrt{\frac{1}{|\mathcal{K}|}\sum_{k\in\mathcal{K}} REW(k,C)^2}$, respectively. Metric abbreviations are defined in the table captions.

Evaluating the Approaches. Besides the proposed functions $D(k,C;L,n)$ and $W(k,C;L,n)$, we refer to the baseline model [11] as $D_b(k,C;L,n)$ and $W_b(k,C;L,n)$ (b denotes baseline). Also, to assess the isolated effect of the constancy assumption of $g_k(C;L,n)$ and $h_k(C;L,n)$ wrt the $corpus$ size, we considered another approach denoted as $D_c(k,C;L,n)$ and $W_c(k,C;L,n)$, for evaluating the baseline model using cross-validation, instead of using the same $corpora$ for training and testing as in [11]. Table 1 shows the mean relative errors, $MRED(k)$, for $k \in \mathcal{K}^D = \{1,2,3\ldots,16\} \cup \{2^5, 2^6, 2^7, 2^8, 2^9, 2^{10}, 2^{11}, 2^{12}\}$. The M^D column shows that the relative errors for $D(k,C;L,n)$ predictions are low across the entire range of k, with global means of 0.7%, 0.6% and 3.3% for 1-grams, 3-grams and 6-grams, respectively. Generally, for each k, M^D and S^D are relatively close, as the relative error remains stable across the different $corpora$. However, two outliers appear for 6-grams: 13.6% and 11.6% for $k = 2^{10}$ and $k = 2^{12}$, respectively. This is due to the relatively low empirical values for higher n-gram sizes and larger k values, becoming more sensitive to small variations.

By comparison, the significantly higher values in M_b^D show that the baseline is not able to handle such a large range of $corpora$ sizes, as global means surpass 30% for these n-gram sizes. The baseline [11] does not present $D_b(k,C;L,n)$ values for $k > 16$. The M_c^D column shows that, after modifying the baseline to use cross-validation, while maintaining the assumption of constancy of $g_k(C;L,n)$ and $h_k(C;L,n)$ wrt C, the global means of the relative errors are still higher (reaching 16.8% for 6-grams) than those obtained by our approach (M^D). This highlights that the high relative errors of the baseline in a wide range of $corpora$ are due to two issues: the inadequate estimation based on the same $corpora$ set for both training and testing, and the constancy assumption of $g_k(C;L,n)$

Table 1. Mean relative errors, $MRED(k)$, for each k, denoted M^D, M_b^D and M_c^D, respectively, for models $D(k,C;L,n)$, $D_b(k,C;L,n)$ [11] and $D_c(k,C;L,n)$. $SRED(k)$ is represented by S^D. A global mean (GM) for each column (except S^D) is shown. Values shown for English test set (in percentage).

English

k	1-grams				3-grams				6-grams			
	M^D	S^D	M_b^D	M_c^D	M^D	S^D	M_b^D	M_c^D	M^D	S^D	M_b^D	M_c^D
1	**1.0**	1.3	87.4	4.5	**0.8**	1.0	20.6	6.0	**1.4**	1.6	27.6	1.7
2	**1.0**	1.1	72.0	3.3	**1.1**	1.3	35.0	0.4	**3.5**	4.2	46.0	2.7
3	**0.6**	0.7	67.7	3.2	**0.3**	0.4	35.3	1.0	**2.0**	2.5	40.1	5.2
4	**0.6**	0.9	64.1	3.0	**0.2**	0.3	35.3	1.0	**2.0**	2.5	40.1	5.2
5	**0.6**	0.8	61.3	2.9	**0.1**	0.1	35.7	1.3	**1.9**	2.3	38.2	5.6
6	**0.6**	0.8	57.9	2.8	**0.0**	0.1	35.7	1.8	**1.9**	2.2	37.1	4.3
7	**0.6**	0.7	56.6	2.7	**0.1**	0.6	36.6	2.6	**1.6**	1.8	34.5	2.7
8	**0.4**	0.5	54.1	2.6	**0.4**	0.6	35.6	3.2	**1.3**	1.5	33.5	5.1
9	**0.6**	0.7	53.0	2.4	**0.3**	0.4	35.7	4.2	**0.9**	1.2	30.5	10.0
10	**0.5**	0.6	52.1	2.3	**0.3**	0.4	35.3	5.0	**1.1**	1.2	29.2	13.5
11	**0.4**	0.6	51.4	2.2	**0.2**	0.3	35.2	5.9	**1.7**	1.8	31.9	18.0
12	**0.4**	0.6	50.1	2.2	**0.2**	0.3	35.2	6.5	**1.8**	2.0	33.5	20.7
13	**0.4**	0.6	49.5	2.2	**0.4**	0.5	35.2	7.0	**1.4**	1.9	35.0	22.6
14	**0.4**	0.6	48.3	2.1	**0.4**	0.6	35.3	7.5	**1.6**	2.1	36.1	25.1
15	**0.5**	0.6	47.5	2.1	**0.4**	0.5	35.3	8.1	**2.0**	2.6	38.4	28.7
16	**0.5**	0.6	46.6	2.1	**0.5**	0.5	35.5	8.5	**2.1**	2.8	39.6	30.1
2^5	**0.7**	0.8		2.1	**0.5**	0.6		12.4	**3.9**	5.3		37.1
2^6	**1.1**	1.7		2.5	**1.8**	2.7		12.2	**4.5**	5.4		21.8
2^7	**0.7**	0.8		3.7	**1.2**	1.5		12.9	**6.8**	9.5		17.8
2^8	**0.7**	0.9		4.5	**1.2**	1.2		14.2	**3.7**	6.2		32.8
2^9	**0.6**	0.8		4.8	**0.6**	0.9		16.7	**2.9**	3.5		46.7
2^{10}	**0.8**	1.2		4.1	**0.9**	1.4		17.9	**13.6**	15.5		26.1
2^{11}	**1.1**	2.0		3.6	**0.9**	1.2		19.3	**5.1**	6.3		9.2
2^{12}	**1.2**	2.0		4.2	**2.5**	4.6		19.4	**11.6**	17.2		10.7
GM	**0.7**		57.5	3.2	**0.6**		34.5	8.1	**3.3**		35.8	16.8

and $h_k(C;L,n)$ wrt *corpora* sizes. Although not shown, 2-grams, 4-grams and 5-grams exhibit similar values.

Table 2 shows mean relative errors, $MRED(C)$ for the English *corpora*. For each case, all the $k \in \mathcal{K}^D$ were used. The values of M^D and S^D are relatively close, showing that the $D(k,C;L,n)$ predictions have low relative errors and are stable for each *corpus* across the values of k. This is true for all n-gram sizes

Table 2. Mean relative errors, MRED(C), for each *corpus* C, denoted M^D, M_b^D and M_c^D, respectively, for models $D(k,C;L,n)$, $D_b(k,C;L,n)$ [11] and $D_c(k,C;L,n)$. SRED(C) represented by S^D. A global mean (GM) for each column (except S^D) is shown. Values shown for English test set (in percentage).

	English											
	1-grams				2-grams				3-grams			
C	M^D	S^D	M_b^D	M_c^D	M^D	S^D	M_b^D	M_c^D	M^D	S^D	M_b^D	M_c^D
366 Mw	1.2	1.4	31.0	8.5	0.9	1.2	34.7	13.6	1.2	2.2	43.3	26.7
11.3 Gw	0.5	0.6	61.7	2.0	0.5	0.8	18.4	1.3	0.8	1.4	36.7	2.4
31.5 Gw	0.3	0.4	66.4	2.0	0.1	0.2	12.6	1.2	0.3	0.4	31.8	2.6
82.7 Gw	0.3	0.5	66.0	0.4	0.4	0.4	6.2	0.3	0.3	0.4	26.1	0.6
172 Gw	0.7	0.8	62.5	2.1								
172 Gw	1.2	1.7	57.1	4.4								
GM	0.7		57.5	3.2	0.4		18.0	4.1	0.9		33.5	8.1
	4-grams				5-grams				6-grams			
366 Mw	2.5	5.6	32.4	36.7	3.9	7.9	22.3	47.3	4.6	9.0	24.4	54.7
11.3 Mw	1.0	1.5	41.2	3.5	4.9	5.8	35.6	6.1	3.3	4.1	35.8	6.3
31.5 Mw	0.8	1.7	40.2	3.5	1.4	2.5	39.9	3.0	1.7	2.9	39.7	4.7
82.7 Mw	0.4	0.7	38.5	0.8	2.7	4.1	41.5	0.9	3.8	5.9	43.3	1.4
GM	1.2		38.1	11.1	3.2		34.8	14.3	3.3		35.8	16.8

($1 \leq n \leq 6$). The GM values range from 0.4% (2-grams) to 3.3% (6-grams). In comparison, the errors in M_b^D show significant errors for the baseline across the various test *corpora* and n-gram sizes, with GM values ranging from 18.0% (2-grams) to 57.5% (1-grams). The values of M_c^D show that the constancy assumption of $g_k(C;L,n)$ and $h_k(C;L,n)$ wrt C exhibits significant relative errors, namely for the smaller *corpora* in this large range set, reaching 54.7% (6-grams). For *corpora* sizes 172 Gw and 373 Gw, only 1-gram results are shown (Sect. 5.1).

Table 3 shows mean relative errors, MRED(C), for each of the German *corpora* set. $D_b(k,C;L,n)$ results for German are not included, since German is not reported in the baseline [11]. Again, $D(k,C;L,n)$ predictions generally show low values for the relative errors (M^D, S^D, and GM), similar to those obtained for English. Although for the smallest *corpus* (308 Mw), the error value is 8.2% (5-gram) and 9.7% (6-grams). Likely, these outliers could disappear if the training set were larger. In comparison to $D(k,C;L,n)$, for this *corpus* (308 Mw), the M_c^D approach reaches errors of 47.9% (5-grams) and 61.9% (6-grams).

From Sect. 4, the reliability of $W(k,C;L,n)$ evaluation imposes restrictions on the k value. So, for each k for which $g_k(C;L,n)$ and $h_k(C;L,n)$ are trained, all training *corpora* should be used. Since $W(k,C;L,n)$ predictions should not apply to $k > k$-threshold, the k-threshold value for evaluating $W(k,C;L,n)$ is determined by the *corpus* with the smallest k-threshold, typically the smallest

Table 3. Mean relative errors, $MRED(C)$, for each *corpus* C, denoted M^D and M_c^D, respectively, for models $D(k, C; L, n)$ and $D_c(k, C; L, n)$. $SRED(C)$ represented by S^D. A global mean (GM) for each column (except S^D) is shown. Values shown for the German test set (in percentage).

German

C (Gw)	1-grams			2-grams			3-grams			4-grams			5-grams			6-grams		
	M^D	S^D	M_c^D	M^D	S^D	M_c^D	M^D	S^D	M_c^D	M^D	S^D	M_c^D	M^D	S^D	M_c^D	M^D	S^D	M_c^D
.308	2.3	2.6	6.8	2.3	2.6	15.3	3.2	3.6	22.8	5.8	6.5	30.3	8.2	9.6	47.9	9.7	11.4	61.9
4.93	0.3	0.5	1.4	0.8	1.3	2.1	1.4	2.6	2.4	2.0	3.3	1.8	3.1	4.4	4.4	3.6	4.9	3.9
24.3	0.2	0.2	0.0	0.2	0.2	0.1	0.2	0.4	0.2	0.3	0.6	0.3	0.6	1.0	0.5	0.5	0.8	1.8
48.9	0.1	0.1	0.0	0.1	0.4	0.0	0.2	0.5	0.0	0.3	0.7	0.0	0.6	1.4	0.2	0.5	0.7	0.3
GM	0.7		2.1	0.9		4.4	1.3		6.4	2.1		8.1	3.1		13.2	3.6		17.0

Table 4. Mean relative errors, $MREW(k)$, for each k, denoted M^W and M_b^W, respectively, for models $W(k, C; L, n)$ and $W_b(k, C; L, n)$ [11]. $SREW(k)$ is represented by S^W. A global mean (GM) for each column (except S^W) is shown. Values shown for the English test set (in percentage).

English

k	1-grams			2-grams			3-grams			4-grams			5-grams			6-grams		
	M^W	S^W	M_b^W	M^W	S^W	M_b^W	M^W	S^W	M_b^W	M^W	S^W	M_b^W	M^D	S^W	M_b^W	M^W	S^W	M_b^W
1	1.4	1.9	97.8	1.6	2.1	29.5	1.3	1.9	13.8	2.0	2.4	22.9	2.2	2.7	27.5	2.2	2.5	23.9
2	1.9	2.4	79.8	2.9	4.1	9.4	2.1	2.4	34.5	2.3	3.2	44.7	4.5	6.3	49.1	5.0	6.2	49.2
3	0.5	0.6	80.8	0.6	0.9	9.8	0.6	0.8	34.2	1.1	1.4	44.0	2.0	2.7	46.3	2.0	2.2	44.3
4	1.1	1.5	76.8	0.7	0.8	12.2	0.9	1.2	35.8	1.1	1.5	45.2	2.9	3.5	47.1	3.0	3.6	44.7
5	0.6	0.8	82.8	0.3	0.4	12.3	0.3	0.4	34.6	0.6	0.9	44.0	2.1	2.7	45.3	1.9	2.5	41.8
6	1.4	1.7	67.2	0.5	0.8	16.8	0.5	0.7	37.9	1.0	1.5	47.2	2.7	3.4	48.9	2.7	3.7	46.0
7	1.8	2.3	79.7	1.0	1.4	13.5	1.5	2.6	34.6	2.8	5.3	42.6	4.8	8.3	42.0	6.8	10.6	38.0
8	1.3	1.9	65.8	0.8	1.3	18.3	1.0	1.5	37.7	1.7	2.6	46.2	2.2	3.4	47.0	4.6	5.4	44.5
9	1.2	1.6	63.2	0.3	0.4	15.9	0.3	0.5	35.3	0.5	0.6	41.3	0.9	1.2	38.7	2.5	3.0	34.9
10			63.2	0.5	0.7	17.3	0.7	1.2	35.8	1.3	2.1	43.1	2.7	3.3	41.2	5.0	5.4	39.5
11			70.2	0.3	0.3	15.8	0.3	0.4	33.5	2.9	3.4	38.6	1.8	2.0	33.2	3.7	3.9	30.3
12			60.5	0.9	1.2	17.9	1.5	2.0	35.3	6.2	7.7	40.8	4.8	7.3	36.6	7.0	9.9	35.7
13			70.5	0.5	0.6	14.8	0.5	0.5	33.3	1.0	1.1	36.5	2.0	2.2	28.7	2.7	3.2	27.0
14			63.1	1.1	1.3	16.8	1.9	2.4	33.6	3.7	5.0	38.3	4.9	8.1	32.6	6.8	10.9	33.5
15			66.9	0.6	0.6	16.8	0.8	0.9	32.7	1.3	1.4	35.8	1.9	1.9	26.1	1.3	1.8	25.4
16				1.0	1.2													
GM	1.2		72.5	0.9		15.8	1.0		33.5	2.0		40.7	2.8		39.4	3.8		37.2

Table 5. Mean relative errors, $MREW(C)$, for each *corpus* C, denoted M^W and M_b^W, respectively, for models $W(k, C; L, n)$ and $W_b(k, C; L, n)$ [11]. $SREW(C)$ represented by S^W. A global mean (GM) for each column (except S^W) is shown. Values shown for the English test set (in percentage).

English

C (Gw)	1-grams			2-grams			3-grams			4-grams			5-grams			6-grams		
	M^W	S^W	M_b^W	M^W	S^W	M_b^W	M^W	S^W	M_b^W	M^W	S^W	M_b^W	M^W	S^W	M_b^W	M^W	S^W	M_b^W
.366	2.3	2.8	43.5	1.7	2.3	32.6	1.9	2.4	47.9	4.1	5.6	45.5	5.6	7.7	38.5	7.2	10.0	34.2
11.3	1.1	1.7	82.7	1.0	1.6	14.3	1.2	1.6	33.8	2.1	2.6	40.5	2.8	4.1	36.3	3.6	4.5	34.0
31.5	0.4	0.5	86.4	0.3	0.4	10.2	0.4	0.6	29.1	0.6	0.8	39.7	0.7	1.0	40.1	0.9	1.2	38.4
82.7	0.6	0.8	83.4	0.4	0.5	6.1	0.3	0.5	23.3	1.1	2.1	37.4	2.2	2.4	41.9	3.6	3.7	42.5
172	1.2	1.5	75.6															
373	1.8	2.1	63.5															
GM	1.2		72.5	0.9		15.8	0.9		33.5	2.0		40.7	2.8		39.4	3.8		37.2

Table 6. Mean relative errors, $MREW(C)$, for each *corpus* C, denoted M^W for model $W(k, C; L, n)$. $SREW(C)$ represented by S^W. A global mean (GM) for column M^W is shown. Values shown for the German test set (in percentage).

German

C (Gw)	1-grams		2-grams		3-grams		4-grams		5-grams		6-grams	
	M^W	S^W	M^W	S^W	M^W	S^W	M^W	S^W	M^W	S^W	M^W	S^W
.308	2.4	3.0	3.6	4.4	4.5	5.9	6.3	8.9	9.1	12.7	12.2	16.0
4.93	0.9	1.1	0.8	0.9	1.8	2.4	1.1	1.6	2.4	4.6	7.3	20.7
24.3	0.4	0.4	0.2	0.2	0.2	0.4	0.2	0.2	0.3	0.4	0.5	0.7
48.9	0.1	0.2	0.1	0.1	0.5	1.0	0.1	0.2	0.3	0.6	1.0	2.1
GM	1.0		1.2		1.8		1.9		3.0		5.2	

corpus. The k-threshold values, given by (6), found for each n-gram size in each training set, are: 9, 16, 15, 15, 15, 15 for English 1-grams,...,6-grams, respectively, and 9, 15, 23, 17, 17, 17 for German 1-grams,..., 6-grams, respectively.

Table 4 shows the mean relative errors, $MREW(k)$, for $k \leq k$-threshold for each n-gram size. M^W and S^W values, and their relative proximity, show, for all n-gram sizes, $W(k, C; L, n)$ predictions with low relative errors, stable for each k across the *corpora* set, with GM from 0.9% to 3.8%. In contrast, $W_b(k, C; L, n)$ predictions (M_b^W) show much higher relative errors: GM from 15.8% to 72.5% (1-grams). The 1-grams evaluation, by including the largest *corpora*, 172 Gw and

373 Gw, stresses the ability to handle large *corpora* scales. The high errors for 1-grams, by standing out from the other errors, highlight the baseline limitations.

For each English test *corpus* Table 5 shows the mean relative errors $MREW(C)$ for $k \leq k$-threshold and each n-gram size. M^W and S^W values, being relatively close, indicate stable $W(k, C; L, n)$ predictions across the k values, for all n-gram sizes, with GM from 0.9% to 3.8%. In contrast, M_b^W shows $W_b(k, C; L, n)$ predictions with much higher relative errors, GM reaching 72.5% for 1-grams. For German *corpora* set, Table 6 shows similar values for the $W(k, C; L, n)$ predictions relative errors. However, the outliers in M^W for 5-grams and 6-grams (9.1% and 12.2%) suggest that a larger training set could likely eliminate them.

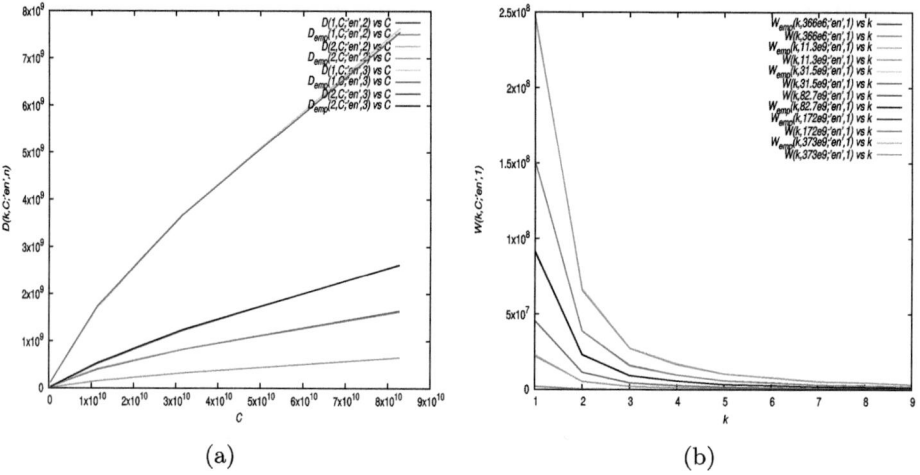

Fig. 2. (a) Predicted and empirical values, $D(k, C; L, n)$ and $D_{emp}(k, C; L, n)$ versus C, for 2-grams and 3-grams, and $k \in \{1, 2\}$, in the English test *corpora* set. (b) Predicted and empirical values, $W(k, C; L, n)$ and $W_{emp}(k, C; L, n)$ versus k, for the 1-grams in the English test *corpora* set.

Figure 2a compares $D(k, C; L, n)$ prediction curves with corresponding empirical values for the English *corpora* test set, for 2-grams and 3-grams. The curves overlap illustrates the low relative errors. Figure 2b shows $W(k, C; L, n)$ predictions, for 1-grams, and the corresponding empirical values, for the same test set, from 366 Mw to 373 Gw, for $k \leq k$-threshold. The curve overlap for each *corpus* reveals the low relative errors of the $W(k, C; L, n)$ predictions.

6 Conclusions

We aim to address the scalability issues raised by the need to predict the effect of the *corpus* size on n-gram frequency distributions when wide range of large natural language *corpora* are considered, encompassing sizes from hundreds of million words to hundreds of billion words. We propose a novel approach to handle the dependence of the model parameters on the *corpora* sizes. This was supported by a sound methodology for estimating the proposed model parameters, based on a state-of-the art for *corpora* training and testing, with cross-validation and generalisation through *spline*-based regression. Our goal is to achieve very low relative errors in the model predictions, and keeping them stable across the entire *corpora* size range. We focus on a prediction model applying uniformly to multi-words of different sizes, from 1-grams to 6-grams, considering the distribution of n-grams with low occurrence frequencies. In contrast to an approach assuming the parameter constancy wrt the *corpora* sizes, the conducted experimentation showed that the proposed approach led to very low relative errors (circa 2%) for the predictions of n-grams frequency distributions ($1 \leq n \leq 6$) in the range of low occurrence frequencies starting from 1 (singletons), and kept stable across a significant wide range of *corpora* sizes (from several hundred millions up to a maximum of 373 billion words in English), in two languages. This suggests that the proposed approach is promising to address the challenges posed by very large scale *corpora* sizes, and opens possibilities for handling relevant low occurrence multi-words in emerging and compelling applications, namely based on LLM.

Acknowledgments. This work has the financial support of FCT.IP: by UID/04516/ NOVA Laboratory for C omputer Science and Informatics (NOVA LINCS); and by the FCT.IP project "Modelling the Statistical Distribution of n-grams in Large Natural Language Corpora", DOI 10.54499/2024.07024.CPCA.A1.

Disclosure of Interests. The authors have no competing interests to declare that are relevant to the content of this article.

References

1. Bernhardsson, S., da Rocha, L.E.C., Minnhagen, P.: The meta book and size-dependent properties of written language. CoRR arxiv.org/abs/0909.4385 (2009)
2. Brants, T., Popat, A.C., Xu, P., Och, F.J., Dean, J.: Large language models in machine translation. In: Joint Conference on Empirical Methods in NLP and Computational Natural Language Learning, pp. 858–867. ACL (2007)
3. Buck, C., Heafield, K., van Ooyen, B.: N-gram counts and language models from the common crawl. In: LREC 2014, pp. 3579–3584 (2014)
4. Chierichetti, F., Kumar, R., Pang, B.: On the power laws of language: word frequency distributions. In: ACM SIGIR Conference, pp. 385–394 (2017)
5. Goncalves, C., Silva, J.F., Cunha, J.C.: n-gram cache performance in statistical extraction of relevant terms in large *Corpora*. In: Rodrigues, J.M.F., et al. (eds.) ICCS 2019. LNCS, vol. 11537, pp. 75–88. Springer, Cham (2019). https://doi.org/10.1007/978-3-030-22741-8_6
6. Ha, L.Q., Hanna, P., Ming, J., Smith, F.: Extending Zipf's law to n-grams for large corpora. Artif. Intell. Rev. **32**, 101–113 (2009)
7. Jones, E., et al.: SciPy: open source scientific tools for Python (2001). https://www.scipy.org/. https://doi.org/10.5281/zenodo.1913564
8. Lü, L., Zhang, Z., Zhou, T.: Deviation of zipf's and heaps' laws in human languages with limited dictionary sizes. Sci. Rep. **3**(1082) (2013)

9. Newman, M.E.J.: Power laws, pareto distributions and zipf's law. Contemp. Phys. **46**(5), 323–351 (2005)
10. Silva, J.F., Cunha, J.C.: An empirical model for n-gram frequency distribution in large corpora. In: Lauw, H.W., Wong, R.C.-W., Ntoulas, A., Lim, E.-P., Ng, S.-K., Pan, S.J. (eds.) PAKDD 2020. LNCS (LNAI), vol. 12085, pp. 840–851. Springer, Cham (2020). https://doi.org/10.1007/978-3-030-47436-2_63
11. Silva, J., Cunha, J.: How large corpora sizes influence the distribution of low frequency text n-grams. In: Advances in Knowledge Discovery and Data Mining: PAKDD 2024. LNCS, pp. 210–222. Springer (2024)
12. Simon, H.: On a class of skew distribution functions. Biometrika **42**(3/4), 425–440 (1955)
13. Zipf, G.K.: Human Behavior and the Principle of Least-Effort. Addison-Wesley, Cambridge (1949)

FinCPRG: A Bidirectional Generation Pipeline for Hierarchical Queries and Rich Relevance in Financial Chinese Passage Retrieval

Xuan Xu[1], Beilin Chu[1], Qinhong Lin[1], Yixiao Zhong[1], Fufang Wen[2], Jiaqi Liu[2], Binjie Fei[2], Yu Li[2(✉)], Zhongliang Yang[1(✉)], and Linna Zhou[1(✉)]

[1] Beijing University of Posts and Telecommunications, Beijing 102206, China
{sh22xuxuan,beilin.chu,greenred99,050922zyx,yangzl,zhoulinna}@bupt.edu.cn
[2] Beijing Value Simplex Technology Co., Ltd., Beijing 100026, China
{wenfufang,liujiaqi,feibj,liyu}@entropyreduce.com

Abstract. In recent years, large language models (LLMs) have demonstrated significant potential in constructing passage retrieval datasets. However, existing methods still face limitations in expressing cross-doc query needs and controlling annotation quality. To address these issues, this paper proposes a bidirectional generation pipeline, which aims to generate 3-level hierarchical queries for both intra-doc and cross-doc scenarios and mine additional relevance labels on top of direct mapping annotation. The pipeline introduces two query generation methods: bottom-up from single-doc text and top-down from multi-doc titles. The bottom-up method uses LLMs to disassemble and generate structured queries at both sentence-level and passage-level simultaneously from intra-doc passages. The top-down approach incorporates three key financial elements-industry, topic, and time-to divide report titles into clusters and prompts LLMs to generate topic-level queries from each cluster. For relevance annotation, our pipeline not only relies on direct mapping annotation from the generation relationship but also implements an indirect positives mining method to enrich the relevant query-passage pairs. Using this pipeline, we constructed a Financial Passage Retrieval Generated dataset (FinCPRG) from almost 1.3k Chinese financial research reports, which includes hierarchical queries and rich relevance labels. Through evaluations of mined relevance labels, benchmarking and training experiments, we assessed the quality of FinCPRG and validated its effectiveness as a passage retrieval dataset for both training and benchmarking (https://github.com/valuesimplex/FinCPRG).

Keywords: Passage retrieval datasets · Query generation · Relevance annotation

1 Introduction

In the domain of dense retrieval (DR), passage retrieval datasets are typically composed of three fundamental elements: queries, passages, and relevance labels.

Due to the high cost of collecting queries and relevance labels [15], as well as challenges in ensuring quality and diversity, traditional methods heavily rely on internal search business data accumulation and crowdsourcing [9,20], as well as dataset collection [8,12,14], leading to slow progress in low-resource and highly specialized scenarios. In recent years, LLMs have revolutionized traditional data engineering practices, such as (semi-)automated dataset construction, due to their strong generalization capabilities in natural language processing tasks [1,11]. A surge of work has emerged around LLM-based synthetic data generation, covering pretraining corpora, instructions, question-answering, and other data types. Correspondingly, many studies [19] have attempted to synthesize and augment passage retrieval datasets using LLMs. These methods can be classified according to focus on synthesizing or augmenting one of the key elements, specifically: a) Query or Document synthesis and augmentation [5,6,10,18]; b) Automatic Labeling such as Positives or negatives relevance label mining [10,13,16]. These approaches have demonstrated the potential of synthetic data in terms of effectiveness. However, there are two core issues in using LLMs to synthesize high-quality retrieval datasets. First, due to the limited context window of LLMs, generated queries are often confined to individual documents, lacking global information across the document set, and failing to synthesize complex queries spanning multiple paragraphs (e.g., issues exposed in datasets like [2,13,18]). Second, previous designs of synthesis pipelines are relatively simplistic, failing to comprehensively leverage traditional methods and various neural models, resulting in insufficient quality and diversity control [17,22]. Especially, these models are not tailored to any specific domain, which may result in the overlooking of key semantic elements pertinent to the domain. Consequently, this can lead to a relatively high rate of false positives or false negatives [3] in relevance labels. For instance, in the financial sector, elements such as industry, company entities, and time play crucial roles.

To address these challenges, we propose a bidirectional generation pipeline for automated passage retrieval dataset construction. This pipeline combines bottom-up (for intra-doc queries) and top-down (for cross-doc queries) approaches to generate hierarchical queries while employing an indirect positives mining method to balance efficiency and coverage of relevance label mining.

The core of the bottom-up approach for intra-doc queries is generating sentence-level and passage-level queries simultaneously given a specific passage of a document, which are then completed and hierarchically organized. The preprocess process involves segmenting document text into paragraphs and sentences. Subsequently, low-quality passages are filtered using a BERT-based quality scorer and regex rules. Then we use LLMs to disassemble and generate structured queries at both levels simultaneously. Subsequently, extract company entity names from metadata to resolve issues of ambiguous references in the generated query. Finally, we organize queries from different paragraphs within the same document into larger hierarchical query sets for subsequent indirect relevance mining.

The top-down approach for cross-doc queries is inspired by human report reading processes: people typically approach document collections with specific interests and intentions within certain industries and topics, scanning index-type text (usually chapter titles or paragraph topic sentences) to locate relevant passages for detailed reading. Building on this insight, we leverage industry classification models and topic modeling techniques to divide clusters for report titles, incorporating three core semantic dimensions: industry, topic, and temporal factors. Subsequently, we utilize LLM to generate the intention to consult the documents and then decompose it into fine-grained query sets, guided by a list of representative titles within each cluster.

What's more, we propose a comprehensive automatic relevance annotation strategy combining direct mapping annotation with indirect positives mining. The direct mapping annotation, similar to previous work, is derived directly from the generation relationships of LLMs, where queries are mapped to their source passages. However, relying solely on direct associations overlooks the relevance between the generated queries and other adjacent passages. To address this, we indirectly determine the relevance between queries and passages through localized traversal of query pairs using a reranker, which identifies a large number of additional relevance labels, alleviating the false negative issue in synthetic datasets. We sampled approximately 1,300 Chinese financial research reports across 19 categories, including company reports, industry reports, and fund reports. Using our pipeline, we synthesized queries at three granularity levels, ultimately constructing FinCPRG, a financial Chinese passage retrieval generated dataset comprising five subsets (sentence, sentence-mined, passage, passage-mined, and topic).

We conducted various experiments on FinCPRG: first analyzing the quality of relevance labels through interval sampling inspection, then evaluating common Chinese open-source retrieval models using FinCPRG as a test set. The evaluation results showed high consistency with two true financial retrieval benchmarks, validating the synthetic dataset's utility as an evaluation set. Additionally, we explored the framework's potential for generating effective training data for low-resource domains. We use FinCPRG as a training set and test on a third-party financial retrieval benchmark. We significantly observe an improvement in its financial domain retrieval capabilities (Fig. 1).

Specifically, our contributions are:

1. We propose a bidirectional generation pipeline that combines both bottom-up and top-down approaches for generating intra-doc and cross-doc queries. Additionally, we introduce an automated positives mining method to construct a rich annotated dataset while ensuring a balance between efficiency and coverage.
2. We construct the FinCPRG dataset using our proposed pipeline-a comprehensive Chinese financial passage retrieval dataset. It is derived from approximately 1,300 financial research reports sampled from a collection of 17 types of reports. The dataset features hierarchical queries along with rich relevance labels.

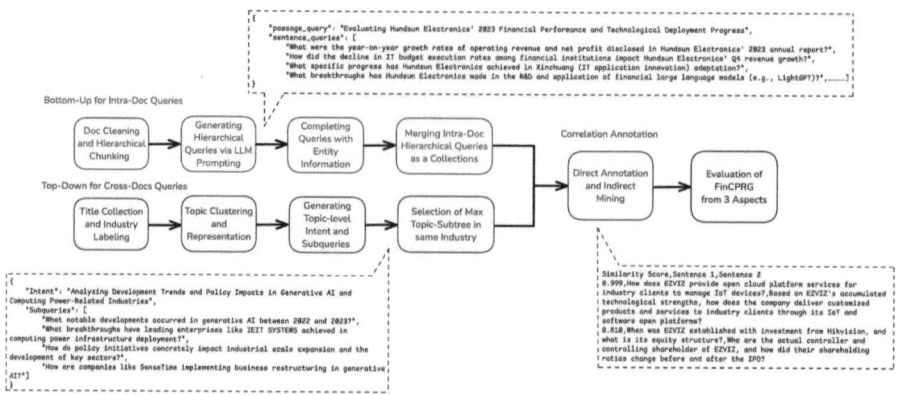

Fig. 1. Overview of the FinCPRG pipeline along with intermediate examples.

3. We evaluate the FinCPRG dataset through multiple types of experiments, assessing relevance labels' quality and validating its effectiveness as both an evaluation benchmark and a training dataset.

2 Related Work

2.1 Fully Synthetic Datasets for DR

"Fully synthetic" refers to synthesizing retrieval datasets from raw corpora alone, or even without any corpora. It typically involves the complete pipeline of query synthesis, relevance label mining, quality control, and other processes. E5 [17] uses a two-step prompt template to generate synthetic data, first prompting GPT-4 to brainstorm retrieval tasks, then generating (query, positive, hard negative) triplets for each task. In contrast, AIR-Bench [3] generates characters who would find the document useful and scenarios where they might use it, then creates queries based on specific characters and scenarios, using embedding models, multiple rerankers, and LLMs for quality control. Chuxin-Embedding [13] generates queries similarly with E5 after a choice of the roles, scenarios, and categories and refines query quality using the LLMs, hard negative mining, and reranking techniques. Additionally, Rahmani et al. [10] validate the reliability of fully synthetic datasets, demonstrating their effectiveness for retrieval evaluation. However, these synthetic datasets have the disadvantages of the absence of cross-document queries and the challenging trade-off between cost and quality.

2.2 Partly Synthetic Datasets (Data Augmentation) for DR

Partly synthetic typically refers to original data that contains some elements of retrieval datasets, such as queries and partial relevance labels. It uses LLMs for data augmentation to improve retrieval systems, including query rewriting, label mining/cleaning, document enhancement, and so forth. Works like Inpars-v2 [6] and Query2doc [18] leverage LLMs for query and document synthesis, while Precise Zero-Shot Dense Retrieval [5] proposes to pivot through Hypothetical Document Embeddings (HyDE). Another critical aspect of synthetic techniques is the generation of relevance labels. Generative Pseudo Labeling (GPL) [16] introduces an unsupervised method for pseudo-relevance label generation. These approaches reduce reliance on costly human annotations and scale retrieval systems efficiently. However, these methods are fragmented and scattered, requiring integration and adaptation to specific domains.

3 Methodology

3.1 Bottom-Up for Intra-Doc Queries

The bottom-up approach operates on the passages which are chunked from the doc, leveraging the language understanding and generation capabilities of LLMs to synthesize sentence-level and passage-level queries simultaneously, whose semantic connotations are precisely aligned with the original text chunks. By carefully prompting LLMs to generate queries of two different granularities, comprehensive coverage of all possible queries related to the passage is ensured.

Document Cleaning and Hierarchical Chunking. Our initial step involves passage-level segmentation (500 character length) of research reports, employing rule-based matching to eliminate passages containing extensive tables and privacy information such as organization and personal introduction. Given that our original research report data was obtained through PDF recognition, we still encountered various noise elements, including URLs, table/figure captions, and inadvertently recognized text from images. To address this, we annotated a set of low-quality samples and fine-tuned BERT to automatically detect and remove low-quality passages. After cleaning (removing approximately 15% of the content), we performed secondary chunking (100 length) on the remaining passages, segmenting each passage chunk into sentence-level sub-chunks. This hierarchical chunking structure facilitates the subsequent generation of hierarchical queries.

Generating Hierarchical Queries via LLMs Prompting. We designed a complex LLM prompt to generate hierarchical inner-doc queries. Specifically, given an input document chunk, the model generates queries at two distinct granularity levels: passage-level queries that capture broader thematic content and sentence-level queries that focus on fine-grained information. It takes full advantage of LLM's instruction-following capabilities to perform more challenging tasks (instead of generating a list of queries, we're more likely to generate a query tree), thus reducing LLM's inference costs. What's more, creating queries at different levels facilitates indirect relevance mining among queries in the same level, as explained in Chap. 4. The specific prompt design for query generation is as follows:

> **Prompt:** Given a passage from a financial report (provided as a list of sentences), generate hierarchical queries including both passage-level and sentence-level queries. Follow these requirements strictly and return results in JSON format.
> **Input:** ["Sentence 1.", "Sentence 2.", ..., "Sentence N."]
> **Requirements:** 1. Ignore disclaimers, copyright notices, or sensitive information 2. Include passage-specific information (company names, events, data) 3. Use empty string ("") for unclear sentences 4. Return in specified JSON format
> **Output Format:** {"passage_query": "query 0", "sentence_queries": ["Query 1", "Query 2", ..., "Query N"]}

Query Completion and Merging. Some generated queries use fuzzy references as their subject. For example, 'How is the company's financial situation this year?' is an invalid query that requires entity completion. Therefore, we have introduced a query rewriting mechanism to address the issue of incomplete entity names. We employ regular expressions to extract company names from report document titles and use these to replace ambiguous references in the synthesized queries (e.g., replacing generic terms like "company" with specific names like "XX Technology"). After query completion, we collect and organize queries from different passages within the same document to create merged intra-doc hierarchical query collections.

3.2 Top-Down for Cross-Doc Queries

The top-down approach for cross-doc queries draws inspiration from human reading behavior: readers typically approach document collections with specific interests and intentions within particular industries or topics, scanning index-type text (such as chapter titles or topic sentences) to locate relevant passages for detailed reading. Following this insight, we leverage industry classification models and topic modeling techniques to divide clusters for report titles, incorporating three key semantic elements: industry, topic, and temporal factors. We then prompt LLMs to generate intentions as topic-level queries based on representative documents and decompose these intentions into fine-grained subqueries simultaneously that will be used in follow-up relevance mining.

Title Collection and Industry Labeling. During the data preprocessing phase, we extracted report titles from the metadata of sampled research reports and filtered out titles with fewer than five Chinese characters (e.g., "Daily Morning Report" or "Morning Meeting Digest"), as such short titles typically lack substantive thematic information. Then we performed deduplication to retain only one instance. Subsequently, we employed FinBERT2-IC, an industry classifier fine-tuned on FinBERT2 [21] to annotate each title with its corresponding industry label. This classifier adheres to the CITIC Securities primary industry classification standard, encompassing 28 distinct industry categories.

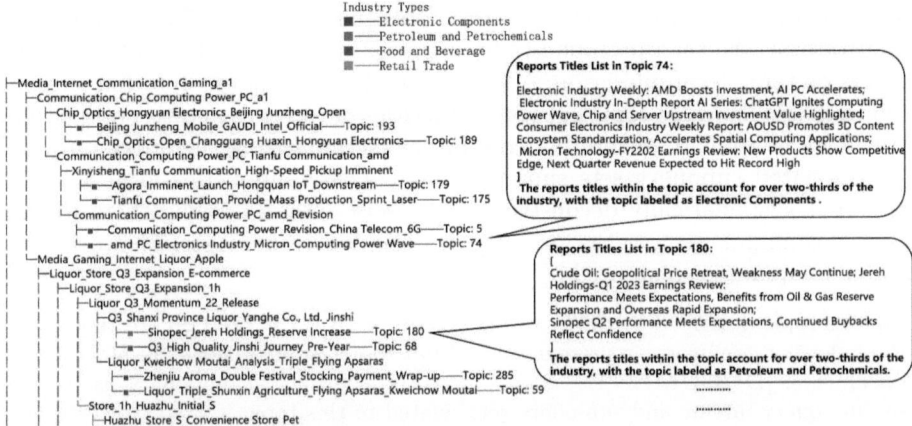

Fig. 2. The demonstration of the topic tree from the Topic Clustering and Representation phase, highlighting the hierarchical organization of topics. Each topic comprises a set of research report titles. Additionally, two annotation examples of the dominant industry within a specific topic are provided during the phase of selection of the maximum topic subtree within the same industry.

Topic Clustering and Representation. This part builds on the BERTopic framework, which is a popular topic modeling tool. Rather than using a general embedding model to extract vectors, which would overlook subtle yet critical differences leading to high similarity- for example, deeming the two titles "Company A is growing rapidly" and "Company B is growing rapidly" as highly similar when, in reality, Company A and Company B belong to different industries- we used a fine-tuned industry classification model, FinBERT2-IC, to encode report titles into embeddings that capture both semantic and industry-specific information.

Furthermore, to incorporate temporal information from report metadata into the clustering representations, we implement a periodic temporal encoding scheme inspired by Time2Vec [7]. This approach maps temporal information into a continuous vector space while preserving the periodic nature of temporal patterns, specifically by encoding the temporal displacement between each document's timestamp and a reference date into a 6-dimensional vector, which is concatenated into the previous embeddings.

Based on these embeddings, we apply the HDBSCAN (Hierarchical Density-Based Spatial Clustering of Applications with Noise) algorithm for unsupervised clustering to construct hierarchical clusters. Consistent with BERTopic, we employ c-TF-IDF (Class-Based Term Frequency-Inverse Document Frequency) to identify statistically significant keywords within each cluster and take the keywords list as the topic description. The demonstration of the topic tree from the Topic Clustering and Representation phase is shown in Fig. 2.

Generating Topic-Level Intent and Subqueries from Representative Documents. We then prompt LLMs to generate intentions to read these title clusters as topic-level queries and decompose these intentions into fine-grained subqueries. Specifically, topic keywords and titles most representative of the topic are passed as input to generate a core intent (summarizing the query purpose) and associated subquery sets simultaneously. These subqueries form a logical chain that systematically deconstructs the users' intent, guiding them to construct meaningful query paths for retrieving the desired passages. The translated prompt template is structured as follows:

> I have a topic described by the following keywords: **[KEYWORDS]** For this topic, the following documents represent a small but representative subset of all relevant documents: **[DOCUMENTS]** Please generate a formatted dictionary list representing query intents and sub-query sets related to this topic.
> **Output Format:** [{ "intent": "brief description of the core purpose for querying this topic", "subqueries": ["subquery 1: first question to address the intent", "subquery 2: second question to address the intent", ...] }]

Selection of Maximum Topic Subtree Within Same Industry. Although we generated topic queries with the most fine-grained cluster partitions previously, there is a topic over-segmentation problem, which is not conducive to the subsequent sufficient indirect mining. So we identify the largest subtree that shares the same industry type as a new cluster unit. Specifically, we analyze the industry distribution of document titles within each topic. A topic is labeled with a dominant industry if more than two-thirds of its document titles belong to that industry; otherwise, it is labeled as 'none'. If even the smallest topic does not share the same industry as the title, we default to selecting the smallest topic as its maximum topic subtree. We select the largest corresponding topic subtree sharing the same industry for each title to prepare for subsequent positives mining.

4 Correlation Annotation

4.1 Positive Annotation Strategy

We first distinguish three types of relationships between queries and passages:

1. Subset Query (sentence-level queries, $Q < D$): The document contains all information required by the query, along with additional redundant information
2. Equivalent Query (passage-level queries, $Q = D$): The document and query contain approximately equivalent information
3. Superset Query (topic-level queries, $Q > D$): Multiple documents are needed to fully cover the information required by the query

Our annotation strategy combines direct mapping annotation with the indirect positives mining method. The direct mapping annotation is based on LLM-based hierarchical query generation: passage-level queries naturally correspond to equivalent relationships (Q = D), while sentence-level queries correspond to subset relationships (Q < D). In addition to direct mapping annotation, there are still two broad cases of possible positives that exist. Firstly, both passage-level and sentence-level queries may still have relevant passages in adjacent sections. Secondly, since prompts for generating topic-level queries only incorporate information from titles, the generated queries cannot be directly mapped to specific passages. Therefore, we introduce the indirct positives mining method, whose core is to indirectly determine the relevance between queries and passages through localized traversal of query pairs using a reranker model.

4.2 Positives Mining via Localized Traversal Between Queries

Our indirect positive mining method adopts a localized traversal strategy using a reranker to mine equivalent query pairs. Different from the embedding model, the reranker can get a relevance score by taking two pieces of text as input. To balance efficiency and coverage of the mining process, we set different traversal spaces for queries of different granularities. Then we identify equivalent pairs through threshold filtering, which is set empirically at 0.99. This space constraint also helps mitigate false positive labels caused by semantically similar queries that differ in key semantic elements. The three levels of traversal space are defined as follows:

- For each sentence-level query, the reranker evaluates its similarity with sentence-level queries from other passages within the same document.
- For each passage-level query, the reranker evaluates its similarity with other passage queries under the same maximum topic subtree within the same industry.
- For each topic intent, the reranker evaluates the similarity between subqueries decomposed from the topic intent and the passage-level queries within the same topic hierarchy.

Compared to previous asymmetric query-document mining methods, our symmetric query-pair mining approach offers several advantages:

1. While document texts are cleaned, their quality remains uncertain, whereas queries are more concise with less noise.
2. Compared to query+document pairs, query pairs are shorter, facilitating more efficient model inference and easier manual verification.
3. The reranker will perform full-attention over the input pair, which is more accurate than embedding model (i.e., bi-encoder) but more time-consuming. As a result, a localized traversal strategy addresses the time complexity constraint.

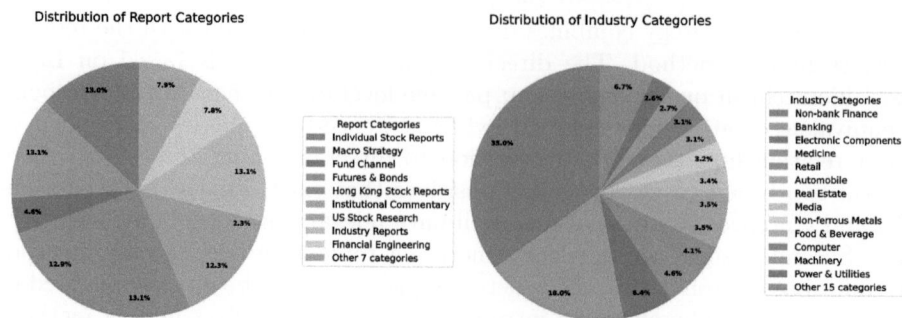

Fig. 3. Pie charts illustrating the distribution of report types (left) and industry categories (right) in the seed research reports dataset.

5 Implementation Setup and Results

5.1 Raw Dataset

To ensure the diversity of the synthetic dataset, we sampled from a research reports collection spanning from 2022 to January 2024. These reports cover subcategories of more than twenty types, including individual stock analysis, industry analysis, futures, and bonds. For each report type, we conducted independent random sampling, with sampling rules set to extract a minimum of 10 samples per category (or all samples if less than 10) and a maximum of 200 samples. Finally, we obtained a dataset containing 1,317 research reports. The categories and industry distribution of the raw dataset are shown in the Fig. 3.

5.2 Implementation Details

Any steps that involve using LLM are implemented by calling the gpt-4o-2024-11-20 API. Industry classification tasks were performed using FinBERT2-IC[1]. The hierarchical clustering and topic representation in our pipeline were implemented based on the BERTopic[2], and the generation of intentions and subqueries also utilized the LLM-based custom topic representation module in the BERTopic library. For indirect positives mining, we employed the BGE-reranker-v2-m3[3] from the BGE (BAAI General Embedding) series.

5.3 Final Dataset Statistics

By integrating the aforementioned synthesis and annotation methods, we obtained five types of query-passage relevance labels. Among these, sentence-level and passage-level were direct mapping annotated, while sentence-level-mined, passage-level-mined, and topic-level were derived through indirect positives mining. Along with the passages from all of our research reports as the

---

[1] https://github.com/valuesimplex/FinBERT2.
[2] https://github.com/MaartenGr/BERTopic.
[3] https://huggingface.co/BAAI/bge-reranker-v2-m3.

Table 1. Statistic of FinCPRG, FinCPRG-all is the collection of other five subsets.

Subset Name	Avg. Query Length	Avg. Doc. Length	Avg. Rel. Docs per Query	Count of Pairs
FinCPRG-sentence	37.18	448.70	1.00	45,457
FinCPRG-sentence-mined	39.95	457.73	2.65	19,464
FinCPRG-passage	45.43	564.47	1.00	10,624
FinCPRG-passage-mined	46.14	635.25	9.06	18,216
FinCPRG-topic	21.84	579.39	2.95	1,113
FinCPRG-all	38.63	564.47	1.71	94,874

corpus, we ultimately constructed five paragraph retrieval datasets. Statistics of each subset in FinCPRG are shown in Table 1.

6 Experiments and Evaluation

6.1 Evaluation of Mined Relevance Labels

Methods. Although we used a localized traversal method to evaluate the relevance of each query pair in the search space, our arbitrary threshold-setting approach for determining relevance and the label quality require further analysis. Therefore, we first analyzed the distribution of similarity scores from the reranker to gain insights into the model's scoring preferences. Subsequently, we designed an evaluation framework based on both LLM and human assessments to further measure the quality of similarity scores obtained from the reranker. While cost considerations prevented us from employing LLM and human methods during the mining process, we sampled a subset of data for evaluation purposes to provide valuable insights into the reasonableness of our threshold settings and the quality of our mined labels.

In the evaluation of query pairs scored by the reranker with different similarity, we randomly sampled 50 pairs from 8 high-similarity intervals (0.99–1.00, 0.97–0.99, 0.95–0.97, and so on down to 0.85). A five-level scoring criterion was developed, and the LLM was prompted with the following instructions to rescore

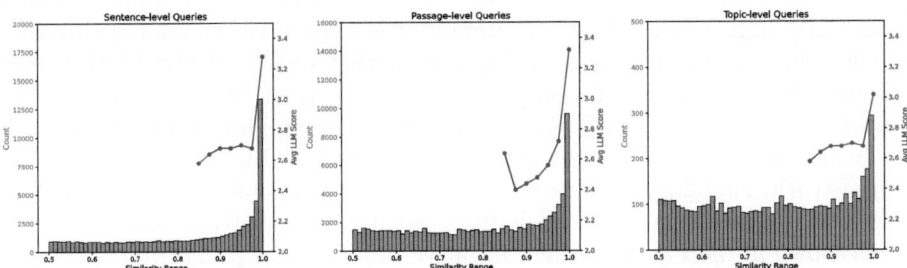

Fig. 4. The distribution of similarity labels from the re-ranker and the average LLM score across different intervals.

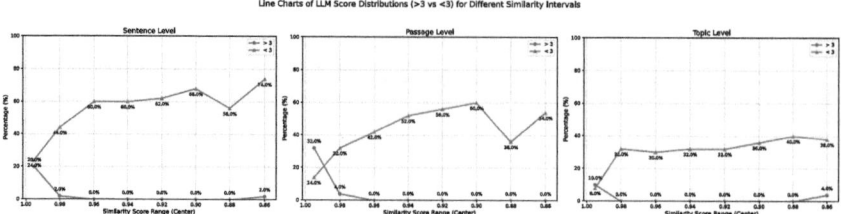

Fig. 5. Line charts showing the distributions of LLM scores (>3 vs. <3) across different similarity intervals. We can probe the approximate percentage of false positive and false negative rate in the relevant labels from our indirect positives mining.

the selected samples. This allowed us to compare the consistency and differences between the two sets of scores.

> Please evaluate the synonymy between the following two sentences on a scale from 5 (completely synonymous) to 1 (not synonymous) and provide the score along with a brief explanation: {sentence1} and {sentence2}.
> **Scoring Criteria as follows:**
> **Completely Synonymous (5 points):** The core meaning of both sentences is identical, with only differences in expression.
> **Highly Synonymous (4 points):** The core meaning is the same, but there are slight extensions, omissions, or differences in emphasis.
> **Partially Synonymous (3 points):** The core meaning overlaps partially, but there are significant differences in focus or interpretation.
> **Low Synonymy (2 points):** Only some keywords or parts of the content are similar, but the overall meaning is unrelated.
> **Not Synonymous (1 point):** The core meanings of the two sentences are entirely different, with no semantic connection.

Results and Analysis. As shown in the Fig. 4, we observe that the similarity distribution from the reranker peaked in the 0.99 to 1 interval. This means that the 0.99 cut-off is an important feature of the model's discrimination ability. At the same time, the average LLM scores for samples in this interval were significantly higher than others. Therefore, it is reasonable we set the threshold at 0.99. Our manual review to verify the scoring results of the LLM showed that over 90% of the LLM's judgments were accepted by human evaluators. Considering potential human errors and the inherent limitations of the task, which may not be scored absolutely, we can assume LLM judgments as the ground truth, enabling us to estimate the approximate false positive and false negative rates in the relevant labels from our indirect positives mining.

As shown in the Fig. 5, the false negative rate (i.e., the proportion of samples with a similarity score below 0.99 threshold but with a rating >3) remains low across all levels (4%), demonstrating effective retention of high-quality relevance samples. For the false positive rate (i.e., the proportion of samples with a similarity score above threshold 0.99 but with a rating <3), the topic level (10%)

and passage level (14%) performed well, while the sentence level was relatively higher (24%). This stratified difference can be attributed to the characteristics of LLM in synonymy judgment. Through manual review, we find that LLMs apply stricter semantic detail comparisons than human evaluators, particularly at the sentence level. Since sentence-level queries often contain more specific details, minor semantic differences are amplified in LLM scoring, leading to a higher false positive rate. In contrast, the topic-level and passage-level queries, with their higher degree of abstraction and greater semantic tolerance, achieved a relatively lower false positive rate.

6.2 Evaluation of FinCPRG

Our evaluation includes experiments where FinCPRG is utilized both as a benchmark and a training dataset. The first component directly compares the evaluation results before and after replacing the benchmark in open-source financial retrieval evaluations with FinCPRG. The second component fine-tunes open-source models on our FinCPRG and evaluates their performance on other financial retrieval benchmarks to assess the pipeline's potential of generating training sets for low-resource domains.

Table 2. We evaluate models on FinCPRG tasks using Recall@10, maximally aligning with the metric (Recall@k) adopted in FIR-Bench for consistent benchmarking.

Model	FinCPRG					
	All	Sentence	Sentence-mined	Passage	Passage-mined	Topic
bge-base	0.719	0.696	0.649	0.865	0.695	0.381
bce-embedding-base	0.757	0.743	0.658	0.889	0.639	0.232
FinRetriever-base	0.780	0.768	0.715	0.896	0.704	0.391
FinRetriever-large	0.795	0.787	0.724	0.893	0.708	0.349

Serving as a Benchmark. To ensure the fairness of comparations, we evaluated on FinCPRG while aligning with the original baselines and metric settings with two Chinese financial retrieval benchmarks, i.e. FinMTEB [12] (BGE-Large-zh-v1.5, Paraphrase-multilingual-MiniLM-L12-v2, All-MiniLM-L12-v2, and BGE-M3) and FIR-Bench [21] (bge-base-zh-v1.5, bce-embedding-base-v1, FinRetriever-base, and FinRetriever-large). The evaluation was implemented based on Cocktail [4], which includes a user-friendly evaluation tool. The results are shown in Table 2 and Table 3.

Then we calculated the Pearson correlation coefficient for the evaluation results of shared models between FinCPRG and FIR-Bench as well as the results of shared models between FinCPRG and FinMTEB. As shown in the Fig. 6, we observe that most values are high, which reflects the utility consistency between

Table 3. We evaluate models on FinCPRG tasks using NDCG@10, aligning with the metric adopted in FinMTEB for consistent benchmarking.

Model	FinCPRG					
	All	Sentence	Sentence-mined	Passage	Passage-mined	Topic
bge-base	0.588	0.541	0.440	0.745	0.447	0.277
bge-large	0.546	0.506	0.415	0.678	0.402	0.279
bge-m3	0.706	0.667	0.527	0.832	0.475	0.265
all-MiniLM	0.116	0.114	0.087	0.120	0.052	0.022
multilingual-MiniLM	0.266	0.252	0.195	0.312	0.149	0.075
text2vec-base	0.403	0.392	0.304	0.430	0.237	0.129

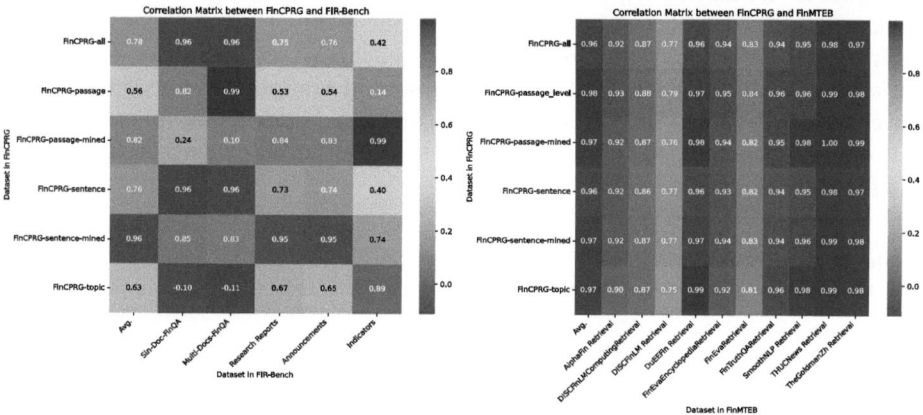

Fig. 6. Correlation matrices of FinCPRG with two financial retrieval benchmarks, FIR-Bench (left) and FinMTEB (right). Each value of the correlation matrix represents the Pearson correlation between the test results of certain subset of our FinCPRG and the test results of certain subset of the real financial benchmark.

FinCPRG and the real financial benchmark. Due to the narrow performance gap among the officially selected models in FIR-Bench and the inconsistent benchmarking metrics (i.e., varying k in Recall@k) used in FIR-Bench compared to our dataset, the correlation coefficients show fluctuations. In contrast, the large performance gap among the officially selected models in FinMTEB results in highly consistent test outcomes across different datasets.

Serving as Training Dataset. To evaluate the effectiveness of synthetic datasets as a training dataset, we conducted fine-tuning experiments using FinCPRG and tested the results on FinMTEB. Specifically, we fine-tuned three models: bge-base-zh-v1.5, bge-large-zh-v1.5, and paraphrase-multilingual-MiniLM-L12-v2. The fine-tuning process employed the CoSENT

Table 4. Performance comparison of models fine-tuned on FinCPRG and evaluated on various datasets within the FinMTEB benchmark. The results are reported using NDCG@10. The suffix "ft" is the abbreviation for "fine-tuned".

Model	Avg.	Dataset in FinMTEB									
		AlphaFin	DISCFinLLM-C	DISCFinLLM	DuEEFin	FinEva-E	FinEva	FinTruthQA	SmoothNLP	THUCNews	TheGoldmanZh
bge-base	0.458	0.676	0.941	0.671	0.018	0.539	0.962	0.370	0.105	0.187	0.108
bge-base-ft	0.640	0.678	0.926	0.660	0.223	0.860	0.965	0.419	0.632	0.604	0.429
bge-large	0.607	0.664	0.948	0.672	0.243	0.432	0.955	0.433	0.695	0.588	0.442
bge-large-ft	0.619	0.694	0.915	0.687	0.222	0.785	0.962	0.404	0.619	0.542	0.365
MiniLM	0.379	0.487	0.807	0.646	0.036	0.316	0.878	0.242	0.049	0.140	0.195
MiniLM-ft	0.533	0.628	0.710	0.879	0.093	0.752	0.954	0.311	0.333	0.403	0.269

loss function and mean pooling strategy without hard negative mining. The experimental results are summarized in the Table 4.

Overall, all three models achieved an average performance improvement across ten evaluation datasets after fine-tuning. The BGE model's strong performance on certain financial retrieval evaluation sets can be attributed to its good generalization capabilities or possibly to data leakage in some of the evaluation datasets. We observed that if the model initially performed well on a particular dataset, its performance would show slight fluctuations after our fine-tuning. Conversely, if the model has not been adequately trained, fine-tuning would lead to a significant improvement in its performance. Notably, the models that initially exhibited lower performance experienced the most significant gains. For instance, MiniLM achieved an average improvement of approximately 15%. This indicates that our pipeline is well suited for low-resource areas to improve domain capabilities.

7 Discussions

7.1 Estimation About Computational Cost and Scalability

We evaluate the computational cost of each stage in our multi-stage pipeline, where costs comprise inference from three model types: BERT-based models, LLMs, and reranker models. For the raw corpus, we assume n documents with an average of t tokens each, resulting in NC_1 sentence-level chunks and NC_2 passage-level chunks total, where NC_1 is calculated as $\frac{nt}{100}$ and NC_2 as $\frac{nt}{500}$.

BERT inference costs for document cleaning ($\frac{t}{500} \times n$), industry labeling (n), and topic clustering (n) yield a total cost proportional to NC_2.

LLM inference costs for query generation scale with token count: intra-document generation ($2 \times t \times n$) and cross-document generation ($n \times L_2 \times 3$), making the total cost approximately proportional to corpus tokens.

Reranker mining costs vary in different parts. Sentence-level: $n \times (\frac{t}{100})^2 \propto NC_1$ Passage-level: Within topic subtrees with m clusters, cost scales as $\frac{n^2 t^2}{m 500^2} \propto NC_2^{1.5}$ (using empirical formula for clustering $m = \sqrt{n}$). Topic-level: $m \times \frac{n}{m} \times \frac{t}{500} \propto NC_2$.

Overall, the pipeline demonstrates favorable scalability, with costs scaling linearly to sub-quadratically with corpus size.

7.2 Limitations and Future Work

Coverage and Scale of Raw Data. Our dataset comprises 39w financial research reports spanning 2022 to January 2024, distributed across 20+ report categories. Despite this broad coverage, the relatively limited samples per category (<100) may not fully capture domain-specific nuances. Future research could benefit from focused sampling within specific subdomains of finance and increasing sample quantities in high-priority categories.

Stability of Pipeline. The multi-stage nature of our approach-incorporating various language models including API of commercial LLMs, complex manual sequential operations, and vast hyperparameter configurations-introduces inherent variability. This complexity affects model output consistency and cross-run reproducibility. Addressing these stability issues requires systematic evaluation of model robustness and development of standardized benchmarking procedures.

Quality Constraints in Pipeline. The quality of generated data faces several inherent inadequacies in the design of the pipeline, such as limited context in cross-doc query synthesis, insufficient utilization of doc metadata and inadequate incorporation of temporal context. Additionally, there can be non-conforming outputs at every step of the pipeline, such as wrong reasoning of BERT-based cleaning and labeling, inherited biases from LLM generation, bad cases in rule-based entity completion, and threshold-based relevance judgment. Future improvements could focus on enhanced prompt engineering, model optimization, and development of automated verification mechanisms for synthetic data.

8 Conclusion

We proposed a bidirectional generation pipeline to construct hierarchical queries and enrich relevance labels for financial passage retrieval. Using this method, we created FinCPRG, a financial Chinese passage retrieval generated dataset with hierarchical queries and rich relevance annotations. Evaluations of mined relevance labels and experiments as both a benchmark and training dataset confirmed our proposed pipeline's effectiveness, showcasing its potential for generating effective passage retrieval datasets for low-resource domains.

Acknowledgments. This work was supported in part by the National Key Research and Development Program of China under Grant 2023YFC3305402, Grant 2023YFC3305401 and in part by the National Natural Science Foundation of China (Nos.62302059 and 62172053).

References

1. Brown, T., et al.: Language models are few-shot learners. Adv. Neural. Inf. Process. Syst. **33**, 1877–1901 (2020)
2. Chen, J., et al.: FinTextQA: a dataset for long-form financial question answering. In: Ku, L.W., Martins, A., Srikumar, V. (eds.) Proceedings of the 62nd Annual Meeting of the Association for Computational Linguistics (Volume 1: Long Papers), Bangkok, Thailand, pp. 6025–6047. Association for Computational Linguistics (2024). https://doi.org/10.18653/v1/2024.acl-long.328
3. Chen, J., et al.: Air-bench: Automated heterogeneous information retrieval benchmark (2024). https://arxiv.org/abs/2412.13102
4. Dai, S., et al.: Cocktail: a comprehensive information retrieval benchmark with LLM-generated documents integration. In: Ku, L.W., Martins, A., Srikumar, V. (eds.) Findings of the Association for Computational Linguistics: ACL 2024, Bangkok, Thailand, pp. 7052–7074. Association for Computational Linguistics (2024). https://doi.org/10.18653/v1/2024.findings-acl.421
5. Gao, L., Ma, X., Lin, J., Callan, J.: Precise zero-shot dense retrieval without relevance labels. In: Rogers, A., Boyd-Graber, J., Okazaki, N. (eds.) Proceedings of the 61st Annual Meeting of the Association for Computational Linguistics (Volume 1: Long Papers), Toronto, Canada, pp. 1762–1777. Association for Computational Linguistics (2023). https://doi.org/10.18653/v1/2023.acl-long.99
6. Jeronymo, V., et al.: Inpars-v2: large language models as efficient dataset generators for information retrieval. arXiv preprint arXiv:2301.01820 (2023)
7. Kazemi, S.M., et al.: Time2vec: learning a vector representation of time. In: NeurIPS (2019)
8. Muennighoff, N., Tazi, N., Magne, L., Reimers, N.: MTEB: Massive text embedding benchmark. In: Vlachos, A., Augenstein, I. (eds.) Proceedings of the 17th Conference of the European Chapter of the Association for Computational Linguistics, Dubrovnik, Croatia, pp. 2014–2037. Association for Computational Linguistics (2023). https://doi.org/10.18653/v1/2023.eacl-main.148, https://aclanthology.org/2023.eacl-main.148/
9. Qiu, Y., et al.: DuReader-retrieval: a large-scale Chinese benchmark for passage retrieval from web search engine. In: Goldberg, Y., Kozareva, Z., Zhang, Y. (eds.) Proceedings of the 2022 Conference on Empirical Methods in Natural Language Processing, Abu Dhabi, United Arab Emirates, pp. 5326–5338. Association for Computational Linguistics (2022). https://doi.org/10.18653/v1/2022.emnlp-main.357
10. Rahmani, H.A., Craswell, N., Yilmaz, E., Mitra, B., Campos, D.: Synthetic test collections for retrieval evaluation. In: Proceedings of the 47th International ACM SIGIR Conference on Research and Development in Information Retrieval, pp. 2647–2651 (2024)
11. Schick, T., Schütze, H.: It's not just size that matters: small language models are also few-shot learners. In: Proceedings of the 2021 Conference of the North American Chapter of the Association for Computational Linguistics: Human Language Technologies. pp. 2339–2352. Association for Computational Linguistics (2021). https://doi.org/10.18653/v1/2021.naacl-main.185
12. Tang, Y., Yang, Y.: Finmteb: finance massive text embedding benchmark (2025). https://arxiv.org/abs/2502.10990
13. Team, C.L.: Chuxin-embedding: a Chinese text retrieval enhancement embedding model (2024). https://github.com/chuxin-llm/Chuxin-Embedding. accessed: 2024-03

14. Thakur, N., Reimers, N., Rücklé, A., Srivastava, A., Gurevych, I.: Beir: a heterogeneous benchmark for zero-shot evaluation of information retrieval models. In: Vanschoren, J., Yeung, S. (eds.) Proceedings of the Neural Information Processing Systems Track on Datasets and Benchmarks, vol. 1 (2021)
15. Wang, J., et al.: CSPRD: a financial policy retrieval dataset for Chinese stock market. In: Strauss, C., Amagasa, T., Manco, G., Kotsis, G., Tjoa, A.M., Khalil, I. (eds.) DEXA 2024. LNCS, vol. 14910, pp. 3–17. Springer, Cham (2024). https://doi.org/10.1007/978-3-031-68309-1_1
16. Wang, K., Thakur, N., Reimers, N., Gurevych, I.: GPL: generative pseudo labeling for unsupervised domain adaptation of dense retrieval. arXiv preprint arXiv:2112.07577 (2021)
17. Wang, L., Yang, N., Huang, X., Yang, L., Majumder, R., Wei, F.: Improving text embeddings with large language models. In: Ku, L.W., Martins, A., Srikumar, V. (eds.) Proceedings of the 62nd Annual Meeting of the Association for Computational Linguistics (Volume 1: Long Papers), Bangkok, Thailand, pp. 11897–11916. Association for Computational Linguistics (2024). https://aclanthology.org/2024.acl-long.642/
18. Wang, L., Yang, N., Wei, F.: Query2doc: query expansion with large language models. arXiv preprint arXiv:2303.07678 (2023)
19. Weller, O., et al.: When do generative query and document expansions fail? a comprehensive study across methods, retrievers, and datasets. In: Findings of the Association for Computational Linguistics: EACL 2024, St. Julian's, Malta, pp. 1987–2003. Association for Computational Linguistics (2024). https://aclanthology.org/2024.findings-eacl.134
20. Xie, X., et al.: T2ranking: a large-scale Chinese benchmark for passage ranking. In: Proceedings of the 46th International ACM SIGIR Conference on Research and Development in Information Retrieval. SIGIR '23, New York, NY, USA, pp. 2681–2690. Association for Computing Machinery (2023). https://doi.org/10.1145/3539618.3591874
21. Xu, X., et al.: Finbert2: a specialized bidirectional encoder for bridging the gap in finance-specific deployment of large language models. In: Proceedings of the 31st ACM SIGKDD Conference on Knowledge Discovery and Data Mining. ACM (2025). https://doi.org/10.1145/3711896.3737219
22. Zhang, J., Lan, Z., He, J.: Contrastive learning of sentence embeddings from scratch. In: Bouamor, H., Pino, J., Bali, K. (eds.) Proceedings of the 2023 Conference on Empirical Methods in Natural Language Processing, Singapore, pp. 3916–3932. Association for Computational Linguistics (2023). https://doi.org/10.18653/v1/2023.emnlp-main.238

Speech-to-Visualization: Toward End-to-End Speech-Driven Data Visualization Generation from Natural Language Questions

Haodi Zhang[1], Xinhe Zhang[1], Jihua Zhou[1], Kaishun Wu[4], Yuanfeng Song[2(✉)], and Raymond Chi-Wing Wong[3]

[1] Shenzhen University, Shenzhen, China
[2] AI Group, WeBank Co., Ltd, Shenzhen, China
songyf@outlook.com
[3] The Hong Kong University of Science and Technology, Hong Kong, China
[4] The Hong Kong University of Science and Technology (Guangzhou), Guangzhou, China

Abstract. Data visualization (DV) has evolved rapidly, transforming intricate datasets into accessible visual re presentations. However, the intricate grammar of DV languages, such as Vega-Lite, presents a substantial barrier for beginners and users without technical backgrounds. To address this challenge, extensive research has focused on developing models that can translate natural language questions (NLQs) into DV languages, a process formally known as text-to-visualization in the field. With the recent development of speech-related technologies, particularly Acoustic Speech Recognition (ASR), voice-based interaction has become a growing trend in real-world applications. In this paper, we introduce speech-to-vis, a novel task that translates speech-form NLQs into data visualizations. To address the scarcity of relevant datasets, we present *Speech-NVBench*, the first manually annotated dataset specifically designed for this field. Our research reveals that the intuitive cascaded approach (i.e., ASR followed by text-to-vis) suffers from error propagation issues, where small errors in earlier stages lead to larger errors in subsequent stages. In response, we introduce *SpeechVisNet*, the first end-to-end neural architecture that directly translates speech-form NLQs into DVs. SpeechVisNet incorporates advanced structures like a DV-aware decoder to ensure reliable output. Furthermore, to mitigate the modality gap between speech-modality questions and text-modality data schema, we explore bridging techniques to align them. Experimentation on our proposed dataset demonstrates SpeechVisNet's competitive edge against various strong baselines. This work aims to drive innovation in human-machine interfaces, enhancing the efficiency and accessibility of DV tools across various domains.

Keywords: Data Visualization · Data Analysis · Speech-Driven Visualization System · Neural Architecture · Speech-to-Visualization

1 Introduction

With the rapid growth of available data in today's digital world, the capacity of transforming complex data into meaningful visual representations has become essential for rational decision-making and eff communication. Data visualization (DV) is a cornerstone in this process, leveraging visual elements such as bar charts, scatter plots, and histograms to convey data information to readers in a straight-forward and intuitive manner [24]. By enhancing the comprehension of data, DV enables users to grasp intricate concepts and patterns with greater ease and clarity. Recognizing its transformative impact, DV plays an indispensable role in a wide range of academic and commercial fields, including but not limited to data mining, databases, recommendation systems, and data analysis [17,23,34,41]. In recent years, there have been numerous DV-related studies published in top database conferences and journals such as ICDE [15,28] and SIGMOD [18,33], VLDB [35,39], and TKDE [17,42]. For example, Sevi [32], published in SIGMOD'22, proposed an automatic DV generation system that processes natural language questions in speech form.

The creation of DVs is usually achieved by composing specifications using the DV languages. These DV languages, such as Vega-Lite [26], ggplot2 [36], ZQL [27], ECharts [16], and VizQL [13], defined in form of complicated grammars, where a json configuration file can be executed to produce a visualization chart. They empower professionals and seasoned scholars to craft sophisticated visualizations tailored to their needs, while also presenting substantial challenges for common users due to the complexity and steep learning curves. To bridge the gap, text-to-visualization (*text-to-vis*) techniques have been proposed to automate the translation of natural language questions (NLQs) into DVs, unlocking the power of databases and visualization systems for users with limited technical skills [18]. In this context, a significant body of work has contributed to the field's progress [18,31].

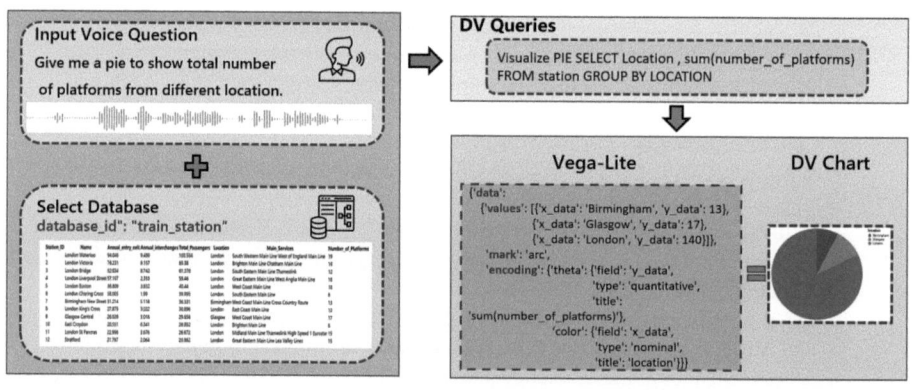

Fig. 1. Speech-to-Vis Process: From Voice Query to Data Visualization. This chart illustrates the workflow of converting a speech-based natural language question and database schema into a corresponding data visualization. It demonstrates how spoken queries can be transformed into visual representations of data, bridging the gap between verbal communication and visual analytics.

On the other hand, with the widespread utilization of smartphones and tablets, applications like voice search, AI assistants, and chatbots have gained popularity. Thus, the evolution of speech-based input systems has presented new avenues for the field of data querying and analysis. Several substantial studies published in top database venues have addressed speech-based data querying [19,29,30] and DV [32]. While current endeavors in DV have predominantly focused on textual natural language inputs, the potential of speech-based natural language inputs remains largely untapped. Compared to text-based inputs, speech interfaces offer superior user-friendliness and convenience, holding potential in areas such as voice search, hands-free operation, smart home control, and enhancing virtual and augmented reality experiences. In response to the demand for Speech-based DV systems and models, a task named speech-to-visualization (*speech-to-vis*) (Fig. 1) has been proposed to generate DV queries from spoken NLQs automatically.

The few existing speech-to-vis work (e.g., Sevi [32]) in the DV domain, simply cascades an Automatic Speech Recognition (ASR) model and a text-to-vis model [18,31]. However, these systems and approaches suffer from the error propagation problem [29,30] (i.e., *a small error in the ASR module leads to a much larger error in the following text-to-vis module*) and demand high-quality ASR models for good performance. Designing an end-to-end speech-to-vis system is necessary but challenging. Firstly, the scarcity of speech-to-vis datasets poses a fundamental obstacle, restricting the development and evaluation of end-to-end speech-to-vis models. Secondly, the modality gap between the speech-based query inputs and the textual-based database information presents a tough technical challenge for the neural network.

In response to these challenges, we present the speech-to-vis dataset *SpeechNVBench*, and a novel model named *SpeechVisNet*. To our knowledge, SpeechVisNet is the first end-to-end speech-to-vis model. Our training regimen is structured into three distinct phases: alignment pre-training, weakly supervised data pre-training, and model fine-tuning, each designed to enhance the model's performance and adaptability. Specifically, to alleviate the first challenge, we manually labeled a new speech-to-vis dataset named SpeechNVBench by leveraging the public text-to-vis dataset named NVBench [18], considering factors such as difficulty, length, and domain. Additionally, to further mitigate the situation where the amount of data is insufficient to fully engage model training, we utilized a weakly supervised data pre-training approach to provide preliminary processing before model fine-tuning. To address the second challenge, we designed the sophisticated *SpeechVisNet* model and further employed a methodology, utilizing a teacher-student paradigm for the pre-training step to map the speech-based inputs and textual-based database information into a unified hidden space. SpeechVisNet also employed a DV grammar-aware decoder to generate more rigorous and reliable output. Experiment results show that our model could surpass existing SOTA cascaded baselines.

In summary, our main contributions include:

- We have formalized a novel task named speech-to-vis and have accordingly established the first human-labeled *SpeechNVBench* dataset. As the first manually annotated dataset in this domain, it offers greater possibilities and convenience for following research on this task.
- We introduced SpeechVisNet, a novel model specifically designed for the speech-to-vis task. As the first end-to-end neural network model in its field, this framework

eschews the need for an intermediate text phase, pioneering the capability to directly convert speech into DV.
- We have designed innovative model training methodologies for our designed end-to-end approach, encompassing dual pre-training phases and fine-tuning. The *Alignment Pre-training* aligns the representational spaces of speech and text inputs through a teacher-student framework. Concurrently, the *Weakly Supervised Data Pre-training* enriches the model's training by incorporating labels that bypass manual verification. This synergistic approach of pre-training stages followed by fine-tuning notably boosts the model's capabilities, presenting a valuable blueprint for future reference and in-depth exploration.
- Our SpeechVisNet model has demonstrated exceptional performance in experiments, achieving state-of-the-art (SOTA) results in the task. It outperforms existing baselines by a margin, with an improvement of 9.00% in precision.

2 Task Formulation

In this section, we begin by introducing several preliminary concepts that are instrumental in fostering a deeper understanding of the work that follows, and then we proceed to provide a formal definition of the text-to-vis task.

Natural Language Question. In this paper, an NLQ serves as a comprehensible discourse for humans that describes the desired DV, aligning with people's natural habits of expression and reading. For non-specialists and novices in the field of DV, utilizing NLQs to manipulate and process data is a more user-friendly approach, particularly when the required DV is complex and esoteric.

Visualization Specification. Composing visualization specifications is a crucial step for visualizing data as graphical charts. Declarative visualization languages (DVLs) available in the market are Vega-Lite [26], ggplot2 [36], ZQL [27], ECharts [16], and VizQL [13], each with its grammar. These DVLs detail the visualization's construction, such as chart type, color, size, mapping functions, and properties for marks including canvas size and legends, and thus, determine the visualization specifications. In Fig. 1, a specification in Vega-Lite [26] is given, defining attributes such as data path, mark, and encoding.

Data Visualization Query. The DV query concept, proposed to abstract all possible DVLs, allows for the execution of queries on databases to retrieve data, akin to SQL queries. It also provides details necessary for data visualization. In Fig. 1, the DV query specifies a "PIE" type chart and defines the data range and aggregation method. This query can be easily converted into a visualization specification in DVLs, which the visualization engine then uses to render the chart. The example in Fig. 1 shows this conversion in Vega-Lite, and it is noted that transforming the query for other DVLs, such as ECharts, is straightforward.

Speech-to-Vis Task. Suppose we have a dataset $\mathcal{D}$ with I examples, denoted as $\mathcal{D} = \{\mathbf{d}^1, \cdots, \mathbf{d}^I\}$, where $\mathbf{d}^i$ ($i \in 1, \cdots, I$) refers to the i-th example. Every training example $\mathbf{s}^i$ is structured as $\{x, y, V\}$, with x representing a speech-form NLQ,

y denotes its DV query (which can be further executed to obtain the DV chart), and V refers to the schema of the corresponding database needed to execute y. Here, the database schema V_i contains a set of tables $T = \{t_1, \cdots, t_{M_i}\}$, where M_i represents the count of tables in database schema V_i. For each table t_j ($j \in 1, \cdots, M^i$), it includes a set of columns denoted as $C = \{c_1, \cdots, c_{N_j}\}$, where N_j signifies the count of columns for the table t_j. The goal of the speech-to-vis task is to build a learning-based model that can accurately generate the correct DV query y' from an unseen NLQ-schema pair $\{x', V'\}$. An example is illustrated in Fig. 1 to elucidate the task.

3 Speech-To-Vis Dataset

Within this section, we present one of our key contributions: the *SpeechNVBench* dataset. Our presentation will detail its creation methodology, provide an overview of its statistical properties, and elucidate the criteria used for its partitioning.

3.1 Dataset Creation Process

To address the data scarcity problem in the speech-to-vis domain, we manually created a dataset named *SpeechNVBench* by refining a subset of 12,000 samples from the NVBench dataset [18]. NVbench introduced a novel synthesizer (nl2sql-to-nl2vis) that transforms the nl-to-SQL (nl2sql) benchmarks into nl-to-vis (nl2vis) benchmarks by analyzing and processing the Abstract Syntax Tree (AST). Furthermore, on this foundation, the data is validated and annotated by experts and crowd workers. On the foundation of this nl2vis benchmark, we meticulously evaluate and filter the data by considering a range of factors including its complexity, length, category, and relevance to specific domains. Specifically, in NVbench, where a one-to-many relationship exists between (NLQs, DVs) pairs, we first guarantee the inclusion of every DV instance within our dataset. Then we endeavor to expand our dataset to a suitable scale while preserving the original benchmark's proportionate distribution of difficulty and types. Subsequently, leveraging the contributions of 32 crowd workers who provided voice recordings, and dedicated 100 h of meticulous work, we have labeled and constructed the speech-to-vis dataset. In this context, the workers encompass English learners from a wide range of ages, genders, and proficiency levels. They deliver voiceovers in English that, with fluent and largely standard, are characterized by their unique accents, contributing to the rich diversity of the audio data within the dataset. Further details regarding these individuals are available in the appendix.

This process involved a comprehensive assessment of factors such as hardness, length, and domain relevance. Subsequently, we enlisted the assistance of 32 crowd workers, diverse in age and gender, dedicating around 100 h to annotate and construct this speech-to-vis dataset meticulously.

3.2 Dataset Analysis

Dataset Overview. The SpeechNVBench dataset encompasses 153 distinct databases, comprising a total of 780 tables spanning 105 domains. The 153 databases within the

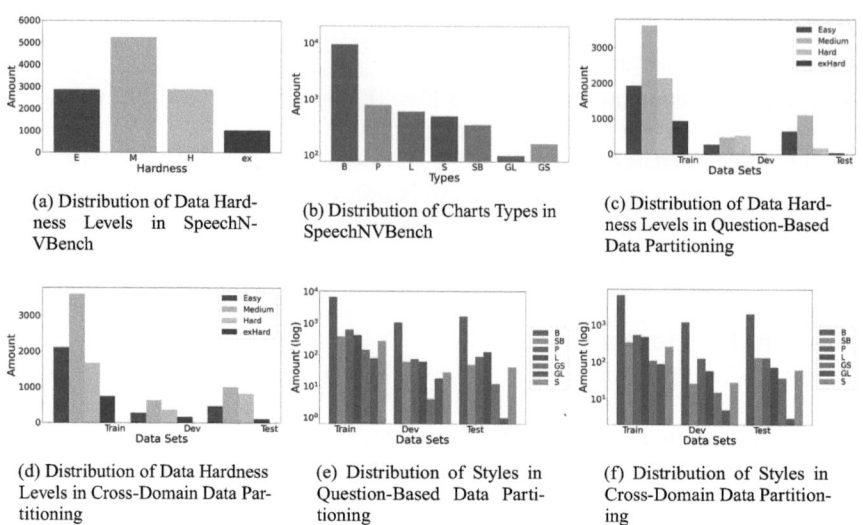

Fig. 2. Statistical overview of the complete dataset and its partitioned subsets, including hardness and styles, Categorized by hardness levels Easy(E), Medium(M), Hard(H), and Extra Hard(ex) and Style Types Bar(B), Pie(P), Line(L), Scatter(S), Stacked Bar(SB), Grouping Line (GL), Grouping Scatter (GS).

dataset contain 780 tables, 4,017 columns, and 1,000,572 rows. So the average number of columns/rows in the 780 tables is 5.15/1,282.78. Ranging from the minimal to the maximal, the dataset includes a table with just two columns and one row, contrasting with another that spans 48 columns and features 183,978 rows.

(SPEECH, DV) Statistics. The WAV2VIS dataset, similar to NVBench [18], encompasses 12,000 pairs of (Speech-form questions, DVs), sharing 7,274 DVs with the NVBench dataset. Each DV in the SpeechNVBench dataset corresponds to one or more Speech-from questions. Among these 12,000 pairs of (Speech-form questions, DVs), they encompass 7 types of charts, further classified into four difficulty levels. The detailed difficulty statistics of this dataset can be found in Fig. 2.

3.3 Dataset Partitioning

Two recommended dataset partitioning approaches are available. The first, known as the question-based method, ensures that identical audio inputs are not shared between the test set and the training/validation sets while allowing for the possibility of identical DVs appearing in both. This method is straightforward for model training. The second method termed the cross-domain method, prohibits the presence of the same database in both the test and training/validation sets, requiring stronger model performance and cross-domain transferability. Both approaches are provided within the dataset for users' convenience. We also present specific details regarding the two methodologies of dataset partitioning in Fig. 2. Following [31], we use the second approach in our experiments.

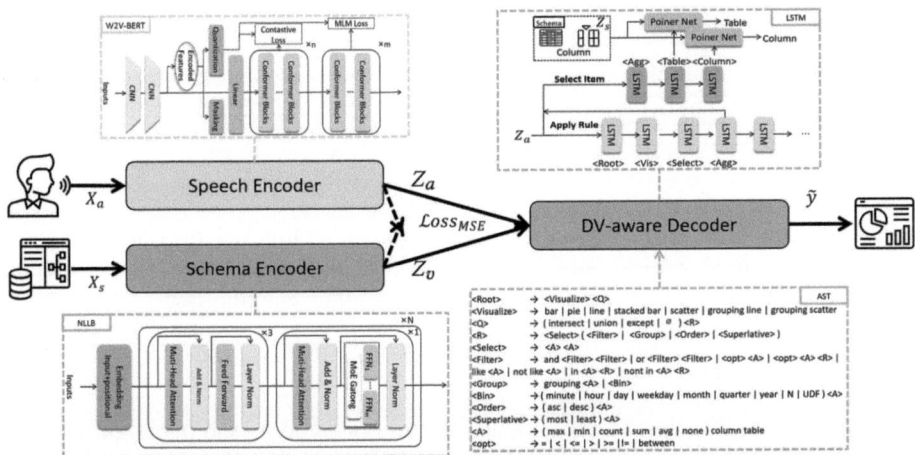

Fig. 3. The network structure of our proposed SpeechVisNet model, which consists of a speech encoder, a schema encoder, and a DV grammar-based decoder to achieve end-to-end speech-to-vis translation. To bridge the modality gap between the speech query (i.e., speech modality) and the database schema (i.e., text modality), a novel pre-training approach is also utilized to align the representations of both speech and text into the same hidden space.

4 Our Proposed Model: SpeechVisNet

In this section, we delve into our SpeechVisNet model, tailored for the speech-to-vis task, beginning with a comprehensive overview of the framework and then proceeding to elucidate the specifics of each constituent part.

4.1 Framework Overview

Due to the significant modality gap between speech NLQ and DV, developing an end-to-end speech-to-vis model presents considerable challenges. Our proposed SpeechVisNet model comprises three main components: a speech encoder, a schema encoder, and a DV-aware decoder. Our speech encoder harnesses the capabilities of the W2V-BERT model [3]. It employs a CNN neural network to process input and leverages the masked language model (MLM) pre-training task of the BERT model to enhance the transformation of speech signals into hidden representations. Simultaneously, information about the tables, columns, and values of the required database is integrated as a natural language input and fed into the schema encoder. We then adopt a pre-training approach inspired by SONAR [9], aligning the representations of both speech and text inputs into the same vector space. Drawing inspiration from existing architectures for Speech-to-SQL tasks [29,30] and text-to-vis [31] tasks, the DV-aware decoder first predicts an intermediate AST tree using SemQL [12], which then can be translated into a DV query to obtain the final chart. The overall structure of the model is illustrated in Fig. 3.

4.2 Schema Encoder

We have adopted the architecture of the NLLB [4] to serve as our schema encoder, which ingests pertinent database information, encompassing table and column names. Specifically, this component is designed with a foundation in transformer mechanisms and is enhanced by the strategic intercalation of a Mixture of Experts (MoE) layer at every three layers, effectively supplanting the traditional Feed-Forward Network (FFN) sublayers. Each MoE layer within the architecture is composed of 128 specialized experts and is paired with a gating mechanism that directs the allocation of tokens. Through the speech encoder, we derived the schema representation Z_v.

4.3 Speech Encoder

We have constructed a speech encoder architecture inspired by the paradigm of w2v-BERT [3], which adopts conformer layers [11] for constructing the network. As referenced in [11], the conformer architecture-integrated with convolutional neural networks (CNNs) and transformer mechanisms-offers a superior approach to speech modeling. This integration effectively captures the nuanced interplay between the local and global contextual relationships within audio sequences, outperforming a standalone transformer or CNN layers. Upon processing through the speech encoder, we have obtained the speech representation Z_a.

4.4 DV-Aware Decoder

Given that DV languages are essentially executable statements grounded in syntactic structures, we opted to design a structured decoder that leverages the syntactic prior knowledge inherent in these languages. In alignment with the established approach in the text-to-SQL field, as delineated in [12], which integrates the SemQL grammar and constructs a corresponding decoder, we have tailored a similar grammar-aware neural architecture. The intricacies of the grammar are illustrated in the lower right corner of Fig. 3. Specifically, our DV-aware decoder utilizes an LSTM architecture to generate data visualizations by selecting a sequence of actions represented as $\tilde{y}$. Mathematically, the generation process of a SemQL DV query $\tilde{y}$ can be formalized as follows:

$$p(\tilde{y}|x, V) = \prod_{i=1}^{K} p(act_i|x, V, act_{<i}), \quad (1)$$

where x and V have already been defined in Sect. 2, and act_i represents an action taken at step i, $act_{<i}$ denotes all actions preceding step i, and K is the total number of actions required to predict $\tilde{y}$. To specify, 'actions' refers to the grammar reasonings in the Rules Application or Schema Selection phase mentioned later. The processes encompassed within the formulation of the equation are delineated into two steps:(i) *Rules Application*: This step involves the application of a production rule to progressively develop the current grammar tree, culminating in the completion of the DV sketch. (ii) *Schema Selection*: This step involves selecting specific column and table elements from the schema to generate the DV query from the sketch (Fig. 4).

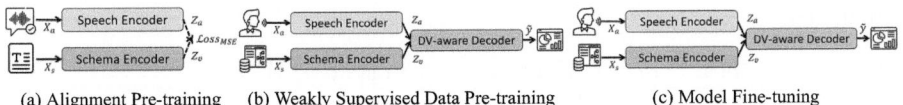

(a) Alignment Pre-training (b) Weakly Supervised Data Pre-training (c) Model Fine-tuning

Fig. 4. The flowchart of the model training process. Figure (a) corresponds to the alignment pre-training phase, where X_a and X_s signify the speech and textual inputs that correspond to identical content. The outputs of the two encoders are indicated by Z_a and Z_b. Utilizing these, we calculate the MSE Loss, which guides our pre-training process. Furthermore, in Figures (b) and (c), X_a corresponds to the speech query inputs that are crafted in the weakly supervised pre-training stage and the inputs used in the formal training sessions. On the other hand, X_s signifies the text inputs related to the pertinent database information.

Rules Application. The *Rules Application* phase is designed to formulate a context-free grammar tree that underpins the structure of a DV query, following the approach outlined in [12]. In this iterative process, we strategically identify the most likely branch at each juncture, leveraging an LSTM-driven framework to navigate the construction. In this iterative process, we discern and opt for the branch with the highest likelihood based on the established route, utilizing an LSTM-based network. Specifically, for each predictive interval i, the LSTM's internal state is updated, contingent upon the previous state $h_{i-1} \in \mathbb{R}^{d_m}$, previous action embedding $act_{i-1} \in \mathbb{R}^{d_a}$ (d_a is the size of the action embedding), previous action type embedding $n_{i-1} \in \mathbb{R}^{d_t}$ (d_t is the size of the action type embedding), and previous context representation of LSTM c_{i-1}. Here, d_a denotes the dimensionality of the action embedding, and d_t denotes the dimensionality of the action type embedding, respectively. Subsequently, the attention context across the encoder's temporal dimensions can be computed, and the production rule can be evaluated using a softmax probability distribution, as presented in Eq. 5.

$$h_i = \text{LSTM}([act_{i-1}; n_{i-1}; c_{i-1}], h_{i-1}), \tag{2}$$

$$c_i = \text{Softmax}(h_i^T W_a Z_a^T) Z_a, \tag{3}$$

$$u_i = \tanh([h_i; c_i] W_u + b_u), \tag{4}$$

$$p(\tilde{y}_i = act_i | x, S, act_{<i}) = \text{Softmax}(\tanh(u_i^T W_p + b_p)), \tag{5}$$

where $W_a \in \mathbb{R}^{d_m \times d_m}$, $W_u \in \mathbb{R}^{2d_m \times d_m}$ are the learnable weights. When n_a denotes the total number of actions associated with the specified grammar, $W_p \in \mathbb{R}^{d_m \times n_a}$ b_c is trainable bias, and the initial state h_0 is obtained by a max-pooling operation of the speech embedding Z_a.

Schema Selection. To address the task of populating the specific elements within a DV query, we have integrated an LSTM-driven component. The main objective of this module is to decide which item is involved in the text in the condition of the given schema. Items to be decided include tables, columns, and operations like max, min, count, etc. Different from the "rules application" step, the schema exhibits variability across individual cases, with the desired items also lacking a fixed nature. Accordingly, we have utilized a pointer network, as referenced in Pointer networks [37], to address this challenge. The probability of selecting a schema item is determined through the following computation:

$$p(\tilde{y}_i = act_i | x, V, act_{<i}) = \text{Softmax}(u_i^T W_v Z_v^T), \quad (6)$$

where $W_v \in \mathbb{R}^{d_m \times d_m}$ is a learnable weight matrix. Specifically, the selection of table options is confined to those tables that possess the corresponding selected column.

5 Model Training

To bridge the gap between the embedding vector representations of the two modalities and maximize the model's capabilities, we propose a training framework consisting of two pre-training steps followed by fine-tuning: alignment pre-training (Sect. 5.1), weakly supervised data pre-training (Sect. 5.2), and model fine-tuning (Sect. 5.3). We will now delve into a detailed exposition of these components.

5.1 Alignment Pre-training

Following SONAR [9], we use a pre-trained w2v-bert 600 million parameter model to initialize the speech encoders and train them on training sets such as Common Voice 12 ASR [1], Must-C [6], Voxpopuli [38], and Librispeech [22]. After reviewing prior research [8,9] and conducting a thorough analysis, we opted for Attention-pooling as our ultimate pooling methodology. We chose the Mean Squared Error (MSE) as the objective loss function for our training regimen because it effectively minimizes the average squared difference between the predicted embeddings and the actual ones, thereby ensuring a more accurate representation in the sentence embedding space. This choice aligns with its proven success in prior studies for fostering model performance in multilingual and multimodal contexts [14,25], as well as in applications involving multilingual speech processing [8]. In particular, we adopted the teacher-student approach, fixing the parameters of the schema encoder, which takes text as input, as the teacher model and minimizing the MSE loss between the two to train the student model, which takes speech as input. The loss function is defined as:

$$L_{\text{MSE}} = \frac{1}{N} \sum_{i=1}^{N} (h_i^{\text{text}} - h_i^{\text{speech}})^2, \quad (7)$$

where h_i^{text} and h_i^{speech} represent the embeddings of the text and speech inputs at the same timestep, respectively.

To better aggregate information and obtain embeddings of the same size, we employed an attention-pooling mechanism. The output of the attention-pooling layer is calculated as follows:

$$z_i = \sum_{j=1}^{L} \alpha_{ij} h_j, \quad (8)$$

where α_{ij} is the attention weight, computed as:

$$\alpha_{ij} = \frac{\exp(e_{ij})}{\sum_{k=1}^{L} \exp(e_{ik})}. \quad (9)$$

The attention score e_{ij} is determined by:

$$e_{ij} = \tanh(W_a h_j + b_a), \tag{10}$$

where W_a and b_a are learnable weight matrix and bias vector, respectively. Here, L represents the number of timesteps in the input sequence, i denotes the index of the output embedding, and j denotes the index of the input timestep.

After completing this pre-training phase, we have effectively mapped the two disparate modalities into a unified vector space, establishing a robust groundwork for the following stages of pre-training and the fine-tuning process.

5.2 Weakly Supervised Data Pre-training

Post its preliminary alignment pre-training phase, we generated a significant volume of synthetic data to enhance the model's pre-training process, aiming to unlock its utmost potential for performance. During the weakly supervised data generation phase, we employed Baidu's text-to-speech (TTS) model to provide vocalization for most of the data in NVBench. This approach allowed us to amass a considerable volume of unlabeled weakly supervised data. To elaborate, the synthetic data generated in this phase includes four distinct AI voice profiles, amassing more than 20,000 dubbing outcomes per profile. However, this synthetic dataset intentionally excludes the data from the test and validation sets that are reserved for fine-tuning in the next phase of our process. Given that the training strategies and methodologies applied in this pre-training phase mirror those utilized in the fine-tuning stage, we refrain from repeating them here. For comprehensive insights, one can refer to the section dedicated to fine-tuning for a detailed explanation.

5.3 Model Fine-Tuning

Following the pre-training phases previously described, we acquire pre-trained weights for both the speech encoder and the schema encoder. In this subsequent fine-tuning phase, we initially load the pre-existing weights from the pre-training phase, if available. Subsequently, we conduct comprehensive training of the model using speech-to-vis data. This training is aimed at maximizing the log-likelihood of the ground truth action sequences, which are defined as follows:

$$\begin{aligned}\mathcal{L} = \max &\sum_{(x,V,y)\in\mathcal{D}} \sum_{act_i \in ApplyRule} \log p(\tilde{y}_i = act_i | x, V, act_{<i}) \\ &+ \sum_{act_i \in SelectSchema} \log p(\tilde{y}_i = act_i | x, V, act_{<i})).\end{aligned} \tag{11}$$

The whole network is trained in an end-to-end style with stochastic gradient descent methods.

6 Experiment

This section presents an in-depth assessment of the performance of our proposed framework, focusing on quantitative metrics. Here, we illustrate the superiority of our framework by juxtaposing its performance with that of several robust baselines.

6.1 Experimental Setup

Datasets. We use the same training set of the *SpeechNVBench* dataset, which is detailed in Sect. 3, to train all the models, tune their parameters with the same validation set, and finally, evaluate the performance on the same testing set. Considering that the data partitioning based on question-based methods presents a lower difficulty level for our model as well as for existing baseline models, and thus does not effectively reflect performance differences. We employ a unified cross-domain approach for dataset partitioning, ensuring that (SPEECH, DV) pairs from the same database do not simultaneously appear in the training/validation sets and the test set. In this scenario, the quantities of the training set, validation set, and test set are 8121, 1442, and 2408 respectively. Concurrently, we strive to ensure an equitable distribution of data hardness and diversity of visualization chart types across all subsets.

Baselines. Current approaches addressing the speech-to-vis task are predominantly based on a cascaded methodology, integrating ASR models with text-to-vis models, with a significant lack of end-to-end solutions. In our experiments, we selected four methods as baseline models, comprising both existing cascaded approach models and ASR integrated with existing text-to-vis models. Each model was thoroughly trained under the premise of utilizing the same dataset and adopting an identical dataset partitioning strategy. For our ASR model, we selected the Paraformer [10], a parallel transformer model for non-autoregressive, end-to-end speech recognition. Utilizing the SequenceMatcher class within Python's difflib library, we calculated the degree of similarity between the ASR results and the correct labels, obtaining a notable similarity score of 0.89. It matches the performance of autoregressive models and enhances inference speed through a Lookahead Language Model sampler and minimum word error rate training.

- **ASR-Transformer.** The Transformer architecture has demonstrated its effectiveness in seq2seq tasks. Since the speech-to-vis task falls within the scope of seq2seq tasks, we aim to adopt this most classic model as the fundamental baseline and compare its results with our model's.
- **Sevi (i.e., ASR-ncNet).** Alongside the introduction of the NVBench dataset, Luo et al. [18] also proposed ncNet, a model based on the Transformer architecture that leverages templates and incorporates some manual processing techniques. Then they introduced Sevi [32], which integrates ASR and ncNet in a cascading manner.
- **ASR-IRNet.** IRnet [12] is an advanced text-to-SQL model that enhances the traditional direct approach by representing SQL statements in the SemSQL syntax as an AST. We modified IRNet to generate a DV query to adapt to our task.
- **ASR-RGVisNet.** RGVisNet [31] embodies an integration of retrieval and generation modules into a new framework, demonstrating impressive efficacy in addressing the task.
- **SpeechVisNet.** This is the first end-to-end neural model proposed by us that can generate visualizations directly from speech-based questions.

Evaluation Metrics. Our experimental validation leverages three well-established metrics from this domain, selected for their capacity to affirm the effectiveness of our innovative model. The first two metrics are applicable to all models within the speech-to-vis domain, while the last one is particularly suited for models that generate intermediate sketches.

- **Exact Match Accuracy.** According to common practice [40], we assess performance through exact match accuracy, where exact match accuracy measures whether the predicted query is equivalent to the gold query as a whole. This stringent metric implies that all elements, such as visualization chart types, x, y, and z-axis, and data with transformations from the according database, must match accurately.
- **Average Time Per Query (TPQ).** This particular metric evaluates the average time expended on inferring a query through various methodologies, thereby reflecting the swiftness with which a model can handle and interpret speech queries.
- **Sketch Match Accuracy.** Our model's decoder generates the final output in two stages: rules application and schema selection. Upon completing the "rules application", we arrive at a sketch that conforms to the DV grammar; think of it as a blueprint for a DV, devoid of specific table column names and values. We assess the alignment of this sketch with the correct one from the labels. The metric, sketch match accuracy, reflects the ratio of accurately generated sketches among the outputs for all queries in the test set. This metric is instrumental in gauging the model's detailed performance, highlighting both its capabilities and areas for improvement.

6.2 Comparison of Accuracy and TPQ

Table 1 displays the accuracy of our proposed model as well as the baselines for the validation and test datasets, from which we can analyze the experimental results.

In our main experiment, the SpeechVisNet model has delivered impressive accuracy, showcasing its competitive edge. Specifically, it surpassed the top-performing baseline model by a notable margin of 9.00% in terms of exact match accuracy on the test dataset. The grammatical intricacies of DV queries prove too sophisticated for the original Transformer architecture, leading to outputs that are vague and devoid of accurate queries. Sevi, which employs templates and some detailed processing, performs relatively better. However, the open-domain dataset's requirement for cross-domain capabilities still limits its performance. The IR-net model and the RGvisnet model, due to their reliance on the accuracy of the ASR component to generate intermediate text-based NLQs, do not perform as impressively as they do in text-to-vis tasks. Overall, our model achieved the highest accuracy and demonstrated the most competitive performance in the main experiments. It does not rely on ASR models and demonstrates robust cross-domain adaptability and flexibility.

Turning our attention to the TPQ, our model demonstrates a markedly shorter processing time for each query compared to other cascaded models, whether they are based on seq2seq or grammar-based approaches. This efficiency stems from the fact that our model operates as an end-to-end, cohesive unit, in contrast to cascaded models which are segmented into distinct components-an ASR module and a text-to-vis module (Table 2).

Table 1. Performance Comparison

Models	Acc. (↑)	TPQ(s)(↓)
ASR-IRNet	0.1582	0.3575
ASR-Transformer	0.0	0.6048
ASR-RGVisNet	0.1238	0.3375
Sevi (ASR-ncNet)	0.3095	0.4471
SpeechVisNet(Ours)	**0.3995**	**0.2547**

Table 2. Ablation Experiment

Models	Sketch Acc.	Exact Acc.
SpeechVisNet	0.7243	0.3995
w/o alignment pre-training	0.2317	0.0
w/o weakly supervised pre-training	0.2552	0.0021

7 Related Work

Our work bridges three key research directions: voice-driven systems, text-to-vis techniques, and speech representation learning.

7.1 Voice-Driven Data Querying Systems

Voice-driven systems have evolved significantly in both industry and academia. Early systems like Dragon NaturallySpeaking laid the foundation, while modern platforms (e.g., Siri and Alexa) expanded voice interaction to broader applications. In database querying, EchoQuery [19] pioneered translating specialized voice commands into SQL. Subsequent works like SpeechSQLNet [29] and VoiceQuerySystem [30] generalized this to natural language inputs, enabling intuitive data retrieval for non-experts. For visualization, Sevi [32] introduced a cascaded system combining ASR with a text-to-vis model. However, existing approaches rely on error-prone cascaded pipelines, leaving end-to-end speech-to-vis solutions unexplored-a gap addressed by our work.

7.2 Text-to-Vis Techniques

Text-to-vis research aims to democratize visualization creation. Early systems like Text-to-viz [5] generated infographics from simple textual statistics, while Draco-Learn [20] formalized design constraints. Deep learning approaches emerged with Data2Vis [7], framing visualization as a sequence-to-sequence task. NVBench [18] advanced the field by adapting text-to-SQL benchmarks, enabling transformer-based models like ncNet. Subsequent work integrated retrieval mechanisms (e.g., RGVisNet [31]) and speech inputs (e.g., Sevi [32]), but retained cascaded architectures. Our end-to-end SpeechVisNet eliminates intermediate text conversion, directly mapping speech to visualizations.

7.3 Speech Representation Learning

Self-supervised speech representation learning underpins modern speech systems. CPC [21] pioneered contrastive predictive coding, while Wav2Vec 2.0 [2] integrated transformers for context-aware embeddings. w2v-BERT [3] further unified contrastive and masked language modeling. These advances enabled robust speech encoders critical to our model. By leveraging w2v-BERT's architecture, SpeechVisNet effectively aligns speech signals with textual schema representations, overcoming modality gaps inherent in end-to-end learning.

8 Conclusion and Discussion

In this paper, we introduce a novel speech-driven model for data visualization, along with the associated speech-to-vis task and the SpeechNVBench dataset, aimed at directly converting human-natural language into DV queries. As the pioneering end-to-end solution in its field, our model has been rigorously tested and proven to excel in generating DV queries from spoken inputs. It also exhibits a strong competitive edge when juxtaposed with a multitude of established baselines.

Moving forward, we plan to investigate additional pre-training strategies for systems that operate on voice input. Our ablation experiments revealed a marked decrease in performance when the model was not pre-trained. It is meaningful to examine the causes in-depth, provide a comprehensive analysis, and search for more efficacious pre-training techniques. Furthermore, our SpeechVisNet demonstrates the practicality of a speech-based approach to data visualization, leveraging the methodologies outlined in this research. We are keen to pursue further development in this direction, focusing on crafting more accessible speech-driven systems, particularly for specialized fields such as AI interaction and data analysis fields.

Acknowledgments. We thank the reviewers for their valuable comments.

References

1. Ardila, R., et al.: Common voice: a massively-multilingual speech corpus. In: LREC, Marseille, France, pp. 4218–4222. European Language Resources Association (2020). https://aclanthology.org/2020.lrec-1.520
2. Baevski, A., Zhou, Y., Mohamed, A., Auli, M.: wav2vec 2.0: a framework for self-supervised learning of speech representations. In: Advances in Neural Information Processing Systems, vol. 33, pp. 12449–12460 (2020)
3. Chung, Y.A., et al.: W2v-Bert: combining contrastive learning and masked language modeling for self-supervised speech pre-training. In: ASRU, pp. 244–250. IEEE (2021)
4. Costa-jussà, M.R., et al.: No language left behind: scaling human-centered machine translation. arXiv preprint arXiv:2207.04672 (2022)
5. Cui, W., et al.: Text-to-viz: automatic generation of infographics from proportion-related natural language statements. IEEE Trans. Visual Comput. Graphics **26**(1), 906–916 (2019)
6. Di Gangi, M.A., Cattoni, R., Bentivogli, L., Negri, M., Turchi, M.: Must-c: a multilingual speech translation corpus. In: NAACL-HLT, pp. 2012–2017. Association for Computational Linguistics (2019)
7. Dibia, V., Demiralp, Ç.: Data2vis: automatic generation of data visualizations using sequence-to-sequence recurrent neural networks. IEEE Comput. Graphics Appl. **39**(5), 33–46 (2019)
8. Duquenne, P.A., Gong, H., Schwenk, H.: Multimodal and multilingual embeddings for large-scale speech mining. Adv. Neural. Inf. Process. Syst. **34**, 15748–15761 (2021)
9. Duquenne, P.A., Schwenk, H., Sagot, B.: Sonar: sentence-level multimodal and language-agnostic representations. arXiv e-prints pp. arXiv–2308 (2023)
10. Gao, Z., Zhang, S., McLoughlin, I., Yan, Z.: Paraformer: fast and accurate parallel transformer for non-autoregressive end-to-end speech recognition. In: Proceedings of the Interspeech 2022, pp. 2063–2067 (2022). https://doi.org/10.21437/Interspeech.2022-9996

11. Gulati, A., et al.: Conformer: convolution-augmented transformer for speech recognition. In: Interspeech 2020 (2020)
12. Guo, J., et al.: Towards complex text-to-SQL in cross-domain database with intermediate representation. In: ACL. Association for Computational Linguistics (2019)
13. Hanrahan, P.: VIZQL: a language for query, analysis and visualization. In: SIGMOD, pp. 721–721 (2006)
14. Heffernan, K., Çelebi, O., Schwenk, H.: Bitext mining using distilled sentence representations for low-resource languages. In: EMNLP, pp. 2101–2112 (2022)
15. Krommyda, M., Kantere, V.: Visualization systems for linked datasets. In: ICDE, pp. 1790–1793. IEEE (2020)
16. Li, D., et al.: Echarts: a declarative framework for rapid construction of web-based visualization. Vis. Inform. **2**(2), 136–146 (2018)
17. Luo, Y., Qin, X., Chai, C., Tang, N., Li, G., Li, W.: Steerable self-driving data visualization. IEEE Trans. Knowl. Data Eng. **34**(1), 475–490 (2020)
18. Luo, Y., Tang, N., Li, G., Chai, C., Li, W., Qin, X.: Synthesizing natural language to visualization (nl2vis) benchmarks from nl2sql benchmarks. In: SIGMOD, pp. 1235–1247 (2021)
19. Lyons, G., Tran, V., Binnig, C., Cetintemel, U., Kraska, T.: Making the case for query-by-voice with echoquery. In: SIGMOD, pp. 2129–2132 (2016)
20. Moritz, D., et al.: Formalizing visualization design knowledge as constraints: actionable and extensible models in DRACO. IEEE Trans. Visual Comput. Graphics **25**(1), 438–448 (2018)
21. Oord, A.V.D., Li, Y., Vinyals, O.: Representation learning with contrastive predictive coding. arXiv preprint arXiv:1807.03748 (2018)
22. Panayotov, V., Chen, G., Povey, D., Khudanpur, S.: Librispeech: an ASR corpus based on public domain audio books. In: ICASSP, pp. 5206–5210. IEEE (2015)
23. Qian, X., et al.: Learning to recommend visualizations from data. In: KDD, pp. 1359–1369 (2021)
24. Qin, X., Luo, Y., Tang, N., Li, G.: Making data visualization more efficient and effective: a survey. VLDB J. **29**(1), 93–117 (2020)
25. Reimers, N., Gurevych, I.: Making monolingual sentence embeddings multilingual using knowledge distillation. In: EMNLP. Association for Computational Linguistics (2020)
26. Satyanarayan, A., Moritz, D., Wongsuphasawat, K., Heer, J.: Vega-lite: a grammar of interactive graphics. IEEE Trans. Visual Comput. Graphics **23**(1), 341–350 (2016)
27. Siddiqui, T., Kim, A., Lee, J., Karahalios, K., Parameswaran, A.: Effortless data exploration with zenvisage: an expressive and interactive visual analytics system. Proc. VLDB Endow. **10**(4), 457–468 (2016). https://doi.org/10.14778/3025111.3025126
28. Song, Y., Lu, J., Zhao, X., Wong, R.C.W., Zhang, H.: Demonstration of fevisqa: Free-form question answering over data visualization. In: ICDE. pp. 5417–5420. IEEE (2024)
29. Song, Y., Wong, R.C.W., Zhao, X.: Speech-to-SQL: toward speech-driven SQL query generation from natural language question. VLDB J. 1–23 (2024)
30. Song, Y., Wong, R.C.W., Zhao, X., Jiang, D.: Voicequerysystem: a voice-driven database querying system using natural language questions. In: SIGMOD, pp. 2385–2388 (2022)
31. Song, Y., Zhao, X., Wong, R.C.W., Jiang, D.: Rgvisnet: a hybrid retrieval-generation neural framework towards automatic data visualization generation. In: KDD, pp. 1646–1655 (2022)
32. Tang, J., Luo, Y., Ouzzani, M., Li, G., Chen, H.: SEVI: speech-to-visualization through neural machine translation. In: SIGMOD, pp. 2353–2356 (2022)
33. Tang, N., Wu, E., Li, G.: Towards democratizing relational data visualization. In: Proceedings of the 2019 International Conference on Management of Data, pp. 2025–2030 (2019)
34. Vartak, M., Huang, S., Siddiqui, T., Madden, S., Parameswaran, A.: Towards visualization recommendation systems. ACM SIGMOD Rec. **45**(4), 34–39 (2017)

35. Vartak, M., Rahman, S., Madden, S., Parameswaran, A., Polyzotis, N.: SeeDB: efficient data-driven visualization recommendations to support visual analytics. In: VLDB, vol. 8, p. 2182. NIH Public Access (2015)
36. Villanueva, R.A.M., Chen, Z.J.: ggplot2: elegant graphics for data analysis (2019)
37. Vinyals, O., Fortunato, M., Jaitly, N.: Pointer networks. In: Advances in Neural Information Processing Systems, vol. 28 (2015)
38. Wang, C., et al.: VoxPopuli: a large-scale multilingual speech corpus for representation learning, semi-supervised learning and interpretation. In: ACL-IJCNLP, pp. 993–1003. Association for Computational Linguistics (2021)
39. Xie, Y., Luo, Y., Li, G., Tang, N.: Haichart: Human and AI paired visualization system. In: VLDB (2024)
40. Yu, T., et al.: Spider: a large-scale human-labeled dataset for complex and cross-domain semantic parsing and text-to-SQL task. In: EMNLP, Brussels, Belgium. Association for Computational Linguistics (2018)
41. Yuan, H., Li, G.: A survey of traffic prediction: from spatio-temporal data to intelligent transportation. Data Sci. Eng. **6**(1), 63–85 (2021)
42. Zhang, W., et al.: Natural language interfaces for tabular data querying and visualization: a survey. IEEE Trans. Knowl. Data Eng. (2024)

Text-Guided Dual Interaction for Multimodal Relation Extraction in Social Media

Yachuan Zhang[1] and Yi Guo[1,2,3]([✉])

[1] East China University of Science and Technology, Shanghai 200237, China
Y10220122@mail.ecust.edu.cn, guoyi@ecust.edu.cn
[2] Shanghai Engineering Research Center of Big Data and Internet Audience, Shanghai, China
[3] Business Intelligence and Visualization Research Center, National Engineering Laboratory for Big Data Distribution and Exchange Technologies, Shanghai, China

Abstract. Multimodal relation extraction is essential for information extraction and knowledge graph construction. In social media, in some situations, text and images often lack relevance or have weak connections, which can mislead models. While many current approaches focus on modality alignment and fusion, they overlook the role of domain-specific modality in mitigating information bias. Moreover, significant gaps between modalities make it challenging to establish deep associative relationships. To tackle these challenges, we propose the Text-Guided Dual Interaction (TGDI) model, which incorporates a Modal Dual-Interaction mechanism. Specifically, the Cross-Modal Interaction module performs global level fusion to achieve initial alignment, while the Text-Oriented Interaction module refines this integration by preserving essential visual information under textual guidance. Additionally, the Text Modulated Matching Gate regulates visual contributions and evaluates image-text similarity to minimize visual noise. Finally, the fusion function adapts to various text-image scenarios, ensuring effective relation extraction. Extensive experiments on the Twitter dataset demonstrate that TGDI not only surpasses state-of-the-art baselines but also robustly suppresses the influence of irrelevant visual content in real-world multimodal settings.

Keywords: Multimodal relation extraction · Modality preference · Multimodal fusion · Cross-modal alignment

1 Introduction

In the era of big data, the vast amount of information available on the Internet presents significant challenges for data analysis and information extraction. Relation extraction is a crucial subtask within information extraction that effectively identifies structured data and valuable insights. This process advances search engine technology and enhances and enriches knowledge graphs. Text-based relation extraction has yielded excellent results in previous studies. Recently, there has been a substantial increase in text, visual, and audio content on social media. The vast surge in multimodal information benefits social media relation extraction, enabling public opinion monitoring, user relationship mining, and personalized content recommendations.

Therefore, multimodal relation extraction (MRE) has garnered increasing attention. MRE aims to classify the relationships between two given entities by utilizing visual information as supplementary evidence, thereby enhancing extraction performance. A notable characteristic of social media is the limited word count of text, resulting in concise messages that often provide few details and context. In contrast, visual content such as images and videos can provide essential background information, thereby enhancing the effectiveness of relation extraction. Previous work has extensively explored the alignment and fusion between images and text. The MEGA [25] model combines a parsed scene graph from the image with a syntactic dependency tree and textual semantics derived from the alignment of representations to learn mappings between visual and textual relationships. To fully leverage image information, most researchers use object images to align with the entity. Prior work has aimed to find correlations between entity-entity and object-object relationships [21], and explored alignment between entities and objects [6]. In addition, some studies [2] [12] leverage visual prefixes, such as object or image features, to enhance multimodal fusion. How to establish in-depth interactions among complex modality-specific semantic information and bridge the gap between modalities remains a long-term challenge that requires continuous efforts.

Another often-overlooked phenomenon is that many studies are based on the assumption that images and text are aligned. However, this is not always the case. Research data shows that images and text do not always correspond perfectly, with only 18.5% of cases where the text is already represented and the image provides additional information [15]. In Fig. 1, if the image and tweet are not highly relevant, visuals cannot provide rich supplementary information. Furthermore, in multimodal named entity recognition [7] [19], it has been observed that the performance of multimodal models is not always better than that of unimodal approaches. Researches in multimodal sentiment analysis [8] and [27] also indicate that the contributions of different modalities can vary significantly. While previous works have demonstrated good performance, MRE models often assign equal importance to text and images, even though different modalities should hold varying significance in social media. When the provided entity pairs are textual, excessive reliance on visual information can introduce visual bias.

Inspired by the above, this paper introduces an innovative Text-Guided Dual Interaction (TGDI) model designed for multimodal relation extraction in social media. The TGDI model focuses on filtering out unnecessary visual information, leveraging text guidance to enhance multimodal relation extraction. To achieve this, the Cross-Modal Interaction module conducts a global level fusion for initial alignment. Meanwhile, the Text-Oriented Interaction module refines this

Fig. 1. On Twitter, the relevance between text and images may vary. Here are two different scenarios: (a) High text-image relevance. When the text and image are highly relevant, visual information can serve as an auxiliary cue to aid relation extraction. In this case, the visual objects "a person and a trophy" correspond to the textual entities "Kobe Bryant" and "NBA MVP, facilitating the extraction of the textual relation "Awarded." (b) Low text-image relevance. The attached image simply shows a group of people dining at a restaurant, lacking any explicit Spanish food or cultural elements. The visual objects mainly consist of "person," which provides little help in identifying the "Held_on" relation between "theTaste" and "Spain."

process by preserving key visual information guided by the text. Additionally, the Text Modulated Matching Gate plays a crucial role in regulating the contributions of visual data and assessing image-text similarity to minimize any visual noise. Finally, the fusion function is adaptable to various text-image scenarios, paving the way for effective relation extraction. In summary, here are the main contributions of our paper:

- We propose a Text-Guided Dual Interaction (TGDI) model that takes text as the dominant modality and introduces a dual-interaction mechanism to capture fine-grained cross-modal features, adapting to varying degrees of text-image relevance.
- We design a Text Modulated Matching Gate to filter out irrelevant visual content, improving the alignment precision of multimodal relation extraction.
- We conduct extensive experiments on the Twitter dataset, demonstrating the effectiveness of TGDI and highlighting the importance of text dominance in MRE for social media contexts.

2 Related Work

Multimodal relation extraction is a key branch of information extraction that has garnered increasing attention in recent years. Particularly in social media, researchers have discovered that visual information can supplement the semantic details missing from the text, leading to significant improvements in extraction performance [26]. Chen et al. [2] designed a hierarchical multi-scaled visual representation as visual guidance for fusion, utilizing both object images and whole images as visual prefixes for each self-attention layer in BERT. Dai et al. [3] developed an image-text matching approach to enhance the model's ability to capture different semantic correspondences by constructing hard negatives for improvement. Li et al. [12] proposed two types of prefix tuning, entity-oriented prefix and object-oriented prefix, to integrate deeper associations between intra-modal and inter-modal data. They also designed a dual-gated fusion module that identifies and suppresses irrelevant interaction data through local and global visual contexts. Hu et al. [6] introduced a pretraining task for entity-object and relation-image alignment, extracting self-supervised signals from large numbers of unlabeled image-caption pairs and providing soft pseudo-labels to guide the pretraining process. Wu et al. [16] utilized visual and textual scene graph structures to represent input data, integrating them into a cross-modal graph. They refined the structure guided by the graph information bottleneck principle and introduced latent multimodal topic features to tackle the challenges of internal and external information utilization in multimodal relation extraction. Yuan et al. [21] identified correlations between object-object and entity-entity relationships and introduced an edge-enhanced graph alignment network that aligns nodes and edges across graphs to improve joint multimodal entity-relation extraction. Xu et al. [17] proposed a reinforcement learning-based data segmentation approach to determine whether social media posts are better suited for multimodal or unimodal models. Shen et al. [13] argued that previous methods overlooked textual information within images, resulting in performance degradation when handling text-intensive images. They incorporated cross-attention in the textual evidence integration process to extract entity-related information from image captions and OCR text.

Unlike the above studies, we treat different modalities unequally. We aim to explore modality preferences and guide modal interaction through the dominant textual modality. Additionally, we aim to correct the bias introduced by visual information.

3 Methodology

3.1 Problem Definition

Given a short sentence $T = \{t_1, t_2, \ldots, t_m\}$ that contains an entity pair (e_s, e_o) and associates with an image I. The main objective of MRE is to identify the semantic relationship $r \in R = \{r_1, r_2, \ldots, r_n\}$ between the entities. The process is defined as a function $F : (e_s, e_o, T, I) \to R$.

The overall architecture of TGDI for multimodal relation extraction in social media is illustrated in Fig. 2, with a detailed explanation of each module provided in the following section.

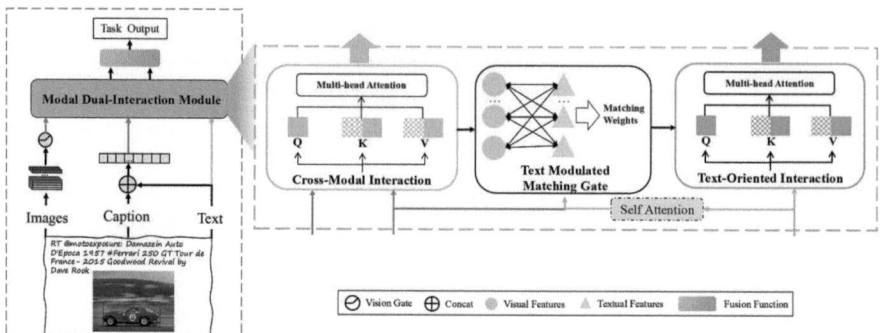

Fig. 2. The overall framework of our proposed TGDI introduces a modal dual-interaction module designed to minimize the interference of visual noise while preserving highly relevant fused features for textual relations. Additionally, we employ a result fusion function to accommodate different text-image relevance scenarios.

3.2 Feature Extraction

Visual Representation. Global image features mainly capture comprehensive information in the image, including abstract concepts such as scenes and themes. The objects typically refer to a specific entity and serve as key features in an image, making them well-aligned with textual entities. The object image $O = (o_1, o_2, \ldots, o_m)$ is obtained by extracting m salient objects from the entire image using the Visual Grounding Toolkit [18]. Combining both global and object image features can effectively leverage the potential value of visual modality. The vision transformer(ViT) [5] as the visual encoder, global image I and object image O are rescaled to 224×224 pixels and fed to ViT to obtain the hierarchical visual semantic representation as $V = \{V_0, V_1, \ldots, V_{12}\}, V_i \in \mathbb{R}^{n \times d}$. To ensure that the visual features obtained align with the structure of the textual information, we apply a mapping function to transform the visual features accordingly.

$$V_i = Conv_{(1 \times 1)}(MLP(Pool(V))), \tag{1}$$

where $Pool$ is a global average pooling layer that reduces the dimensions of visual features, then a 1×1 kernel size convolution module to align with textual features. The dynamic vision gate function generates i-th layer probability vector $g(l)$, which is applied to hierarchical global visual features to obtain the final visual features that match the i-th layers in the fusion model. Then we allocate visual information from different hierarchies to specific layers, enabling the effective fusion of information to enhance the model's text and image fusion capabilities. The vision gate is calculated as follows:

$$s^{(l)} = L(W_l(\frac{1}{c}\sum_{i=1}^{c} P(V_i))), \tag{2}$$

$$g^{(l)} = softmax(s^{(l)}), \tag{3}$$

where l denotes the index of each layer, L is activate function Leaky_ReLU, P denotes pooling layer. Then the final aggregated hierarchical visual feature V obtained with $g^{(l)}$ to match the l-th layer $V = g^{(l)}V^{(l)}$. Global visual features and object features are fused together as $\tilde{V}$ for subsequent steps.

Text Representation. Image captions serve as an essential source of information, helping models better understand the content of images and their relationship with text. Visual context can be directly integrated by utilizing captions to expand and enhance the original text, thereby reducing the semantic gap caused by differences in modalities across various spaces. Caption (C) generated by the image-to-text generation model of Bilp2 [9] extends the textual content and integrates comprehensive semantic information from the image, thereby offering rich background evidence for text. For text modality, we use BERT [4] as an encoder to obtain text representations. Each input includes text and caption as textual modal information $T_e = \{t_0, t_1, t_2, \ldots, t_m, t_{m+1}, t_{c1}, \ldots, t_{cn}, t_{cn+1}\}$, where t_0 represent begin token [CLS], t_{m+1} and t_{cn+1} represent end tokens [SEP], t_1 to t_m as the textual sequence, t_{c1} to t_{cn} as the caption sequence. Therefore, the enhanced textual representation of the input is obtained through BERT: $H_e = BERT(T_e)$. Similarly, the input text T is processed through BERT to obtain its representation $H = BERT(T)$.

3.3 Modal Dual-Interaction Module

To better align and integrate images and text, we propose a Modal Dual-Interaction module. Specifically, visual and textual information are fused at a global level through Cross-Modal Interaction (CMI). Subsequently, the Text Modulated Matching Gate computes matching weights based on both visual and textual features. The refined features, after mitigating visual bias, are fed into the Text-Oriented Interaction (TOI) module to generate well-aligned multimodal representations for relation extraction.

Cross-Modal Interaction. In multimodal fusion, hierarchical visual features are used as visual prompts appended with the textual sequence at each BERT attention layer, aiming to guide the fusion with layer-level textual representations. For input sequence T_e, the context representation of $H_e^{l-1} \in \mathbb{R}^{n \times d}$:

$$Q^l = H_e^{l-1} W_Q^l, K^l = H_e^{l-1} W_K^l, V^l = H_e^{l-1} W_V^l, \qquad (4)$$

W_Q^l, W_K^l, W_V^l are mapping parameters of attention. For the l-th visual representation, we use a linear transformation W_l^α to project $\tilde{V}^{(l)}$ into the same embedded space as the text representation to get the visual prompt vector:

$$\{\alpha_l^k, \alpha_l^v\} = \tilde{V}_l W_l^\alpha. \qquad (5)$$

The hidden features at the l-th layer of the fusion encoder based on CMI are calculated as:

$$f_1^l = softmax(\frac{Q^l[\alpha_l^k; K^l]^\top}{\sqrt{d}})[\alpha_l^v; V^l]. \qquad (6)$$

Text Modulated Matching Gate. The TMMG module enables a finer-grained computation of the similarity between each patch in an image and each token in the text. This module captures more precise local cross-modal alignment, enhancing the correspondence between modalities while reducing visual noise, thereby improving the accuracy of cross-modal matching. The textual representation H is then fed into a self-attention mechanism to capture the dependencies and syntactic relationships within the text, resulting in a deeper understanding of the textual information.

$$H_s = softmax(\frac{HW_Q(HW_K)^\top}{\sqrt{d}})HW_V, \tag{7}$$

where W_Q, W_K, and $W_V \in \mathbb{R}^{d \times d}$ are query, key, and value trainable weight matrices, respectively.

To minimize the impact of noise from irrelevant images, we regulate the contributions of visual information through a matching gate mechanism that assesses the matching degree between the image and the text. The Text Modulated Matching Gate between textual features $H_s \in \mathbb{R}^{b \times l \times d}$ and visual features $V \in \mathbb{R}^{b \times n \times d}$ is calculated as:

$$A = softmax(VH_s), \tag{8}$$
$$C' = AH_s, \tag{9}$$
$$m = M\left(\frac{1}{N}\sum_{i=1}^{N}[V; C'; V \odot C']\right), \tag{10}$$

where $\odot$ represents Hadamard product, $M(\cdot)$ is an MLP. Based on the similarity gate, we can obtain the final visual-aware fusion representations:

$$f_2 = m \odot f_1. \tag{11}$$

Tex-Oriented Interaction. In TOI, the textual features interact with the fusion representation obtained from above module, allowing the text to rectify any inaccurate fusion information. This process ultimately results in a text representation that effectively incorporates relevant visual content. For text representation of $H_s^{l-1} \in \mathbb{R}^{n \times d}$:

$$Q^l = H_s^{l-1}W_Q^l, K^l = H_s^{l-1}W_K^l, V^l = H_s^{l-1}W_V^l. \tag{12}$$

Then, f_2 is reshaped and split into key-value prefixes $\{\beta_l^k, \beta_l^v\}$ of each layer, enabling layer-specific injection of enhanced fusion context into the attention computation. And the hidden state at l-th layer of TOI is calculated as follows:

$$f_3^l = softmax(\frac{Q^l[\beta_l^k; K^l]^\top}{\sqrt{d}})[\beta_l^v; V^l]. \tag{13}$$

3.4 Result Fusion and Classification

Considering the varying amounts of information contained in the two interaction results, we design a weighted fusion function to merge them, yielding a more reliable output. The output f_3 from TOI is the primary foundation for adjustment. The core computational process can be stated as follows:

$$\mathbf{R} = \lambda \cdot f_3 + (1 - \lambda) \cdot f_1, \tag{14}$$

where $\lambda \in [0, 1]$. MRE aims to predict r when the input consists of a post T and an image I. Ultimately, the MRE loss equation is given below, where W and b are learnable parameters.

$$p(r|e_o, e_s, T) = softmax(W\mathbf{R} + b), \tag{15}$$
$$\mathcal{L} = -log(p(r|e_o, e_s, T)). \tag{16}$$

4 Experiments

4.1 Experiment Settings

Dataset and Evaluation Metrics. Regarding the dataset, we utilized MNRE[1] (see in Table 1) from Twitter to experiment, which comprises 9201 images and 30970 entities across 23 relations, with a split of 12247/1624/1614 samples for the train/validation/test sets. The metrics used in experiments include Accuracy (Acc%), Precision (P%), Recall (R%), and F1 score (F1%).

$$Acc = \frac{TP + TN}{TP + TN + FP + FN} \tag{17}$$

$$P = \frac{TP}{TP + FP} \tag{18}$$

$$R = \frac{TP}{TP + FN} \tag{19}$$

$$F1 = 2 \times \frac{P \times R}{P + R} \tag{20}$$

Table 1. The statistics of MNER dataset

Dataset	#Image	#Sentence	#Instance	#Entity	#Relation
MNRE	9201	9201	15485	30970	23

---

[1] The dataset is available at https://github.com/thecharm/MNRE.

Experiments Setup. Our model, which utilizes PyTorch 2.0.0, is trained on a NVIDIA RTX A6000 GPU. All input images are resized to a standard resolution of 224×224 pixels. Both visual and textual modalities are transformed into 768-dimensional hidden representations through CLIP-ViT-B/32 and BERT-base-uncased, respectively. We employ the AdamW optimizer with a learning rate of 3e-5 and a batch size of 16. The number of object images (m) is set to 3. The hyperparameter λ is set to 0.5 to balance the fusion strategy. To mitigate overfitting, we apply a dropout rate of 0.01 during training.

Baselines. We compare our model with well-known MRE baselines as follows:
- **Text Baseline:**
  1. Glove + CNN [23]: A CNN-based model for relation extraction.
  2. PCNN [22]: A distantly supervised model that uses external knowledge graphs to assign labels to sentences containing the same entities automatically.
  3. MTB [14]: A relation extraction model that enhances BERT pre-training by incorporating entity masking.
- **Multimodal Baseline:**
  1. VisualBERT [11]: A pre-trained visual-language model for capturing rich semantics in images and associated text.
  2. UMT [20]: A unified multimodal transformer integrating a multimodal interaction module and an entity span detection module for prediction.
  3. UMGF [24]: A unified multimodal graph framework capturing multimodal semantic relationships via graph-based fusion layers.
  4. BERT + SG [25]: Combines fine-tuned BERT representations with visual features extracted from a pre-trained scene graph (SG).
  5. BERT + SG + Att [25]: Incorporates an attention mechanism to compute semantic similarity between visual graphs and textual contents.
  6. MEGA [25]: A multimodal neural network with efficient graph alignment, considering the structural similarity and semantic agreement between visual and textual graphs.
  7. IFAformer [10]: A dual-transformer architecture introducing a visual prefix for modal fusion to reduce sensitivity to errors.
  8. HVPNeT [2]: A hierarchical visual prefix fusion network leveraging hierarchical visual features to alleviate error sensitivity from irrelevant images.
  9. MKGformer [1]: Employs a correlation-aware fusion module to mitigate the impact of noisy information.

4.2 Overall Results

Main Results. The experimental results demonstrate that our model outperforms the baseline across all metrics, validating the effectiveness of our approach, as shown in Table 2. Notably, the following points deserve attention: First, not all multimodal methods outperform unimodal methods; however, it is undeniable that images can effectively enhance certain context information in social media. Second, while the MEGA model attempts to leverage image and text alignment through parsed scene graphs, we observed that irrelevant images often introduce visual noise. TGDI enhances performance by minimizing noise and facilitating deep interaction between the two modalities. Finally, compared to models HVP-NeT, MKGformer, and IFAformer, which also focus on reducing visual error sensitivity, TGDI prioritizes text-oriented relational extraction while decreasing visual bias. This strategy enhances performance and highlights the critical role of text modality in extraction within social media contexts.

Table 2. Performance comparison of previous SOTA baseline models for multimodal RE on MNRE dataset

Modal	Methods	Precision	Recall	F1
Text	Glove + CNN	57.81	46.25	51.39
	PCNN	62.85	49.69	55.49
	MTB	64.46	57.81	60.86
Multimodal	VisualBERT	57.15	59.48	58.30
	BERT + SG	62.95	62.65	62.80
	BERT + SG + Att	60.97	66.56	63.64
	UMT	62.93	63.88	63.46
	UMGF	64.38	66.23	65.29
	MEGA	64.51	68.44	66.41
	IFAformer	82.59	80.78	81.67
	HVPNeT	83.64	80.78	81.85
	MKGformer	82.67	81.25	81.95
	TGDI	**84.18**	**83.13**	**83.65**
Ablation	w/o caption	83.86	82.81	83.33
	w/o TMMG	83.36	83.75	83.55
	w/o CMI	81.75	81.87	81.81
	w/o TOI	82.28	81.25	81.76
	w/o R	81.75	81.88	81.81

At the same time, Fig. 3 compares extraction accuracy across several models, clearly indicating that TGDI achieves the highest accuracy. Unlike the coarse-grained fusion between modalities, our model fully leverages modality information through deep interactions and text-oriented corrections. It strategically integrates representations from the two interaction modules, considering the extraction results under varying scenarios.

Ablation Study. To assess the contribution of each module to MRE, we conducted an ablation study using consistent parameters to confirm their effectiveness. Specifically, we removed the following components: "image caption," "Text Modulated Matching Gate," "Cross-Modal Interaction," "Text-Oriented Interaction," and "Fusion Function," represented as "w/o caption," "w/o TMMG," "w/o CMI," "w/o TOI," and "w/o R". The detailed results are shown in Table 2.

After removing the caption, Precision, Recall, and F1 each decreased by 0.32%. This suggests that captions are a direct means of incorporating visual information into the textual modality. By doing so, they help bridge the semantic gap between modalities, reducing the impact of modality differences on performance. The decline in Precision and F1 for the TMMG highlights its primary function of assessing the relevance between images and texts. Without CMI in result fusion, all metrics show a noticeable decline, indicating that visual information is an important component that provides supplementary visual cues. In removing the TOI, Recall decreased by 1.88% and F1 by 1.89%, demonstrating that global level fusion of image and text yields poor results. Regarding the result fusion function R, using the TOI output representation for extraction directly results in a decrease in Precision by 2.43%, Recall by 1.25%, and F1 by 1.84%. This decline suggests that integrating results from different interaction levels helps combine perspectives from relevant and irrelevant scenarios, leading to more stable and robust outcomes.

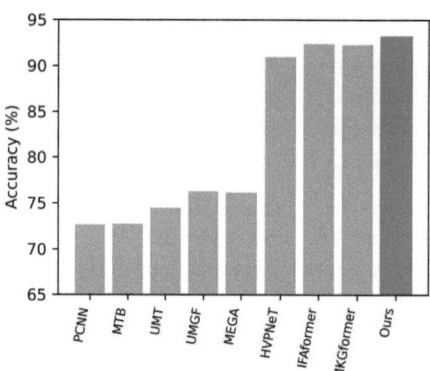

Fig. 3. Comparison extraction accuracy of different models.

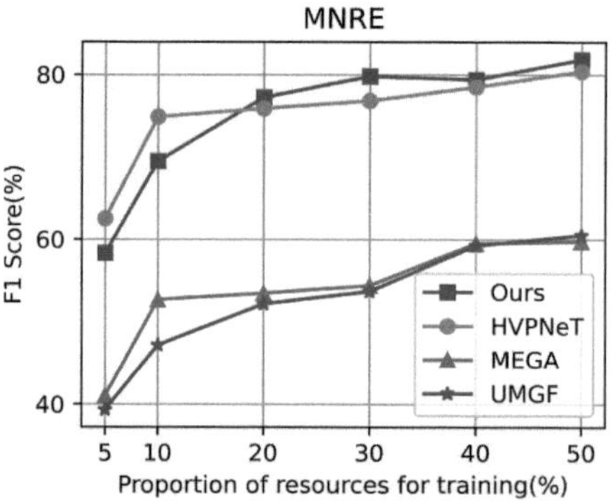

Fig. 4. Performances on low-resource setting on MNER.

Analysis. Based on our analysis, we conclude that deep interaction and fine-grained fusion between text and images are essential, confirming the dominant role of the text modality. Captions enhance the contextual information of images, reduce ambiguity, and minimize visual bias. Furthermore, the lack of sufficient interaction between images and text necessitates a more profound fusion. TOI can effectively improve this interaction, align text with image information, and demonstrate its effectiveness in a text-oriented manner. Reducing visual noise minimizes visual bias, leading to more accurate fusion outcomes. Because irrelevant images and text are often shared on social media, the TMMG helps balance these relationships in multimodal fusion, enabling better control of visual information and reducing excessive noise, which enhances detail in interactions. Regarding result fusion, the decrease in values indicates that the fusion of results from two different interaction levels can combine outcomes from both learning phases. It ensures that suitable image information is fully fused while preventing mismatched image-text pairs from interfering with the extraction results, thus avoiding unstable interaction fluctuations and resulting in more stable and robust outcomes.

4.3 Case Study and Discussion

Performance on Categories. Compared with HVPNeT, our model achieves significant performance improvements in most of the six main categories of the MNRE test set (Table 3). It effectively integrates both text and visual content. For categories like "person," where clear objects are present, the text aligns well with the images, allowing relevant visual information to aid in relation extraction. In contrast, for categories such as "location," "organization," and certain "misc" types that do not correspond to regional images, our model relies more on textual information to make accurate judgments.

Table 3. Our results compared with HVPNeT on the six main categories of the test set (HVPNeT results are based on our reproduction).

Category	Count	HVPNeT(F1.)	TGDI(F1.)
/per/per/peer	156	88.96	91.69
/per/org/member_of	110	80.33	83.70
/loc/loc/contain	99	93.88	96.55
/per/misc/present_in	74	75.00	83.69
/org/loc/locate_at	46	85.06	83.72
/per/loc/place_of_residence	29	63.16	64.41

Low Resource. We conducted experiments in low-resource settings, randomly sampling 5% to 50% from the original training set in a low-resource scenario. Figure 4 shows a comparison of our model with several baselines. It is clear that in most low-resource scenarios, reducing visual noise can effectively mitigate bias and yield better results. However, when the training set is particularly small, excessive reliance on textual information can lead to a significant loss of contextual background, resulting in poorer performance.

High relevance

Sentence: RT @Bellagio: No pool day is complete without gelato. Photo by Instagram user Shooo_matcha.

Caption: a green ice cream sitting on a table next to a pool

Relation: /per/org/member_of

Ours: ✓

Medium relevance

Sentence: RT @France3MidiPy: Montauban: les Gilets Jaunes lancent leur web radio

Caption: a close up of a microphone and some cables

Relation: /org/loc/locate_at

Ours: ✓

Low relevance

Sentence: RT @Ravens: We feel the need, the need IV Snead @Willie_Snead4 G

Caption: baltimore ravens wide receiver jimmy graham catches a pass during practice

Relation: /per/org/member_of

Ours: ✓

Fig. 5. A selection of image-text pairs with varying relevance is analyzed, including images and text from Twitter, a similarity heatmap between the text and the image, a caption generated from the image, and predefined relationship labels between entities. (Red represents the head entity, while blue represents the tail entity.) (Color figure online)

Case Study. To validate our model, we selected several relevant image-text pairs for analysis in the MNRE task (Fig. 5). In these image-text posts, excessive visual information can mislead the model, resulting in incorrect predictions and interfering with judgment. Building on our previous analyses, this finding reinforces that abundant visual information does not always lead to better model performance; instead, it can introduce noise and hinder accurate predictions. This highlights the importance of our proposed text-guided approach, prioritizing textual information to effectively integrate visual cues, ensuring a more reliable and meaningful multimodal representation.

5 Conclusion

In this paper, we propose the Text-Guided Dual Interaction Multimodal Relation Extraction (TGDI) model to address the weak correlation between text and images in social media relation extraction. At its core, TGDI employs a Modal Dual-Interaction mechanism. The interaction module consists of a Cross-Modal Interaction, which performs global fusion of text and image features, and a Text-Oriented Interaction, which eliminates irrelevant visual information, reduces visual noise, and enhances the relevance of visually perceptive text representations. And the Text Modulated Matching Gate regulates visual contributions and evaluates image-text similarity to minimize visual noise. To effectively integrate the outcomes of both modules, we introduce a fusion function that balances predictions based on image-text alignment and those relying solely on textual information. Extensive experiments demonstrate that TGDI significantly improves relation extraction performance, highlighting the effectiveness of our approach.

6 Limitations

Our model focuses on low text-image relevance and is text-dominant, evaluated on a single benchmark dataset. Its performance may be restricted in multimodal applications where text and image correlation is high, and visual information supplements text. We will explore this in future work.

References

1. Chen, X., et al.: Hybrid transformer with multi-level fusion for multimodal knowledge graph completion. In: Proceedings of the 45th International ACM SIGIR Conference on Research and Development in Information Retrieval, pp. 904–915 (2022)
2. Chen, X., et al.: Good visual guidance make a better extractor: hierarchical visual prefix for multimodal entity and relation extraction. In: Findings of the Association for Computational Linguistics: NAACL 2022, Seattle, United States, pp. 1607–1618. Association for Computational Linguistics (2022). https://doi.org/10.18653/v1/2022.findings-naacl.121
3. Dai, Y., Gao, F., Zeng, D.: An alignment and matching network with hierarchical visual features for multimodal named entity and relation extraction. In: Luo, B., Cheng, L., Wu, Z.G., Li, H., Li, C. (eds.) ICONIP 2023. LNCS, vol. 1966, pp. 298–310. Springer, Cham (2023). https://doi.org/10.1007/978-981-99-8148-9_24
4. Devlin, J.: Bert: pre-training of deep bidirectional transformers for language understanding. arXiv preprint arXiv:1810.04805 (2018)
5. Dosovitskiy, A.: An image is worth 16x16 words: transformers for image recognition at scale. arXiv preprint arXiv:2010.11929 (2020)
6. Hu, X., Chen, J., Liu, A., Meng, S., Wen, L., Yu, P.S.: Prompt me up: unleashing the power of alignments for multimodal entity and relation extraction. In: Proceedings of the 31st ACM International Conference on Multimedia, pp. 5185–5194 (2023)

7. Jia, M., et al.: MNER-QG: an end-to-end MRC framework for multimodal named entity recognition with query grounding. In: Proceedings of the AAAI Conference on Artificial Intelligence, pp. 8032–8040 (2023)
8. Lei, Y., Yang, D., Li, M., Wang, S., Chen, J., Zhang, L.: Text-oriented modality reinforcement network for multimodal sentiment analysis from unaligned multimodal sequences. In: Fang, L., Pei, J., Zhai, G., Wang, R. (eds.) CICAI 2023. LNCS, vol. 14474, pp. 189–200. Springer, Cham (2023). https://doi.org/10.1007/978-981-99-9119-8_18
9. Li, J., Li, D., Savarese, S., Hoi, S.: Blip-2: bootstrapping language-image pretraining with frozen image encoders and large language models. In: International Conference on Machine Learning, pp. 19730–19742. PMLR (2023)
10. Li, L., Chen, X., Qiao, S., Xiong, F., Chen, H., Zhang, N.: On analyzing the role of image for visual-enhanced relation extraction (student abstract). In: Proceedings of the AAAI Conference on Artificial Intelligence, pp. 16254–16255 (2023)
11. Li, L.H., Yatskar, M., Yin, D., Hsieh, C.J., Chang, K.W.: Visualbert: a simple and performant baseline for vision and language. arXiv preprint arXiv:1908.03557 (2019)
12. Li, Q., Guo, S., Ji, C., Peng, X., Cui, S., Li, J.: Dual-gated fusion with prefix-tuning for multi-modal relation extraction. arXiv preprint arXiv:2306.11020 (2023)
13. Shen, Q., Lin, H., Liu, H., Lin, Z., Wang, W.: Watch and read! a visual relation-aware and textual evidence enhanced model for multimodal relation extraction. In: 2024 27th International Conference on Computer Supported Cooperative Work in Design (CSCWD), pp. 2491–2496 (2024)
14. Soares, L.B., FitzGerald, N., Ling, J., Kwiatkowski, T.: Matching the blanks: distributional similarity for relation learning. arXiv preprint arXiv:1906.03158 (2019)
15. Vempala, A., Preoţiuc-Pietro, D.: Categorizing and inferring the relationship between the text and image of twitter posts. In: Proceedings of the 57th Annual Meeting of the Association for Computational Linguistics, pp. 2830–2840 (2019)
16. Wu, S., Fei, H., Cao, Y., Bing, L., Chua, T.S.: Information screening whilst exploiting! multimodal relation extraction with feature denoising and multimodal topic modeling. arXiv preprint arXiv:2305.11719 (2023)
17. Xu, B., Huang, S., Du, M., Wang, H., Song, H., Sha, C., Xiao, Y.: Different data, different modalities! reinforced data splitting for effective multimodal information extraction from social media posts. In: Proceedings of the 29th International Conference on Computational Linguistics, pp. 1855–1864 (2022)
18. Yang, Z., Gong, B., Wang, L., Huang, W., Yu, D., Luo, J.: A fast and accurate one-stage approach to visual grounding. In: Proceedings of the IEEE/CVF International Conference on Computer Vision, pp. 4683–4693 (2019)
19. Yu, J., Jiang, J., Yang, L., Xia, R.: Improving multimodal named entity recognition via entity span detection with unified multimodal transformer. In: Proceedings of the 58th Annual Meeting of the Association for Computational Linguistics, pp. 3342–3352. Association for Computational Linguistics (2020)
20. YU, J., JIANG, J., YANG, L., XIA, R.: Improving multimodal named entity recognition via entity span detection with unified multimodal transformer. In: Proceedings of the 58th Annual Meeting of the Association for Computational Linguistics, pp. 3342–3352 (2020)
21. Yuan, L., Cai, Y., Wang, J., Li, Q.: Joint multimodal entity-relation extraction based on edge-enhanced graph alignment network and word-pair relation tagging. In: Proceedings of the AAAI Conference on Artificial Iintelligence, pp. 11051–11059 (2023)

22. Zeng, D., Liu, K., Chen, Y., Zhao, J.: Distant supervision for relation extraction via piecewise convolutional neural networks. In: Proceedings of the 2015 Conference on Empirical Methods in Natural Language Processing, pp. 1753–1762 (2015)
23. Zeng, D., Liu, K., Lai, S., Zhou, G., Zhao, J.: Relation classification via convolutional deep neural network. In: Proceedings of COLING 2014, the 25th International Conference on Computational Linguistics: Technical Papers, pp. 2335–2344 (2014)
24. Zhang, D., Wei, S., Li, S., Wu, H., Zhu, Q., Zhou, G.: Multi-modal graph fusion for named entity recognition with targeted visual guidance. In: Proceedings of the AAAI Conference on artificial intelligence, pp. 14347–14355 (2021)
25. Zheng, C., Feng, J., Fu, Z., Cai, Y., Li, Q., Wang, T.: Multimodal relation extraction with efficient graph alignment. In: Proceedings of the 29th ACM International Conference on Multimedia, pp. 5298–5306 (2021)
26. Zheng, C., Wu, Z., Feng, J., Fu, Z., Cai, Y.: MNRE: a challenge multimodal dataset for neural relation extraction with visual evidence in social media posts. In: 2021 IEEE International Conference on Multimedia and Expo (ICME), pp. 1–6 (2021). https://doi.org/10.1109/ICME51207.2021.9428274
27. Zhou, M., Quan, W., Zhou, Z., Wang, K., Wang, T., Yan, D.M.: TCAN: text-oriented cross attention network for multimodal sentiment analysis. arXiv preprint arXiv:2404.04545 (2024)

Time Series

Time Series

MotiPlus and MotiSet: Discovering the Best Set of Motiflets in Time Series

Len Feremans[1]($\boxtimes$), Patrick Schäfer[2], and Wannes Meert[3]

[1] Department of Computer Science, University of Antwerp, Antwerpen, Belgium
len.feremans@uantwerpen.be
[2] Department of Computer Science, Humboldt-Universität zu Berlin, Berlin, Germany
patrick.schaefer@hu-berlin.de
[3] Department of Computer Science, KU Leuven, Leuven, Belgium
wannes.meert@kuleuven.be

Abstract. Motif discovery algorithms find repeating patterns in time series with high similarity. Many methods exist for this important task, which has numerous applications. This work is guided by the following two ambitious questions: What is the "perfect" motif? What is the "perfect" set of motifs? To answer the first question, we consider all motifs of a certain size and rank them based on a robust measure of similarity. To determine the optimal size of a motif, we assess the quality of a motif relative to a lattice of sub- and supermotifs and define two novel quality constraints. To answer the second question, we balance multiple contrastive quality criteria for a set of motifs. The set of motifs should be diverse, non-redundant, and include highly similar motifs of varying sizes. Due to the exponential search space, the exact search for the best motif and set of motifs is a major concern. We leverage the lattice structure of time series and prune most candidate motifs and sets of motifs. For discovering a set of motifs, we propose two variations. The first is based on a greedy search and filters using the aforementioned quality constraints. The second algorithm is based on A* search, by directly measuring the quality of thousands of candidate sets of motifs. We evaluate our method qualitatively on music datasets and quantitatively on a time series motif discovery benchmark. The proposed algorithms achieve state-of-the-art results, improving precision by 27.9% and recall by 10.1% over LoCoMotif, and significantly outperforming strong baselines like GrammarViz, MMotif, and Motiflets.

1 Introduction

Time series (TS) consist of sequences of continuous values that are typically recorded over time. In the last two decades, research has focused on the automatic discovery of motifs, i.e. identifying a set of repeating subsequences in

Supplementary Information The online version contains supplementary material available at https://doi.org/10.1007/978-3-032-06109-6_27.

TS [8]. Motif discovery algorithms efficiently enumerate frequently occurring patterns and provide these insights to experts, enhancing interpretability in AI systems. Furthermore, motifs are used for downstream tasks such as TS clustering, classification, segmentation, and anomaly detection, and have applications in smart devices, financial monitoring, healthcare, studying natural phenomena in astronomy, and more [1,3]. Unlike clustering, motif discovery does not aim to comprehensively describe the entire TS; instead, it seeks to identify multiple relevant patterns, distinguishing them from the remaining TS. Many motif discovery algorithms have been proposed. A natural trade-off arises between reporting a few large (i.e., frequently repeating) motifs with lower similarity and many smaller motifs with higher similarity. Evaluating a single method is challenging because changing hyperparameters produces multiple alternative sets of motifs. A common practice is to perform a qualitative evaluation, however authors can cherry-pick parameters and present favorable examples of motifs on only a few TS. Recently, a benchmark and evaluation measure for comparing motif discovery methods was introduced, the *tsmd-benchmark* [15]. It provides a more comprehensive evaluation than existing metrics, and more challenging benchmark than earlier ones. The authors compare 11 different methods based on F1-score, precision, and recall across 14 datasets. They find that LOCOMOTIF performs best, followed by MOTIFLETS, MMOTIF, and GRAMMARVIZ [6,13,14].

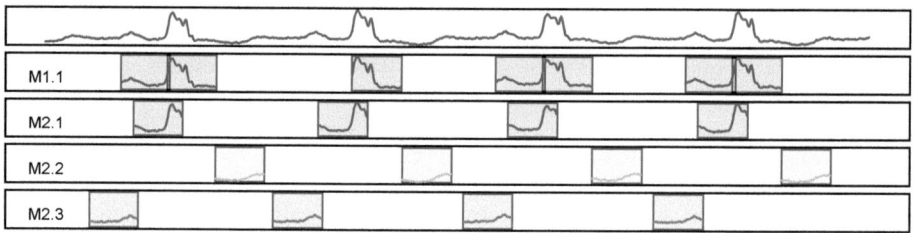

Fig. 1. An example of motifs discovered by MOTIFLETS and MOTIPLUS. MOTIFLETS identifies a single motiflet of size 7 (M1.1), which lacks self-sufficiency and should be split. In contrast, MOTIPLUS finds three similar local motiflets of size 4 (M2.1–3), which Motiflets cannot detect due to its one-motif-per-size limitation.

In this context, we introduce two novel algorithms for identifying a high-quality set of highly similar motifs: MOTIPLUS and MOTISET. Both methods address the limitation that most motif discovery methods rely on heuristics and identify only a single set of motifs. Depending on the parameter settings and heuristics used, the quality and robustness of the resulting set can vary significantly. MOTIPLUS and MOTISET first identify local motiflets, which are motifs of a certain size with the highest overall similarity. We define two key quality constraints for motifs: k-closedness and self-sufficiency. Both constraints help determining the correct size of the motifs. Specifically, if adding a subsequence leads to only a minor increase in similarity, the motif is not k-closed. Likewise, if a motif can be decomposed into two distinguishable smaller motifs, it is not self-sufficient. MOTIPLUS uses greedy search and in Fig. 1 we present an example output of MOTIPLUS and MOTIFLETS [12]. MOTISET searches for the optimal set of motifs thereby evaluating thousands of candidate sets using A* search [4]. Using A* search, we prioritize sets of motifs with the highest value, allowing us to stop MOTISET at any time and report the best solution found so far. We compute the value by balancing high intra-motif similarity with low inter-motif similarity. In the search for the "perfect" motif and the "perfect" motif size, a major challenge is the *exponential* size of the search space. Given n subsequences of length l in a time series, there are n^k possible motifs of size k. For sets of motifs, the search space is even larger, with $n^{k \cdot m}$ possible sets of motifs of size m. We design efficient algorithms that leverage the *lattice* structure of the time series to prune most candidate motifs and sets of motifs, reducing the number of possibilities by an order of magnitude. In summary, we make the following key contributions:

- We identify the best motifs, referred to as *local motiflets*, which are defined as motifs with the highest local similarity, measured by *extent*. Additionally, we introduce two new quality constraints, *k-closedness* and *self-sufficiency*, to select the best motif of varying size.
- We present a tighter *approximate* algorithm and a more efficient *exact* algorithm to discover high-quality motifs.
- We introduce a novel greedy algorithm, MOTIPLUS, which efficiently identifies the top-m non-redundant motifs across various motif sizes.
- We develop a novel A*-based algorithm MOTISET that *optimizes* the selection of a diverse, non-redundant motif set with high intra-motif and low inter-motif similarity.
- We conduct a case study on music datasets and find that MOTIPLUS identifies more motifs with higher similarity, and outperforms existing motif discovery methods on detecting repeating lyrical segments.
- We demonstrate that MOTIPLUS and MOTISET achieve state-of-the-art accuracy on the *tsmd-benchmark*, attaining the highest F1 score, precision, and recall [15].

The paper is organized as follows. Section 2 reviews related work; Sect. 3 introduces preliminaries. Sections 4 and 5 describe MOTIPLUS and MOTISET, respectively. Section 6 presents the experimental evaluation, and Sect. 7 concludes.

2 Related Work

Challenges addressed by recent motif discovery methods include: (i) eliminating hyperparameters, such as the length and distance thresholds, (ii) reporting varying-length motifs, (iii) reporting larger motifs instead of motif pairs, (iv) adopting alternatives to Euclidean distance, such as Dynamic Time Warping, and (v) clustering motifs to increase accuracy. Recent motif discovery methods include MMOTIF, GRAMMARVIZ, MOTIFLETS, LOCOMOTIF, SNIPPETS, HIME, SWAMP, SPIKELET, VALMOD, and FRM-MINER [1,6,11–14]. Many motif discovery methods have complementary quality objectives and definitions of motif representations, which makes it difficult to compare all methods.

GRAMMARVIZ, EMMA, and FRM-MINER first convert TS to discrete sequences and use discrete pattern mining to enumerate candidate motifs [11,13]. Discretisation can impede the exact discovery of high-quality continuous motifs and require carefully selection of parameters such as alphabet size and word length. Many recent methods are based on the Matrix Profile [17]. MMOTIF finds the most similar subsequence pairs under z-normalized Euclidean distance (z-ED) [6,8]. Next, larger motifs are created by selecting all subsequences within a specified radius. MOTIFLETS searches for the top-1 motif, or motiflet, with the lowest extent while varying the size of the motif. A disadvantage of MOTIFLETS is that it discovers fewer motifs and does not search recursively for non-redundant motifs. More recently, LOCOMOTIF proposed discovering varying-length motifs using Dynamic Time Warping. A disadvantage of LOCOMOTIF and MMOTIF is that they are sensitive to the similarity or distance threshold parameter, which leads to variability in the quality of the resulting set of motifs.

MOTIPLUS is related to MMOTIF because we perform a recursive search, thereby excluding regions in the TS covered by previously discovered motifs. MOTIPLUS is also related to the TS clustering that uses Minimum Description Length to evaluate motifs during search [10]. However, the self-sufficiency measure is not based on information theory. The concept of closed motifs was defined earlier, but relates motifs of different subsequence lengths, not of different sizes [9]. MOTIPLUS and MOTISET both search for motifs with low extent, similar to MOTIFLETS. Our algorithm for finding the exact motiflet is related to frequent pattern mining in transaction databases, such as APRIORI and ECLAT [18]. In contrast to the aforementioned greedy motif discovery methods, MOTISET evaluates many possible sets of motifs. The proposed value function is related to clustering algorithms such as K-MEANS and DBSCAN. However, we consider a variable number of clusters and do not aim to cluster all points in the TS [2,5].

3 Background and Definitions

In this section, we introduce some background terminology for time series analysis and motif discovery.

3.1 Time Series and Motifs

A continuous *time series* T is a sequence of n real-valued measurements $(x_1, x_2, \ldots, x_n)$. A *subsequence* $T_{i,l} = (x_i, x_{i+1}, \ldots, x_{i+l-1})$ consists of l measurements starting at index i. A subsequence $T_{i,l}$ overlaps, or *trivially matches*, another subsequence $T_{j,l}$ if $\lceil i - l \cdot \alpha \rceil \leq j \leq \lceil i + l \cdot \alpha \rceil$ where $\alpha \in [0,1]$. By default, we set $\alpha = 0.5$, ignoring subsequences that share more than $l/2$ values. We enumerate all subsequences using a sliding window of size l over T, denoted as $P^l = \{T_{i,l} \mid 1 \leq i \leq n - l + 1\}$. The *normalized Euclidean distance* between two subsequences $T_{i,l}$ and $T_{j,l}$, with means μ and standard deviations σ, is:

$$z\text{-}ED(T_{i,l}, T_{j,l}) = \sqrt{\sum_{t=1}^{l} \left(\frac{x_{i+t-1} - \mu_i}{\sigma_i + \epsilon} - \frac{x_{j+t-1} - \mu_j}{\sigma_j + \epsilon} \right)^2}.$$

where we add ϵ to the denominator to avoid division by zero. Given a TS T and length l, a *motif* S_k is a subset of k non-overlapping subsequences, i.e., $S_k = \{T_{i_1,l}, T_{i_2,l}, \ldots, T_{i_k,l}\} \subseteq \mathcal{P}(P^l)$, where $k \geq 2$. We note that there are $\hat{n} = n - l + 1$ subsequences and $\hat{n}^k$ motifs of size k, assuming trivial matching subsequences are ignored.

3.2 Motiflets

We search for the most similar motif of a given size and provide the following relevant definitions from MOTIFLETS [12]. The main idea behind MOTIFLETS is straightforward: it searches for motiflets of varying sizes up to k_{max} and selects the maximal motiflets, typically fewer than three.

Definition 1. *Extent: The extent of a motif S_k with motif length l is defined as the maximum pairwise distance between any two subsequences in S_k, i.e., extent(S_k) = $max(\{z\text{-}ED(T_{i,l}, T_{j,l}) \mid (T_{i,l}, T_{j,l}) \in S_k \times S_k\})$.*

The extent measures the cluster diameter in normalized space and is at most twice the radius to a subsequence, where the radius is the large distance between a selected subsequence (the core) and other subsequences.

Definition 2. *k-motiflet: A k-motiflet is the motif of size k with the lowest extent: S_k is the k-motiflet $\iff \nexists S'_k \subseteq \mathcal{P}(P^l) : extent(S'_k) < extent(S_k)$.*

The extent function is used to compare motiflets of different sizes and to tune the motif length l.

Definition 3. *Extent function: Given a TS T and length l, let S_k be the k-motiflet. The extent function of T is defined as $EF(k) = extent(S_k)$ where $k \geq 2$, i.e. $EF^l = extent(S_2^l), extent(S_3^l), \ldots, extent(S_{k_{max}}^l)$.*

Definition 4. *A k-motiflet is maximal if there is an elbow point at k in the EF:*

$$elbow(k) = \frac{EF(k+1) - EF(k) + \epsilon}{EF(k) - EF(k-1) + \epsilon} > \beta.$$

Here, ϵ is a small constant used to prevent division by zero, and β is a hyperparameter that governs the sensitivity of detecting elbow points, which we set to 1 by default.

4 MotiPlus: Discovering the Top-m Motifs in Time Series

In this section, we define the desirable properties of motifs and sets of motifs. Next, we introduce MOTIPLUS, a greedy algorithm designed to discover a set of m motifs. Finally, we present both an approximate and an exact algorithm for identifying motifs with the highest local similarity.

4.1 Desirable Properties Motifs and Set of Motifs

We define the optimal motifs as local motiflets, which have the smallest extent among all non-redundant motifs. Next, we introduce a quality constraint on a motif and examine whether adding or removing a subsequence affects its similarity, i.e., whether the motif is *k-closed*. Additionally, we check if a motif can be decomposed into smaller submotifs, each with higher similarity, i.e., if the motif is *self-sufficient*. These concepts are illustrated in Fig. 2.

Definition 5. *Local k-motiflet: Given a candidate motif S_k and a set of motifs $\mathbf{S}$, S_k is the local k-motiflet if it has the lowest extent of all non-redundant motifs:*

$$S_k \in \mathcal{C}_k \text{ is the local } k\text{-motiflet} \iff \nexists S'_k \in \mathcal{C}_k : extent(S'_k) < extent(S_k) \text{ where}$$
$$\mathcal{C}_k = \{S_i | S_i \in \mathcal{P}(P^l) \land |S_i| = k \land \text{not-redundant}(S_i, \mathbf{S})\}$$

Two motifs S_i and S_j are redundant if a subsequence $T_{k,l} \in S_i$ trivially matches with any subsequence in S_j.

We note that a known *blind spot* in MOTIFLETS is that it discovers only a single highly similar motif repeating k times. A second goal is to determine the optimal size of a motif.

Definition 6. *Submotif and supermotif: For a motif, we define a submotif $S' \subset S_k$ of $S_k = \{T_{i_1,l}, \ldots, T_{i_k,l}\}$ as any proper subset of subsequences. Likewise, we define a supermotif as any proper superset.*

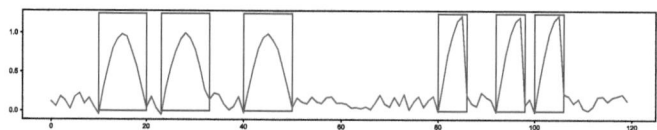

Fig. 2. A synthetic TS with two motifs, each of size 3, in red and green. Both motifs are local motiflets, i.e. the green motif has the lowest extent, and the red non-redundant motif the second lowest extent. Both motifs are k-closed, i.e. the extent increases significantly upon any addition of a non-trivially matching subsequence. Finally, we note that the union of both motifs of size 6 is k-closed, but not self-sufficient. (Color figure online)

Definition 7. *Maximal submotif and supermotif: The maximal supermotif S_{k+1} of a motif S_k is the supermotif with the lowest extent. Formally, $S_k \subset S_{k+1}$ is maximal $\iff \nexists S'_{k+1} : S_k \subset S'_{k+1} \land extent(S'_{k+1}) < extent(S_{k+1})$. A similar definition holds for submotifs.*

By suppressing motifs that are not k-closed, we avoid reporting motifs that are either too small or too large, as illustrated in Fig. 2.

Definition 8. *k-closed: A motif S_k is k-closed if there is a maximal submotif S_{k-1} and maximal supermotif S_{k+1} such that*

$$elbow(S_k) = \frac{extent(S_{k+1}) - extent(S_k) + \epsilon}{extent(S_k) - extent(S_{k-1}) + \epsilon} > \beta.$$

Another issue, illustrated in Figs. 1 and 2, occurs when motif discovery methods mistakenly combine discernible smaller motifs into a single supermotif. Therefore, we define self-sufficient motifs, inspired by a quality measure used in discrete pattern mining [16].

Definition 9. *Self-sufficient motif: A motif S of size 4 or higher is self-sufficient if there is no partitioning of S into two disjoint subsets $S = S_A \cup S_B$ of size 2 or higher such that $extent(S_A) + extent(S_B) < extent(S)$.*

To verify self-sufficient motifs, we use an approximate solution based on the *Minimum Spanning Tree* (MST). The MST is a tree where each of the k subsequences in a motif represents a node, and the k nodes are connected by adding edges with the smallest distances. Using the MST enables efficient enumeration of partitions consisting of two submotifs with high similarity. A limitation of using the MST for verifying self-sufficiency is that it may result in *false positives*, where a motif that is not self-sufficient is erroneously included in the discovered set of motifs. The algorithm for verifying self-sufficiency is described in the Appendix. Finally, the task of enumerating the top-m non-redundant motifs within a TS is defined as follows:

Definition 10. *Top-m enumeration: Given a TS T, a top-m enumeration aims to identify the top-m set of non-redundant motifs $\mathbf{S} = \{S_1, S_2, \ldots, S_m\}$, having high similarity.*

4.2 Enumerating Top-M Motifs in a Time Series

In this section, we define MOTIPLUS, a greedy algorithm for discovering the m best motifs. The algorithm iteratively searches for the best motif that: (i) has the locally lowest extent, (ii) is not redundant, (iii) satisfies the k-closed and *self-sufficiency* constraints, and (iv) has the maximal elbow value for varying size. We note that the algorithm is efficient by using an *index* of local motiflets, which is pruned at each iteration. It has hyperparameters l, the length of subsequence occurrences; the maximum motif size k_{max}; and m, the maximum number of motifs to return. The worst-case time complexity is $\mathcal{O}(k^2 \cdot n^2)$.

Algorithm. In Algorithm 1, we present the procedures MOTIPLUS and BEST-MOTIFLET. We begin by computing the distance matrix $D \in \mathbb{R}^{\hat{n} \times \hat{n}}$, where $\hat{n} = n - l + 1$ (line 2). In the distance matrix, each cell $D_{i,j}$ contains the z-ED between subsequences starting at indices i and j of length l. Next, we compute local motiflets using the algorithm described in Sect. 4.3. That is, we call K_MOTIFLETS_HEAP once with the maximum size of a motif (k_{max}) and return an index with at most $\hat{n} \times k_{max}$ varying-sized local motiflets. The main loop in MOTIPLUS calls the subroutine BESTMOTIFLET at most m times (lines 5-9). Early termination is possible if no additional motif is discovered (line 7). BESTMOTIFLET has two additional parameters: the index of candidate motiflets and the current set of motifs, **S**. We iterate over each value of k and retrieve candidate motifs ordered by extent from the index (lines 13-14). Next, we iterate over at most $\hat{n}$ motifs and verify whether each motif is not *redundant* and satisfies the *k-closed* and *self-sufficiency* constraints (line 15). The first motif of size k that satisfies the constraints is added to the list of local motiflets of varying size (line 16). Motifs that do not satisfy the constraints are *pruned* from the index. Finally, we use the elbow-based heuristic to return the *maximal* local motiflet (line 22). As a special case, we return ∅ if no motif satisfying the constraints is discovered.

Time Complexity. The complexity of MOTIPLUS is dominated by calling K_MOTIFLETS_HEAP once, which has a complexity of $\mathcal{O}(k^2 \cdot n^2)$, and computing the distance matrix. The time complexity for computing the distance matrix naively is $\mathcal{O}(l \cdot n^2)$. Using MASS [17], this can be reduced to $\mathcal{O}(n \cdot \log n)$. In the worst case, we verify the constraints of all candidates in the index, regardless of the value of m, where there are at most $\mathcal{O}(n \cdot k)$ candidates in the index. The overall worst-case complexity is thus given by $\mathcal{O}(k^2 \cdot n^2 + n \cdot k \cdot n) = \mathcal{O}(k^2 \cdot n^2)$.

4.3 Discover the Motif with the Overall Highest Similarity

In this section, we discuss both an approximate and exact algorithm for local motiflet discovery. The approximate algorithm directly optimizes extent, resulting in higher fidelity to the exact solution, and returns many motifs of the same size with the lowest extent. The exact algorithm applies admissible pruning of supermotifs based on the *monotonicity of extent* inspired by related work in discrete pattern mining [18]. We note this is the first feasible solution that considers all n^k motifs.

A Tighter Approximate k-Motiflets Algorithm. For local motiflets discovery we return a list of n motifs of size k ranked by extent. We use *greedy search* with *extent* as a heuristic. We note that greedy search evaluates $k \times \hat{n}$ subsequence candidates, whereas related work focuses on the non-trivially matching nearest subsequences [6,12]. An advantage is that by evaluating extent we take all pairwise distances into account, leading to lower extent. An interesting property of greedy search, is that any submotif of size $2, \ldots, k_{max} - 1$ also has the lowest extent. Hence, we only have to search for the local motiflets once with

Algorithm 1: MOTIPLUS: Discovering the top-m motifs

Input: A time series T, motif length l, number of motifs m, the maximum motif size k_{max}
Result: Set **S** with up to m motifs

1 **procedure** MOTIPLUS(T, l, m, k_{max})
2     $D \leftarrow$ CALC_DISTANCE_MATRIX(T, l)
3     $index \leftarrow$ K_MOTIFLETS_HEAP(T, D, l, k_{max})
4     $\mathbf{S} \leftarrow \{\}$
5   **for** $i \leftarrow 1$ **to** m **do**
6        $S_i \leftarrow$ BESTMOTIFLET($T, index, \mathcal{S}, k_{max}$)
7   **if** $S_i = \emptyset$ **then**
8   **break**
9        $\mathbf{S} \leftarrow \mathbf{S} \cup \{S_i\}$
10   **return S**

11 **procedure** BESTMOTIFLET($T, index, \mathbf{S}, k_{max}$)
12    $\mathcal{C} \leftarrow \{\}$
13   **for** $k \leftarrow 2$ **to** k_{max} **do**
14   **for** $S_k \in index[k]$ *sorted on extent* **do**
15   **if** *non-redundant*($S_k, \mathbf{S}$) $\wedge$ *k-closed*(S_k) $\wedge$ *self-sufficient*(S_k) **then**
16             $\mathcal{C} \leftarrow \mathcal{C} \cup \{S_k\}$
17   **break**
18   **else**
19             $index[k] \leftarrow index[k] \setminus \{S_k\}$
20   **if** $\mathcal{C} = \{\}$ **then**
21   **return** $\emptyset$
22    $S \leftarrow \underset{S_k \in \mathcal{C}}{\operatorname{argmax}} \; elbow(k)$
23   **return** S

size k_{max}. For brevity, we discuss the pseudo-code in the Appendix. The proposed greedy search optimization using extent requires $\mathcal{O}(k^2 \cdot n)$ time and the total complexity is $\mathcal{O}(k^2 \cdot n^2)$. In contrast, the nearest-neighbor search has a complexity of $\mathcal{O}(k \cdot n^2)$.

An Efficient Exact k-Motiflets Algorithm. Next, we present a novel exact algorithm for the discovery of k-motiflets. The main goal is to design an algorithm that is efficient in time and space by applying *pruning* using the *lattice* of motifs. We represent a motif $S_k = \{T_{i_1,l}, T_{i_2,l}, \ldots, T_{i_k,l}\}$ as $\hat{S}_k = \{i_1, i_2, \ldots, i_k\}$ where each subsequence $T_{i,l}$ is represented by its starting index $i \in [1, \hat{n}]$. Using this representation we enumerate all subsets of size $1, 2, \ldots k$, and finally return the subset of size k having the lowest extent. The following theorem is used to prune motifs during exact search.

Theorem 1. *Given a motif $\hat{S}'$ and supermotif $\hat{S}$, we find that extent is monotonically increasing, that is, for all $\hat{S} : \hat{S}' \subset \hat{S}$: $extent(\hat{S}') \leq extent(\hat{S})$.*

Proof: The proof is trivial, i.e. $extent(\hat{S}) = max(z\text{-}ED(T_{a,l}, T_{b,l})|\ a, b \in \hat{S}\}) = max(\{z\text{-}ED(T_{a,l}, T_{b,l})|\ a, b \in \hat{S}'\} \cup \{z\text{-}ED(T_{a,l}, T_{b,l})|\ a \in \hat{S} \setminus \hat{S}' \wedge b \in \hat{S}\}) \geq extent(\hat{S}')$.

We leverage *depth-first search* to create candidate motifs of growing size bottom-up and prunes all supermotifs based on Theorem 1. We initialise the lower bound of extent using the approximate solution. If any motif subset (possible of small size) already has an extent higher than the approximate solution, we do not have to evaluate any supermotif. Additionally, we make use of a second theorem for initial pruning of motif pairs having a large distance. For brevity, the pseudo-code is discussed in the Appendix.

5 MotiSet: Discover the Best Set of Motifs

One disadvantage of most motif discovery methods is that greedy search is sub-optimal. In contrast, MOTISET searches for an optimal solution using A* and measures the value of thousands of candidate sets of motifs. To evaluate a set of motifs, we propose a new value function that balances contrasting aspects of motifs. MOTISET has the same hyper-parameters as MOTIPLUS, however the maximal number of motifs to return (m) is optional. In theory, the worst-case complexity of MOTISET is $O((\hat{n} \cdot k_{max})^m)$. However, we prune redundant motifs thereby achieving an order-of-magnitude reduction in the number of possible candidate sets. Moreover, the A* search is an anytime algorithm and we suggest to stopping after a fixed number of candidate sets of motifs have been evaluated.

Definition 11. *Optimal set of motifs: Given a set of candidate motifs* $\mathcal{S} \subseteq \mathcal{P}(P^l)$, *and a value function f, we define that the set of motifs* $\mathbf{S}$ *is optimal* $\iff \forall \mathbf{S}' \subseteq \mathcal{S} : f(\mathbf{S}) \leq f(\mathbf{S}')$.

Definition 12. *For a set of motifs,* $\mathbf{S} = \{S_1, S_2, \ldots, S_m\}$, *we seek high intra-motif and low inter-motif similarity. We define the value as the difference between the sum of the minimal pairwise distances (smpd), and the sum of the minimal outer distances (smod):*

$$f(\mathbf{S}) = norm(smpd(\mathbf{S})) - \gamma \cdot norm(smod(\mathbf{S}))$$

$$smpd(\mathbf{S}) = \frac{\sum_{k=1}^{m} \sum_{i=1}^{|S_k|} min\_dist\_in(T_{i,l}, S_k)^2}{\sum_{k=1}^{m} |S_k|}$$

$$smod(\mathbf{S}) = \sum_{k=1}^{m} min\_dist\_out(S_k, T)^2$$

$$min\_dist\_in(T_{i,l}, S_k) = min(\{z\text{-}ED(T_{i,l}, T_{j,l})\ |\ T_{j,l} \in S_k \wedge T_{i,l} \neq T_{j,l}\})$$

$$min\_dist\_out(S_k, T) = min(\{z\text{-}ED(T_{i,l}, T_{j,l})\ |\ T_{i,l} \in S_k \wedge T_{j,l} \in T\})$$

For smaller motifs the intra-motif similarity (*smpd*) will be high, while for larger motifs that inter-motif similarity (*smod*) will be low. The rationale behind the value function is that we want larger motifs, at least if they are semantically similar. *Smpd* compute the squared minimal distance between each subsequence $T_{i,l}$ and every other subsequence $T_{j,l}$ within each motif. The rationale for aggregating minimal distances inter-motif is that the extent (and radius) ignores the variability in distances within a motif. We normalize the *smpd* values by the total number of subsequences in the set of motifs. For *smod* we compute the minimal distance between any subsequence $T_{i,l}$ in a motif and any non-trivially matching subsequence $T_{j,l}$ outside the motif. Finally, we normalize the *smpd* and *smod* values across all candidate sets of motifs between 0 and 1. Based on our experiments, we found that setting $\gamma = 0.2$ yields good performance.

Algorithm. Using A* search we prioritize the expansion for sets of motifs with the current lowest value. To limit the search space, we start with local motiflets, which are restricted to $\hat{n} \times k_{max}$ motifs (see Sect. 4.3). In the first phase, *vertical pruning* is applied, because many local motiflets of the same size are redundant, i.e., they share trivially matching subsequences. During search, we apply *horizontal pruning*, because many motifs of different sizes are submotifs, supermotifs or partially overlapping. Additionally, we enforce an ordering between motifs to avoid enumeration of all possible orders of motifs within each candidate set. By combining both types of pruning, we achieve an order-of-magnitude reduction in the number of possible candidate sets of motifs. For brevity, we define the pseudo-code for the A* algorithm in the Appendix.

6 Experiments

In this section, we answer the following research questions[1]: **Q1:** What is the quality of the approximate algorithm and the runtime of the exact algorithm for discovering motiflets? **Q2:** How does MOTIPLUS compare to existing motif discovery methods qualitatively on music datasets? **Q3:** How do MOTIPLUS and MOTISET compare to existing motif discovery methods on the tsmd-benchmark?

6.1 The Runtime and the Quality for Discovering Motiflets Using the Exact and Approximate Algorithm (Q1)

In the first experiment, we measure the quality of the approximate solution and the runtime of the exact algorithm against the brute-force algorithm. We use a benchmark dataset of 12 pairs of univariate TS of the same class from [7].

Quality of the Approximate Algorithm. We compare the approximate algorithm proposed in Sect. 4.3 with the original algorithm from MOTIFLETS which finds the nearest subsequences to the core. The goal of both methods is to achieve high fidelity to the exact solution at a fraction of the cost. We measure the quality of the approximate solutions as the *ratio* of the extents of the approximate to the exact solution (i.e. values close to 1 indicate the extent is close to the

---

[1] MOTIPLUS and MOTISET are implemented in Python; motiflet search is in Java. Data and code are available at https://bitbucket.org/len_feremans/kmotiflets.

exact solution). The motif length $l \in [25, 200]$ is selected based on the minimum area under the curve of the extent function, and we set k to 7. The proposed approximate algorithm discovers a k-motiflet in all 12 time series, achieving an extent ratio of 0.9 or higher. The approximate algorithm from [12] achieves an extent ratio of 0.9 or higher in only 8 out of 12 time series.

Runtime of the Exact Algorithm. We compare the runtimes for discovering the exact k-motiflet using the algorithm proposed in Sect. 4.3 against the brute-force algorithm from MOTIFLETS. We vary k between 2 and 15 and stop execution if computation exceeds 30 min. As expected, the brute-force algorithm fails for relatively small values of k (as low as 6) due to the exponential number of candidates. In contrast, the exact algorithm based on depth-first search completes execution within 30 min for all TS for k up to 15. We conclude that the proposed exact algorithm is an *order-of-magnitude* more efficient and feasible to run in practice for reasonable values of k. However, given the additional computational cost, and the high quality of the approximate method, we prefer the approximate method in further experiments. For brevity, we report detailed plots in the Appendix.

6.2 How Does MotiPlus Qualitatively Compare to Existing Motif Discovery Methods on Music Data? (Q2)

In this experiment, we compare MOTIPLUS with MMOTIF, LOCOMOTIF, and MOTIFLETS. We collected six songs with synchronized lyrics from an online audio streaming platform. We evaluate the discovered set of motifs by measuring the *Jaccard similarity* between each ground truth (GT) motif and its best-matching counterpart.

Experimental Setup. We preprocess raw audio samples using the second Mel-Frequency Cepstral Coefficient (MFCC) channel sampled 100 Hz [17]. Each song is about four minutes long. After preprocessing, a time series (TS) consists of approximately $n = 50,000$ values, which is large. Each song contains between 3 and 12 repeating lyric segments synchronized to the TS, which we use as GT motifs. For MMOTIF, we use the implementation from STUMPY [6]. For each method, we selected the best parameters using grid search. For MMOTIF, the radius is set to 2. For LOCOMOTIF, we set the minimum and maximum lengths to the same value, *rho* to 0.5, and *warping* to False. For MOTIPLUS and MOTIFLETS, we set the maximum motif size k_{max} to 15. For all methods we set the number of motifs, m, to 50. We select the motif length $l \in [100, 400]$ based on the minimum area under the curve of the extent function.

Results. In Table 1, we report the mean Jaccard similarity with ground-truth lyrics and statistics such as the mean extent, and coverage, the percentage of time series values covered by motif subsequences. We find that MOTIPLUS has a higher Jaccard similarity than MMOTIF on four out of six datasets. MMOTIF achieves higher accuracy on two datasets. However, MMOTIF primarily searches for top motif pairs and only secondarily for larger motifs, resulting in lower extent. MOTIFLETS has the lowest average extent, which we expect since it finds the top-1 motiflets. However, it fails to detect many GT motifs. For LOCO-MOTIF, the accuracy is quite low, and the average extent is highest, which is surprising. We inspected whether discovered motifs align with meaningful lyrical or instrumental phrases. MOTIPLUS generally produces motifs that better follow musical structure. Its coverage is also more evenly distributed over each song. In contrast, LOCOMOTIF and MMOTIF sometimes return repetitive background patterns—such as sustained chords or rhythmic noise—that do not correspond to meaningful musical or lyrical segments[2]. Regarding run-time, we find that MMOTIF and MOTIFLETS are the fastest, requiring approximately 30s per dataset. The bottleneck is the computation of the distance matrix, which is required by all methods. MOTIPLUS requires approximately 60s per dataset. Finally, we note that LOCOMOTIF is somewhat slower and has a high memory consumption, taking several minutes and exceeding the 16 GB limit.

Table 1. Comparing the mean *Jaccard similarity* between known lyrics and discovered counterpart motifs for each method on the music datasets. We also report the extent and coverage averaged across all datasets.

Dataset	LOCOMOTIF	MMOTIF	MOTIFLETS	MOTIPLUS
Ice ice baby	0.118	**0.336**	0.092	0.271
Beverly hills	0.185	0.538	0.331	**0.570**
La Isla Bonita	0.105	**0.451**	0.069	0.326
Billie Jean	0.123	0.000	0.011	**0.442**
The Chain	0.085	0.175	0.012	**0.204**
The Pretender	0.178	0.275	0.152	**0.358**
Mean Jaccard Sim.	0.132	0.296	0.113	**0.362**
Mean extent	17.4	13.0	**7.6**	10.0
Mean coverage	45.4%	**83.2%**	15.3%	76.4%

6.3 How Do MotiPlus and MotiSet Compare to Existing Motif Discovery Methods on the Tsmd-Benchmark? (Q3)

We adopt the evaluation metrics, labeled TS datasets, and experimental setup from the *tsdm-benchmark* [15]. We compare MOTIPLUS and MOTISET with the four best-performing methods in the *tsdm-benchmark*, namely LOCOMOTIF, MMOTIF, GRAMMARVIZ, and MOTIFLETS[3]. We evaluate on TS datasets with

---

[2] For brevity, we report all discovered motifs, including instrumental motifs, on our website.
[3] We do not compare with motif discovery methods that performed worse, namely EMMA, MRMOTIF, SETFINDER, LATENTMOTIFS, VALMOD, and VONSEM.

fixed-length GT motifs namely Ecg5000, Fungi, Mallat, Plane and Symbols. Each dataset consists of 200 TS instances with a variable number of GT motifs that differ in length and size. We evaluate the F1 score, precision and recall using the PROM matrix. We penalize off-target motifs, i.e., methods that discover more motifs than are present in the GT set.

Table 2. We report the average F1-score, precision, recall, and standard deviation across six datasets from the tsmd-benchmark. We find that MOTISET achieves the highest F1-score and precision, while MOTIPLUS attains the highest recall.

Dataset	F1	Precision	Recall
GRAMMARVIZ	0.234 (+-0.097)	0.264 (+-0.196)	0.321 (+-0.088)
MMOTIF	0.314 (+-0.058)	0.400 (+-0.106)	0.323 (+-0.061)
MOTIFLETS	0.498 (+-0.104)	0.719 (+-0.125)	0.403 (+-0.094)
LOCOMOTIF	0.565 (+-0.232)	0.604 (+-0.268)	0.564 (+-0.195)
MOTIPLUS	0.552 (+-0.094)	0.543 (+-0.125)	**0.621** (+-0.087)
MOTISET	**0.586** (+-0.097)	**0.773** (+-0.068)	0.531 (+-0.108)

Experimental Setup. We make the following adjustments to the experimental setup in the *tsdm-benchmark*. We include a Mixed dataset, which constitutes a heterogeneous collection by combining TS instances from the aforementioned datasets (excluding Mallat due to its longer motif length). We combine test and validation TS instances and add noise to TS segments not covered by any GT motif resulting in TS datasets having a longer length and a larger set of GT motifs, making the task more challenging[4]. We tune parameters using grid search, thereby using the last 50 TS instances for validation and report the accuracy on the first 50 TS instances. For LOCOMOTIF, we set *warping* to True and search for the optimal value of *rho*. For GRAMMARVIZ and MMOTIF we search for the best parameters as suggested in [15]. For MOTIFLETS, MOTIPLUS and MOTISET we optimize the maximal motif size k_{max} within the range $[k_{gt} - 3, k_{gt} + 3]$, where k_{gt} is the maximum size of GT motifs. For MOTISET we set the maximum number of iterations to 10 000. Finally, we set the motif length l and number of motifs m to match the GT length and maximum count.

Results. Our study replicates the findings of the original study. We report two major differences in reported accuracy. First, we observe a much lower accuracy for GRAMMARVIZ. GRAMMARVIZ typically discovers a much larger set of motifs than other methods since it does not have a parameter m, resulting in an unfair advantage, which we correct by penalizing off-target motifs. Secondly, we find that tuning k_{max} increases the accuracy of MOTIFLETS substantially.

---

[4] The generator from the tsmd-benchmark creates motifs based on different TS classes within each TS dataset. However, it uses distinct subsets of the available classes to generate test and validation instances.

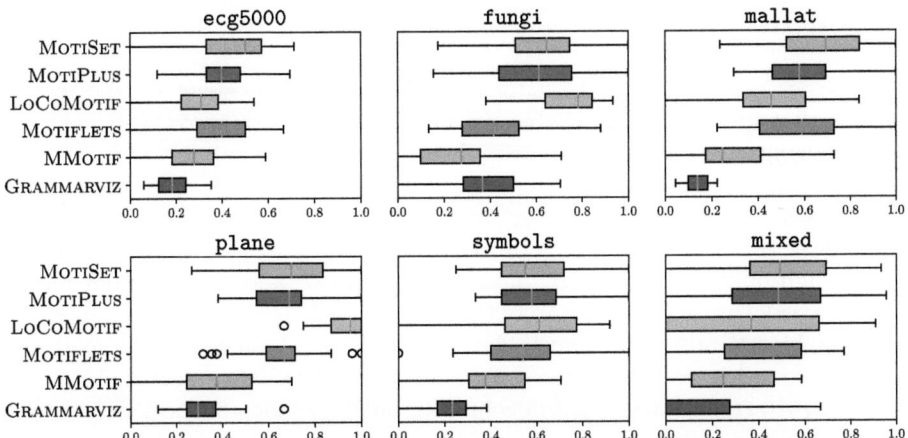

Fig. 3. The distribution of F1-scores for each method on the tsmd-benchmark datasets shows that either LoCoMotif or MotiSet performs best on each dataset. MotiPlus improves upon Motiflets. Grammarviz and MMotif perform significantly worse.

The average F1 score, precision, and recall across all datasets are shown in Table 2. We find that MotiSet achieves the highest overall F1 score and precision. MotiPlus achieves the highest overall recall, but has lower precision than LoCoMotif and Motiflets. In Fig. 3, we show the distribution of F1 scores for each dataset. We find that LoCoMotif performs best on Plane, Fungi, and Symbols, while MotiSet performs best on Ecg5000, Mallat, and Mixed, suggesting that both methods are complementary in terms of F1 score. We argue that the increased performance of LoCoMotif on certain datasets, such as Plane, is likely due to the use of Dynamic Time Warping, which is known to be more accurate than Euclidean distance on certain TS datasets [1]. We find that MotiPlus improves on LoCoMotif in 3 out of 6 datasets and in 5 out of 6 datasets compared to Motiflets. We observe that the increase in accuracy compared to Motiflets is correlated with the number of GT motifs in each dataset, i.e., Fungi has the most motifs. MotiPlus requires setting the maximum motif size, however this parameter mainly affects runtime. In contrast, LoCoMotif and MMotif rely on sensitive similarity and distance thresholds, which vary across datasets and hinder reproducibility, leading to high variability on the Mixed dataset. Concerning runtime, we find that Grammarviz, MMotif, Motiflets, and MotiPlus are generally faster, completing each dataset under two minutes. The runtime of LoCoMotif is slightly longer, taking approximately 10 min. Finally, we note that MotiSet requires about 30 min. The runtime varies significantly for each time series (TS) instance and depends on the number of iterations, which ranges from 100 to the upper limit of 10,000.

7 Conclusion

In this paper, we presented MOTIPLUS and MOTISET, two novel motif discovery methods that identify the top-m motifs in time series data across varying motif sizes, ensuring high internal similarity. Both methods are supported by efficient algorithms for scalable motif discovery. We approximate local motiflets using extent as a heuristic and propose an exact method for k-motiflet discovery that is significantly faster than existing approaches. MOTIPLUS iteratively searches for diverse, high-quality motiflets by filtering for k-closed and self-sufficient motifs, while MOTISET uses A* search to optimize motif set selection. We qualitatively evaluated MOTIPLUS on six music datasets with synchronized lyrics as ground truth and found it uncovers lyrical segments missed by MOTIFLETS, MMOTIF, and LOCOMOTIF. On the tsmd-benchmark, both methods outperform state-of-the-art baselines, with MOTISET and MOTIPLUS improving precision by 27.9% and recall by 10.1% over LOCOMOTIF. While MOTIPLUS runs comparably to baselines, MOTISET is up to three times slower depending on the number of iterations. In future work, we aim to explore variable-length motiflets, improve robustness, and study ensemble methods and their use in downstream time series tasks.

Acknowledgements. This research received funding from the Flemish Government (AI Research Program), and L.F. is funded on project 12B0V24N by Research Fund Flanders.

References

1. Alaee, S., Mercer, R., Kamgar, K., Keogh, E.: Time series motifs discovery under dtw allows more robust discovery of conserved structure. Data Min. Knowl. Disc. **35**, 863–910 (2021)
2. El-Sonbaty, Y., Ismail, M.A., Farouk, M.: An efficient density based clustering algorithm for large databases. In: 16th IEEE International Conference on Tools with Artificial Intelligence, pp. 673–677. IEEE (2004)
3. Feremans, L., Cule, B., Goethals, B.: Petsc: pattern-based embedding for time series classification. Data Min. Knowl. Disc. **36**(3), 1015–1061 (2022)
4. Hart, P.E., Nilsson, N.J., Raphael, B.: A formal basis for the heuristic determination of minimum cost paths. IEEE Trans. Syst. Sci. Cybern. **4**(2), 100–107 (1968)
5. Jain, A.K., Dubes, R.C.: Algorithms for clustering data. Prentice-Hall, Inc (1988)
6. Law, S.M.: Stumpy: a powerful and scalable python library for time series data mining. J. Open Source Softw. **4**(39), 1504 (2019)
7. Lin, J., Khade, R., Li, Y.: Rotation-invariant similarity in time series using bag-of-patterns representation. J. Intell. Inf. Syst. **39**, 287–315 (2012)
8. Lonardi, J., Patel, P.: Finding motifs in time series. In: 2nd Workshop on Temporal Data Mining, pp. 53–68 (2002)
9. Nguyen, H.L., Ng, W.K., Woon, Y.K.: Closed motifs for streaming time series classification. Knowl. Inf. Syst. **41**(1), 101–125 (2014)

10. Rakthanmanon, T., Keogh, E.J., Lonardi, S., Evans, S.: Time series epenthesis: Clustering time series streams requires ignoring some data. In: 2011 IEEE 11th International Conference on Data Mining, pp. 547–556. IEEE (2011)
11. Rotman, S., Čule, B., Feremans, L.: Efficiently mining frequent representative motifs in large collections of time series. In: BigDataprocee, pp. 66–75. IEEE (2023)
12. Schäfer, P., Leser, U.: Motiflets: simple and accurate detection of motifs in time series. PVLDB **16**(4), 725–737 (2022)
13. Senin, P., et al.: Grammarviz 3.0: Interactive discovery of variable-length time series patterns. TKDD **12**(1), 1–28 (2018)
14. Van Wesenbeeck, D., Yurtman, A., Meert, W., Blockeel, H.: Locomotif: Discovering time-warped motifs in time series. Data Mining and Knowledge Discovery, pp. 1–30 (2024)
15. Van Wesenbeeck, D., Yurtman, A., Meert, W., Blockeel, H.: Quantitative evaluation of motif sets in time series. arXiv preprint arXiv:2412.09346 (2024)
16. Webb, G.I.: Self-sufficient itemsets: an approach to screening potentially interesting associations between items. TKDD **4**(1), 1–20 (2010)
17. Yeh, C.C.M., Zhu, Y., Ulanova, L., Begum, N., Ding, Y., Dau, H.A., Zimmerman, Z., Silva, D.F., Mueen, A., Keogh, E.: Time series joins, motifs, discords and shapelets: a unifying view that exploits the matrix profile. Data Min. Knowl. Disc. **32**, 83–123 (2018)
18. Zaki, M.J., Meira, W.: Data mining and analysis: fundamental concepts and algorithms. Cambridge University Press (2014)

Right on Time: Revising Time Series Models by Constraining Their Explanations

Maurice Kraus[1](✉), David Steinmann[1,2](✉), Antonia Wüst[1], Andre Kokozinski[5], and Kristian Kersting[1,2,3,4]

[1] Artificial Intelligence and Machine Learning Group, TU Darmstadt, Darmstadt, Germany
{maurice.kraus,david.steinmann}@cs.tu-darmstadt.de
[2] Hessian Center for Artificial Intelligence (hessian.AI), Darmstadt, Germany
[3] Centre for Cognitive Science, TU Darmstadt, Darmstadt, Germany
[4] German Center for Artificial Intelligence (DFKI), Landwehrstraße 50A, 64293 Darmstadt, Germany
[5] Institute for Production Engineering and Forming Machines, TU Darmstadt, Darmstadt, Germany

Abstract. Deep time series models often suffer from reliability issues due to their tendency to rely on spurious correlations, leading to incorrect predictions. To mitigate such shortcuts and prevent "Clever-Hans" moments in time series models, we introduce Right on Time (RioT), a novel method that enables interacting with model explanations across both the *time* and *frequency* domains. By incorporating feedback on explanations in both domains, RioT constrains the model, steering it away from annotated spurious correlations. This dual-domain interaction strategy is crucial for effectively addressing shortcuts in time series datasets. We empirically demonstrate the effectiveness of RioT in guiding models toward more reliable decision-making across popular time series classification and forecasting datasets, as well as our newly recorded dataset with naturally occurring shortcuts, P2S, collected from a real mechanical production line.

1 Introduction

Time series data is ubiquitous in today's world. Everything that is measured over time generates some form of time series, for example, energy load [15], sensor measurements in industrial machinery [21] or recordings of traffic data [18]. Complex time series data is often analyzed using various neural models [3,28].

M. Kraus and D. Steinmann—Equal contribution.

Supplementary Information The online version contains supplementary material available at https://doi.org/10.1007/978-3-032-06109-6_28.

© The Author(s), under exclusive license to Springer Nature Switzerland AG 2026
R. P. Ribeiro et al. (Eds.): ECML PKDD 2025, LNAI 16019, pp. 490–507, 2026.
https://doi.org/10.1007/978-3-032-06109-6_28

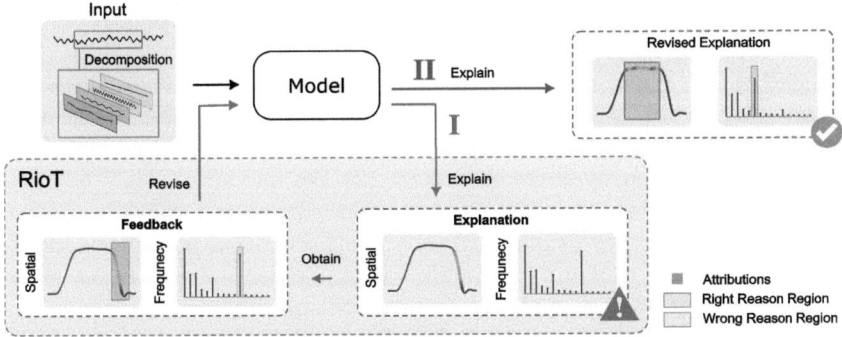

Fig. 1. Explanations reveal that the model relies on spurious factors in the input (red region) instead of relevant features (blue region). With RioT, the model can be guided away from these misleading patterns, whether they appear in the *spatial* or *frequency* domain. For this, RioT leverages feedback on incorrect explanations to steer the model toward more meaningful and reliable reasoning.

However, as in other domains, these can be subject to spurious factors ranging from simple noise or artifacts to complex shortcuts [16]. Intuitively, a shortcut, also called "Clever-Hans" moment, is a spurious pattern in the data that correlates with the target task during training but lacks true relevance. If a model learns to rely on such patterns rather than meaningful features, its generalizability suffers, performing well on data with the shortcut but failing on data without it, which poses a significant challenge in real-world deployment [11]. While model explanations can help uncover these shortcuts, they do not resolve the issue on their own (cf. Fig. 1 **I**). Despite extensive research in other domains [36], shortcuts in time series models remain underexplored. Existing studies often have specific assumptions about settings and data [4], leaving a gap in understanding and mitigating shortcut learning in broader time series applications. To address this, we introduce Right on Time (RioT), a new method grounded in the principles of explanatory interactive learning (XIL) [38], which leverages feedback on explanations to mitigate shortcuts (cf. Fig. 1 **II**). RioT uses traditional explanation methods, such as Integrated Gradients (IG) [37], to assess whether the model attends to the correct time steps. It then incorporates feedback on shortcut areas to refine the model, improving robustness and generalization.

However, spurious factors in time series data extend beyond the time domain. For example, a consistent noise frequency in an audio signal can act as a shortcut without being tied to a specific point in time. RioT can handle these types of shortcuts by incorporating feedback in the frequency domain. To highlight the importance of shortcuts in time series data, we introduce a new real-world dataset with naturally occurring shortcuts, called PRODUCTION PRESS SENSOR DATA (P2S). The dataset includes sensor measurements from an industrial high-speed press, essential to many manufacturing processes in the sheet metal working industry. The sensor data for detecting faulty production contains shortcuts and thus provokes incorrect predictions after training. Next to its industrial relevance, P2S is the first time series dataset that contains explicitly annotated shortcuts, enabling the evaluation of mitigation strategies on real data.

Altogether, we make the following contributions: (1) We show both on our newly introduced real-world dataset P2S and on several other datasets with manual shortcuts that SOTA neural networks on time series classification and forecasting are affected by these shortcuts. (2) We introduce RioT to mitigate shortcuts for time series data. The method can incorporate feedback on the time domain and the frequency domain. (3) By incorporating explanations and feedback in the frequency domain, we enable a new perspective on XIL, overcoming the important limitation that shortcuts must be spatially separable.

The paper is structured as follows: Sect. 2 provides a brief overview of related work on explaining time series and correcting model mistakes. Section 3 introduces our approach, while Sect. 4 describes our decoy methods and P2S. We then present a detailed evaluation and discussion in Sect. 5. Finally, Sect. 6 concludes the paper and outlines directions for future research.

2 Related Work

Explanations for Time Series. Explainable artificial intelligence offers various techniques to interpret machine learning models, many of which originated in image or text data before being adapted for time series [26]. Attribution methods explain models directly in the input space, while approaches like symbolic aggregation [17] and shapelets [42] provide higher-level insights (cf. [26,29] for a broader discussion on time series explanations). While explanation methods help identify shortcuts, they alone do not enable model revision. Thus, our approach begins with explanations to detect shortcuts and integrates feedback to mitigate them. Specifically, we use Integrated Gradients (IG) [37], which computes attributions via model gradients and is widely used for time series data [22,39].

Explanatory Interactive Learning (XIL). Research on shortcuts and their mitigation is growing, though it primarily focuses on visual data [36]. One direction is explanatory interactive learning (XIL), which entails methods that revise a model's decision-making based on human feedback [30,38]. A core aspect of XIL is using model explanations to correct mistakes, particularly to prevent Clever-Hans-like behavior, where models rely on spurious shortcuts [9,35]. Several XIL methods have been applied to image data. Right for the Right Reasons (RRR) [27] and Right for Better Reasons [32] penalize incorrect attributions, while HINT [31] rewards correct focus and [10] explore using multiple explainers. Despite their success in vision tasks, XIL approaches remain largely unexplored for time series. To address this, we introduce RioT, adapting XIL principles to the unique challenges of time series data.

Unconfounding Time Series. Apart from interactive learning approaches, some methods address confounding in time series models through causal inference [8]. Techniques like the Time Series Deconfounder [4], SqeDec [13], and LipCDE [5] estimate data while mitigating confounders in covariates of the target variable. They rely on causal analysis and specific assumptions about data

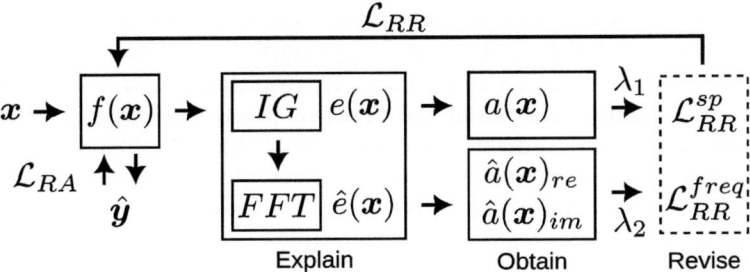

Fig. 2. RioT's explanation-based revision process. Input data x passes through the model $f(x)$ to generate explanations $e(x)$, receives annotated feedback $a(x)$, and is then fed back into the model. Integrated Gradients (IG) provides spatial explanations, while Fourier Transform (FFT) converts them into frequency-based explanations. Annotations can be applied in either or both domains and are leveraged by the right-reason loss ($\mathcal{L}_{RR}^{sp}$ and $\mathcal{L}_{RR}^{freq}$) to steer the model away from shortcuts in time or frequency.

generation. In contrast, our method focuses on shortcuts within the target variable itself, requiring no assumptions beyond the shortcut being detectable in model explanations - an area where existing causal methods are less applicable.

3 Right on Time (RioT)

The core idea of Right on Time (RioT) is to use feedback on model explanations to guide the model away from incorrect reasoning. Following the XIL paradigm, RioT is designed for seamless integration with other XIL methods. To ensure compatibility, we structure RioT around the four key steps identified by [9]: *Select, Explain, Obtain* and *Revise*. In *Select*, samples for feedback and model revision are selected. Following previous methods, we select all samples by default but also explore using subsets of the data. Afterwards, *Explain* covers model explanations before feedback is provided in *Obtain*. Lastly, in *Revise*, the feedback is integrated into the model to overcome the shortcuts. We introduce RioT along these steps in the following (as illustrated in Fig. 2).

Given a dataset $(\mathcal{X}, \mathcal{Y})$ and a model $f(\cdot)$ for time series classification or forecasting. The dataset consists of D many pairs of x and y. Thereby, $x \in \mathcal{X}$ is a time series of length T, i.e., $x \in \mathbb{R}^T$. For K class classification, the ground-truth output is $y \in \{1, \ldots, K\}$ and for forecasting, the ground-truth output is the forecasting window $y \in \mathbb{R}^W$ of length W. The ground-truth output of the full dataset is described as $\mathcal{Y}$ in both cases. For a datapoint x, the model generates the output $\hat{y} = f(x)$, where the dimensions of $\hat{y}$ are the same as of y.

3.1 Explain

Given a pair of input x and model output $\hat{y}$ for time series classification, the explainer generates an explanation $e_f(x) \in \mathbb{R}^T$ in the form of attributions to explain $\hat{y}$ w.r.t. x, where a large attribution value means a large influence on the output. In the remainder of the paper, explanations refer to the model f, but we drop f from the notation to declutter it, resulting in $e(x)$. We use IG [37] (Eq. 1) as an explainer, an established gradient-based attribution method. This method integrates the gradient along the path (using the integration variable α) from a baseline $\bar{x}$ to the input x. It multiplies the result with the difference between baseline and input. However, we make some adjustments to the base method to make it more suitable for time series and model revision, namely taking the absolute value of the difference between x and $\bar{x}$ (further details in Appx. A.1). In the following, we introduce the modifications to use attributions for forecasting and to obtain explanations in the frequency domain.

$$e(x) = |x - \bar{x}| \cdot \int_0^1 \frac{\partial f(\tilde{x})}{\partial \tilde{x}}\bigg|_{\tilde{x}=\bar{x}+\alpha(x-\bar{x})} d\alpha \quad (1) \quad e(x) = \frac{1}{W} \sum_{i=1}^{W} e'_i(x) \quad (2)$$

Attributions for Forecasting. In a classification setting, attributions are generated by propagating gradients back from the model output (of its highest activated class) to the model inputs. However, there is often no single model output in time series forecasting. Instead, the model simultaneously generates one output for each timestep of the forecasting window. Naively, one could use these W outputs and generate as many explanations $e'_1(x), \ldots e'_W(x)$, where each $e'_i(x)$ is the IG explanation using the i-th time step from the forecasting window as a target instead of a classification label. This number of explanations would, however, make it even harder for humans to interpret the results, as the size of the explanation increases with W [23]. Therefore, we propose aggregating the individual explanations by averaging in Eq. 2. Averaging attributions over the forecasting window provides a simple yet robust aggregation of the explanations. Other means of combining them, potentially even weighted based on distance of the forecast in the future are also imaginable. Overall, this allows attributions for time series classification and forecasting to be generated similarly.

Attributions in the Frequency Domain. Time series data is often given in the frequency representation, and this format can sometimes be more intuitive for humans to understand than the typical spatial representation. Thus, providing explanations in this domain is essential. [40] showed how to obtain frequency attributions of the method Layerwise Relevance Propagation [1], even if the model does not operate directly on the frequency domain. We adapt this idea to IG: for an input sample x, we generate attributions with IG, resulting in $e(x) \in \mathbb{R}^T$ (Eq. 1 for classification or Eq. 2 for forecasting). We then interpret the explanation as a time series, with the attribution scores as values. To obtain the frequency explanation, we perform a Fourier transformation of $e(x)$, resulting in the frequency explanation $\hat{e}(x) \in \mathbb{C}^T$ with $\hat{E}$ for the entire set.

3.2 Obtain

The next step of RioT is to obtain feedback on shortcuts. For an input x, feedback marks input parts via a binary mask $a(x) \in \{0,1\}^T$, where a 1 signals a potential shortcut at this time step. Thereby, masks $a(x) = (0, \ldots, 0)^T$ corresponds to no feedback for a sample. Similarly, feedback can also be given on the frequency explanation, marking which elements in the frequency domain are potential shortcuts. The resulting feedback mask $\hat{a}(x) = (\hat{a}(x)_{re}, \hat{a}(x)_{im})$ can be different for the real $\hat{a}(x)_{re} \in \{0,1\}^T$ and imaginary part $\hat{a}(x)_{im} \in \{0,1\}^T$. For the whole dataset, we then have spatial annotations A and frequency annotations $\hat{A}$. Obtaining annotated feedback masks can become costly, particularly if the feedback comes from human experts. However, as shortcuts often occur systematically, it can be possible to apply annotations to many samples, drastically reducing the number of annotations required in practice.

3.3 Revise

The last step of RioT is integrating the feedback into the model. We apply the general idea of using a loss-based model revision [27,30,35] based on the explanations and the annotation mask. Given the input data $(\mathcal{X}, \mathcal{Y})$, we define the original task (or right-answer) loss as $\mathcal{L}_{RA}(\mathcal{X}, \mathcal{Y})$. This loss measures the model performance and is the primary learning objective. To incorporate the feedback, we further use the right-reason loss $\mathcal{L}_{RR}(A, E)$. This loss aligns model explanations $E = \{e(x) | x \in \mathcal{X}\}$ and user feedback A by penalizing the model for explanations in the annotated areas. To achieve model revision and a good task performance, both losses are combined, where λ is a hyperparameter to balance both parts of the combined loss $\mathcal{L}(\mathcal{X}, \mathcal{Y}, A, E) = \mathcal{L}_{RA}(\mathcal{X}, \mathcal{Y}) + \lambda \mathcal{L}_{RR}(A, E)$. Together, the combined loss simultaneously optimizes the primary training objective (e.g. accuracy) and feedback alignment.

Time Domain Feedback. Masking parts of the time domain is an easy way to mitigate spatially locatable shortcuts (Fig. 1, left). We use the explanations E and annotations A in the spatial version of the right-reason loss:

$$\mathcal{L}_{RR}^{sp}(A, E) = \frac{1}{D} \sum_{x \in \mathcal{X}} (e(x) * a(x))^2 \quad (3)$$

As the explanations and the feedback masks are element-wise multiplied, this loss minimizes the explanation values in marked parts of the input. This effectively trains the model to disregard the marked parts for its computation. Thus, using the loss in Eq. 3 as right-reason component for the combined loss allows to effectively steer the model away from points or intervals in time.

Frequency Domain Feedback. However, feedback in the time domain is insufficient to handle every type of shortcut. If the shortcut is not locatable in time, giving spatial feedback cannot be used to revise the models' behavior. Therefore, we utilize explanations and feedback in the frequency domain to tackle shortcuts like in Fig. 1, (right). Given the frequency explanations $\hat{E}$ and annotations $\hat{A}$, the right-reason loss for the frequency domain is:

$$\mathcal{L}_{RR}^{fr}(\hat{A}, \hat{E}) = \frac{1}{D} \sum_{x \in \mathcal{X}} \left((\text{Re}(\hat{e}(x)) * \hat{a}_{re}(x))^2 + (\text{Im}(\hat{e}(x)) * \hat{a}_{im}(x))^2 \right) \quad (4)$$

The Fourier transformation is invertible and differentiable, so we can backpropagate gradients to parameters directly from this loss. Intuitively, the frequency right-reason loss causes the masked frequency explanations of the model to be small while not affecting any specific point in time.

Depending on the problem, it is possible to use RioT either in the spatial or frequency domain. Moreover, it is also possible to combine feedback in both domains, including two right-reason terms in the final loss. This results in two parameters λ_1 and λ_2 to balance the right-answer and both right-reason losses.

$$\mathcal{L}(\mathcal{X}, \mathcal{Y}, A, E) = \mathcal{L}_{\text{RA}}(\mathcal{X}, \mathcal{Y}) + \lambda_1 \mathcal{L}_{\text{RR}}^{sp}(A, E) + \lambda_2 \mathcal{L}_{\text{RR}}^{fr}(\hat{A}, \hat{E}) \qquad (5)$$

It is important to note that giving feedback in the frequency domain allows a new form of model revision through XIL. Even if we effectively still apply masking in the frequency domain, the effect in the original input domain is entirely different. Masking out a single frequency affects all time points without preventing the model from looking at any of them. In general, having an invertible transformation from the input domain to a different representation allows to give feedback more flexible than before. The Fourier transformation is a prominent example but not the only possible choice for this. Using other transformations like wavelets [12], is also possible.

Computational Costs. Including RioT in the training of a model increases the computational cost. Computing the right reason loss term requires the computation of a mixed partial derivative: $\frac{\partial^2 f_\theta(x)}{\partial \theta \partial x}$. Even though this is a second-order derivative, it does not result in any substantial cost increases, as the second-order component of our loss can be formalized as a Hessian-vector product (cf. Appx. A.3), which is known to be fast to compute [20]. We also observed this in our experimental evaluation, as even the naive implementation of our loss in PyTorch scales to large models.

Source of Feedback. A key aspect of RioT is the feedback incorporated in the *Obtain* step, which can come from various sources, including automated methods, rule-based systems, foundation models, or human annotations. Automated approaches, such as rule-based heuristics or pre-trained foundation models, provide scalable and consistent feedback, reducing the reliance on manual labeling. However, human annotations remain valuable for ensuring accuracy, especially in complex cases where automated methods may introduce biases or fail to capture nuanced patterns. RioT is agnostic to the feedback source, allowing flexibility in its application.

4 Shortcuts in Time Series

Shortcuts, like those in images, naturally occur in time series data but are often less apparent. Developing effective mitigation methods requires datasets where shortcuts are explicitly annotated, yet no existing datasets provide such annotations, despite known biases in popular datasets [2]. To address this gap, we introduce several time series dataset decoy variants inspired by prior work on decoy data [27], allowing for controlled evaluation of shortcut mitigation strategies. To further evaluate shortcut mitigation under real-world conditions, we present P2S, a real-world dataset where shortcuts arise from sensor recording processes.

4.1 Decoy Shortcuts

Classification. For both spatial and frequency cases, we introduce the shortcut as a class-specific pattern embedded in each training sample. The **spatial** pattern *replaces* m time steps with a sine wave defined as $s := \sin(t \cdot (2+j)\pi) \cdot A$ where $t \in \{0, 1, \ldots, m\}$ are the respective time steps, j represents the class index and A is the amplitude. In contrast, the **frequency** pattern is a similar sine wave, but it is *additively* applied to the full sequence ($m = T$).

Forecasting. For forecasting datasets, spatial decoys are more challenging due to window-based sampling and the complexity of the target. To address this, we design the shortcut as a "back-copy" of the forecast, where the decoy is equivalent to the actual solution. Due to the windowed sampling, the shortcut appears in every second sample. Given a sample of *lookback window* $\boldsymbol{x} \in \mathbb{R}^T$ and the *forecast horizon* $\boldsymbol{y} \in \mathbb{R}^W$. In the shortcut samples, we overwrite the first W entries of the lookback window with the future horizon values, yielding:

$$\boldsymbol{x}^s = (\underbrace{y_1, \ldots, y_W}_{\text{future horizon}}, \underbrace{x_{W+1}, \ldots, x_T}_{\text{remaining lookback}}).$$

while y remains unchanged. While this setting may seem constructed, similar patterns can emerge in real-world scenarios. For instance, in data transmission, glitches such as packet losses or duplications can subtly introduce irregularities into time series data, inadvertently creating forecasting shortcuts.

We model the forecasting frequency decoy as a recurring Dirac impulse with a specific frequency, added every k time steps: $i \in \{n \cdot k | n \in \mathbb{N} \land n \cdot k \leq T + W\}$ with a strength of A: $interference := A \cdot \Delta_i$. The impulse is present within the lookback and forecasting window during training, representing an effective decoy distracting the model from the actual forecast.

4.2 Real-World Shortcuts: Production Press Sensor Data (P2S)

RioT aims to mitigate shortcuts in time series data. While the decoys above provide a controlled evaluation setting, they do not capture the complexity of real-world shortcuts. To rectify this, we introduce PRODUCTION PRESS SENSOR DATA (P2S)[1], a dataset of sensor recordings with naturally occurring shortcuts.

The sensor data stems from a high-speed press production line for metal parts, one of the sheet metal working industry's most economically significant processes. Based on the sensor data, the task is to predict whether a run is defective. The recordings include different production speeds, which, although

---

[1] https://huggingface.co/datasets/AIML-TUDA/P2S.

not affecting part quality, influence process friction, and applied forces. Figure 3 shows samples recorded at different speeds from normal and defect runs, highlighting variations even within the same class. A domain expert identified regions in the time series that vary with production speed, potentially distracting models from relevant features, especially when no defect and normal runs of the same speed are in the training data. In these cases, the run's speed is a shortcut and makes it difficult to generalize to other speeds than those present in training. P2S also includes a specifically curated setup that matches run speeds during training to avoid the shortcut. Further details on the dataset are available in Sec. B.

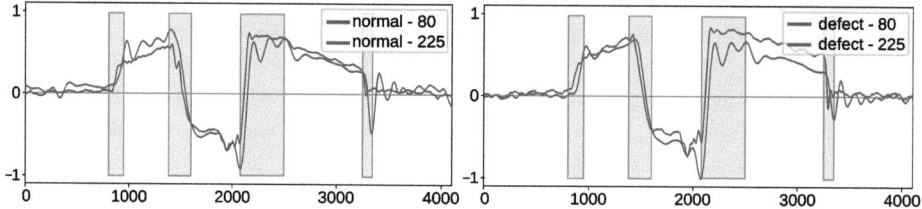

Fig. 3. Samples of P2S from normal (left) and defect (right) class at 80 and 225 strokes per minute. Areas of the time series that are especially sensitive to the stroke rate are considered a shortcut and marked red.

5 Experimental Evaluations

In this section, we investigate the effectiveness of RioT[2] to mitigate shortcuts in time series classification and forecasting, including revision in the spatial domain (RioT$_{sp}$) and the frequency domain (RioT$_{freq}$), as well as both jointly.

5.1 Experimental Setup

Data. For classification, we use datasets from the UCR/UEA repository [7]. We select available datasets of a minimal size (cf. Appx. A.2), which results in FAULT DETECTION A, FORD A, FORD B, and SLEEP. For time series forecasting, we evaluate on three popular datasets from the Darts repository [14]: ETTM1, ENERGY, and WEATHER. We split the data into training and test sets using a 70/30 ratio and 20% of the training set are used for validation. We apply the previously described decoys to the training sets and simulate feedback based on the shortcuts to generate annotation masks. In the real-world experiment, we utilize our newly introduced dataset P2S. The mask is applied to all samples except in our feedback scaling experiment. For the real-world test case, we consider our

---

[2] https://github.com/ml-research/RioT.

newly introduced dataset P2S. We standardize all datasets as suggested by [41], i.e., rescaling the distribution to zero mean and a standard deviation of one.

Models. For time series classification, we use the FCN model of [19], with a slightly modified architecture for Sleep to achieve better performance (cf. Appx. A.1). Additionally, we use the OFA model [43]. For forecasting, we use TiDE [6], PatchTST [24] and NBEATS [25] to highlight the applicability of our method to a variety of model classes.

Metrics. In our evaluations, we compare model performance on datasets with and without shortcuts, as well as with and without RioT. For classification, we report balanced (multiclass) accuracy (ACC), and mean squared error (MSE) for forecasting. The respective mean absolute error (MAE) results can be found in Appx. A.5. We report average and standard deviation over 5 runs.

Table 1. Applying RioT mitigates shortcuts in time series classification. Performance before and after applying RioT for spatial (Base$_{sp}$) and frequency (Base$_{freq}$) shortcuts. High training and low test accuracies indicate overfitting to the shortcut, which RioT successfully mitigates. *No Shortcut* represents the ideal scenario where the model is not affected by any shortcut.

Model	Config (ACC ↑)	Fault Detection A Train	Test	FordA Train	Test	FordB Train	Test	Sleep Train	Test
FCN	No Shortcut	0.99 ± 0.00	0.99 ± 0.00	0.92 ± 0.01	0.91 ± 0.00	0.93 ± 0.00	0.76 ± 0.01	0.68 ± 0.00	0.62 ± 0.00
	Base$_{sp}$	1.00 ± 0.00	0.74 ± 0.06	1.00 ± 0.00	0.71 ± 0.08	1.00 ± 0.00	0.63 ± 0.03	1.00 ± 0.00	0.10 ± 0.03
	+ RioT$_{sp}$	0.98 ± 0.01	0.93 ± 0.03	0.99 ± 0.01	0.84 ± 0.02	0.99 ± 0.00	0.68 ± 0.02	0.60 ± 0.06	0.54 ± 0.05
	Base$_{freq}$	0.98 ± 0.01	0.87 ± 0.03	0.98 ± 0.00	0.73 ± 0.01	0.99 ± 0.01	0.60 ± 0.01	0.98 ± 0.00	0.27 ± 0.02
	+ RioT$_{freq}$	0.94 ± 0.00	0.90 ± 0.03	0.83 ± 0.02	0.83 ± 0.02	0.94 ± 0.00	0.65 ± 0.01	0.67 ± 0.05	0.45 ± 0.07
OFA	No Shortcut	1.00 ± 0.00	0.98 ± 0.02	0.92 ± 0.01	0.87 ± 0.04	0.95 ± 0.01	0.70 ± 0.04	0.69 ± 0.00	0.64 ± 0.01
	Base$_{sp}$	1.00 ± 0.00	0.53 ± 0.02	1.00 ± 0.00	0.50 ± 0.00	1.00 ± 0.00	0.52 ± 0.01	1.00 ± 0.00	0.21 ± 0.05
	+ RioT$_{sp}$	0.96 ± 0.08	0.98 ± 0.01	0.92 ± 0.03	0.85 ± 0.02	0.94 ± 0.01	0.65 ± 0.04	0.52 ± 0.22	0.58 ± 0.05
	Base$_{freq}$	1.00 ± 0.00	0.72 ± 0.02	1.00 ± 0.00	0.65 ± 0.01	1.00 ± 0.00	0.56 ± 0.02	0.99 ± 0.00	0.24 ± 0.03
	+ RioT$_{freq}$	0.96 ± 0.02	0.98 ± 0.02	0.78 ± 0.04	0.85 ± 0.04	1.00 ± 0.00	0.64 ± 0.03	0.50 ± 0.16	0.49 ± 0.04

5.2 Evaluations

Removing Shortcuts for Time Series Classification. We evaluate the effectiveness of RioT (spatial: RioT$_{sp}$, frequency: RioT$_{freq}$) in addressing shortcuts in classification tasks by comparing balanced accuracy with and without RioT. As shown in Table 1, without RioT, both FCN and OFA overfit to shortcuts, achieving ≈100% training accuracy, while having poor test performance. Applying RioT significantly improves test performance for both models across all datasets. In some cases, RioT even reaches the performance of the ideal reference (no shortcut) scenario as if there would be no shortcut in the data. Even on FordB, where the drop in training-to-test performance highlights the distribution shift of that dataset [2], RioT$_{sp}$ is still beneficial. Similarly, RioT$_{freq}$ enhances performance on data with frequency shortcuts, though the improvement is less pronounced for FCN on Ford B, suggesting essential frequency information is sometimes obscured by RioT$_{freq}$. In summary, RioT successfully mitigates shortcuts in both domains, enhancing test generalization for FCN and OFA models.

Removing Shortcuts for Time Series Forecasting. Shortcuts are not exclusive to time series classification and can significantly impact other tasks, such as forecasting. In Table 2, we outline that spatial shortcuts cause models to overfit, but applying RioT$_{sp}$ reduces MSE across datasets, especially for Energy, where MSE drops by up to 56%. In the frequency-shortcut setting, the training data includes a recurring Dirac impulse as a decoy (cf. Appx. A.4 for details). RioT$_{freq}$ alleviates this distraction and improves the test performance significantly. For example, TiDE's test MSE on ETTM1 decreases by 14% compared to the decoy setting.

In general, RioT effectively addresses spatial and frequency shortcuts in forecasting tasks. Interestingly, for TiDE on the Energy dataset, the performance with RioT$_{freq}$ even surpasses the no shortcut model. Here, the added frequency acts as a form of data augmentation, enhancing model robustness. A similar behavior can be observed for NBEATS and ETTM1, where the decoy setting actually improves the model slightly, and RioT even improves upon that.

Table 2. RioT can successfully overcome shortcuts in time series forecasting. MSE values (MAE values cf. Table 7) on the training set with and test set without shortcuts. *No Shortcut* is the ideal scenario where the model is not affected by shortcuts.

Model	Config (MSE ↓)	ETTM1		Energy		Weather	
		Train	Test	Train	Test	Train	Test
NBEATS	No Shortcut	0.30 ± 0.02	0.47 ± 0.02	0.34 ± 0.03	0.26 ± 0.02	0.08 ± 0.01	0.03 ± 0.01
	Base$_{sp}$	**0.24** ± 0.01	0.55 ± 0.01	**0.33** ± 0.03	0.94 ± 0.02	**0.09** ± 0.01	0.16 ± 0.04
	+ RioT$_{sp}$	0.30 ± 0.01	**0.50** ± 0.01	0.45 ± 0.03	**0.58** ± 0.01	0.11 ± 0.01	**0.09** ± 0.02
	Base$_{freq}$	**0.30** ± 0.02	0.46 ± 0.01	**0.33** ± 0.04	0.36 ± 0.04	**0.11** ± 0.02	0.32 ± 0.09
	+ RioT$_{freq}$	0.31 ± 0.02	**0.45** ± 0.01	**0.33** ± 0.04	**0.34** ± 0.04	0.81 ± 0.48	**0.17** ± 0.01
PatchTST	No Shortcut	0.46 ± 0.03	0.47 ± 0.01	0.26 ± 0.01	0.23 ± 0.00	0.26 ± 0.03	0.08 ± 0.01
	Base$_{sp}$	**0.40** ± 0.02	0.55 ± 0.01	**0.29** ± 0.01	0.96 ± 0.03	**0.20** ± 0.03	0.19 ± 0.01
	+ RioT$_{sp}$	**0.40** ± 0.03	**0.53** ± 0.01	0.44 ± 0.00	**0.45** ± 0.01	0.55 ± 0.20	**0.14** ± 0.01
	Base$_{freq}$	0.45 ± 0.03	0.91 ± 0.16	**0.04** ± 0.00	0.53 ± 0.05	**0.63** ± 0.09	0.24 ± 0.04
	+ RioT$_{freq}$	0.91 ± 0.07	**0.66** ± 0.04	0.71 ± 0.10	**0.38** ± 0.06	0.96 ± 0.02	**0.17** ± 0.00
TiDE	No Shortcut	0.27 ± 0.01	0.47 ± 0.01	0.27 ± 0.01	0.26 ± 0.02	0.25 ± 0.02	0.03 ± 0.00
	Base$_{sp}$	**0.22** ± 0.01	0.54 ± 0.03	**0.28** ± 0.01	1.19 ± 0.03	**0.22** ± 0.03	0.15 ± 0.01
	+ RioT$_{sp}$	0.23 ± 0.01	**0.48** ± 0.01	0.53 ± 0.02	**0.52** ± 0.02	0.25 ± 0.03	**0.11** ± 0.01
	Base$_{freq}$	**0.06** ± 0.01	0.69 ± 0.08	**0.07** ± 0.01	0.34 ± 0.08	**0.79** ± 0.09	0.31 ± 0.09
	+ RioT$_{freq}$	0.07 ± 0.01	**0.49** ± 0.07	**0.07** ± 0.01	**0.21** ± 0.02	1.12 ± 0.36	**0.22** ± 0.01

Removing Shortcuts in the Real-World. So far, our experiments have demonstrated RioT's ability to counteract shortcuts within controlled environments. However, real-world shortcuts, as in our new dataset P2S, often have

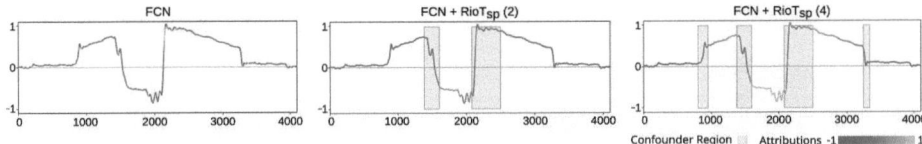

Fig. 4. Applying RioT lets the model ignore shortcut areas. While FCN primarily focuses on shortcuts, applying RioT with partial feedback (middle) or full feedback (bottom) causes the model to ignore the shortcut and focus on the remaining input.

more complex structures. The model explanations in Fig. 4 (top) reveal a focus on distinct regions of the sensor curve, specifically the two middle regions. With domain knowledge, it is clear that these regions should not affect the model's output. By applying RioT, we can redirect the model's attention away from these regions. New model explanations highlight that the model still focuses on (other) incorrect regions, which can be mitigated by extending the annotated area. In Table 3, the model performance (exemplarly with FCN) in these settings is presented. Without RioT, the model overfits to the shortcut. the test performance improves already with partial feedback (2) and even more with full feedback (4). These results highlight the effectiveness of RioT in real-world scenarios where not all shortcuts are initially known.

Removing Multiple Shortcuts at Once. In the previous experiments, we illustrated that RioT is suitable for addressing individual shortcuts, whether spatial or frequency-based. However, real-world time series data often presents a blend of multiple shortcuts that simultaneously influence model performance.

Table 3. Applying RioT overcomes shortcuts in P2S. Performance on the train set with and test set without shortcuts. FCN learns the train shortcut, resulting in lower test performance. Applying RioT with partial feedback (2) already yields good improvements, while adding feedback on the full shortcut area (4) is even better. *No Shortcut* is the ideal scenario, specifically curated so that there is no shortcut.

P2S (ACC ↑)	Train	Test
$FCN_{NoShortcut}$	0.97 ± 0.01	0.95 ± 0.01
FCN_{sp}	0.99 ± 0.01	0.66 ± 0.14
$FCN_{sp} + RioT_{sp}$ (2)	0.96 ± 0.01	0.78 ± 0.05
$FCN_{sp} + RioT_{sp}$ (4)	0.95 ± 0.01	$\mathbf{0.82} \pm 0.06$

Table 4. RioT can combine spatial and frequency feedback. If the data contains time and frequency shortcuts, RioT can combine feedback on both domains to mitigate them, superior to feedback on only one domain. *No Shortcut* represents the ideal scenario when the model is not affected by any shortcuts.

Sleep (Classification ACC ↑)	Train	Test
$FCN_{NoShortcut}$	0.68 ± 0.00	0.62 ± 0.00
$FCN_{freq,sp}$	1.00 ± 0.00	0.10 ± 0.04
$FCN_{freq,sp} + RioT_{sp}$	0.94 ± 0.00	0.24 ± 0.02
$FCN_{freq,sp} + RioT_{freq}$	1.00 ± 0.00	0.04 ± 0.00
$FCN_{freq,sp} + RioT_{freq,sp}$	0.47 ± 0.00	$\mathbf{0.48} \pm 0.03$
Energy (Forecasting MSE ↓)	Train	Test
$TiDE_{NoShortcut}$	0.28 ± 0.01	0.26 ± 0.02
$TiDE_{freq,sp}$	0.16 ± 0.01	0.74 ± 0.02
$TiDE_{freq,sp} + RioT_{sp}$	0.20 ± 0.01	0.61 ± 0.02
$TiDE_{freq,sp} + RioT_{freq}$	0.22 ± 0.01	0.55 ± 0.02
$TiDE_{freq,sp} + RioT_{freq,sp}$	0.25 ± 0.01	$\mathbf{0.47}$ v± 0.01

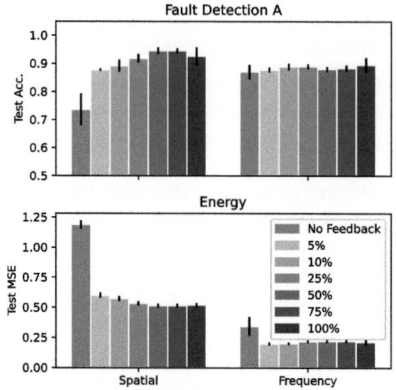
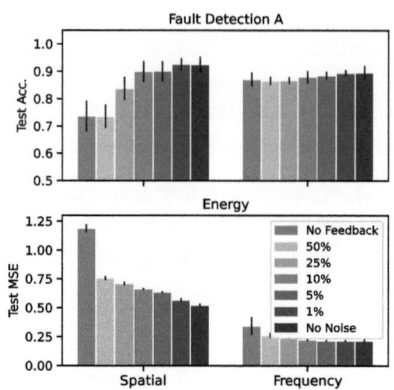

Fig. 5. RioT uses feedback efficiently. Even with feedback on only a small percentage of the data, RioT can overcome shortcuts.

Fig. 6. RioT is robust against invalid feedback. Even with some percentage of random feedback, RioT overcomes the shortcuts.

Thus, we investigate the impact of applying RioT to both spatial and frequency shortcuts simultaneously (cf. Table 4), exemplarily using FCN and TiDE. When Sleep contains shortcuts in both domains, FCN without RioT overfits and fails to generalize. Addressing only one shortcut does not mitigate the effects, as the model adapts to the other. However, combining the respective feedback from both domains ($\text{RioT}_{freq,sp}$) significantly improves test performance, matching the frequency-shortcut scenario (cf. Table 1). Table 4 (bottom) shows the impact of multiple shortcuts on the Energy dataset, where the lower training MSE indicates overfitting. While applying either spatial or frequency feedback individually shows some effect, utilizing both types of feedback simultaneously ($\text{RioT}_{freq,sp}$) results in the largest improvements, as both decoys are addressed. The performance gap between $\text{RioT}_{freq,sp}$ and the no shortcut setting is more pronounced than in single shortcut cases (cf. Table 2). This highlights again the known challenge of removing multiple shortcuts at once, which is generally more complex than individual shortcuts [36].

Handling Feedback. As the annotations are a crucial component of RioT, we conduct two different ablation studies to evaluate its impact using the classification data set Fault Detection A and the forecasting data set Energy. The first experiment examines the required amount of feedback, while the second assesses robustness to noisy feedback. In particular if the feedback stems from domain experts, making excessive feedback requests is impractical. Thus our first experiment evaluates the performance of RioT when feedback is provided on only a portion of the dataset (Fig. 5). The findings reveal that full annotations are unnecessary. Even with minimal feedback, such as annotating just 5% of the samples, RioT significantly outperforms scenarios with no feedback. While previous experiments assumed entirely accurate feedback, real-world applications often involve some degree of error. Therefore, we test the resilience of RioT to increas-

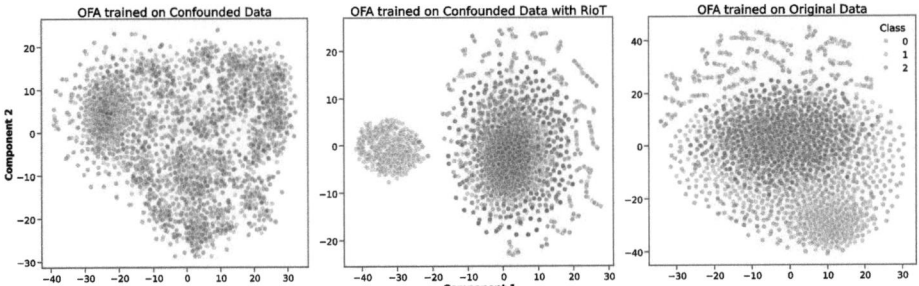

Fig. 7. t-SNE plots of OFA encodings for Fault Detection A. The left plot shows that a model trained with shortcuts shows minimal class separation. The middle plot shows the same setup but after RioT regularization, while the far right plot shows a model without shortcuts with clear class separation. Both RioT-regularized and model without shortcuts exhibit similar structures, highlighting the effectiveness of RioT.

ing levels of incorrect feedback (Fig. 6). Instead of accurately marking shortcut areas, random time steps or frequency components are incorrectly labeled as shortcuts. The results show that RioT maintains strong performance even with up to 10% invalid feedback, presenting only slight performance declines. In certain cases, like forecasting with spatial shortcuts, RioT can still achieve notable improvements despite high levels of feedback noise. To further evaluate whether annotations in different settings can also be incorporated via RioT, we conduct an additional ablation where the feedback is based on shaplets instead of the input domain directly (cf. Table 11 in the appendix). The results show that RioT can be effective in this setup as well, and is not limited to the specific explanation method and annotation modality shown in the other experiments (more details in Appx. A.5). In summary, RioT effectively generalizes from small subsets of feedback and remains robust against a moderate amount of annotation noise. Additionally, RioT can incorporate feedback in other settings with other types of explanations as well. These qualities demonstrate that RioT is well-equipped to manage the practical challenges associated with incorporating feedback.

Qualitative Insights into Model Encodings. Lastly, we examine the inner workings of a model by analyzing its latent representations under various configurations. In Fig. 7, t-SNE plots show OFA's feature encodings on Fault Detection A in three settings: trained on shortcut data (left) with poor class separation; after RioT regularization (center), where structure and separation improve; and trained on clean data (right), yielding clear clusters. This reflects the scores of the models (Table 1): the shortcut model reaches ≈50% accuracy, whereas RioT boosts it to nearly 100%, matching the reference scenario with clean data. This further demonstrates RioT's ability to mitigate shortcuts and restore robust performance.

Limitations. A key aspect of RioT is the incorporation of feedback. While this is a major advantage of RioT, obtaining feedback can also present some challenges. Although we demonstrate that only a small fraction of annotated samples is needed, annotations remain essential. Moreover, like many interactive learning approaches, RioT assumes accurate feedback, making it important to consider potential issues from inaccuracies in practical applications. To reduce the need of manual feedback, one could explore automated feedback strategies instead or alongside manual feedback [34] (e.g., using an LLM to provide feedback or automated clustering of explanations to identify outliers). Such approaches may alleviate annotation costs but inevitably trade off some precision and can introduce new failure modes if the surrogate feedback is misaligned with task requirements. Another drawback of RioT is the increased training cost. Optimizing model explanations with gradient-based attributions requires computing a mixed-partial derivative. However, this can be efficiently handled using a Hessian-vector product, keeping the additional overhead manageable.

6 Conclusion

In this work, we present Right on Time (RioT) a method to mitigate shortcuts in time series data with the help of feedback. By revising the model, RioT significantly diminishes the influence of these factors, steering the model to align with the correct reasons. Using popular time series models on several controlled decoy datasets and the newly introduced, real-world dataset P2S with naturally occurring shortcuts, showcases that SOTA models are indeed subject to shortcuts. Our results demonstrate that applying RioT to these models can mitigate shortcuts in the data. Furthermore, we have unveiled that addressing solely the time domain is insufficient for fully steering the model toward the correct reasons. To overcome this, we extended our method to incorporate feedback in the frequency domain, offering an additional mechanism for reducing reliance on shortcuts. Logical next steps are the extension of RioT to multivariate time series and the integration of various explainer types. Furthermore, exploring the usage of adaptive feedback mechanisms could prove to be beneficial, in particular in the context of multiple simultaneous shortcuts. Beyond time series, the application of RioT, especially $RioT_{freq}$, can also allow for a more nuanced approach to shortcut mitigation in other modalities.

Acknowledgments. This work was partly funded by the Federal Ministry of Education and Research (BMBF) project "XEI" (FKZ 01IS24079B), received funding by the EU project EXPLAIN, funded by the Federal Ministry of Education and Research (grant 01—S22030D). Additionally, it was funded by the project "The Adaptive Mind" from the Hessian Ministry of Science and the Arts (HMWK), the "ML2MT" project from the Volkswagen Stiftung, and the Priority Program (SPP) 2422 in the subproject "Optimization of active surface design of high-speed progressive tools using machine and deep learning algorithms" funded by the German Research Foundation (DFG). The latter also contributed the data for the P2S dataset. Furthermore, this work benefited from the HMWK project "The Third Wave of Artificial Intelligence – 3AI".

Disclosure of Interests. The authors have no competing interests to declare that are relevant to the content of this article.

References

1. Bach, S., et al.: On pixel-wise explanations for non-linear classifier decisions by layer-wise relevance propagation. PLoS ONE **10**(7), e0130140 (2015)
2. Bagnall, A., Davis, L., Hills, J., Lines, J.: Transformation based ensembles for time series classification. In: Proceedings of the SIAM International Conference on Data Mining (SDM) (2012)
3. Benidis, K., et al.: Deep learning for time series forecasting: tutorial and literature survey. ACM Comput. Surv. **55**(6), 1–36 (2023)
4. Bica, I., Alaa, A.M., Van Der Schaar, M.: Time series deconfounder: estimating treatment effects over time in the presence of hidden confounders. In: Proceedings of the International Conference on Machine Learning (ICML) (2020)
5. Cao, D., et al.: Estimating treatment effects from irregular time series observations with hidden confounders. In: Proceedings of the AAAI Conference on Artificial Intelligence (AAAI) (2023)
6. Das, A., Kong, W., Leach, A., Mathur, S., Sen, R., Yu, R.: Long-term Forecasting with TiDE: Time-series Dense Encoder. Trans. Mach. Learn. Res. (TMLR) (2023)
7. Dau, H.A., et al.: The UCR time series archive. ArXiv:1810.07758 (2018)
8. Flanders, W.D., et al.: A method for detection of residual confounding in time-series and other observational studies. Epidemiology **22**(1), 59–67 (2011)
9. Friedrich, F., Stammer, W., Schramowski, P., Kersting, K.: A typology for exploring the mitigation of shortcut behaviour. Nature Mach. Intell. **5**(3), 319–330 (2023)
10. Friedrich, F., Steinmann, D., Kersting, K.: One explanation does not fit XIL. ArXiv:2304.07136 (2023)
11. Geirhos, R., et al.: Shortcut learning in deep neural networks. Nature Mach. Intell. **2**(11), 665–673 (2020)
12. Graps, A.: An introduction to wavelets. IEEE Comput. Sci. Eng. **2**(2), 50–61 (1995)
13. Hatt, T., Feuerriegel, S.: Sequential deconfounding for causal inference with unobserved confounders. In: Proceedings of the Conference on Causal Learning and Reasoning (CLeaR) (2024)
14. Herzen, J., et al.: Darts: user-friendly modern machine learning for time series. J. Mach. Learn. Res. (JMLR) **23**(124), 1–6 (2022)
15. Koprinska, I., Wu, D., Wang, Z.: Convolutional neural networks for energy time series forecasting. In: Proceedings of the International Joint Conference on Neural Networks (IJCNN) (2018)
16. Lapuschkin, S., et al.: Unmasking clever hans predictors and assessing what machines really learn. Nat. Commun. **10**(1), 1096 (2019)
17. Lin, J., Keogh, E., Lonardi, S., Chiu, B.: A symbolic representation of time series, with implications for streaming algorithms. In: Proceedings of the ACM SIGMOD workshop on Research Issues in Data Mining and Knowledge Discovery (DMKD) (2003)
18. Ma, C., Dai, G., Zhou, J.: Short-term traffic flow prediction for urban road sections based on time series analysis and LSTM_bilstm method. IEEE Trans. Intell. Transp. (T-ITS) **23**(6), 5615–5624 (2022)
19. Ma, Q., Liu, Z., Zheng, Z., Huang, Z., Zhu, S., Yu, Z., Kwok, J.T.: A survey on time-series pre-trained models. ArXiv:2305.10716 (2023)
20. Martens, J.: Deep learning via hessian-free optimization. In: Proceedings of the International Conference on Machine Learning (ICML) (2010)
21. Mehdiyev, N., Lahann, J., Emrich, A., Enke, D., Fettke, P., Loos, P.: Time series classification using deep learning for process planning: a case from the process industry. Procedia Comput. Sci. **114**, 242–249 (2017)

22. Mercier, D., Bhatt, J., Dengel, A., Ahmed, S.: Time to focus: a comprehensive benchmark using time series attribution methods. ArXiv:2202.03759 (2022)
23. Miller, T.: Explanation in artificial intelligence: insights from the social sciences. Artif. Intell. (AIJ) **267**, 1–38 (2019)
24. Nie, Y., H. Nguyen, N., Sinthong, P., Kalagnanam, J.: A time series is worth 64 words: long-term forecasting with transformers. In: Proceedings of the International Conference on Learning Representations (ICLR) (2023)
25. Oreshkin, B.N., Carpov, D., Chapados, N., Bengio, Y.: N-BEATS: Neural basis expansion analysis for interpretable time series forecasting. In: Proceedings of the International Conference on Learning Representations (ICLR) (2020)
26. Rojat, T., Puget, R., Filliat, D., Del Ser, J., Gelin, R., Díaz-Rodríguez, N.: Explainable Artificial Intelligence (XAI) on TimeSeries Data: A Survey. ArXiv:2104.00950 (2021)
27. Ross, A.S., Hughes, M.C., Doshi-Velez, F.: Right for the right reasons: training differentiable models by constraining their explanations. In: Proceedings of the International Joint Conference on Artificial Intelligence (IJCAI) (2017)
28. Ruiz, A.P., Flynn, M., Large, J., Middlehurst, M., Bagnall, A.: The great multivariate time series classification bake off: a review and experimental evaluation of recent algorithmic advances. Data Mining Knowl. Discov. (DMKD) **35**(2), 401–449 (2021)
29. Schlegel, U., Arnout, H., El-Assady, M., Oelke, D., Keim, D.A.: Towards a Rigorous Evaluation of XAI Methods on Time Series. ArXiv:1909.07082 (2019)
30. Schramowski, P., et al.: Making deep neural networks right for the right scientific reasons by interacting with their explanations. Nature Mach. Intell. **2**(8), 476–486 (2020)
31. Selvaraju, R.R., et al.: Taking a HINT: leveraging explanations to make vision and language models more grounded. In: Proceedings of the International Conference on Computer Vision (ICCV) (2019)
32. Shao, X., Skryagin, A., Stammer, W., Schramowski, P., Kersting, K.: Right for better reasons: training differentiable models by constraining their influence functions. In: Proceedings of the AAAI Conference on Artificial Intelligence (AAAI) (2021)
33. Shrikumar, A., Greenside, P., Shcherbina, A., Kundaje, A.: Not Just a Black Box: Learning Important Features Through Propagating Activation Differences. ArXiv:1605.01713 (2017)
34. Stammer, W., Friedrich, F., Steinmann, D., Brack, M., Shindo, H., Kersting, K.: Learning by self-explaining. Trans. Mach. Learn. Res. (TMLR) (2024)
35. Stammer, W., Schramowski, P., Kersting, K.: Right for the right concept: Revising neuro-symbolic concepts by interacting with their explanations. In: Proceedings of the Conference on Computer Vision and Pattern Recognition (CVPR) (2020)
36. Steinmann, D., et al.: Navigating Shortcuts, Spurious Correlations, and Confounders: From Origins via Detection to Mitigation. ArXiv:2412.05152 (2024)
37. Sundararajan, M., Taly, A., Yan, Q.: Axiomatic attribution for deep networks. In: Proceedings of the International Conference on Machine Learning (ICML) (2017)
38. Teso, S., Kersting, K.: Explanatory Interactive Machine Learning. In: Proceedings of the AAAI/ACM Conference on AI, Ethics, and Society (AIES) (2019)
39. Veerappa, M., Anneken, M., Burkart, N., Huber, M.F.: Validation of xai explanations for multivariate time series classification in the maritime domain. J. Comput. Sci. **58**, 101539 (2022)
40. Vielhaben, J., Lapuschkin, S., Montavon, G., Samek, W.: Explainable AI for Time Series via Virtual Inspection Layers. ArXiv:2303.06365 (2023)

41. Wu, H., Xu, J., Wang, J., Long, M.: Autoformer: Decomposition transformers with Auto-Correlation for long-term series forecasting. In: Proceedings of the Conference on Neural Information Processing Systems (NeurIPS) (2021)
42. Ye, L., Keogh, E.: Time series shapelets: a novel technique that allows accurate, interpretable and fast classification. Data Mining Knowl. Discovery (DMKD) **22**, 149–182 (2011)
43. Zhou, T., Niu, P., Wang, X., Sun, L., Jin, R.: One fits all: Power general time series analysis by pretrained LM. In: Proceedings of the Conference on Neural Information Processing Systems (NeurIPS) (2023)

C³DE: Causal-Aware Collaborative Neural Controlled Differential Equation for Long-Term Urban Crowd Flow Prediction

Yuting Liu[1], Qiang Zhou[1(✉)], Hanzhe Li[1], Chenqi Gong[2], and Jingjing Gu[1]

[1] Nanjing University of Aeronautics and Astronautics, Nanjing, China
{yuting_liu,zhouqnuaacs,lihanzhe,gujingjing}@nuaa.edu.cn
[2] Chongqing University, Chongqing, China
gcq@stu.cqu.edu.cn

Abstract. Long-term urban crowd flow prediction suffers significantly from cumulative sampling errors, due to increased sequence lengths and sampling intervals, which inspired us to leverage Neural Controlled Differential Equations (NCDEs) to mitigate this issue. However, regarding the crucial influence of Points of Interest (POIs) evolution on long-term crowd flow, the multi-timescale asynchronous dynamics between crowd flow and POI distribution, coupled with latent spurious causality, poses challenges to applying NCDEs for long-term urban crowd flow prediction. To this end, we propose Causal-aware Collaborative neural CDE (C³DE) to model the long-term dynamic of crowd flow. Specifically, we introduce a dual-path NCDE as the backbone to effectively capture the asynchronous evolution of collaborative signals across multiple time scales. Then, we design a dynamic correction mechanism with the counterfactual-based causal effect estimator to quantify the causal impact of POIs on crowd flow and minimize the accumulation of spurious correlations. Finally, we leverage a predictor for long-term prediction with the fused collaborative signals of POI and crowd flow. Extensive experiments on three real-world datasets demonstrate the superior performance of C³DE, particularly in cities with notable flow fluctuations.

Keywords: Long-Term Urban Crowd Flow Prediction · Neural Controlled Differential Equation · Counterfactual Inference

1 Introduction

Urban development is a dynamic process driven by population growth, economic activities, and infrastructure development. As a key indicator of urban operations, urban crowd flow exhibits a significant continuous evolution trend. Exploring its long-term evolution helps reveal urban operating patterns and provides valuable insights for traffic management and sustainable urban development.

Existing researches on long-term prediction [15,32,34] typically employed coarse-grained data with hourly or even longer intervals, in contrast to the high-frequency, minute-level data commonly used. Such coarse-grained data obscures the important urban dynamics and trends, leading to information loss and making it harder for models to capture crowd flow dynamics, resulting to suboptimal prediction performance. Consequently, we introduce a continuous modeling approach to better capture urban dynamics from coarse-grained data, enhancing prediction stability and accuracy. Intuitively, it is essential to consider the evolution of urban structure in urban crowd flow prediction, which is mainly reflected in the changes of POI distribution [19,33]. For example, the construction of a new commercial center may attract higher pedestrian flow, while the renovation of an old residential area may affect the surrounding traffic flow.

However, modeling the impact of POI distribution on crowd flow (also referred to as collaborative signals) from a continuous-time perspective poses the following two challenges: *i) The multi-timescale asynchronous dynamics of collaborative signals increase the difficulty of modeling spatio-temporal dependencies in urban dynamic systems.* The evolution of collaborative signals occurs across different time scales, with their dynamic changes unsynchronized. Specifically, changes in low-frequency POI distributions gradually manifest in the high-frequency crowd flow patterns. This cross-scale influence is often reflected in significant crowd flow variations across multiple timestamps, which significantly increases the difficulty of modeling the multi-scale asynchronous dynamic and revealing dynamic patterns in a urban system. *ii) The accumulation of spurious correlations between collaborative signals complicates the identification of true causal relationships in continuous modeling.* POI distribution and urban crowd flow often exhibit statistically spurious correlations, which may mislead the model. From a discrete-time perspective, spurious correlations can be easily identified and removed through statistical methods like calculating correlation coefficients or Granger causality tests [7]. However, in continuous-time modeling, where time is treated as a continuous variable and dynamics are learned through differential equations [4], spurious correlations can be amplified during long-term integration. Moreover, minor perturbations in continuous time can significantly impact the overall system, further complicating the accurate identification of true causality.

To this end, we propose a **C**ausal-aware **C**ollaborative Neural **C**ontrolled **D**ifferential **E**quations framework (C^3DE) for long-term urban crowd flow prediction. Specifically, we propose a collaborative neural controlled differential equation (NCDE) with a dual-path architecture to capture the dynamic evolution of collaborative signals across different timescales in continuous time. With the continuous-time integration property of NCDE, the asynchronous dynamics of collaborative signals can be effectively modeled. Furthermore, we design a counterfactual-based causal effect estimator to simulate urban dynamics under different POI distribution interventions, enabling a quantitative assessment of each POI category's direct impact on crowd flow. To mitigate the accumulation of spurious correlations among collaborative signals, we incorporate causal effect values into the NCDE framework and introduce a causal effect-based dynamic correction mechanism. By computing causal influences across multiple time steps and feeding them back into POI representations, the mechanism effectively minimizes interference from spurious POIs, alleviates the amplification of spurious correlations, and enhances the model's robustness and reliability in the long-term prediction task.

Overall, our contributions can be summarized as follows:

- To the best of our knowledge, C^3DE, is the first to simulate the evolution of collaborative signals and explore the underlying causal mechanisms for long-term urban crowd flow prediction.
- We propose a collaborative NCDE with a dual-path architecture to effectively capture the asynchronous evolution of collaborative signals across multiple timescales.
- We design a counterfactual-based causal effect estimator to quantify the causal impact of POIs on crowd flow and introduce a causal effect-based dynamic correction mechanism to reduce the accumulation of spurious correlations.
- Extensive experiments on three real-world datasets demonstrate that C^3DE offers a significant advantage in modeling crowd flow dynamics, particularly in cities with notable flow fluctuations.

2 Related Work

Urban Crowd Flow Prediction. Recently, urban crowd flow prediction [2,21] has become a critical research topic, relying on historical flow data and using Gated Recurrent Unit (GRU) and Graph Neural Networks (GNNs) to learn spatio-temporal features. Traditional spatio-temporal GNNs, like STGCN [31] and STSGCN [26], used predefined graph structures to capture spatial dependencies but often fail to capture the hidden ones. To address this, methods based on adaptive graph structures introduced learnable adaptive adjacency matrices, enabling capturing the dynamics of node relationships [1,25,30]. In addition, considering that urban structure, i.e., POI distribution, significantly affect crowd mobility patterns, some works have incorporated it into flow pattern modeling [20,23]. For example, GeoMAN [20] treated POI as a spatial feature to capture spatial correlations within regions. GSTE-DF [23] utilizes POI data to uncover differences and similarities between regions for inferring origin-destination flows. Although these works achieved some success, they treated POI as a static feature and ignored the dynamics of POI distribution in cities.

Neural Ordinary Differential Equations. [4] first combined neural networks with Ordinary Differential Equations (ODE) and proposed Neural ODEs to model continuous dynamics, which has been widely used in the fields of time series prediction [11,16], continuous dynamic systems [12,13]. [10] proposed tensor-based ODEs to capture spatio-temporal dynamics, overcoming the limitations of graph convolutions in modeling long-range spatial dependencies and semantic connections. [5] designed two types of Neural Controlled Differential Equations to handle temporal and spatial dependencies separately. Additionally, [22] proposed STDDE, which incorporates delayed states into NCDE, allowing it to model time delays in spatio-temporal information propagation.

Counterfactual Inference. The main goal of counterfactual inference is to analyze potential outcomes through hypothetical interventions and answer "What would have happened if the situation had been different?" [3,27]. For example, [18] proposed a counterfactual data augmentation-based causal explanation framework that identifies the true causal factors by constructing counterfactual data. [24] introduced a counterfactual explanation method based on causal intervention, using a causal director to capture causal relationships in the distribution and guide counterfactual generation. In this paper, We address the spurious correlations between collaborative signals from a counterfactual perspective.

3 Preliminary

3.1 Definitions and Problem Statement

Definition 1 (Urban Network). The urban network is represented as a directed graph $G = (V, X, A)$, where $V = \{V_1, V_2, ..., V_N\}$ denotes N regions in the city. $X \in \mathbb{R}^{t' \times N \times C}$ denotes the urban crowd flow across N regions at t' time steps, where t' is measured in days and C capturing hourly features. $A \in \mathbb{R}^{N \times N}$ is the adjacency matrix, which encodes the relationships between regions.

Definition 2 (POI Distribution). The POI distribution is denoted as $P \in \mathbb{R}^{t'' \times N \times K}$, where t'' is the time steps, measured in months. K represents the number of POI categories, such as restaurants, shops and public facilities.

Problem Statement (Long-Term Urban Crowd Flow prediction). Given the crowd flow for the past T time steps and POI distribution for the past M time steps, our goal is to learn a map function $\mathcal{F}(\cdot)$ that capture the causal evolutionary relationship and predict the urban crowd flow for the next S time steps. It can be formulated as follows:

$$\mathcal{F}^* = arg\min_{\mathcal{F}} \sum_S \ell(\mathcal{F}(X_{t'-T+1:t'}, P_{t''-M+1:t''}), X_{t'+1:t'+S}), \tag{1}$$

where $\mathcal{F}^*$ denote the function with the learned optimal parameters, and $\ell(\cdot)$ is the loss function.

In this work, we divide the map function $\mathcal{F}(\cdot)$ into two stages, i.e., a representation part $F(\cdot)$ to model the collaborative causal evolutionary relationship and a predictor $G(\cdot)$ to predict the future crowd flow.

3.2 Neural Differential Equation

Neural ODEs. Neural ODEs [4] extend residual networks into the continuous time domain. Given the input X, neural ODEs define a hidden state $h(t)$ that evolves over time t, as described by the following Riemann integral:

$$h(t) = h(0) + \int_0^t \frac{dh}{dt} dt = h(0) + \int_0^t f(h(t), t; \theta) dt, \qquad (2)$$

where a neural network $f(\cdot)$ with parameter θ parameterize the derivative of the hidden state, i.e., $\frac{dh}{dt} := f(h(t), t; \theta)$. The evolution process is computed using ODE solvers, such as the Euler method and Runge-Kutta. To improve efficiency, the adjoint sensitivity method is often employed to compute the parameter gradients via the adjoint equations, rather than direct backpropagation.

Neural CDEs. Neural CDEs [17] are the extension of neural ODEs. Neural CDEs introduces an external control signal X_t, which drives the evolution of the hidden state $h(t)$, making it dependent on both its own dynamics and the control signal. Specifically, it can be expressed as:

$$h(t) = h(0) + \int_0^t f(h(t), t; \theta) dX_t, \qquad (3)$$

where X_t is a continuous path defined in a Banach space, representing the external control signal. Different from Eq. 2, it represents a Riemann–Stieltjes integral, allowing to model the influence of control signal on system's evolution.

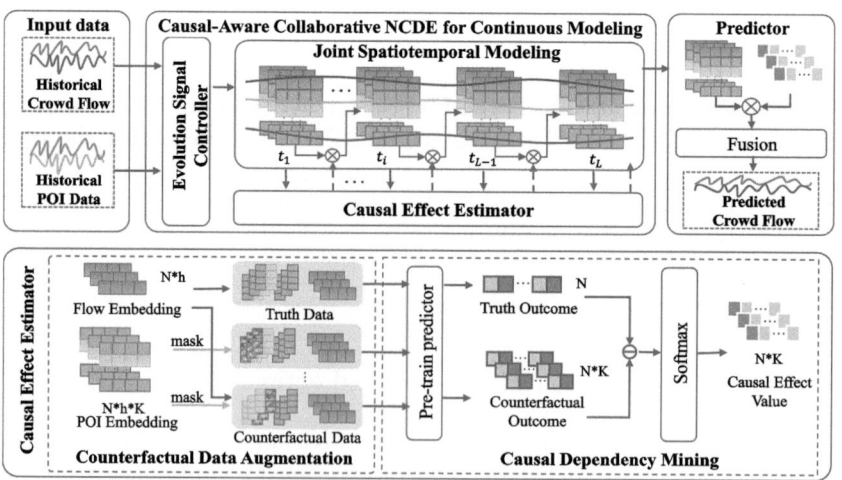

Fig. 1. Framework overview of C^{3}DE.

4 Methodology

In this section, we introduce the proposed C³DE framework, as shown in Fig. 1. It comprises two main modules. The first is the main pipeline of causal-aware collaborative neural CDE, which models the continuous evolution of collaborative signals while uncovering their potential causal impacts. The second is the well-designed causal effect estimator, consisting of counterfactual data augmentation and causal dependency mining, designed to explore the causal relationships between collaborative signals.

4.1 Dual Neural CDE

We first introduce a naive dual neural CDE as $F(\cdot)$ for modeling both the crowd flow and the POI distribution data simultaneously. It is formulated as:

$$\begin{cases} h_x(t') = h_x(0) + \int_0^{t'} f(h_x(t), t; \theta) \mathrm{d}X_t, & t' \in [0, T], \\ h_p(t'') = h_p(0) + \int_0^{t''} f(h_p(t), t; \theta) \mathrm{d}P_t, & t'' \in [0, M], \end{cases} \quad (4)$$

where $h_x(t')$ and $h_p(t'')$ represent the hidden states of crowd flow and POI distribution at t' and t'' respectively, which can be computed by an adaptive step-size solver or a fixed step-size solver like Runge-Kutta and Euler methods [14]. The control signals X_t and P_t guide the dynamic evolution process of the dual neural CDE, which are derived from the urban crowd flow and the POI distribution, respectively. Given the crowd flow $X_{t'-T+1:t'} \in \mathbb{R}^{T \times N \times C}$ and POI distribution $P_{t''-M+1:t''} \in \mathbb{R}^{M \times N \times K}$, we use the natural cubic spline [5] to create continuous paths which are needed in a neural CDE for control signals:

$$X_t = Spline(X_{t'-T+1:t'}), \quad P_t = Spline(P_{t''-M+1:t''}), \quad (5)$$

where $Spline(\cdot)$ denotes the natural cubic spline function, which generates continuous, smooth, and twice-differentiable paths for a given input, ensuring accurate and stable gradient computation.

Exemplification. In Eq.(4), the function $f(\cdot)$, which deals with the spatio-temporal features of signals, can be applied with any model for processing sequential data.

Without loss of generality, we leverage Gated Recurrent Unit (GRU) [6] as an example to illustrate the derivation of $f(\cdot)$ in Eq.(4).

To extend the state update of GRU to the continuous time domain, we introduce the state change $\triangle h_t$ over the time interval $\triangle t$, defined as:

$$\triangle h_t = h_t - h_{t-\triangle t} = (1 - z_t) \odot (\tilde{h}_t - h_{t-\triangle t}), \quad (6)$$

where z_t and $\tilde{h}_t$ are the intermediate vectors of GRU. As the time interval $\triangle t$ tends to 0, it can be transformed into the differential form of continuous time:

$$\frac{\mathrm{d}h(t)}{\mathrm{d}t} = (1 - z_t) \odot (\tilde{h}_t - h_{t-\triangle t}). \quad (7)$$

Similarly to the GRU model, the state update of any function $f(\cdot)$ for processing sequential data can be extended to the continuous time domain.

4.2 Causal-Aware Collaborative Neural CDE (C³DE)

Intuitively, there is a tight interaction between long-term evolution of the urban crowd flow and that of the POI distribution. These mutual causalities result in the insufficient modeling in the dual neural CDE which deals with the two collaborative signals respectively. To explore causal impacts of collaborative signals, we integrate the causal awareness mechanism and propose the causal-aware collaborative neural CDE. Regarding the accumulation of spurious correlations during continuous evolution, we employ a dynamic correction mechanism in $F(\cdot)$ and rewrite the Eq.(4) to alleviate spurious correlations as follows:

$$\begin{cases} h_x(t') = h_x(0) + \int_0^{t'} f(h_x(t), t; \theta) \mathrm{d}X_t, & t' \in [0, T], \\ h_p(t'') = h_p(0) + \int_0^{t''} \mathcal{C} \cdot f(h_p(t), t; \theta) \mathrm{d}P_t, & \mathcal{C} \in [\mathcal{C}_1, ..., \mathcal{C}_L], t'' \in [0, M]. \end{cases} \quad (8)$$

where $\mathcal{C} \in \mathbb{R}^{N \times K}$ is the causal impact weight, used to correct the biased POI representations, and L is the number of observation points during the evolution. We design a counterfactual-based causal effect estimator $g(\cdot)$ to compute $\mathcal{C}$. Specifically, it takes the hidden states of collaborative signals at observation points during the evolution as input to quantify:

$$\mathcal{C}_i = g(h_x(t_i'), h_p(t_i'')), i \in \{1, ..., L\}, \quad (9)$$

where $\{t_1', ..., t_i', ..., t_L'\} \subset [0, T]$ and $\{t_1'', ..., t_i'', ..., t_L''\} \subset [0, M]$ are the evenly spaced observation time points within their intervals. $\mathcal{C}_i$ denotes the causal impact weight of i-th observation point. Next, we introduce the design of $g(\cdot)$.

Counterfactual-Based Causal Effect Estimator. Inspired by the success of counterfactual data augmentation in natural language processing [35] and dynamic system [28], we explore the causal impact of POI on crowd flow from a counterfactual perspective, which aims to answer: "How would crowd flow change if a certain POI were changed?".

Specifically, the causal effect estimator consists of two modules: counterfactual data augmentation and causal dependency mining.

Counterfactual Data Augmentation. To answer the above question, we propose a counterfactual data augmentation method based on category-level perturbation, simulating various scenarios of POI changes. Specifically, given the POI representation $h_p(t_i'') \in \mathbb{R}^{N \times K \times H}$ at the i-th observation points, where H denotes the hidden space dimension, the counterfactual data for the k-th POI category is constructed as $h_{p^*}^k(t_i'')$:

$$h_{p^*}^k(t_i'') = h_p(t_i'') \odot M_k, \quad (10)$$

where M_k is a perturbation matrix, such as zero-setting, random perturbation, or mean replacement, that controls the category-level perturbation on the k-th POI category. Take the zero-setting perturbation as an example, the perturbation matrix M_k can be defined as:

$$(M_k)_{n,j,h} = \begin{cases} 0, & \text{if } j = k \\ 1, & \text{otherwise,} \end{cases} \quad (11)$$

where n is the region index, j is the POI category index, and h is the hidden space dimension index.

We can generate a set of counterfactual POI data by applying perturbations to the K POI categories: $\{h_{p*}^1(t_i''), ..., h_{p*}^k(t_i''), ..., h_{p*}^K(t_i'')\}$, where each represents the POI representation under a specific POI category's perturbation. Next, we pair the generated counterfactual POI representation $h_{p*}^k(t_i'')$ with the crowd flow representation $h_x(t_i')$ to obtain K pairs of counterfactual samples $\mathfrak{D}_{cf}$:

$$\mathfrak{D}_{cf} = \left\{ \left(h_x(t_i'), h_{p*}^k(t_i'')\right) \mid h_{p*}^k(t_i'') \in \{h_{p*}^1(t_i''), ..., h_{p*}^K(t_i'')\} \right\}, \quad (12)$$

the unperturbed POI representation $h_p(t_i'')$ and $h_x(t_i')$ are paired to form the factual sample $\mathfrak{D}_{fact}$:

$$\mathfrak{D}_{fact} = \{(h_x(t_i'), h_p(t_i''))\}. \quad (13)$$

Causal Dependency Mining. To evaluate the dynamic impacts of collaborative signals and reveal their causal dependency, we propose a causal dependency mining module based on factual and counterfactual samples.

We first pre-train a predictor $\mathcal{T}(\cdot)$ with the loss function $\ell(\cdot)$. Notably, $\mathcal{T}(\cdot)$ can be any spatiotemporal model, and here we use MTGNN [29] as the backbone:

$$\mathcal{T}^* = \arg\min_{\mathcal{T}} \ell(\mathcal{T}(X_{t-T+1:t}, P_{t'-M+1:t'}), X_{t+1:t+S}). \quad (14)$$

Next, we sequentially input the counterfactual samples into the predictor $\mathcal{T}(\cdot)$ to obtain the counterfactual output $O_{x,p*}^k$:

$$O_{x,p*}^k = \mathcal{T}(h_x(t_i'), h_{p*}^k(t_i'')) \in \mathbb{R}^N, \quad \forall (h_x(t_i'), h_{p*}^k(t_i'')) \in \mathfrak{D}_{cf}. \quad (15)$$

Meanwhile, we input the factual samples $\{(h_x(t_i'), h_p(t_i''))\} \in \mathfrak{D}_{fact}$ into the same $\mathcal{T}(\cdot)$ to obtain the factual output $O_{x,p}^k$, which is considered as an anchor:

$$O_{x,p}^k = \mathcal{T}(h_x(t_i'), h_p(t_i'')) \in \mathbb{R}^N. \quad (16)$$

We quantify the causal impact of a specific POI category on crowd flow by the absolute difference between the anchor and counterfactual outputs. For the k-th category of POI, the causal effect value is computed as followed:

$$\mathcal{C}_k(i) = |O_{x,p}^k - O_{x,p*}^k| \in \mathbb{R}^N. \quad (17)$$

A larger causal effect value $\mathcal{C}_k(i)$ indicates significant fluctuations in crowd flow with the changes in k-th POI category, suggesting its key role in flow variation.

To evaluate the causal impacts of all categories, we apply *Softmax* function to normalize all causal effect values, obtaining the overall causal effect value at i-th observation point:

$$\mathcal{C}(i) = Softmax(\mathcal{C}_1(i), ..., \mathcal{C}_K(i)) \in \mathbb{R}^{N \times K}. \tag{18}$$

By performing the above operation at L observation points, we can capture the dynamic causal impacts of POI on crowd flow.

4.3 Predictor and Overall Objective

Predictor. Through the modeling process of C³DE, we obtain the crowd flow representation $h_x(t')$ and POI distribution representation $h_p(t'')$, capturing historical evolution and the key causal features for the prediction task. We fuse their representations to explore the evolution of collaborative signals between POI and crowd flow, resulting in a comprehensive representation H that captures the multidimensional features of crowd flow changes:

$$H = \sigma(h_x(t') \cdot W_x + b_x) \odot (h_p(t'') \cdot W_p + b_p), \tag{19}$$

where W_x and W_p are the learnable weight matrices, b_x and b_p are learnable bias, and $\sigma(\cdot)$ denotes the *sigmod* function.

Subsequently, the fused representation H is fed into a multilayer perceptron-based predictor $G(\cdot)$ to predict the next S time steps, as shown below:

$$\hat{X}_{t+1:t+S} = G(H; \theta_g) \in \mathbb{R}^{S \times N \times C}, \tag{20}$$

where $\hat{X}_{t+1:t+S}$ denotes the predicted values.

Overall Objective. Finally, we adopt the Huber loss as the objective function $\ell(\cdot)$. Compared to the traditional squared error loss, it exhibits greater robustness in handling outliers. For simplicity, we use Y and $\hat{Y}$ to represent $X_{t'+1:t'+S}$ and $\hat{X}_{t'+1:t'+S}$, respectively. The learning objective is expressed as:

$$\ell(Y, \hat{Y}) = \begin{cases} \frac{1}{2}(Y - \hat{Y}), & |Y - \hat{Y}| \leq \delta \\ \delta|Y - \hat{Y}| - \frac{1}{2}\delta^2, & \text{otherwise,} \end{cases} \tag{21}$$

where δ is a hyperparameter that controls the sensitivity to outliers.

4.4 Complexity Analysis of C³DE

In the solving process of C³DE, we adopt the adjoint sensitivity method [8] to compute gradients efficiently. Unlike traditional backpropagation, this method solves an auxiliary adjoint differential equation to trace gradients backward in time, requiring only the storage of the final state rather than the entire forward trajectory. This leads to a space complexity of $O(N \cdot d)$, where N denotes the number of nodes and d is the dimension of the hidden state, significantly lower

Table 1. Statistics of urban crowd flow dataset.

Description	NYC-1	NYC-2	Beijing
time spanning	2012.06~ 2014.05	2014.09~2016.12	2018.07 ~ 2019.10
# of time steps	16,128	17,424	10,241
# of records	2,322,432	2,787,840	1,894,585
# of nodes	144	160	185

Table 2. Statistics of POI distribution dataset.

Description	NYC-1	NYC-2	Beijing
time spanning	2011.10~ 2014.05	2014.01~2016.12	2017.10 ~ 2019.10
# of records	23,040	28,800	32,375
# of nodes	144	160	185
# of types	5	5	7

than that of standard backpropagation. However, this advantage in space comes at the cost of additional computation time. Since the adjoint method requires an extra backward integration, the time complexity is approximately $O(2 \cdot N_{fe} \cdot C_f)$, where N_{fe} is the number of times the CDE solver calls the function $f(\cdot)$, and C_f is the time cost of the spatio-temporal modeling function $f(\cdot)$. Given that our task focuses on long-term crowd flow prediction, where prediction accuracy and stability are prioritized over real-time inference, this trade-off in computation cost is acceptable. The advantages in storage space and model performance make our approach both practical and deployable in real-world urban management applications.

5 Experiments

5.1 Experimental Setup

Dataset. We evaluate the proposed framework on three real-world urban crowd flow datasets and their corresponding POI datasets: *NYC-1* and *NYC-2*, collected from NYC OpenData[1], and *Beijing* [34]. We summarize the statistics for three datasets in Table 1 and Table 2.

Baselines. To evaluate the effectiveness of our C^3DE, we compare it with the following baselines:

- Traditional methods: **HA** predicts future values by averaging historical data from the same time period. **SVR** is a regression method based on support vector machines.

---

[1] https://opendata.cityofnewyork.us/.

Table 3. Overall performance comparison on three real-world datasets. Highlighting denotes the best results and **bolding** denotes the second-best results.

Dataset	Method	Horizon 7			Horizon 14			Average		
		MAE	RMSE	MAPE	MAE	RMSE	MAPE	MAE	RMSE	MAPE
Beijing	HA	289.40	756.21	81.4%	289.40	756.21	81.4%	289.40	756.21	81.4%
	VAR	280.41	724.90	74.2%	285.71	731.12	79.5%	283.06	728.01	76.8%
	STGCN	271.55	669.84	77.3%	283.85	692.63	80.1%	277.70	681.24	78.7%
	GWNET	170.33	414.13	39.0%	208.77	503.38	47.7%	189.55	458.76	43.4%
	STSGCN	198.82	507.28	50.7%	221.04	546.77	53.3%	209.93	527.02	52.0%
	MTGNN	196.19	483.25	**38.9%**	232.93	561.09	48.2%	214.56	522.17	43.6%
	STWave	212.40	522.14	48.6%	242.89	588.74	54.4%	227.65	555.44	51.5%
	STGODE	209.26	498.13	58.1%	234.87	560.02	59.2%	222.07	529.08	58.7%
	STG-NCDE	**159.56**	**404.01**	39.2%	**202.23**	**491.81**	**47.0%**	**180.89**	**447.91**	**43.1%**
	MTGODE	218.85	572.61	75.1%	222.38	594.06	76.4%	220.61	583.33	75.7%
	C³DE	117.56	245.20	35.3 %	124.05	248.39	41.9 %	120.81	246.80	38.6 %
NYC-1	HA	39.065	106.79	34.42%	39.065	106.79	34.42%	39.065	106.79	34.42%
	VAR	36.186	101.18	32.70%	37.393	104.03	33.80%	36.789	102.60	33.25%
	STGCN	28.777	63.783	26.68%	30.316	77.264	26.99%	29.546	70.524	26.84%
	GWNET	25.060	60.958	17.40%	24.970	61.039	17.96%	25.015	60.999	17.68%
	STSGCN	26.143	62.917	26.19%	26.943	63.592	26.14%	26.543	63.255	26.17%
	MTGNN	24.165	57.958	18.94%	24.899	58.121	20.30%	24.532	58.040	19.62%
	STWave	24.354	57.839	16.90%	24.824	58.256	17.35%	24.589	58.047	17.13%
	STGODE	24.868	58.664	20.01%	25.095	58.777	20.75%	24.982	58.721	20.38%
	STG-NCDE	24.693	58.289	19.53%	24.988	58.479	20.52%	24.841	58.384	20.03%
	MTGODE	**24.141**	**57.771**	**16.37%**	**24.758**	**57.726**	**17.06%**	**24.449**	**57.748**	**16.72%**
	C³DE	23.997	55.598	14.16 %	24.050	56.208	14.31 %	24.024	55.903	14.24 %
NYC-2	HA	24.963	63.686	24.73%	24.963	63.686	24.73%	24.963	63.686	24.73%
	VAR	23.908	61.967	16.46%	24.232	62.761	16.22%	24.070	62.364	16.34%
	STGCN	19.969	34.225	11.63%	20.619	36.281	11.64%	20.294	35.253	11.64%
	GWNET	11.043	27.509	8.73%	11.665	29.120	8.90%	11.354	28.314	8.82%
	STSGCN	11.424	27.697	8.84%	11.736	29.163	8.92%	11.580	28.430	8.88%
	MTGNN	10.699	26.470	**8.18%**	11.102	28.049	8.36%	10.901	27.260	8.27%
	STWave	10.933	26.074	8.37%	11.676	28.056	8.45%	11.304	27.065	8.41%
	STGODE	12.780	28.357	11.55%	12.780	29.633	11.43%	12.780	28.995	11.49%
	STG-NCDE	10.876	27.601	8.22%	11.342	28.970	8.78%	11.109	28.286	8.50%
	MTGODE	**10.545**	**26.028**	**8.18%**	**10.816**	**28.023**	**8.33%**	x**10.681**	**27.026**	**8.26%**
	C³DE	10.159	25.619	7.98 %	10.115	27.257	8.07 %	10.137	26.438	8.03 %

- Discrete methods: **STGCN** [31] learns spatio-temporal dependencies with a graph convolutional structure. **GWNET** [30] uses an adaptive adjacency matrix to capture hidden spatial dependencies. **STSGCN** [26] captures localized correlations via the synchronous mechanism. **MTGNN** [29] is a general GNN for modeling multivariate time series. **STWave** [9] is a decomposition-based framework that decouples flow using wavelet transform.

- Continuous methods: **STGODE** [10] extends GNNs with tensor-based ODEs to build deeper networks. **STG-NCDE** [5] designs two NCDEs to model temporal and spatial dependencies. **MTGODE** [16] uses NODEs and dynamic graph structure learning to model continuous dynamics.

Evaluation Metrics. We use Mean Absolute Error (MAE), Root Mean Square Error (RMSE) and Mean Absolute Percentage Error (MAPE) to evaluate performance. Lower values of these metrics indicate better performance.

Implementation Details. We implemented C^3DE in PyTorch using the Adam optimizer with a learning rate $lr = 0.001$, weight decay of 5×10^{-4}, and batch size $B = 64$. The representation size was fixed to 64 for all methods. We set the historical observation length to $T = 14$, $M = 4$, and the future prediction length to $S = 14$. For the Beijing, NYC-1 and NYC-2 datasets, we set the number of observation points to $L = 10/8/8$, respectively. For counterfactual data augmentation, we applied zero-setting perturbation by default. We used an adaptive solver for the Beijing and NYC-2 datasets and the 4th order Runge-Kutta (RK4) solver with a step size of 1.2 for NYC-1. The codes are available at https://github.com/Sonder-arch/C3DE.

5.2 Overall Performance

We evaluate C^3DE on three real-world datasets for the task of long-term urban crowd flow prediction, with results in Table 3. We observe: (1) Statistical methods HA and VAR perform the worst, as relying solely on historical data fails to capture complex and dynamic spatiotemporal patterns, leading to significant prediction errors. (2) MTGODE performs sub-optimally on the NYC-1 and NYC-2 datasets but experiences a sharp performance drop on the Beijing dataset. While its continuous-time modeling and dynamic graph structure can effectively capture long-term dependencies in the stable NYC data, it struggles with the complex temporal dynamics of the more volatile Beijing dataset, resulting in instability. In contrast, STG-NCDE achieves the second-best performance on the Beijing dataset, likely due to its NCDEs-based independent spatio-temporal modeling, which better captures sudden flow changes and intricate temporal dynamics. (3) Continuous methods do not always outperform discrete methods. MTGNN consistently surpasses STGODE across all three datasets, likely because while STGODE employs a continuous GNN with residual connections to avoid over-smoothing, it still relies on a fixed graph structure, limiting its ability to capture potential correlations. MTGNN overcomes this limitation with node-adaptive graph convolution. (4) C^3DE consistently outperforms all baselines, especially on the Beijing dataset, demonstrating its superior generalization and stability. It is due to its ability to uncover complex data changes through counterfactual inference. When handling highly volatile collaborative signals, it more accurately models their continuous evolution, demonstrating stronger robustness and generalization in complex scenarios.

5.3 Ablation Study

In this section, we further validate the effectiveness of the proposed modules in C^3DE, with a particular focus on the continuous modeling and causal mining modules. Specifically, we design the following variants, and the experimental results on Beijing and NYC-2 datasets are shown in Fig. 2.

- *w/o MS-NCDE*: Remove the NCDE continuous modeling module.
- *w/o CA-Att*: Replacing counterfactual-based causal effect values with attention mechanism-based values.
- *w/o CA*: Remove the counterfactual-based causal effect estimator module totally, only simply fuse POI and flow final representations.
- *All*: It is our complete framework.

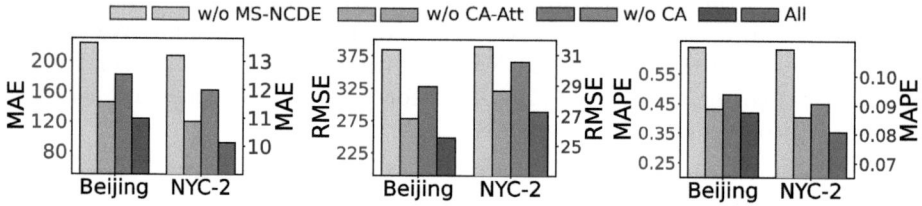

Fig. 2. Ablation study on Beijing and NYC-2 datasets.

Effectiveness of Dynamic Continuous Modeling. Experimental results show that *w/o MS-NCDE* performs the worst across the three datasets, highlighting the effectiveness of collaborative NCDE in continuous collaborative signals modeling. Specifically, collaborative NCDE, formulated as differential equations, can smoothly capture the fine-grained continuous spatio-temporal evolution of collaborative signals, thereby effectively learning potential changes beyond the observation points.

Effectiveness of Causal Dependency Mining. From the results, we can see that the *All* outperforms the *w/o CA* and *w/o CA-Att*, which demonstrates the effectiveness of the counterfactual-based causal effect estimator in capturing and eliminating spurious correlations. Further, we also find that: first, the *w/o CA* variant performs worst among the three variants, indicating that relying solely on POI distribution for prediction is insufficient. While POI distribution can partially reflect flow dynamics, not all POI have a substantive causal relationship with crowd flow. Many POIs exhibit only superficial correlations, which introduce spurious relationships and weaken the model's expressiveness, leading to the performance degradation of *w/o CA*. Second, *w/o CA-Att* models collaborative signals based on attention, dynamically assigning weights to POI distributions to highlight key signals. However, it fundamentally relies on data correlations, making it challenging to distinguish true causal relationships. Third, *All* employs a counterfactual framework for causal inference, capturing more interpretable causal dependencies and mitigating spurious correlations, leading to superior modeling of collaborative signal evolution.

Table 4. The impact of different counterfactual strategies on Beijing dataset.

Method	Horizon 7			Horizon 14			Average		
	MAE	RMSE	MAPE	MAE	RMSE	MAPE	MAE	RMSE	MAPE
baseline (w/o CA)	160.66	291.87	41.8%	182.26	327.58	47.9%	171.46	309.73	44.9%
C^3DE-*random*	123.12	252.36	35.9%	136.08	271.18	42.7%	129.60	261.77	39.3%
C^3DE-*zero*	117.56	245.20	35.3%	124.04	248.39	41.9%	120.81	246.80	38.6%
C^3DE-*mean*	128.53	266.86	36.2%	142.66	278.08	43.4%	135.60	272.47	39.8%

5.4 The Impact of Different Counterfactual Strategies

In this section, we explore the impact of different counterfactual strategies on prediction performance. Specifically, we employ three strategies: "*random*", "*zero*", and "*mean*", against the baseline *w/o CA*, which removes the causal effect estimator module. Table 4 presents the results on Beijing dataset, leading to the following findings: (1) The "*zero*" strategy performs best. As a stringent intervention, it sets the target POI representation to zero, effectively removing its feature information to explore its direct causal impact on crowd flow. (2) Unlike "*zero*", the "*random*" strategy introduces random noise to replace the target POI representation. However, this may introduce uncertainty into the model's causal inference process, leading to suboptimal performance. (3) The "*mean*" strategy averages all POIs representations except the target and uses this average as its counterfactual representation. However, it achieves the lowest performance, possibly because the averaged spatial distribution information blurs the target POI's unique causal effect, making it challenging for the model to capture its true impact. (4) Notably, all three strategies outperform the baseline "*w/o CA*", demonstrating that our framework effectively mines the true causality and thus enhances performance regardless of the intervention strategy.

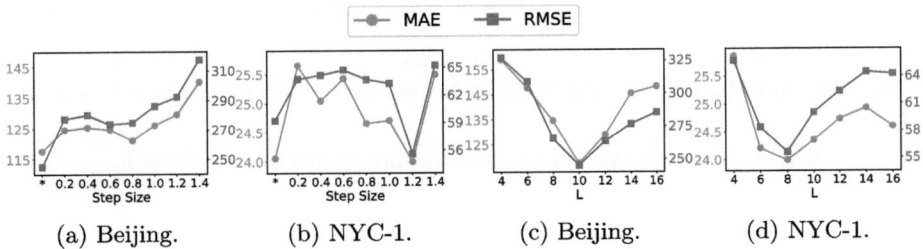

(a) Beijing. (b) NYC-1. (c) Beijing. (d) NYC-1.

Fig. 3. The impacts of *Step Size* and L on two datasets.

5.5 Impacts of Hyper-Parameters

We conduct experiments to validate the impacts of different solvers and the number of observation points L in the dynamic correction mechanism. First, we choose the adaptive solver and the commonly used fixed-step RK4 solver with different step sizes. Note that, smaller step sizes yield finer data fitting. As illustrated in Fig. 3a and Fig. 3b, the adaptive solver (marked with *) and RK4 solver with a step size of 1.2 perform best on the Beijing and NYC-1 datasets, respectively. Performance improves as the step size decreases, as larger step sizes hinder the model to capture precise dynamic changes. However, beyond a threshold, further reducing the step size offers no gains, as the variation between each step becomes negligible. Second, the impacts of varying L from 4 to 16 are shown in Fig. 3c and Fig. 3d. The best results are achieved with $L = 10$ for Beijing and $L = 8$ for NYC-1. A small L limits the model's ability to detect and reduce spurious correlations between collaborative signals, while a large L hinders its capacity to capture dynamic signal variations.

5.6 Visualization of Prediction Results

We conduct a case to demonstrate the advantages of our method over the continuous modeling baseline, STG-NCDE. Specifically, C^3DE excels at capturing the early-stage changes in fluctuations, which are critical for accurate prediction. As shown in Fig. 4, it can not only accurately identify the growth trend at the beginning of the fluctuation(Fig. 4a) but also capture the subsequent decline(Fig. 4b and Fig. 4c), which is due to C^3DE's ability to accurately model the relationships between collaborative signals. These results indicate that C^3DE effectively captures the dynamic changes in the system, precisely tracks the early stages of fluctuations, and accurately predicts the future flow variation trends.

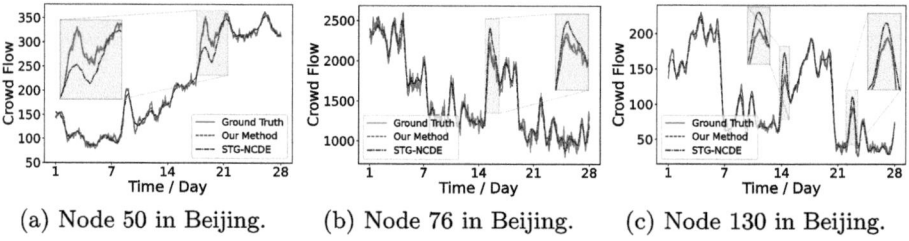

(a) Node 50 in Beijing. (b) Node 76 in Beijing. (c) Node 130 in Beijing.

Fig. 4. Visualization of prediction results on the Beijing dataset.

6 Conclusion

In this paper, we proposed C^3DE, a framework with causal-aware collaborative neural controlled differential equations for long-term urban crowd flow prediction. We first introduced the neural CDE with a dual-path architecture to capture the asynchronous dynamic evolution of collaborative signals. Next, we designed a counterfactual inference-based causal effect estimator to simulate urban dynamics under different POI distribution scenarios and mine the direct impact of different POIs on crowd flow. Moreover, we incorporated causal effect values into neural CDE. By introducing a causal effect-based dynamic correction mechanism, C^3DE can mitigate the accumulation of spurious correlations among collaborative signals. Extensive experiments on three real-world datasets demonstrated the significant superiority of C^3DE. Future work will focus on enhancing causal relationship mining efficiency by integrating causal priors based on domain knowledge in urban dynamics.

Acknowledgments. This work was supported by the Natural Science Foundation of China (Grant No. 62072235) and the Young Scientists Fund of the Natural Science Foundation of Jiangsu Province, China (Grant No. BK20241402). We would also like to thank the anonymous reviewers for giving us useful and constructive comments. Additionally, we are grateful to the community and everyone who made their datasets and source codes publicly accessible. These datasets and source codes are valuable and have greatly facilitated this research.

References

1. Bai, L., Yao, L., Li, C., Wang, X., Wang, C.: Adaptive graph convolutional recurrent network for traffic forecasting. Adv. Neural. Inf. Process. Syst. **33**, 17804–17815 (2020)
2. Chen, C., Liu, Y., Chen, L., Zhang, C.: Multivariate traffic demand prediction via 2d spectral learning and global spatial optimization. In: Joint European Conference on Machine Learning and Knowledge Discovery in Databases, pp. 72–88. Springer (2024)
3. Chen, G., Li, J., Lu, J., Zhou, J.: Human trajectory prediction via counterfactual analysis. In: Proceedings of the IEEE/CVF International Conference on Computer Vision, pp. 9824–9833 (2021)
4. Chen, R.T., Rubanova, Y., Bettencourt, J., Duvenaud, D.K.: Neural ordinary differential equations. Advances in neural information processing systems **31** (2018)
5. Choi, J., Choi, H., Hwang, J., Park, N.: Graph neural controlled differential equations for traffic forecasting. In: Proceedings of the AAAI Conference on Artificial Intelligence, pp. 6367–6374 (2022)
6. Dey, R., Salem, F.M.: Gate-variants of gated recurrent unit (gru) neural networks. In: 2017 IEEE 60th International Midwest Symposium on Circuits and Systems (MWSCAS), pp. 1597–1600. IEEE (2017)
7. Diks, C., Panchenko, V.: A new statistic and practical guidelines for nonparametric granger causality testing. J. Econ. Dyn. Control **30**(9–10), 1647–1669 (2006)
8. Errico, R.M.: What is an adjoint model? Bull. Am. Meteor. Soc. **78**(11), 2577–2592 (1997)
9. Fang, Y., et al.: When spatio-temporal meet wavelets: disentangled traffic forecasting via efficient spectral graph attention networks. In: 2023 IEEE 39th International Conference on Data Engineering (ICDE), pp. 517–529. IEEE (2023)
10. Fang, Z., Long, Q., Song, G., Xie, K.: Spatial-temporal graph ode networks for traffic flow forecasting. In: Proceedings of the 27th ACM SIGKDD Conference on Knowledge Discovery & Data Mining, pp. 364–373 (2021)

11. Gravina, A., Zambon, D., Bacciu, D., Alippi, C.: Temporal graph odes for irregularly-sampled time series. In: Proceedings of the Thirty-Third International Joint Conference on Artificial Intelligence (2024)
12. Huang, Z., Sun, Y., Wang, W.: Learning continuous system dynamics from irregularly-sampled partial observations. Adv. Neural. Inf. Process. Syst. **33**, 16177–16187 (2020)
13. Huang, Z., Sun, Y., Wang, W.: Coupled graph ode for learning interacting system dynamics. In: Proceedings of the 27th ACM SIGKDD Conference on Knowledge Discovery & Data Mining, pp. 705–715 (2021)
14. Islam, M.A., et al.: A comparative study on numerical solutions of initial value problems (ivp) for ordinary differential equations (ode) with euler and runge kutta methods. Am. J. Comput. Math. **5**(03), 393 (2015)
15. Jiang, J., Han, C., Zhao, W.X., Wang, J.: Pdformer: propagation delay-aware dynamic long-range transformer for traffic flow prediction. In: Proceedings of the AAAI Conference on Artificial Intelligence, pp. 4365–4373 (2023)
16. Jin, M., Zheng, Y., Li, Y.F., Chen, S., Yang, B., Pan, S.: Multivariate time series forecasting with dynamic graph neural odes. IEEE Trans. Knowl. Data Eng. **35**(9), 9168–9180 (2022)
17. Kidger, P., Morrill, J., Foster, J., Lyons, T.: Neural controlled differential equations for irregular time series. Adv. Neural. Inf. Process. Syst. **33**, 6696–6707 (2020)
18. Li, H., et al.: Beyond relevance: factor-level causal explanation for user travel decisions with counterfactual data augmentation. ACM Trans. Inf. Syst. **42**(5), 1–31 (2024)
19. Li, H., Gu, J., Ying, H., Lu, X., Yang, J.: User multi-behavior enhanced poi recommendation with efficient and informative negative sampling. In: Asia-Pacific Web (APWeb) and Web-Age Information Management (WAIM) Joint International Conference on Web and Big Data, pp. 149–165. Springer (2022)
20. Liang, Y., Ke, S., Zhang, J., Yi, X., Zheng, Y.: Geoman: Multi-level attention networks for geo-sensory time series prediction. In: IJCAI, vol. 2018, pp. 3428–3434 (2018)
21. Liu, Z., Ding, J., Zheng, G.: Frequency enhanced pre-training for cross-city few-shot traffic forecasting. In: Joint European Conference on Machine Learning and Knowledge Discovery in Databases, pp. 35–52. Springer (2024)
22. Long, Q., Fang, Z., Fang, C., Chen, C., Wang, P., Zhou, Y.: Unveiling delay effects in traffic forecasting: a perspective from spatial-temporal delay differential equations. In: Proceedings of the ACM on Web Conference 2024, pp. 1035–1044 (2024)
23. Rong, C., Li, T., Feng, J., Li, Y.: Inferring origin-destination flows from population distribution. IEEE Trans. Knowl. Data Eng. **35**(1), 603–613 (2021)
24. Shao, X., Wang, H., Chen, X., Zhu, X., Zhang, Y.: Cube: causal intervention-based counterfactual explanation for prediction models. IEEE Trans. Knowl. Data Eng. (2023)
25. Shao, Z., et al.: Decoupled dynamic spatial-temporal graph neural network for traffic forecasting. Proceedings of the VLDB Endowment **15**(11), 2733–2746 (2022)
26. Song, C., Lin, Y., Guo, S., Wan, H.: Spatial-temporal synchronous graph convolutional networks: A new framework for spatial-temporal network data forecasting. In: Proceedings of the AAAI Conference on Artificial Intelligence, pp. 914–921 (2020)
27. Tian, B., Cao, Y., Zhang, Y., Xing, C.: Debiasing nlu models via causal intervention and counterfactual reasoning. In: Proceedings of the AAAI Conference on Artificial Intelligence, pp. 11376–11384 (2022)

28. Wang, Z., et al.: Counterfactual data-augmented sequential recommendation. In: Proceedings of the 44th International ACM SIGIR Conference on Research and Development in Information Retrieval, pp. 347–356 (2021)
29. Wu, Z., Pan, S., Long, G., Jiang, J., Chang, X., Zhang, C.: Connecting the dots: multivariate time series forecasting with graph neural networks. In: Proceedings of the 26th ACM SIGKDD International Conference on Knowledge Discovery & Data Mining, pp. 753–763 (2020)
30. Wu, Z., Pan, S., Long, G., Jiang, J., Zhang, C.: Graph wavenet for deep spatial-temporal graph modeling. In: Proceedings of the 28th International Joint Conference on Artificial Intelligence, pp. 1907–1913 (2019)
31. Yu, B., Yin, H., Zhu, Z.: Spatio-temporal graph convolutional networks: a deep learning framework for traffic forecasting. In: Proceedings of the 27th International Joint Conference on Artificial Intelligence, pp. 3634–3640 (2018)
32. Yu, C., Wang, F., Shao, Z., Sun, T., Wu, L., Xu, Y.: Dsformer: a double sampling transformer for multivariate time series long-term prediction. In: Proceedings of the 32nd ACM International Conference on Information and Knowledge Management, pp. 3062–3072 (2023)
33. Zeng, J., Zhang, G., Rong, C., Ding, J., Yuan, J., Li, Y.: Causal learning empowered od prediction for urban planning. In: Proceedings of the 31st ACM International Conference on Information & Knowledge Management, pp. 2455–2464 (2022)
34. Zheng, Z., Gu, J., Zhou, Q., Lu, X.: Prediction in long-term evolution: Exploiting the interaction between urban crowd flow variation and poi transition patterns. In: 2023 IEEE International Conference on Data Mining (ICDM), pp. 1559–1564. IEEE (2023)
35. Zmigrod, R., Mielke, S.J., Wallach, H., Cotterell, R.: Counterfactual data augmentation for mitigating gender stereotypes in languages with rich morphology. In: Proceedings of the 57th Annual Meeting of the Association for Computational Linguistics, pp. 1651–1661 (2019)

Bridging Neural Networks and Dynamic Time Warping for Adaptive Time Series Classification

Jintao Qu[1(✉)], Zichong Wang[2], Chenhao Wu[1], Wenbin Zhang[2], and Dongmei Li[3]

[1] University of Southern California, Los Angele 90089, CA, USA
{jintaoqu,wuchenha}@usc.edu
[2] Florida International University, Miami 33199, FL, USA
{zwang114,wenbin.zhang}@fiu.edu
[3] Beijing Forestry University, Beijing 100083, China
lidongmei@bjfu.edu.com

Abstract. Neural networks have achieved remarkable success in time series classification, but their reliance on large amounts of labeled data for training limits their applicability in cold-start scenarios. Moreover, they lack interpretability, reducing transparency in decision-making. In contrast, dynamic time warping (DTW) combined with a nearest neighbor classifier is widely used for its effectiveness in limited-data settings and its inherent interpretability. However, as a non-parametric method, it is not trainable and cannot leverage large amounts of labeled data, making it less effective than neural networks in rich-resource scenarios. In this work, we aim to develop a versatile model that adapts to cold-start conditions and becomes trainable with labeled data, while maintaining interpretability. We propose a dynamic length-shortening algorithm that transforms time series into prototypes while preserving key structural patterns, thereby enabling the reformulation of the DTW recurrence relation into an equivalent recurrent neural network. Based on this, we construct a trainable model that mimics DTW's alignment behavior. As a neural network, it becomes trainable when sufficient labeled data is available, while still retaining DTW's inherent interpretability. We apply the model to several benchmark time series classification tasks and observe that it significantly outperforms previous approaches in low-resource settings and remains competitive in rich-resource settings.

Keywords: Time series · Dynamic time warping · Interpretability

1 Introduction

Time Series Classification (TSC) is a subfield of machine learning concerned with assigning categorical labels to time series data. Owing to the remarkable success of deep learning in fields such as image recognition and natural language processing, researchers have increasingly explored deep learning-based approaches for TSC [8,11,31]. Existing research primarily focuses on leveraging the parallelization and feature extraction capabilities of deep learning to improve scalability and classification accuracy. For instance, InceptionTime [9], inspired by the Inception-v4 architecture [28], achieves high classification accuracy while enhancing scalability through an ensemble of Convolutional Neural Networks. Similarly, Rocket [5] attains state-of-the-art performance by utilizing random convolutional kernels. Despite their superior accuracy, deep learning-based TSC methods often suffer from significant limitations. In particular, they typically require large amounts of labeled data to generalize effectively [19], which poses challenges in real-world scenarios where labeled data is scarce [37]. For example, in the medical domain, ethical constraints and data collection biases may lead to severe data imbalances, where common conditions are well-represented while rare diseases lack sufficient samples [21]. Moreover, while state-of-the-art deep learning models employ complex ensembles to improve classification performance, these intricate architectures often compromise interpretability [14]. In critical applications such as medical diagnosis [33], where transparency and explainability are essential, this trade-off remains a major concern. However, deep learning is not the only effective approach. Traditional instance-based methods, such as DTW, remain highly competitive due to their robustness against temporal misalignment and ability to perform well in low-resource settings.

DTW is widely used in time series classification for its capability to align sequences with temporal distortions, for many years, the nearest neighbor classifier with DTW (NN-DTW) has been the predominant approach for time series classification [1]. Despite extensive research efforts to develop alternative similarity measures [20,26,30], NN-DTW remains one of the most competitive approaches on the UCR Archive [4], which serves as the standard benchmark for evaluating TSC performance. As an instance-based approach, NN-DTW provides inherent interpretability by explicitly aligning time series instances. Additionally, unlike deep learning models that require extensive labeled data, NN-DTW can be deployed with only a few instances, making it particularly effective in cold-start scenario [36]. However, NN-DTW lacks trainability, which limits its ability to improve as more data becomes available. This limitation is particularly critical in domains such as medical diagnosis, where models must operate effectively in both cold-start scenarios with scarce patient data and data-rich environments where large-scale labeled datasets are progressively accumulated [29]. In such settings, a adaptive approach is required–one that can ensure reliable classification under low-resource conditions while continuously improving through data-driven optimization when sufficient labeled data is available.

Incorporating the strengths of both neural networks and instance-based approaches is crucial for many applications. However, several fundamental challenges prevent existing techniques from achieving this goal, including: **1) Bridging Instance-Based and Neural Paradigms.** Instance-based methods such as DTW offer strong performance in low-resource scenarios, while neural networks excel in learning from large-scale data through end-to-end optimization. However, combining these advantages in a single model is non-trivial. It requires a trainable architecture that not only supports alignment-based reasoning but also enables gradient-based learning, allowing the model to adapt across diverse data regimes without sacrificing generalization or flexibility. **2) Reducing the Computational Overhead of Alignment.** Dynamic Time Warping involves recursive dynamic programming, which is inherently sequential and difficult to parallelize. This hinders scalability and integration with modern GPU-accelerated deep learning frameworks. To bridge this gap, an effective approach must restructure DTW-like alignment operations into differentiable, parallelizable forms without losing their alignment interpretability–thus enabling fast training and inference in large-scale settings. **3) Learning Robust Representations under Structural Variability.** Time series often exhibit significant variability in length, local distortions, and structural patterns. While DTW handles alignment, it does not provide a robust representation that generalizes across such variations. Neural networks, on the other hand, may overfit to noise or irrelevant patterns without explicit structural guidance. Designing a representation that captures salient alignment structures while ignoring redundant or misleading variations is crucial. This requires a mechanism to extract prototypical patterns that are not only discriminative but also compact and resilient to temporal noise.

This paper proposes a universal model that preserves the structured alignment behavior of DTW while enabling trainability within a neural network framework, all while maintaining interpretability. Specifically, we introduce a length-shortening algorithm that transforms time series into prototypes while preserving key structural patterns, thereby establishing a formal equivalence between DTW and recurrent neural networks (RNNs). Building on this foundation, we design a trainable architecture that mimics DTW's alignment process, allowing it to handle cold-start scenarios effectively while continuously improving as labeled data becomes available. At the same time, the model retains the instance-based reasoning of DTW, ensuring a transparent decision-making process and preserving interpretability. Overall, our main contributions are as follows:

- A versatile model that not only leverages DTW's alignment properties in a trainable setting but also adapts to both cold-start scenarios with limited data and rich-resource settings, bridging the gap between instance-based methods and deep learning.
- A dynamic length-shortening algorithm that converts time series into prototypes while preserving key structural patterns, enabling the DTW recurrence relation to be reformulated as an equivalent recurrent neural network.
- A novel framework that reformulates DTW as an equivalent recurrent neural network, making it trainable while preserving its alignment behavior.
- Extensive experiments and case studies demonstrating the effectiveness of our approach across multiple benchmark time series classification tasks.

2 Preliminaries

Time series classification is the task of assigning a class label to a given time series based on its temporal patterns. Formally, let $\mathbf{x} = \langle x_1, x_2, \ldots, x_N \rangle$ be a time series of length N, where each time step $x_i \in \mathbb{R}^D$ represents a D-dimensional feature vector. The goal of TSC is to learn a mapping function $f : \mathbb{R}^{N \times D} \to \mathcal{L}$ that assigns a label from a predefined set $\mathcal{L} = \{l_1, l_2, \ldots, l_c\}$, where $|\mathcal{L}| = c$ denotes the number of distinct classes.

In distance-based methods for TSC, a fundamental challenge lies in designing effective similarity measures, as variations in sequence length, local distortions, and temporal misalignments often undermine the effectiveness of Euclidean distance. Dynamic Time Warping (DTW) mitigates this issue by computing an optimal warping path, enabling flexible alignments between time series.

Formally, given two time series $\mathbf{x} = \langle x_1, x_2, \ldots, x_N \rangle$ and $\mathbf{y} = \langle y_1, y_2, \ldots, y_M \rangle$, DTW defines a cost matrix $\Delta(\mathbf{x}, \mathbf{y}) = [\delta(x_i, y_j)]_{ij} \in \mathbb{R}^{N \times M}$, where each element $\delta(x_i, y_j)$ represents the alignment cost between time steps x_i and y_j, typically computed using a predefined distance function, such as the squared Euclidean distance. A valid alignment between $\mathbf{x}$ and $\mathbf{y}$ can be represented as a warping path $p = [(e_1, f_1), (e_2, f_2), \ldots, (e_s, f_s)]$ which traces a valid path through the cost matrix Δ, connecting the upper-left entry $(1,1)$ to the lower-right entry (N, M) via permitted moves: downward ($\downarrow$), rightward ($\rightarrow$), or diagonally downward-right ($\searrow$).

To quantify the overall alignment cost of a given warping path, we define the DTW distance as the minimum cumulative alignment cost over all valid warping paths:

$$dtw(\mathbf{x}, \mathbf{y}) = \min_{p \in \mathcal{A}(\mathbf{x}, \mathbf{y})} \sum_{i=1}^{s} \Delta(\mathbf{x}, \mathbf{y})[e_i, f_i], \quad (1)$$

where $\mathcal{A}(\mathbf{x}, \mathbf{y})$ denotes the set of all valid warping paths, and each alignment cost $\Delta(\mathbf{x}, \mathbf{y})[e_i, f_i]$ is accumulated along the path p.

Given the prohibitive complexity of exhaustively searching all possible warping paths, DTW is conventionally computed via dynamic programming. Let $h \in \mathbb{R}^{N \times M}$ denote the cumulative cost matrix, where each entry $h[i, j]$ represents the DTW distance between subsequences $x_{1..i}$ and $y_{1..j}$. The computation of $h[i, j]$ follows the recursive relation:

$$h[i, j] = \Delta(\mathbf{x}, \mathbf{y})[i, j] + \min \begin{pmatrix} h[i-1, j], \\ h[i, j-1], \\ h[i-1, j-1] \end{pmatrix}, \quad (2)$$

where $0 < i \leq N$, $0 < j \leq M$, and $h[0, :] = h[:, 0] = \infty$. The final result is $h[n, m]$. After computing the entire matrix, the final DTW distance is given by $h[N, M]$, and the corresponding optimal warping path can be retrieved via backtracking.

3 The Proposed Method

Here we show step-by-step how we initialize a trainable recurrent neural network with sample instances and apply to time series classification.

3.1 Optimization of DTW via Dynamic Length Shortening

DTW-based methods for TSC often suffer from excessive computational complexity when dealing with long sequences. The traditional DTW alignment retains the full sequence length, leading to increased storage requirements and high computational costs. Furthermore, as this study seeks to reformulate DTW-based methods into an equivalent recurrent neural network, preserving the full sequence in its original form could potentially expand the parameter space, leading to a higher risk of overfitting, increased memory usage, and slower training convergence. In this context, a natural question arises: whether the sequences used as templates for DTW comparison can be shortened without compromising their discriminative capability (i.e., without significantly increasing alignment inertia).

With this in mind, we propose a dynamic length-shortening method that iteratively reduces the sequence length while preserving the essential structural characteristics required for DTW alignment. The core idea is to merge the closest successive coordinates, effectively compressing redundant information while minimizing distortions in the temporal structure, thereby achieving a more compact yet representative sequence.

To illustrate how dynamic length shortening works, let us consider a simple example shown in Fig. 1. Specifically, Fig. 1(a) illustrates the DTW alignment between two sequences, where the bottom sequence (marked in orange) initially contains two separate coordinates aligned to multiple points in the top sequence. According to dynamic length-shortening, these two coordinates can be merged into a single coordinate due to their similarity. Figure 1(b) demonstrates the resulting alignment after applying length shortening, where the two original coordinates in the bottom sequence are merged into one. Despite this reduction in length, the DTW alignment distance remains nearly unchanged, indicating that the shortened sequence effectively preserves the temporal information of the original sequence.

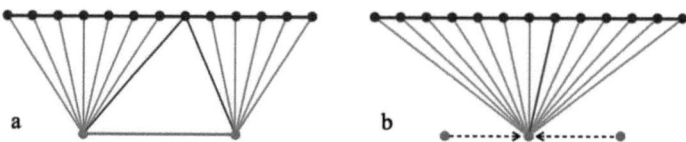

Fig. 1. Illustration of the dynamic length-shortening process. (a) The original alignment, where the bottom sequence contains redundant consecutive coordinates, (b) the alignment after adaptive length shortening, where redundant coordinates are merged.

Furthermore, as illustrated by the green-marked correspondences in Fig. 1, the shortening process tends to eliminate many instances of one-to-many alignments between the sample sequence (blue) and the prototype sequence (orange). In this case, the DTW warping path tends to consist only of downward ($\downarrow$) and diagonal ($\searrow$) moves, eliminating horizontal ($\rightarrow$) transitions. In other words, after appropriately scaling the prototype sequence, the state transition equation of DTW can be approximately optimized as Eq. 3.

$$h[i,j] = \Delta(\mathbf{x},\mathbf{y})[i,j] + \min\begin{pmatrix} h[i-1,j], \\ h[i-1,j-1] \end{pmatrix}, \quad (3)$$

In the context of TSC, the primary objective is to quantify the similarity between the sample sequence and the shortened prototype sequence. Consequently, it is unnecessary to retain the entire cost matrix for backtracking to determine the optimal warping path. Thus, Eq. 3 can be further reformulated into a more space efficient form, as presented in Eq. 4.

$$h_t[j] = \Delta_t(\mathbf{y})[j] + \min\begin{pmatrix} h_{t-1}[j], \\ h_{t-1}[j-1] \end{pmatrix}, \quad (4)$$

where $h_t \in \mathbb{R}^{N+1}$ denotes the states at time step t, and $\Delta_t(\mathbf{y}) = [\delta(x_t, y_j)]_j \in \mathbb{R}^L$ denotes the pairwise distance between the sequences at step t. The indices satisfy $0 < t \leq N$ and $0 < j \leq L$, with boundary conditions $h_0[:] = \infty$ and $h_t[0] = \infty$. The final cost is given by $h_N[L]$.

3.2 From Optimized DTW to Recurrent Neural Network

In the classification task, computing the DTW distance between a given sample sequence $\mathbf{x}$ and multiple prototype sequences from different classes requires evaluating DTW distances in a batch-wise manner. To achieve this, we define the set of prototype sequences as $S = \{\mathbf{y}^1, \mathbf{y}^2, ..., \mathbf{y}^K\}$, where K is the number of prototypes. The pairwise distance matrix between the sample sequence and all prototype sequences at time step t is given by $\Delta_t(S) = [\delta(\mathbf{x}_t, \mathbf{y}_j^i)]_{ij} \in \mathbb{R}^{K \times L}$. Similarly, let $h_t \in \mathbb{R}^{K \times L}$ represent the accumulated DTW cost matrix, where $h_t[i,j]$ denotes the DTW distance between $\mathbf{x}_{1..t}$ and $\mathbf{y}_{1..j}^i$.

By extending Equation (4) to batch computation, the recursive update for DTW distances can be expressed as follows:

$$h_t[i,j] = \Delta_t(S)[i,j] + \min\begin{pmatrix} h_{t-1}[i,j], \\ h_{t-1}[i-1,j] \end{pmatrix}, \quad (5)$$

where $0 < i \leq K$, $0 < j \leq L$. The boundary conditions are defined as $h_t[:,0] = \infty$, and the initialization at $t = 0$ is set as $h_0[:,:] = \infty$. The final DTW distances for classification are obtained as $h_N[:,L]$, representing the DTW costs between the sample sequence and all prototype sequences across different classes.

At this point, Equation (5) can be regarded as a recurrent neural network of the form $h_t = f(h_{t-1})$. In this context, the first term, $\Delta_t(S)[i,j]$, can be interpreted as an input-dependent transformation at time step t, serving as an input transformation that reflects the similarity between the sample sequence at time step t and the prototype sequence features.

To integrate the DTW-based recurrence into a trainable neural network model, we represent the computation in terms of standard tensor operations. The structured recurrence defined in Equation (5) can be reformulated within a deep learning framework using a sequence of differentiable operators, allowing gradient-based optimization.

The proposed recurrent neural network is parameterized by a set of trainable variables, denoted as $\Theta = \langle P, h_t, O, W, b \rangle$, where:

- $P \in \mathbb{R}^{K \times L \times D}$ represents the prototype tensor constructed by directly concatenating K prototype sequences. Here, L corresponds to the sequence length after length shortening, and D is the feature dimension at each time step. Specifically, $P[i,t] \in \mathbb{R}^D$ denotes the feature vector at time step t of the $i-th$ prototype sequence.
- $h_t \in \mathbb{R}^{K \times L}$ represents the hidden state matrix at time step t, corresponding to the recursive cost aggregation in Equation (5).
- $O \in \mathbb{R}^L$ is a static one-hot vector with $O[L] = 1$, enabling the extraction of the final alignment cost. The network output is computed as $h_t O \in \mathbb{R}^K$, representing the final cost for each prototype.
- $W \in \mathbb{R}^{K \times D}$ and $b \in \mathbb{R}^K$ parameterize a linear transformation applied to the input signal, ensuring feature alignment before feeding into the recurrent structure.

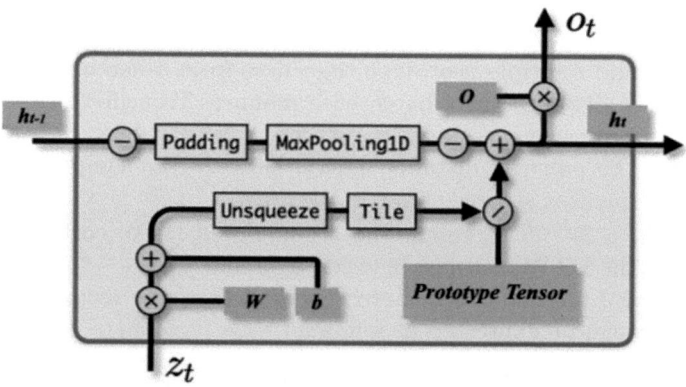

Fig. 2. Illustration of the computation flow in the proposed neural model.

Based on the aforementioned model definition, the overall computational flow is illustrated in Fig. 2. Referring to the equivalent transformation in Equation (5), this computation can be decomposed into following two parts:

(1) Computation of $\Delta_t(S)$. At time step t, the model takes the sample's feature representation $\mathbf{x}_t \in \mathbb{R}^D$ as input, along with the hidden state from the previous step h_{t-1}. To ensure compatibility with the prototype tensor P, $\mathbf{x}_t$ undergoes a linear transformation and is then broadcasted across all prototype sequences, enabling pairwise distance computation between the transformed sample representation and each prototype, which is computed as:

$$\Delta_t(S) = \|(W\mathbf{x}_t + b)\mathbf{1}^\top - P\|^2, \tag{6}$$

where $\mathbf{1} \in \mathbb{R}^L$ is an all-ones vector that enables replication along the second dimension. The notation $\|\cdot\|^2$ represents the pairwise squared Euclidean distance computed across the feature dimension. In practice (as illustrated in Fig. 2), the replication induced by $\mathbf{1}^\top$ can be implemented using tensor operations, where Unsqueeze introduces an additional dimension and Tile expands it along the second axis to align with the prototype tensor.

(2) Computation of $\min\begin{pmatrix} h_{t-1}[i,j], \\ h_{t-1}[i-1,j] \end{pmatrix}$. At time step t, computing the minimum between $h_{t-1}[i,j]$ and $h_{t-1}[i-1,j]$ can be rewritten using the identity $\min(a,b) = -\max(-a,-b)$. To ensure consistency with DTW's alignment mechanism, we first apply a padding operation to the previous hidden state h_{t-1}, producing $h'_{t-1} \in \mathbb{R}^{M \times (L+1)}$ with $h'_{t-1}[:,0] = \infty$. This initialization follows the DTW recurrence formulation, ensuring that the boundary conditions are correctly handled. With this transformation, the minimum operation can be reformulated as:

$$\min\begin{pmatrix} h_{t-1}[i,j], \\ h_{t-1}[i-1,j] \end{pmatrix} = -\max\begin{pmatrix} -h_{t-1}[i,j], \\ -h_{t-1}[i-1,j] \end{pmatrix}$$
$$= -\text{MaxPooling1D}\Big(-h'_{t-1}\Big), \tag{7}$$

here max-pooling is performed using a 1D max-pooling layer with a kernel size of 2 and a stride of 1, which is functionally equivalent to the max function. This design ensures that the recurrence relation of DTW is efficiently computed within deep learning frameworks while maintaining differentiability.

3.3 Logical Aggregation Layer for Classification

Building upon the neuralized dynamic time warping computation introduced in the previous section, we obtain a set of similarity scores between the input sequence $\mathbf{x}$ and the prototype set S, where each prototype represents a reference sequence for a specific class. These similarity scores, derived from softmax-normalized DTW distances, serve as intermediate alignment measures between the input sequence and various class prototypes.

To facilitate classification, we introduce an aggregation mechanism that consolidates similarity scores into a class-level decision. Given an input sequence **x**, we first compute softmax-normalized alignment scores between **x** and its corresponding prototypes. Each class is represented by a collection of prototypes, where $S_{l_c} = \{y^1, y^2, \ldots, y^k\}$ denotes the set of k prototypes corresponding to class l_c. The classification probability is computed by aggregating these similarity scores, which can be interpreted as a differentiable approximation of logical disjunction ($\bigvee$). Prior work [17] has shown that first-order logic principles can be integrated into neural networks by approximating discrete logical rules with trainable functions. Following this approach, we approximate the logical disjunction of prototype alignments using a soft aggregation function as shown in Eq. 8:

$$Score(l_c) = \bigvee_{y^i \in S_{l_c}} \sigma(-h_N O)_i \approx \min\left(1, \sum_{y^i \in S_{l_c}} \sigma(-h_N O)_i\right), \quad (8)$$

where $\sigma(\cdot)$ denotes the softmax function. The final predicted class is the one with the highest aggregated score:

$$\hat{l} = \arg\max_{l \in \mathcal{L}} Score(l). \quad (9)$$

This computation can be efficiently implemented using a two-layer MLP, following the framework in [17], where logical operations are approximated by neural transformations similar to those used for mapping hidden representations to label logits in traditional neural networks.

3.4 Interpretability

Our model inherently preserves the interpretability advantages of instance-based methods while benefiting from the flexibility of trainable representations. Unlike black-box deep learning models that rely solely on abstract feature extraction, our approach enables a direct alignment between input sequences and learned prototypes, making the decision process more transparent. Since the learned prototypes function similarly to nearest neighbors in a transformed space, classification outcomes can be traced back to specific reference sequences, allowing for clear instance-based reasoning. This makes it easier to understand why a particular sample was assigned to a given class, which is especially valuable in high-stakes applications such as medical diagnosis. Furthermore, our model allows for the visualization of learned prototypes, providing deeper insights into how it distinguishes between different categories and adapts to new data over time, which is particularly relevant in real-world applications where understanding model updates and decision boundaries is critical for reliability.

4 Experiments

In this section, we evaluate the proposed method through three dimensions: (1) comparative benchmarking with state-of-the-art approaches in Sect. 4.2, and

(2) performance analysis under varying training data scales in Sect. 4.3. We provided our code and complete results with standard deviations in Github, and it is available at: https://anonymous.4open.science/r/Neurlized-Dynamic-Time-Warping-CBE5.

4.1 Experimental Settings

Datasets. To provide a broad evaluation, we assess our proposed model on all the 85 benchmark datasets from the UCR Time Series Archive [4]. Given that the effectiveness of classification algorithms varies across time series domains, we further highlight 40 datasets that are particularly relevant to distance-based methods. These datasets are characterized by temporal misalignment, dynamic pattern variability, and class separability that is better captured by similarity-based measures rather than purely statistical features. By focusing on this subset, we aim to provide deeper insights into how our method performs in scenarios where alignment-based similarity plays a critical role, allowing for a more targeted comparison against traditional baselines. For the low-resource and full-training experiments (Sect. 4.3), we simulate cold-start conditions by randomly subsampling the training data at rates ranging from 1% to 100%. This enables us to examine the model's performance under different levels of data availability. The 1% sampling rate represents an extreme low-resource setting, where very few labeled instances are available, while the 100% sampling rate corresponds to a fully data-rich scenario, serving as a baseline for evaluating the model's learning capacity when ample training data is provided. To ensure a consistent training setup across different resource levels, we apply a unified data augmentation strategy to all sampled subsets. This approach allows us to assess the model's performance under varying degrees of data availability while maintaining comparable preprocessing procedures.

Training. All models in this study were implemented in Python 3.8 with CUDA 11.1, using PyTorch 1.10.0 as the primary deep learning framework. Additionally, some baseline models were constructed using existing time series analysis libraries - sktime and tsai, to ensure fair and reproducible comparisons. For hyperparameter selection, we adopted a grid search strategy to explore optimal configurations for most model parameters. Specifically, we varied the number of prototypes per class across {5, 10, 15, 20} and the sequence shortening ratio within {0.3, 0.5, 0.8, 0.9} to identify the optimal hyperparameters. A complete list of hyperparameter configurations and additional details are provided in the source code.

Baselines. To ensure a comprehensive evaluation of our approach, we select a diverse range of baselines that allow us to assess its effectiveness against both classical and state-of-the-art models. Following the latest survey on time series classification [22], we include two state-of-the-art deep learning-based methods,

Rocket and InceptionTime [9], both of which have demonstrated strong performance on diverse benchmark datasets. Additionally, since our proposed model adopts a recurrent structure, we incorporate LSTM [7] as a baseline to provide a direct comparison with other recurrent neural network-based approaches. Given that our model is fundamentally DTW-based, we also adopt the Nearest Neighbor classifier with DTW (NN-DTW) as a baseline, as it remains one of the most widely used methods in time series classification. To further enrich the comparison, we include two ensemble-based methods, BOSS [24] and Elastic Ensemble (EE) [18], which have been shown to perform well on various datasets by leveraging multiple similarity measures and transformation-based features.

4.2 Benchmarking Against State-of-the-Art Models

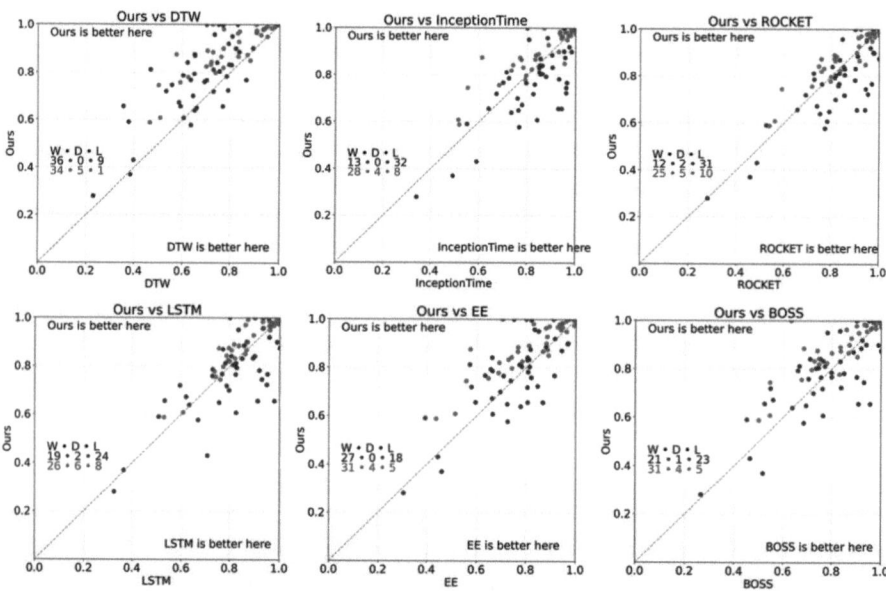

Fig. 3. Accuracy comparison between our model and various baselines. Each point represents a dataset, with the x-axis showing baseline accuracy and the y-axis showing our model's accuracy. Red points indicate datasets where distance-based methods are preferred. Points above the diagonal represent cases where our model outperforms the baseline.

We compare our model with various baseline methods to verify its effectiveness in time series classification. For fairness, we take the best performance of each method for comparison. Figure 3 presents the accuracy comparison across all 85 datasets from the UCR archive. Each point represents a dataset, where the x-axis shows the accuracy of the baseline model and the y-axis shows the accuracy of our proposed model. Points above the diagonal line indicate cases where our model outperforms the corresponding baseline, while points below the line indicate cases where the baseline achieves higher accuracy.

From Fig. 3, we observe that our model demonstrates consistent superiority over DTW-kNN, particularly in distance-based datasets, winning on 34 datasets, drawing on 5, and losing on only 1, highlighting that our method effectively retains DTW's alignment benefits while improving trainability. Against LSTM, which shares a recurrent structure, our model outperforms in 26 distance-based datasets, with 6 draws and 8 losses, demonstrating superior generalization capabilities. Comparing with deep learning-based methods, our model remains highly competitive. Against InceptionTime, we achieve 28 wins, 4 draws, and 8 losses in distance-based datasets, while against ROCKET, the numbers are 25 wins, 5 draws, and 10 losses. For ensemble-based methods, our model demonstrates strong robustness. Against EE, we achieve 31 wins, 4 draws, and 5 losses in distance-based datasets, while against BOSS, the results are 31 wins, 4 draws, and 5 losses as well, showing that our model achieves comparable accuracy with these state-of-the-art architectures.

Overall, these results confirm that our model achieves state-of-the-art performance in distance-based datasets while remaining highly competitive across general datasets. The significant wins over DTW-kNN and LSTM validate its alignment efficiency and generalization capabilities, while the comparable results against deep learning and ensemble methods highlight its ability to balance accuracy and interpretability.

4.3 Low-Resource and Full Training

In this experiment, we simulate low-resource scenarios by randomly sampling 1% to 100% of the training data to examine model performance under varying degrees of data scarcity. Some datasets contain very few training samples per class, making it difficult to perform balanced subsampling across all categories. To ensure a fair and consistent evaluation, we focus on 6 datasets where each class in the training set contains at least 300 samples, enabling controlled subsampling while preserving class balance. Moreover, to mitigate the potential impact of limited data and maintain consistency across different sampling levels, we apply a unified data augmentation strategy to all subsets used in this experiment. The experimental results are shown in Table 1.

In low-resource settings (1% and 10%), NN-DTW demonstrates strong performance across multiple datasets, particularly on ECG5000, Strawberry, and Wafer, where it achieves accuracy close to the highest. This is expected, as NN-DTW does not require training and can perform well even with limited labeled data. However, our model outperforms NN-DTW on four of the six datasets at the 1% sampling rate and on all six datasets at the 10% sampling rate, demonstrating its strong adaptability in data-scarce scenarios. Notably, our model achieves the highest accuracy in ECG5000 (10% and 100%), HandOutlines (1%), StarLightCur (1%, 10%), Strawberry (10%, 100%), and Wafer (1%, 10%), demonstrating its robustness in different classification tasks.

Table 1. Accuracy results in low- and rich-resource settings on six UCR datasets. Bold values indicate the best performance for each setting, while redder colors represent higher accuracy.

	ECG5000 (5-class)			HandOutlines (2-class)			MidPhaCorr (2-class)		
	1%	10%	100%	1%	10%	100%	1%	10%	100%
NN-DTW	**0.842**	0.912	0.924	0.827	0.838	0.881	0.622	0.687	0.711
InceptionTime	0.726	0.850	0.942	0.722	0.854	**0.954**	0.694	0.759	0.818
ROCKET	0.742	0.826	0.948	0.749	**0.876**	0.943	**0.704**	0.738	**0.842**
LSTM	0.702	0.834	0.932	0.700	0.821	0.886	0.691	**0.763**	0.808
Ours	0.840	**0.916**	**0.956**	**0.832**	0.867	0.892	0.663	0.756	0.825

	StarLightCur (3-class)			Strawberry (2-class)			Wafer (2-class)		
	1%	10%	100%	1%	10%	100%	1%	10%	100%
NN-DTW	0.841	0.887	0.907	**0.827**	0.919	0.941	0.887	0.926	0.980
InceptionTime	0.830	0.881	0.979	0.730	0.827	0.984	0.757	0.799	**0.999**
ROCKET	0.826	0.850	**0.981**	0.768	0.854	0.981	0.723	0.811	0.998
LSTM	0.822	0.855	0.975	0.754	0.814	0.957	0.707	0.809	0.997
Ours	**0.844**	**0.890**	0.968	0.816	**0.930**	**0.986**	**0.895**	**0.962**	0.991

In rich-resource settings (100%), our model consistently achieves competitive or the highest accuracy compared to deep learning baselines across most datasets. Notably, in ECG5000 and Strawberry, our model significantly outperforms all baselines, demonstrating its ability to effectively utilize labeled data for training and improve prediction accuracy in data-rich scenarios. Furthermore, we observe that our model, even when trained on only 10% of the available data, can achieve performance comparable to some fully trained baselines. This demonstrates its strong generalization ability from limited training instances, effectively bridging the gap between instance-based approaches and deep learning models. By leveraging the strengths of both paradigms, our model consistently delivers state-of-the-art performance in low-resource scenarios while remaining highly competitive in data-rich environments.

5 Related Works

Low-resource Learning for TSC. Real-world time series data is often scarce or highly imbalanced, presenting a fundamental challenge for supervised learning. Addressing this limitation is essential in domains where large-scale labeled data is difficult to obtain. [3]. A common approach to address this issue is data augmentation, such as over-sampling techniques [2]. On the other hand, instance-based methods, such as k-NN with dynamic time warping (DTW), have been widely used for decades and naturally perform well in low-resource environments [10]. More recently, meta-learning techniques, such as prototypical networks [25], have been developed to mitigate the data-hungry nature of deep learning models. In the context of low-resource time series classification, prior works have explored different meta-learning strategies: cross-branch attention mechanisms for prototypical networks [27], prototype embedding frameworks for capturing class discrepancies [35], and residual neural networks trained as meta-learning agents for low-resource classification. These methods generally enhance neural network performance in low-resource settings by using prototypes or extracted features to initialize model parameters. In contrast, our approach directly reformulates DTW into a trainable neural network, leveraging its inherent suitability for low-resource scenarios while enabling adaptation through learning. This eliminates the need for prototype-based initialization and provides a unified framework that bridges instance-based and deep learning methods.

Interpretable Neural Network for TSC. While neural networks achieve state-of-the-art performance in time series classification, their decision-making process remains opaque. Existing interpretability methods for TSC can be broadly categorized into three types. Instance-based explanations highlight representative subsequences relevant to classification decisions [6,32]. Similarity-based reasoning retrieves similar time series that influenced the classification outcome [15,34]. Feature attribution methods, such as twin systems, map learned feature representations to k-NN retrieval steps, enhancing both accuracy and interpretability [13,16,23]. A comprehensive survey on these approaches is provided in [12]. However, existing methods primarily focus on post-hoc interpretability, explaining the model's classification behavior without allowing direct modification of the decision process. Moreover, twin-system-based approaches require labeled data and do not support manual instance specification to refine the model. In contrast, our model provides a higher level of interpretability by not only enabling parameter visualization but also allowing fine-grained human intervention before and after training. Through our proposed model editing technique, users can modify model parameters to explicitly adjust classification behavior, making the model adaptable to evolving task specifications with minimal retraining.

6 Conclusions

Despite the growing interest in time series classification, existing methods often lack interpretability and struggle to generalize across both low-resource and data-rich scenarios. In this work, we address these challenges by introducing a novel interpretable recurrent neural network derived from the formal equivalence between DTW and RNN. Our approach enables instance-efficient initialization, making it effective in cold-start settings while also allowing training with labeled data to enhance predictive accuracy without compromising interpretability. To the best of our knowledge, this is the first work to neuralize DTW for time series classification. To validate our approach, we conduct extensive empirical evaluations across cold-start and data-rich settings. Experimental results demonstrate that our model outperforms existing methods in low-resource scenarios while remaining highly competitive in data-rich environments.

References

1. Bagnall, A., Lines, J., Bostrom, A., Large, J., Keogh, E.: The great time series classification bake off: a review and experimental evaluation of recent algorithmic advances. Data Min. Knowl. Disc. **31**, 606–660 (2017)
2. Cerqueira, V., Moniz, N., Inácio, R., Soares, C.: Time series data augmentation as an imbalanced learning problem. In: EPIA Conference on Artificial Intelligence, pp. 335–346. Springer (2024)
3. Chu, Z., Wang, Z., Zhang, W.: Fairness in large language models: a taxonomic survey. ACM SIGKDD Explorations Newsl **26**(1), 34–48 (2024)
4. Dau, H.A., et al.: The UCR time series archive (2018). https://doi.org/10.48550/ARXIV.1810.07758, https://arxiv.org/abs/1810.07758
5. Dempster, A., Petitjean, F., Webb, G.I.: Rocket: exceptionally fast and accurate time series classification using random convolutional kernels. Data Min. Knowl. Disc. **34**(5), 1454–1495 (2020)
6. Early, J., Cheung, G., Cutajar, K., Xie, H., Kandola, J., Twomey, N.: Inherently interpretable time series classification via multiple instance learning. In: The Twelfth International Conference on Learning Representations (2024)
7. Hochreiter, S., Schmidhuber, J.: Long short-term memory. Neural Comput. **9**(8), 1735–1780 (1997)
8. Ismail Fawaz, H., et al.: Inceptiontime: finding alexnet for time series classification. Data Min. Knowl. Disc. **34**(6), 1936–1962 (2020)
9. Ismail Fawaz, H., et al.: Inceptiontime: finding alexnet for time series classification. Data Min. Knowl. Disc. **34**(6), 1936–1962 (2020)
10. Jeong, Y.S., Jeong, M.K., Omitaomu, O.A.: Weighted dynamic time warping for time series classification. Pattern Recogn. **44**(9), 2231–2240 (2011)
11. Jia, Z., Lin, Y., Wang, J., Wang, X., Xie, P., Zhang, Y.: Salientsleepnet: multimodal salient wave detection network for sleep staging. In: Zhou, Z.H. (ed.) Proceedings of the Thirtieth International Joint Conference on Artificial Intelligence, IJCAI-21, pp. 2614–2620. International Joint Conferences on Artificial Intelligence Organization (2021). https://doi.org/10.24963/ijcai.2021/360, https://doi.org/10.24963/ijcai.2021/360, main Track
12. Keane, M.T., Kenny, E.M.: How case-based reasoning explains neural networks: A theoretical analysis of xai using post-hoc explanation-by-example from a survey of ann-cbr twin-systems. In: International Conference on Case-Based Reasoning, pp. 155–171. Springer (2019)
13. Kenny, E.M., Keane, M.T.: Twin-systems to explain artificial neural networks using case-based reasoning: Comparative tests of feature-weighting methods in ANN-CBR twins for xai. In: Twenty-Eighth International Joint Conferences on Artifical Intelligence (IJCAI), Macao, 10-16 August 2019, pp. 2708–2715 (2019)
14. Kook, L., Götschi, A., Baumann, P.F., Hothorn, T., Sick, B.: Deep interpretable ensembles. arXiv preprint arXiv:2205.12729 (2022)

15. Labaien, J., Zugasti, E., Carlos, X.D.: Contrastive explanations for a deep learning model on time-series data. In: International Conference on Big Data Analytics and Knowledge Discovery, pp. 235–244. Springer (2020)
16. Leonardi, G., Montani, S., Striani, M.: Deep feature extraction for representing and classifying time series cases: towards an interpretable approach in haemodialysis. In: The Thirty-Third International Flairs Conference (2020)
17. Li, T., Srikumar, V.: Augmenting neural networks with first-order logic. In: Proceedings of the 57th Annual Meeting of the Association for Computational Linguistics, pp. 292–302. Association for Computational Linguistics, Florence, Italy (2019). https://doi.org/10.18653/v1/P19-1028, https://aclanthology.org/P19-1028
18. Lines, J., Bagnall, A.: Time series classification with ensembles of elastic distance measures. Data Min. Knowl. Disc. **29**, 565–592 (2015)
19. Marcus, G.: Deep learning: a critical appraisal. arXiv preprint arXiv:1801.00631 (2018)
20. Marteau, P.F.: Time warp edit distance with stiffness adjustment for time series matching. IEEE Trans. Pattern Anal. Mach. Intell. **31**(2), 306–318 (2008)
21. Rolando, M., Raggio, V., Naya, H., Spangenberg, L., Cagnina, L.: A labeled medical records corpus for the timely detection of rare diseases using machine learning approaches. Sci. Rep. **15**(1), 6932 (2025)
22. Ruiz, A.P., Flynn, M., Large, J., Middlehurst, M., Bagnall, A.: The great multivariate time series classification bake off: a review and experimental evaluation of recent algorithmic advances. Data Min. Knowl. Disc. **35**(2), 401–449 (2021)
23. Sani, S., Wiratunga, N., Massie, S.: Learning deep features for knn-based human activity recognition. CEUR Workshop Proceedings (2017)
24. Schäfer, P.: The boss is concerned with time series classification in the presence of noise. Data Min. Knowl. Disc. **29**, 1505–1530 (2015)
25. Snell, J., Swersky, K., Zemel, R.: Prototypical networks for few-shot learning. In: Proceedings of the 31st International Conference on Neural Information Processing Systems, pp. 4080–4090. NIPS'17, Curran Associates Inc., Red Hook, NY, USA (2017)
26. Stefan, A., Athitsos, V., Das, G.: The move-split-merge metric for time series. IEEE Trans. Knowl. Data Eng. **25**(6), 1425–1438 (2012)
27. Sun, J., Takeuchi, S., Yamasaki, I.: Prototypical inception network with cross branch attention for time series classification. In: 2021 International Joint Conference on Neural Networks (IJCNN), pp. 1–7 (2021). https://doi.org/10.1109/IJCNN52387.2021.9533440
28. Szegedy, C., Ioffe, S., Vanhoucke, V., Alemi, A.A.: Inception-v4, inception-resnet and the impact of residual connections on learning. In: Proceedings of the Thirty-First AAAI Conference on Artificial Intelligence, pp. 4278–4284. AAAI'17, AAAI Press (2017)
29. Tan, Y., et al.: Metacare++: Meta-learning with hierarchical subtyping for cold-start diagnosis prediction in healthcare data, pp. 449–459 (2022). https://doi.org/10.1145/3477495.3532020
30. Vlachos, M., Hadjieleftheriou, M., Gunopulos, D., Keogh, E.: Indexing multidimensional time-series. VLDB J. **15**, 1–20 (2006)
31. Wang, T., Liu, Z., Zhang, T., Hussain, S.F., Waqas, M., Li, Y.: Adaptive feature fusion for time series classification. Knowl.-Based Syst. **243**, 108459 (2022). https://doi.org/10.1016/j.knosys.2022.108459, https://www.sciencedirect.com/science/article/pii/S0950705122001903

32. Wang, Y., et al.: Learning interpretable shapelets for time series classification through adversarial regularization. arXiv preprint arXiv:1906.00917 (2019)
33. Wang, Y.: Designing Deep Methods to Improve Machine Learning Interpretability. Ph.D. thesis, Washington State University (2022)
34. Wen, Y., Ma, T., Luss, R., Bhattacharjya, D., Fokoue, A., Julius, A.A.: Shedding light on time series classification using interpretability gated networks. In: The Thirteenth International Conference on Learning Representations
35. Zhang, B., Li, L., Liang, G., Tan, C., Dong, F.: Elastic slow feature prototypical network for few-shot fault diagnosis of industrial processes. IEEE Sens. J. (2024)
36. Zhang, X., Gao, Y., Lin, J., Lu, C.T.: Tapnet: Multivariate time series classification with attentional prototypical network. In: Proceedings of the AAAI Conference on Artificial Intelligence. vol. 34, pp. 6845–6852 (2020)
37. Zhou, X., Liu, X., Zhai, D., Jiang, J., Gao, X., Ji, X.: Prototype-anchored learning for learning with imperfect annotations. In: Chaudhuri, K., Jegelka, S., Song, L., Szepesvari, C., Niu, G., Sabato, S. (eds.) Proceedings of the 39th International Conference on Machine Learning. Proceedings of Machine Learning Research, vol. 162, pp. 27245–27267. PMLR (2022). https://proceedings.mlr.press/v162/zhou22f.html

Author Index

B
Bajaj, Chandrajit 273
Balar, Nishilkumar 21
Barddal, Jean Paul 327
Beer, Anna 308
Bender, Andreas 74
Bernabeu-Pérez, Pablo 3
Berthou, Céline 111
Bischl, Bernd 74
Borras, Hendrik 147
Bouveyron, Charles 290

C
Cai, Qi 219
Chen, Huaming 164
Chen, Jingyuan 235
Chen, Wei 345
Chevaleyre, Yann 39
Chu, Beilin 419
Coelho, Cecília 252
Cunha, Jose C. 402

D
Dai, Xinyi 183
Dang, Xilin 345
Do, Thanh-Toan 383
Durani, Walid 308

E
Ellendula, Aditya S. 273
Ellison, Noel 56
Enembreck, Fabrício 327

F
Fei, Binjie 419
Feremans, Len 473
Fieback, Laura 21
Fröning, Holger 147
Fu, Lingyue 183

G
Gao, Xin 219
Garcia-Gasulla, Dario 3
Gasevic, Dragan 383
Gnecco Heredia, Lucas 39
Gong, Chenqi 508
Gottschalk, Hanno 21
Granese, Federica 290
Gu, Jingjing 508
Guo, Yi 454
Gupta, Vaibhav 252

H
Han, Wenkang 235
Huynh, Tuan-Luc 383

I
Islam, Md Athikul 56

J
Jahn, Philipp 308
Jalaian, Brian 92
Jin, Zhibo 164

K
Kersting, Kristian 490
Klein, Bernhard 147
Kokozinski, Andre 490
Kopper, Philipp 74
Kraus, Maurice 490

L
Lakha, Bishal 56
Le, Trung 383
Leiber, Collin 308
Li, Dongmei 526
Li, Hanzhe 508
Li, Weichuang 345
Li, Yu 419
Li, Yuan-Fang 383

Liang, Yuxuan 345
Liao, Silin 164
Lin, Fudong 92
Lin, Jianghao 183
Lin, Qinhong 419
Liu, Hengyu 201
Liu, Jiaqi 419
Liu, Xu 345
Liu, Yuting 508
Liu, Zhenghao 201
Long, Ting 183
Lopez-Cuena, Enrique 3
Lou, Jiadong 92

M
Maleshkova, Maria 252
Meert, Wannes 473

N
Najjar, Ghassan 111
Navet, Benjamin 290
Negrevergne, Benjamin 39
Niggemann, Oliver 252
Nordhausen, Klaus 362
Nowak Assis, Daniel 327

Q
Qu, Jintao 526

R
Ruan, Weilin 345
Rügamer, David 74

S
Salim, Flora 164
Schäfer, Patrick 473
Seidl, Thomas 308
Serra, Edoardo 56
Shao, Mingxing 201
Sheinkman, Alisa 129
Silva, Joaquim F. 402
Sipilä, Mika 362
Sonabend, Raphael 74
Song, Yuanfeng 437
Spiegelberg, Jakob 21
Steinmann, David 490

T
Tang, Ruiming 183
Tang, Shaojie 219
Taskinen, Sara 362

V
Villata, Serena 290
Vorobieva, Héléna 111
Vu, Thuy-Trang 383

W
Wade, Sara 129
Wang, Hao 92
Wang, Weiqing 383
Wang, Xiao 147
Wang, Xinyi 164
Wang, Yasheng 183
Wang, Zichong 526
Wei, Yinwei 383
Wen, Fufang 419
Wong, Raymond Chi-Wing 437
Wu, Chenhao 526
Wu, Kaishun 437
Wüst, Antonia 490

X
Xia, Wei 183
Xu, Xuan 419

Y
Yang, Zhongliang 419
Yin, Yifang 201
Yu, Ge 201
Yu, Minghe 201
Yu, Yong 183
Yuan, Jing 219
Yuan, Xu 92

Z
Zhang, Haodi 437
Zhang, Jiayu 164
Zhang, Tiancheng 201
Zhang, Weinan 183
Zhang, Wenbin 526
Zhang, Xinhe 437
Zhang, Yachuan 454
Zhong, Yixiao 419
Zhou, Jianxiang 345
Zhou, Jihua 437
Zhou, Linna 419
Zhou, Qiang 508
Zhou, Yiyun 235
Zhu, Zhiyu 164
Zimmering, Bernd 252

MIX
Papier aus verantwortungsvollen Quellen
Paper from responsible sources
FSC® C105338

If you have any concerns about our products,
you can contact us on
ProductSafety@springernature.com

In case Publisher is established outside the EU,
the EU authorized representative is:
**Springer Nature Customer Service Center GmbH
Europaplatz 3, 69115 Heidelberg, Germany**

Printed by Libri Plureos GmbH
in Hamburg, Germany